THE
College Exp

MW00814203

THRIVING AT NORTHEAST IOWA COMMUNITY COLLEGE AND BEYOND

Fourth Edition

Customized Version of Thriving in the Community College and Beyond, Third Edition
by Joseph B. Cuseo, Aaron Thompson, Julie McLaughlin

NORTHEAST IOWA
COMMUNITY COLLEGE

Kendall Hunt
publishing company

Book Team

Chairman and Chief Executive Officer   Mark C. Falb
President and Chief Operating Officer   Chad M. Chandlee
Vice President, Higher Education   David L. Tart
Director of Publishing Partnerships   Paul B. Carty
Vice President, Operations   Timothy J. Beitzel
Developmental/Product Supervisor   Lynnette M. Rogers
Senior Project Coordinator   Stefani DeMoss
Senior Production Editor   Stefani DeMoss
Permissions Coordinator   Caroline Kieler
Cover Designer   Faith Walker

Kendall Hunt
publishing company

www.kendallhunt.com
Send all inquiries to:
4050 Westmark Drive
Dubuque, IA 52004-1840

Customized version of Thriving in the Community College and Beyond,
Third Edition by Joseph B. Cuseo, Aaron Thompson, and Julie A. McLaughlan.

PAK ISBN: 978-1-5249-3421-7
Text alone ISBN: 978-1-5249-3881-9

Published in the United States of America

Brief Contents

Contents

Preface

WELCOME TO NORTHEAST IOWA COMMUNITY COLLEGE (NICC)

Plan and Purpose of This Book and NICC's College Experience Course

This course, along with this book is designed to help you make a smooth transition to NICC as well as equip you with strategies for success that you can use throughout college and beyond. Its aim is to promote the academic excellence and personal development of all students—whether you're a student who is (a) transitioning to college directly from high school or from a full-time or part-time job, (b) living on or off campus, or (c) attending college on a full-time or part-time basis. Whatever your previous educational record may have been, college is a new ball game played on a different field with different rules and expectations. If you haven't been a particularly successful student in the past, this book will help you become a successful student in the future. If you have been a successful student in high school, this book will make you an even stronger student in college.

One of the book's major goals is to help you put into practice a powerful principle of human learning and personal success: *mindfulness*. When you're mindful, you're aware of *what* you're doing and *if* you're doing it in the most effective way. Mindfulness or self-awareness is the critical first step toward self-improvement and success in any aspect of your life. If you develop the habit of remaining aware of whether you're "doing college" strategically (e.g., by using the key strategies identified in this book), you will have taken a huge step toward college success.

Rather than trying to figure out how to do college on your own through random trial-and-error, this book gives you a game plan for getting it right from the start and an inside track for getting off to a fast start. Its plan is built on a solid foundation of research that equips you with a comprehensive set of well-documented strategies for doing college successfully.

Specific action strategies make up the heart of this book. You will find that these practical strategies aren't presented simply as a laundry list of what-to-do tips dispensed by authority figures who think they know what's best for you. Instead, the recommendations are accompanied by evidence-based reasons for *why* they're effective and they're organized into broader *principles* that tie the strategies together into a meaningful plan. It's not only important for you to know *what* to do, but also *why* to do it. If you understand the reason behind a suggested strategy, you're more likely to take that strategy seriously and implement it effectively.

When specific strategies are organized into general principles, they become more powerful because you're able to see how the same principle may be generalized and applied across different subjects and situations. Understanding the key principles that underlie effective strategies also empowers you to create additional strategies of your own that follow or flow from the same general principle. This promotes deeper, more powerful learning than simply collecting a bunch of tips about what you should or shouldn't do in college. We believe that you're ready and able to meet the challenge of deeper learning.

> "More than 30 years of research has shown that mindfulness is figuratively and literally enlivening. It's the way you feel when you're feeling passionate."
>
> —Dr. Ellen Langer, Harvard University, mindfulness researcher and author of The Power of Mindful Learning

> "Important achievements require a clear focus, all-out-effort, and a bottomless trunk full of strategies."
>
> —Carol Dweck, Stanford professor, and author of Mindset: The New Psychology of Success

> "The man who also knows why will be his own boss. As to methods there may be a million and then some, but principles are few. The man who grasps principles can successfully select his own methods. The man who tries methods, ignoring principles, is sure to have trouble."
>
> —Ralph Waldo Emerson, 19th-century author, poet, and philosopher

Since the strategies cited in this book are research-based, you'll find references cited regularly throughout all the chapters and a sizable reference section at the end of each chapter. Your professors will expect you to think critically and support your ideas with evidence. As authors, we should do the same and model that behavior for you.

You will find that the references cited represent a balanced blend of older, "classic" studies and more recent "cutting edge" research from a variety of fields. The time span of references cited serves to highlight the long-standing relevance of the ideas presented and their power to withstand the test of time. It also underscores the fact that the subject of success in college and beyond, like any other academic subject in the college curriculum, rests on a solid body of research and scholarship that spans multiple decades.

Preview of Content

Chapter 1

College Knowledge
Effective College Behavior In Class and Online

This chapter identifies top tips for academic success you can implement immediately, including what to do inside and outside the classroom. It also alerts you to in-class and out-of-class behavior that should be avoided in college.

Chapter 2

Making Connections: Four Steps to College Success
Using Powerful Student-Success Principles & Key Campus Resources

This chapter focuses on the "big picture"—the most powerful principles you can implement to promote your own success and the key campus resources you can to use to help you succeed. It describes *what* these key principles and resources are, *why* they're effective, and *how* to capitalize on them.

Chapter 3

Goal Setting and Motivation
Moving from Intention to Action

The path to personal success begins with goals and finding the means (succession of steps) to reach those goals. People who set specific goals are more likely to succeed than people who simply tell themselves they're going to try hard and do their best. This chapter lays out the key steps involved in the process of setting effective goals, identifies key self-motivational strategies for staying on track and sustaining progress toward our goals, and describes how personal qualities such as self-efficacy, grit, and growth mindset are essential for achieving goals.

Chapter 4

Time Management
Prioritizing Tasks, Preventing Procrastination, and Promoting Productivity

Time is a valuable personal resource—if you gain greater control of it, you gain greater control of your life. Time managed well not only enables you to get work done in a timely manner, it also enables you to set and attain personal priorities and maintain balance in your life. This chapter offers a comprehensive set of strategies for managing time, combating procrastination, and ensuring that you spend time in a way that aligns with your educational goals and priorities.

"I could really relate to everything we talked about. It is a great class because you can use it in your other classes."

"Everything we learned we will apply in our lives."

"This is the only course I've ever taken that was about me."

—*Comments made by students when evaluating their first-year experience course*

"In high school, a lot of the work was done while in school, but in college all of your work is done on your time. You really have to organize yourself in order to get everything done."

—*First-year student's response to a question about what was most surprising about college life*

Chapter 5
Higher-Level Thinking
Moving Beyond Basic Knowledge to Critical and Creative Thinking

National surveys consistently show that the primary goal of college faculty is teaching students how to think critically. This chapter will help you understand what critical thinking is and empower you to think critically and creatively. You will acquire thinking strategies that move you beyond memorization to higher levels of thought and learn ways to demonstrate higher-level thinking on college tests and assignments.

Chapter 6
Deep Learning
Strategic Note-Taking, Reading, and Studying

This chapter helps you apply research on human learning and the human brain to become a more effective and efficient learner. It takes you through three key stages of the learning process—from the first stage of acquiring information through lectures and readings, through the second stage of studying and retaining the information you've acquired, to the final stage of retrieving (recalling) the information you studied. The ultimate goal of this chapter is to supply you with a set of powerful strategies that makes your learning *deep* (not surface-level memorization), *durable* (long-lasting), and *retrievable* (accessible to you when you need it).

Chapter 7
Test-Taking Skills and Strategies
What to do Before, During, and After Tests

This chapter supplies you with a systematic set of strategies for improving your performance on different types of tests, including multiple-choice and essay. It identifies strategies that can be used before, during, and after tests, as well as practical tips for becoming more "test wise" and less "test anxious."

Chapter 8
Diversity and the Community College Experience
Learning about and from Human Differences

This chapter clarifies what "diversity" really means and demonstrates how experiencing diversity can deepen learning, promote critical and creative thinking, and contribute to your personal and professional development. Strategies are provided for overcoming cultural barriers and biases that block our development of rewarding relationships with diverse people and learning from others whose cultural backgrounds differ from our own. Simply stated, we learn more from people who are different from us than we do from people similar to us. There's more diversity among college students today than at any other time in history. This chapter will help you capitalize on this learning opportunity.

Chapter 9
Financial Literacy
Managing Money and Minimizing Debt

Research shows that accumulating high levels of debt in college is associated with higher stress, lower academic performance, and greater risk of withdrawing from college. The good news is that research also shows that students who learn to use effective money management strategies are able to minimize unnecessary spending, reduce accumulation of debt and stress, and improve the quality of their academic performance. This chapter identifies effective strategies for tracking income and expenses, minimizing and avoiding debt, balancing time spent on schoolwork and employment, and making wise financial choices in college.

Chapter 10

Social and Emotional Intelligence
Relating to Others and Regulating Our Emotions

This chapter identifies effective strategies for communicating with and relating to others, as well as strategies for understanding and managing our emotions—such as stress, anxiety, anger, and depression. Implementing the strategies discussed in this chapter will enhance the quality of your college experience and your overall quality of life.

Chapter 11

Health and Wellness
Body, Mind, and Spirit

Humans cannot reach their full potential without attending to their physical well-being. Sustaining health and attaining peak levels of performance depend on how well we treat our *body*—what we put into it (healthy food), what we keep out of it (unhealthy substances), what we do with it (exercise), and how well we rejuvenate it (sleep). This chapter examines strategies for maximizing wellness by maintaining a balanced diet, attaining quality sleep, promoting total fitness, and avoiding risky behaviors that jeopardize our health and impair our performance.

Think About It—Journal Entry P.1

What does being "well-rounded" and living a "well-balanced" life mean to you?

_____

_____

_____

_____

_____

Chapter 12

Educational and Career Planning & Decision-Making
Making Wise Choices about a College Major, College Transfer, and a Future Career

Making strategic choices about your courses and your major is essential to reaching your educational goals. You want to be sure your choice of a major is compatible with your personal interests, talents, and values. You should also have a strategic plan in mind (and in hand) to explore your options and decide on a major field of study and possible transfer to a four-year campus.

Even though career entry may be years away, career exploration and preparation should begin in the first term of college. Career planning gives you a practical, long-range goal to strive for and gets you thinking about how the skills you're using and developing in college align with the skills that promote your professional success beyond college. This chapter will help you develop a plan for making educational and career decisions that will best enable you to reach your long-term goals.

> It is hard to know how any student could truly understand whom [he or she] wants to be without thinking carefully about what career to pursue."
> —Derek Bok, president emeritus, Harvard University

 ## Think About It—Journal Entry P.2

What percentage of first-year college students do you think have already decided on a major?

What percentage of these "decided" students do you think will eventually change their mind and end up with a different major by the time they graduate?

(See Chapter 12, p. 346 for answers to these questions.)

Sequence of Chapter Topics

The chapters in this book are arranged in an order that allows you to ask and answer the following sequence of questions:

1. Why am I here?
2. Where do I want to go?
3. What must I do to get there?
4. How do I know when I've arrived?

The early chapters help you get oriented to the college environment, excite you about the college experience, and help you decide where college will take you. These chapters provide a mental map of your trip through college, help you set educational goals, and increase your awareness of key campus resources to get you there. Once you get a clear sense of why college is worth doing and where it will take you, you should become more enthused about taking action on the strategies suggested throughout the remainder of the book.

The middle chapters are devoted to helping you handle the practical, daily responsibilities you encounter in college and getting these day-to-day tasks done. The body of the book equips you with strategies for note-taking, reading, writing, learning, thinking, and test-taking.

The book's concluding chapters move you beyond specific day-to-day academic responsibilities and move you toward future planning and promoting your social, emotional, and physical well-being.

Process and Style of Presentation

As important as *what* information is contained in a book is *how* that information is presented. When writing this text, we made an intentional attempt to present information in a way that would: (a) stimulate your motivation to learn, (b) deepen your understanding of what you're learning, and (c) strengthen your retention (memory) for what you've learned.

We attempted to do this by incorporating the following principles of motivation, learning, and memory throughout the text.

- Each chapter begins with a **Preview** of the chapter's key goals and content, followed by a **Thought Starter**—a question designed to stimulate your thoughts and feelings about the upcoming material. This pre-reading exercise is designed to "warm up" or "tune up" your brain, preparing it to connect the ideas you're about to encounter in the chapter with the ideas you already have in your head. It's an instructional strategy that implements one of the most powerful principles of learning: we learn most effectively by relating what we're going to learn to what we've already learned and stored in our brain.

- Within each chapter, we periodically interrupt your reading with opportunities for *reflection*—**Think About It** questions that prompt you to pause and think about the material you've just read. These timely pauses for thought should keep you alert and mentally active throughout the reading process. They serve to intercept "attention drift" that normally takes place when the brain continually receives and processes information for an extended period, such as it does when reading (Willis, 2007). These reflections also deepen your understanding of the material because they ask you to *write* in response to your reading. Writing stimulates deeper learning and higher levels of thinking than simply underlining or highlighting sentences. We recommend keeping a record of your written responses to the textbook's reflection questions in a *learning journal*.

- **Exercises** at the *end* of each chapter ask you to reflect further on the knowledge you've acquired and transform that knowledge into informed action. We achieve *wisdom* when we move beyond simply acquiring knowledge to *applying* the knowledge—putting it into practice to help us become more wise, effective, and successful human beings (Staudinger, 2008).

  The strategic positioning of the *Thought Starter* questions at the beginning of each chapter, the *Think About It* reflections interspersed throughout the chapter, and the application *Exercises* at the end of the chapter will keep you actively involved at three key stages of the reading process: the beginning, middle, and end.

- **End-of-Chapter Reflections** ask you questions that allow you to reflect on what you learned in the chapter and how you can apply it to your success in college and life.

- Information is presented through **multiple modes of input**, which include: diagrams, pictures, cartoons, words of wisdom from famous and successful people, advice from current and former college students, and personal stories drawn from the authors' experiences. When you receive information through different formats, you process that information through multiple sensory modalities (input channels). This deepens learning by enabling your brain to lay down multiple memory tracks (traces) of the information it's taking in (Willis, 2007).

What follows is a list of the book's seven key instructional features. *As you read these features, make a quick note in the side margin about how effective you think this feature will be in terms of motivating you to read and learn from the book.*

1. Research and Scholarly Support

The book's ideas and recommendations are grounded in research and scholarship drawn from a variety of academic fields. You will find references cited regularly throughout the chapters and a sizable reference section at the end of each chapter. The sheer quantity of references cited serves as testimony to the fact that the subject matter of this book is built on a solid body of research and scholarship, just like any other academic subject studied in the college curriculum. You'll also find that the references include a balanced blend of older, "classic" scholarship and more recent "cutting edge" research.

2. Boxed Summaries

At different points in the text, you will find boxes containing summaries of top tips for success. These summaries pull together key strategies relating to the same concept and organize them in the same place physically, which will help you organize and retain them mentally.

3. Quotes

Throughout the book, quotes from successful and influential people appear in the side margins that relate to and reinforce ideas covered at that point of the chapter. You'll find quotes from famous individuals who have lived in different historical periods and who have specialized in a variety of fields, including politics, philosophy, religion, science, business, music, art, and athletics. The wide-ranging time frames, cultures, and fields of study represented by the people quoted demonstrate that their words of wisdom are timeless and universal. It's our hope that the words of these highly successful and respected individuals will inspire you to put their words in practice.

You can also learn a lot from the firsthand experiences of current and former students. Throughout the book, you'll find comments and advice from students at different stages of the college experience, including college graduates (alumni). Studies show that students can learn a great deal from their peers—especially from more experienced peers who've "been there, done that." By hearing about their success stories and stumbling blocks, you can benefit from their college experiences to improve your college experience.

4. Authors' Experiences

In each chapter, you will find at least one author's experience related to the chapter topic. We share our own experiences as college students, our professional experiences working with students as instructors and advisors, and our personal experiences in other areas of our lives. Studies show that when people hear stories shared by others, their understanding and memory for key ideas contained in the stories is deepened and strengthened (McDrury & Alterio, 2002). We share our stories for the purpose of personalizing the book and with the hope that you'll learn from our experiences—including learning from our mistakes!

Think About It—Journal Entry P.3

Have you received any tips or advice from friends or family about what to do, or what not to do in college?

_____

If you have, what kind of advice did you receive and who gave it to you?

_____

_____

_____

If you haven't, why do you think none of your friends or family members have offered you any advice?

_____

_____

_____

_____

_____

5. Concept Maps (Graphic Organizers): Verbal-Visual Aids

Throughout the book, you will find ideas visually organized into diagrams, charts, and figures. When important concepts are represented in a visual-spatial format, we're more likely to retain them because two different memory traces are recorded in our brain: verbal (words) and visual (images).

6. Cartoons: Emotional-Visual Aids

You will find cartoons sprinkled throughout the text to lighten up the reading and provide you with a little entertainment. More importantly, the cartoons relate to an important concept and are also intended to strengthen your retention of that concept by reinforcing it with a visual image (drawing) and an emotional experience (humor). If the cartoon triggers at least a snicker, your body will release adrenaline—a hormone that facilitates memory formation. If it generates actual laughter, it will also stimulate your brain to release endorphins—natural, morphine-like chemicals that lower stress and elevate mood.

7. Learning More through the World Wide Web

At the end of each chapter are web-based resources containing additional information relating to the chapter's major ideas. One of the major goals of a college education is to prepare students to become independent, self-directed learners. We hope that the information presented in each chapter's topic will stimulate your interest and motivation to learn more about the topic. If it does, you can use the online resources cited at the end of the chapter to access additional information.

Think About It—Journal Entry P.4

Look back at the seven features of this book that have just been described. Which of these features do you think will be most effective for stimulating your interest in reading and learning from the book?

_____

_____

_____

_____

_____

We firmly believe that the content of this book, and the manner in which the content is delivered, will empower you not only to survive college, but to *thrive* in college and beyond. The skills and strategies found on the following pages promote success throughout life. Self-awareness, effective planning and decision making, learning deeply and remembering longer, thinking critically and creatively, managing time and money effectively, communicating and relating effectively with others, and maintaining health and wellness are more than college success skills—they are *life* success skills.

Introduction

Welcome to Community College

In the introduction to this book, you'll learn why college has the potential to be the most enriching experience of your life and one will benefit you throughout life. The first year of college is a particularly critical stage of your educational development. It's a transitional stage during which students encounter the greatest challenges, the most stress, the most academic difficulties, and the highest risk of dropping out. However, it's also the year when students experience the greatest amount of learning and personal growth. These findings highlight the power of the first-year experience, the value of first-year courses designed to promote college success, and the importance of books like this.

In the introduction, you'll find convincing evidence that new students who participate in first-year experience courses (college-success courses) are more likely to stick with college, complete their degree, and get the most out of their college experience.

Summary and Conclusion

It is our hope that the content of this book and the manner in which the content is presented will motivate and empower you to make the most of your community college experience. Don't forget that the skills and strategies discussed are relevant to life beyond college. Effective planning and decision making, learning deeply and remembering longer, thinking critically and creatively, managing time and money

"

I've gotten a better sense of how to manage my life."

"

I know that I have a lot to learn, but this class has given me the stepping stones to help me become the person that I want to be."

—Comments made by first-year students in a course that used this book

responsibly, communicating and relating effectively with others, and maintaining health and wellness are more than just college skills: they are life skills.

> Learning doesn't stop after college; it's a lifelong process. If you strive to apply the ideas in this book, you'll develop habits that will enable you to thrive in college and beyond.

AUTHOR'S EXPERIENCE

I've learned a lot from teaching the first-year seminar (college success course) and from writing this book. Before I taught this course, I didn't have a clear idea about the meaning, purpose, and value of a college education, or why general education was so important for achieving personal and professional success. By preparing for this course, I also learned new strategies for improving my memory and my writing, as well as for managing my time, money, and health. I continue to use these strategies in my personal and professional life. My only regret is that I didn't take a course like this when I was a college freshman. If I had, I would have been able to apply these life success skills earlier in my life.

—*Joe Cuseo*

Note

This is more than just a textbook for first-term students. It's a college success and life success book; it contains principles and strategies that can promote your success in college and improve the quality of your life.

Sincerely,

Joe Cuseo, Aaron Thompson, & Julie McLaughlin

References

McDrury, J., and Alterio, M. G. (2002). *Learning through Storytelling: using reflection and experience in higher education contexts*. Palmerston North: Dunmore Press.

Staudinger, U. M. (2008). A psychology of wisdom: History and recent developments. *Research in Human Development*, 5, 107–120.

Willis, J. (2007). *Brain-friendly strategies for the inclusion classroom*. Alexandria, VA: Association for Supervision and Curriculum Development.

Acknowledgments

I'd like to take this opportunity to thank several people who have played an important role in my life and whose positive influence made this book possible. My parents, Mildred (nee, Carmela) and Blase (nee, Biaggio) Cuseo, for the many sacrifices they made to support my education. My wife, Mary, for her patience, love, and meticulous editorial feedback. My uncle, Jim Vigilis, for being a second father and life coach to me during my formative years. Jim Cooper, my best friend, for being a mentor to me in graduate school. My students, who taught me a lot and contributed their insightful perspectives, poignant poems, and illustrations to this book. Finally, thanks to all the author-centered professionals at Kendall Hunt who gave me the freedom to write a book I believe in and reflect who I am.

—Joe Cuseo

I would like to thank all of the teachers, community leaders, friends, and others that I have never met (e.g., Judge Thurgood Marshall) who have had profound impact on my life as mentors. I would especially like to thank my siblings who have loved me unconditionally. I dedicate this edition of the book to my brother Perry who did far more good for humanity than ever can be understood. RIP brother. Thanks to Joe and Jules for being my partners in this endeavor. Thanks to Kendall Hunt (especially my close friend Paul) for allowing us to build a book with fidelity. Lastly, my true heartfelt thanks to those institutions (Lexington Community College, University of Kentucky, University of Missouri-Columbia, The Kentucky Council on PostSecondary Education, and my beloved Eastern Kentucky University) that gave me an opportunity to live out my autonomy as a professor and educational leader.

—Aaron Thompson

I would like to thank my parents, O.J. and Karen McLaughlin, for the unconditional love and support they have given me throughout the years. I would also like to thank my sister, Jaime Chandler, as well as my parents for believing in me, especially when I did not believe in myself. Thanks to the entire Cincinnati State FYE community—we could not be successful in what we do without the hard work and support of ALL involved. Although there are too many to name, I thank all of those who have mentored me throughout my career (special thanks to Diane Stump and Joyce Rimlinger)! In addition, I thank Paul Carty (and all at Kendall Hunt who support this project) for this incredible opportunity and for trusting us to do the job right. Aaron and Joe, thanks for mentoring me (and making me laugh). I have learned so much from you both. Most importantly, I thank my students, who inspire me every day. I would like to dedicate this edition of the book to the memory of my dear friend, mentor, and "big sis," Bobbi Madison. I love you Bobbi and miss you every day.

—Julie McLaughlin

About the Authors

Joe Cuseo holds a doctoral degree in Educational Psychology and Assessment from the University of Iowa and is Professor Emeritus of Psychology. For more than 25 years, he directed the first-year seminar—a core college success course required of all new students.

He's a 14-time recipient of the "faculty member of the year award" on his home campus—a student-driven award based on effective teaching and academic advising; a recipient of the "Outstanding First-Year Student Advocate Award" from the National Resource Center for The First-Year Experience and Students in Transition; and a recipient of the "Diamond Honoree Award" from the American College Personnel Association (ACPA) for contributions made to student development and the Student Affairs profession.

Currently, Joe serves as an educational advisor and consultant for AVID—a nonprofit organization whose mission is to promote the college access and success of underserved student populations. He has delivered hundreds of campus workshops and conference presentations across North America, as well as Europe, Asia, Australia, and the Middle East.

Aaron Thompson is the executive vice president and chief academic officer for the Kentucky Council on Postsecondary Education. He is also a professor of Sociology in the Department of Educational Leadership and Policy Studies at Eastern Kentucky University. Thompson has a Ph.D. in Sociology in areas of organizational behavior and race and gender relations. Dr. Thompson has over 27 years of leadership experience in higher education and business. In addition, he has spent numerous years serving on nonprofit boards in leadership roles. Thompson has researched, taught, and/or consulted in areas of diversity, leadership, ethics, multicultural families, race and ethnic relations, student success, first-year students, retention, cultural competence, and organizational design throughout his personal career. He has over 30 publications and numerous research and peer-reviewed presentations. Thompson has traveled throughout the Unite States and has given more than 700 workshops, seminars, and invited lectures in areas of race and gender diversity, living an unbiased life, overcoming obstacles to gain success, creating a school environment for academic success, cultural competence, workplace interaction, leadership, organizational goal setting, building relationships, the first-year seminar, and a variety of other topics. He has been or is a consultant to educational institutions (elementary, secondary, and postsecondary), corporations, nonprofit organizations, police departments, and other governmental agencies. His latest authored or co-authored books are: *Changing Student Culture from the Ground Up, The Sociological Outlook, Infusing Diversity and Cultural Competence into Teacher Education, Peer to Peer Leadership: Changing Student Culture from the Ground Up*. In addition to this text, he also co-authored *Thriving in College and Beyond: Research-Based Strategies for Academic Success, Diversity and the College Experience, Focus on Success*, and *Black Men and Divorce*.

Julie McLaughlin is department chair and professor of the First-Year Experience (FYE) courses, as well as co-chair of the FYE Advisory Committee, at Cincinnati State Technical and Community College. She has an M.A. in College Student Personnel from Eastern Michigan University. Julie is responsible for assisting in the creation of the three FYE courses that are offered at Cincinnati State, as well as the Psychology of Leadership course whose students serve as peer mentors in FYE courses. She is also responsible for overseeing the FYE curriculum and Instructor Development Program, with the assistance of full-time FYE faculty. McLaughlin is a five-time House-Bruckmann Faculty Excellence Award nominee. Julie previously served as an academic advisor and co-created the Athletic Advising Program at Cincinnati State which has been recognized as an exemplary practice by the National Academic Advising Association (NACADA), and she contributed to the NACADA monograph *Advising Student-Athletes: A Collaborative Approach to Success.* McLaughlin has presented at multiple national conferences for FYE and NACADA. She has also served as faculty for the Institute on First-Year Student Success in the Community College and the Institute on Developing and Sustaining First-Year Seminars presented by The National Resource Center for First-Year Experience and Students in Transition.

A letter from the President of Northeast Iowa Community College

At NICC, our students have hopes for and dreams of a better future through education and training. For the hopes to be realized and dreams to come true, the learning must be purposeful and meaningful in building a strong foundation for success. Every course is a critical piece that builds that foundation for success.

Therefore, your understanding of the importance of each course and learning as much as possible from each course is crucial. This particular course was created with your success in mind. Education is a journey and it requires you to stay on track and build upon what you have learned. It is critical for you to start well and stay engaged.

This course is like a compass that will guide your way and the chapters will provide you with the useful information and tools that you will need along your learning journey. During the course, share what you know with other students and learn from them also. Remember that your professor is here to help you. Together, gain the maximum benefits from this course.

I encourage you to use what you will learn in this course to prepare for other courses and experiences coming your way in life. Your success is very important to us.

Best wishes to you,
Liang Chee Wee, Ph.D.
President of NICC

Introduction

WHY COMMUNITY COLLEGE?

Congratulations! We applaud your decision to continue your education. Your previous enrollment in school was required, but your decision to continue your education in college is entirely *your choice*. By choosing to enter *higher education*, you've chosen to learn and think at a higher level than you did in high school. You're about to begin an exciting and challenging journey that has the potential to be the most enriching experience of your life.

 Think About It—Journal Entry I.1

Why have you decided to attend college?

_____

_____

_____

What are you most *looking forward to* about college?

_____

_____

_____

History of Northeast Iowa Community College

In 1966, the State Board of Education approved the formation of the Area One–Vocational-Technical School with Calmar as its administrative headquarters. This included the public school districts in Allamakee, Chickasaw, Clayton, Fayette, Howard and Winneshiek counties, as well as sections of Bremer, Buchanan and Mitchell counties.

On September 5, 1967, career education programs in Calmar began with 170 students enrolled in 12 programs. The school also broke ground on construction of college facilities on the 210-acre Calmar campus, which now include Darwin L.

Ready for takeoff, On my adventure today, As I take a seat in my chair And clear the way.

Eager people around, With destinations to go, As a woman at the front says, "Please find a seat in any row."

Some people are anxious, Waiting to take flight, To soar above the rest, With aspirations in sight

Our first day of college, A chance to start anew, To find out who we are, And learn what is true.

—Waiting to Take Flight, *a poem by Kimberly Castaneda, first-year student*

People often ask me why I prefer to teach at a community college when I have degrees from more elite institutions. I chose to teach at a community college because it celebrates committed, passionate teachers. Teaching at a community college is the best thing that ever happened to me."

—*Professor Ellen Olmstead, "It's the Community-College Life for Me,"* The Chronicle of Higher Education

Schrage Administration, Max Clark Hall, Wilder Business Center, Industrial Technologies, Student Center, Agricultural Technologies, Child Development Center and Iowa's Dairy Center, a $4.1 million dairy education center and applied research laboratory built in 2000.

The merged Area One Vocational-Technical School was enlarged in 1970 to include the public school districts in Dubuque and Delaware counties and sections of Jones and Jackson counties. In 1971, career education programs in Dubuque began at several locations throughout the city including the Roshek building.

In April 1979, the Area One Vocational-Technical School changed its name to Northeast Iowa Technical Institute. This same year, the Peosta campus was established. The Peosta campus currently includes the main building, the Gas Utilities and Construction building, a child development center, the National Education Center for Agricultural Safety and most recently the Industrial Technologies building, which opened in August 2010.

In 1988, the College was authorized by the Iowa Board of Education to award the Associate of Arts, Associate of Science and Associate of Applied Science degrees as well as diplomas and certificates. The College also changed its name from Northeast Iowa Technical Institute to Northeast Iowa Community College (NICC).NICC has since expanded to include centers and service locations in Cresco, Dubuque, New Hampton, Manchester, Oelwein and Waukon. The purpose of these centers is to bring education and training to students where they live and to serve as a catalyst for economic development.

In 2008, the Town Clock Business Center in Dubuque was expanded to include a one-stop center with Iowa Workforce Development (IWD) and East Central Intergovernmental Association (ECIA).In December of 2007, taxpayers passed, by supermajority, a $35 million renovation and construction bond levy for NICC. The funds supported construction and renovation of the industrial technologies buildings on each campus, the student center on the Calmar campus, renovations to the health and science labs and a new library on the Peosta campus, Darwin L. Schrage Administration building in Calmar, and the Wilder Business Center, which opened in January 2013.

In fall 2011, the Aspen Institute Community College Excellence Program named NICC to the top ten of community colleges in the nation for the College's successful graduate outcomes, academic excellence and community impact.

Under the leadership of its current President, Dr. Liang Chee Wee, Northeast Iowa Community College celebrated its 50th anniversary and the staff and faculty are committed than ever to transforming and honoring its communities one student at a time. We invite you to join us as we continue to make history.

The Community College Experience

You're about to join approximately 8 million (4,900,000 part-time and 3,120,000 full-time) students enrolled at more than 1,000 community colleges in the United States today. Student enrollment at community colleges has been growing faster than all other types of colleges and universities in the United States (Desrochers, Lenihan, & Wellman, 2010); the diversity of students enrolled in America's community colleges makes it the most diverse system of education in the world. (See **Box I.1** for a snapshot summary of student diversity at America's community colleges today.) According to the American Association of Community Colleges (2014), 52% of your peers are white and 48% are nonwhite; 36% of you are first in your family to attend college; 17% of you are single parents; 17% of you are non-U.S. citizens; 7% of you are veterans; and 4% of you are students with disabilities. As you will learn in Chapter 8, a diverse student body represents a golden *educational* opportunity for enhancing learning, personal development, and career preparation. The diversity found at teaching-oriented community colleges represents a unique learning environment that's tough to match at other types of colleges and universities.

Box I.1

Student Diversity in America's Community Colleges

- There are approximately 13 million students currently enrolled in approximately 1,132 community colleges in the United States; they account for almost half of all first-year college students in America today.
- More than 770,000 community college students will earn an associate degree this year, and more than 436,000 will earn a certificate.
- Most first-year community college students are employed either part- or full-time and attend college part-time.
- The average age of the American community college student is 28.
- Almost 36% of all community college students are the first in their family to attend college.

- More than 45% of community college students are members of minority racial or ethnic groups.
- Close to 6% of international students attend America's community colleges.

Source: American Association of Community Colleges (2014).

There are two other groups of students that are growing in number and adding to the student diversity found in America's community colleges:

- Veterans returning from the war in the Middle East who have been afforded the opportunity to attend college with the help of generous financial aid provided by a GI Bill passed in 2009.
- Displaced workers over the age of 20 who have lost full-time jobs due to job layoffs and company closings triggered by the current economic recession.

PERSONAL EXPERIENCE

There are some challenges us vets do face when we get out and go to college. There is that natural gap in maturity [between] the regular college student versus the veteran student. While some students come in late on a regular basis, veteran students are often early to class. Also some students talk during a lecture, while a veteran student gives the instructor the utmost attention. But these are things that are drilled into our heads being raised in the military. Things like loyalty, respect, and integrity.

—*Veteran student*

"

The scariest thing for me to have done was to get out [of the military] and not have a plan. I firmly believe that you have to plan for success. Success doesn't just happen; you have to work for it."

—*First-year veteran student*

PERSONAL EXPERIENCE

Many of these new students [displaced workers] feel that going back to school was the best thing that they have ever done. They feel better about themselves because of the daily challenges, making contacts and developing new relationships with classmates, and the thrill of learning helps them to believe in themselves and feel successful. I hear these comments: "This is a wonderful opportunity for me." "I realized what was important to me." "I've wanted to go back to school for a long time."

—*Community College counselor*

"

I am very impressed by the displaced workers who are returning to school. While one would expect the workers to be down and depressed, most of them are viewing this as an opportunity to pursue an opportunity [and] a dream delayed."

—*Community college counselor*

The community college has been called "America's college" (Cohen, Brawer, & Kisker, 2014) because it's an American invention. It's also referred to as "democracy's college" (Topper & Powers, 2013) because its open-door admissions policy embodies the democratic principle of equal opportunity for all people—regardless of their age, gender, ethnicity, race, religion, prior educational history, or family income. The community college system provides accessible, affordable higher education for all people who want to improve their quality of life and pursue the American dream. America's community colleges are the "Ellis Island" of higher education because they embody the American ideal of providing equal educational opportunity and a gateway to success for all people.

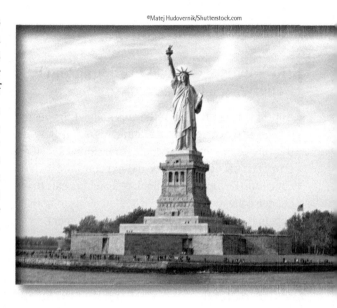

©Matej Hudovernik/Shutterstock.com

⊜ Think About It—Journal Entry I.2

Why are you attending NICC now?

_____

_____

_____

> "
> Community colleges are the 'unsung heroes' of the nation's education system. They may not get the credit they deserve, they may not get the same resources as other schools, but they provide a gateway to millions of Americans to good jobs and a better life."
>
> —*Barack Obama, 44th president of the United States*

Studies show that compared to high school graduates, students who earn a community college credential—whether it be a certificate or an associate degree—have higher rates of employment, earn higher wages (approximately $400,000 more over a course of a lifetime), and have children who are more likely to complete a college degree (Gagliardi & Hiemstra, 2013; Ganzglass, 2014; Mullin & Phillippe, 2013; Tinto, 2012). For community college students who eventually transfer to a four-year college and complete a bachelor's degree, they experience additional benefits similar to students who start their college education at four-year campuses (Pascarella & Terenzini, 2005). These benefits are summarized in **Box I.2**.

Box I.2

The Power of College: Economic and Personal Benefits of a College Education

Approximately 31% of Americans hold a four-year (bachelor's) degree (Lumina Foundation, 2015). When they are compared with people from similar social and economic backgrounds who did not continue their education beyond high school, research reveals that a college education is well worth it—in terms of both personal development and career advancement.

Summarized below are positive outcomes associated with a college education and a college degree. Their wide-ranging impact on the whole person and society at large serve as testimony to the power of the college experience.

1. Economic and Career Benefits
- Job security and stability—college graduates have lower rates of unemployment and lower risk of being laid off work
- Higher income—the gap between the earnings of high school and college graduates is large and *growing*. Individuals holding a bachelor's degree earn an average salary that's $17,500 higher than high school graduates. When these differences are calculated over a lifetime, the income of families headed by people with a bachelor's degree earn an income that's over a

million dollars more than families headed by people with a high school diploma. (See Figure I.1.)

> It's an irrefutable fact that college gives you a significant and persistent advantage decade after decade."
> —*Mary C. Daly, vice president of the Federal Reserve Bank of San Francisco (quoted in the Los Angeles Times, April 15, 2015)*

- Better retirement and pension benefits
- Career versatility and mobility—greater ability to move out of one position into another (a college graduate has more job options)
- Career advancement—greater opportunity to move up to higher-level professional positions (in other words, a college graduate has more opportunities for job promotions)
- Career satisfaction—college graduates are more likely to be in careers that interest them and in positions they find stimulating, challenging, and personally fulfilling
- Career autonomy—college graduates have more opportunities to work independently (without supervision) and make their own on-the-job decisions
- Career prestige—college graduates are more likely to hold higher status positions, (i.e., jobs considered to be desirable and highly regarded by society)

FIGURE I.1

(continued)

Box I.2 *(continued)*

2. Advanced Intellectual Skills

College graduates possess:

- Greater knowledge
- More effective problem-solving skills—better ability to deal with complex and ambiguous (uncertain) problems
- Greater openness to new ideas
- More advanced levels of moral reasoning
- More effective consumer choices and decisions
- Wiser long-term investments
- Clearer sense of self-identity—greater awareness and knowledge of personal talents, interests, values, and needs
- Greater likelihood of learning continually throughout life

> Without exception, the observed changes [during college] involve greater breadth, expansion, and appreciation for the new and different . . . and the evidence for their presence is compelling."
>
> —*Ernest Pascarella and Pat Terenzini,* How College Affects Students

3. Physical Health Benefits

- Better health insurance—college graduates are more likely to have insurance coverage and have more comprehensive coverage
- Better dietary habits
- Exercise more regularly
- Have lower rates of obesity
- Live longer and healthier lives

4. Social Benefits

- Greater social self-confidence
- Better ability to understand and communicate effectively with others
- Greater popularity
- More effective leadership skills
- Higher levels of marital satisfaction

5. Emotional Benefits

- Lower levels of anxiety
- Higher levels of self-esteem
- Greater sense of self-efficacy—college graduates believe they have more influence or control over the outcomes of their lives
- Higher levels of psychological well-being
- Higher levels of life satisfaction and happiness

6. Effective Citizenship

- Greater interest in national issues—both social and political
- Greater knowledge of current events
- Higher voting participation rates
- Higher rates of participation in civic affairs and community service

7. Higher Quality of Life for Their Children

- Less likely to smoke during pregnancy
- Provide better health care for their children
- Spend more time with their children
- More likely to involve their children in stimulating educational activities that advance their cognitive (mental) development
- More likely to save money for their children to go to college
- More likely to have children who graduate from college
- More likely that their children attain higher status, higher salary careers

> My three-month-old boy is very important to me, and it is important I graduate from college so my son, as well as I, live a better life".
>
> —*First-year student's response to the question: "What is most important to you?"*

Sources: Andres & Wyn (2010); Astin (1993); Bowen (1977, 1997) ; Baum, Ma,, & Payea (2013); Carnevale, Strohl, & Melton (2011); Dee (2004); Feldman & Newcomb (1994); Hamilton (2011, 2014); Knox, Lindsay, & Kolb (1993); Lumina Foundation (2013, 2015); Pascarella & Terenzini (2005); Pew Research Center (2014); Seifert, et al. (2008); SHEEO (2012); The Hamilton Project (2014); Tomsho (2009); U.S. Bureau of Labor Statistics (2015).

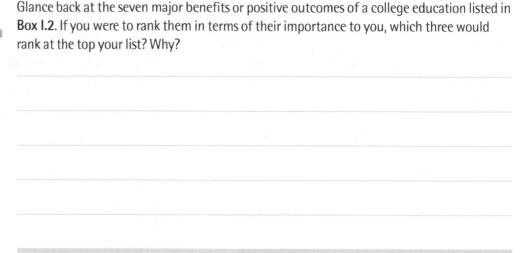

Think About It—Journal Entry I.3

Glance back at the seven major benefits or positive outcomes of a college education listed in **Box I.2**. If you were to rank them in terms of their importance to you, which three would rank at the top your list? Why?

> "For the individual, having access to and successfully graduating from an institution of higher education has proved to be the path to a better job, to better health and to a better life."
>
> —The College Board

> "One of the major transitions from high school to college involves the unlearning of past attitudes, values, and behaviors and the learning of new ones. This represents a major social and psychological transition and a time when students may be more ready to change than at any other point in their college career."
>
> —Ernest Pascarella & Patrick Terenzini, How College Affects Students

After college, it's probably safe to say that you will never again be a member of an organization or community with as many resources and services available to you that have been intentionally designed to promote your learning, development, and success. If you capitalize on the resources available to you, and if you utilize effective college-going strategies—such as those suggested in this book—you can create a life-changing experience for yourself that will enhance your quality of life for the remainder of your life.

Northeast Iowa Community College Profile

Northeast Iowa Community College is a student-driven, community-focused educational institution serving eight counties in northeast Iowa and surrounding areas. Offering over 85 academic https://www.nicc.edu/collegeprograms/ programs of study, as well as "https://www.nicc.edu/distancelearning/" distance learning, "https://www.nicc.edu/trainingandoutreach/" customized business and industry training, short-term certification options and "https://www.nicc.edu/admissions/adulteducationandliteracy/" adult education and literacy, NICC is committed to high-quality education and training at an affordable price to ensure the growth and vitality of northeast Iowa.

Mission Statement

Northeast Iowa Community College provides accessible, affordable, quality education and training to meet the needs of our communities.

Vision Statement

The Northeast Iowa Community College educational community will live the values of service, respect, innovation, stewardship and integrity within a culture of continuous improvement.

Service: Dedication to meet the ever-changing educational needs of our stakeholders

Respect: Recognition of individual dignity by promoting trust and cooperation

Innovation: An open climate fostering collaboration, improvement and advancement of ideas

Stewardship: Responsible management that sustains resources for the common good

Integrity: Policies, practices and actions reflecting responsible citizenship

The Importance of the First Year of College

Your transition into higher education represents an important life transition. Somewhat similar to an immigrant moving to a new country, you're moving into a new culture with unfamiliar expectations, regulations, customs, and language (Chaskes, 1996). (For definitions and "translations" of the new language you'll encounter in college, see the *Glossary and Dictionary of College Vocabulary*, **pp. 411–418.**)

The *first* year of college is undoubtedly the most important year of the college experience because it's a *transitional* stage. Students report the most change, the most learning, and the most development during their first year of college (Flowers, et al., 2001; HERI, 2014; Light, 2001). Other research suggests that the academic habits students develop in their first year are likely to persist throughout their remaining years of college (Schilling, 2001). When graduating seniors look back at their college experience, many of them say that their first year was the time of greatest change and the time when they made the most significant improvements in their approach to learning. Here's how one senior put it during a personal interview:

Interviewer: What have you learned about your approach to learning [in college]?

Student: I had to learn how to study. I went through high school with a 4.0 average. I didn't have to study. It was a breeze. I got to the university and there was no structure. No one took attendance to make sure I was in class. No one checked my homework. No one told me I had to do something. There were no quizzes on the readings. I did not work well with this lack of structure. It took my first year and a half to learn to deal with it. But I had to teach myself to manage my time. I had to teach myself how to study. I had to teach myself how to learn in a different environment (Chickering & Schlossberg, 1998, p. 47).

In some ways, the first-year experience in college is similar to ocean surfing or downhill skiing: It can be filled with the most exciting thrills—greatest learning and development, but also the most dangerous spills—it's the year when students experience the most stress, the most academic difficulties, and the highest college withdrawal rates (American College Testing, 2012; Bartlett, 2002; Sax, Bryant, & Gilmartin, 2004). The ultimate goal of downhill skiing and surfing is to experience the thrills, avoid the spills, and finish the run on your feet and feeling exhilarated. The same can be said for the first year of college; studies show that if students complete their first-year experience in good standing, their chances for successfully completing college increase dramatically (American College Testing, 2009).

You'll find that the research cited and the advice provided in this book point to one major conclusion: Success in college depends on you—you make it happen by what you do and how well you capitalize on the resources available to you. Don't let college happen *to* you; make it happen *for* you—take charge of your college experience and take advantage of the college resources that are at your command.

> "One of the major transitions from high school to college involves the unlearning of past attitudes, values, and behaviors and the learning of new ones. This represents a major social and psychological transition and a time when students may be more ready to change than at any other point in their college career."
>
> —*Ernest Pascarella & Patrick Terenzini*, How College Affects Students

> "What students do during college counts more than who they are or where they go to college."
>
> —*George Kuh, author*, Student Success in College

After reviewing 40 years of research on how college affects students, two distinguished researchers reached the following conclusion:

> *The impact of college is largely determined by individual effort and involvement in the academic, interpersonal, and extracurricular [co-curricular] offerings on a campus. Students are not passive recipients of institutional efforts to "educate" or "change" them, but rather bear major responsibility for any gains they derive from their postsecondary [college] experience* (Pascarella & Terenzini, 2005, p. 602).

Compared to your previous experiences in school, college will provide you with a broader range of courses to choose from, more resources to capitalize on, and more decision-making opportunities. Your particular college experience will end up being different than any other college student because you have the freedom to actively shape and create it in a way that's uniquely your own.

" Being in this class has helped me a lot. What I learned I will apply to all my other classes."

" I feel like I have so much to take away from this class and will continue to keep it with me the rest of my college career."

" This course will be a hard act to follow. This is one of the most valuable classes I will ever take."

—Comments made by students when evaluating their first-year experience course

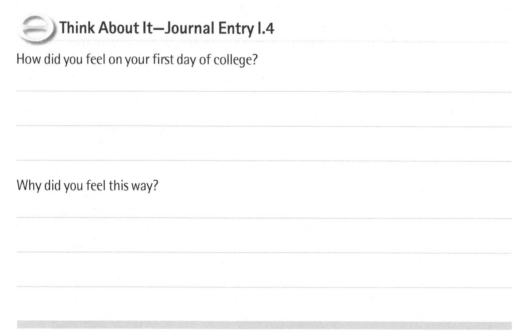

Think About It—Journal Entry I.4

How did you feel on your first day of college?

_____

_____

_____

Why did you feel this way?

_____

_____

_____

_____

Importance of the College Experience Course (also known as a First-Year Seminar)

If you're reading this book, you are already beginning to take charge of your college experience because you're likely to be enrolled in a course that's designed to promote your college success. Research strongly indicates that new students who participate in first-year experience courses are more likely to continue in college until they complete their degree and perform at a higher level. These positive effects have been found for:

- All types of students (under-prepared and well-prepared, minority and majority, residential and commuter, male and female),
- Students at all types of colleges (two-year and four-year, public and private),
- Students attending colleges of all sizes (small, mid-sized, and large), and
- Students attending college in all locations (urban, suburban, and rural).

(Sources: Barefoot, et al., 1998; Boudreau & Kromrey, 1994; Cuseo, 2011; Cuseo & Barefoot, 1996; Fidler & Godwin, 1994; Glass & Garrett, 1995; Grunder & Hellmich, 1996; Hunter & Linder, 2005; Porter & Swing, 2006; Shanley & Witten, 1990; Sidle & McReynolds, 1999; Starke, Harth, & Sirianni, 2001; Thomson, 1998; Tobolowsky, 2005).

There has been more research on the first-year experience course and more evidence supporting its positive impact on student success than any other course in the college curriculum. Give this course your best effort and take full advantage of what it has to offer. If you do, you'll take an important first step toward excelling in college and in life beyond college.

Enjoy the trip!

"Being in this class has helped me a lot. What I learned I will apply to all my other classes."

"I feel like I have so much to take away from this class and will continue to keep it with me the rest of my college career."

"This course will be a hard act to follow. This is one of the most valuable classes I will ever take."
—Comments made by students when evaluating their first-year experience course

Student Perspective

"This is a class where even if you know the answers you can still learn something new provided you show up."
—NICC Fall 2014 student evaluating her College Experience Course

Introduction Reflection

After reading the Introduction, how do you think this course will benefit you?

List and briefly describe three things you hope to learn or accomplish as a result of success-fully completing this course.

References

American Association of Community Colleges. (2014). FACT SHEET. Washington, DC: Author.

American College Testing (2015). *College student retention and graduation rates from 2000 through 2015*. Retrieved from http://www.act.org/research/policymakers/pdf/retain_2015.pdf.

Andres, L., & Wyn, J. (2010). *The making of a generation: The children of the 1970s in adulthood*. Buffalo, NY: University of Toronto Press.

Astin, A. W. (1993). *What matters in college?* San Francisco: Jossey-Bass.

Barefoot, B. O., Warnock, C. L., Dickinson, M. P., Richardson, S. E., & Roberts, M. R. (Eds.). (1998). *Exploring the evidence: Vol. 2. Reporting outcomes of first-year seminars* (Monograph No. 29). Columbia: National Resource Center for the First-Year Experience and Students in Transition, University of South Carolina.

Bartlett, T. (2002). Freshman pay, mentally and physically, as they adjust to college life. *Chronicle of Higher Education, 48*, 35–37.

Baum, S., Ma, J., & Payea, K. (2013). *Education pays 2013: The benefits of higher education for individuals and society*. Washington DC: The College Board. Retrieved from http://trends.collegeboard.org/sites/default/files/education-pays-2013-full-report-022714.pdf.

Boudreau, C., & Kromrey, J. (1994). A longitudinal study of the retention and academic performance of participants in a freshman orientation course. *Journal of College Student Development, 35*, 444–449.

Bowen, H. R. (1977). *Investment in learning: The individual and social value of American higher education*. San Francisco: Jossey-Bass.

Bowen, H. R. (1997). *Investment in learning: The individual and social value of American higher education* (2nd ed.). Baltimore: Johns Hopkins Press.

Carnevale, A. P., Strohl, J., & Melton, M. (2011). *What's in worth? The economic value of college majors*. Washington DC: Center on Education and the Workforce, Georgetown University. Retrieved from http:cew.georgetown.edu/whatsitworth/

Chaskes, J. (1996). The first-year student as immigrant. *Journal of The Freshman Year Experience & Students in Transition, 8*(1), 79–91.

Chickering, A. W., & Schlossberg, N. K. (1998). Moving on: Seniors as people in transition. In J. N. Gardner, G. Van der Veer, et al. (Eds.), *The senior year experience* (pp. 37–50). San Francisco: Jossey-Bass.

Cohen, A, M., Brawer, F. B., & Kisker, C. B. (2014). *The American Community College*. San Francisco: Jossey-Bass.

Cuseo, J. B., & Barefoot, B. O. (1996). A natural marriage: The extended orientation seminar and the community college. In J. Henkin (Ed.), *The community college: Opportunity and access for America's first-year students* (pp. 59–68). Columbia: National Resource Center for the First-Year Experience and Students in Transition, University of South Carolina.

Dee, T. (2004). Are there civic returns to education? *Journal of Public Economics, 88*, 1697–1720.

Desrochers, D. M., Lenihan, C. M., & Wellman, J. V. (2010). *Trends in college spending 1998-2008: Where does the money come from? Where does it go? What does it buy?* Washington, DC: Delta Project on Postsecondary Education Costs, Productivity, and Accountability.

Feldman, K. A., & Newcomb, T. M. (1994). *The impact of College on students*. New Brunswick: Transaction Publishers.

Fidler, P., & Godwin, M. (1994). Retaining African-American students through the freshman seminar. *Journal of Developmental Education, 17*, 34–41.

Flowers, L., Osterlind, S., Pascarella, E., & Pierson, C. (2001). How much do students learn in college? Cross-sectional estimates using the College Basic Academic Subjects Examination. *Journal of Higher Education, 72*, 565–583.

Gagliardi, J. & Hiemstra, H. (2013). *College still pays*. Kentucky Postsecondary Education Policy Brief. Retrieved from http://cpe.ky.gov/NR/rdonlyres/8DE2CF1E-51A2-4C27-8C2B-41FB126252FE/0/CollegeStillPayspolicybrief.pdf.

Ganzglass, E. (2014). Scaling "stackable credentials": Implications for implementation and policy. Center for Postsecondary and Economic Success. Retrieved from http://www.clasp.org/resources-and-publications/files/2014-03-21-Stackable-Credentials-Paper-FINAL.pdf

Glass, J., & Garrett, M. (1995). Student participation in a college orientation course: Retention, and grade point average. *Community College Journal of Research and Practice, 19*, 117–132.

Grunder, P., & Hellmich, D. (1996). Academic persistence and achievement of remedial students in a community college's success program. *Community College Review, 24*, 21–33.

Hamilton, W. (2011, December 29). "College still worth it, study says." *Los Angeles Times*, p. B2.

Hamilton, W. (2014, June 25). "College still good bet, study says." *Los Angeles Times*, p. B4.

HERI (Higher Education Research Institute) (2014). *Your first college year survey 2014*. Los Angeles, CA: Cooperative Institutional Research Program, University of California-Los Angeles.

Hunter, M. A., & Linder, C. W. (2005). First-year seminars. In M. L. Upcraft, J. N. Gardner, B. O. Barefoot, et al. (Eds.), *Challenging and supporting the first-year student: A handbook for improving the first year of college* (pp. 275–291). San Francisco: Jossey-Bass.

Knox, W. E., Lindsay, P., & Kolb, M. N. (1993). Does college make a difference? Long-term changes in activities and attitudes. Westport, CT: Greenwood.

Light, R. J. (2001). *Making the most of college: Students speak their minds*. Cambridge, MA: Harvard University Press.

Lumina Foundation (2013). *A stronger nation through higher education*. Indianapolis IN: Author. Retrieved from http://www.pesc.org/library/docs/about_us/whitepapers/a-stronger-nation-2013lumina.pdf.

Lumina Foundation (2015). *A stronger nation through higher education*. Indianapolis IN: Author. Retrieved from http://www.luminafoundation.org/files/publications/A_stronger_nation_through_higher_education-2015.pdf.

Mullin, C., & Phillippe, K. (2013). *Community college contributions* (No. AACC Policy Brief 2013-01PB). American Association of Community Colleges. Retrieved from http://www.aacc.nche.edu/Publications/Briefs/Documents/2013PB_01.pdf.

Pascarella, E., & Terenzini, P. (2005). *How college affects students: A third decade of research* (Vol. 2). San Francisco: Jossey-Bass.

Pew Research Center (2014, February). *The rising cost of not going to college*. Retrieved from http://www.pewsocialtrends.org/2014/02/11/the-rising-cost-of-not-going-to-college/.

Porter, S. R., & Swing, R. L. (2006). Understanding how first-year seminars affect persistence. *Research in Higher Education, 47*(1), 89–109.

Sax, L. J., Bryant, A. N., & Gilmartin, S. K. (2004). A longitudinal investigation of emotional health among male and female first-year college students. *Journal of the First-Year Experience, 16*, 39–65.

Schilling, K. (2001, August). *Plenary address*. Presented at The Summer Institute on First-Year Assessment, Asheville, North Carolina.

Seifert, T. A., Goodman, K. M., Lindsay, N., Jorgensen, J. D., Wolniak, G. C., Pascarella, E. T., & Blaich, C. (2008). The effects of liberal arts experiences on liberal arts outcomes. *Research in Higher Education, 49*, 107–125.

Shanley, M., & Witten, C. (1990). University 101 freshman seminar course: A longitudinal study of persistence, retention, and graduation rates. *NASPA Journal, 27*, 344–352.

SHEEO (State Higher Education Executive Officers) (2012). *State higher education finance, FY 2011*. Retrieved from http://www.sheeo.org/sites/default/files/publications/SHEF_FY11.pdf.

Sidle, M., & McReynolds, J. (1999). The freshman year experience: Student retention and student success. *NASPA Journal, 36*, 288–300.

Starke, M. C., Harth, M., & Sirianni, F. (2001). Retention, bonding, and academic achievement: Success of a first-year seminar. *Journal of the First-Year Experience and Students in Transition, 13*(2), 7–35.

The Hamilton Project (2014). *Major decisions: What graduates earn over their lifetimes*. Washington, DC: Brookings Institution. Retrieved from http://www.hamiltonproject.org/papers/major_decisions_what_graduates_earn_over_their_lifetimes/

Thomson, R. (1998). University of Vermont. In B. O. Barefoot, C. L. Warnock, M. P. Dickinson, S. E. Richardson, & M. R. Roberts (Eds.). (1998). *Exploring the evidence: Vol. 2. Reporting outcomes of first-year seminars* (Monograph No. 29, pp. 77–78). Columbia: National Resource Center for the First-Year Experience and Students in Transition, University of South Carolina.

Tinto, V. (2012). *Completing college: Rethinking institutional action*. Chicago: The University of Chicago Press.

Tobolowsky, B. F. (2005). *The 2003 national survey on first-year seminars: Continuing innovations in the college curriculum* (Monograph No. 41). Columbia, SC: University of South Carolina, National Resource Center for the First-Year Experience and Students in Transition.

Tomsho, R. (2009, April 22). Study tallies education's gap on GDP. Wall Street Journal. Retrieved from http://www.wsj.com/articles/SB124040633530943487

Topper, A. M., & Powers, J. M. (2013). Democracy's college: The american community college in the 21st century: Framing the issue. *Educational Policy Analysis Archives, 21*(14), 1–12.

U.S. Bureau of Labor Statistics (2015). *Employment projections*. United States of Department of Labor. Retrieved from http://www.bls.gov/emp/ep_chart_001.htm.

College Knowledge

EFFECTIVE COLLEGE BEHAVIOR IN CLASS AND ONLINE

This chapter identifies top tips for academic success you can implement immediately, including what to do inside and outside the classroom. It also alerts you to in-class and out-of-class behavior that should be avoided in college.

Chapter Preview

Equip you with key academic strategies for getting off to a good start in college, and increase your awareness of behaviors that reflect academic incivility and lack of academic integrity.

Learning Goal

 Think About It—Journal Entry 1.1

Thought Starter

1. In what three major ways do you think college will differ from high school? If you have been out of high school for a while and are just now returning to school, what are the biggest changes you see?

2. What three personal characteristics, qualities, or strategies do you think will be most important for college success?

Box 1.1

Birds of a Different Feather: High School vs. College

High School	*College*
Your classes are mostly arranged for you.	You arrange your own schedule in consultation with your advisor. Schedules tend to look lighter than they really are.
Your time is structured by others.	You manage your own time.
You go from one class directly to another, spending six hours per day—30 hours per week—in class.	You have free time between classes; class times vary throughout the day and evening; and you spend 12–16 hours each week in class if you are a full-time student.
The school year is 36 weeks long; some classes extend over both semesters, and some do not.	The academic year may be divided into separate semesters or quarters.
Teachers monitor class attendance.	Professors may not formally monitor class attendance; you're expected to have the self-discipline to show up and get down information that's presented in class.
Teachers often write information on the board for you to put in your notes.	Professors may lecture nonstop, expecting you to identify and write down important information in your notes. Professors don't record all their key points on the board. Notes that professors write on the board are used to supplement or complement the lecture, not to summarize for the lecture.
Teachers provide you with information you missed when you were absent.	Professors expect you to get information you missed from classmates.
You are given short reading assignments that are then discussed, and often reviewed, in class.	You're assigned substantial amounts of reading and writing that may not be directly addressed in class.
You seldom need to read anything more than once and sometimes listening in class is enough.	You need to review class notes and read material regularly.
Teachers present material to help you understand the textbook.	Professors may not follow the textbook, but you may be expected to relate class sessions to textbook readings.
You may have studied outside of class for zero to two hours per week.	You need to study for at least two to three hours outside of class for each hour spent in class.
Teachers remind you of assignments and due dates.	Professors expect you to consult the course syllabus for assignments and deadlines.

Source: Southern Methodist University (2006).

College teachers don't tell you what you're supposed to do. They just expect you to do it. High school teachers tell you about five times what you're supposed to do."
—*College sophomore (Appleby, 2008)*

If you have been out of school for a while, consider what has changed in your life since high school. You probably have more and different responsibilities now (e.g., a mortgage, children, etc.). Reflect on how you will manage these responsibilities with your college work (Chapter 4 on time management will give you some strategies). You will also notice the classroom environment has changed quite a bit over the years. You will rely on technology much more to assist with your education than you did years ago. If you need help with your technology skills, see if your school offers a basic technology course or has a technology help desk. You might also want to ask some of your more tech savvy classmates for some technology tips.

Think About It—Journal Entry 1.2

Look back at the differences between high school and college listed in **Box 1.1**.

Which differences were you least aware or were most surprised to see?

_____

_____

_____

_____

_____

_____

Why?

_____

_____

_____

_____

_____

_____

Top Tips for Academic Success

1. Read the course syllabus carefully when you first receive it and refer to it throughout the term. (See **Box 1.2** for details and strategies.)

Box 1.2

Reading and Understanding a Syllabus

What's in a syllabus? A course syllabus is a document created by instructors that will probably be given to you on the first day of class. The syllabus has been called a contract between the student and the instructor. Please pay careful attention to all parts of the syllabus and make a copy to keep with you at all times. You are responsible for adhering to this contract. However, your instructor can change the syllabus as he/she deems necessary. A syllabus usually contains the following components (not necessarily in this order):

1. Course department, prefix, number, title, credit hours, semester and year, and course reference number.
2. Meeting times and location, instructor information (name, office location, office hours, contact information).
3. Catalog course description, including prerequisites and/or corequisites (courses students need to have taken before this one or at the same time); prerequisite skill sets (e.g., programming languages, familiarity with software).
4. Text(s) with dates, supplemental text(s), other required readings, and references readings (books, reserve readings, course readers, software, and supplies with information about where they can be obtained). You are expected to have these on the first day or soon after the first day.
5. Student learning outcomes and/or course objectives (this is what the instructor is telling you that he or she will work the lectures around, and you will have learning opportunities around them throughout the course). The tests, quizzes, papers, etc., are based on these objectives.
6. Skills and knowledge students will gain. These are the new items you will have learned after the course is completed. You may hear these referred to as competencies.
7. Course organization. This tells you step-by-step how this course will be taught.
8. Explanation of the topical organization of the course. This will give you an idea of the specific topics that will be covered in class.
9. Course requirements (what students will have to do in the course: assignments, exams, projects, performances, attendance, participation, etc.). Usually the nature and format of assignments and the expected length of written work, as well as due dates for assignments and dates for exams, will be explained.
10. Evaluation and grading policy: what grades are based on, especially your final grade. Always keep up on what grade you have in class and discuss how to improve it with the instructor on a regular basis.
11. Course policies and expectations: may include policies on attendance, participation, tardiness, academic integrity, missing homework, missed exams, recording classroom activities, food in class, laptop use, cell phone use, etc.
12. Other expectations such as student behavior (e.g., respectful consideration of one another's perspectives, open-mindedness, creative risk-taking).
13. Course calendar/schedule (sometimes the instructor will put "tentative" before these words, letting you know it is subject to change). However, this is a class-to-class breakdown of topics and assignments (readings, homework, project due dates).

As a college student, you are responsible for knowing the contents of the course syllabus. It is not the instructor's responsibility to go over it with you. Be sure you read and understand your syllabi for all your courses. If you have any questions, be sure to ask your instructor right away.

My biggest recommendation: GO TO CLASS. I learned this the hard way my first semester. You'll be surprised what you pick up just by being there. I wish someone would have informed me of this before I started school."

—Advice to new students from a college sophomore (Walsh, 2005)

2. **Don't miss class.** Not surprisingly, the total amount of time you spend on learning is associated with how much you learn and how deeply you learn. This association leads to a straightforward recommendation: Attend all your classes in all your courses. It may be tempting to skip or cut classes because college professors are less likely to monitor your attendance or take roll than high school teachers. However, don't let this new freedom fool you into thinking that missing classes will not affect your course grades. Over the past 75 years, numerous studies have shown a direct relationship between class attendance and course grades—as one goes up or down, so does the other (Credé, Roch, Kieszczynka, 2010; Launius, 1997; Shimoff & Catania, 2001; Tagliacollo, Vol-

pato, & Pereira, 2010). **Figure 1.1** depicts the results of a study conducted at the City Colleges of Chicago, which shows the relationship between students' class attendance during the first five weeks of the term and their final course grades.

Note

Look at going to class like going to work. If you miss work days, it lowers your pay; if you miss classes, it lowers your grades.

3. **Adopt a seating location in class that maximizes attention and minimizes distraction.** Many years of research show that students who sit in the front and center of class tend to earn higher test scores and course grades (Benedict & Hoag, 2004; Rennels & Chaudhair, 1988; Tagliacollo, Volpato, & Pereira, 2010). These results have been found even when students are assigned seats by their instructor, so it's not just a matter of more motivated and studious students sitting in the front of the room. Instead, the better academic performance achieved by students sitting front and center stems from learning advantages associated with this seating location.

FIGURE 1.1: **Percentage of Classes Attended and Final Course Grades**

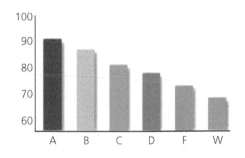

City Colleges of Chicago

Front-and-center seating benefits your academic performance by improving your vision of material written on the board or screen and your ability to hear the instructor's lectures. In addition, sitting in the front means you don't have to peer over or around the heads of other students. This results in more direct eye contact with the instructor, which increases your focus of attention, reduces your sense of anonymity, and increases your level of involvement in class.

Lastly, sitting in the front of class can also reduce your level of anxiety about speaking in class because you will not have numerous classmates sitting in front of you turning around to look at you when you speak.

The *bottom line:* When you enter a classroom, get in the habit of heading for a seat in the front and center of class. In large classes, it's even more important to get to know your instructors—not only to improve your attention, note taking, and class participation—but also to improve your instructors' ability to remember who you are and how well you performed in class. This will work to your advantage when you ask your instructors for letters of recommendation later in your college career.

> Eighty percent of success is showing up."
>
> *—Woody Allen, Oscar & Golden Globe winning film director, writer, and author*

> I like to sit up front so I am not distracted by others and I don't have to look around people's heads to see the chalkboard."
>
> *—First-year college student*

> I tend to sit at the very front of my classrooms. It helps me focus and take notes better. It also eliminates distractions."
>
> *—First-year college student*

4. **Sit by people who will enable (not disable) your ability to listen and learn.** Intentionally sit near classmates who will not distract you or interfere with the quality of your note taking. The human attention span has a limited capacity; we can give all or part of our attention to whatever task we're performing. Actively listening to and taking notes on lecture information is a demanding task that demands undivided attention.

Note

When you enter class, you have a choice about where you're going to sit. Choose wisely by selecting a location that will maximize your attentiveness to the instructor and your effectiveness as a note-taker.

Think About It—Journal Entry 1.3

When you enter a classroom, where do you usually sit?

_____

_____

Why do you sit there? Is it a conscious choice or more like an automatic habit?

_____

_____

_____

Do you think that the seat you usually choose places you in the best possible position for listening and learning in the classroom? Why or why not?

_____

_____

_____

_____

5. **Adopt a seating posture that screams attention.** Sitting upright and leaning forward increases attention because these signs of physical alertness reach the brain and stimulate mental alertness. If your body is in an alert and ready position, your mind picks up these physical cues and follows your body's lead. Baseball players get into a ready position before a pitch is delivered to ready themselves to catch batted balls; similarly, learners who assume a ready position in the classroom put themselves in a better position to catch ideas batted around in class. Studies show that when humans are mentally alert and ready to learn, a greater amount of C-kinase (a brain chemical) is released at the connection point between brain cells, which increases the likelihood that neurological (learning) connections are formed between them (Howard, 2014).

Another advantage to being attentive in class is that it sends a clear message to your instructor that you're a courteous and conscientious student. This can influence your instructor's perception and evaluation of your academic performance; if at the end of the course you're on the border between a higher and lower grade, you're more likely to get the benefit of the doubt.

6. **Be a self-aware learner.** One characteristic of successful learners is that they self-monitor (check themselves) while learning to remain aware of:

   - Whether they're using effective learning strategies (e.g., if they're giving their undivided attention to what they're learning)
   - Whether they're truly comprehending what they are learning (e.g., if they're understanding it at a deep level or memorizing it at a surface level)
   - How they're regulating or adjusting their learning strategies to meet the demands of different academic tasks and subjects (e.g., if they're reading technical material in a science textbook, they read at a slower rate and check their understanding more frequently than when reading a novel) (Pintrich & Schunk, 2002).

   You can begin to establish good self-monitoring habits by getting in the routine of periodically pausing to reflect on the strategies you're using to learn and how you "do" college. For instance, you can ask yourself the following questions:

   - Am I listening attentively to what my instructor is saying in class?
   - Am I comprehending what I'm reading outside of class?
   - Am I effectively using campus resources designed to support my success?
   - Am I interacting with campus professionals who can contribute to my current success and future development?
   - Am I interacting and collaborating with peers who can support (not sabotage) my learning and development?
   - Am I effectively implementing college success strategies (such as those identified in this book)?

> We learn neither by thinking nor by doing; we learn by thinking about what we are doing."
>
> *—George Stoddard, Professor Emeritus, University of Iowa*

Note

Successful students and successful people are mindful—they watch what they're doing and remain aware of whether they're doing it effectively and to the best of their ability.

 Think About It—Journal Entry 1.4

How would you rate your academic self-confidence at this point in your college experience? (Circle one.)

very confident   somewhat confident   somewhat unconfident   very unconfident

Why?

The Importance of Time Spent on Coursework outside of Class

In college, you will spend much less time sitting in class than you did in high school; however, you will be expected to spend much more time working on your courses outside of class. Less than 40% of beginning college students report having studied six or more hours per week during their final year in high school (Pryor, et al., 2012) and only one-third expect to spend more than 20 hours per week preparing for class in college (National Survey of Student Engagement, 2009).

Unfortunately, less than 10% of beginning college students say they will study at least two hours out of class for every hour spent in class—which is what most college faculty believe is necessary to do well in college (Kuh, 2005). This has to change if college students are to earn good grades. Just as successful athletes need to put in time and effort to improve their physical performance, successful students need to do the same to improve their academic performance. Studies repeatedly show that the more time college students spend on academic work outside of class, the higher grades they earn in their college courses (National Survey of Student Engagement, 2009). In one study of more than 25,000 college students it was found that the percentage of students receiving "A" grades was almost three times higher for students who spent 40 or more hours per week on academic work than it was for students who spent between 20 and 40 hours. For students who spent 20 or fewer hours per week on academic work, the percentage of them receiving a grade of "C" or below was almost twice as high as it was for students who spent 40 or more hours on academic work (Pace, 1990, 1995).

If you need further motivation to achieve good grades, keep in mind that higher grades earned in college translates into career success after college. Research on college graduates indicates that the higher their grades were in college, the higher is: (a) their starting salary, (b) the status (prestige) of their first job, and (c) their career mobility (ability to change jobs or move into different positions). This relationship between higher college grades and greater career advantages exists for students at all types of colleges and universities—regardless of the reputation or prestige of the institution the students attended (Pascarella & Terenzini, 1991, 2005). In other words, how well students do in college matters more to their career success than where they went to college.

> "I thought I would get a better education if the school had a really good reputation. Now, I think one's education depends on how much effort you put into it."
>
> —First-year college student

 Think About It—Journal Entry 1.5

During your senior year in high school, about how many hours per week did you spend on schoolwork outside of class? What do you think you'll have to do differently in college?

AUTHOR'S EXPERIENCE

When I went to college, I had to work to assist my family and to assist in paying for college. Although I was an 18-year-old, I came from a very poor family and it was part of my obligation to assist them financially, while it was more important to me to go to school and graduate so I could have a higher standard of living in comparison to my mother and father. Juggling my work life and school life quickly became a reality to which I had to adjust. Thus, I made sure I made the time to study and attend class as my first priority and worked with my employer to adjust my work hours around my classes. By placing my future above my immediate present, I was able to get my college degree and increase my earnings substantially beyond the earnings I had in college and way beyond my parents' earnings.

—Aaron Thompson

Effective Classroom Behavior: The Fundamentals

In college, there will be expectations regarding appropriate behavior inside and outside the classroom. These expectations will vary, depending on the type of course you're taking—traditional face-to-face, online, technology-enhanced, or hybrid. With a few exceptions (e.g., you can wear pajamas while participating in an online course at home), the following expectations apply to all college courses.

Regardless of the type of course you take, you will be expected to know basic computer skills such as how to save, download, and send documents, etc. If you have minimal computer skills refer to the Learn Free Basic Computer Skills website (http://www.gcflearnfree.org/basic-computer-skills) for helpful information.

1. **Avoid inappropriate and "uncivil" classroom behavior.** The following behaviors indicate to the instructor and to your classmates that you're an unmotivated student. In addition, they create a classroom climate that disturbs or disrupts the learning process. Be sure not to engage in any of them.
   - Coming to class late and/or leaving early
   - Walking in and out of the classroom during class
   - Talking with classmates while the instructor (or other classmates) is speaking
   - Disregarding deadlines set by your instructor
   - Using electronic devices for personal purposes
   - Acting disinterested in class (e.g., looking at the window or putting your head on your desk)
   - Doing homework during class time
   - Sleeping in class
   - Using electronic devices. (See **Box 1.3**)

Box 1.3

Guidelines for Civil and Responsible Use of Personal Technology in the College Classroom

Behavior that interferes with the right of others to learn or teach in the classroom is referred to as *classroom incivility*. Listed below are forms of classroom incivility that involve student use of personal technology. Be sure to avoid them.

Using Cell Phones

Keeping a cell phone on in class is a clear form of classroom incivility because it can interfere with the right of others to learn. In a study of college students who heard a cell phone ringing during class and were later tested on information presented in class, they scored approximately 25% lower for information that was presented at the time a cell phone rang. This drop in performance was found

(continued)

Box 1.3 *(continued)*

even if the material was covered by the professor just prior to the cell phone ringing and if it was projected on a slide while the phone rang. The study also showed that students' attention to information presented in class is significantly reduced when classmates frantically search through handbags or pockets to find and silence a ringing (or vibrating) phone (Shelton, et al., 2009). These findings clearly suggest that cell phone use in class disrupts the learning process and the civil thing to do is:

The right to do something does not mean that doing it is right."

—*William Safire, American author, journalist, and presidential speech writer*

- Turn your cell phone off before entering class, or keep it out of the classroom altogether. (You can use *studiousapp.com* to automatically silence your phone at times of the day when you're in class.) In rare cases where you may need to leave class to respond to an emergency, ask your instructor for permission in advance.
- Don't check your cell phone during the class period by turning it off and on.

- Don't look at your cell phone at any time during a test because your instructor may suspect that you're looking up answers to test questions.

Text Messaging

Although this form of electronic communication is silent, it still can distract or disturb your classmates. It's also discourteous or disrespectful to instructors when you put head down and turn your attention away from them while they're speaking in class. The bottom line: Be sensitive to your classmates and your instructor—don't text in class!

Surfing the Web

Although this can be done without creating distracting sounds, it still can still create visual distractions. Unless you're taking class notes on it, keep your laptop closed to avoid distracting your classmates and raising your instructors' suspicion that you're a disinterested or disrespectful student.

Final Note: In addition to technological incivilities, other discourteous classroom behaviors include personal grooming, holding side conversations, and doing home-work for other classes. Even if your attendance is perfect, "little things" you do in class that reflect inattention or disinterest can send a strong message to your instructors that you're an unmotivated and discourteous student.

 Think About It—Journal Entry 1.6

Have you observed any recent examples of classroom incivility that you thought were particularly distracting or discourteous? What was the uncivil behavior and what consequences did it have on others?

Technology should be used sensitively and civilly not only inside the classroom, but outside the classroom as well. There are common rules of courtesy for Internet use (referred to as "netiquette") that should be used in social media. These rules are summarized in **Box 1.4**.

Box 1.4

Top 20 Rules to Follow for Appropriate Netiquette

1. The Internet is not private. What goes out on the airwaves stays on the airwaves! Do not post pictures to the Internet that you would not want your mom or younger cousin to see.
2. Avoid saying anything that could be interpreted as derogatory (e.g., no cursing).
3. Do not say harsh or mean things to someone over e-mail or text (this could be considered cyber bullying) and do not post nasty, mean, or insulting items about someone.
4. Do not respond to nasty e-mails sent to you.
5. Do not break up with a significant other via text or e-mail.
6. When you receive an e-mail that says to forward it to everyone you know, please don't.
7. Do not use ALL CAPITALS. IT IMPLIES YOU ARE SHOUTING!!!
8. When you send messages online, make sure you proofread and correct mistakes before sending.
9. Do not forward other people's e-mails without their permission.
10. Do not forward virus warnings. They are generally hoaxes.
11. Ask before you send huge attachments.
12. Keep your communications short and to the point.
13. Do not leave the subject field blank in e-mails.
14. Avoid posting personal messages to a listserv.
15. Avoid using texting language for e-mails or social media sites (use correct spellings and correct language mechanics).
16. Remember to treat others online as you would like to be treated.
17. Use the Internet in ways that do not take away from your learning, but add to it.
18. Allow an appropriate amount of time for a person to respond to a message (24–48 business hours).
19. Be sure to have an appropriate salutation (i.e., *good morning, hello*) and closing (i.e., *goodbye, see you tomorrow*, etc.) in your e-mails.
20. Avoid slang (i.e., *wha's up, yo*, etc.) and acronyms (*btw, lol*, etc.)

Also, be sure your communication with your instructor, both in and out of the classroom is appropriate, particularly when e-mailing your instructor. E-mailing and text messaging are very different forms of communication. Texting is very informal. E-mail, especially to an instructor, etc. is considered a professional form of communication. Be sure to treat it that way. First, be sure to send the e-mail from your school e-mail address. Other e-mails often go to spam or junk folders. Do not leave the subject line blank and be sure the subject pertains to your e-mail. Address your instructor appropriately. State your question or concern (be aware of your tone). Avoid all slang and close your e-mail appropriately. Appropriate response time for an e-mail is 24 business hours. Give your instructor enough time to respond to your e-mail and do not inundate their inbox with multiple e-mails about the same issue. See box below for an example of an appropriate e-mail to an instructor and one that could use some work.

How to E-mail (or not) your Instructor

An example of what not to do:

To: instructor@communitycollege.edu

From: pimpdaddy@bade-mail.com

Subject: WHATEVER!

Yo teach! Wha's up?
I know you did not give me an F on that test!!!! WTH!?!? I studied all night for that and I know I should not have failed. Tell me how you are gonna fix this cuz I gotta pass your class.

Peace!

An example of an appropriate e-mail:

To: instructor@communitycollege.edu

From: concernedstudent@communitycollege.edu

Subject: My test grade

Good morning instructor (name),
I am concerned about my grade on the last test. I got an F and I don't know what I did wrong. I studied all night for that test! Can I meet with you to discuss some strategies about how I might do better on the next test? I really want to pass this class.

Please let me know when you are available to meet. I appreciate your time.

Sincerely,

Concerned Student

It is important to pay attention to your behavior on social media (i.e. Facebook, Instagram, Twitter, etc.) as well. Once you post something on the Internet it is always out "in the cloud." Even when you delete a post, highly skilled people can find it. Coaches, potential employers, graduate schools, etc. are taking a closer look at social media profiles to aid in their decision making process. Just as you think before you speak, you should think before you post. Refrain from posting anything illegal, rude, disrespectful, or in poor taste. Also be sure to refrain from cyberbullying. People tend to be much more brave when they can hide behind a computer. Don't post anything online that you would not say in person. All of these things could affect your future in far more ways than you realize.

2. Avoid plagiarism. Plagiarism is a violation of academic integrity that involves intentional or unintentional use of someone else's work without acknowledging it, which gives the reader the impression that it's your own work. Listed below are common forms of plagiarism.
   - Paying someone, or paying a service, for a paper and turning it in as your own work.
   - Submitting an entire paper, or portion thereof, that was written by someone else.
   - Copying sections of someone else's work and inserting it into your own work.

- Cutting paragraphs from separate sources and pasting them into the body of your own paper.
- Paraphrasing or rewording someone else's words or ideas without citing that person as a source. (Good strategies for paraphrasing without plagiarizing may be found at: http://www.upenn.edu/academicintegrity/ai_paraphrasing.html.)
- Placing someone else's exact words in the body of your paper and not placing quotation marks around them.
- Failing to cite the source of factual information in your paper that's not common knowledge.

Good examples of different forms of plagiarism may be found at: http://www.princeton.edu/pr/pub/integrity/pages/plagiarism/

Two other things to keep in mind:
- If you include information in your paper and just list its source in your reference (works cited) section—without citing the source in the *body* of your paper—this still qualifies as plagiarism.
- Be sure only to include sources in your reference section that you actually used and cited in the body of your paper. Although including sources in your reference section that aren't cited in your paper isn't technically a form of plagiarism, it may be viewed as being deceitful because you're "padding" your reference section, giving the reader the impression that you incorporated more sources into your paper than you actually did.

> When a student violates an academic integrity policy no one wins, even if the person gets away with it. It isn't right to cheat and it is an insult to everyone who put the effort in and did the work, and it cheapens the school for everyone. I learned my lesson and have no intention of ever cheating again."
> —First-year student's reflection on an academic integrity violation.

> I understood what I did was morally wrong and now I have to overcome it and move on living morally and ethically. It's really amazing that integrity is in everything we do in our lives."
> —First-year student's reflection on an academic integrity violation

 ## Think About It—Journal Entry 1.7

Reflect back at the different forms of plagiarism just described. Were there any you were surprised to see, or didn't realize were plagiarism?

_____

_____

_____

_____

_____

_____

Chapter Summary and Highlights

This chapter highlighted the fact that successful students understand:

1. The differences between high school and college
2. The syllabus and class policies
3. What constitutes responsible classroom behavior
4. The dos and don'ts of technology

More specifically, this chapter suggested a number of "top tips" for getting off to a good start in college. These tips are summarized below.

Read the course syllabus. Review it carefully when you first receive it, save it, and refer to it throughout the term.

Don't miss class. Attend all your classes in all your courses. Studies repeatedly show that students who go to class earn higher grades. Look at going to class like going to work. If you miss work, you get lower pay; if you cut class, you get lower grades.

Intentionally choose a seat in class that maximizes attention and minimizes distraction. When you enter class, you have a choice about where you're going to sit. Choose wisely by selecting a location that will maximize your attentiveness to the instructor and your effectiveness as a note-taker. Many years of research show that students who sit in the front and center of class tend to earn higher exam scores and course grades.

Sit by people who will enable your ability to listen and learn. Intentionally sit near classmates who will not distract you or interfere with the quality of your note taking.

Be a self-aware learner. Successful students and success people are *mindful*—they watch what they're doing and remain aware of whether they're doing it effectively and to the best of their ability. You can be a self-aware learning by asking yourself questions such as:

- Am I listening attentively to what my instructor is saying in class?
- Am I comprehending what I'm reading outside of class?
- Am I effectively using campus resources designed to support my success?
- Am I interacting with campus professionals who can contribute to my current success and future development?
- Am I interacting and collaborating with peers who can support (not sabotage) my learning and development?
- Am I effectively implementing college success strategies (such as those identified in this book)?

Spend at least two hours on schoolwork out of class for every hour you spend in class. This is what most college faculty believe is necessary to succeed in college.

Avoid inappropriate classroom behavior, such as the following:

- Coming to class late and/or leaving early
- Walking in and out of the classroom during class
- Talking with classmates while the instructor is speaking
- Disregarding deadlines set by your instructor
- Using electronic devices for personal purposes
- Acting disinterested in class (e.g., looking at the window or putting your head on your desk)
- Doing homework during class time
- Using electronic devices in class (e.g., texting or surfing the web)

Avoid plagiarism. Plagiarism is a violation of academic integrity that involves intentional or unintentional use of someone else's work without acknowledging it, which gives the reader the impression that it's your own work. Common forms of plagiarism include:

- Paying someone, or paying a service, for a paper and turning it in as your own work.
- Submitting an entire paper, or portion thereof, that was written by someone else.
- Copying sections of someone else's work and inserting it into your own work.
- Cutting paragraphs from separate sources and pasting them into the body of your own paper.
- Paraphrasing or rewording someone else's words or ideas without citing that person as a source. (Good strategies for paraphrasing without plagiarizing may be found at: http://www.upenn.edu/academicintegrity/ai_paraphrasing.html.)
- Placing someone else's exact words in the body of your paper and not placing quotation marks around them.
- Failing to cite the source of factual information in your paper that's not common knowledge.

Learning More through the World Wide Web: Internet-Based Resources

For additional information on strategies for college success, see the following websites:

Using the College Syllabus
http://www.mycollegesuccessstory.com/academic-success-tools/course-syllabus.html

Classroom Etiquette & Civility
http://college.usatoday.com/2012/12/07/5-rules-for-college-classroom-etiquette/

Academic Integrity:
http://www.calea.org/calea-update-magazine/issue-100who-s-watching-character-and-integrity-21st-century

References

Appleby, D. C. (2008, June). *Diagnosing and treating the deadly 13th grade syndrome*. Paper presented at the Association of Psychological Science Convention, Chicago, IL.

Benedict, M. E., & Hoag, J. (2004). Seating location in large lectures: Are seating preferences or location related to course performance? *Journal of Economics Education, 35,* 215–231.

Credé, M., Roch, S. G., & Kieszczynka, U. M. (2010). Class attendance in college: A meta-analytic review of the relationship of class attendance with grades and student characteristics. *Review of Educational Research, 80*(2), 272–295.

Howard, P. J. (2014). *The owner's manual for the brain: Everyday applications of mind-brain research* (4th ed.). New York: HarperCollins.

Kuh, G. D. (2005). Student engagement in the first year of college. In M. L. Upcraft, J. N. Gardner, B. O. Barefoot, & Associates, *Challenging and supporting the first-year student: A handbook for improving the first year of college* (pp. 86–107). San Francisco: Jossey-Bass.

Launius, M. H. (1997). College student attendance: Attitudes and academic performance. *College Student Journal, 31*(1), 86–93.

National Survey of Student Engagement. (2009). *NSSE Annual Results 2009. Assessment for improvement: Tracking student engagement over time.* Bloomington, IN: Author.

Pace, C. (1990). *The undergraduates: A report of their activities.* Los Angeles: University of California, Center for the Study of Evaluation.

Pace, C. (1995, May). *From good processes to good products: Relating good practices in undergraduate education to student achievement.* Paper presented at the meeting of the Association for Institutional Research, Boston.

Pascarella, E., & Terenzini, P. (1991). *How college affects students: Findings and insights from twenty years of research.* San Francisco: Jossey-Bass.

Pascarella, E., & Terenzini, P. (2005). *How college affects students: A third decade of research* (Vol. 2). San Francisco: Jossey-Bass.

Pintrich, P. R., & Schunk, D. H. (2002). *Motivation in education: Theory, research, and applications.* Upper Saddle River, NJ: Merrill-Prentice Hall.

Pryor, J. H., De Angelo, L., Palucki-Blake, B., Hurtado, S., & Tran, S. (2012) *The American freshman: National norms fall 2011.* Los Angeles: Higher Education Research Institute, UCLA.

Rennels, M. R., & Chaudhair, R. B. (1988). Eye-contact and grade distribution. *Perceptual and Motor Skills, 67* (October), 627–632.

Shelton, J. T., Elliot, E. M., Eaves, S. D., & Exner, A. L. (2009). The distracting effects of a ringing cell phone: An investigation of the laboratory and the classroom setting. *Journal of Environmental Psychology,* (March). Retrieved from http://news-info.wustl.edu/news/page/normal/14225.html.

Shimoff, E., & Catania, C. A. (2001). Effects of recording attendance on grades in Introductory Psychology. *Teaching of Psychology, 23*(3), 19–195.

Tagliacollo, V. A., Volpato, G. L., & Pereira, A., Jr. (2010). Association of student position in classroom and school performance. *Educational Research, 1*(6), 198–201.

Walsh, K. (2005). *Suggestions from more experienced classmates.* Retrieved from http://www.uni.edu/walsh/introtips.html.

Chapter 1 Exercises

1.1 Quote Reflections

Review the sidebar quotes contained in this chapter and select two that were especially meaningful or inspirational to you.

For each quote, provide a three- to five-sentence explanation why you chose it.

1.2 Reality Bite

Crime and Punishment: Plagiarism and Its Consequences

In an article that appeared in an Ohio newspaper, titled "Plagiarism persists in classrooms," an English professor is quoted as saying: "Technology has made it easier to plagiarize because students can download papers and exchange information and papers through their computers. But technology has also made it easier to catch students who plagiarize." This professor works at a college that subscribes to a website that matches the content of students' papers with content from books and online sources. Many professors now require students to submit their papers through this website. If students are caught plagiarizing, for a first offense, they typically receive an F for the assignment or the course. A second offense can result in dismissal or expulsion from college, which has already happened to a few students.

Reflection and Discussion Questions

1. What do you suspect are their primary motives or reasons why students plagiarize from the web?

2. What would you say is a fair or just penalty for those found guilty of a first plagiarism violation? What do you think would be fair penalty for a second violation?

3. How might web-based plagiarism be minimized or prevented from happening in the first place?

1.3 Syllabus Review

Review the syllabus (course outline) for all classes you're enrolled in this term, and complete the following information for each course.

Self-Assessment Questions

1. Is the overall workload what you expected? Are your surprised by the amount of work required in any particular course(s)?

2. At this point in the term, what do you see as your most challenging or demanding course or courses? Why?

3. Do you think you can handle the total workload required by the full set of courses you're enrolled in this term?

4. What adjustments or changes do you think you'll make to your previous learning and study habits to accommodate your academic workload this term?

1.4 Is it or is it Not Plagiarism?

The following four incidents were brought to a judicial review board to determine if plagiarism had occurred and, if so, what the penalty should be. After reading each case, answer the questions listed below it.

Case 1. A student turned in an essay that included substantial material copied from a published source. The student admitted that he didn't cite the sources properly, but argued that it was because he misunderstood the directions, not because he was attempting to steal someone else's ideas.

Is this Plagiarism?

How severe is it? (Rate it on a scale from 1 = low to 5 = high)

What should the consequence or penalty be?

How could the accusation of plagiarism been avoided?

Case 2. A student turned in a paper that was identical to a paper submitted by another student for a different course.
Is this plagiarism?

How severe is it? (Rate it on a scale from 1 = low to 5 = high)

What should the consequence or penalty be?

How could the accusation of plagiarism been avoided?

Case 3. A student submitted a paper he wrote in a previous course as an extra credit paper for a current course.
Is this plagiarism?

How severe is it? (Rate it on a scale from 1 = low to 5 = high)

What should the consequence or penalty be?

How could the accusation of plagiarism been avoided?

Case 4. A student submitted a paper in an art history that contained some ideas from art critics she read about and whose ideas she agreed with. The student didn't cite the critics as sources, but claimed it wasn't plagiarism because their ideas were merely their own subjective judgments or opinions, not facts or findings; furthermore, they were opinions she agreed with.
Is this plagiarism?

How severe is it? (Rate it on a scale from 1 = low to 5 = high)

What should the consequence or penalty be?

How could the accusation of plagiarism been avoided?

1.5 Chapter 1 Reflection

List five strategies discussed in this chapter that you intend to use to achieve college success, and explain HOW you plan to put them into practice.

Making Connections: Four Steps to Your Success

USING POWERFUL PRINCIPLES OF STUDENT SUCCESS AND KEY CAMPUS RESOURCES

Chapter Preview

This chapter focuses on the "big picture": powerful principles you can implement to promote your own success and key campus resources you can use to help you succeed. It describes what these key principles and resources are, why they're effective, and how to capitalize on them.

Learning Goal

Alert you to the most powerful strategies and resources that you can use immediately to get off to a fast start in college and continually to achieve excellence throughout your college experience.

Thought Starter

 Think About It—Journal Entry 2.1

1. What excites you about starting college?

2. What concerns do you have about starting college?

Four Steps to College Success

Research points to four powerful principles of college success:

1. Active Involvement (Engagement)
2. Capitalizing on Campus Resources (Resourcefulness)
3. Interpersonal Interaction and Collaboration (Social Integration)
4. Reflection and Self-Awareness (Mindfulness)

(Sources: Astin, 1993; Kuh, et al., 2005; Light, 2001; Pascarella & Terenzini, 1991, 2005; Tinto, 1993.)

These four principles are presented in the beginning of this book because they represent the foundational basis for all success strategies discussed throughout the book.

FIGURE 2.1: The Diamond of College Success

© Kendall Hunt Publishing Company

First Step of College Success: Active Involvement (Engagement)

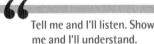

> Tell me and I'll listen. Show
> me and I'll understand.
> Involve me and I'll learn.
>
> *—Teton Lakota Indian saying*

Research indicates that active involvement may be the most powerful principle of human learning and college success (Astin, 1993; Kuh, et al., 2005). To succeed in college, you can't be a passive spectator; you need to be an active player.

Active involvement includes the following key components:

- The amount of *time* you devote to the college experience—inside and outside the classroom
- The degree of *effort or energy* (mental and physical) you invest in the learning process.

Think of something you do with intensity, passion, and commitment. If you were to approach college in the same way, you would be faithfully implementing the principle of active involvement. Here's how you can apply both key components of active involvement— time and energy—to the major learning challenges you'll face in college.

Active Involvement in the Learning Process

College success will require that you work harder (put in more time than high school) and smarter (learn more strategically and effectively). Probably the most powerful principle of effective learning is active involvement (engagement); there's simply no such thing as "passive learning." You can ensure you're actively involved in the learning process by engaging in some form of *action* on what you're learning, such as the actions listed below.

* *Writing.* For example, when reading, take notes on what you're reading rather than passively highlighting sentences.
* *Speaking.* For example, rather than studying silently, explain what you're learning to a study group partner.
* *Organizing.* For example, create an outline, diagram, or concept map that pulls together the ideas you're learning.

Active Listening and Note Taking in Class

You will find that many college professors rely heavily on the lecture method—they profess their knowledge by speaking for long stretches of time and expect students to listen and take notes on the knowledge they dispense. This method of instruction places great demands on your ability to listen actively and take notes that are both accurate and complete. Research consistently shows that most test questions on college exams come from professors' lectures and students who take better class notes get better grades (Brown, 1988; Cuseo, et al., 2013; Kiewra, 2000).

The best way to apply the principle of active involvement during a class lecture is to engage in the physical action of writing notes. Writing down what your instructor is saying in class "forces" you to pay closer attention to what is being said and reinforces your retention of what was said. By taking notes, you not only hear the information (auditory memory), you also see it on paper (visual memory) and feel it in the muscles of your hand as you write it (motor memory).

> ”
> I never had a class before where the teacher just stands up and talks to you. He says something and you're writing it down, but then he says something else."
> —*First-year college student (Erickson, Peters, and Strommer, 2006)*

Note

Your role in the college classroom is not that of a passive spectator or an absorbent sponge who sits back and soaks up information through osmosis. Instead, it's like being an aggressive detective or investigative reporter on a search-and-record mission. Your job is to actively search for information by picking your instructor's brain, picking out the instructor's key points, and recording your "pickings" in your notebook.

> ”
> All genuine learning is active, not passive. It is a process in which the student is the main agent, not the teacher."
> —*Mortimer Adler, American professor of philosophy and educational theorist*

Box 2.1 contains a summary of top strategies for classroom listening and note taking that you can put into action right now.

Box 2.1

Top Tips for Active Listening and Note Taking in the College Classroom

One task that you'll be expected to perform during the very first week of college is taking notes in class. Studies show that professors' lecture notes are the number one source of test questions (and test answers) on college exams. You can improve the quality of your note taking and your course grades by using the following strategies.

1. Get to every class. Whether or not your instructors take roll, you're responsible for all material covered in class. Remember that a full load of college courses (12 units) only requires that you be in class about 13 hours per week. If you consider your class work to be a full-time job, any job that requires you to show up for only 13 hours a week is a pretty sweet deal; it's a deal that supplies you with much more educational freedom than you had in high school. To miss classes in college when you're required to spend so little time in class per week is an abuse of this educational freedom. It's also an abuse of the money that you, your family, and taxpaying American citizens are paying to support your college education.

(continued)

Box 2.1 *(continued)*

2. **Get to every class on time.** During the first few minutes of a class session, instructors often share valuable information—such as important reminders, reviews, and previews.

3. **Get organized.** Bring the right equipment to class. Get a separate notebook for each class, write your name on it, date each class session, and store all class handouts in it.

4. **Get in the right position.**
   - The ideal place to sit in class is at the front and center of the room—where you're in the best position to hear and see what's going on.
   - The ideal posture to adopt is sitting upright and leaning forward—because your body influences your mind; if your body is in an alert and ready position, your mind is likely to follow.
   - The ideal social position to occupy in class is near motivated classmates who will not distract you, but motivate you to listen actively and take notes aggressively.

Note

These attention-focusing strategies are particularly important in large classes where you're likely to feel more anonymous, less accountable, and less engaged.

5. **Get in the right frame of mind.** Come to class with the attitude that you're there to pick your instructor's brain, pick up answers to test questions, and pick up points to elevate your course grade.

6. **Get it down (in writing).** Actively look, listen, and record important points at all times in class. Pay special attention to whatever information instructors put in writing, whether it appears on the board, on a slide, or in a handout.

7. **Don't let go of your pen (or keyboard).** When in doubt, write it out (or type it out); it's better to have it and not need it than to need it and not have it.

Note

Most college professors don't write all important information on the board for you; instead, they expect you to listen carefully and write it down yourself.

8. **Finish strong.** During the last few minutes of class, instructors often share valuable information, such as timely reminders, reviews, and previews.

9. **Stick around.** When class ends, don't bolt out of the room; instead, hang out for a few moments and quickly review your notes (by yourself or with a classmate). This quick end-of-class review will help your brain retain the information it just received. If you detect any gaps or confusing points in your notes, try to consult with your instructor immediately after class.

For more detailed ideas and strategies on listening and note taking, see Chapter 6, **p. 127.**

Finish class with a rush of attention, not a rush out the door!

Think About It—Journal Entry 2.2

When you enter a classroom, where do you usually sit?

Why do you sit there? Is it a conscious choice or more like an automatic habit?

Do you think that the seat you usually choose places you in the best possible position for listening and learning in the classroom?

Active Class Participation

You can implement the principle of active involvement in the college classroom by not only taking notes in class, but also by being an engaged participant who comes to class well prepared (e.g., having done the assigned reading), asks relevant questions, and contributes thoughtful comments during class discussions. Class participation increases your ability to stay alert and attentive in class, and it sends a clear message to your instructors that you are a motivated student who wants to learn. Class participation is also likely to account for a portion of your grade in many courses, so your attentiveness and involvement in class can have a direct, positive effect on your college grades.

Active Reading

Note-taking not only promotes active listening in class, it also promotes active reading out of class. Taking notes on what you're reading (or on information you've highlighted while reading) keeps you actively involved in the reading process because it requires more mental and physical energy than merely reading the material or passively highlighting sentences.

College professors also expect you to relate or connect what they talk about in class to the reading they've assigned. Thus, it's important to start developing good reading habits now. You can do so by using the top tips suggested in **Box 2.2**.

Box 2.2

Top Tips for Strengthening Textbook Reading Comprehension and Retention

1. Get the textbooks required for your courses as soon as possible and get your reading assignments done on time. Information from reading assignments ranks right behind lecture notes as a source of test questions on college exams. Many professors deliver their lectures with the expectation that you've done the assigned reading and assume you can build on that knowledge to understand their lectures. If you haven't done the reading, you'll have more difficulty following what your instructor is saying in class. Thus, by not doing the assigned reading you pay a double penalty: you miss information from the reading that's not covered in class which will likely appear on exams, and you miss understanding ideas presented in class that build on the reading.

I recommend that you read the first chapters right away because college professors get started promptly with assigning certain readings. Classes in college move very fast because, unlike high school, you do not attend class five times a week but two or three times a week."

—Advice to new college students from a first-year student

2. Read with the right equipment.
    - Bring a writing tool (pen, pencil, or keyboard) to record important information and a storage space (notebook or computer) in which you can save and later retrieve information acquired found in your reading for later use on tests and assignments.
    - Have a dictionary nearby to quickly find the meaning of unfamiliar words that may interfere with your ability to comprehend what you're reading. Looking up definitions of unfamiliar words helps you understand what you're reading and also builds your vocabulary. A strong vocabulary will improve your reading comprehension in all college courses, as well as your performance on standardized tests, such as those required for admission to graduate and professional schools.
    - Check the back of your textbook for a glossary (list) of key terms included in the book. Each

college subject and academic discipline has its own special language, and decoding it is often the key to understanding the concepts covered in the course. The glossary that appears at the end of your textbook is more than an ancillary add-on, it's a valuable tool that you can use to improve your comprehension of course concepts. Consider making a photocopy of the glossary at the back of your textbook so you can access it easily while you're reading—without having to repeatedly stop, hold your place, and go to the back of the text to find it.

3. Get in the right position. Sit upright and have light coming from behind you, over the side of your body opposite your writing hand. This will reduce the distracting and fatiguing effects of glare and shadows.

4. Get a sneak preview. Approach the chapter by first reading its boldface headings and any chapter outline, summary, or end-of-chapter questions that may be provided. This will supply you with a mental map of the chapter's important ideas before you start your trip through it. Getting an overview of the chapter will help you keep track of its chapter's major ideas (the "big picture") and reduce your risk of getting lost in all the smaller details you encounter along the way.

5. Finish each of your reading sessions with a short review. Rather than using the last few minutes of a reading session to cover a few more pages, end it with a review of what you've highlighted or noted as important information. Since most forgetting takes place immediately after you stop processing (taking in) information and start doing something else, it's best to use your last minutes of reading time to "lock in" the most important information you've just read.

Note

When reading, your goal should be to discover or uncover the most important ideas, so the final step in the reading process should be to review (and lock in) the most important ideas you've discovered.

Note: For a more detailed discussion of reading comprehension and retention, see Chapter 6 (pp. 139–140).

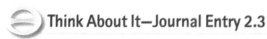
Think About It—Journal Entry 2.3

Which of the five reading strategies listed in **Box 2.2** have you used in the past? Which of these strategies do you intend to use in the future?

Second Step for College Success: Capitalizing on Campus Resources (Resourcefulness)

Successful people are *resourceful*; they seek out and take advantage of resources to help them reach their goals. Your campus is chock full of resources that have been intentionally designed to support your quest for educational and personal success. Studies show that students who utilize campus resources report higher levels of satisfaction with college and get more out of the college experience (Pascarella & Terenzini, 1991, 2005).

Note

Capitalizing on campus services is not only valuable, it's also "free"; the cost of these services has already been covered by your college tuition. By investing time and energy in campus resources, you maximize the return on your financial investment in college— you get a bigger bang for your buck.

Utilizing campus resources is a natural extension of the principle of active involvement. Successful students are *involved* students, both inside and outside the classroom. Out-of-class involvement includes involvement with campus resources. The first step toward making effective use of campus resources is becoming aware of the full range of resources available to you and what they can do for you. Listed below are key campus services that are likely to be available to you and what they can do for you.

For information on campus resources, consult your college catalog or your iNdex. These publications are available online at www.nicc.edu/catalog or www.nicc.edu/iNdex for electronic copies. The student portal, MyCampus, also provides additional resources.

Learning Center

The Learning Center is designed to strengthen your academic performance. The individual and group tutoring provided here will help you master difficult course concepts and assignments, and the people working here are professionally trained to help you learn *how to learn*. Just as instructors are experts in the subjects they teach, learning resource professionals are experts in the process of learning. They are professionals who can equip you with effective learning strategies that can be used in all courses, as well as specific strategies for dealing with the demands of certain courses and teaching styles. You're also likely to find trained peer tutors in this

> "Do not be a PCP (Parking Lot→ Classroom→Parking Lot) student. The time you spend on campus will be a sound investment in your academic and professional success."
> —Drew Appleby, professor of psychology

> "The impact of college is not simply the result of what a college does for or to a student. Rather, the impact is a result of the extent to which an individual student exploits the people, programs, facilities, opportunities, and experiences that the college makes available."
> —Ernest Pascarella and Patrick Terenzini, How College Affects Students

> "Where I learn the material best is tutoring because they go over it and if you have questions, you can ask. They have time for you or will make time for you."
> —First-year college student

center who can often help you understand concepts better than more experienced professionals because they're closer to you in age and experience.

Studies show that college students who capitalize on academic support services outside the classroom achieve higher grades and are more likely to complete their college degree, particularly if they begin their involvement with these support services during their first year of college (Bailey, 2009; Cuseo, 2003). Students who seek and receive assistance from the Learning Center also show significant improvement in academic self-efficacy—that is, they develop a stronger sense of personal control over their academic performance and higher expectations for academic success (Smith, Walter, & Hoey, 1992).

Despite the powerful advantages associated with student use of academic support services, these services are typically underused by college students—especially by students who need them the most (Cuseo, 2003; Walter & Smith, 1990). Unfortunately, some college students believe that seeking academic help is admitting they're not smart, self-sufficient, or able to succeed on their own. Don't buy into this myth. In high school, students may only go to an office on campus if they're required to (e.g., if they forgot to do something or did something wrong). In college, students go to campus offices to enhance their success by taking advantage of the services and support they provide.

> "At colleges where I've taught, we found that the grade point average of students who used the Learning Center was higher than the college average, and honors students were more likely to use the center than other students."
>
> —*Joe Cuseo, professor of psychology and lead author of this text*

Note

Using the Learning Center doesn't mean you're helpless, need remedial repair work, or require academic life support because you're on the verge of flunking out. Instead, it's a sign that you're a motivated and resourceful student who is striving for academic excellence.

Disability Services (a.k.a. Office for Students with Accommodations)

If you have a physical or learning disability that's interfering with your performance in college, or you think you may have such a disability, Disability Services is the campus resource to consult for assistance and support. Programs and services typically provided by this office include:

- Assessment for learning disabilities;
- Verification of eligibility for disability support services;
- Authorization of academic accommodations for students with disabilities; and
- Specialized counseling, advising, and tutoring.

College Library

> "The next best thing to knowing something is knowing where to find it."
>
> —*Dr. Samuel Johnson, English literary figure and original author of the* Dictionary of the English Language *(1747)*

This is your campus resource for finding information and completing research assignments (e.g., term papers and group projects). Librarians are professional educators who provide instruction outside the classroom; you can learn from them just as you can learn from faculty inside the classroom. They can help you develop research skills for accessing, retrieving, and evaluating information. These are life-long learning skills that promote your educational success at all stages of the college experience as well as your professional and personal success beyond college. Many NICC Library resources can be accessed electronically off-campus as well.

Academic Advising

Your academic advisor is a personal resource who can help guide you through the educational planning and decison-making process. The Academic Advising Center is your campus resource for help with course selection, educational planning, and choosing or changing a major. You may also be assigned a faculty advisor. Studies show that students who develop clear educational and career goals are more likely to persist in college and complete their college degree (Lotkowski, Robbins, & Noeth, 2004). Research also indicates that most beginning college students need help clarifying their educational goals, deciding on a major, and identifying career options (Cuseo, 2005; Tinto, 2012). As a first-year college student, being undecided or uncertain about your educational and career goals is nothing to be embarrassed about. However, you should start thinking about your future now. Connect early and often with your assigned academic advisor to help you clarify your educational goals and choose a field of study that best complements your interests, talents, and values.

Student Life: iMPACT

This is your campus resource for involvement in student life outside the classroom, including student clubs and organizations, recreational programs, leadership activities, and volunteer experiences. Research consistently shows that experiential learning outside the classroom contributes as much to your personal development and career success as class work (Kuh, 1995; Kuh, et al., 1994; Pascarella & Terenzini, 2005). This is one reason why most campuses no longer refer to out-of-class experiences as "*extra*curricular" activities; instead they are referred to as "*co*-curricular" experiences—which conveys the message they're equally important as classroom-based learning. Studies show that students who become actively involved in campus life are more likely to:

- Enjoy their college experience;
- Graduate from college; and
- Develop leadership skills that enhance career performance beyond college (Astin, 1993).

Note

Co-curricular experiences are also resume-building experiences, and campus professionals with whom you interact regularly while participating in co-curricular activities (e.g., director of student activities or dean of students) can be valuable resources for personal references and letters of recommendation.

Devoting some out-of-class time to co-curricular experiences should not interfere with your academic performance. Keep in mind that in college you'll be spending much less time in the classroom than you did in high school. As mentioned previously, a full load of college courses (12 units) requires that you be in class for about 13 hours per week. This can leave you with sufficient time to become involved in learning experiences on or off campus. Research indicates that students' academic performance and progress to degree completion aren't impaired if they spend 20 or fewer hours on co-curricular and part-time work experiences (Advisory Committee on Student Financial Assistance, 2008). In fact, they earn higher grades than students who don't get involved in any out-of-class activities (Pascarella, 2001; Pascarella & Terenzini, 2005).

Although co-curricular involvement is valuable, limit your involvement to no more than two or three major campus organizations at a time. Restricting the number of your out-of-class activities will not only enable you to keep up with your studies, it will be more impressive to future schools or employers because a long list of involvement in numerous activities may send the message that you're padding your resume with activities you participated in superficially (or never participated in at all).

> Just a [long] list of club memberships is meaningless; it's a fake front. Remember that quality, not quantity, is what counts."
>
> —*Lauren Pope, former director of the National Bureau for College Placement*

Think About It—Journal Entry 2.4

If you were to join one campus club or student organization, what would it be? How would participating in this club or organization contribute to your educational development?

_____

_____

_____

_____

_____

Financial Aid

If you have questions concerning how to obtain assistance in paying for college, the staff in this office can guide you through the application process. The paperwork needed to apply for and secure financial aid can sometimes be confusing or overwhelming. Don't let the process of applying for financial aid intimidate you or prevent you from seeking financial aid because professional financial aid counselors can walk you through the process. They can also help you find:

- Part-time employment on campus through a work–study program;
- Low-interest student loans;
- Grants and scholarships.

If you have any doubt about whether you're using the most effective plan for financing your college education, make an appointment to see a professional in your Financial Aid Office right now.

Counseling

Here's where you can get ideas and strategies for managing college stress, gaining greater self-awareness, and reaching your full potential. NICC's counselors are professionals who do more than just help students maintain mental health; they also develop students' emotional intelligence, interpersonal skills, and personal growth.

Third Step for College Success: Interpersonal Interaction and Collaboration (Social Integration)

Students who become socially integrated or connected with other members of the college community are more likely to complete their first year of college and go on to complete their college degree (Pascarella & Terenzini, 2005; Tinto, 1993). (For effective ways to make interpersonal connections with key members of your college community, see **Box 2.3**.)

Box 2.3

Social Integration: Making Connections with Members of Your College Community

Listed below are top tips for making key social connections in college. Start developing these relationships right now so you can build a base of social support to help you succeed during the critical first year of college.

- Connect with a student development professional you may have met during orientation.
- Join a college club, student organization, campus committee, intramural team, or volunteer service group whose members share the same personal or career interests as you. If you can't find a club or organization you were hoping to join, consider starting it on your own. For example, if you're an English major, consider starting a Writing Club or a Book Club.
- Connect with a peer leader who has been trained to assist new students (e.g., orientation week leader, peer tutor, or peer mentor).
- Connect with classmates and team up with them to take notes, complete reading assignments, study for exams, or take classes together. Look especially to team

up with a peer who may be in more than one class with you. (For more detailed information on forming collaborative learning teams, see Chapter 6, pp. 131–132.)
- Connect with peers who live near you or who commute to school from the same community in which you live. If your schedules are similar, consider carpooling together.
- Connect with faculty members—particularly in a field that you're considering as a major. Visit them during office hours, converse briefly with them after class, or communicate with them via e-mail.
- Connect with an academic advisor to discuss and develop your educational plans.
- Connect with academic support professionals in your college's Learning Center for personalized academic assistance or tutoring related to any course in which you'd like to improve your performance or achieve academic excellence.
- Connect with a college librarian to get early assistance or a head start on any research
- Connect with a personal counselor or campus minister to discuss college adjustment or personal challenges you may be experiencing.

Four particular forms of interpersonal interaction have been found to promote student learning and motivation in college:

1. Student–faculty interaction,
2. Student–advisor interaction,
3. Student–mentor interaction, and
4. Student–student (peer) interaction.

Strategies for capitalizing on each of these key forms of interaction are provided below.

Interacting with Faculty Members

College success is strongly influenced by the frequency and quality of student–faculty interaction *outside the classroom*. Out-of-class contact with faculty is associated with the following positive outcomes for college students:

- Improved academic performance;
- Increased critical thinking skills;
- Greater satisfaction with the college experience;
- Increased likelihood of completing a college degree; and
- Stronger desire to pursue education beyond a four-year degree (Astin, 1993; Pascarella & Terenzini, 1991, 2005).

These positive outcomes are so powerful, strong, and widespread that we encourage you to immediately begin making connections with your professors outside of class time. Here are some of the easiest ways to do so.

> [In high school] the teacher knows your name. But in college they don't know your name; they might see your face, but it means nothing to them unless you make yourself known."
>
> —First-year college student

> I wish that I would have taken advantage of professors' open-door policies when I had questions, because actually understanding what I was doing, instead of guessing, would have saved me a lot of stress and re-doing what I did wrong the first time."
>
> —College sophomore (Walsh, 2005)

1. **Seek contact with your instructors right after class.** If something covered in class captures your interest, approach your instructor to discuss it further. You could ask a quick question about something you weren't sure you understood, or have a short conversation about how the material covered in class really hit home for you or connected with something you learned in another course. Interacting briefly with instructors after class can help them get to know you as an individual and help you gain the confidence to approach them during office hours.

2. **Connect with course instructors during their office hours.** One of the most important pieces of information you'll find on a course syllabus is your instructor's office hours. College instructors specifically reserve times in their weekly schedule to be available to students in their office. (Make note of them and make an earnest attempt to capitalize on them.) Try to visit the office of each of your instructors at least once, preferably early in the term, when quality time is easier to find. Don't wait until later in the term when major exams and assignments start piling up. Even if your early contact with instructors is only for a few minutes, it can be a valuable icebreaker that helps them get to know you as a person and helps you feel more comfortable interacting with them in the future.

3. **Connect with your instructors through e-mail.** Electronic communication is another effective tool for experiencing the benefits of student–faculty interaction outside the classroom, particularly if your professor's office hours conflict with your class schedule, work responsibilities, or family commitments. If you're a commuter student who doesn't live on campus, or if you're an adult student juggling family and work commitments along with your academic schedule, e-mail communication may be an especially effective and efficient way to interact with faculty. E-mail may also be a good way to initially communicate with instructors and build self-confidence to eventually seek out face-to-face interaction with them. In one national survey, almost half of college students reported that e-mail enabled them to communicate their ideas with professors on subjects they would not have discussed in person (Pew Internet & American Life Project, 2002). However, if you miss class, don't use e-mail to ask such questions as:
   - Did I miss anything important in class today?
   - Could you send me your PowerPoint slides from the class I missed?

   Also, when using e-mail to communicate with your instructors, be sure to:
   - Include your full name in the message.
   - Mention the class or course in which you're enrolled.
   - Use complete sentences, correct grammar, and avoid informal "hip" expressions (e.g., "yo," "whatup").
   - Spell check and proofread your message before sending it.
   - Include your full contact information. (If you're communicating via Facebook, watch your screen name; for example, names like "Sexsea" or "Studly" wouldn't be appropriate.)
   - Give your instructor time to reply. (Don't expect an immediate response, particularly if you send your message in the evening or on a weekend.) (See Chapter 1, **pp. 9–10**, for more netiquette guidelines.)

Interacting with Academic Advisors

If you need some help understanding college policies and procedures, or navigating the organizational maze of course options and course requirements, an academic advisor is the person to see. Advisors also serve as key referral agents who can direct you to, and connect you with, key campus support services that best meet your educational needs and career goals.

Your academic advisor should be someone whom you feel comfortable speaking with, someone who knows your name, and someone who's familiar with your personal interests and abilities. Give advisors the opportunity to get to know you personally, and seek their input on courses, majors, and any academic difficulties you may be experiencing.

If you've been assigned a specific advisor and cannot develop a good relationship with this person, ask the director of advising or academic dean if you could make a change. Consider asking your peers or peer leaders for their recommendations.

If your college does not assign you a personal advisor, but offers advising services in an Advising Center on a drop-by or drop-in basis, you may see a different advisor each time you visit the center. If you're not comfortable working with different advisors from one visit to the next, find one you like and make that person your advisor by scheduling appointments in advance. This will enable you to consistently connect with the same advisor and develop a close, ongoing relationship with that person.

Note

Advisors can be much more than course schedulers; they can be mentors. Unlike your course instructors—who may change from term to term—your academic advisor may be the one professional on campus with whom you have regular contact and a continuous relationship throughout your college experience.

 Think About It—Journal Entry 2.5

Do you have a personally assigned advisor?

_____

If yes, do you know who this person is and where he or she can be found?

_____

If you don't have a personally assigned advisor, where will you go if you have questions about your class schedule or educational plans?

_____

_____

_____

Interaction with Peers (Student–Student Interaction)

Your peers can be more than competitors or a source of negative peer pressure; they can also be collaborators, a source of positive social influence, and a resource for

FIGURE 2.2: Maslow's Theory of Self-Actualization

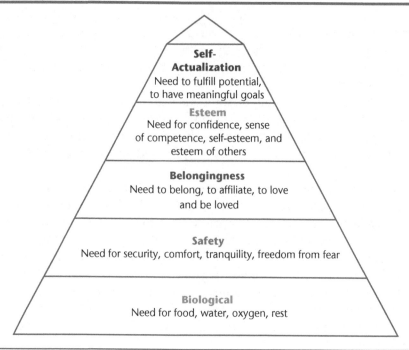

© Kendall Hunt Publishing Company

college success. Peer support is important at any stage of the college experience, but it's especially valuable during the first term of college. It's at this stage when new students have a strong need for belongingness and social acceptance because they're in the midst of a major life transition. As a new student, it may be useful to view your first-year experience through the lens of psychologist Abraham Maslow's hierarchy of human needs (see **Figure 2.2**). According to Maslow, humans only reach their full potential and achieve peak performance after their more basic emotional and social needs have been met (e.g., needs for personal safety, social acceptance, and self-esteem). Making early connections with your peers helps you meet these basic human needs, provides you with a base of social support that eases your integration into the college community, and prepares you to move up to higher levels of the need hierarchy (e.g., achieving academic excellence and reaching your educational goals).

Getting involved with campus organizations or activities is one way to connect with other students. Also, try to interact with experienced students who have spent more time at college than you. Sophomores, juniors, and seniors can be valuable social resources for a new student. In particular, seek out contact with students who have been selected and trained as peer mentors or peer leaders.

Research clearly demonstrates that college students learn as much from peers as they do from instructors and textbooks (Astin, 1993; Pascarella, 2005). One study of more than 25,000 college students revealed that when peers interact with one another while learning, they achieve higher levels of academic performance and are more likely to persist to degree completion (Astin, 1993).

Be observant—keep an eye out for peers who are successful. Start building your social support network by surrounding yourself with success-seeking and success-achieving students. Learn from them, emulate their productive habits and strategies, and use them as a social resource to promote your own success.

Surround yourself with only people who are going to lift you higher."

—Oprah Winfrey, actress and talk-show host

Collaborative Learning

Simply defined, collaborative learning is the process of two or more people working *interdependently* to advance each other's success—as opposed to working independently or competitively. Learning is strengthened when it takes place in a social context that involves interpersonal interaction. As scholars put it, human knowledge is "socially constructed" or built up through dialogue and an exchange of ideas; conversations with others become internalized as ideas in your mind and influence your way of thinking (Bruffee, 1993). Thus, by having frequent, intelligent conversations with others, you broaden your knowledge base, deepen your learning, and elevate the quality of your thinking.

Research from kindergarten through college shows that students who learn collaboratively in teams experience significant gains in both academic performance and interpersonal skills (Cross, Barkley, & Major, 2005; Cuseo, 1996; Gilles & Adrian, 2003; Johnson, Johnson, & Smith, 1998). In one national study that involved in-depth interviews with more than 1,600 college students, it was discovered that almost all students who struggled academically had one particular study habit in common: they always studied alone (Light, 2001).

To maximize the power of collaboration, use the following pair of guidelines to choose teammates who will enhance the quality and productivity of your learning team:

1. Observe your classmates with an eye toward identifying potentially good teammates. Look for motivated students who will actively contribute to your team's success (rather than those whom you suspect may just be hitchhikers looking for a free ride).
2. Don't team up exclusively with peers who are familiar with or similar to you in terms of their personal characteristics, backgrounds, and experiences. This familiarity can actually interfere with your team's performance by turning your learning team into a social group or gabfest that gets off track and onto topics that have nothing to do with studying (e.g., what you did last weekend or what you're planning to do next weekend). Instead, include teammates who differ from you with respect to such characteristics as: age, gender, race or ethnicity, and cultural or geographical background. Such variety brings different life experiences, styles of thinking strategies, and learning styles to your team, which enriches your team's diversity and learning capacity.

Note

Capitalize on the advantages of collaborating with peers of varied backgrounds and lifestyles. Studies show that we learn more from people who are different from us than from people similar to us (Pascarella, 2001; Thompson & Cuseo, 2014).

Keep in mind that collaborative learning can be much more than just forming study groups the night before an exam. You can team up with classmates more regularly to work on a variety of academic tasks, such as those listed below.

Note-Taking Teams. Immediately after class sessions end, take a couple of minutes to team up with other students to compare and share notes. Since listening and note-taking are demanding tasks, it's likely that a classmate will pick up an important point you missed and vice versa. By teaming up *immediately after class*, if you and your teammates find missing or confusing information, quickly consult with the instructor before leaving the room.

> If you want to go quickly, go by yourself—if you want to go farther, go in a group."
> —*African proverb*

> TEAM = <u>T</u>ogether <u>E</u>veryone <u>A</u>chieves <u>M</u>ore"
> —*Author unknown*

During my first term in college, I was having difficulty taking complete notes in my biology course because the instructor spoke rapidly and with an unfamiliar accent. I noticed another student (Alex) sitting in the front row who was trying to take notes as best he could; however, he was experiencing the same difficulty as me. Following one particularly fast and complex lecture, we looked at each other and noticed we were both shaking our heads in frustration. We started talking about how frustrated we were and decided to join forces after every class to compare notes and identify points we missed or found confusing. First, we helped each other by comparing and sharing our notes in case one of us got something the other missed. If there were points we both missed or couldn't figure out, we went to the front of class together to consult with the instructor before he left the room. At the end of the course, Alex and I finished with the highest grades in the course.

—Joe Cuseo

Reading Teams. After completing reading assignments, team up with classmates to compare your highlighting and margin notes. See what you both identified as the most important material to be studied for upcoming exams.

Writing Teams. Students can provide each other with feedback to revise and improve their own writing. Studies show that when peers assess each other's writing, the quality of their individual writing gets better and they develop a more positive attitude about the writing process (Topping, 1998). You can form peer writing teams to help at any or all of the following stages in the writing process:

1. Topic selection and refinement: to help one another come up with a list of possible topics and subtopics to write about;
2. Pre-writing: to clarify your writing purpose and audience;
3. First draft: to improve your general writing style and tone; and
4. Final draft: to proofread, detect, and correct clerical errors before submitting your written work.

Library Research Teams. Many first-year students are unfamiliar with the process of using a college or university library to conduct academic research. Some experience "library anxiety" and avoid even stepping foot into the library, particularly if it's a large and intimidating place (Malvasi, Rudowsky, & Valencia, 2009). Forming library research teams is an effective way to develop a social support group that can make library research less intimidating by converting it from a solitary experience done alone to a collaborative venture done as a team. Working together with peers on any research task can reduce anxiety, create collective energy, and result in a final product that's superior to what could have been produced by a single person working independently.

Note

It's perfectly acceptable and ethical to team up with others to search for information and share resources. This isn't cheating or plagiarizing—as long as your final product is completed individually and what you turn into the instructor represents your own work.

" I would suggest students get to know [each] other and get together in groups to study or at least review class material. I find it is easier to ask your classmates with whom you are comfortable 'dumb' questions."

—Advice to first-year students from a college sophomore (Walsh, 2005)

Study Teams. When seniors at Harvard University were interviewed, nearly every one of them who had participated in study groups considered the experience to be crucial to their academic progress and success (Light, 1990, 1992, 2001).

Additional research on study groups indicates that they are effective only if each member has done the required course work in advance of team meetings—for example, if all teammates attended class consistently and completed required readings (Light, 2001). To fully capitalize and maximize the power of study teams, each team member should study individually *before* studying with the group and come to the group prepared with answers and ideas to share with teammates, as well as specific questions or points of confusion about which they hope to receive help from other members of the team. This ensures that all team members are individually account-able for their own learning and equally responsible for contributing to their team-mates' learning.

Note

Don't forget that team learning goes beyond late-night study groups. Students could and should form learning teams in advance of exams to help each other with other academic tasks—such as note-taking, reading, writing, and library research.

Test Review Teams. After receiving your results on course examinations (and as-signments) you can collaborate with peers to review your performance as a team. When you compare your answers to the answers of other students, you're better able to identify what you did well and where you lost points. By seeing the answers of teammates who received maximum credit on certain questions, you get a clearer picture of what went wrong and what you can do next time to get it right next time.

Think About It—Journal Entry 2.6

Think about classmates in courses you're taking this term. Would you be willing to ask any of them if they'd like to form a learning team? Why?

_____

_____

_____

_____

_____

_____

_____

Fourth Step for College Success: Reflection and Self-Awareness (Mindfulness)

The final step in the learning process, whether it be learning in the classroom or learning from experience, is to step back from the process, thoughtfully review it, and connect it to what you already know. Reflection is the flip side of active in-volvement; both processes are necessary for learning to be complete. Active in-volvement ensures attention—it enables information to enter your brain—and re-flection ensures consolidation—it converts that information into knowledge and remains in your brain on a long-term basis (Bligh, 2000; Roediger, Dudai, & Fitz-patrick, 2007).

Research reveals that different brain wave patterns are associated with each of these two key mental states (Bradshaw, 1995). In **Figure 2.3**, the electrical pattern on the left shows the brain waves of someone actively involved in the learning pro-cess, indicating that information is being attended to and processed by the brain.

FIGURE 2.3

| High-Amplitude Brain Waves Associated with a Mental State of *Active Involvement*. | High-Frequency Brain Waves Associated with a Mental State of *Reflective Thinking*. |

© Kendall Hunt Publishing Company

The electrical pattern on the right shows the brain waves of a person reflecting on information after it's been actively processed and moving that information into long-term memory. The brain wave patterns in these two different stages of the learning process indicate that deep, long-lasting learning takes place through a combination of (a) active involvement, characterized by high-amplitude "beta" brain waves; and (b) thoughtful reflection, characterized by high-frequency "alpha" brain waves (similar to someone in a meditative state).

Self-Awareness

In addition to reflecting on what you're learning, it's also important to reflect on yourself. This process is known as *introspection*—it involves turning inward to gain deeper self-awareness and understanding of who you are, what you're doing, and where you're going. Two forms of self-awareness are particularly important for success in college: (a) self-monitoring and (b) self-assessment.

Self-Monitoring

One characteristic of successful learners is that they self-monitor (check themselves) while learning to remain aware of:

> "We learn neither by thinking nor by doing; we learn by thinking about what we are doing."
>
> —*George Stoddard, Professor Emeritus, University of Iowa*

- Whether they're using effective learning strategies (e.g., if they're giving their undivided attention to what they're learning);
- Whether they're truly comprehending what they are learning (e.g., if they're understanding it at a deep level or memorizing it at a surface level);
- How they're regulating or adjusting their learning strategies to meet the demands of different academic tasks and subjects (e.g., if they're reading technical material in a science textbook, they read at a slower rate and check their understanding more frequently than when reading a novel) (Pintrich & Schunk, 2002).

You can begin to establish good self-monitoring habits by getting in the routine of periodically pausing to reflect on the strategies you're using to learn and how you "do" college. For instance, you can ask yourself the following questions:

- Am I listening attentively to what my instructor is saying in class?
- Am I comprehending what I'm reading outside of class?
- Am I effectively using campus resources designed to support my success?
- Am I interacting with campus professionals who can contribute to my current success and future development?
- Am I interacting and collaborating with peers who can support (not sabotage) my learning and development?
- Am I effectively implementing college success strategies (such as those identified in this book)?

Note

Successful students and successful people are mindful—*they watch what they're doing and remain aware of whether they're doing it effectively and to the best of their ability.*

Self-Assessment

Simply defined, self-assessment is the process of reflecting on and evaluating your personal characteristics. The following are key target areas for self-assessment because they enable you to accurately identify and achieve your educational and personal goals:

- **Personal interests.** What you like to do or enjoy doing.
- **Personal values.** What's important to you and what you care about doing.
- **Personal abilities or aptitudes.** What you do well or have the potential to do well.
- **Learning habits.** What approaches, methods, or techniques you use to learn.
- **Learning styles.** How you like or prefer to learn.
- **Personality traits.** Your temperament, emotional characteristics, and social tendencies (e.g., whether you lean toward being outgoing or reserved).

> "Successful students know a lot about themselves."
>
> —*Claire Weinstein and Debra Meyer, professors of educational psychology at the University of Texas*

 Think About It—Journal Entry 2.7

How would you rate your academic self-confidence at this point in your college experience? (Circle one.)

very confident   somewhat confident   somewhat unconfident   very unconfident

Why?

_____

_____

_____

_____

Chapter Summary and Highlights

The key ideas contained in this chapter are summarized in the following self-assessment checklist of success promoting principles and practices.

A Checklist of Success Promoting Principles and Practices

1. **Active Involvement (Engagement)**
   Inside the classroom, I will:
   - ☑ *Get to class.* I'll treat it like a job and be there on all days I'm expected to.
   - ☑ *Get involved in class.* I'll come prepared, listen actively, take notes, and participate. Outside the classroom, I will:

☑ *Read actively*. I'll take notes while I read to increase attention and retention.
☑ *Double up*. I'll spend twice as much time on academic work outside of class as I spend in class. If I'm a full-time student, I'll make it a full-time job and put in a 40-hour workweek (with occasional "overtime" as needed).

2. **Capitalizing on Campus Resources**
   I will capitalize on academic and student support services available to me, such as the:
   ☑ Learning Center
   ☑ College Library
   ☑ Academic Advising
   ☑ Student Life and iMPACT
   ☑ Financial Aid
   ☑ Counseling Center

3. **Interpersonal Interaction & Collaboration (Social Integration)**
   I will interact and collaborate with the following members of my college community:
   ☑ Peers. I'll join student clubs and participate in campus organizations.
   ☑ Faculty members. I'll connect with my course instructors and other faculty members after class, in their offices, or via e-mail.
   ☑ Academic advisors. I'll see an advisor for more than course registration, and I'll find an advisor whom I can relate to and develop an ongoing relationship.

4. **Reflection & Self-Awareness (Mindfulness)**
   I will engage in:
   ☑ Reflection. I'll step back from what I'm learning, review it, and connect it to what I already.
   ☑ Self-Monitoring. I'll maintain self-awareness of how I'm learning in college and if I'm using effective strategies.
   ☑ Self-Assessment. I'll reflect on and evaluate my personal interests, talents, learning styles, and learning habits.

In short, successful students are:
- Involved. They *get into* it by investing time and effort in the college experience;
- Interactive. They *team up* for it by interacting and collaborating with others;
- Resourceful. They *get help* with it by capitalizing on their surrounding resources; and
- Reflective. They *step back* from it to think about their performance and themselves.

Think About It—Journal Entry 2.8

Identify one way in which you will put each of the following four principles of college success into practice during the next few weeks.

1. Active Involvement (Engagement)

2. Utilizing Campus Resources (Resourcefulness)

_____

_____

_____

3. Interpersonal Interaction and Collaboration (Social Integration)

_____

_____

_____

4. Reflection and Self-awareness (Mindfulness)

_____

_____

_____

_____

Learning More through the World Wide Web: Internet-Based Resources

For additional information on strategies for college success, see the following websites:

http://www.cgcc.edu/success

http://www.dartmouth.edu/~acskills/success/

www.studygs.net

References

Advisory Committee on Student Financial Assistance (2008, September). *Apply to succeed: Ensuring community college students benefit from need-based financial aid*. Washington DC: Author. Retrieved from https://www2.ed.gov/about/bdscomm/list/acsfa/applytosucceed.pdf

Astin, A. W. (1993). *What matters in college?* San Francisco: Jossey-Bass.

Bailey, G. (2009). *University of North Carolina, Greensboro application for NADE certification, tutoring program*. NADE Certification Council Archives. Searcy, AR: Harding University.

Bligh, D. A. (2000). *What's the use of lectures?* San Francisco: Jossey Bass.

Bradshaw, D. (1995). Learning theory: Harnessing the strength of a neglected resource. In D. C. A. Bradshaw

(Ed.), Bringing learning to life: *The learning revolution, the economy and the individual* (pp. 79–92). London: Falmer Press.

Brown, R. D. (1988). Self-quiz on testing and grading issues. Teaching at UNL (*University of Nebraska–Lincoln*), 10(2), 1–3.

Bruffee, K. A. (1993). *Collaborative learning: Higher education, interdependence, and the authority of knowledge*. Baltimore: Johns Hopkins University Press.

Cross, K. P., Barkley, E. F., & Major, C. H. (2005). *Collaborative learning techniques: A handbook for college faculty*. San Francisco: Jossey-Bass.

Cuseo, J. B. (1996). *Cooperative learning: A pedagogy for addressing contemporary challenges and critical issues in higher education*. Stillwater, OK: New Forums Press.

Cuseo, J. B. (2003). Comprehensive academic support for students during the first year of college. In G. L. Kramer et al. (Eds.), *Student academic services: An integrated approach* (pp. 271–310). San Francisco: Jossey-Bass.

Cuseo, J. B. (2005). "Decided," "undecided," and "in transition": Implications for academic advisement, career counseling, and student retention. In R. S. Feldman (Ed.), *Improving the first year of college: Research and practice* (pp. 27–50). Mahwah, NJ: Lawrence Erlbaum.

Cuseo, J. B., & Thompson, A., Campagna, M., & Fecas, V. S. (2013). *Thriving in college & beyond: Research-based strategies for academic success and personal development* (3rd ed.). Dubuque, IA: Kendall Hunt.

Erickson, B. L., Peters, C. B., & Strommer, D. W. (2006). *Teaching first-year college students.* San Francisco: Jossey-Bass.

Gilles, R. M., & Adrian, F. (2003). *Cooperative learning: The social and intellectual outcomes of learning in groups.* London: Farmer Press.

Gordon, V. N., & Steele, G. E. (2003). Undecided first-year students: A 25-year longitudinal study. *Journal of the First-Year Experience and Students in Transition, 15*(1), 19–38.

Johnson, D., Johnson, R., & Smith, K. (1998). Cooperative learning returns to college: What evidence is there that it works? *Change, 30*, 26–35.

Kiewra, K. A. (2000). Fish giver or fishing teacher? The lure of strategy instruction. *Teaching at UNL (University of Nebraska–Lincoln), 22*(3), 1–3.

Kuh, G. D. (1995). The other curriculum: Out-of-class experiences associated with student learning and personal development. *Journal of Higher Education, 66*(2), 123–153.

Kuh, et al. (2005). Student engagement in the first year of college. In M. L. Upcraft, J. N. Gardner, B. O. Barefoot, & Associates (Eds.), *Challenging and supporting the first-year student: A handbook for improving the first year of college* (pp. 86–107). San Francisco: Jossey-Bass.

Kuh, G. D., Douglas, K. B., Lund, J. P., & Ramin-Gyurnek, J. (1994). *Student learning outside the classroom: Transcending artificial boundaries.* ASHE-ERIC Higher Education Report No. 8. Washington, DC: George Washington University, School of Education and Human Development.

Light, R. L. (1990). *The Harvard assessment seminars.* Cambridge, MA: Harvard University Press.

Light, R. L. (1992). *The Harvard assessment seminars, second report.* Cambridge, MA: Harvard University Press.

Light, R. J. (2001). *Making the most of college: Students speak their minds.* Cambridge, MA: Harvard University Press.

Lotkowski, V. A., Robbins, S. B., & Noeth, R. J. (2004). *The role of academic and non-academic factors in improving student retention.* ACT Policy Report. Retrieved from https://www.act.org/research/policymakers/pdf/college_retention.pdf.

Malvasi, M., Rudowsky, C., & Valencia, J. M. (2009). *Library Rx: Measuring and treating library anxiety, a research study.* Chicago: Association of College and Research Libraries.

Pascarella, E. T. (2001, November/December). Cognitive growth in college: Surprising and reassuring findings from the National Study of Student Learning. *Change*, pp. 21–27.

Pascarella (2005). *How College Affects Students: Ten Directions for Future Research.*

Pascarella, E., & Terenzini, P. (1991). *How college affects students: Findings and insights from twenty years of research.* San Francisco: Jossey-Bass.

Pascarella, E., & Terenzini, P. (2005). *How college affects students: A third decade of research* (Vol. 2). San Francisco: Jossey-Bass.

Pew Internet & American Life Project. (2002). *The Internet goes to college: How students are living in the future with today's technology.* Retrieved from http://www.pewinternet.org/files/old-media/Files/Reports/2002/PIP_College_Report.pdf.pdf.

Pintrich, P. R., & Schunk, D. H. (2002). *Motivation in education: Theory, research, and applications.* Upper Saddle River, NJ: Merrill-Prentice Hall.

Roediger, H. L., Dudai, Y., & Fitzpatrick, S. M. (2007). *Science of memory: concepts.* New York, NY: Oxford University Press.

Smith, J. B., Walter, T. L., & Hoey, G. (1992). Support programs and student self-efficacy: Do first-year students know when they need help? *Journal of the Freshman Year Experience, 4*(2), 41–67.

Thompson, A., & Cuseo, J. (2014). *Diversity and the college experience.* Dubuque, IA: Kendall Hunt.

Tinto, V. (1993). *Leaving college: Rethinking the causes and cures of student attrition* (2nd ed.). Chicago: University of Chicago Press.

Tinto, V. (2012). *Completing college: Rethinking institutional action.* Chicago: The University of Chicago Press.

Topping, K. (1998). Peer assessment between students in colleges and universities. *Review of Educational Research, 68*(3), 249–276.

Walsh, K. (2005). *Suggestions from more experienced classmates.* Retrieved from http://www.uni.edu/walsh/introtips.html

Walter, T. L., & Smith, J. (1990, April). *Self-assessment and academic support: Do students know they need help?* Paper presented at the annual Freshman Year Experience Conference, Austin, Texas.

Chapter 2 Exercises

2.1 Quote Reflections

Review the sidebar quotes contained in this chapter and select two that were especially meaningful or inspirational to you.

For each quote, provide a three- to five-sentence explanation why you chose it.

2.2 Reality Bite-Case Study

Alone and Disconnected: Feeling like Calling It Quits

Josephine is a first-year student in her second week of college. She doesn't feel like she's fitting in with other students on her campus. She also feels a little guilty about the time she's taking time away from family and friends, and she fears that her ties with them will be weakened or broken if she continues spending so much time at school and on schoolwork. Josephine is feeling so torn between college, her family, and her old friends that she's beginning to have second thoughts about coming back next term.

Reflection and Discussion Questions

1. What would you say to Josephine that might persuade or motivate her to stay in college?

2. What could Josephine do to get more connected with her college community and feel less disconnected from her family and hometown friends?

3. What could Josephine do for herself right now to minimize the conflict she's experiencing between her commitment to college and her commitment to family and high school friends?

4. Can you relate to Josephine's situation? If yes, in what way? If no, why not?

2.3 Creating a Master List of Resources on Your Campus

1. Construct a master list of all support services that are available to you on your campus by consulting the following sources:

    *   Information published in your college catalog and iNdex
    *   Information posted at www.nicc.edu and MyCampus.
    *   Information obtained by visiting with a professional in different offices or centers on your campus

2. Your final product will be a list that includes the following:

Learning Center	Type of Support Provided	Contact Person	Campus Location
_____	_____	_____	_____
_____	_____	_____	_____
_____	_____	_____	_____
_____	_____	_____	_____

etc.

- You can team up with other classmates to work collaboratively on this assignment. Members of your team could identify different campus resources to research and then share their findings with teammates.
- After completing this assignment, save your master list of support services for future use.

2.4 Utilizing Campus Resources

Look back at the campus resources you identified in the previous exercise, or those described on **pp. 27–30** of this chapter. Which of these resources do you plan to use this term?

Why did you identify these resources as your top priorities right now?

Ask your course instructor for recommendations about what campus resources you should consult during your first term on campus. Compare their recommendations with your selections.

2.5 Chapter 2 Reflection

WHAT do you believe is the most important principle of community college success?

WHY do you believe this is the most important one?

Explain HOW you will use this principle to assist you in being successful in college.

Goal Setting and Motivation

MOVING FROM INTENTION TO ACTION

The path to success begins with goals and finding the means (succession of steps) to reach those goals. People who set specific goals are more likely to experience success than people who simply tell themselves they're going to try hard and do their best. This chapter lays out the key steps involved in the process of setting effective goals, identifies key self-motivational strategies for staying on track and sustaining progress toward goals, and describes how personal qualities such as self-efficacy, grit, and growth mindset are essential for achieving goals.

Help you set meaningful goals and maintain motivation to achieve your goals.

Think About It—Journal Entry 3.1

Complete the following sentence:

For me, success is . . .

_____

_____

_____

_____

The Relationship between Goal Setting and Success

Achieving success begins with setting goals. Research shows that people who set goals and develop plans to reach them are more likely to reach them (Halvorson, 2010), and successful people set goals on a regular basis (Locke & Latham, 1990). In fact, the word *success* derives from the Latin root *successus*—meaning "to follow or come after"—as in the word *successive*. Thus, by definition, success involves a sequence of actions that leads to a desired outcome; the process starts with identifying an end (goal) and then finding a means (sequence of steps) to reach that goal.

Motivation begins with dreams and great intentions that get turned into realistic goals. Depending on the length of time it takes to reach them and the order in which they are to be achieved, goals may be classified into three general categories: long-range, mid-range, and short-range. Short-range goals need to be completed before a mid-range goal can be reached, and mid-range goals must be reached before a long-range goal can be achieved. For example, if your long-range goal is a successful career that requires a college degree, your mid-range goal is completing all the coursework required for a degree that will allow you entry into that career. To reach your mid-range goal of a college degree, you need to start by successfully completing the courses you're taking this term (your short-range goal).

This goal-setting process is called *means-end analysis*; it involves working backward from your long-range goal (the end) and identifying what mid-range and short-range subgoals (the means) must be reached in order to achieve your long-range goal (Brooks, 2009; Newell & Simon, 1959). Engaging in this process doesn't mean you're locking yourself into a premature plan that will restrict your flexibility or options. It's just a process that (a) gets you to think about where you want to go, (b) provides some sense of direction about how to get there, and (c) starts moving you in the right direction.

> "You've got to be careful if you don't know where you're going because you might not get there."
> —Yogi Berra, Hall of Fame baseball player

Characteristics of a Well-Designed Goal

Studies show that people who set specific, well-designed goals are more likely to succeed than are people who simply tell themselves they're going to try hard and do their very best (Halvorson, 2010; Latham & Locke, 2007). The acronym "SMART" is a well-known mnemonic device (memory strategy) for recalling all the key components of a well-designed goal (Doran, 1981; Meyer, 2003). **Box 3.1** describes the different components of a SMART goal.

Box 3.1

The *SMART* Method of Goal Setting

A *SMART* goal is one that's:

Specific—it states precisely what the goal is, targets exactly what needs to be done to achieve it, and provides a clear picture of what successfully reaching the goal looks like.

Example: By spending 25 hours per week on my coursework outside of class and by using the effective learning strategies (such as those recommended in this book), I'll achieve at least a 3.0 grade point average this term. (Note that this is a much more specific goal than saying, "I'm really going to work hard this term.")

Meaningful (and Measurable)—the goal really matters to you (not someone else) and the progress you're making toward the goal can be clearly measured (tracked).

> "Dreams can be fulfilled only when they've been *defined*."
> —Ernest Boyer, former United States Commissioner of Education

Example: Achieving at least a 3.0 grade point average this term is important to me because it will enable me to get into the field I'd like to major in. I'll measure my progress toward this goal by calculating the grade I'm earning in each of my courses this semester at regular intervals throughout the term.

Note: At *www.futureme.org* you can set up a program to send future e-mails to yourself that remind you to check and reflect on whether you're making steady progress toward the goals you set.

Actionable (i.e., Action-Oriented) —the actions or behaviors that will be taken to reach your goal are clearly specified.

Example: I will achieve at least a 3.0 grade point average this term by (a) attending all classes, (b) taking detailed notes in all my classes, (c) completing all reading assignments before their due dates, and (d) avoiding cramming by studying in advance for all my major exams.

Realistic—there is a good chance of reaching the goal, given the time, effort, and skills needed to get there.

(continued)

Box 3.1 *(continued)*

Example: Achieving a 3.0 grade point average this term is a realistic goal because my course load is manageable, I will be working no more than 15 hours per week at my part-time job, and I'll be able to get help from campus support services for any academic skills or strategies that need to be strengthened.

*T*ime-framed—the goal has a deadline plus a timeline or timetable that includes short-range (daily), mid-range (weekly), and long-range (monthly steps).

Example: To achieve at least a 3.0 grade point average this term, first I'll acquire all the information I need to learn by taking complete notes in my classes and complete all reading assignments (short-range step). Second, I'll learn the information I've acquired from my notes and readings, break it into parts and study the parts in separate sessions in advance of major exams (mid-range step). Third, on the day before exams, I'll review all the

information I previously studied in parts so I avoid cramming and get a good night's sleep (long-range step).

Note: The SMART process can be used to set goals in any area of your life or dimension of personal development, such as:

- self-management (e.g., time management and money management goals),
- physical development (e.g., health and fitness goals),
- social development (e.g., relationship goals),
- emotional development (e.g., stress management or anger management goals),
- intellectual development (e.g., learning and critical thinking goals),
- career development (e.g., career exploration and preparation goals),
- any other element of holistic (whole-person) development discussed in Chapters 11.

Think About It—Journal Entry 3.2

If you were to set a SMART goal for some aspect of your life right now, what would it be and why would you set it?

In addition to the effective goal-setting properties associated with the SMART method, research reveals that the following goal-setting features characterize people who set and reach important goals.

1. Effective goal-setters set *improvement (get-better) goals* that emphasize progress and growth, rather than perfection (be-good) goals. Studies show that when people pursue get-better goals, they pursue them with greater interest and intensity, and they are more likely to enjoy the process (Halvorson, 2010). This is likely because get-better goals give us a sense of accomplishment about how far we've come—even when we still have a long way to go.

2. Effective goal-setters focus on outcomes they have *influence or control over*, not on outcomes that are beyond their control. For example, a controllable goal for

Nothing ever comes that is worth having, except as a result of hard work."

—*Booker T. Washington, born-in-slavery Black educator, author, and advisor to Republican presidents* an aspiring actress would be to improve her acting skills and opportunities, rather than to become a famous movie star—which will depend on factors that are beyond her control.

3. Effective goal-setters set goals that are *challenging and effortful*. Goals worth achieving require that we stretch ourselves and break a sweat; they require endurance, persistence, and resiliency. Studies of successful people in all occupations indicate that when they set goals that are attainable but also *challenging*, they pursue those goals more strategically, with more intensity, and with greater commitment (Latham & Locke, 2007; Locke & Latham, 2002). There's another advantage of setting challenging goals: Achieving them supplies us with a stronger sense of accomplishment, satisfaction, and self-esteem.

4. Effective goal-setters anticipate *obstacles* they may encounter along the path to their goal and have a plan in place for dealing with them. Successful people often imagine what things will be like if they don't reach their goals, which drives them to anticipate problems and setbacks before they arise (Gilbert, 2006; Harris, Griffin, & Murray, 2008). They're optimistic about succeeding, but they're not blind optimists; they realize the road will be tough and they have a realistic plan in place for dealing with the rough spots (Oettingen, 2000; Oettingen & Stephens, 2009). Thus a well-designed goal should not only include specific information about how the goal will be achieved, but also specific plans to handle anticipated impediments along the way—for example, identifying what resources and social support networks may be used to keep you on track and moving forward.

Capitalize on resources that can help you stay on track and moving toward your goal. Research indicates that success in college involves a combination of what students do for themselves (personal responsibility) and how they to capitalize on resources available to them (Pascarella & Terenzini, 1991, 2005). Successful people are resourceful; they seek out and take advantage of resources to help them reach their goals. Use your campus (and community) resources to help you achieve your long-range goals (e.g., academic advising and career counseling).

Don't forget that your peers can serve as a resource to help you reach your goals. Much has been said about the dangers of "peer pressure," but much less attention has been paid to the benefits of "peer power." The power of social support groups for helping people achieve personal goals is well documented by research in different fields (Brissette, Cohen, & Seeman, 2000; Ewell, 1997). There's also a long historical trail of research pointing to the power of peers for promoting the development and success of college students (Astin, 1993; Feldman & Newcomb, 1994; Pascarella & Terenzini, 2005). Be sure to ask yourself: Who can help me stick to my plan and complete the steps needed to reach my goal? You can harness the power of social support by surrounding yourself with peers who are committed to successfully achieve their educational goals and by avoiding "toxic" people who are likely to poison your plans or dampen your dreams.

Find motivated peers with whom you can make mutually supportive "pacts" to help one another reach your respective goals. These mutual support pacts may be viewed as "social contracts" signed by "co-witnesses" who help them stay on track and moving toward their long-range goals. Studies show that making a commitment to a goal in the presence of others increases our commitment to that goal because our successful pursuit of it is viewed not only through our own eyes, but through the eyes of others as well (Hollenbeck, Williams, & Klein, 1989; Locke, 2000).

Think About It—Journal Entry 3.3

What *obstacles* or *impediments* do you anticipate may interfere with your goal of succeeding in college and completing your college degree?

What *campus resources* do you think would be most helpful for dealing with your anticipated obstacles?

What *social support networks* (family members, friends, or mentors) do you think could help you overcome your anticipated obstacles?

Strategies for Maintaining Motivation and Progress toward Your Goals

The word *motivation* derives from the Latin *movere*, meaning "to move." Success comes to those who overcome inertia—they start moving toward their goal; then they maintain momentum until their goal is reached. Goal-setting only creates the potential for success; it takes motivation to turn this potential into reality by converting intention into action. We can have the best designed goals and know the way to succeed, but if we don't have the *will* to succeed, there's no way we will succeed. Studies show that goal-setting is just the first step in the process; it must be accompanied by a strong commitment to achieve the goal that has been set (Locke, 2000; Locke & Latham, 1990).

> You can lead a horse to water, but you can't make him drink."
> —*Author unknown*

Reaching challenging goals requires that you maintain motivation and sustain effort over an extended period of time. Listed below are strategies for doing so.

Put your goals in writing and make them visible. Written goals can serve almost like a written contract that holds you accountable for following through on your commitments.

By placing written goals where you can't help but see them on a daily basis (e.g., your laptop, refrigerator, and bathroom mirror), you're less likely to "lose sight" of them and more likely to continue pursuing them. What's kept in sight is kept in mind.

Note

The next best thing to doing something you intend to do is to write down your intention to do it.

Keep your eye on the prize. Visualize reaching your long-range goals; picture it by creating vivid mental images of your future success. For example, if your goal is to achieve a college degree, visualize a crowd of cheering family, friends, and faculty at your graduation. (You could even add musical accompaniment to your visualization by playing a motivational song in your head—e.g., "We are the Champions" by Queen.) Imagine cherishing this proud memory for the rest of your life and being in a career your college degree enabled you to enter. Picture a typical workday going something like this: You wake up on a Monday morning and are excited about the upcoming workweek. When you're at work, time seems to fly by; before you know it, the day is over. When you go home after work and reflect on your day, you feel great about what you did and how well you did it.

In addition to visualizing the positive consequences of achieving your goal, you can also motivate yourself by visualizing the negative consequences of not achieving it—as illustrated by the following experience.

AUTHOR'S EXPERIENCE

My father, who spent 50 years working in the coal mines of eastern Kentucky, always had a simple, motivating statement for me to gain more education than he had. He would always say, "Son, I did not have the chance to go to school, so I have to write my name with an X and work in the coal mines. You have the opportunity to get an education and you do not have to break your back in those mines." What my father was telling me was that education would give me options in life that he did not have and that I should take advantage of those options by going to college. My dad's lack of education supplied me with drive and dedication to pursue education. My experience suggests that when you are developing your goals and motivating yourself to achieve them, it may be as important to know what you don't want as it is to know what you do want.

—*Aaron Thompson*

"Whether you think you can or you can't, you're right."

—*Henry Ford, founder of Ford Motor Co. and one of the richest people of his generation.*

Visualize completing the steps leading to your goal. For visualization to be really effective, you need to visualize not just the success itself (the end goal), but also the steps you'll take along the way. "Just picturing yourself crossing the finish line doesn't actually help you get there—but visualizing how you run the race (the strategies you will use, the choices you will make, the obstacles you will face) not only will give you greater confidence, but also leave you better prepared for the task ahead" (Halvorson, 2010, p. 208).

Thus, reaching a long-term goal requires focusing on the prize—your dream and *why* it's important to you; this "big picture" view provides the inspiration. At the same time, however, you have to focus on the little things—*what* it will take to get there—the nitty-gritty of due dates, to-do lists, and day-to-day tasks. This is the perspiration that transforms inspiration into action, enabling you to plug away and stay on track until your goal is achieved.

It could be said that successfully achieving a long-term goal requires two lenses, each of which provides you with a different focus point: (a) a wide-angle lens that gives you a big picture view of a future that's far ahead of you (your ultimate goal), and (b) a narrow-angle lens that allows you to focus intently on the here and now—on the steps that lie immediately ahead of you. Alternating between these two perspectives allows you to view your small, short-term chores and challenges (e.g., completing an assignment that's due next week) in light of the larger, long-range picture (e.g., college graduation and a successful future).

> "You've got to think about 'big things' while you're doing small things, so that all the small things go in the right direction."
>
> —*Alvin Toffler, American futurologist and author who predicted the future effects of technology on our society*

AUTHOR'S EXPERIENCE

I once helped coach a youth soccer team (five to six year olds) and noticed that many of the less successful players tended to make one of either two mistakes when they tried to advance the ball toward the goal. Some spent too much time looking down, focusing on the ball at their feet, trying to be sure that they didn't lose control of it. By not occasionally lifting their head and looking ahead, they often missed open territory, open teammates, or an open goal. Other unsuccessful players made the opposite mistake: They spent too much time with their heads up, trying to see where they were headed. By not periodically glancing down at the ball in front of them, they often lost control of it, moved ahead without it, or sometimes stumbled over it and fell flat on their face. In contrast, the more successful players had developed the habit of shifting their focus between looking down to maintain control of the ball immediately in front of them and lifting their eyes to see where they were headed.

The more I thought about how these successful soccer players alternated their perspective between looking at the ball right in front of them and looking at the goal farther ahead, it struck me that this was a metaphor for success in life. Successful people alternate between long-range and short-range perspectives; they don't lose sight of how executing the tasks immediately in front of them connect with the ultimate goal further ahead of them.

—Joe Cuseo

Note

Keep pursuit of your future dreams and completion of your current tasks in dual focus. Integrating these two perspectives provides you with the inspiration to set goals and the determination to reach them.

Keep a record of your progress. Research indicates that the mere act of monitoring and recording progress toward your goals increases your motivation to continue pursuing them (Locke & Latham, 2005; Matsui, Okada, & Inoshita, 1983). Keeping a regular record of your personal progress increases motivation by providing you with frequent *feedback* about whether you're on track and positive *reinforcement* for staying on track (Bandura & Cervone, 1983; Schunk, 1995).

Mark down your accomplishments in red on a calendar, or keep a journal of the short- and mid-range goals you've reached. These markings serve as benchmarks, supplying you with concrete evidence and a visible reminder of your progress. You can also mark your progress on a chart or graph, or list your achievements in a resume or portfolio. Place these displays of progress where you can see them on a daily basis and use them as a source of motivation to keep striving toward your ultimate goal (Halvorson, 2010).

> "Writing my resume was a real ego booster—I've actually done stuff!"
>
> —*College student (quoted in Brooks, 2009)*

This practice of ongoing (daily) assessment of our personal progress toward goal completion is a simple, yet powerful form of self-reflection that's associated with success. Research on successful people reveals that they reflect regularly on their daily progress to ensure they're on track and progressing steadily toward their goals (Covey, 1990).

Reward yourself for reaching milestones on the path toward your goal. Reaching a long-range goal is clearly rewarding because it marks the end of the trip and arrival at your desired destination. However, reaching short- and mid-range goals are not as self-rewarding because they're merely the means to the end. Thus, you need to make intentional attempts to reward yourself for climbing these smaller, yet essential stepping stones on the path to the mountain peak.

The behaviors needed to persist and persevere through all the intermediate steps needed to reach a long-range goal is more likely to take place if these behaviors are followed by reward (positive reinforcement). The process of setting small goals, moving steadily toward them, and rewarding yourself for reaching them is a simple, yet powerful self-motivational strategy. It helps you maintain momentum over an extended period of time, which is exactly what's required to reach a long-range goal. When you achieve short- and mid-range goals, check them off as milestones and reward yourself for reaching them (e.g., celebrate successful completion of midterms or finals by treating yourself to something you really enjoy).

"Whoever wants to reach a distant goal must take many small steps."

—Helmut Schmidt, former chancellor of West Germany

Think About It—Journal Entry 3.4

For you, what would be effective rewards for making progress toward your goals and serve as motivators to keep you going?

_____

_____

_____

_____

_____

Characteristics of Successful People

Achieving success involves effective use of goal-setting and motivational strategies, but it takes something more. Ultimately, success emerges from the inside out; it flows from personal qualities and attributes found within a person. Studies of successful people who achieve their goals reveal they possess the following personal characteristics. Keep these characteristics in mind as you set and pursue your goals.

Internal Locus of Control

"If you do not find it within yourself, where will you go to get it?"

—Zen saying (Zen is a branch of Buddhism that emphasizes seeing deeply into the nature of things and ongoing self-awareness)

Successful people have what psychologists call an "internal locus of control"; they believe that the locus (location or source) of control for events in their life is *internal*—"inside" them and within their control—rather than *external*—outside them and beyond their control. They believe that success is influenced more by attitude, effort, commitment, and preparation than by inherited ability, inborn intelligence, luck, chance, or fate (Carlson, et al., 2009; Jernigan, 2004; Rotter, 1966).

Research shows that individuals with a strong internal locus of control display the following positive qualities:

1. Greater independence and self-direction (Van Overwalle, Mervielde, & De Schuyer, 1995),

2. More accurate self-assessment of strengths and weaknesses (Hashaw, Hammond, & Rogers, 1990), and
3. Higher levels of learning and achievement (Wilhite, 1990).

Self-Efficacy

An internal locus of control contributes to the development of another positive trait that psychologists refer to as *self-efficacy*—the belief that you have power to produce a positive effect on the *outcomes* of your life (Bandura, 1994). People with low self-efficacy tend to feel helpless, powerless, and passive; they think (and allow) things to happen to them rather than taking charge and making things happen for them. College students with a strong sense of self-efficacy believe they're in control of their educational success and can shape their future, regardless of their past experience or current circumstances.

People with a strong sense of self-efficacy initiate action and exert effort. They believe success is something that's earned and the harder they work at it, the more likely they'll get it. If they encounter setbacks or bad breaks along the way, they don't give up or give in; they persevere and push on (Bandura, 1986, 1997).

Students with a strong sense of *academic self-efficacy* have been found to:

1. Put considerable effort into their studies;
2. Use active learning strategies;
3. Capitalize on campus resources; and
4. Persist in the face of obstacles (Multon, Brown, & Lent, 1991; Zimmeman, 1995, 2000).

Students with a strong sense of self-efficacy also possess a strong sense of personal responsibility. As the breakdown of the word "responsible" implies, they are "response" "able"—they believe they're able to respond to personal challenges, including academic challenges.

> "I'm a great believer in luck, and I find the harder I work the more I have of it."
>
> —*Thomas Jefferson, third president of the United States*

 Think About It—Journal Entry 3.5

In what area or areas of your life do you feel that you've been able to exert the most control and achieve the most positive results?

_____

_____

_____

_____

In what area(s) do you wish you had more control and were achieving better results?

_____

_____

What strategies have you used in the area of your life where you've been able to exert the most personal control and achieve the most positive outcomes?

_____

_____

_____

_____

Could you apply any of these same strategies to those areas in which you need to gain more control? How?

_____

_____

_____

_____

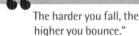

> "Grit is perseverance and passion for long-term goals. Sticking with your future day in, day out, not just for the week, not just for the month, but for years and working really hard to make that future a reality."
>
> —_Angela Duckworth, psychologist, University of Pennsylvania_

> "How smart you are will influence the extent to which you experience something as difficult (for example, how hard a math problem is), but it says nothing about how you will deal with difficulty when it happens. It says nothing about whether you will be persistent and determined or feel overwhelmed and helpless."
>
> —_Heidi Grant Halvorson, social psychologist, and author of_ Succeed: How We Can Reach Your Goals

> "The harder you fall, the higher you bounce."
>
> —_Chinese proverb_

Grit

When you expend significant effort, energy, and sacrifice over a sustained period of time to achieve a goal, you're demonstrating grit (Stoltz, 2014). People with grit have been found to possess the following qualities (Duckworth, et al., 2007).

Persistence. They hang in there and persevere effort until they reach their goals. When the going gets tough, they don't give up—they step it up. They have the fortitude to persist in the face of frustration and adversity.

Tenacity. They pursue their goals with relentless determination. If they encounter something along the way that's hard to do, they work harder to do it.

Resilience. They bounce back from setbacks and keep striving to reach their goals. They adopt the mindset that they'll bounce back from setbacks and turn them into comebacks. How you react mentally and emotionally to a setback affects what action you take in response to it. For instance, you can react to a poor test grade by knocking yourself down with self-putdowns ("I'm a loser") or by building yourself back up with positive self-talk ("I'm going to learn from my mistakes on this test and rebound with a stronger performance on the next one").

As you can see in **Figure 3.1**, information passes through the emotional center of the human brain (lower, shaded area) before reaching the center responsible for rational thinking and future planning (upper area). As a result, when we encounter setbacks, our initial (and subconscious) tendency is to react emotionally and defensively. To counteract this tendency, we need to slow down, calm down, and make a conscious attempt to respond rationally to setbacks—thinking about how we can overcome them, learn from them, and make use of them to continue progressing toward our goal.

FIGURE 3.1: The Brain's Emotional Filter

Information entering the human brain is first processed emotionally (lower shaded area)
before reaching higher areas of rational thinking and future planning.

©Kendall Hunt Publishing Company

It's noteworthy that the word *problem* derives from the Greek root *proballein*, meaning "to throw forward." This suggests that a problem is an opportunity to move ahead. You can take this approach to problems by rewording or rephrasing the problem you're experiencing in terms of a positive goal statement. (For example, "I'm flunking math" can be reframed as: "My goal is to get a grade of C or better on the next test to pull my overall course grade into passing territory.")

Similarly, the root of the word *failure* is *fallere*—meaning to "trip or fall." Thus, failing at something doesn't mean we've been defeated, it just means we've stumbled and taken a temporary spill. Success can still be achieved after a fall if we don't give up, but get up and get back to taking the next step needed to reach our goal. By viewing poor academic performances and other setbacks (particularly those occurring early in your college experience) not as failures but as learning opportunities, you put yourself in a position to bounce back and transform your setbacks into comebacks. Here are some notable people who did so:

* Louis Pasteur, famous bacteriologist, failed his admission test to the University of Paris;
* Albert Einstein, Nobel Prize–winning physicist, failed math in elementary school;
* Thomas Edison, prolific inventor, once expelled from school as "uneducable";
* Johnny Unitas, Hall of Fame football player, cut twice from professional football teams early in his career;
* Michael Jordan, Hall of fame basketball player, cut from his high school team as a sophomore.

Note

Don't let early setbacks bring you down emotionally or motivationally. Reflect on them, learn from them, and make sure they don't happen again.

> What happens is not as important as how you react to what happens."
>
> —*Thaddeus Golas*, Lazy Man's Guide to Enlightenment

> When written in Chinese, the word 'crisis' is composed of two characters. One represents danger, and the other represents opportunity."
>
> —*John F. Kennedy, 35th president of the United States*

Think About It—Journal Entry 3.6

What would you say is the biggest setback or obstacle you've overcome in your life thus far?

_____

_____

_____

_____

How did you overcome it? (What enabled you to get past it, or what did you do to prevent it from stopping you?)

_____

_____

_____

_____

_____

_____

> " Self-discipline is the ability to make yourself do the thing you have to do, when it ought be done, whether you like it or not."
>
> —_Thomas Henry Huxley, 19th-century English biologist_

Self-Discipline. People with grit have the _self-control_—they keep their actions aligned with their goal, staying on course and moving in the right direction—despite distractions and temptations (Halvorson, 2010). They resist the impulse to pursue instant gratification and do what they feel like doing instead of what needs to be done to reach their goal. They're able to sacrifice immediate, short-sighted needs and desires to do what has to be done to get where they want to be in the long run.

The ability to delay short-term (and short-sighted) gratification is distinctive human characteristic that sets us apart from other animals. As can be seen in **Figure 3.2**, the upper front part of the human brain, which is responsible for long-range planning and impulse control, is much larger in humans than chimpanzees—one of the most intelligent of all nonhuman animals.

Setting long-range goals is important but having the self-discipline to reach them is another matter. Each day, whether we're aware of it or not, we're tempted to make choices and decisions that interfere with our ability to reach our goals. We need to remain mindful about whether these choices are moving us in the direction of our goals or taking us off course.

FIGURE 3.2: **Where Thoughts, Emotions, and Drives are Experienced in the Brain**

The part of the brain responsible for long-range planning and controlling emotions and impulses is much larger in humans than in other animals, including the highly intelligent chimpanzee.

©Kendall Hunt Publishing Company.

AUTHOR'S EXPERIENCE

When I entered college in the mid-1970s, I was a first-generation student from an extremely impoverished background. Not only did I have to work to support my education, I also needed to assist my family financially. I stocked grocery store shelves at night during the week and waited tables at a local country club on the weekends. Managing my time, school, work, and life required a lot of self-discipline. However, I always understood that my goal was to graduate from college and all of my other commitments supported that goal. One of my greatest achievements in life was to keep my mind and body focused on the ultimate prize of getting a college education. That achievement has paid off for me many times over the course of my life.

—Aaron Thompson

Note

Doing what you have to do now allows you to do what you want to do later. Sacrifices made for a short time can bring benefits that last a lifetime.

Think About It—Journal Entry 3.7

Think about something in your life that you sacrificed for and persisted at for the longest period of time before getting there. What is it? Do you see ways in which you could apply the same approach to achieving your goals in college? Explain.

Growth Mindset

A *mindset* is a powerful belief. People with a *growth mindset* believe that intelligence and other positive qualities can be grown or developed. People with a *fixed mindset* believe just the opposite: they think that intelligence and personal characteristics are deep-seated traits that are set and unlikely to change (Dweck, 2006).

Listed below are opposing pairs of traits—one representing a fixed mindset (FM) and the other representing a growth mindset (GM). As you read through them, honestly assess whether you lean more toward a fixed or growth mindset by circling either FM or GM for each pair of traits.

I try to get better at what I do. (GM)
I try to show others (including myself) how good I am. (FM)

I try to validate myself by proving how smart or talented I am. (FM)
I validate myself by stretching myself to become smarter and more talented. (GM)

I believe that if I cannot learn to do something easily, I'm not smart. (FM)
I believe that I can learn to do something well even if it doesn't come easily at first. (GM)

I evaluate my performance by comparing it to the performance of others. (FM)
I evaluate my performance by comparing it to my past performances. (GM)

I believe I have a certain amount of intelligence and not much can be done to change it. (FM)
I believe that the amount of intelligence I start with isn't the amount I'll end up with. (GM)

I think that intelligence and personal qualities are inherited and hard to change. (FM)
I think that intelligence and personal qualities are learned and changeable. (GM)

I think success is a matter of having ability. (FM)
I think success is a matter of getting ability. (GM)

I focus on demonstrating my skills to others. (FM)
I focus on developing my skills. (GM)

I focus on proving myself (as being good or smart). (FM)
I focus on improving myself (by getting better). (GM)

I feel smart when I complete tasks quickly and without mistakes. (FM)
I feel smart when I work on something for awhile before figuring it out. (GM)

I avoid seeking constructive criticism from others because it will expose my weaknesses. (FM)
I seek out constructive criticism from others to improve myself. (GM)

I feel threatened by the success of others. (FM)
I feel I can be inspired by and learn from the success of others. (GM)

I tend to peak early and don't continually progress to higher levels of achievement. (FM)
I tend to keep progressing toward increasingly higher levels of achievement. (GM)

I think success should be effortless. (FM)
I think success should be effortful. (GM)

I view challenges as threatening because they may prove I'm not smart. (FM)
I view challenges as opportunities to develop new skills. (GM)

> "If you believe you can develop yourself, then you're open to accurate information about your current abilities, even if it's unflattering."
>
> —*Carol Dweck*, Growth Mindset: The New Psychology of Success

I believe effort creates talent. (GM)
I believe effort is for those who can't make it on talent. (FM)

I focus on self-improvement—about becoming the best I can be. (GM)
I focus on self-validation—about proving I'm already good. (FM)

I look at grades as labels that judge or measure my intelligence. (FM)
I look at grades as a source of feedback for improving my performance. (GM)

Think About It—Journal Entry 3.8

Look back at the above pairs of statements and compare the total number of fixed mindset (FM) and growth mindset (GM) statements you circled.

Do your totals suggest that, in general, you lean more toward a growth or fixed mindset?

Do you see any patterns in your responses that suggest you're more likely to hold a growth mindset for certain characteristics or situations and a fixed mindset for others?

> "No matter what your ability is, effort is what ignites that ability and turns it into accomplishment."
> —Carol Dweck, Stanford psychologist and author of Mindset

> SUCCESS is peace of mind which is a direct result of self-satisfaction in knowing you made the effort to become the best that you are capable of becoming."
> —John Wooden, college basketball coach and author of the Pyramid of Success

Numerous studies show that a growth mindset is strongly associated with goal achievement and personal success (Dweck, 2006). In one study, the mindset of pre-med students taking a difficult chemistry course was measured at the start of the semester and their performance was tracked throughout the term. Students with a growth mindset consistently earned higher grades in the course. Even when students with a growth mindset did poorly on a particular test, they improved on the next one. In contrast, the performance of students with a fixed mindset showed no pattern of improvement from one exam to the next (Dweck, 2006).

In another study, students with a growth mindset (who believed their goal in college courses was to improve their grade as the course progressed) were compared to students with a fixed mindset (who believed their goal was to prove how smart they were). Students with a growth mindset achieved higher overall course grades and did so because they improved with each exam. They didn't have higher grades on the first exam, but began earning higher grades on later exams. The opposite pattern was true for fixed mindset students—their performance actually remained the same or declined over time—particularly if their first exam score was low (Halvorson, 2010).

It's been found that students can have different mindsets for different subjects and situations. Some students may have a fixed mindset for learning math, but a growth mindset for learning other subjects. However, the most important thing to remember about mindsets is that, although they're powerful, they're just beliefs held in our mind. Thus, mindsets can be changed from fixed to growth for any subject or situation. By so doing, we increase the likelihood of achieving our goals and reaching our full potential (Dweck, 2006).

> "When we change the way we look at things, the things we look at change."
>
> —Max Planck, Nobel Prize–winning physicist

Chapter Summary and Highlights

A key to success is challenging ourselves to set ambitious, yet realistic goals. Studies consistently show that goal-setting is a more effective self-motivational strategy than simply telling ourselves to "try hard" or "do our best." Achieving success begins with setting goals and successful people set goals on a regular basis.

The acronym "SMART" is a popular mnemonic device (memory strategy) for recalling all the key components of a well-designed goal. A *SMART* goal is one that is:

Specific—it states precisely what the goal is and what you will do to achieve it.

Meaningful (and Measurable)—it's a goal that really matters to you and your progress toward reaching it can be steadily measured or tracked.

Actionable (or Action-Oriented) —it identifies concrete actions and specific behaviors you'll engage in to reach the goal.

Realistic—the goal is attainable and you're aware of the amount of time, effort, and skill it will take to attain it, as well as obstacles you'll need to overcome along the way.

Time-framed—the goal has a deadline and a timeline that includes a sequence of short-range, mid-range, and long-range steps.

In addition to the effective goal-setting properties associated with the SMART method, research reveals that the following goal-setting features characterize people who set and reach important goals.

1. Effective goal-setters set *improvement (get-better) goals* that emphasize progress and growth, rather than perfection (be-good) goals.
2. Effective goal-setters focus on what outcomes can *influence or control*, not on outcomes that are beyond their control.
3. Effective goal-setters set goals that are *challenging and effortful*.
4. Effective goal-setters anticipate *obstacles* they may encounter along the path to their goal and have a plan in place for dealing with them.

Setting goals ignites motivation, but maintaining motivation after it's been ignited requires use of effective self-motivational strategies. You can maintain your motivation by using such strategies as:

- Visualizing reaching your long-range goals;
- Putting your goals in writing;
- Creating a visual map of your goals;

- Keeping a record of your progress toward your goals;
- Rewarding yourself for milestones you reach along the path to your goals;
- Converting setbacks into comebacks by learning from mistakes and maintaining positive expectations.

Studies of successful people who achieve their goals reveal they possess the following personal characteristics.

Internal Locus of Control. They believe that the locus (location or source) of control for events in their life is *internal*—"inside" them and within their control—rather than *external*—outside them and beyond their control.

Self-Efficacy. They believe they have power to produce a positive effect on the *outcomes* of their lives. They believe success is something that's earned and the harder they work at it, the more likely they'll get it.

Grit. They expend significant effort, energy, and sacrifice over an extended period of time to achieve their goals. People with grit have been found to possess the following qualities:

- *Persistence*—when the going gets tough, they don't give up, they step it up; they have the fortitude to persist in the face of frustration and adversity.
- *Tenacity*—they pursue their goals with relentless determination; if they encounter something along the way that's hard to do, they work harder to do it.
- Resilience—they bounce back from setbacks and turn them into comebacks.
- *Self-Discipline*—they have *self-control*—they resist the impulse to pursue instant gratification and do what they feel like doing instead of what should be done to reach their goal; they're able to sacrifice immediate, short-sighted needs and desires to do what has to be done to get where they want to be in the long run.

Growth Mindset. They believe that intelligence and other positive qualities can be grown or developed. In contrast, people with a "fixed mindset" believe that intelligence and personal characteristics are deep-seated traits that are set and unlikely to change.

Note

Achieving success isn't a short sprint; it's a long-distance run that takes patience and perseverance. Goal-setting is the key that gets us off the starting blocks and motivation is the fuel that keeps us going until we cross the finish line.

Learning More through the World Wide Web: Internet-Based Resources

For additional information on goal-setting and motivation, see the following websites.

Goal Setting:
https://www.mindtools.com/page6.html

Self-Motivational Strategies:
www.selfmotivationstrategies.com

Self-Efficacy:
www.psychologytoday.com/blog/flourish/201002/
if-you-think-you-can-t-think-again-the-sway-self-efficacy

Grit & Resilience:
https://undergrad.stanford.edu/resilience

Growth Mindset:
www.ted.com/talks/carol_dweck_the_power_of_believing_that_you_can_
improve?language=en

References

Astin, A. W. (1993). *What matters in college?* San Francisco: Jossey-Bass.

Bandura, A. (1986). *Social foundations of thought and action: A social cognitive theory.* Englewood Cliffs, NJ: Prentice Hall.

Bandura, A. (1994). Self-efficacy. In V. S. Ramachaudran (Ed.), *Encyclopedia of human behavior* (Vol. 4, pp. 71–81). New York: Academic Press.

Bandura, A. (1997). *Self-efficacy: The exercise of control.* New York: Freeman.

Bandura, A., & Cervone, D. (1983). Self-evaluative and self-efficacy mechanisms governing the motivational effects of goal systems. *Journal of Personality and Social Psychology, 45*(5), 1017–1028.

Brissette, I., Cohen, S., & Seeman, T. E. (2000). Measuring social integration and social networks. In S. Cohen, L. G. Underwood, & B. H. Gottlieb (Eds.), *Social support measurement and intervention* (pp. 53–85). New York: Oxford University Press.

Brooks, K. (2009). *You majored in what? Mapping your path from chaos to career.* NY: Penguin.

Carlson, N. R., Miller, H., Heth, C. D., Donahoe, J. W., & Martin, G. N. (2009). *Psychology: The science of behaviour* (7th ed.). Toronto, ON: Pearson Education Canada.

Covey, S. R. (1990). Seven habits of highly effective people (2nd ed.). New York: Fireside.

Doran, G. T. (1981). "There's a S.M.A.R.T. Way to Write Management's Goals and Objectives", Management Review, Vol. 70, Issue 11, pp. 35–36.

Duckworth, A. L., Peterson, C., Matthews, M. D., & Kelly, D. R. (2007). Grit: Perseverance and passion for long-term goals. *Journal of Personality and Social Psychology, 92*(6), 1087–1101.

Dweck, C. S. (2006). *Mindset: The new psychology of success.* New York: Random House.

Ewell, P. T. (1997). Organizing for learning. *AAHE Bulletin, 50*(4), 3–6.

Feldman, K. A., & Newcomb, T. M. (1994). *The impact of college on students.* New Brunswick, NJ: Transaction Publishers. (Original work published 1969).

Gilbert, P. T. (2006). *Stumbling on happiness.* New York: Alfred A. Knopf.

Halvorson, H. G. (2010). *Succeed: How we can reach our goals.* New York: Plume.

Harris, P., Griffin, D., & Murray, S. (2008). Testing the limits of optimistic bias: Event and person moderators in a multilevel framework. *Journal of Personality and Social Psychology, 95*, 1225–1237.

Hashaw, R. M., Hammond, C. J., & Rogers, P. H. (1990). Academic locus of control and the collegiate experience. *Research & Teaching in Developmental Education, 7*(1), 45–54.

Hollenbeck, J. R., Williams, C. R., & Klein, H. J. (1989). An empirical examination of the antecedents of commitment to difficult goals. *Journal of Applied Psychology, 74*(1), 18–23.

Jernigan, C. G. (2004). What do students expect to learn? The role of learner expectancies, beliefs, and attributions for success and failure in student motivation. *Current Issues in Education* [On-line], 7(4). Retrieved January 16, 2012, from cie.asu.edu/ojs/index.php/cieatasu/article/download/824/250

Latham, G., & Locke, E. (2007). New developments in and directions for goal-setting research. *European Psychologists, 12*, 290–300.

Locke, E. A. (2000). Motivation, cognition, and action: An analysis of studies of task goals and knowledge. *Applied Psychology: An International Review, 49*, 408–429.

Locke, E. A., & Latham, G. P. (1990). *A theory of goal setting and task performance.* Englewood Cliffs, NJ: Prentice Hall.

Locke, E. A., & Latham, G. P. (2002). Building a practically useful theory of goal setting and task motivation. *American Psychologist, 57*, 705–717.

Locke, E. A., & Latham, G. P. (2005). Goal setting theory: Theory building by induction. In K.G. Smith & M.A. Mitt (Eds.), *Great minds in management: The process of theory development.* New York: Oxford.

Matsui, T., Okada, A., & Inoshita, O. (1983). Mechanism of feedback affecting task performance. *Organizational Behavior and Human Performance, 31*, 114–122.

Meyer, P. J. (2003). "What would you do if you knew you couldn't fail? Creating S.M.A.R.T. Goals". *In Attitude Is Everything: If You Want to Succeed Above and Beyond.* Meyer Resource Group, Incorporated.

Multon, K. D., Brown, S. D., & Lent, R. W. (1991). Relation of self-efficacy beliefs to academic outcomes: A meta-analytic investigation. *Journal of Counseling Psychology, 38*(1), 30–38.

Newell, A., & Simon, H. A. (1959). *The simulation of human thought*. Santa Monica, CA: Rand Corporation.

Oettingen, G. (2000). Expectancy effects on behavior depend on self-regulatory thought. *Social Cognition, 14*, 101–129.

Oettingen, G., & Stephens, E. (2009). Mental contrasting future and reality: A motivationally intelligent self-regulatory strategy. In G. Moskowitz & H. Grant (eds.), *The psychology of goals*. New York: Guilford.

Pascarella, E., & Terenzini, P. (1991). *How college affects students: Findings and insights from twenty years of research*. San Francisco: Jossey-Bass.

Pascarella, E., & Terenzini, P. (2005). *How college affects students: A third decade of research* (Vol. 2). San Francisco: Jossey-Bass.

Rotter, J. (1966). Generalized expectancies for internal versus external controls of reinforcement. *Psychological Monographs: General and Applied, 80*(609), 1–28.

Schunk, D. H. (1995). Self-efficacy and education and instruction. In J. E. Maddux (Ed.), *Self- efficacy, adaptation, and adjustment: Theory, research, and application* (pp. 281–303). New York: Plenum Press.

Snyder, C. R. (1995). Conceptualizing, measuring, and nurturing hope. *Journal of Counseling and Development, 73* (January/February), 355–360.

Stoltz, P. G. (2014). *Grit: The new science of what it takes to persevere, flourish, succeed*. San Luis Obispo: Climb Strong Press.

Van Overwalle, F. I., Mervielde, I., & De Schuyer, J. (1995). Structural modeling of the relationships between attributional dimensions, emotions, and performance of college freshmen. *Cognition and Emotion, 9*(1), 59–85.

Wilhite, S. (1990). Self-efficacy, locus of control, self-assessment of memory ability, and student activities as predictors of college course achievement. *Journal of Educational Psychology, 82*(4), 696–700.

Zimmerman, B. J. (1995). Self-efficacy and educational development. In A. Bandura (Ed.), *Self-efficacy in changing societies*. New York: Cambridge University Press.

Zimmerman, B. J. (2000). Self-efficacy: An essential motive to learn. *Contemporary Educational Psychology 25*, 82–91.

Chapter 3 Exercises

3.1 Quote Reflections

Review the sidebar quotes contained in this chapter and select two that were especially meaningful or inspirational to you.

For each quote, write a three- to five-sentence explanation why you chose it.

3.2 Reality Bite

Goals and Motivation

Lorraine has decided to go to her local community college to become an RN. She knows that nurses make good money and it is easy to get a job in the profession right now. All she really cares about is having a good job and making money. She did not realize the classes would be difficult and she has a hard time getting through them since she really is not that interested in them. She started her clinicals and HATED what she was being asked to do. She was not prepared for all the bodily fluids she would see in one day. Lorraine decides nursing is not for her and is angry that no one told her she would hate it this much! She has to find a different major now that will still make a lot of money, but she is angry that she wasted more than a year of her life as well as the money she has spent on her education.

1. Why do you think Lorraine is really unhappy with the events that have unfolded during the past year?

2. What could Lorraine have done differently to avoid this situation?

3. What goals would you suggest Lorraine set for herself?

Lorraine is clearly motivated by money; is that what is going to make her happy? Why or why not?

3.3 Clarifying Your Goals

*   Take a moment to answer the following questions as honestly as possible:
*   What are my highest priorities?
*   What competing needs and priorities do I need to keep in check?
*   How will I maintain balance across different aspects of my life?
*   What am I willing and able to give up in order to achieve my educational and personal goals?
*   How can I maintain motivation on a day-to-day basis?
*   Who can I collaborate with to reach my goals and what will that collaboration involve?

3.4 Setting a SMART Goal to Reduce the Gap between Your Ideal Future and Your Current Reality

Think of an aspect of your life where there's a significant gap between what you'd like it to be (the ideal) and where you are (the reality).

Use the following form to identify a goal you could pursue to reduce this gap.

Goal: _____

What specific *actions* will be taken?

When will these actions be taken?

What *obstacles or roadblocks* do you anticipate?

What *resources* could you use to overcome your anticipated obstacles or roadblocks?

How will you *measure your progress*?

How will you know when you *reached or achieved* your goal?

3.5 Converting Setbacks into Comebacks: Transforming Pessimism into Optimism through Positive Self-Talk

In Hamlet, Shakespeare wrote: "There is nothing good or bad, but thinking makes it so." His point was that experiences have the potential to be positive or negative, depending on how people interpret them and react to them.

Listed below is a series of statements representing negative, motivation-destroying interpretations and reactions to a situation or experience:

a)   "I'm just not good at this."

b)   "There's nothing I can do about it."

c)   "Nothing is going to change."

d)   "This always happens to me."

e)   "Everybody is going to think I'm a loser."

For each of the preceding statements, replace the negative statement with a statement that represents a more positive, self-motivating interpretation or reaction.

3.6 Self-Assessment of Hope

Studies of people who have changed their lives in productive ways indicate they exhibit "high hope" by engaging in certain behaviors that enable them to find the will and the way to reach their personal goals (Snyder, 1995). A sample of hopeful behaviors is listed below. Assess yourself on these behaviors, using the following scale:

1 = Never
2 = Rarely
3 = Frequently
4 = Almost Always

Behavior Exhibited by People Possessing High Levels of Hope

___ When I think of goals, I think of challenges, rather than setbacks and failures.

___ I seek out stories about how other people have succeeded to inspire me and give me new ideas on how to be successful.

___ I find role models I can emulate and who can advise, guide, or mentor me.

___ I tell my friends about my goals and seek their support to help me reach my goals.

___ I use positive self-talk to help me succeed.

___ I think that mistakes I make along the way to my goals are usually the result of using a wrong strategy or making a poor decision, rather than lack of talent or ability on my part.

___ When I struggle, I remember past successes and things I did that worked.

___ I reward myself when reaching smaller, short-term goals I accomplish along the way to larger, long-term goals.

Adapted from: Snyder, C. R. (1995). Conceptualizing, measuring, and nurturing hope. *Journal of Counseling and Development*, 73 (January/February), 355–360.

Self-Assessment Reflections

For any item you rated "1" or "2," explain:

(a) *Why* you "rarely" or "never" engage in the practice;

(b) *If* you intend to engage in the practice more frequently in the future;

(c) *How likely* is it that you'll engage in the practice more frequently in the future;

(d) *When do* you plan to begin engaging in the practice.

3.7 Chapter 3 Reflection

What is the one thing that motivates you the most in college?

HOW and WHY does this motivate you?

What is the one obstacle that gets in the way of your success?

How can you use your motivation to overcome your obstacle(s)?

Time Management

PRIORITIZING TASKS, PREVENTING PROCRASTINATION, AND PROMOTING PRODUCTIVITY

Chapter Preview

Time is a valuable personal resource—if you gain greater control of it, you can greater control of your life. Time managed:

- Enables you to get work done in a timely manner,
- Enables you to attain personal priorities, and
- Maintain balance in your life.

This chapter offers a comprehensive set of strategies for managing time, combating procrastination, and ensuring that your time-spending habits are aligned with your educational goals and priorities.

Learning Goal

Equip you with a powerful set of strategies for setting priorities, planning time, and completing tasks in a timely and productive manner.

Thought Starter

 Think About It—Journal Entry 4.1

Complete the following sentence with the first thought that comes to your mind:

For me, time is . . .

_____

_____

_____

_____

The Importance of Time Management

For many first-year students, the beginning of college means the beginning of more independent living and self-management. Even if you've lived on your own for some time, managing time is an important skill to possess because you're likely juggling multiple responsibilities, including school, family, and work. Studies show that most first-year community college students are attending classes while working either part-time or full-time (American Association of Community Colleges, 2009). To have any realistic chance of achieving our goals, we need an intentional and strategic plan for spending our time in a way that aligns with our goals and enables us to make steady progress toward them. Thus, setting goals, reaching goals, and managing time are interrelated skills.

Most college students struggle to at least some extent with time management, particularly first-year students who are transitioning from the lockstep schedules of high school to the more unstructured time associated with college course schedules. National surveys indicate that almost 50% of first-year college students report difficulty managing their time effectively (HERI, 2014). In college, time management skills grow in importance because students' time is less structured or controlled by school authorities or family members and more responsibility is placed on students to make their own decisions about how their time will be spent. Furthermore, the academic calendar and class scheduling patterns in college differ radically from high school. There's less "seat time" in class each week and college students are expected to do much more academic work on their courses outside of class time, which leaves them with a lot more "free time" to manage.

Simply stated, college students who have difficulty managing their time have difficulty managing college. One study compared college sophomores who had an outstanding first year (both academically and personally) with sophomores who struggled in their first year. Interviews with both groups revealed there was one key difference between them: sophomores who experienced a successful first year repeatedly brought up the topic of time during the interviews. The successful students said they had to think carefully about how they spent their time and that they needed to budget their time. In contrast, sophomores who experienced difficulty in their first year of college hardly talked about the topic of time during their interviews, even when they were specifically asked about it (Light, 2001).

Studies also indicate that people of all ages report time management to be a critical element of their life. Working adults report that setting priorities and balancing multiple responsibilities (e.g., work and family) can be a stressful juggling act (Harriott & Ferrari, 1996). For them, time management and stress management are interrelated.

These findings suggest that time management is more than just a college success skill; it's also as a life management and life success skill. When we gain greater control of our time, we gain greater control of our life. Studies show that people who manage their time well report being happier (Myers, 1993, 2000).

> "The major difference [between high school and college] is time. You have so much free time on your hands that you don't know what to do for most of the time."
>
> —*First-year college student (Erickson & Strommer, Teaching College Freshmen)*

> "I cannot stress enough that you need to intelligently budget your time."
>
> —*Advice to new college students from a student finishing his first year in college*

AUTHOR'S EXPERIENCE

I started the process of earning my doctorate a little later in life than other students. I was a married father with a pre-school daughter (Sara). Since my wife left for work early in the morning, it was always my duty to get up and get Sara's day going in the right direction. In addition, I had to do the same for myself. Three days of my week were spent on campus in class or in the library. (We didn't have quick access to research on home computers then as you do now.) The other two days of the workweek and the weekend were spent on household chores, family time, and studying.

I knew that if I was to have any chance of finishing my Ph.D. in a reasonable amount of time, I had to adopt an effective schedule for managing my time. Each day of the week, I held to a strict routine. I got up in the morning, ate breakfast while reading the paper, got Sara ready for school, and got her to school. Once I returned home, I put a load of laundry in the washer, studied, wrote, and spent time concentrating on what I needed to do to be successful from 8:30 a.m. to 12:00 p.m. every day. At lunch, I had a pastrami and cheese sandwich and a soft drink while rewarding myself by watching *Perry Mason* reruns until 1:00 p.m. I then continued to study until it was time to pick up Sara from school. Each night I spent time with my wife and daughter and then prepared for the next day. I lived a life that had a preset schedule. By following that schedule, I was able to successfully complete my doctorate in a reasonable amount of time while giving my family the time they needed. (By the way, I still watch *Perry Mason* reruns.)

—*Aaron Thompson*

Strategies for Managing Time and Tasks

Effectively managing our time and our tasks involves three key processes:

1. **Analysis**—breaking down time to see how much of it we have and what we're spending it on;
2. **Itemizing**—identifying and listing the tasks that we need to complete and when we need to complete them; and
3. **Prioritizing**—ranking our tasks in terms of their importance and attacking them in order of their importance.

The following strategies can be used to implement these three processes and should help you open up more time in your schedule, enabling you to discover new ways to use your time more productively.

Think About It—Journal Entry 4.2

1. What is your greatest time waster?

_____

_____

_____

_____

2. Is there anything you can do right now to stop or eliminate it?

_____

_____

_____

_____

Become more aware of how your time is spent by breaking it into smaller units. How often have you heard someone say, "Where did all the time go?" or "I just can't seem to find the time!" One way to find out where all our time goes and find more time to get things done is by doing a *time analysis*—a detailed examination of how much total time we have and where we're spending it—including patches of wasted time when we get little done and nothing accomplished. This time analysis only has to be done for a week or two to give us a pretty good idea of where our time is going and to find better ways to use our time productively.

Identify *what* specific tasks you need to accomplish and when you need to accomplish them. When we want to remember items we need to buy at the grocery store or people we want to invite to a party, we make a list. This same list-making strategy can be used for tasks we need to complete so we don't forget about them, or forget to do them on time. One characteristic of successful people is that they are list makers; they make lists for things they want to accomplish each day (Covey, 2004).

Note

When we write out things we need to do, we're less likely to block them out and forget to do them.

 Think About It—Journal Entry 4.3

Do you make a to-do list of things you need to get done each day? (Circle one.)

never   seldom   often   almost   always

If you circled "never" or "seldom," why don't you?

_____

_____

_____

_____

Take advantage of time planning and task management tools, such as the following:

- *Small, portable planner.* You can use this device to list all your major assignments and exams for the term, along with their due dates. By pulling together all work tasks required in each of your courses and getting them in one place, it will be much easier to keep track of what you have to do and when you have to do it throughout the entire term.
- *Large, stable calendar.* In the calendar's date boxes, record your major assignments for the term. The calendar should be posted in a place you can see every day (e.g., bedroom or refrigerator). If you repeatedly see the things you have to do, you're less likely to overlook them, forget about them, or subconsciously push them out of your mind because you'd really prefer not to do them.
- *Smartphone.* These devices can be used for more than checking social networking sites and sending or receiving text messages. They can be used as a calendar tool to record due dates and set up alert functions to remind you of deadlines. Many smartphones also allow you to set up task or to-do lists and set priorities for each item entered. A variety of apps are now available for planning tasks and tracking time spent on tasks (e.g., see: http://www.rememberthemilk.com; other apps available include cozi, an organization app, and pomodoro, an app intended to boost productivity). Take advantage of cutting edge tools, but at the same time, keep in mind that planners don't plan time, people do. Effectively planning time and tasks flows from a clear vision of your goals and priorities.

My mom ensured I got up for school on time. Once I got to school the bell would ring to let me know to move on to the next class. When I returned home, I had to do my homework and chores. My daily and weekly schedules were dictated by someone else.

When I entered college, I quickly realized that I needed to develop my own system for being organized, focused, and productive without the assistance of my mother or school authorities. Since I came from a modest background, I had to work my way through college. Juggling schedules became an art and science for me. I knew the things that I could not miss, such as work and school, and the things I could miss—TV and girls. (OK, TV, but not girls.)

After college, I spent 10 years in business—a world where I was measured by being on time and delivering a productive "bottom line." It was during this time that I discovered a scheduling book. When I became a professor, I had other mechanisms to make sure I did what I needed to do when I needed to do it. This was largely based on when my classes were offered. Other time was dedicated to working out and spending time with my family. Now, as an administrator, I have an assistant who keeps my schedule for me. She tells me where I am going, how long I should be there, and what I need to accomplish while I am there. Unless you take your parents with you or have the luxury of a personal assistant, it's important to schedule your time. Use a planner!

—*Aaron Thompson*

Think About It—Journal Entry 4.4

Do you have a calendar that you carry with you or use the calendar tool on your cell phone?

If yes, why? If no, why not?

Prioritize: rank tasks in order of their importance. After you itemize your work tasks by identifying and listing them, the next step is to *prioritize* them—determine the order or sequence in which they get done. Prioritizing basically involves ranking tasks in terms of their importance, with the highest priority tasks placed at the top of the list to ensure they're tackled first.

How do you decide on what tasks are to be ranked highest and tackled first? Here are two key criteria (standards of judgment) for determining your highest priority tasks:

- **Urgency.** Tasks that are closest to their deadline or due date should receive highest priority. Finishing an assignment that's due tomorrow should receive higher priority than starting an assignment that's due next month.
- **Gravity.** Tasks that carry the greatest weight (count the most) should receive highest priority. If an assignment worth 100 points and an assignment worth 10 points are due at the same time, the 100-point task should receive higher prior-

> Things that matter most must never be at the mercy of things that matter least."
>
> —*Johann Wolfgang von Goethe, German poet, dramatist, and author of the epic* Faust

ity. We want to be sure to invest our work time on tasks that matter most. Similar to investing money, we should invest our time on tasks that yield the greatest pay-off.

Note

Put first things first: Plan your work by identifying your most important and most urgent tasks, and work your plan by attacking these tasks first.

An effective strategy for prioritizing tasks is to divide them into "A," "B," and "C" lists (Lakein, 1973; Morgenstern, 2004). The "A" list is reserved for *essential* (nonnegotiable) tasks—those that that *must* be done now. The "B" list is for *important* tasks—those that *should* be done soon. The "C" list is for *optional* tasks—those that *could* or *might* be done if there's time remaining after the more important tasks on lists A and B have been completed. Organizing tasks and time in this fashion helps you decide how to divide your labor in a way that ensures you "put first things first." You shouldn't waste time doing unimportant things to deceive yourself into thinking that you're "getting stuff done"—when, in reality, all you're doing is "keeping busy" and distracting yourself (and subtracting time) from doing the things that should be done.

>
> When I have lots of homework to do, I suddenly go through this urge to clean up and organize the house. I'm thinking, 'I'm not wasting my time. I'm cleaning up the house and that's something I have to do.' But all I'm really doing is avoiding school work."
>
> —*College sophomore*

AUTHOR'S EXPERIENCE

My mom is a schoolteacher, and when my sister and I were growing up she had a strict policy: when we came home from school we could have a snack, but after that we were not allowed to do anything else until our homework was finished. I remember that on days when it was really nice outside, I would beg and plead (and sometimes even argue) with my mom about going outside to play. She always won, and often I had wasted so much time arguing that I completely missed out on the opportunity to play at all. At the time I thought my mom was really mean. As I grew older (in high school and college), though, it became easy to put my homework first. My mom had taught me the importance of prioritizing and completing important things (like homework) before things that were not as important.

—*Julie McLaughlin*

Note

Developing awareness of how our time is spent is more than a brainless, clerical activity. When it's done well, it becomes an exercise in self-awareness and values clarification—how we spend our time is a true test of who we are and what we really value.

> Time = Life. Therefore waste your time and waste your life, or master your time and master your life."
>
> —*Alan Lakein, international expert on time management and author of the bestselling book How to Get Control of Your Time and Your Life (1973)*

> If you fail to plan, you are planning to fail."
>
> —*Benjamin Franklin, renowned author, inventor, civic activist, and a founding father of the United States*

Creating a Time-Management Plan

You may have heard of the old proverb, "A stitch in time saves nine." Planning your time represents the "stitch" (unit of time) that saves you nine additional stitches (units of time). Similar to successful chess players, successful time managers plan ahead and anticipate their next moves.

Don't buy into the myth that taking time to plan takes time away from getting started and getting things done. Time management experts estimate that the amount of time planning your total work actually reduces your total work time by a factor of three: for every one unit of time you spend planning, you save three units of time working (Goldsmith, 2010; Lakein, 1973). For example, 5 minutes of planning time will typically save you 15 minutes of total work time, and 10 minutes of planning time will save you 30 minutes of work time.

Planning your time saves you time because it ensures you start off in the right direction. If you have a plan of attack, you're less vulnerable to "false starts"—starting your work and then discovering you're not on the right track or not doing things in the right sequence, which forces you to retreat and start all over again.

Once you have accepted the idea that taking time to plan your time will save you time in the long run, you're ready to create a plan for effectively managing time. Listed below are specific strategies for doing so.

Be mindful of time by wearing a watch or carrying a phone that can accurately and instantly tell you the date and time. This may seem like an obvious "no-brainer", but time can't be managed if we don't know what time it is, and we can't plan a schedule if we don't know what day it is. Consider setting the time on your watch or phone slightly ahead of the actual time to help ensure that you arrive to class, work, or meetings on time. You can also equip your phone with apps to remind you of times when tasks are to be completed (e.g., *remindme.com* or *studiousapp.com*).

Carry a *small calendar, planner,* or *appointment book* at all times. This will allow you to record appointments that you may make on the run as well as enable you to jot down creative ideas or memories of things you need to do—which can sometimes pop into your mind at the most unexpected times.

Take *portable work* with you during the day that you can work at any place at any time. This will enable you to take advantage of "dead time" such as time spent sitting and waiting for appointments or transportation. Portable work allows you to resurrect dead time and transform it into productive work time. Not only is this a good time management strategy, it's a good stress management strategy because you replace the frustration and boredom associated with having no control over "wait time" with a sense of accomplishment.

> Only boring people get bored."
> —*Graffiti appearing in a bathroom stall at the University of Iowa, circa 1977*

Make good use of your *free time between classes* by working on assignments and studying in advance for upcoming exams. See **Box 4.1** for a summary of how you can use your out-of-class time to improve your academic performance and course grades.

Note

College professors are more likely than high school teachers to expect you to rely on your course syllabus to keep track of what you have to do and when you have to do it. Your instructors may not remind you about upcoming papers, tests, quizzes, assignments, etc.

Box 4.1

Making Productive Use of "Free Time" Outside the Classroom

Students' class schedules in college differ radically from high school. College students are often pleasantly surprised by how much "free time" they have because they're spending much less time in class. However, students are expected to spend two or more hours outside of class for every hour they spend in class. Thus, using out-of-class time strategically and productively is critical to ensuring college success.

Compared to high school, "homework" in college often doesn't involve turning in assignments on a daily or weekly basis. Academic work assigned to be done outside the college classroom may not even be collected and graded. Instead, it's often done for your own benefit to help you prepare for upcoming exams and complete written reports (e.g., assigned reading and assigned

(continued)

Box 4.1 *(continued)*

problems in math and science). Rather than formally assigning and collecting this work as homework, your professors expect that you will do this work on your own and without supervision.

> In high school we were given a homework assignment every day. Now we have a large task assigned to be done at a certain time. No one tells [us] when to start or what to do each day."
>
> —*First-year college student*

Listed in this box are strategies for working independently and in advance of college exams and assignments. By building time for each of these activities into your regular schedule, you'll make more productive use of out-of-class time, decrease your level of stress, and strengthen your academic performance.

Doing Out-of-Class Work in Advance of Exams

- **Complete reading assignments** relating to lecture topics *before* the topic is discussed in class. This will make lectures easier to understand and enable you to participate intelligently in class (e.g., by asking meaningful questions and making informed comments during class discussions).
- **Review class notes** from your last class before the next class to build a mental bridge from one class to the next. Many students don't look at their class notes until they study them right before an exam. Don't be one of those students; instead, review your notes before the next class. Rewrite any class notes that may have been sloppily written the first time. If you find notes related to the same point all over the place, reorganize them into the same section. Lastly, if you find any information gaps or confusing points in your notes, seek out the course instructor or a trusted classmate to clear them up before the next class takes place.

    By reviewing your class notes on a regular basis, you will improve your ability to understand each upcoming lecture and reduce the total time you'll need to spend studying your notes the night before an exam.
- **Review your reading notes and highlights** to improve retention of important material. If you find certain

points in your reading to be confusing, discuss them with your course instructor during office hours or with a fellow classmate outside of class.

- **Integrate class material with reading material.** Connect related information from your lecture notes and reading notes and get them in the same place (e.g., on the same index card).
- **Use a "part-to-whole" study method** whereby you study material from your class notes and assigned reading in small pieces (parts) during short, separate study sessions in advance of the exam; then make your last study session before the exam a longer review session during which you re-study all the small parts (the whole) at the same time. Don't buy into the myth that studying in advance is a waste of time because you'll forget everything you studied by test time. As will be fully explained in Chapter 6, material studied in advance of an exam remains in your brain and is still there when you later review it. Even if it doesn't immediately come back to mind when you first start reviewing it, you'll relearn it much faster than you did the first time.

Doing Out-of-Class Work in Advance of Term Papers and Research Reports

Work on large, long-range assignments due at the end of the term by breaking them into smaller, short-term tasks completed at separate times during the term. For instance, a large term paper may be broken up into the following smaller tasks and completed in separate installments.

1. Search for and decide on a topic.
2. Locate sources of information on the topic.
3. Organize information obtained from your sources into categories.
4. Develop an outline of your paper's major points and the order or sequence in which you plan to present them.
5. Construct a first draft of your paper (and, if necessary, a second or third draft).
6. Write a final draft of your paper.
7. Proofread your final draft for spelling and grammatical errors before turning it in.

⊜ Think About It—Journal Entry 4.5

Do you have time gaps between your classes this term? If you do, what have you been doing during these "free" periods between classes?

_____

_____

_____

_____

What would you say is your greatest between-class time waster?

_____

_____

_____

_____

Do you see a need to stop or eliminate it?

_____

If yes, what could you do to convert your wasted time into productive time?

_____

_____

_____

_____

_____

A good time management plan transforms intention into action. Once you've planned the work, the next step is to work the plan. A time management plan turns into an action plan when you: (a) preview what you intend to do, (b) review whether you actually did what you intended to do, and (c) close the gap between your intentions and actions. The action plan begins with your *daily to-do list*, bringing that list with you as the day begins, and checking off items on the list as they're completed during the day. At the end of the day, the list is reviewed to determine what got done and what still needs to be done. The uncompleted tasks then become high priorities on the following day's to-do list.

If, at the end of each day, you find many unchecked items still remaining on your daily to-do list, this probably means you're spreading yourself too thin by trying to do too many things in a single day. You may need to be more realistic about how much you can accomplish per day by shortening your daily to-do lists. Not being able to complete many of your intended daily tasks may also mean that you need to modify your time management plan by adding more work time or subtracting some non-work activities that are drawing time and attention away from your work (e.g., responding to phone calls and text messages during your planned work times). If you're consistently falling short of achieving your daily goals, honestly ask yourself if you're spending too much time on less important things (e.g., TV, video games, Facebook).

 Think About It—Journal Entry 4.6

At the end of a typical day, how often do you find that you accomplished most of the tasks you intended to accomplish? (Circle one.)

never   seldom   often   almost   always

If you circled "never" or "seldom," what strategies could you use to move the bar toward "often" or "almost always"?

_____

_____

_____

_____

Murphy's Laws:

1. Nothing is as simple as it looks.
2. Everything takes longer than it should.
3. If anything can go wrong, it will.

—Author unknown (Murphy's Laws were named after Captain Edward Murphy, a naval engineer)

It is important to allow time for things you enjoy doing because this is what will keep you stable."

—Advice to new college students from a first-year student

A good time management plan includes reserving time for the unexpected. Always hope for the best, but prepare for the worst. Your plan should include a buffer zone or safety net that contains extra time in case you encounter unforeseen developments or unexpected emergencies. Just as you should plan to have extra funds in your account to pay for unexpected expenses (e.g., auto repair), you should plan to have extra time in your schedule for unexpected events (e.g., personal illness or family emergency).

A good time management plan contains time for work and play. Your plan shouldn't consist solely of a daunting list of work tasks you have to do; it should also include fun things you like to do. Plan time to relax, refuel, and recharge. Your overall time management plan shouldn't turn you into an obsessive-compulsive workaholic. Instead, it should represent a balanced blend of work and play, including activities that promote your mental and physical wellness—such as relaxation, recreation, and reflection. Consider following the daily "8-8-8 rule"—8 hours for sleep, 8 hours for school, and 8 hours for other activities.

If you schedule things you like to do, you're more likely do to the things you have to do. You're much more likely to faithfully execute your plan if play time is scheduled along with work time, allowing play activities to serve as a reward for completing your work tasks.

Note

An effective time management plan helps you stress less, learn more, and earn higher grades while reserving time for other things that are important to you, enabling you to attain and maintain balance in your life.

⊜ Think About It—Journal Entry 4.7

What activities do you engage in for fun or recreation?

What do you do to relax or relieve stress?

Do you build these activities into your daily or weekly schedule?

A good time management plan has some flexibility. A time management plan shouldn't enslave you to a rigid work schedule. The plan should be flexible enough to allow you to occasionally bend it without breaking it. Just as work commitments and family responsibilities can crop up unexpectedly, so, too, can opportunities for fun and enjoyable activities. Your plan should allow you the freedom to modify your schedule to take advantage of these enjoyable opportunities and experiences. However, you should plan to make up the work time you lost. In other words, you can borrow or trade work time for play time, but don't "steal" it; plan to pay back the work time you borrowed by substituting it for play time that was planned for another time. If you decide not to do work you planned, the next best thing to do is re-plan when you'll do it.

Note

When you create a personal time management plan, remember it's your plan—you own it and you run it. It shouldn't run you.

Dealing with Procrastination

A major enemy of effective time management is procrastination. Procrastinators don't abide by the proverb: "Why put off till tomorrow what can be done today?" Instead, their philosophy is just the opposite: "Why do today what can be put off till tomorrow?" Adopting this philosophy promotes a perpetual pattern of postponing what needs to be done until the last possible moment, forcing the procrastinator to rush frantically to finish work on time and turn in work that's inferior or incomplete (or not turn anything in at all).

©Kendall Hunt Publishing Company.

Next time I'll start sooner!

A procrastinator's idea of planning ahead and working in advance often boils down to this scenario.

Research shows that 80% to 95% of college students procrastinate (Steel, 2007) and almost 50% report that they procrastinate consistently (Onwuegbuzie, 2000). Procrastination is such a serious issue for college students that some campuses have opened "procrastination centers" to help them (Burka & Yuen, 2008).

AUTHOR'S EXPERIENCE

During my early years in college, I was quite a procrastinator. During my sophomore year, I waited to do a major history paper until the night before it was due. Back then, I had a word processor that was little more than a typewriter; it allowed you to save your work to a floppy disk before printing. I finished writing my paper around 3:00 a.m. and hit "print," but halfway through the printing I ran out of paper. I woke up my roommate to ask if she had paper, but she didn't. So, at 3:00 a.m. I was forced to get out of my pajamas, get into my street clothes, get into my car, and drive around town to find someplace open at three in the morning that sold typing paper. By the time I found a place, got back home, printed the paper, and washed up, it was time to go to class. I could barely stay awake in any of my classes that day, and when I got my history paper back, the grade wasn't exactly that I was hoping for. I never forgot that incident. My procrastination on that paper caused me to lose sleep the night before it was due, lose attention in all my other classes on the day it was due, and lose points on the paper that I managed to do. Thereafter, I was determined not to let procrastination get the best of me.

—Julie McLaughlin

Myths That Promote Procrastination

To have any hope of putting a stop to procrastination, procrastinators need to let go of two popular myths or misconceptions about time and performance.

Myth 1. "I work better under pressure" (e.g., on the day or night before something is due). Procrastinators often confuse desperation with motivation. Their belief that they work better under pressure is usually a rationalization to justify the fact that they *only* work under pressure—when they have to work because they've run out of time and are under the gun of a looming deadline.

It's true that when people are under pressure, they will start working and work with frantic energy, but that doesn't mean they're working more *effectively* and producing work of better *quality*. Because procrastinators are playing "beat the clock," they focus less on doing the job well and more on beating the buzzer. This typically results in a work product that's incomplete or inferior to what could have been produced if they had begun the work process sooner.

Myth 2. "Studying in advance is a waste of time because you will forget it all by test time." This myth is used by procrastinators to justify putting off all studying until the night before an exam. As will be discussed in Chapter 6, studying that's distributed (spread out) over time is more effective than massed (crammed) studying all at one time. Furthermore, last minute studying before exams often involves pulling "late-nighters" or "all-nighters" that result in sleep loss. This fly-by-night strategy deprives the brain of dream sleep (a.k.a. REM sleep), which it needs to retain information and manage stress (Hobson, 1988; Voelker, 2004). Research indicates that procrastinators suffer from higher rates of stress-related physical disorders, such as insomnia, stomach problems, colds, and flu (McCance & Pychyl, 2003). Working under time pressure also increases performance pressure by leaving the procrastinators with (a) no margin of error to correct mistakes, (b) no time to seek help on their work, and (c) no chance to handle random catastrophes or setbacks that may arise at the last minute.

Psychological Causes of Procrastination

Sometimes, procrastination has deeper psychological roots. People may procrastinate for reasons that relate more to emotional issues than poor time management habits. Studies show that some people procrastinate as a psychological strategy to protect their self-esteem. Referred to as *self-handicapping* (Rhodewalt & Vohs, 2005), this strategy is used by some procrastinators, often unconsciously, to give themselves a "handicap," or disadvantage. By starting their work at the last possible moment, if their performance turns out to be less than spectacular, they can always conclude (rationalize) that it was because they were performing under a handicap— lack of time rather than lack of ability (Chu & Cho, 2005).

For example, if they receive a low grade on a test or paper, they can "save face" (self-esteem) by concluding that it was because they waited until the last minute and didn't put much time or effort into it. In other words, they had enough ability or intelligence to earn a high grade, they just didn't put in enough time. Better yet, if they happen to get a good grade—despite their last-minute, last-ditch effort—it proves just how smart they are. It shows they were able to earn a high grade, even without putting in much time at all. Thus, self-handicapping creates a fail-safe or win–win scenario that always protects the procrastinators' self-image.

> Haste makes waste."
> —Benjamin Franklin

> Procrastinators would rather be seen as lacking in effort than lacking in ability."
> —Joseph Ferrari, professor of psychology and procrastination researcher

Think About It—Journal Entry 4.8

Do you tend to put off work for so long that getting it done turns into an emergency or panic situation?

_____

If your answer is yes, why do you think you put yourself in this position?

_____

_____

_____

_____

If your answer is no, what motivates or enables you to avoid this scenario?

_____

_____

_____

_____

_____

_____

In addition to self-handicapping, other psychological factors have been found to contribute to procrastination, including the following:

- **Fear of failure.** The procrastinator feels better about not turning in work than turning it in and getting negative feedback (Burka & Yuen, 2008; Solomon & Rothblum, 1984);
- **Perfectionism.** The procrastinator has unrealistically high personal standards or expectations, which leads to the belief that it's better to postpone work or not do it than to risk doing it less than perfectly (Kachgal, Hansel, & Nuter, 2001);
- **Fear of success.** The procrastinator fears that doing well will show others that he has the ability to achieve success, leading others to expect him to maintain those high standards in the future (Beck, Koons, & Milgram, 2000; Ellis & Knaus, 2002);
- **Indecisiveness.** The procrastinator has difficulty making decisions, including decisions about what to do first, when to do it, or whether to do it (Anderson, 2003; Steel, 2007), so they delay doing it or don't do it at all; and
- **Thrill seeking.** The procrastinator is hooked on the adrenaline rush triggered by rushing around to get things done just before a deadline (Szalavitz, 2003).

> Striving for excellence motivates you; striving for perfection is demoralizing."
>
> —Harriet Braiker, psychologist and best-selling author

If these psychological issues are at the root of procrastination, they must be uprooted and dealt with before the problem can be solved. This may take some time and assistance from a counseling psychologist (either on or off campus) who is professionally trained to deal with emotional issues, including those that underlie procrastination.

Think About It—Journal Entry 4.9

How often do you procrastinate? (Circle one.)

rarely   occasionally   frequently   consistently

When you do procrastinate, what's the usual cause?

_____

_____

_____

_____

_____

Strategies for Preventing and Overcoming Procrastination

Consistently use effective time management strategies. When effective time management practices (such as those cited in this chapter) are implemented consistently, they turn into regular habits. Research indicates that procrastinators are less likely to procrastinate when they convert their intentions or vows ("I swear I'm going to start tomorrow") into concrete action plans (Gollwitzer, 1999; Gollwitzer & Sheeran, 2006). When they repeatedly practice effective time management strategies with respect to tasks they tend to procrastinate on, their bad procrastination habits gradually fade and are replaced by good time management habits (Ainslie, 1992; Baumeister, Heatherton, & Tice, 1994).

> We are what we repeatedly do. Excellence, then, is not an act, but a habit."
> —*Aristotle, influential Ancient Greek philosopher*

Make the start of work as inviting or appealing as possible. Starting work—getting off the starting blocks—is often the major stumbling block for procrastinators. It's common for procrastinators to experience what's known as "start-up stress"—when they're about to start a task, they start having negative feelings about it, expecting it to be difficult, stressful, or boring (Burka & Yuen, 2008).

> The secret to getting ahead is getting started."
> —*Mark Twain (Samuel Clemens), American humorist and author of the Adventures of Huckleberry Finn (1885), a.k.a. "the Great American Novel"*

If you have trouble starting your work, sequence your work tasks in a way that allows you to start on tasks you find more interesting or are more likely to do well. Beginning with these tasks can give you a "jump start," enabling you to overcome inertia and create momentum. You can ride this initial momentum to motivate you to attack less appealing or more daunting work tasks that come later in your work sequence, which often turn out not to be as unpleasant or time-consuming as you thought they would be. Like many events in life, anticipation of the event turns out to be worse than the event itself. In one study of college students who didn't start a project until just before its due date, it was found that they experienced anxiety and guilt while they were procrastinating, but once they began working, these negative

> Did you ever dread doing something, then it turned out to take only about 20 minutes to do?"
> —*Conversation between two college students overheard in a coffee shop*

emotions subsided and were replaced by more positive feelings of progress and accomplishment (McCance & Pychyl, 2003).

You can also reduce start-up stress by beginning your work in an environment you find pleasant and relaxing (e.g., working in your favorite coffee shop while sipping your favorite beverage). In other words, if you have trouble starting work, start it in a place you enjoy while doing something you enjoy.

Organization matters. Research indicates that disorganization is a factor that contributes to procrastination (Steel, 2007). How well you organize your workplace and manage your work materials can reduce your tendency to procrastinate. Having the right materials in the right place at the right time can make it easier to get started. Once you decide to start working, you don't want to delay acting on that decision by looking for the tools you need to work with. If you're a procrastinator, this slight delay may provide the time (and excuse) to change your mind and not start working.

Note

The less time and effort it takes to start working, the more likely the work will be started.

One simple, yet effective way to organize academic materials is to develop your own filing system. Start by filing (storing) materials from different courses in different colored folders or notebooks. This not only enables you to keep all materials related to the same course in the same place, it also gives you immediate access to them when you need them. A filing system helps get you organized, gets rid of the stress associated with having things all over the place, and reduces your risk of procrasting by reducing the time and effort it takes to get started.

Location matters. *Where* you choose to work can influence *whether* your work gets done. Research indicates that distractions promote procrastination (Steel, 2007). Thus, working in an environment that minimizes distraction and maximizes concentration will reduce the risk of procrastination.

Arrange your work environment in a way that minimizes social distractions (e.g., people nearby who are not working), and media distractions (e.g., cell phones, e-mails, text messages, music, and TV). Remove everything from your work site that's not relevant or directly related to the work you're doing.

Your concentration will also improve if you work in an environment that allows you easy access to (a) work-support materials— (e.g., class notes, textbooks, and a dictionary), and (b) social support networks (e.g., working with a group of motivated students who help you stay focused, on task, and on track toward completing your work).

> "To reduce distractions, work at a computer on campus rather than using one in your room or home."
>
> —*Advice to new college students from a student finishing her first year in college*

 Think About It—Journal Entry 4.10

List your two most common sources of distraction while working. Next to each distraction, identify a strategy you might use to reduce or eliminate it.

Source of Distraction   *Strategy for Reducing this Distraction*

1.

2. _____

    _____

    _____

    _____

If you have difficulty maintaining or sustaining commitment to your work until it's finished, schedule easier and more interesting work tasks *in the middle or toward the end* of your planned work time. Some procrastinators have difficulty starting work, others have trouble continuing and completing the work they've started (Lay & Silverman, 1996). As previously mentioned, if you have trouble starting work, it might be best for you to start with tasks you find most interesting or easiest. In contrast, if you tend to experience procrastination by not completing your work once you've started, it might be better to schedule tasks of greater interest and ease at later points during your work session. Doing so can restore or revive your interest and energy. Tackling enjoyable and easier tasks last can also provide you with an incentive or reward for completing your less enjoyable and more difficult tasks first.

If you're close to completing a task, don't stop until you complete it. Just do it! Completing a task that's almost done allows you to build on the momentum you've already generated. In contrast, postponing work on a task that's near completion means that you have to overcome inertia and regenerate momentum all over again. As the old saying goes, "There's no time like the present."

    Furthermore, finishing a task gives you a sense of *closure*—the feeling of personal accomplishment and self-satisfaction that comes from knowing you've "closed the deal." Checking off a completed task can motivate you to keep going and complete the unfinished tasks ahead of you.

Divide large work tasks into smaller, bite-sized pieces. Work becomes less overwhelming and stressful when it's handled in small chunks or segments. You can conquer procrastination for large tasks by using a "divide and conquer" strategy: divide the large task into smaller, more manageable subtasks, then tackle and complete these subtasks one at a time.

    Don't underestimate the power of short work sessions. They're often more effective than longer sessions because it's easier to maintain concentration and momentum for shorter periods of time. By dividing work into short sessions, you can take quick jabs at a tall task, poke holes in it, and shrink its overall size with each successive jab. This reduces the pressure of having to deliver one, big knockout punch right before the final bell (deadline date).

> "I'm very good at starting things but often have trouble keeping a sustained effort."
> —*First-year college student*

> "Just do it."
> —*Commercial slogan of Nike, athletic equipment company named after the Greek goddess of victory*

> "To eat an elephant, first cut it into small pieces."
> —*Author unknown*

AUTHOR'S EXPERIENCE

The two biggest projects I've had to complete in my life were writing my doctoral the-sis and writing this book. The strategy that enabled me to complete both of these large tasks was to set short-term deadlines for myself (e.g., complete five to ten pages each week). I psyched myself into thinking that these little, self-imposed due dates were re-ally drop-dead deadlines that I had to meet. This strategy allowed me to divide one monstrous chore into a series of smaller, more manageable mini-tasks. It was like tak-ing a huge, indigestible meal and breaking it into small, bite-sized pieces that could be easily ingested and gradually digested over time.

—*Joe Cuseo*

> I long to accomplish some great and noble task, but it is my chief duty to accomplish small tasks as if they were great and noble."
>
> —*Helen Keller, seeing- and hearing-impaired author and activist for the rights of women and the handicapped*

Chapter Summary and Highlights

Effective goal-setting gets you going, but effective time management gets things done. To manage time effectively, we need to

- *Analyze* it. Break down time and become aware of how we spend it;
- *Itemize* it. Identify the tasks we need to accomplish and their due dates; and
- *Prioritize* it. Tackle our tasks in order of their importance.

Developing a comprehensive time management plan for academic work involves long-, mid-, and short-range steps that involve:

- Planning the total term (long-range step);
- Planning your week (mid-range step); and
- Planning your day (short-range step).

A good time management plan includes the following features:

- It transforms intention to action.
- It includes time to take care of unexpected developments.
- It contains time for work and play.
- It gives you the flexibility to accommodate unforeseen opportunities.

The enemy of effective time management is procrastination. Overcoming it in-volves letting go of two major myths:

- Better work is produced "under pressure"—on the day or night before it's due.
- Studying in advance is a waste of time—because you'll forget it all by test time.

Effective strategies for beating the procrastination habit include the following:

- Organize your work materials to make it easy and convenient for you to start working.
- Organize your work place or space so that you work in a location that mini-mizes distractions and temptations not to work.
- Intentionally arrange your work schedule so that you are working on more en-joyable or stimulating tasks at times when you're less vulnerable to procrastination.
- If you're close to finishing a task, finish it, because it's often harder to restart a task than to complete one that's already been started.
- Divide large tasks into smaller, more manageable units and tackle them in sepa-rate work sessions.

Mastering the skill of managing time is critical for success in college and beyond. Time is one of our most powerful personal resources; the better we manage it, the more likely we are to achieve our goals and gain control of our life.

> Doesn't thou love life? Then do not squander time, for that is the stuff life is made of."
>
> —Benjamin Franklin, 18th-century inventor, newspaper writer, and cosigner of the Declaration of Independence

Learning More through the World Wide Web: Internet-Based Resources

For additional information on managing time, and preventing procrastination, see the following websites:

Time-Management Strategies for All Students:
www.studygs.net/timman.htm

www.pennstatelearning.psu.edu/resources/study-tips/time-mgt

Time-Management Strategies for Adult Students:
www.essortment.com/lifestyle/timemanagement_sjmu.htm

Beating Procrastination:
www.mindtools.com/pages/article/newHTE_96.htm

http://success.oregonstate.edu/learning-corner/time-management/managing-procrastination

References

Ainslie, G. (1992. Specious reward: A behavioral theory of impulsiveness and impulse control. *Psychological Bulletin, 82*, 463–496.

American Association of Community Colleges 2009 Fact Sheet. (2009). Retrieved from http://www.aacc.nche.edu/About/Documents/factsheet2009.pdf.

Anderson, C. J. (2003). The psychology of doing nothing: Forms of decision avoidance result from reason and emotion. *Psychological Bulletin, 129*, 139–167.

Baumeister, R. F., Heatherton, T. F., & Tice, D. M. (1994). *Losing control: How and why people fail at self-regulation.* San Diego, CA: Academic Press.

Beck, B. L., Koons, S. R. & Milgram, D. L. (2000). Correlates and consequences of behavioural procrastination: The effects of academic procrastination, self-consciousness, self-esteem and self-handicapping [Special issue], *Journal of Social Behaviour & Personality, 15*(5) (2000), pp. 3–13Burka, J. B., & Yuen, L. M. (2008). *Procrastination: Why you do it, what to do about it now.* Cambridge, MA: De Capo Press.

Chu, A. H. C., & Cho, J. N. (2005). Rethinking procrastination: Positive effects of "active" procrastination behavior on attitudes and performance. *The Journal of Social Psychology, 145*(3), 245–264.

Covey, S. R. (2004). *Seven habits of highly effective people* (3rd ed.). New York: Fireside.

Ellis, A., & Knaus, W. J. (2002). *Overcoming procrastination* (Rev. ed.). New York: New American Library.

Goldsmith, E. B. (2010). *Resource management for individuals and families.* (4th ed.). Upper Saddle River, NJ: Prentice Hall.

Gollwitzer, P. M. (1999). Implementation intentions: Strong effects of simple plans. *American Psychologist, 54*(7), 493–503.

Gollwitzer, P. M., & Sheeran, P. (2006). Implementation intentions and goal achievement: A meta-analysis of effects and processes. *Advances in Experimental Social Psychology, 38*, 69–119.

Harriot, J. & Ferrari, J. R. (1996). Prevalence of procrastination among samples of adults. *Psychological Reports, 78* (1996), pp. 611–616.

HERI (Higher Education Research Institute) (2014). *Your first college year survey 2014.* Los Angeles, CA: Cooperative Institutional Research Program, University of California-Los Angeles.

Hobson, J. A. (1988). *The dreaming brain.* New York: Basic Books.

Kachgal, M. M., Hansen, L. S., & Nutter, K. T. (2001). Academic procrastination prevention/intervention: Strategies and recommendations. *Journal of Developmental Education, 25*(1), 2–12.

Lakein, A. (1973). *How to get control of your time and your life.* New York: New American Library.

Lay, C. H., & Silverman, S. (1996). Trait procrastination, time management, and dilatory behavior. *Personality & Individual Differences, 21*, 61–67.

Light, R. J. (2001). *Making the most of college: Students speak their minds.* Cambridge, MA: Harvard University Press.

McCance, N., & Pychyl, T. A. (2003, August). *From task avoidance to action: An experience sampling study of undergraduate students' thoughts, feelings and coping strategies in relation to academic procrastination.* Paper presented at the Third Annual Conference for Counseling Procrastinators in the Academic Context, University of Ohio, Columbus.

Morgenstern, J. (2004). *Time management from the inside out: The foolproof system for taking control of your schedule—and your life* (2nd ed.). New York: Henry Holt & Co.

Myers, D. G. (1993). *The pursuit of happiness: Who is happy—and why?* New York: Morrow.

Myers, D. G. (2000). *The American paradox: Spiritual hunger in an age of plenty.* New Haven, CT: Yale University Press.

Onwuegbuzie, A. J. (2000). Academic procrastinators and perfectionistic tendencies among graduate students. *Journal of Social Behavior and Personality, 15,* 103–109

Rhodewalt, F., & Vohs, K. D. (2005). Defensive strategies, motivation, and the self. In A. Elliot & C. Dweck (Eds.), *Handbook of competence and motivation* (pp. 548–565). New York: Guilford Press.

Solomon, L. J., & Rothblum, E. D. (1984). Academic procrastination: Frequency and cognitive-behavioral correlates. *Journal of Counseling Psychology, 31*(4), 503–509.

Steel, P. (2007). The nature of procrastination: A meta-analytic and theoretical review of quintessential self-regulatory failure. *Psychological Bulletin, 133*(1), 65–94.

Szalavitz, M. (2003, July/August). Tapping potential: Stand and deliver. *Psychology Today,* 50–54.

Voelker, R. (2004). Stress, sleep loss, and substance abuse create potent recipe for college depression. *Journal of the American Medical Association, 291,* 2177–2179.

Chapter 4 Exercises

4.1 Quote Reflections

Review the sidebar quotes contained in this chapter and select two that were especially meaningful or inspirational to you.

For each quote, provide a three- to five-sentence explanation why you chose it.

4.2 Reality Bite

You have a paper due tomorrow for your 10:00 a.m. class. You stay up late writing the paper, and then your friends call and ask you to go out. The paper is finished, and you decide you can print it off when you get to school tomorrow. You have a great time with your friends and oversleep, waking at 9:45 a.m. You go straight to the computer lab and experience difficulties printing off your paper. You find a lab technician to help you, but it takes him 40 minutes to retrieve the paper. You run into class (45 minutes late) and give the paper to your instructor, who informs you that she will take the paper for late credit because the class policy states that any papers handed in after the beginning of class are considered late.

1. Who is primarily responsible for this paper being late? Why?

2. How could the situation have been avoided or handled differently?

4.3 Term at a Glance

Review the syllabus (course outline) for each course you're enrolled in this term, and complete the following information for each:

Term _____Year _____

Course	Professor	Exams	Projects & Papers	Other Assignments	Attendance Policy	Late & Makeup Assignment Policy

1. Is the overall workload what you expected? Are you surprised by the amount of work required in any particular course or courses?

2. At this point in the term, what do you see as your most challenging or demanding course or courses? Why?

3. Do you think you can handle the total workload required for the full set of courses you're enrolled in this term?

4. What adjustments or changes could you make to your personal schedule that would make it easier to accommodate your academic workload this term?

4.4 Developing a Task Management Plan for Your First Term in College

1. Review the *course syllabus (course outline)* for each class you are enrolled in this term and highlight all major exams, tests, quizzes, assignments, and papers and the dates on which they are due.

2. Obtain a *large calendar* for the academic term (available at your campus bookstore or learning center) and record all the highlighted information for your exams and assignments for all your courses in the calendar boxes that represent their due dates. To fit this information within the calendar boxes, use creative abbreviations to represent different tasks, such as RA for reading assignment, E for exam, and TP for term paper. When you're done, you'll have a detailed chart or map of deadline dates and a master schedule for the entire term. There are several online calendars that can assist in managing your schedule (e.g., http://www.cozi.com/family-calendar.htm and http://pomodorotechnique.com/).

3. Activate the calendar and task lists functions on your PDA or smartphone. Enter your schedule, important dates, deadlines, and set alert reminders. By carrying your PDA or cell phone with your regularly, you will always have this information at your fingertips.

Reflections

1. Is your overall workload what you expected? Are your surprised by the amount of work time you will need to devote to your courses?

2. At this point in the term, what course is demanding the greatest amount of out-of-class work time? Have you been able to put in this time?

3. What adjustments or changes (if any) could you make to your personal schedule this term to create more time to handle your academic workload?

4.5 Time Analysis Inventory

1. Go to the following website: *pennstatelearning.psu.edu/resources/study-tips/time-mgt* Click on the link for the "time-management exercise."

2. Complete the time management exercise at this site. The exercise asks you to estimate the hours per day or week that you engage in various activities (e.g., sleeping, employment, and commuting). When you enter the amount of time devoted to each activity, this website will automatically compute the total number of remaining hours you have available in the week for academic work.

3. After completing your entries, answer the following questions (or provide your best estimate).

   a) How many hours per week do you have available for academic work?

   b) Do you have two hours available for academic work outside of class for each hour you spend in class? If you don't, what activities could be eliminated or reduced to create more time for academic work outside of class?

4.6 Developing a Time Management Plan for Your First Term in College

Keep in mind the task management plan you developed in Exercise 4.3, use the following *Week-at-a-Glance Grid* to map out your typical or average week for this term. Start by recording what you usually do on these days, including the times you're in class, when you work, and when you relax or recreate. You can use abbreviations (e.g., CT for class time, HW for homework, J for job, and R&R for rest and relaxation). List the abbreviations you created at the bottom of the page so that your instructor can follow them.

> "
> The amount of free time you have in college is much more than in high school. Always have a weekly study schedule to go by. Otherwise, time slips away and you will not be able to account for it."
>
> —*Advice to new college students from a first-year student (Rhoads, 2005)*

If you're a *full-time* student, plan for 25 *hours* in your week for homework (HW). (If you're a *part-time* student, find 2 *hours* you could devote to homework *for every hour* you're in class—i.e., if you're in class 9 hours per week, find 18 hours of homework time).

These homework hours could take place at any time during the week, including weekends. If you combine 25 hours per week of out-of-class school work with the amount of time you spend in class each week, you'll end up with a 40-hour academic workweek—comparable to a full-time job—which is how college should be viewed.

Week-at-a-Glance Grid

	Sunday	Monday	Tuesday	Wednesday	Thursday	Friday	Saturday
7:00 a.m.							
8:00 a.m.							
9:00 a.m.							
10:00 a.m.							
11:00 a.m.							
12:00 p.m.							
1:00 p.m.							
2:00 p.m.							
3:00 p.m.							
4:00 p.m.							
5:00 p.m.							
6:00 p.m.							
7:00 p.m.							
8:00 p.m.							
9:00 p.m.							
10:00 p.m.							
11:00 p.m.							

Reflections:

1. How likely are you to put this time management plan into practice? Circle one: Definitely Probably Unlikely

2. What would *promote or encourage* you to put this plan into practice?

3. What would *prevent or discourage* you from putting this plan into practice?

4. How do you think other students would answer the above three questions?

4.7 Ranking Priorities

Look at the tasks below and decide if they are A, B, or C priorities:

_____ Going for a run

_____ Writing a paper that is due tomorrow

_____ Paying your electric bill that is due next week

_____ Checking out what your friends are doing on Facebook

_____ Getting your haircut

_____ Making an appointment with your academic advisor to register for classes

_____ Playing your favorite video game

_____ Making it to your doctor's appointment

_____ Helping your sister plan her wedding

_____ Picking up your child's prescription from the pharmacy

_____ Studying for your final exams

_____ Calling your cousin to catch up on family gossip

_____ Making reservations for your vacation

_____ Going to see the hot new movie that has come out

_____ Getting your oil changed in your car

_____ Getting your car washed

4.8 Reality Bite

Procrastination: The Vicious Cycle

Delayla has a major paper due at the end of the term. It's now past midterm and she still hasn't started to work on it. She keeps telling herself, "I should have started sooner," but she continues to postpone her work and is becoming increasingly anxious and guilty. To relieve her growing anxiety and guilt, Delayla starts doing other tasks instead, such as cleaning her room and returning e-mails. This makes her feel a little better because these tasks keep her busy, take her mind off the term paper, and give her the feeling that at least she's getting something accomplished. Time continues to pass; the deadline for the paper grows dangerously close. Delayla now finds herself in the position of having lots of work to do and little time in which to do it.

Adapted from *Procrastination: Why You Do It, and What to do about It* (Burka & Yuen, 2008)

Reflection and Discussion Questions

1. What do you expect Delayla will do at this point? Why?

2. What grade do you think she'll end up receiving on her paper?

3. Other than simply starting sooner, what else could Delayla (and other procrastinators like her) do to break the cycle of procrastination?

4. Can you relate to this student's predicament, or do you know other students who often find themselves in this predicament?

4.9 Time Management PEPS Reflection

Look back at your PEPS Learning Style Inventory Report and answer the following questions.

1. Is your time of day preference late day, early day, or did you have no preference? Knowing this, when is the best time of day for you to take classes? To study?

2. How can you make your time of day preference part of your time management plan?

Chapter 4 Reflection

Looking back on suggestions from this chapter, what are three things you can do start managing your time better?

1.

2.

3.

Explain how you are going to make this happen.

Higher-Level Thinking

MOVING BEYOND BASIC KNOWLEDGE TO CRITICAL AND CREATIVE THINKING

National surveys consistently show that the primary goal of college faculty is teaching students how to think critically. This chapter will help you understand what critical thinking is and empower you to think in this way. You will be provided with thinking strategies that move you beyond memorization to higher levels of thinking and learn how to demonstrate higher-level thinking on college exams and assignments.

Equip you with higher-level thinking skills for achieving excellence in college and beyond.

Think About It—Journal Entry 5.1

To me, critical thinking is . . .

_____

_____

_____

_____

(At a later point in this chapter, we'll ask you to flashback to the response you made here.)

What Is Higher-Level Thinking?

Contestants on TV quiz shows like *Jeopardy* are asked questions that call for knowledge of facts: Who? What? When? or Where? If game show contestants were asked higher-level thinking questions, they'd be responding to questions such as: "Why?" "How?" "What if?" Higher-level thinking (a.k.a. higher-order thinking) refers to a more advanced level of thought than that used to acquire factual knowledge. It involves reflecting on knowledge and taking it to a higher level—evaluating its validity, integrating it with something else you've learned, or creating new ideas. As its name implies, higher-level thinking involves raising the bar and jacking up your thinking to a level that goes beyond merely remembering, reproducing, or regurgitating factual information.

> "
> To me, thinking at a higher level means to think and analyze something beyond the obvious and find the deeper meaning."
>
> —First-year college student

The number one educational goal of college professors is to help students think at a higher or more advanced level. In national surveys of college professors teaching freshman-level through senior-level courses in various academic fields, more than 95% of faculty report that the most important goal of a college education is to develop students' ability to think critically (Gardiner, 2005; Milton, 1982). Similarly, college professors teaching introductory courses for freshmen and sophomores report that the primary educational purpose of their courses is to develop students' critical thinking skills (Higher Education Research Institute, 2009; Stark, et al., 1990). Simply stated, professors are more concerned with teaching you *how* to think than teaching you *what* to think (i.e., what facts to remember).

Compared to high school, college courses focus less on memorizing information and more on thinking about issues, concepts, and principles (Conley, 2005). Remembering information in college may get you a grade of "C," demonstrating comprehension of that information may get you a "B," and going beyond comprehension to demonstrate higher-level thinking will earn you an "A." This is not to say that acquiring knowledge and basic comprehension are unimportant; they provide the stepping stones needed to climb to higher levels of thinking—as illustrated in **Figure 5.1**.

"What is the hardest task in the world? To think."

—*Ralph Waldo Emerson, celebrated 19th-century American essayist and lecturer*

FIGURE 5.1: **The Relationship between Knowledge, Comprehension, and Higher-Level Thinking**

©Kendall Hunt Publishing Company.

Note

College professors expect students to do more than just retain or reproduce information; they want you to demonstrate higher levels of thinking with respect to what you learned (e.g., analyze it, evaluate it, apply it, or integrate it with other concepts you've learned).

Studies show that memory for factual information acquired in college fades quickly with the passage of time. However, higher-level thinking is a *skill* (like learning to ride a bike) that's retained on a long-term basis and used for an entire lifetime (Pascarella & Terenzini, 1991, 2005).

Note

The focus of higher-level thinking is not just to answer questions but also to question answers.

Defining and Describing the Major Forms of Higher-Level Thinking

When your college professors ask you to "think critically," they're usually asking you to use one or more of the eight forms of thinking listed in **Box 5.1**. As you read the descriptions of each form of thinking, note whether you've heard of it before.

Box 5.1

Seven Major Forms of Higher-Level Thinking

1. Analysis (Analytical Thinking). Breaking down information to identify its essential parts and underlying elements.
2. Synthesis (Integrative Thinking). Building up ideas by connecting them to form a larger whole or more comprehensive system.

> In college ... you will be expected to get inside what you are learning to apply it, make comparisons and connections, draw implications, and use ideas."
>
> —Robert Shoenberg, author, Why Do I Have to Take This Course?

3. Application (Applied Thinking). Putting thinking into practice to solve problems and resolve issues.
4. Multidimensional Thinking. Viewing issues from a variety of vantage points to gain a more complete or comprehensive perspective.
5. Balanced Thinking. Carefully considering arguments for and against a particular position or viewpoint.
6. Critical Thinking (Evaluation). Judging the quality of arguments, conclusions, and thought processes—including all forms of thinking on this list.
7. Creative Thinking. Generating ideas that are unique, original, or distinctively different.

Think About It—Journal Entry 5.2

Look back at the seven forms of thinking described in **Box 5.1.** Which of these forms of thinking have you used on high school exams or assignments?

_____

_____

_____

_____

_____

Analysis (Analytical Thinking)

The mental process of analysis is similar to the physical process of peeling an onion. When you analyze something, you take it apart and pick out its key parts, main points, or underlying elements. For example, if you were to analyze a chapter in this book, you would do more than cover its content; you would try to uncover or discover its main ideas by detecting its essential points and distinguishing them from background information or incidental details.

In an art course, you would use analytical thinking to identify the underlying elements or separate components of a painting or sculpture (e.g., its structure, texture, tone, and form). In the natural and social sciences, you would use analysis to identify underlying reasons or causes for natural (physical) phenomena and social events—known as "causal analysis." For instance, a causal analysis of the September 11, 2001, attack on the United States would involve identifying the key factors that led to the attack or the underlying reasons why the attack took place.

> In physics, you have to be analytical and break it [the problem] down into its parts."
>
> —Physics student (quoted in Donald, 2002)

Think About It—Journal Entry 5.3

A TV commercial for a particular brand of liquor (which shall remain nameless) once showed a young man getting out of his car in front of a house where a party is going on. The driver gets out of his car, takes out a knife, slashes his tires, and goes inside to join the party. Using the higher-level thinking skill of analysis, what would you say are the underlying or embedded messages in this commercial?

_____

_____

_____

_____

_____

_____

Synthesis (Integrative Thinking)

When you engage in *synthesis*, you're using a thought process that's basically the opposite of analysis. Instead of breaking down or taking apart ideas, you piece them together to form an integrated whole—like piecing together parts of a puzzle. Connecting ideas learned in different courses is a form of synthesis, such as integrating ethical concepts learned in a philosophy course with marketing concepts learned in a business course to develop a comprehensive set of ethical guidelines for marketing and advertising products.

Although synthesis and analysis are seemingly opposite thought processes, they complement one another. Analysis enables you to disassemble information into its key parts; synthesis allows you to reassemble those parts into a new whole. For instance, when writing this book, we analyzed published material in many fields (e.g., psychology, history, philosophy, and biology) to detect pieces of information in these different fields that were most relevant to promoting the success of college students. We then synthesized or reassembled these parts to create a new whole—the textbook you're now reading.

Note

Synthesis is not just a summary of ideas produced by someone else, it's a thought process that integrates isolated pieces of information to generate a comprehensive product of your own.

Application (Applied Thinking)

When you learn something deeply, you transform information into knowledge; when you translate knowledge into practice, you engage in a higher-level thinking process known as *application*. It's a powerful form of higher-level thinking that allows you to transfer your knowledge to real-life situations and put it to use for practical purposes. For instance, you're engaging in application if you use the knowledge you've acquired about human relations in Chapter 10 to become more assertive, or when you take knowledge acquired in an accounting course to help manage your personal finances.

Always be on the lookout for ways to take action on the knowledge you've acquired by applying it to your personal life experiences and current events or issues. When you use your knowledge for the practical purpose of doing something good, such as bettering yourself or others, you not only demonstrate application, you also demonstrate *wisdom* (Staudinger, 2008).

Multidimensional Thinking

When you view yourself and the world around you from different perspectives or vantage points to gain a comprehensive perspective, you're engaging in *multidimensional thinking*. For instance, multidimensional thinkers are able to think from the following four key perspectives and see how each of them influences, and is influenced by, the issue they're examining.

1. Perspective of **Person (Self):** How does this issue affect individuals on a personal basis?
2. Perspective of **Place:** What impact does this issue have on people living in different parts of the country or world?
3. Perspective of **Time:** How will future generations of people be affected by this issue?
4. Perspective of **Culture:** How is this issue likely to be interpreted or experienced by groups of people who share different social customs and traditions? (the perspective of culture)

Important issues don't exist in isolation but as parts of a complex, interconnected system that involves interplay of multiple factors and perspectives. For example, global warming (climate change) is an issue that involves the gradual thickening and trapping of more heat in the earth's atmosphere as a result of a buildup in gases generated by the burning fossil fuels for industrial purposes (Intergovernmental Council on Climate Change, 2013). The consensus among today's scientists is that this buildup of human-made pollution is causing temperatures to rise (and sometimes fall) around the world, resulting in more extreme weather conditions and more frequent natural disasters—such as droughts, wildfires, hurricanes, and dust storms (Joint Science Academic Statement, 2005; National Resource Defense Council, 2005, 2012). As depicted in **Box 5.2**, understanding and addressing this issue requires understanding interrelationships among the multiple perspectives of person, place, time, and culture,

> "As gold which he cannot spend will make no man rich, so knowledge which he cannot apply will make no man wise."
>
> —Dr. Samuel Johnson, famous English literary figure and original author of the Dictionary of the English Language (1747)

> "To me, thinking at a higher level is when you approach a question or topic thoughtfully, when you fully explore every aspect of that topic from all angles."
>
> —First-year college student

Box 5.2

Understanding Climate Change from Four Key Perspectives

Person

Climate change involves humans at a personal level because individual efforts to conserve energy in our homes and our willingness to purchase energy-efficient products can play a major role in resolving this issue.

Place

Climate change is an international phenomenon that extends beyond the boundaries of any one country; it affects all countries in the world and its solution requires the joint effort of different nations around the world to reduce their level of carbon emissions.

Time

If the current trend toward higher global warming isn't addressed soon, it could seriously threaten the lives of future generations inhabiting the planet.

Culture

Industries in technologically and industrially advanced cultures are primarily responsible for contributing to the problem of climate change, yet its potentially adverse effects will be greater for less technologically advanced cultures because they lack the resources to respond to it (Joint Science Academies' Statement, 2005). Industrially advanced cultures will need to use their advanced resources and technology to devise alternative methods for generating energy in ways that reduce the risk of global warming for all cultures.

 Think About It—Journal Entry 5.4

Think of a current national or international problem (other than climate change) whose solution requires multiple perspective taking or systems thinking.

_____

_____

_____

_____

_____

Balanced Thinking

When we seek out and carefully consider arguments *for* and *against* a particular position, we're engaging in balanced thinking. The process of finding supporting evidence or reasons for a position is referred to as *adduction*—when you adduce, you identify reasons *for* a position; the process of finding evidence or reasons that contradicts a position is called *refutation*—when you refute, you provide a rebuttal *against* a particular position.

Balanced thinking involves both adduction and refutation. Each position's stronger arguments are acknowledged, and its weaker ones are refuted (Fairbairn & Winch, 1996). The goal of a balanced thinker is not to stack up evidence for one position or the other but to be an impartial judge looking at supporting and opposing evidence for both sides of an issue, and striving to draw a conclusion that's neither biased nor one-sided. When you consider the strengths and weaknesses of opposing arguments at the same time, it reduces the likelihood that you'll fall prey to an overly simplistic form of thinking typical of many first-year students—known as *dualistic* thinking—seeking the "truth" in the form of clear-cut, black-or-white answers or solutions to complex issues—where one position or theory is "right" and the others "wrong" (Perry, 1970, 1999).

Don't be surprised and frustrated if you find scholars disagreeing about what particular positions or theories are more accurate or account for most of the "truth" in their field. This is a healthy thought process known as *dialectic* or *dialogic* thinking (deriving from the root "dialogue" or "conversation"). It's a productive form of intellectual dialogue (Paul & Elder, 2014) that acknowledges different sides of a complex issue and results in a more balanced, integrated understanding of it. In a study of leaders who excel in the field of business, it was discovered that one of their distinguishing qualities was their capacity for "integrative thinking"—the ability to hold opposing or conflicting ideas in their head and use that tension to create a new and superior idea—much like how humans use their opposable thumbs to excel at manual tasks (Martin, 2007).

Keep in mind that your first step in the process of solving problems and seeking truth shouldn't be to immediately jump in and take an either-or (for-or-against) position. Instead, take a balanced thinking approach by looking at arguments for and against each position, acknowledge the strengths and weaknesses of both sides of the argument, and seek to integrate the best points of both arguments.

Lastly, balanced thinking involves more than just totaling the number of arguments for and against a position; it also involves *weighing* the strength of each argument. Arguments can vary in terms of their degree of importance or level of support. When weighing arguments, ask yourself, "What is the quality and quantity of evidence supporting it?" Consider whether the evidence is:

1. Definitive—so strong or compelling that a definite conclusion should be reached;
2. Suggestive—strong enough to suggest that a tentative or possible conclusion may be reached; or
3. Inconclusive—too weak to reach any conclusion.

When making class presentations and writing papers or reports, be mindful of how much weight should be assigned to different arguments and explain how their weight has been factored into your conclusion.

In some cases, after reviewing both supporting and contradictory evidence for opposing positions, balanced thinking may lead you to suspend judgment and withhold drawing a conclusion that favors one position over another. A balanced thinker may occasionally reach the following conclusion: "The evidence doesn't strongly favor one position over the other" or "More information is needed before I can make a final judgment or reach a firm conclusion." These aren't wishy-washy answers; they're legitimate conclusions to reach after all the evidence has been carefully considered. In fact, it's better to hold an undecided but informed viewpoint based on balanced thinking than to hold definite opinions that are uninformed, biased, or based on emotion—such as those often expressed by people on radio talk shows.

If you find that the more you learn, the more complicated things seem to become, this is good news. It means you're moving from simplistic to complex thinking that's more multidimensional and balanced.

> "The test of a first-rate intelligence is the ability to hold two opposed ideas in mind at the same time and still retain the ability to function."
>
> —*F. Scott Fitzgerald, regarded as one of the greatest American writers of the 20th century*

> "[Successful] business leaders have the capacity to hold two diametrically opposing ideas in their heads. And then, without panicking or settling for one alternative or the other, they're able to produce a synthesis that is superior to either opposing idea."
>
> —*Roger Martin, dean of the Rotman School of Management, University of Toronto*

> "For years I really didn't know what I believed. I always seemed to stand in the no man's land between opposing arguments, yearning to be won over by one side or the other but finding instead degrees of merit in both. But in time I came to accept, even embrace, what I called "my confusion" and to recognize it as a friend and ally, with no apologies needed."
>
> —*"In Praise of the 'Wobblies,'" by Ted Gup, journalist, who has written for Time Magazine, National Geographic, and The New York Times*

Think About It—Journal Entry 5.5

Consider the following positions:

1. Course requirements should be eliminated; college students should be allowed to choose the classes they want to take for their degree.

2. Course grades should be eliminated; college students should take classes on a pass–fail basis.

Using balanced thinking, identify one or more arguments *for* and *against* each of these positions?

_____

_____

_____

_____

_____

_____

Note

Balanced thinking enables you to become a more complex and comprehensive thinker capable of viewing issues from opposing sides and multiple perspectives.

Critical Thinking (Evaluation)

When we *evaluate* or *judge* the quality of an argument or work product, we're engaging in a form of higher-level thinking known as *critical thinking*. It's a skill highly valued by professors teaching students at all stages in the college experience and all subjects in the college curriculum (Higher Education Research Institute, 2009; Stark, et al., 1990). By working on developing your critical thinking skills as a first-year student, you will significantly improve you academic performance throughout your college experience.

Many students misinterpret critical thinking to mean "being critical"—criticizing something or somebody. Although critical thinking does involving making an evaluation or judgment, the evaluation can be either positive or negative. For instance, a movie critic can give a good (thumbs up) or bad (thumbs down) review of a film.

Critical thinking is used for many purposes beyond critiquing films, art, or music. It's a skill that enables you to "read between the lines" and cut through the fog or smog of ideas and arguments—including your own. Whether the evaluation is positive or negative (or some combination thereof), critical thinking involves backing up your evaluation with specific, well-informed reasons or evidence that support the critique. Failure to do so makes the criticism unfounded—that is, lacking any foundation or basis of support.

You can start developing the mental habit of critical thinking by using the following criteria as standards for evaluating ideas or arguments:

1. **Validity (Truthfulness).** Is it true or accurate?
2. **Morality (Ethics).** Is it fair or just?
3. **Beauty (Aesthetics).** Does it have artistic merit or value?
4. **Practicality (Usefulness).** Can it be put to use for practical or beneficial purposes?
5. **Priority (Order of Importance or Effectiveness).** Is it better than other ideas and alternative courses of action?

Think About It—Journal Entry 5.6

Flash back to **Journal Entry 5.1** on **p. 97.** How does your response compare with the definition of critical thinking just provided?

How are they similar?

_____

_____

_____

_____

_____

_____

How do they differ?

_____

_____

_____

_____

_____

Critical Thinking and Inferential Reasoning

When we make arguments or arrive at conclusions, we use a mental process called *inferential reasoning*. We start with a premise (a statement or observation) and use it to infer (step to) a conclusion. Two major ways in which we use inferential reasoning to make arguments and reach conclusions are: (a) through logical reasoning, and/or (b) citing empirical (observable) evidence.

1. *Logical Reasoning.* Reaching a conclusion by showing that it logically follows from or is logically consistent with an established premise. In other words, if statement "A" is true, it can be concluded that statement "B" is also true.

For example:

Statement A.   The constitution guarantees all U.S. citizens the right to vote. (Premise)

Statement B.   Women and people of color are citizens of the U.S.; therefore, they should have the right to vote. (Conclusion)

2. *Empirical (observable) evidence.* Reaching a conclusion by showing that it is supported with statistical data or scientific research findings. In other words, based on evidence "A," it can be concluded that "B" is true.

For example:

Statement A.   There is statistical evidence that a much higher percentage of people who smoke experience cancer and heart disease. (Premise)

Statement B.   Based on this statistical evidence, smoking is a major health risk. (Conclusion)

Although using logic and empirical evidence are different routes to conclusions, they can be combined to support the same conclusion. For instance, in this book, we use both logical arguments and empirical evidence (research and statistics) to support our conclusions and recommendations. Similarly, advocates for lowering the legal drinking age to 18 have used the following forms of logical reasoning and empirical evidence to support their position:

(a) Logical reasoning: 18-year-olds in the United States are considered to be legal adults with respect to such rights and responsibilities as voting, serving on juries, joining the military, and being held responsible for committing crimes; therefore, 18-year-olds should have the right to drink.

(b) Empirical evidence: In other countries where drinking is allowed at age 18, statistics show that they have fewer binge-drinking and drunk-driving problems than the United States.

Think About It—Journal Entry 5.7

Can you think of arguments *against* lowering the drinking age to 18 that are based on logical reasoning and empirical evidence?

_____

_____

_____

_____

Drawing inferences based on logic and empirical evidence are the primary thought processes that humans use to reach conclusions about themselves and the world around them. Inferential reasoning is also the form of thinking you will use to make arguments and reach conclusions in your college courses. You'll often be required to take positions and support your conclusions with sound reasoning and solid evidence. Adopt the mindset that you're a courtroom lawyer and be ready to prove your case with logical arguments and empirical evidence (exhibit A, exhibit B, etc.).

Logical Fallacies: Inferential Reasoning Errors

Unfortunately, errors can be made in the inferential reasoning process, which are commonly referred to as *logical fallacies*. Listed below is a summary of the major types of logical fallacies. Be mindful of them in your thinking and when evaluating the thinking of others. As you read the following reasoning errors, briefly note in the margin whether you've ever witnessed it or committed it.

- **Non sequitur.** Drawing a conclusion that doesn't follow from or connect with the premise—the initial statement or observation. (*Non sequitur* derives from Latin, which literally means, "it does not follow.") Example: There was a bloody glove found at the murder scene and it doesn't fit the defendant, therefore the defendant must be innocent.

- **Selective Perception.** Seeing only examples and instances that support one's position while overlooking or ignoring those that contradict it. Example: Believers of astrology who only notice and point out people whose personalities happen to fit their astrological sign, but overlook those who don't.

> A very bad (and all too common) way to misread a newspaper: To see whatever supports your point of view as fact, and anything that contradicts your point of view as bias."
> —*Daniel Okrent, first public editor of* The New York Times

- **Dogmatism.** Stubbornly clinging to a personal point of view unsupported by evidence while remaining closed-minded (nonreceptive) to other viewpoints better supported by evidence. Example: Arguing that adopting a national health system is a form of socialism that cannot work in a capitalistic economy, while ignoring the fact that there are many other nations in the world that have both a national health care system and a capitalistic economy.

- **Double Standard.** Having two sets of judgment standards—a higher standard for judging others and a lower standard for judging oneself. Example: Critically evaluating and challenging the opinions of others, but not our own.

> Facts do not cease to exist because they are ignored."
> —*Aldous Huxley, English writer and author of* Brave New World.

- **Wishful Thinking.** Thinking something is true not because of logic or evidence, but because the person *wants* it to be true. Example: A teenage girl who believes she will not become pregnant, even though she and her boyfriend are having sex without any form of contraception.

- **Hasty Generalization.** Reaching a conclusion prematurely on the basis of a limited number of instances or experiences. Example: Concluding that people belonging to a racial or ethnic group are all "that way" on the basis of personal experiences with only one or two individuals.

- **Jumping to a Conclusion.** Making a leap of logic to a conclusion that's based on a single reason or factor while ignoring other possible reasons or contributing factors. Example: A shy person immediately concludes that a person who doesn't make eye contact with her doesn't like her, without considering the possibility that the lack of eye contact may be due to the fact that the other person was distracted or shy himself.

> Belief can be produced in practically unlimited quantity and intensity, without observation or reasoning, and even in defiance of both by the simple desire to believe."
> —*George Bernard Shaw, Irish playwright and Nobel Prize winner for literature*

- **False Cause and Effect (a.k.a. Correlational Error).** Concluding that if two things co-occur at about the same time or in close sequence, one must *cause* the other. Example: The old belief that sexual activity causes acne because when children become teenagers, they are more sexually active and also are more likely to develop acne.

- **False Analogy.** Concluding that because two things are alike in one respect, they must be alike in another respect. This is the classic error of "comparing apples and oranges"—they're both alike in that they are fruits but they're not alike in other ways. Example: People who argue that government is a form of business, therefore it should be run like a business or run by a businessman. While it's true that government and business are societal institutions that have some similarities (e.g., budgets and payrolls), government is not a profit-making enterprise and it has purposes that are not fiscal in nature.

- **Glittering Generality.** Making a positive, general statement that isn't supported by specific details or evidence. Example: A letter of recommendation that describes the recommended person as a "wonderful person" with a "great personality," but provides little or no evidence to back up the claim.

- **Straw Man Argument.** Distorting an opponent's argument position and then attacking it. Example: Attacking an opposing political candidate for restricting civil liberties when, in fact, the opponent only supported a ban on concealed weapons.

- **Ad Hominem Argument.** Attacking the person, not the person's argument. (Literally translated, *ad hominem* means "to the man") Example: discounting a young person's argument by saying: "you're too young and inexperienced to know what you're talking about," or discounting an older person's argument by stating: "you're too old-school to understand this issue."

- **Red Herring.** Bringing up an irrelevant issue that disguises or distracts attention from the real issue being discussed or debated. (The term "red herring" derives from an old practice of dragging a herring—a strong-smelling fish—across a trail to distract the scent of pursuing dogs.) Example: People who responded to criticism of former President Richard Nixon's involvement in the Watergate scandal by arguing, "He was a good president who accomplished many great things while he was in office." (Nixon's effectiveness as a president is an irrelevant issue or a red herring; the real issue being discussed is Nixon's behavior in the Watergate scandal.)

- **Smoke Screen.** Intentionally disguising or camouflaging the truth by providing confusing or misleading explanations. Example: A politician who opposes gun control legislation by arguing that it's a violation of the constitutional right to bear arms, when in reality, the reason for his position is that he's receiving financial support from gun manufacturing companies.

- **Slippery Slope.** Using fear tactics to argue that not accepting a position will result in a "domino effect"—bad things will happen one after another—like a series of falling dominoes. Example: Arguing that "if America allows communism to happen anywhere, it will eventually happen everywhere."

- **Rhetorical Deception.** Using deceptive language to conclude that something is true without actually providing reasons or evidence. Example: Using glib words such as: "*Clearly* this is . . ." "It's *obvious* that . . ." or "Any *reasonable* person can see . . . ", without explaining why it's so "clear," "obvious," or "reasonable."

- **Circular Reasoning (a.k.a. "Begging the Question").** Drawing a conclusion by merely rewording or restating one's position without providing any supporting reasons or evidence, thus leaving the original question unanswered. This logical fallacy basically offers a conclusion that's simply a circular restatement of the premise—it's true because it's true. Example: Concluding that "stem cell research isn't ethical because it's morally wrong."

- **Appealing to Authority or Prestige.** Believing that if an authority figure or celebrity says it's true, it must be true. Example: Buying product X simply because a famous actor or athlete endorses it. Or, concluding that a course of action should be taken simply because the president says so.

- **Appealing to Tradition or Familiarity.** Concluding that if something has been considered to be true for a long time, or has always been done in a certain way, it must be true or must be the best way to do it. Example: "Throughout history, marriage has been a relationship between a man and a woman; therefore, gay marriage should be illegal."
- **Appealing to Popularity or the Majority (a.k.a. Jumping on the Bandwagon).** Believing that if an idea is popular or held by the majority of people, it must be true. Example: "So many people believe in psychics, it must be true; they can't all be wrong."
- **Appealing to Emotion.** Believing in something based on the emotional intensity of our reaction to an argument, rather than the quality of reasoning or evidence used to support the argument. Example: "If I feel strongly about something, it must be true" or believing that I should "always trust my feelings" and "just follow my heart."

> "Political talk shows have become shouting matches designed to push emotional hot buttons and drive us further apart. We desperately need to exchange ideas with one another rationally and courteously."
>
> —David Boren, president, University of Oklahoma and longest-serving chairman of the U.S. Senate Intelligence Committee

 Think About It—Journal Entry 5.8

Glance back at the reasoning errors just discussed. Identify the two most common errors you've witnessed or experienced.

_____

_____

_____

What were the situations in which these errors took place?

_____

_____

_____

_____

Why do you think they took place?

_____

_____

_____

_____

_____

AUTHOR'S EXPERIENCE

When I teach classes or give workshops, I often challenge students or participants to debate me on either politics or religion. I ask them to choose a political party affiliation, a religion or a branch of religion for their debate topic, or their stance on a social issue for which there are political or religious viewpoints. The ground rules are as follows: They choose the topic for debate; they can only use facts to support their argument, rebuttal, or both, and they must respond in a rational manner—without letting emotions drive their answers.

When I conduct this exercise, I usually discover that the topics people feel most strongly about are often those they haven't critically evaluated. For instance, people say they are Democrat, Republican, independent, and so on, and argue from this position; however, few of them have taken the time to critically examine whether their stated affiliation is actually consistent with their personal viewpoints. They almost always answer "no" to the following questions: "Have you read the core document (e.g., party platform) that outlines the party stance?" and "Have you engaged in self-examination of your party affiliation through reasoned discussions with others who say they have the same or a different political affiliation?"

> "Too often we enjoy the comfort of opinion without the discomfort of thought."
> —*John F. Kennedy, 35th U.S. president*

—*Aaron Thompson*

Creative Thinking

> "The principle mark of genius is not perfection but originality, the opening of new frontiers."
> —*Arthur Koestler, Hungarian novelist and philosopher*

> "The blues are the roots. Everything else are the fruits."
> —*Willie Dixon, blues songwriter; commenting on how all forms of contemporary American music contain elements of blues music, which originated among African American slaves*

> "Imagination should give wings to our thoughts, but imagination must be checked and documented by the factual results of the experiment."
> —*Louis Pasteur, French microbiologist, chemist, and founder of pasteurization (a method for preventing milk and wine from going sour)*

> "Creativity isn't 'crazytivity.'"
> —*Edward De Bono, internationally known authority on creative thinking*

Creative thinking leads you to ask the question: "Why not?" (e.g., "Why not do it a different way?"). When you generate something new or different—an original idea, strategy, or work product—you're thinking creatively.

The process of creative thinking may be viewed as an extension or higher form of synthesis. Like synthesis, separate ideas are integrated, but they're combined in a way that results in something distinctively different (Anderson & Krathwohl, 2001). For instance, the musical genre of hard rock was created by combining elements of blues and rock and roll, and folk rock was born when Bob Dylan combined musical elements of acoustic blues and amplified rock (Shelton, et al., 2003). Robert Kearns (subject of the film, "Flash of Genius") combined preexisting mechanical parts to create the intermittent windshield wiper (Seabrook, 2008).

Keep in mind that creative thinking is not restricted to the arts, it can occur in all subject areas—even in fields that seek precision and definite answers. In math, creative thinking involves using new approaches or strategies for arriving at a correct solution to a problem. In science, creativity takes place when a scientist first uses imaginative thinking to create a hypothesis or logical hunch ("What might happen if . . . ?") and then conducts an experiment to test out whether the hypothesis turns out to be true.

It could be said that thinking critically involves looking "inside the box" to evaluate the quality of its content. Thinking creatively involves looking "outside the box" to imagine other packages containing different content. Creative and critical thinking are two of the most important forms of higher-level thinking and they can work together in a cyclical and complementary fashion. Creative thinking is used to ask new questions and generate new ideas; critical thinking is used to evaluate or critique the ideas we generate (Paul & Elder, 2004). For an idea to be truly creative, it must not just be different or unusual, it must also be effective or significant (Runco, 2004; Sternberg, 2001). If our critique of what we've created reveals that it lacks quality or is ineffective, we shift back to creative thinking to generate something new and improved.

Or, the starting points for the cyclical process of creative and critical thinking may be reversed, whereby we begin by using critical thinking to evaluate an old idea or approach. If our evaluation indicates that it's not very good, we turn on the creative thinking process to come up with a quality of the new idea or different approach; then we turn back to critical thinking to evaluate the quality of the new idea we created.

Brainstorming is a problem-solving process that illustrates how creative and critical thinking work hand-in-hand. The steps or stages involved in the process of brainstorming are summarized in **Box 5.3**.

Box 5.3

The Process of Brainstorming

1. Generate as many ideas as you can, jotting them down rapidly without stopping to evaluate their validity or practicality. Studies show that worrying about whether an idea is correct often blocks creativity (Basadur, Runco, & Vega, 2000). So, at this stage of the process, just let your imagination run wild; don't be concerned about whether the idea you generate is impractical, unrealistic, or outrageous.
2. Review the ideas you generated and use them as a springboard to trigger additional ideas, or combine them into larger ideas.
3. After you run out of ideas, critically evaluate the list of ideas you've generated and eliminate those that you think are least effective.
4. From the remaining list of ideas, choose the best idea or best combination of ideas.

Note that the first two steps in the brainstorming process involve *divergent thinking*—a form of creative thinking that allows you to go off in different directions and generate diverse ideas. In contrast, the last two steps in the process involve *convergent thinking*—a form of critical thinking in which you converge (focus in) and narrow down the ideas, evaluating each of them for their effectiveness.

As this multistage process suggests, creativity doesn't just happen suddenly or effortlessly (the so-called "stroke of genius"); instead, it takes sustained mental effort (De Bono, 2007; Paul & Elder, 2004). Although creative thinking may occasionally involve spontaneous or intuitive leaps, it typically involves careful reflection and evaluation of whether any of those leaps actually land you on a good idea.

AUTHOR'S EXPERIENCE

I was once working with a friend to come up with ideas for a grant proposal. We started out by sitting at his kitchen table, exchanging ideas while sipping coffee; then we both got up and began to pace back and forth, walking all around the room while bouncing different ideas off each other. Whenever a new idea was thrown out, one of us would jot it down (whoever was pacing closer to the kitchen table at the moment).

After we ran out of ideas, we shifted gears, slowed down, and sat down at the table together to critique the ideas we generated during our "binge-thinking" episode. After some debate, we finally settled on an idea that we judged to be the best of all the ideas we produced, and we used this idea for the grant proposal—which, ultimately, was awarded to us.

> Creativity is allowing oneself to make mistakes; art is knowing which ones to keep."
>
> —Scott Adams, creator of the Dilbert comic strip and author of The Dilbert Principle

Although I wasn't fully aware of it at the time, the stimulating thought process my friend and I were engaging in was called brainstorming: first we engaged in creative thinking—our fast-paced, idea-production stage—followed by critical thinking—our slower-paced, idea-evaluation stage.

—*Joe Cuseo*

Note

Creative thinking is about generating new answers and solutions. Critical thinking is about evaluating the quality of answers and solutions we generate.

Think About It—Journal Entry 5.9

Do you consider yourself to be a creative thinker? Why?

_____

_____

_____

_____

What could you do to improve your ability to think creatively?

_____

_____

_____

_____

_____

Using Higher-Level Thinking Skills to Improve Academic Performance

Thus far, this chapter has focused primarily on helping you get a clear idea of what higher-level thinking is and what its major forms are. The remainder of the chapter focuses on helping you develop habits of higher-level thinking that can be applied to improve your performance in college and beyond.

Connect ideas you acquire in class with related ideas found in your assigned reading. When you discover information in your reading that relates to something you've learned about in class (or vice versa), make a note of it in the margin of your textbook or your class notebook. By integrating knowledge you've obtained from these two major sources, you're engaging in the higher-level thinking skill of synthesis, which you can then demonstrate on exams and assignments to improve your course grades.

When listening to lectures and completing reading assignments, pay attention not only to the content being covered but also the thought process used to cover the content. Periodically ask yourself what form of higher-level thinking your instructors are using during class presentations and authors are using when you're reading their writing. The more conscious you are of the type of higher-level thinking skills you're being exposed to, the more likely you are to develop those thinking skills yourself and demonstrate them on exams and assignments.

Periodically pause to reflect on your own thinking process. When working on different academic tasks, ask yourself what type of thinking you're doing (e.g., analysis, synthesis, or evaluation). Thinking about and becoming aware of how you're thinking while you're thinking is a mental process called _metacognition_ (Flavell, 1979; Hartman, 2001). It's a mental habit that's associated with higher-level thinking and improved problem-solving skills (Halpern, 2013; Resnick, 1986).

Develop habits of higher-level thinking by asking yourself higher-level thinking questions. One simple yet powerful way to help you reflect on your thinking is through self-questioning. Since thinking often involves talking to ourselves silently (or aloud), if we ask ourselves high-quality, thought-provoking questions, you can train your mind to think at a higher level. A good question can launch you on a quest or voyage to answer it by using higher-level thinking skills. Getting in the habit of asking yourself higher-level thinking questions while learning will increase the likelihood you'll display higher levels of thinking during class discussions, as well as on course exams and assignments.

> "If you do not ask the right questions, you do not get the right answers."
>
> —Edward Hodnett, British poet

 Think About It—Journal Entry 5.10

Critically evaluate the common practice of bars selling alcoholic drinks at reduced prices that's depicted in the preceding cartoon by answering the following questions:

1. What are the assumptions or implications of calling this practice "happy hour"?

2.   What are arguments for and against this practice?

Box 5.4 contains key questions you can use to trigger different forms of higher-level thinking. The questions are constructed as incomplete sentences so you can fill in the blank with any topic or concept you're studying in any course you may be taking. Research indicates that when students get in the habit of using question stems such as these, they develop and demonstrate higher levels of thinking in college courses (King, 1990, 1995, 2002). As you read the questions under each of the seven forms of higher-level thinking in the following box, think about how they may be applied to material you're learning in courses this term.

Box 5.4

Self-Questioning Strategies to Trigger Different Forms of Higher-Level Thinking

1.   ANALYSIS (ANALYTICAL THINKING)—breaking down information into its essential elements or parts.

Trigger Questions:
- What are the main ideas contained in _____?
- What are the important aspects of _____?
- What are the key issues raised by _____?
- What are the major purposes of _____?
- What hidden assumptions are embedded in _____?
- What are the reasons behind _____?

2.   SYNTHESIS (INTEGRATIVE THINKING)—integrating separate pieces of information to form a more complete and coherent product or pattern.

Trigger Questions:
- How can this idea be joined or connected with _____ to create a more complete or comprehensive answer?
- How could these different _____ be grouped together into a more general class or category?
- How could these separate _____ be reorganized

or rearranged to produce a comprehensive understanding of the big picture?

3.   APPLICATION (APPLIED THINKING)—using knowledge for practical purposes to solve problems and resolve issues.

Trigger Questions:
- How can this idea be used to _____?
- How can this theory be put into practice to _____?
- What could be done to improve or strengthen _____?
- What could be done to prevent or reduce _____?

4.   BALANCED THINKING—carefully considering reasons for and against a particular position or viewpoint.

Trigger Questions:
- Have I considered both sides of _____?
- What are the strengths (advantages) and weaknesses (disadvantages) of _____?
- What evidence supports and contradicts _____?
- What are arguments for and counterarguments against _____?

(continued)

Box 5.4 *(continued)*

5. MULTIDIMENSIONAL THINKING—thinking that involves viewing yourself and the world around you from different angles or vantage points.

   Trigger Questions:
   - Have I taken into consideration all factors that could influence _____ or be influenced by _____?
   - How would _____ affect different dimensions of myself (emotional, physical, etc.)?
   - What broader impact would _____ have on the social and physical world around me?
   - How might people living in different times (e.g., past and future) experience _____?
   - How would people from different cultural backgrounds interpret or react to _____?

6. CRITICAL THINKING (EVALUATION)—making critical judgments or assessments.

   Trigger Questions for Evaluating *Empirical Evidence:*
   - What examples support the argument that _____?
   - What research evidence is there for _____?
   - What statistical data document or back up this _____?

   Trigger Questions for Evaluating *Logical Consistency:*
   - If _____ is true, does it follow that _____ is also true?
   - If I believe in _____, should I practice _____?
   - To draw this conclusion means I'm assuming that _____?

   Trigger Questions for Evaluating *Morality (Ethics):*
   - Is _____ fair?
   - Is _____ just?
   - Is this action consistent with the professed or stated values of _____?

   Trigger Questions for Evaluating Beauty (Aesthetics):
   - Does _____ meet established criteria for judging artistic beauty?
   - What is the aesthetic merit or value of _____?

   - Does _____ contribute to or detract from the beauty of the environment?

   Trigger Questions for Evaluating *Practicality (Usefulness):*
   - Will _____ work?
   - What practical value does this _____ have?
   - What potential benefits and drawbacks would result if this _____ were put into practice?

   Trigger Questions for Evaluating *Priority (Order of Importance or Effectiveness):*
   - Which one of these _____ is the most important?
   - Is this _____ the best option or choice available?
   - How do these _____ rank from first to last (best to worst) in terms of their effectiveness?

7. CREATIVE THINKING—generating ideas that are unique, original, or distinctively different.
   Trigger Questions:
   - What could be invented to _____?
   - Imagine what would happen if _____?
   - What might be a different way to _____?
   - How would this change if _____?
   - What would be an innovative approach to _____?

Note: Save these higher-level thinking questions and use them when completing different academic tasks required in your courses (e.g., preparing for exams, writing papers or reports, and participating in class discussions or study group sessions). Get in the habit of periodically stepping back to reflect on your thinking and ask yourself what form of thinking you're engaging in (analysis, synthesis, application, etc.). You could even keep a "thinking log" or "thinking journal" to increase self-awareness of the thinking strategies you're using and developing. This strategy will not only help you acquire higher-level thinking skills, it will also help you communicate these skills in job interviews and letters of application for career positions.

Think About It—Journal Entry 5.11

Review the higher-level thinking skills listed in questions in **Box 5.4** above. Identify one trigger question listed under each of the seven forms of thinking and fill in the blank with an idea or issue being covered in a course you're taking this term.

_____

_____

_____

_____

_____

Strategies for Increasing Creativity

In addition to self-questioning strategies, the following attitudes and practices can be used to stimulate creative thinking.

> "All thinking begins with wonder."
>
> —*Socrates, classic Greek (Athenian) philosopher and founding father of Western philosophy*

- **Be flexible.** Think about ideas and objects in alternative and unconventional ways. The power of flexible and unconventional thinking was well illustrated in the movie "Apollo 13," based on the true story of an astronaut who saved his life by creatively using duct tape as an air filter. The inventor of the printing press (Johannes Gutenberg) made his groundbreaking discovery while watching a machine being used to crush grapes at a wine harvest. He thought that the same type of machine could be used for a different purpose—to press letters onto paper (Dorfman, Shames, & Kihlstrom, 1996).

- **Be experimental.** Play with ideas; try them out to see whether they'll work or work better than the status quo. Studies show that creative people tend to be mental risk-takers who are willing to experiment with different ideas and techniques (Sternberg, 2001). Consciously resist the temptation to settle for the security of familiarity. When people cling rigidly to what's conventional or traditional, they're clinging to the comfort or security of what's most familiar and predictable; this often blocks originality, ingenuity, and openness to change. Tom Kelley, cofounder of the famous IDEO design firm in Palo Alto, California, has found that innovative thinking emerges from an exploratory mindset that's "open to new insights every day" (Kelley & Littman, 2005).

- **Get mobile.** Stand up and move around while you're thinking. Research shows that taking a walk—either inside or outside—stimulates the production of creative ideas (Oppezzo & Schwartz, 2014). Even by standing up, our brain gets approximately 10% more oxygen than it does when sitting down (Sousa, 2011). Since oxygen provides fuel for the brain, our ability to think creatively is energized when we're up on our feet and moving around.

- **Get it down.** Creative ideas can often pop into our mind at the most unexpected times. Scholars refer to the sudden birth of creative ideas as *incubation*—just like incubated eggs can hatch at any time, so too can original ideas suddenly hatch and pop into our consciousness. However, just as great ideas can suddenly come to mind, they can also slip out of mind as soon as we start thinking about something else. You can prevent this slippage from happening by having the right equipment on hand to record your creative ideas before they slip away. Carry a pen and a small notepad, a packet of sticky notes, or a portable electronic recording device at all times to immediately record original ideas the instant you have them.

- **Get diverse.** Seek ideas from diverse social and informational sources. Bouncing your ideas off of different people and getting their feedback about your ideas is a good way to generate mental energy, synergy (multiplication of ideas), and serendipity (accidental discoveries). Studies show that creative people venture well beyond the boundaries of their particular area of training or specialization (Baer, 1993; Kaufman & Baer, 2002). They have wide-ranging interests and knowledge, which they draw upon and combine to generate new ideas (Riquelme, 2002). So, be on the lookout to combine the knowledge and skills you acquire from different subjects and different people, and use them to create bridges to new ideas.

- **Take breaks.** If you're having trouble discovering a solution to a problem, stop working on it for a while and come back to it later. Creative solutions often come to mind after you stop thinking about the problem you're trying to solve. What often happens when you work intensely on a problem or challenging task for a sustained period of time, your attention can get rigidly riveted on just one approach to its solution (German & Barrett, 2005; Maier, 1970). By taking your mind off of it and returning to it later, your focus of attention is likely to shift to a different feature or aspect of the problem. This new focus may enable you to view the problem from a different angle or vantage point, which can lead to a breakthrough idea that was blocked by your previous perspective (Anderson, 2010). Furthermore, taking a break allows the problem to incubate in your mind at a lower level of consciousness and stress, which can sometimes give birth to a sudden solution.

- **Reorganize the problem.** When you're stuck on a problem, try rearranging its parts or pieces. Reorganization can transform the problem into a different pattern that may enable you to suddenly see a solution you previously overlooked—similar to how changing the order of letters in a word jumble can help you find the hidden word. You can use the same strategy to change the wording of any problem you're working on, or by recording ideas on index cards (or sticky notes) and laying them out in different sequences and patterns.

    If you're having trouble solving a problem that involves a sequence of steps (e.g., a math problem), try reversing the sequence and start by working from the end or middle. The new sequence makes you to take a different approach to the problem; this forces you to come at it from a different direction, which can lead you to an alternative path to its solution.

> I make progress by having people around who are smarter than I am—and listening to them. And I assume that everyone is smarter about something than I am."
>
> —Henry Kaiser, successful industrialist, known as the father of American shipbuilding

> Eureka! (literally translated: "I have found it!")
>
> —Attributed to Archimedes, ancient Greek mathematician and inventor when he suddenly discovered (while sitting in a bathtub) how to measure the purity of gold

> Creativity consists largely of re-arranging what we know in order to find out what we do not know."
>
> —George Keller, prolific American architect and originator of the Union Station design for elevated train stations

Think About It—Journal Entry 5.12

The popularity of sticky notes is no doubt due to their versatility—you can post them on almost anything, remove them from where they were stuck (without a mess), and re-stick them somewhere else.

Think creatively for a minute. In what ways might you use sticky notes in a course or to handle a challenge you face in college?

_____

_____

_____

_____

_____

• **Be persistent.** Studies show that creativity takes time, dedication, and hard work (Ericsson, 2006; Ericsson & Charness, 1994). Creative insights typically don't occur effortlessly, but emerge after repeated reflection and sustained commitment.

Chapter Summary and Highlights

Higher-level thinking (also known as higher-order thinking) refers to a more advanced level of thought than that used to acquire factual knowledge. It involves reflecting on knowledge acquired and taking it to a higher level—by performing additional mental action on it—such as evaluating its validity, integrating it with other ideas, or applying it to solve problems.

In this chapter, seven major forms of higher-level thinking skills were identified along with strategies for developing each of them:

1. *Analysis (Analytical Thinking)*—breaking down information to identify its key parts and underlying elements;
2. *Synthesis (Integrative Thinking)*—building up ideas by connecting them to form a larger whole or more comprehensive system;
3. *Application (Applied Thinking)*—putting knowledge into practice to solve problems and resolve issues;
4. *Multidimensional Thinking*—taking multiple perspectives (i.e., viewing issues from different vantage points);
5. *Balanced Thinking*—carefully considering arguments for and against a particular argument or position;
6. *Critical Thinking*—evaluating (judging the quality of) arguments, conclusions, and ideas;
7. *Creative Thinking*—generating ideas that are unique, original, or distinctively different.

Besides achieving academic excellence in college, there are other key benefits of developing higher-level thinking skills.

1. Higher-level thinking is essential for success in today's "information age"—a time when new information is being generated at faster rates than at any other time in human history. The majority of new workers in the

information age no longer work with their hands, they will work with their heads (Miller, 2003). Employers now value college graduates who have inquiring minds and possess higher-level thinking skills (Harvey, et al., 1997; Peter D. Hart Research Associates, 2006).

2. **Higher-level thinking skills are vital for citizens in a democratic nation.** Authoritarian political systems, such as dictatorships and fascist regimes, suppress critical thought and demand submissive obedience to authority. In contrast, citizens of a democracy are able to control their political destiny by making wise choices about the political leaders they elect. Thus, effective use of higher-level thinking skills, such as critical thinking, is an essential civic responsibility for people living in a democratic nation.

3. **Higher-level thinking is an important safeguard against prejudice, discrimination, and hostility.** Racial, ethnic, and national prejudices are often rooted in narrow, self-centered or group-centered thinking (Paul & Elder, 2014). Oversimplified, dualistic thinking can lead individuals to categorizing others into either "in" groups (us) or "out" groups (them). Such dualistic thinking can lead, in turn, to ethnocentrism—the tendency to view one's own racial or ethnic group as the superior "in" group and see other groups as inferior "out" groups. Development of higher-level thinking skills, such as taking multiple perspectives and using balanced thinking, counteracts the type of dualistic, ethnocentric thinking that leads to prejudice, discrimination, and hate crimes.

4. **Higher-level thinking helps preserve mental and physical health.** Simply put: Those who use their mind don't lose their mind. As they age, mentally active people are less likely to suffer memory loss or experience dementia (Wilson, Mendes, & Barnes, 2002). Thinking is not only a mental activity, it's also a physical activity that exercises the brain, much like physical activity exercises muscles in other parts of the body. Thinking requires higher levels of energy, which stimulates biological activity among brain cells, invigorates them, and reduces the likelihood they will deteriorate with age.

©Kendall Hunt Publishing Company.

Contrary to common belief, problem solving and other forms of higher-level thinking will not "fry" your brain but will stimulate and exercise it, reducing the likelihood that you'll experience Alzheimer's disease and other causes of memory loss in later life.

Learning More through the World Wide Web: Internet-Based Resources

For additional information on thinking skills, see the following websites:

Higher-Level Thinking Skills: http://edorigami.wikispaces.com/Bloom%27s+Digital+Taxonomy

Critical Thinking: www.criticalthinking.org

Creative Thinking: www.amcreativityassoc.org

Thinking Errors: www.psychologytoday.com/blog/what-mentally-strong-people-dont-do/201501/10-thinking-errors-will-crush-your-mental-strength

www.factcheck.org (site for evaluating the factual accuracy of statements made by politicians in TV ads, debates, speeches, interviews, and news releases)

References

Anderson, J. R. (2010). *Cognitive psychology and its implications*. New York: Worth Publishers.

Anderson, L. W., & Krathwohl, D. R. (Eds.). (2001). *A taxonomy for learning, teaching, and assessing: A revision of Bloom's taxonomy of educational objectives*. New York: Addison Wesley Longman.

Baer, J. M. (1993). *Creativity and divergent thinking*. Hillsdale, NJ: Erlbaum.

Basadur, M., Runco, M. A., & Vega, L. A. (2000). Under–standing how creative thinking skills, attitudes and behaviors work together: A causal process model. *Journal of Creative Behavior*, Vol. 34, (2), pp 77–100.

Conley, D. T. (2005). *College knowledge: What it really takes for students to succeed and what we can do to get them ready*. San Francisco: Jossey-Bass.

De Bono, E. (2007). *How to have creative ideas*. London, UK: Vermillion.

Donald, J. G. (2002). *Learning to think: Disciplinary perspectives*. San Francisco: Jossey-Bass.

Dorfman, J., Shames, J., & Kihlstrom, J. F. (1996). Intuition, incubation, and insight. In G. Underwood (Ed.), *Implicit cognition* (pp. 257–296). New York: Oxford University Press.

Ericsson, K. A. (2006). The influence of experience and deliberate practice on the development of superior expert performance. In K. A. Ericsson, N. Charness, P. Feltovich, & R. R. Hoffman, (Eds.). *Cambridge handbook of expertise and expert performance* (pp. 685–706). Cambridge, UK: Cambridge University Press.

Ericsson, K. A., & Charness, N. (1994). Expert performance: Its structure and acquisition. *American Psychologist, 49*(8), 725–747.

Fairbairn, G. J., & Winch, C. (1996). *Reading, writing and reasoning: A guide for students* (2nd ed.). Buckingham: OU Press.

Flavell, J. H. (1979). Metacognition and cognitive monitoring: A new area of cognitive- developmental inquiry. *American Psychologist, 34*(10), 906–911.

Gardiner, L. F. (2005). Transforming the environment for learning: A crisis of quality. *To Improve the Academy, 23*, 3–23.

German, T. P., & Barrett, H. C. (2005). Functional fixedness in a technologically sparse culture. *Psychological Science, 16*, 1–5.

Halpern, D. F. (2013). *Thought & knowledge: An introduction to critical thinking* (5th ed.). New York: Psychology Press.

Hartman, H. J. (Ed.) (2001). *Metacognition in learning and instruction: Theory, research and practice*. Dordrecht: Kluwer Academic Publishers.

Harvey, L., Moon, S., Geall, V., & Bower, R. (1997). *Graduates work: Organizational change and students' attributes*, Birmingham, Centre for Research into Quality, University of Central England.

Higher Education Research Institute (HERI) (2009). *The American college teacher: National norms for 2007–2008*. Los Angeles: HERI, University of California, Los Angeles.

Intergovernmental Council on Climate Change (2013). *Climate change 2013: The physical science basis*. Working Group I Contribution to the Fifth Assessment Report of the Intergovernmental Council on Climate Change. Switzerland: Intergovernmental Panel on Climate Change. Retrieved from http://www.ipcc.ch/report/ar5/wg1/.

Joint Science Academies Statement (2005). *Global response to climate change*. Retrieved from http://nationalacademies.org/onpi/06072005.pdf.

Kaufman, J. C., & Baer, J. (2002). Could Steven Spielberg manage the Yankees? Creative thinking in different domains. *Korean Journal of Thinking & Problem Solving, 12*(2), 5–14.

Kelley, T., & Littman, J. (2005). *The ten faces of innovation: IDEO's strategies for beating the devil's advocate & driving creativity throughout your organization.* New York: Currency/Doubleday.

King, A. (1990). Enhancing peer interaction and learning in the classroom through reciprocal questioning. *American Educational Research Journal, 27*(4), 664–687.

King, A. (1995). Guided peer questioning: A cooperative learning approach to critical thinking. *Cooperative Learning and College Teaching, 5*(2), 15–19.

King, A. (2002). Structuring peer interaction to promote high-level cognitive processing. *Theory into Practice, 41*(1), 33–39.

Maier, N. R. F. (1970). *Problem solving and creativity in individuals and groups.* Belmont, CA: Brooks/Cole.

Martin, R. L. (2007). *The opposable mind: How successful leaders win through integrative thinking.* Boston: Harvard Business School Press.

Miller, M. A. (2003, September/October). The meaning of the baccalaureate. *About Campus*, pp. 2–8.

Milton, O. (1982). *Will that be on the final?* Springfield, IL: Charles C. Thomas. National Resources Defense Council (2005). *Global warming: A summary of recent findings on the changing global climate.* Retrieved from http://www.nrdc.org/globalwarming/science/2005.asp.

National Resources Defense Council. (2012). *Global warming: An introduction to climate change.* Retrieved from www.nrdc.org/globalwarming.

Oppezzo, M., & Schwartz, D. L. (2014). Give your ideas some legs: The positive effect of walking on creative thinking. *Journal of Experimental Psychology: Learning, Memory, and Cognition, 40*(4), 1142–1152.

Pascarella, E., & Terenzini, P. (1991). *How college affects students: Findings and insights from twenty years of research.* San Francisco: Jossey-Bass.

Pascarella, E., & Terenzini, P. (2005). *How college affects students: A third decade of research* (Vol. 2). San Francisco: Jossey-Bass.

Paul, R., & Elder, L. (2004). *The nature and functions of critical and creative thinking.* Dillon Beach, CA: Foundation for Critical Thinking.

Paul, R., & Elder, L. (2014). *Critical thinking: Tools for taking charge of your professional and personal life.* Upper Saddle River, NJ: Pearson Education.

Perry, W. G. (1970, 1999). *Forms of intellectual and ethical development during the college years: A scheme.* New York: Holt, Rinehart & Winston.

Peter D. Hart Research Associates, 2006. *How should colleges prepare students to succeed in today's global economy?* The Association of American Colleges and Universities by Peter D. Hart Research Associates, Inc.

Resnick, L. B. (1986). *Education and learning to think.* Washington, DC: National Academy Press.

Riquelme, H. (2002). Can people creative in imagery interpret ambiguous figures faster than people less creative in imagery? *Journal of Creative Behavior, 36*(2), 105–116.

Runco, M. A. (2004). Creativity. *Annual Review of Psychology, 55*, 657–687.

Seabrook, J. (2008). *Flash of genius and other true stories of invention*, New York: St. Martin's Press.

Shelton, et al., 2003 Evaluation of parameters affecting quantitative detection of Escherichia coli O157 in enriched water samples using immunomagnetic electrochemiluminescence. *J. Microbiology Methods, Dec; 55*(3): 717–25.

Sousa, D. A. (2011). *How the brain learns.* Thousand Oaks, CA: Sage.

Stark, J. S., Lowther, R. J., Bentley, M. P., Ryan, G. G., Martens, M. L., Genthon, P. A., et al. (1990). *Planning introductory college courses: Influences on faculty.* Ann Arbor: National Center for Research to Improve Postsecondary Teaching and Learning, University of Michigan. (ERIC Document Reproduction Services No. 330 277 370.)

Staudinger, U. M. (2008). A psychology of wisdom: History and recent developments. *Research in Human Development, 5*, 107–120.

Sternberg, R. J. (2001). What is the common thread of creativity? *American Psychologist, 56*(4), 360–362.

Wilson, R., Mendes, C., Barnes, L., and others (2002). Participation in cognitively stimulating activities and risk of incident Alzheimer's disease. *Journal of the American Medical Association, 287*(6), 742–748.

Chapter 5 Exercises

5.1 Quote Reflections

Review the sidebar quotes contained in this chapter and select two that were especially meaningful or inspirational to you. For each quote, provide a three- to five-sentence explanation why you chose it.

5.2 Reality Bite

Trick or Treat: Confusing Test or Challenging Test?

Students in Professor Plato's philosophy course just got their first exam back and they're going over the test together in class. Some students are angry because they feel the professor deliberately included "trick questions" to confuse them. Professor Plato responds by saying that his test questions were not designed to trick the class but to "challenge them to think."

Reflection and Discussion Questions

1.   What do you think may have led some students to conclude that the professor was trying to trick or confuse them?

2.   What type of test questions do you suspect the professor created to "challenge students to think"?

3.   On future tests, what might the students do to reduce the likelihood that they'll feel tricked again?

4.   On future tests, what might Professor Plato do to reduce the likelihood that students will complain about being asked "trick questions"?

5.3 Faculty Interview

Make an appointment to visit a faculty member on campus, either in a course you're taking this term, or in a field of study you're likely to pursue as your major. During your visit, ask the following questions:

1.   In your field of study, what key questions do scholars ask?

2.   How are answers to these questions investigated and discovered?

3.   How do scholars in your field demonstrate critical and creative thinking?

4.   What types of thinking skills does it take for students to succeed or excel in your field?

5.4 Self-Assessment of Higher-Level Thinking Characteristics

Thinking at a higher level is not just an intellectual process, it's also a personal attribute. Listed below are attributes of higher-level thinkers, accompanied by specific behaviors associated with each attribute. As you read the behaviors under each of the general attributes, place a checkmark (✓) next to any behavior that's true of you now and an asterisk (*) next to any behavior you think you need to work on.

1.   *Tolerant and Accepting*

____ Don't tune out ideas that conflict with your own

____ Keep your emotions under control when someone criticizes your personal viewpoint

____ Feel comfortable discussing controversial issues

____ Try to find common ground with others holding opposing viewpoints

2. *Inquisitive and Open Minded*

     ___ Eager to continue learning new things from different people and different experiences

     ___ Willing to seek out others who hold viewpoints different than your own

     ___ Find differences of opinion and opposing viewpoints to be interesting and stimulating

     ___ Attempt to understand why people have opposing viewpoints

3. *Reflective and Tentative*

     ___ Take time to consider all perspectives or sides of an issue before drawing conclusions, making choices, or reaching decisions

     ___ Give fair consideration to ideas that others may instantly disapprove of or find distasteful

     ___ Acknowledge the complexity, ambiguity and uncertainty of certain issues, and am willing to say: "I need to give this more thought" or "I need more evidence before I can draw a conclusion"

     ___ Periodically reexamine your own viewpoints to determine whether they should be maintained or changed

4. *Honest and Courageous*

     ___ Willing to examine your views to see if they're biased or prejudiced

     ___ Willing to challenge others' ideas that are based on personal bias or prejudice

     ___ Willing to express viewpoints that may not conform to those of the majority

     ___ Willing to change previously held opinions and personal beliefs when they're contradicted by sound arguments or new evidence

Look back at the list and count the number of checkmarks and asterisks you placed in each of the four general areas:

	Checkmarks	Asterisks
Tolerant and Accepting:	_____	_____
Inquisitive and Open Minded:	_____	_____
Reflective and Tentative:	_____	_____
Honest and Courageous:	_____	_____

Reflection questions:

- Under which of the four attributes did you place (a) the most *checkmarks*, (b) the most *asterisks*? What do you think accounts for the difference?

- What could you do in college to strengthen your weakest area (the attribute below which you had the most asterisks)?

5.5 Chapter 5 Reflection

How can you use critical thinking to be a more successful student? Explain. List three action steps you can do to make this happen.

How can you use critical thinking to improve your personal life? Explain.

How can you use creative thinking to be a more successful student? Explain. List three action steps you can do to make this happen.

How can you use creative thinking to improve your personal life? Explain.

CHAPTER 6

Deep Learning

STRATEGIC NOTE-TAKING, READING, AND STUDYING

This chapter will help you apply research on human learning and the human brain to become a more effective and efficient learner. It takes you through three key stages of the learning process—from the first stage of acquiring information through lectures and readings, through the second stage of studying and retaining the information you acquire, through the final stage of retrieving (recalling) the information you studied. The ultimate goal of this chapter is to supply you with a set of powerful strategies that can be used to promote learning that's *deep* (not surface-level memorization), *durable* (long-lasting), and retrievable (accessible to you when you need it).

Chapter Preview

Develop a collection of effective strategies for studying smarter, learning deeply, and retaining longer what you have learned.

Learning Goal

 Think About It—Journal Entry 6.1

Thought Starter

What would you say is the key difference between learning and memorizing?

Learning is the fundamental mission of all colleges and universities. One of the major goals of a college education is to help students become independent, self-directed learners. Learning doesn't stop after college graduation; it's a lifelong process that is essential for success in the 21st century. The ongoing information technology revolution, coupled with global interdependence, is creating a greater need for effective learning skills that can be used throughout life and in different cultural and occupational contexts. Today's employers value job applicants who have "learned how to learn" and will continue to be "lifelong learners" (SECFHE, 2006).

FIGURE 6.1: Network of Brain Cells

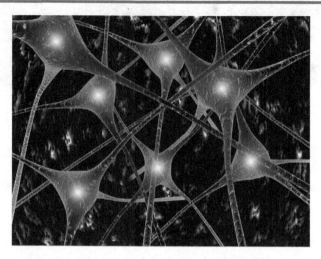

Deep learning involves making connections between what you're trying to learn and what you already know. When you learn something deeply, it's stored in the brain as a link in an interconnected network of brain cells.

©Jurgen Ziewe/Shutterstock.com

What Is Deep Learning?

When students learn deeply, they dive below the surface of shallow memorization; they go further by building mental bridges between what they're trying to learn and what they already know (Piaget, 1978; Vygotsky, 1978). Knowledge isn't acquired by simply pouring information into the brain as if it were an empty jar. It's a matter of attaching or connecting new ideas to ideas that are already stored in the brain. When this happens, facts are transformed into *concepts*—networks of connected or interrelated ideas. In fact, when something is learned deeply, the human brain actually makes a physical (neurological) connection between separate nerve cells (LeDoux, 2002). (See **Figure 6.1.**)

Studies suggest that most college students don't engage in deep learning (Arum & Roksa, 2011; Kuh, 2005; Nathan, 2005). They may show up for class most of the time, cram for their exams, and get their assignments done right before they're due. These learning strategies may enable students to survive college, but not thrive in college and achieve academic excellence.

Stages in the Learning and Memory Process

Learning deeply and retaining what you've learned is a process that involves three key stages:

1. **Sensory input (perception).** Taking information into the brain;
2. **Memory formation (storage).** Transforming that information into knowledge and storing it in the brain;
3. **Memory recall (retrieval).** Bringing that knowledge back to mind when you need it.

These three stages are summarized visually in **Figure 6.2**. These stages of the learning and memory process are similar to the way information is processed by a computer: (1) information is entered onto the screen (input), (2) that information is saved in a memory file (storage), and (3) the saved information is recalled and used

FIGURE 6.2: **Key Stages in the Learning and Memory Process**

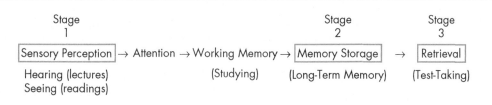

©Kendall Hunt Publishing Company.

when it's needed (retrieval). This three-stage process can serve as a framework for using the two major routes through which knowledge is acquired in college: from lectures and readings.

Effective Lecture-Listening and Note-Taking Strategies

The importance of developing effective listening skills in the college classroom was highlighted in a classic study of more than 400 students who were given a listening test at the start of their college experience. At the end of their first year in college, 49% of those students who scored low on the listening test were on academic probation—compared to only 4.4% of students who scored high on the listening test. On the other hand, 68.5% of students who scored high on the listening test were eligible for the honors program at the end of their first year—compared to only 4.17% of those students who had low listening test scores (Conaway, 1982).

Think About It—Journal Entry 6.2

Do you think writing notes in class helps or hinders your ability to pay attention to and learn from your instructors' lectures?

Why?

Studies show that information delivered during lectures is the number one source of test questions (and answers) on college exams (Brown, 1988; Kuhn, 1988). When lecture information isn't recorded in students' notes and appears on a test, it has only a 5% chance of being recalled (Kiewra, et al., 2000). Students who write notes during lectures achieve higher course grades than students who just listen to lectures (Kiewra, 1985, 2005), and students with a more complete set of lecture notes are more likely to demonstrate higher levels of overall academic achievement (Johnstone & Su, 1994; Kiewra & DuBois, 1998).

Contrary to a popular belief that writing while listening interferes with the ability to listen, students report that taking notes actually increases their attention and concentration in class (Hartley, 1998; Hartley & Marshall, 1974). Studies also show that when students write down information that's presented to them, they're more likely to remember the most important aspects of that information when tested later (Bligh, 2000). One study discovered that students with grade point averages (GPAs) of 2.53 or higher record more information in their notes and retain a larger percentage of the most important information than do students with GPAs of less than 2.53 (Einstein, Morris, & Smith, 1985). These findings aren't surprising when you consider that hearing information, writing it and then seeing it after it's been written produces three different memory traces (tracks) in the brain, thus tripling your chances of remembering it.

Furthermore, when notes are taken, you're left with a written record of lecture information that can be studied later to improve your test performance. In contrast, if you take few or no notes, you're left with little or no information to study for upcoming exams. As previously noted, the majority of questions on professors' exams come from information contained in their lectures. So, come to class with the attitude that your instructors are dispensing answers to test questions as they speak and your job is to pick out and record these answers so you can pick up points on the next exam.

Note

Points your professors make in class that make it into your notes turn into points earned on your exams (and higher grades in your courses).

You can get the most out of lectures by employing effective strategies at three key times: before, during, *and* after *class.*

Pre-Lecture Strategies: What to Do *Before* Class

1. **Check your syllabus to see where you are in the course and determine how the upcoming class fits into the total course picture.** By checking the course syllabus before individual class sessions you'll see how each part (class) relates to the whole (course). This strategy capitalizes on the brain's natural tendency to seek larger patterns and see the "big picture." The human brain is naturally inclined to connect parts into a whole (Caine & Caine, 2011). It looks for meaningful patterns and connections rather than isolated bits and pieces of information (Jensen, 2008). In **Figure 6.3**, notice how your brain naturally ties together and fills in the missing information to perceive a whole pattern that is meaningful.

2. **Get to class early so that you can review your notes from the previous class session and from any reading assignments relating to the day's lecture topic.** Research indicates that when students review information related to an upcoming lecture topic, they take more accurate and complete lecture notes (Jairam & Kiewra, 2009; Kiewra, 2005). Thus, a good way to improve your ability to learn from lectures is to review your notes from the previous class session and read textbook information related to the lecture topic—*before* hearing the lecture. Reviewing previously learned information activates your prior knowledge, enabling you to connect lecture material to what you already know—a powerful way to promote deep learning (Bruner, 1990; Piaget, 1978; Vygotky, 1978).

FIGURE 6.3: **Triangle Illusion**

You perceive a white triangle in the middle of this figure. However, if you use three fingers to cover up the three corners of the white triangle that fall outside the other (background) triangle, the white triangle suddenly disappears. What your brain does is take these corners as starting points and fills in the rest of the information on its own to create a complete or whole pattern that has meaning to you. (Also, notice how you perceive the background triangle as a complete triangle, even though parts of its three sides sides are missing.)

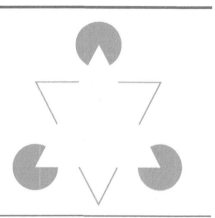

Listening and Note-Taking Strategies: What to Do *During* Class

1. **Give lectures your undivided attention.** As previously noted, research shows that in all subject areas, the majority of test questions appearing on college exams come from the professor's lectures and students who take better class notes get better course grades (Brown, 1988; Cuseo, et al., 2013; Kiewra, 2000). Studies also show that the more time students spend surfing the web or using Facebook during lectures, the lower their test scores. These results hold true for all students, regardless of how they scored on college admissions tests (Ravizza, Hambrick, & Fenn, 2014).

    Remember that like all humans, not all professors are created equal. You'll have some that are more dynamic and easier to pay attention to than others. It's the less dynamic ones that will tempt you to lose attention and stop taking notes. Don't let the less engaging or less entertaining professors lower your course grades. Instead view them as a challenge; step up your focus of attention, continue taking notes to keep yourself engaged, and leave the course with the satisfaction of earning a good grade.

2. **Take your own notes in class.** Don't rely on someone else to take notes for you. Taking notes in your own words focuses your attention and ensures the notes you take make sense to you. Research indicates that students who record and review their own notes on information presented to them earn higher scores on memory tests for that information than do students who review notes taken by others (Jairam & Kiewra, 2009; Kiewra, 2005). Taking your own notes in your own words makes them *meaningful to you*. While it's a good idea to collaborate with classmates to compare notes for completeness and accuracy, or to pick up points you may have missed, you shouldn't rely on someone else to do your note-taking for you.

3. **Take notes in longhand rather than typing them on a laptop.** Studies show that when students use a keyboard to type notes, they're more likely to mindlessly punch in the exact words used by the instructor, rather than transforming the instructor's words into words that are meaningful to them. When tested on understanding and memory for key concepts presented in class, students who took notes in longhand outperformed those who typed notes on a keyboard (Mueller & Oppenheimer, 2014). This may be due to the fact that the movements made during handwriting leave a motor (muscle) memory trace in the brain, which deepens learning and strengthens memory (Herbert, 2014).

4. **Be alert to cues for the most important information contained in lectures.**
Since the human attention span is limited, it's impossible to attend to and make note of everything. Thus, we need to use our attention *selectively* to detect and select information that matters most. Here are some strategies for identifying and recording the most important information delivered by professors during lectures:

- Pay particular attention to information your instructors put *in print*—on the board, on a slide, or in a handout. If your instructor has taken the time and energy to write it out or type it out, this is usually a good clue that the information is important and you'll likely see it again—on an exam.
- Pay special attention to information presented during the *first and last few minutes of class*. Instructors are most likely to provide valuable reminders, reviews, and previews at the start and end of a class session.
- Look for *verbal and nonverbal cues* that signal the instructor is delivering important information. Don't just tune in when your professors are writing something down and tune out at other times. It's been found that students record almost 90% of material written on the board, but less than 50% of important ideas that professors state but don't write on the board (Johnstone & Su, 1994; Locke, 1977; Titsworth & Kiewra, 2004). So, don't fall into the reflex-like routine of just taking notes when you see your instructor writing notes. Instead, listen actively to ideas you *hear* your instructor saying and take notes on these ideas as well. **Box 6.1** contains strategies for detecting clues to important information that professors are delivering orally in class.

Box 6.1

Detecting When Instructors Are Delivering Important Information during Lectures

Look for *verbal* cues, such as:

- Phrases signaling important information (e.g., "The point here is . . ." or "What's most significant about this is . . .").
- Information that's repeated or rephrased in a different way (e.g., "In other words, . . ", or "To put it another way . . . ").
- Stated information that's followed by a question to check understanding (e.g., "Is that clear?" "Do you follow that?" "Does that make sense?" or "Are you with me?").

Watch for *vocal* (*tone of voice*) cues, such as:

- Information delivered in a louder tone or at a higher pitch than usual—which may indicate excitement or emphasis.

- Information delivered at a slower rate or with more pauses than usual—which may be your instructor's way of giving you more time to write down these important ideas.

Keep an eye out for *nonverbal* cues, such as:

- Information delivered by your instructor with more than the usual:
  a. Facial expressiveness (e.g., raised or furrowed eyebrows);
  b. Body movement (e.g., gesticulation and animation);
  c. Eye contact (e.g., looking directly and intently at the faces of students to see if they're following or understanding what's being said).
- Your instructor moving closer to the students (e.g., moving away from the podium or blackboard).
- Your instructor orienting his or her body directly toward the class (i.e., both shoulders directly or squarely facing the class).

5. **Keep taking notes even if you don't immediately understand what your instructor is saying.** If you are uncertain or confused about the material being presented, don't stop taking notes. Having notes on that material will at least leave you with a record to review later—when you have more time to think about it and make sense of it. If you still don't understand it after taking time to review it, seek clarification from your instructor, a classmate, or your textbook.

6. **Take organized notes.** If your instructor continues to make points relating to the same idea, take notes on that idea within the same paragraph. When the instructor shifts to a new idea, skip a few lines and shift to a new paragraph. Be alert to phrases that your instructor may use to signal a shift to a new or different idea (e.g., "Let's turn to . . ." or "In addition to . . ."). Use these phrases as cues for taking notes in paragraph form.

By recording different ideas in different paragraphs, the organizational quality of your notes improves as will your comprehension and retention of them. Be sure to leave extra space between paragraphs (ideas) to give yourself room to add information that you may have initially missed, or to later translate the professor's words into your own words.

Another popular strategy for taking organized notes is the *Cornell Note-Taking System*.

There are several methods to take notes. It is important you find the note-taking method that works best for you. Examples include formal outlining, informal outlining, mapping, charting, and many others. Please refer to: http://www.redlands.edu/docs/Academics/1Five_Methods_of_Notetaking_2015.pdf for more information.

Post-Lecture Strategies: What to Do *After* Class

1. **As soon as class ends, quickly check your notes for missing information or incomplete thoughts.** Information delivered during a lecture is likely to be fresh in your mind immediately after class. A quick check of your notes at this time will allow you to take advantage of your short-term memory. By reviewing and reflecting on your notes, you can help move that information into long-term memory before forgetting takes place. This quick review can be done alone or, better yet, with a motivated classmate. If you both have gaps in your notes, check them out with your instructor before he or she leaves the classroom. Even though it may be weeks before you'll be tested on the material, the quicker you pick up missed points and clear up sources of confusion, the better; it will help you understand upcoming material—especially upcoming material that builds on previously covered material. Catching confusion early in the game also enables you to avoid the mad last-minute rush of students seeking help from the instructor just before test time. You want to reserve the critical time just before exams to study notes you know are complete and accurate, rather than rushing around trying to find missing information and seeking last-minute help on concepts presented weeks earlier.

⊜ Think About It—Journal Entry 6.3

Do you tend to stick around a few minutes after class sessions end to review your notes and clear up missing information or confusing points? Why?

_____

_____

_____

_____

What could you do immediately after class to be a more successful student?

_____

_____

_____

_____

_____

2. **Before the next class session meets, reflect on and review your notes to make sense of them.** Your professors will often lecture on information that you may have little prior knowledge about, so it's unrealistic to expect that you will understand everything that's being said the first time you hear it. Instead, set aside time to reflect on and review your notes as soon as possible after class has ended. During this review process, take notes on your notes by:
    *   Translating technical information into your own words to make it more meaningful to you; and
    *   Reorganizing your notes to get ideas related to the same point in the same place.

    Studies show that students who organize their lecture notes into meaningful categories demonstrate superior recall of that information on memory tests—compared to students who simply review the notes they took in class (Howe, 1970; Kiewra, 2005).

    ### Note

    Effective note taking is a two-stage process: Stage 1 involves actively taking notes in class and stage 2 takes places after class—when you take time to reflect on your notes and process them more deeply.

I spent my first year in college spending a lot of time trying to manipulate my schedule to create large blocks of free time. I took all of my classes in a row without a break to preserve some time at the end of the day for relaxation and hanging out with friends. Seldom did I even look at my notes until it was time to be tested on them. Thus, on the day before the test I was in a panic trying to cram the lecture notes into my head for the upcoming exam. Needless to say, I didn't perform well on many of my first tests. Eventually, a professor told me that if I spent some time each day re-writing my notes I would retain the material longer, increase my grades, and decrease my stress at test time. I employed this system and it worked wonderfully.

—Aaron Thompson

 ## Think About It—Journal Entry 6.4

Rate yourself in terms of how frequently you use these note-taking strategies according to the following scale:

4 = always, 3 = sometimes, 2 = rarely, 1 = never

1.	I take notes aggressively in class.	4	3	2	1
2.	I sit near the front of the class.	4	3	2	1
3.	I sit upright and lean forward while in class.	4	3	2	1
4.	I take notes on what my instructors say, not just what they write on the board.	4	3	2	1
5.	I pay special attention to information presented at the start and end of class.	4	3	2	1
6.	I take notes in paragraph form.	4	3	2	1
7.	I review my notes immediately after class to check that they are complete and accurate.	4	3	2	1

What works for you? What might you try to improve your note-taking skills?

_____

_____

_____

_____

_____

Strategic Reading

Expect to do more reading in college than you did in high school and be ready to be held accountable for the reading you're assigned. Information from assigned readings ranks right behind information from lectures as a source of test questions on college exams (Brown, 1988; Cuseo, et al., 2013). You're likely to find exam questions relating to reading assignments that your professors didn't talk about specifically in class (or even mention in class). College professors often expect you to re-late or connect their lectures with material they've assigned you to read. Furthermore, professors often deliver class lectures with the assumption that students have done the assigned reading, so if you haven't done it, you're more likely to have difficulty following what your instructor is saying in class. Thus, you should do the assigned reading but also do it according to the schedule the instructor has established. By completing assigned reading in a timely manner, you will (a) be better positioned to understand class lectures, (b) acquire information that's likely to appear on exams but not covered in class, and (c) improve the quality of your participation in class.

The following research-based strategies can be used to improve your comprehension and retention of material you read.

Pre-Reading Strategies: What to Do *Before* Reading

1. **Before jumping into your assigned reading, first see how it fits into the overall organizational structure of the book and course.** You can do this efficiently by taking a quick look at the book's table of contents to see where the chapter you're about to read is placed in the overall sequence of chapters. Look especially at its relationship to the chapters that immediately precede and follow it. This strategy will give you a sense of how the particular part you're focusing on connects with the bigger picture. Research shows that if students have advanced knowledge about how material they're about to learn is organized—if they see how its parts relate to the whole before they start learning the specific parts—they're better able to comprehend and retain the material (Ausubel, Novak, & Hanesian 1978; Chen & Hirumi, 2009). Thus, the first step toward improving reading comprehension and retention of a book chapter is to see how it relates to the book as a whole.

 Think About It—Journal Entry 6.5

When you open a textbook to read a chapter, how do you start the reading process? What's the first thing you do? Why?

_____

_____

_____

_____

_____

2. **Preview the chapter by first reading its boldface headings and any chapter outline, objectives, summary, or end-of-chapter questions that may be included.** Before tackling the chapter's specific content, get in the habit of previewing what's in the chapter to get a general sense of its overall organization. If you dive into the specific details first, you may lose sight of how the smaller details relate to the larger picture. Since the brain's natural tendency is to perceive

and comprehend whole patterns rather than isolated bits of information, start by seeing how the parts of the chapter relate to the whole. Just as looking at the whole picture of a completed jigsaw puzzle beforehand helps you connect its parts, so too does getting a picture of the whole chapter before reading its parts.

3. **Take a moment to think about what you may already know that relates to the main topic of the chapter.** This strategy will activate the areas of your brain where your prior knowledge about that topic is stored, thereby preparing it to make meaningful connections with the material you're about to read.

Strategies to Use *During* the Reading Process

1. **Read selectively to locate the most important information.** Effective reading begins with a plan for identifying what should be noted and remembered. Here are three key strategies you can use while reading to help you determine what information you should focus on and retain.

   - **Use boldface or dark-print headings and subheadings as cues for identifying important information.** These headings organize the chapter's major points; you can use them as "traffic" signs to direct you to the most important information in the chapter. Better yet, turn the headings into questions and read to find answers to them. This question-and-answer routine ensures that you read actively and with a purpose. (You can set up this strategy while previewing the chapter by placing a question mark after each heading contained in the chapter.) Creating and answering questions while reading also keeps you motivated because the questions stimulate curiosity and a desire to find answers to them (Walter, Knudsvig, & Smith, 2003). Another advantage of posing and answering questions about what you're reading is that it's an effective way to prepare for exams—you're practicing exactly what you'll be expected to do on exams—answering questions.

   - **Pay close attention to information that's *italicized*, <u>underlined</u>, CAPITALIZED, or bulleted.** These features call attention to key terms that must be understood and built on before you can proceed to understand higher-level concepts covered later in the reading. Don't simply highlight these words because their special appearance suggests they're important. Read these terms carefully and be sure you understand them before you continue reading.

   - **Pay special attention to the first and last sentences in each paragraph.** These sentences provide an important introduction and conclusion to the key point contained in the paragraph. It's a good idea to reread the first and last sentences of each paragraph before you move on to the next paragraph, particularly when reading material that's cumulative (builds on previously covered material), such as science and math.

Note

Your goal when reading is not just to cover the assigned pages, but to uncover the most important ideas contained on those pages.

2. **Take written notes on important information you find in your reading.** A good way to stop and think deeply about key ideas in your reading is to take notes on those ideas in your own words. Research shows that the common student practice of just highlighting the text (the author's words) is not a particularly effective strategy (Dunlosky, et al., 2013). Highlighting is a passive learning process, whereas note-taking actively engages you in the reading process

99

I would advise you to read with a pen in your hand, and enter in a little book of short hints of what you find that is curious, or that might be useful; for this will be the best method of imprinting such particulars in your memory, where they will be ready."

—Benjamin Franklin, 18th-century inventor, newspaper writer, and cosigner of the Declaration of Independence

and enables you to transform the text into your own words. Don't slip into the habit of using your textbook simply as a coloring book in which the artistic process of highlighting information in spectacular, kaleidoscopic colors distracts you from the more important process of learning actively and thinking deeply about what you're reading. Highlighting is okay as long it's not the only thing you do while reading; take time to make notes on the material you've highlighted—in your own words—to ensure that you reflect on it and make it personally meaningful. Taking notes on information delivered during lectures will improve your performance on exams; taking notes on your reading assignments will do the same.

> "I had the worst study habits and the lowest grades. Then I found out what I was doing wrong. I had been highlighting with a black magic marker."
>
> —Jeff Altman, American comedian

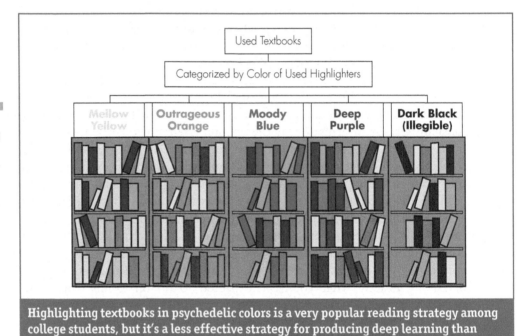

Highlighting textbooks in psychedelic colors is a very popular reading strategy among college students, but it's a less effective strategy for producing deep learning than taking written notes on what you read.

When you transform what someone else has written into your own words, you're implementing a powerful principle of deep learning: relating what you're trying to learn to what you already know (Demmert & Towner, 2003). A good time for pausing and writing a brief summary of what you've read in your own words is when you encounter a boldface heading because it indicates you're about to encounter a new topic; this is the ideal time to deepen your knowledge of what you just finished reading and use that knowledge to help you understand what's coming next.

 Think About It—Journal Entry 6.6

When reading a textbook, do you usually have the following tools on hand?

Highlighter:	yes	no
Pen or pencil:	yes	no
Notebook:	yes	no
Class notes:	yes	no
Dictionary:	yes	no
Glossary:	yes	no

If you don't usually have one or more of the above tools on hand while reading, which one(s) do you plan to have on hand in the future?

_____

_____

_____

_____

3. **Make use of visual aids that accompany the written text.** Don't fall into the trap of thinking that visual aids can or should be skipped because they're merely supplemental or ornamental. Visual aids, such as charts, graphs, diagrams, and concept maps are powerful learning and memory tools for a couple of reasons: (a) they enable you to "see" the information in addition to reading (hearing) it, and (b) they pull together separate ideas into a unified snapshot.

   Visual aids also improve learning and memory of written material by delivering information to the brain through a different sensory modality. In addition, periodically pausing to view visual aids adds variety and a change of pace to the reading process. Breaking up sustained periods of reading with a change of pace and different sensory input helps maintain your interest and attention (Malmberg & Murname, 2002; Murname & Shiffrin, 1991).

4. **Regulate or adjust your reading speed to the type of subject matter you're reading.** As you know, academic subjects vary in terms of their level of technicality and complexity. Reading material in a math or science textbook requires reading at a slower rate with more frequent pauses to check for understanding than reading a novel or a short story.

Post-Reading Strategies: What to Do *After* Reading

1. **End your reading sessions with a short review of the key information you've highlighted and taken notes on.** Rather than ending your reading session by trying to cover a few more pages, reserve the last five minutes to review the key ideas you already covered. Most forgetting of information takes place immediately after we stop focusing on the information and turn our attention to another task (Averell & Heathcote, 2011; Baddeley, 1999). By taking a few minutes at the end of a reading session to review the most important information you've just read, you help your brain "lock" that information into long-term memory before getting involved with another task.

   The graph in **Figure 6.4** represents the results of a classic experiment that tested how well information is recalled at various times after it was originally learned. As you can see on the far left of the graph, most forgetting occurs soon after information has been taken in (e.g., after 20 minutes, more than 60% of it was forgotten). The results of this classic study have been confirmed multiple times (Schacter, 2001) and they underscore the importance of reviewing key information acquired through reading *immediately* after you've read it. By doing so, your memory for that information improves dramatically because you're intercepting the human "forgetting curve" at its steepest point of memory loss—just after information has been taken in.

FIGURE 6.4: **The Forgetting Curve**

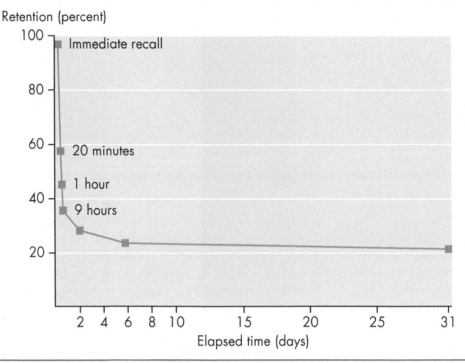

Source: Hermann Ebbinghaus, *Memory: A Contribution to Experimental Psychology*, 1885/1913

2. After completing a reading assignment, if you're still confused about an important idea or concept contained in the reading, go to another source. The problem may not be you—it may be the way the author has presented or explained it. You may be able to clear up your confusion by simply consulting another source or resource, such as those listed below.

   • **Look at how another book explains it.** Not all textbooks are created equal; some do a better job of explaining certain concepts than others. Check to see whether your library or campus bookstore has other texts dealing with the same subject as your course. A different book may be able to explain a hard-to-understand concept much better than your assigned textbook.

   • **Seek help from your instructor.** If you completed the reading assignment and made every effort to understand a particular concept but still can't grasp it, most instructors should be willing to assist you.

   • **Seek help from learning assistance professionals or peer tutors in your Learning Center (Academic Support Center).** This is your key campus resource for help with reading assignments, particularly if your instructor is unavailable or unwilling to provide assistance.

Box 6.2

SQ3R: A Method for Improving Reading Comprehension and Retention

A popular system for organizing and remembering key reading strategies, such as those discussed in this chapter, is the *SQ3R* system. SQ3R is an acronym for five steps that can be taken to increase textbook reading comprehension and retention, particularly when reading highly technical or complex material. The following sequences of steps comprise this method:

1. Survey
2. Question
3. Read
4. Recite
5. Review

S = Survey: Get a preview and overview of what you're about to read.

1. Use the chapter's title to activate your thoughts about the subject and get your mind ready to receive information related to it.
2. Read the introduction, chapter objectives, and chapter summary to become familiar with the author's purpose, goals, and key points.
3. Note the boldface headings and subheadings to get a sense of the chapter's organization before you begin reading. This supplies you with a mental structure or framework for making sense of the information you're about to read.
4. Take note of any graphics—such as charts, maps, and diagrams; they provide valuable visual support and reinforcement for the material you're reading.

5. Pay special attention to reading aids (e.g., italics and boldface font); use them to identify, understand, and remember key concepts.

Q = Question: Stay active and curious.

As you read, use boldface headings to formulate questions and read to find answers to those questions. When your mind is actively searching for answers, it becomes more engaged in the learning process. As you read, add any questions of your own that come to mind.

R = Read: Find answers to questions you've created.

Read one section at a time—with your questions in mind—and search for answers to these questions.

R = Recite: Rehearse your answers.

After you complete reading each section, recall the questions you asked and see if you can answer them from memory. If not, look at the questions again and practice your answers until you can recall them without looking. Don't move onto the next section until you're able to answer all questions in the section you've just completed.

R = Review: Look back and get a second view of the whole picture.

Once you've finished the chapter, review all the questions you've created for different parts or sections. See whether you can still answer them without looking. If not, go back and refresh your memory. Also, read the Chapter Summary. If any of the information in the summary seems unfamiliar, go back and find it and make sure you can relate it to what is in the summary.

 Think About It—Journal Entry 6.7

Rate yourself in terms of how frequently you use the following reading strategies, using the following scale:

4 = always, 3 = sometimes, 2 = rarely, 1 = never

1. I read chapter outlines and summaries before I start reading the chapter content.   4   3   2   1

2. I preview a chapter's boldface headings and subheadings before I begin to read the chapter.   4   3   2   1

3. I adjust my reading speed to the type of subject I am reading.   4   3   2   1

4. I look up the meaning of unfamiliar words and unknown terms that I come across before I continue reading.   4   3   2   1

5. I take written notes on information I read.   4   3   2   1

6. I use the visual aids included in my textbooks.   4   3   2   1

7. I finish my reading sessions with a review of important information that I noted or highlighted.   4   3   2   1

What works for you? What might you do to improve reading strategies?

_____

_____

_____

_____

Strategic Studying: Learning Deeply and Remembering Longer

Studying isn't a short sprint that takes place just before test time. Instead, it's more like a long-distance run that takes place over time. Studying the night before an exam should be the last step in a sequence of test-preparation steps that take place well before test time, which include: (a) taking accurate and complete notes in class, (b) doing the assigned reading, and (c) seeking help from professors or peers along the way for any concepts that are unclear or confusing. After these steps have been taken, you are then well-positioned to study the material you've acquired and learn it deeply.

Described below is a series of study strategies you can use to promote deep and durable (long-lasting) learning.

Give Studying Your Undivided Attention

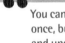

> You can do several things at once, but only if they are easy and undemanding. You are probably safe carrying on a conversation with a passenger while driving on an empty highway [but] you could not compute the product of 17 x 24 while making a left turn into dense traffic, and you certainly should not try."
>
> —*Daniel Kahneman, professor emeritus of Psychology, and author of Thinking Fast and Slow*

The human attention span has limited capacity—we have only so much of it available to us at any point in time and we can give all or part of it to whatever task(s) we're working on. As the phrase "paying attention" suggests, it's like paying money, we only have so much of it to spend. Thus, if attention while studying is spent on other activities at the same time (e.g., listening to music, watching TV, or text messaging friends), there's a deduction in the amount of attention paid to studying. In other words, studying doesn't receive our undivided attention.

Studies show that when people multitask they don't pay equal attention to all tasks at the same time; instead, they divide their attention by shifting it back and forth between tasks (Howard, 2014). Their performance on the task that demands the most concentration or deepest thinking is the one that suffers the most (Crawford & Strapp, 1994). When performing complex mental tasks that cannot be done

Multitasking while studying interferes with learning by dividing up attention and driving down comprehension and retention.

automatically or mindlessly, the brain needs quiet, internal reflection time for permanent connections to form between brain cells—which is what must happen if deep, long-lasting learning is to take place (Jensen, 2008). If the brain must simultaneously engage in other tasks or process other sources of external stimulation, this connection-making process is interfered with and learning is impaired.

So, give study time your undivided attention by unplugging all your electronic accessories. You can even use apps to help you do so (e.g., to silence your phone). Another strategy would be to set aside a short block of time to check electronic messages after you've completed a longer block of study time (e.g., as a study break); this allows you to use social media as a reward *after* putting in a stretch of focused study time. Just don't do both at the *same* time.

AUTHOR'S EXPERIENCE

When I was in college there were so many distractions for me. I had a job that I could work as many hours as I wanted to work. I had organizations where I was offered leadership positions. In addition, there were so many attractive girls. Then there were all these demanding classes that required me to study. To be honest, I enjoyed some of these distractions more than others. Well, that's another story for another day and another book. What I did know was that my education was the most important thing to me so I had to prioritize it. Thus, I had to study, learn, and do well in order to graduate. To do this I had to **REDUCE MY DISTRACTIONS!!** So, I developed Thompson's plan of action. They were: 1. Find a friend or two who also wanted to learn who could be study partners. What I realized was that my primary learning style is auditory (this worked well when I needed to study for a test). 2. If I was studying alone, find a place that was quiet where I could not listen to music or turn on the TV (the library was my favorite place to do this). BTW, in today's terms, that means no internet, text, phone, etc. 3. Never study when I am hungry and tired. 4. Give myself enough time to complete the assigned study task where I did not feel I had to rush through the material.

—Aaron Thompson

Make Meaningful Associations

Deep learning doesn't take place by simply absorbing information like a sponge—in exactly the same, prepackaged form as you received it from a textbook or lecture. Instead, deep learning involves actively translating the information you receive into a form that makes sense to you (Biggs & Tang, 2007; Mayer, 2002).

Note

Deep learning is not about teachers transmitting information to students; it's about students transforming that information into knowledge that's meaningful to them.

The brain's natural learning tendency is to translate unfamiliar information into a familiar form that makes sense and has personal meaning. This is illustrated in the experience.

AUTHOR'S EXPERIENCE

When my son was about three years old, we were riding in the car together and listening to a song by the Beatles titled, *Sergeant Pepper's Lonely Hearts Club Band*. You may be familiar with this tune, but in case you're not, there's a part in it where the following lyrics are sung repeatedly: "Sergeant Pepper's Lonely, Sergeant Pepper's Lonely, Sergeant Pepper's Lonely . . . ."

When this part of the song was being played, I noticed that my three-year-old son was singing along. I thought it was pretty amazing for a boy his age to be able to understand and repeat those lyrics. However, when that part of the song came on again, I listened to him more closely and noticed he wasn't singing "Sergeant Pepper's Lonely, Sergeant Pepper's Lonely . . ." Instead, he was singing: "Sausage Pepperoni, Sausage Pepperoni . . ." (which were his two favorite pizza toppings).

My son's brain was doing what all human brains tend to naturally do. It took unfamiliar information—song lyrics that didn't make any sense to him—and transformed it into a form that was meaningful to him.

—Joe Cuseo

You can experience the brain's natural inclination for meaning-making by reading the following passage, which once appeared anonymously on the Internet.

Aoccdrnig to rscheearch at Cmabridge Uinverstisy, it deos't mattaer in what order the ltteers in a word are, the only iprmoetnt thing is that the frist and lsat ltteer be at the rghit pclae. The rset can be a total mses and you can still raed it wouthit a porbelm. This is bcusae the human mind deos not raed ervey lteter by istlef, but the word as a wlohe. Amzanig huh?

Notice how easily you made meaning out of unfamiliar, misspelled words by naturally transforming them into familiar, meaningful words—which were already stored in your brain. Whenever you're learning something new, capitalize on the brain's natural tendency to find meaning by trying to connect what you're trying to understand to what you already know.

Learning the specialized terminology associated with different academic disciplines may seem like learning a foreign language for a student with little or no experience with these terms. However, before you start brutally beating these terms into your brain through sheer repetition, try to find meaning in them. One way to do so is by looking up the term's word root in the dictionary or by identifying its prefix or suffix, which may give away the term's meaning. For instance, suppose you're taking a biology course and studying the autonomic nervous system—the part of the nervous system that operates without conscious awareness or voluntary control (e.g., your heart and lungs). The meaning of this biological term is found in its prefix "auto," meaning self-controlling or "automatic" (e.g., automatic transmission). Once you find meaning in a term, you can learn it faster and retain it longer than by memorizing it through sheer repetition.

If looking up an academic term's root, prefix, or suffix doesn't reveal its meaning, see if you can make it meaningful to you in some other way. Suppose you looked up the root of the term "artery" and nothing about the origins of this term helped you understand its meaning or purpose. You could create your own meaning for this term by taking its first letter (a), and have it stand for "away"—to help you remember that arteries carry blood away from the heart. By so doing, you take a meaningless term and make it personally meaningful and memorable.

 ## Think About It—Journal Entry 6.8

Think of a technical academic term or concept you're learning in a course this term, and create a meaningful association you could use to remember it.

_____

_____

_____

_____

_____

Another way you can make learning meaningful is by *comparing and contrasting* what you're learning with what you already know. When you're studying, get in the habit of asking yourself the following questions:

1. How is this idea similar or comparable to something that I've already learned? (Compare)
2. How is this idea different from what I've already learned? (Contrast)

Research indicates that this simple strategy is one of the most powerful ways to promote learning of academic information (Marzano, Pickering, & Pollock, 2001). When you ask yourself the question, "How is this similar to and different from concepts I already know?" you make the learning process more meaningful and relevant because you're relating what you're trying to learn to what you already know or have already experienced.

Note

When learning, go for meaning first, memorization last. If you can connect what you're trying to learn to what you already know, the deeper you'll learn it and the longer you'll remember it.

Integrate Information from Lectures and Readings

Connect ideas from your lecture notes and reading assignments that relate to the same concept. Get them in the same place by recording them on the same index card under the same category heading. Index cards can be used like a portable file

> "The extent to which we remember a new experience has more to do with how it relates to existing memories than with how many times or how recently we have experienced it."
>
> *—Morton Hunt*, The Universe Within: A New Science Explores the Human Mind

cabinet, whereby each card functions like the hub of a wheel, around which individual pieces of related information can be attached like spokes. In contrast, when ideas pertaining to the same point or concept are spread all over the place, they're more likely to take that form in your mind—leaving them mentally disconnected and leaving you more confused or overwhelmed (and stressed out).

Note

Deep learners ask questions like: How can this specific piece of information be categorized or classified into a larger concept? How does this particular idea relate to or "fit into" something bigger?

Distribute Study Time across Separate Study Sessions

Learning deeply depends not only on how you learn (your method), but when you learn (your timing). Equally important as how much time you spend studying is how you distribute or spread out your study time. Research consistently shows that for students of all abilities and ages, distributing study time across several shorter sessions results in deeper learning and longer retention than channeling all study time into one long session (Brown, Roediger, & McDaniel, 2014; Carey, 2014; Dunlosky, et al., 2013). Distributed practice improves your learning and memory in two major ways:

- It minimizes loss of attention due to fatigue or boredom.
- It reduces mental interference by giving the brain some downtime to cool down and lock in information it has received before being interrupted by the need to deal with additional information (Malmberg & Murnane, 2002; Murname & Shiffrin, 1991). Memory works like a muscle: after it's been exercised, if given some "cool down" time before it's exerted again, it builds greater strength—that is, stronger memory for what it previously learned (Carey, 2014). On the other hand, if the brain's downtime is interfered with by the arrival of additional information, it gets overloaded and its capacity for handling information becomes impaired. That's what cramming does—it overloads the brain with lots of information in a limited period of time. In contrast, distributed study does just the opposite—it uses shorter sessions with downtime between sessions—giving the brain time to slow down and retain the information it's previously processed (studied) and more time to move that information from short-term to long-term memory (Willis, 2006).

> "Hurriedly jam-packing a brain is akin to speed-packing a cheap suitcase—it holds its new load for a while, then most everything falls out."
>
> *—Benedict Carey, author,* How We Learn: Throw Out the Rule Book and Unlock Your Brain's Potential

Distributed study is also less stressful and more motivating than cramming. You're more likely to start studying when you know you won't be doing it for a long stretch of time (or lose any sleep doing it). It's also easier to sustain attention for tasks that are done for a shorter period of time.

Although cramming just before exams is better than not studying at all, it's far less effective than studying that's spread out across time. Instead of frantically cramming total study time into one long session ("massed practice"), use *distributed practice*—"distribute" or space out your study time over several shorter sessions.

Think About It—Journal Entry 6.9

Are you more likely to study in advance of exams or cram just before exams? Explain.

How do you think most students would answer this question?

Use the "Part-to-Whole" Study Method

A natural extension of distributed practice is the part-to-whole method. This method involves breaking up the material you need to learn into smaller parts and studying those parts in separate sessions in advance of the exam; then you use your last study session just before the exam to review (restudy) the parts you previously studied in separate sessions. Thus, your last session isn't a cram session or even a study session, it's a review session.

Research shows that students of all ability levels learn material in college courses more effectively when it's studied in small units and when progression to the next unit takes place only after the previous unit has been mastered or understood (Pascarella & Terenzini, 1991, 2005).

Don't buy into the myth that studying in advance is a waste of time because you'll forget it all by test time. (Procrastinators often use this argument to rationalize their habit of putting off studying until the very last moment, which forces them to cram frantically the night before exams.) Even if you aren't able to recall what you previously studied when you look at it again closer to test time, research shows that once you start reviewing it, you can relearn it in a fraction of the time it took the first time. Since it takes much less time to relearn the material because the brain still has a memory trace for information studied in the earlier sessions (Kintsch, 1994), it proves you didn't completely forget it and that studying it in advance wasn't a waste of time. Another key advantage of breaking material you're learning into smaller parts and studying those parts in advance of major exams is that it allows you to check your understanding of the part you studied before moving on to learning the next part. This is a particularly important advantage in courses where learning the next unit of material builds on your understanding the previous unit (e.g., math and science).

Capitalize on the Power of Visual Learning

The human brain consists of two hemispheres (half spheres)—left and right (see **Figure 6.5**). Each of these hemispheres specializes in a different type of learning. The left hemisphere specializes in verbal learning; it deals primarily with words. In contrast, the right hemisphere specializes in visual–spatial learning; it deals primarily with perceiving images, patterns, and objects that occupy physical place or space. If you involve both hemispheres of the brain while studying, two different memory traces are recorded—one in each major hemisphere (half) of the brain. This process of laying down dual memory traces (verbal and visual) is referred to as *dual coding* (Paivio, 1990). Since two memory traces are better than one, dual coding results in deeper learning and longer retention.

FIGURE 6.5

The human brain is comprised of two half spheres (hemispheres): the left hemisphere specializes in verbal learning, and the right hemisphere specializes in visual learning.

©JupiterImages Corporation.

To capitalize on the advantage of dual coding, be sure to use all the visual aids available to you, including those found in your textbook and those provided by your instructor in class. You can also create your own visual aids by representing what you're learning in the form of pictures, symbols, or concept maps—such as flow-charts, timelines, spider webs, wheels with hubs and spokes, or branching tree diagrams. (See **Figure 6.6** for an example of a concept map.) Visit https://coggle.it/ for help in creating your own concept/mind maps. When you transform material you're learning into a visual pattern, you're putting it into a form that's compatible with the brain's tendency to store information in neurological networks (Willis, 2006). Drawing also keeps you actively engaged in the process of learning, and by representing verbal information in visual form, you double the number of memory traces recorded in your brain. As the old saying goes, "A picture is worth a thousand words."

Note

Don't forget that drawings and visual illustrations can be more than just forms of artistic expression; they can also be powerful learning tools— you can draw to learn!

FIGURE 6.6: **Concept Map for the Human Nervous System**

ORGANIZATION OF THE HUMAN NERVOUS SYSTEM

©Kendall Hunt Publishing Company

 Think About It—Journal Entry 6.10

Think of a course you're taking this term in which related pieces of information could be joined together to form a concept map. Make a rough sketch of this map that includes the information you need to remember.

Build Variety into the Study Process

Infusing variety and change of pace into your study routine can increase your motivation to study and your concentration while studying. Here are some practical strategies for doing so.

Mix it up: periodically shift the type of academic tasks you perform during a study session. Changing the nature of the academic work you do while studying increases your alertness and concentration by reducing *habituation*—attention loss that occurs after repeatedly engaging in the same type of mental task (Thompson, 2009). You can combat attention loss due to habituation by varying the type of tasks you perform during a study session. For instance, you can shift periodically among tasks that involve reading, writing by hand, typing on a keyboard, reviewing, reciting, and solving problems. Similar to how athletes benefit from mixing different types of drills into their workouts (e.g., separate drills for building strength, speed, and endurance), studies of human learning show that "interleaving" (mixing) different academic subjects or academic skills while studying results in deeper learning and stronger memory (Brown, Roediger, & McDaniel, 2014; Carey, 2014).

Study in different places. In addition to spreading out your studying at different times, it's also a good idea to spread it out in different places. Studying in different locations provides different environmental contexts for learning; this reduces the amount of mental interference that normally builds up when all information is studied in the same place. The great public speakers in ancient Greece and Rome used this method of changing places to remember long speeches by walking through different rooms while rehearsing their speech, learning each major part of their speech in a different room (Higbee, 2001).

Although it's useful to have set times for studying so that you get into a regular work routine, this doesn't mean you learn best by always studying in the same place. Periodically changing the academic tasks you perform while studying, as well as the environment in which you perform them, has been found to improve attention to (and retention of) what you're studying (Carey, 2014; Druckman & Bjork, 1994).

Break up long study sessions with short study breaks that involve physical activity (e.g., a short jog or brisk walk). Study breaks that include physical activity refresh the mind by giving it a rest from studying. Physical activity also stimulates the mind by increasing blood flow to your brain—helping you retain what you've studied and regain concentration for what you'll study next.

Learning Styles: Identifying Your Learning Preferences

Your learning style is another important personal characteristic you should be aware of when choosing your major. Learning styles refer to individual differences in learning preferences—that is, ways in which individuals prefer to perceive information (receive or take it in) and process information (deal with it after taking it in). Individuals may differ in terms of whether they prefer to take it in information by reading about it, listening to it, seeing an image or diagram of it, or physically touching and manipulating it. Individuals may also vary in terms of whether they like to receive information in a structured and orderly format or in an unstructured form that allows them the freedom to explore, play with, and restructure it in their own way. Once information has been received, individuals may also differ in terms of how they prefer to process or deal with it mentally. Some might like to think about it on their own; others may prefer to discuss it with someone else, make an outline of it, or draw a picture of it.

Probably the most frequently used learning styles test is the Myers-Briggs Type Indicator (MBTI; Myers, 1976; Myers & McCaulley, 1985), which is based on the personality theory of psychologist Carl Jung. The test consists of four pairs of opposing traits and assesses how people vary on a scale (low to high) for each of these four sets of traits.

Learning styles are no more or no less common ways that people learn. We all have a mix of multiple learning styles, thus we have different and multiple ways of learning. Many students may find that they have a dominant learning style but using other styles that are less dominant. In many cases, you might use different styles for different learning circumstances. No style is set in concrete. They can change and there is no perfect mix for greater learning. You have the ability to increase your lesser used methods to make them more dominant while strengthening your dominant one. Since students have different learning styles and academic fields emphasize different styles of learning, it's important to consider how your learning style meshes with the style of learning emphasized by the field you're considering as a major. If the match seems to be close or compatible, then the marriage between you and that major could be one that leads to a satisfying and successful learning experience.

Although there are many (multiple) learning styles, the three that are considered most common are:

- Visual-Spatial Learning (learning by seeing),
- Auditory-Sequential Learning (learning by hearing),
- Kinesthetic Learning (learning by doing).

In addition to taking formal tests to assess which or how many of these are your learning style(s), you can gain awareness of your learning styles through some simple introspection or self-examination. Take a moment to complete the following sentences that are designed to stimulate personal reflection on your learning style:

I learn best if . . .
I learn most from . . .
I enjoy learning when . . .

Knowing your preferred learning style can make studying easier for you. Once you discover your dominant learning style, research some ways you can incorporate your learning style into your study routine (i.e., if your learning style is visual, read over notes or use flashcards; if you are an auditory learner, read your notes out loud to yourself; if you are a kinesthetic learner, rewrite your notes).

To sum up, the most important factor to consider when reaching decisions about a major is whether it is compatible with four characteristics of yourself: (1) your learning style, (2) your abilities, (3) your personal interests, and (4) your values. These four pillars provide the foundation for effective decisions about a college major.

The PEPS Learning Styles Inventory that is packaged with your book will help you identify the ways you learn best. Pay close attention to your detailed report and preference chart and reference it as you read through this chapter (and book). Knowing how you learn best can help you maximize your study strategies.

Learn with and through a variety of senses. When memory is formed in the brain, different sensory aspects of it are stored in different areas. For example, if your brain receives auditory input (e.g., hearing your own words or the words of others), visual input (viewing images, maps or charts), and motor input (movement made when writing, drawing, or manipulating), that information reaches your brain through multiple sensory modalities and is better retained because it: (a) creates more interconnections in areas of the brain where that information is stored, and (b) provides multiple cues for retrieving (recalling) the information (Shams & Seitz, 2011; Willis, 2006; Zull, 2002). Different forms of sensory input are stored as multiple neurological tracks in different parts of the brain, which deepens learning and strengthens memory.

Don't forget that movement is also a sensory channel. When you move, your brain receives kinesthetic stimulation—the sensations generated by your muscles. Memory traces for movement are commonly stored in an area of your brain (the cerebellum) that plays a major role for all types of learning (Middleton & Strick, 1994; Jensen, 2005). Thus, incorporating movement into the process of learning improves your ability to retain what you're studying by adding a motor (muscle)

> "I have to *hear* it, *see* it, *write* it, and *talk* about it."
>
> —First-year college student responding to the question: "How do you learn best?"

> "When I have to remember something, it's better for me to do something with my hands so I could physically see it happening."
>
> —First-year college student

memory trace of it to your brain. You can use movement to help you learn and retain academic information by using your body to act out what you're studying or symbolize it with your hands (Kagan & Kagan, 1998). Suppose you're trying to remember five points about something (e.g., five consequences of the Civil War). When you're studying these points, count them on your fingers as you try to recall each of them.

AUTHOR'S EXPERIENCE

I was talking about memory in class one day and mentioned that when I can't recall how to spell a word, its correct spelling comes back to me after I start writing it. One of my students raised her hand and said the same thing happens to her when she forgets a phone number—it comes back to her when she starts punching it in. Both of these experiences point to the power of movement for promoting learning and memory.

—*Joe Cuseo*

AUTHOR'S EXPERIENCE

Often I forget my grocery list when I head to the grocery store. Instead of turning around and heading home to get the list, if I close my eyes, I can usually "see" most of the list in my head. This is because my strongest learning method is visual. Because of this, I often color code my notes, planner, etc. Knowing my dominant learning style has helped me use it to my advantage.

—*Julie McLaughlin*

Also, remember that talking involves muscle movement of your lips and tongue. Thus, speaking aloud when you're studying, either to a friend or to yourself, can improve memory by supplying kinesthetic stimulation to your brain (in addition to the auditory stimulation your brain receives from hearing what you're saying).

Figure 6.7 shows a map of the outer surface of the human brain; you can see how different parts of the brain are specialized to receive input from different sensory modalities. When multiple sensory modalities are used while learning, multiple memory traces of what you're studying are recorded in separate areas of the brain, resulting in deeper learning and stronger memory for what's been studied.

FIGURE 6.7: **A Map of the Functions Performed by the Outer Surface of the Human Brain**

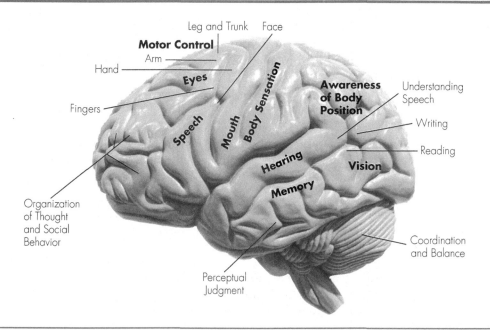

Brain image modified from ©David Huntley/Shutterstock.com

Learn with Emotion

Neural connections run between the emotional and memory centers of the brain (Zull, 1998). Thus, the emotions we're experiencing while learning can affect how deeply we learn. Research indicates that emotional intensity, excitement, and enthusiasm strengthen memory of academic information just as they do for memory of life events and personal experiences. When we're emotionally excited about what we're learning, adrenaline is released and is carried through the bloodstream to the brain. Once adrenaline reaches the brain, it increases blood flow and glucose production, which stimulates learning and strengthens memory (LeDoux, 1998; Rosenfield, 1988). Thus, if you become passionate and enthused about what you're learning, you're more likely to learn it deeply and remember it longer (Howard, 2014; Minninger, 1984).

One way to do this is by keeping in mind the importance or significance of what you're learning. For instance, if you're learning about photosynthesis, remind yourself that you're not just learning a chemical reaction, you're learning about the driving force that underlies all plant life on the planet. If you don't know why the concept you're studying is significant, find out—do a computer search, talk it over with your instructor, or ask an advanced student majoring in the field.

Note

Make learning a "total body experience." Put your whole self into it—your mind, your body, and your heart.

Learn Collaboratively

Simply defined, collaborative learning is the process of two or more people working *interdependently* to advance each other's success—as opposed to working independently or competitively. Learning is strengthened when it takes place in a social

"If you want to go quickly, go by yourself—if you want to go farther, go in a group."
—African proverb

context that involves interpersonal interaction. As scholars put it, human knowledge is "socially constructed" or built up through dialogue and an exchange of ideas; conversations with others become internalized as ideas in your mind and influence your way of thinking (Bruffee, 1993). Thus, by having frequent, intelligent conversations with others, you broaden your knowledge base, deepen your learning and elevate the quality of your thinking. (For specific team-learning strategies, see Chapter 2, **pp. 35–37.**)

AUTHOR'S EXPERIENCE

When I was in my senior year of college, I had to take a theory course by independent study because the course would not be offered again until after I planned to graduate. Another senior found himself in the same situation. The instructor allowed both of us to take this course together and agreed to meet with us every two weeks. My fellow classmate and I studied independently for the first two weeks.

I prepared for the biweekly meetings by reading thoroughly, yet I had little understanding of what I had read. After our first meeting, I left with a strong desire to drop the course but decided to stick with it. Over the next two weeks, I spent many sleepless nights trying to prepare for our next meeting and was feeling pretty low about not being the brightest student in my class of two. During the next meeting with the instructor, I found out that the other student was also having difficulty. Not only did I notice, so did the instructor. After that meeting, the instructor gave us study questions and asked us to read separately then get together to discuss the questions. During the next two weeks, my classmate and I met several times to discuss what we were learning (or attempting to learn). By being able to communicate with each other about the issues we were studying, we both ended up gaining greater understanding. Our instructor was delighted to see that he was able to suggest a collaborative learning strategy that worked for both of us.

—*Aaron Thompson*

"When you know a thing, to recognize that you know it; and when you do not, to know that you do not know; that is knowledge."
—Confucius, influential Chinese thinker and educator

"Most things used to be external to me—out of a lecture or textbook. It makes learning a lot more interesting and memorable when you can bring your experiences into it. It makes you want to learn."
—Returning adult student

Self-Monitor: Reflect on What you're Learning and Assess Whether you're Learning it Deeply

Deep learners are *reflective* learners—they are self-aware and mindful of how well they're learning what they're studying. They reflect, check, and self-assess whether they're really getting it. They monitor their comprehension by asking questions such as: "Am I actually understanding this?" and "Do I really know it?"

How do you know if you really know it? Probably the best answer to this question is: "I find meaning in it—I can relate to it personally or put it in terms that make sense to me" (Ramsden, 2003). Listed below are some strategies for checking whether you're truly (deeply) understanding what you're learning. These strategies can be used as indicators or checkpoints for determining whether you're just memorizing or learning at a deep level. They will help you answer the question: "How do I know if I really know it?"

Can you think of an *analogy* between the concept you're learning and something you already know or understand? (e.g., This concept is like ____ or is similar to ____.)

- Can you paraphrase (restate or translate) what you're learning in your own words? If you can take what you're learning and complete the following sentence: "In other words, . . .", it's very likely you've moved beyond surface memorization (and mental regurgitation) to a deeper level of comprehension, because you've transformed what you're learning into a form that makes sense to you. You know you know it if you're not stating it the same way your instructor or textbook stated it, but restating it in words that are your own.
- Can you explain what you're learning to someone who is unfamiliar with it? One of the best ways to gain awareness of how well we know or don't know

something is to explain it to someone who's never heard it before (just ask any teacher). Studies show that students gain a deeper level of understanding for what they're learning when they're asked to explain it to someone else (Chi, et al., 1994). If you can explain it to someone who's unfamiliar with it, that's a good sign you've moved to deeper comprehension because you're able to translate it into language that's understandable to anyone.

- Can you think of an *example* of what you've learned? If you can come up with an instance or illustration of what you're learning—that's your own—not one given by your instructor or textbook, this is a good sign that you truly understand it. It shows you've taken an abstract academic concept and connected it to a concrete experience (Bligh, 2000).
- Can you apply what you're learning to solve a new problem that you haven't seen before? The ability to apply what you've learned in a different situation is a good indicator of deep learning (Erickson & Strommer, 2005). Learning specialists refer to this mental process as *decontextualization*—taking what you learned in one context (situation) and transferring it to another context (Bransford, Brown, & Cocking, 2000). For instance, you know you've learned a mathematical concept deeply when you can use that concept to solve math problems different from those solved by your instructor or textbook. This is why math instructors rarely include on exams the exact problems they solved in class or were solved in your textbook. They're not trying to "trick" you at test time; they're trying to see whether you've learned the concept deeply.

> "You do not really understand something unless you can explain it to your grandmother."
> —Albert Einstein, considered the Father of Modern Physics

> "I learn best through teaching. When I learn something and teach it to someone else, I find that it really sticks with me a lot better."
> —College sophomore

 ## Think About It—Journal Entry 6.11

Rate yourself in terms of how frequently you use the following learning strategies:

4 = always, 3 = sometimes, 2 = rarely, 1 = never

1. I block out all distracting sources of outside stimulation when I study.   4   3   2   1

2. I try to find meaning in technical terms by looking at their prefix or suffix, or by looking up their etymology (word origin).   4   3   2   1

3. I compare and contrast what I'm currently studying with what I've already learned.   4   3   2   1

4. I organize the information I'm studying into categories or classes.   4   3   2   1

5. I pull together information from my class notes and readings that relate to the same concept or general category.   4   3   2   1

6. I distribute (spread out) my study time over several short sessions in advance of exams and use my last study session before the test to review the information I previously studied.   4   3   2   1

7. I participate in study groups with my classmates.   4   3   2   1

Which works best for you? Why?

_____

_____

_____

_____

_____

_____

Chapter Summary and Highlights

This chapter identified key principles of human learning and supplied specific strategies for learning effectively in college and throughout life. Deep learning goes beyond surface-level memorization. It's connecting new ideas to ideas that have already been learned. Deep learners build mental bridges between what they're trying to learn and what they already know.

Information delivered during lectures is the information that's most likely to appear as items on college exams. Students who don't take good lecture notes have a slim chance of recalling the information at test time. Thus, effective note taking is critical to successful academic performance in college.

Information from reading assignments is the second most common source of test questions on college exams. Professors often don't discuss information in class that's contained in assigned reading. Thus, doing the assigned reading, and doing it in a way that maximizes comprehension and retention, is essential for academic success in college.

Learning from lectures requires active involvement (e.g., actively taking notes while listening to lectures) as does learning from reading (e.g., actively taking notes while reading). Active involvement during the learning process engages your attention and enables information to enter the brain. Reflection on what you have learned keeps it in the brain by locking it into memory. Self-awareness also promotes deep learning. By reflecting on whether you truly understand what you're studying, you become a more self-aware learner and a more successful student.

Cramming total study time into one long session ("massed practice") immediately before exams doesn't promote deep learning or long-term retention. Research consistently shows that *distributed practice*, whereby study time is "distributed" or spread out over several shorter sessions, is more effective—particularly if the last study session just before an exam is used to review (restudy) the parts that were previously studied in separate sessions. Learning is also deepened by engaging as many senses as possible during the learning process.

Lastly, deep learning is enhanced when done *collaboratively*. Research from kindergarten through college shows that students who learn in teams experience significant gains in both academic performance and interpersonal skills.

Learning More through the World Wide Web: Internet-Based Resources

For additional information on learning deeply and strategically, see the following websites:

Strategic Learning & Study Strategies:
https://www.khanacademy.org/coach-res/reference-for-coaches/case-studies-hied/a/help-students-build-study-plans

http://www.dartmouth.edu/~acskills/success/

http://www.isu.edu/success/strategies/handouts.shtml

Brain-Based Learning: http://www.brainrules.net/the-rules

Learning Math and Overcoming Math Anxiety:
www.mathacademy.com/pr/minitext/anxiety

www.onlinemathlearning.com/math-mnemonics.html

References

Anderson, C. J. (2003). The psychology of doing nothing: Forms of decision avoidance result from reason and emotion. *Psychological Bulletin, 129,* 139–167.

Arum, R., & Roska, J. (2011). *Academically adrift: Limited learning on college campuses.* Chicago: The University of Chicago Press.

Ausubel, D., Novak, J., & Hanesian, H. (1978). *Educational psychology: A cognitive view* (2nd ed.). New York: Holt, Rinehart & Winston.

Averell, L., & Heathcote, A. (2011). The form of the forgetting curve and the fate of memories. *Journal of Mathematical Psychology, 55*(1), 25–35

Baddeley, A. D. (1999). *Essentials of human memory.* Hove: Psychology.

Biggs, J., & Tang, C. (2007) *Teaching for quality learning at university* (3rd ed.) Buckingham: SRHE and Open University Press.

Bligh, D.A. (2000). *What's the use of lectures?* San Francisco: Jossey Bass.

Bransford, J. D., Brown, A. L., & Cocking, R. R. (2000). *How people learn: Brain, mind, experience and school.* Washington, DC: National Academies Press.

Brown, R. D. (1988). Self-quiz on testing and grading issues. *Teaching at UNL (University of Nebraska–Lincoln), 10*(2), 1–3.

Brown, P. C., Roediger III, H. L., & McDaniel, M. A. (2014). *Make it stick: The science of successful learning.* Cambridge, MA: The Belknap Press of Harvard University Press.

Bruffee, K. A. (1993). *Collaborative learning: Higher education, interdependence, and the authority of knowledge.* Baltimore: Johns Hopkins University Press.

Bruner, J. (1990) *Acts of Meaning* Cambridge, MA: Harvard University Press.

Caine, R., & Caine, G. (2011). *Natural learning for a connected world: Education, technology and the human brain.* New York, NY. Teachers College Press

Carey, B. (2014). *How we learn.* London: Random House.

Chen, B., & Hirumi, A. (2009). Effects of advance organizers on learning for differentiated learners in a fully Web-based course. *International Journal of Instructional Technology & Distance Learning.* Retrieved from http://itdl.org/Journal/Jun_09/article01.htm

Chi, M., de Leeuw, N., Chiu, M. H., & LaVancher, C. (1994). Eliciting self-explanations improves understanding. *Cognitive Science, 18,* 439–477.

Conaway, M. S. (1982). Listening: Learning tool and retention agent. In A. S. Algier & K. W. Algier, (Eds.), *Improving reading and study skills,* (pp. 51–63). San Francisco: Jossey-Bass.

Crawford, H. J., & Strapp, C. H. (1994). Effects of vocal and instrumental music on visuospatial and verbal performance as moderated by studying preference and personality. *Personality and Individual Differences, 16*(2), 237–245.

Cuseo, J. B., Thompson, A., Campagna, M., & Fecas, V. S. (2013). *Thriving in college & beyond: Research-based strategies for academic success and personal development* (3rd ed.). Dubuque, IA: Kendall Hunt.

Demmert, W. G., Jr., & Towner, J. C. (2003). *A review of the research literature on the influences of culturally based education on the academic performance of Native American students.* Retrieved from the Northwest Regional Educational Laboratory, Portland, Oregon, website: http://educationnorthwest.org/sites/default/files/cbe.pdf.

Druckman, D., & Bjork, R. A. (Eds.). (1994). *Learning, remembering, believing: Enhancing human performance.* Washington, DC: National Academies Press.

Dunlosky, J., Rawson, K. A., Marsh, E. J., Nathan, M. J., & Willingham, D. T. (2013). Improving students' learning with effective learning techniques: Promising directions from cognitive and educational psychology. *Psychological Science in the Public Interest, 14*(1), 4–58.

Einstein, G. O., Morris, J., & Smith, S. (1985). Note-taking, individual differences, and memory for lecture information. *Journal of Educational Psychology*, 77(5), 522–532.

Erickson, B. L., & Strommer, D. W. (2005). Inside the fist-year classroom: Challenges and constraints. In J. L. Upcraft, J. N. Gardner, & B. O. Barefoot, *Challenging and supporting the first-year student* (pp. 241–256). San Francisco: Jossey-Bass.

Hartley, J. (1998). *Learning and studying: a research perspective*. London: Routledge.

Hartley, J., & Marshall, S. (1974). On notes and note taking. *Universities Quarterly*, 28, 225–235.

Hartman, H. J. (2001). *Metacognition in learning and instruction: Theory, research and practice*. Dordrecht: Kluwer Academic Publishers.

Herbert, W. (2014). Ink on paper: Some notes on note taking. Association for Psychological Science (APS). Retrieved from http://www.psychologicalscience.org/index.php/news/were-only-human/ink-on-paper-some-notes-on-note-taking.html

Higbee, K. L. (2001). *Your memory: How it works and how to improve it*. New York: Marlowe.

Howard, P. J. (2014). *The owner's manual for the brain: Everyday applications of mind-brain research* (4th ed.). New York: HarperCollins.

Howe, M. J. (1970). Note-taking strategy, review, and long-term retention of verbal information. *Journal of Educational Psychology*, 63, 285.

Jairam, D., & Kiewra, K. A. (2009). An investigation of the SOAR study method. *Journal of Advanced Academics* (August), 602–629.

Jensen, E. (2005). *Teaching with the brain in mind* (2nd ed.). Alexandria, VA: ASCD.

Jensen, E. (2008). *Brain-based learning*. Thousand Oaks, CA: Corwin Press.

Johnstone, A. H., & Su, W. Y. (1994). Lectures: a learning experience? *Education in Chemistry*, 31(1), 65–76, 79.

Kagan, S., & Kagan, M. (1998). *Multiple intelligences: The complete MI book*. San Clemente, CA: Kagan Cooperative Learning.

Kiewra, K. A. (1985). Students' note-taking behaviors and the efficacy of providing the instructor's notes for review. *Contemporary Educational Psychology*, 10, 378–386.

Kiewra, K. A. (2000). Fish giver or fishing teacher? The lure of strategy instruction. *Teaching at UNL (University of Nebraska–Lincoln)*, 22(3), 1–3.

Kiewra, K. A. (2005). *Learn how to study and SOAR to success*. Upper Saddle River, NJ: Pearson Prentice Hall.

Kiewra, K. A., & DuBois, N. F. (1998). *Learning to learn: Making the transition from student to lifelong learner*. Needham Heights, MA: Allyn and Bacon.

Kiewra, K. A., Hart, K., Scoular, J., Stephen, M., Sterup, G., & Tyler, B. (2000). Fish giver or fishing teacher? The lure of strategy instruction. *Teaching at UNL (University of Nebraska–Lincoln)*, 22(3).

Kintsch, W. (1994). Text comprehension, memory, and learning. *American Psychologist*, 49, 294–303.

Kuh, G. D, (2005). Student engagement in the first year of college. In M. L. Upcraft, J. N. Gardner, B. O. Barefoot, & Associates, *Challenging and supporting the first-year student: A handbook for improving the first year of college* (pp. 86–107). San Francisco: Jossey-Bass.

Kuhn, L. (1988). What should we tell students about answer changing? *Research Serving Teaching*, 1(8).

LeDoux, J. (1998). *The emotional brain: The mysterious underpinnings of emotional life*. New York: Simon & Schuster.

LeDoux, J. (2002). *Synaptic self: How our brains become who we are*. New York: Penguin Books.

Locke, E. (1977). An empirical study of lecture note-taking among college students. *Journal of Educational Research*, 77, 93–99.

Malmberg, K. J., & Murnane, K. (2002). List composition and the word-frequency effect for recognition memory. *Journal of Experimental Psychology: Learning, Memory, and Cognition*, 28, 616–630.

Marzano, R. J., Pickering, D. J., & Pollock, J. (2001). *Classroom instruction that works: Research-based strategies for increasing student achievement*. Alexandria, VA: Association for Supervision and Curriculum Development.

Mayer, R. E. (2002). Rote versus meaningful learning. *Theory into Practice*, 41(4), 226–232.

Middleton, F., & Strick, P. (1994). Anatomical evidence for cerebellar and basal ganglia involvement in higher brain function. *Science*, 226(51584), 458–461.

Minninger, J. (1984). *Total recall: How to boost your memory power*. Emmaus, PA: Rodale.

Mueller, P. A. & Oppenheimer, D. M (2014). The pen is mightier than the keyboard: Advantages of longhand over laptop note taking. *Psychological Science*, 25(6), 1159–1168.

Murname, K., & Shiffrin, R. M. (1991). Interference and the representation of events in memory. *Journal of Experimental Psychology: Learning, Memory, & Cognition*, 17, 855–874.

Nathan, R. (2005). *My freshman year: What a professor learned by becoming a student*. Ithaca, New York: Cornell University Press.

Paivio, A. (1990). *Mental representations: A dual coding approach*. New York: Oxford University Press.

Pascarella, E., & Terenzini, P. (1991). *How college affects students: Findings and insights from twenty years of research*. San Francisco: Jossey-Bass.

Pascarella, E., & Terenzini, P. (2005). *How college affects students: A third decade of research* (Vol. 2). San Francisco: Jossey-Bass.

Piaget, J. (1978). *Success and understanding*. Cambridge, MA: Harvard University Press.

Ramsden, P. (2003). *Learning to teach in higher education* (2nd ed.). London: RoutledgeFalmer.

Ravizza, S. M., Hambrick, D. Z.. & Fenn, K. M. (2014). Non-academic internet use in the classroom is negatively related to classroom learning regardless of intellectual ability. *Computers & Education, 78,* 109–114.

Rosenfield, I. (1988). *The invention of memory: A new view of the brain.* New York: Basic Books.

Schacter, D. L. (2001). *The seven sins of memory: how the mind forgets and remembers.* Boston: Houghton Mifflin.

SECFHE (2006). *A national dialogue: The Secretary of Education's Commission on the future of higher education.* (U.S. Department of Education Boards and Commissions: A Draft Panel Report). Retrieved from http://www.ed.gov/about/bdscomm/list/hiedfuture/reports/0809-draft.pdf

Shams, W., & Seitz, K. (2011). Influences of multisensory experience on subsequent unisensory processing. *Frontiers in Perception Science, 2*(264), 1–9.

Thompson, R. F. (2009). Habituation: A history. *Neurobiology of Learning and Memory, 92*(2), 127–134.

Titsworth, S., & Kiewra, K. A. (2004). Organizational lecture cues and student notetaking. *Contemporary Educational Psychology, 29,* 447–461.

Vygotsky, L. S. (1978). Internalization of higher cognitive functions. In M. Cole, V. John-Steiner, S. Scribner, & E. Souberman (Eds. & Trans.), *Mind in society: The development of higher psychological processes* (pp. 52–57). Cambridge, MA: Harvard University Press.

Walter, T. W., Knudsvig, G. M., & Smith, D. E. P. (2003). *Critical thinking: Building the basics* (2nd ed.). Belmont, CA: Wadsworth.

Willis, J. (2006). *Research-based strategies to ignite student learning: Insights from a neurologist and classroom teacher.* Alexandria, VA: ASCD.

Zull, J. E. (1998). The brain, the body, learning, and teaching. *The National Teaching & Learning Forum, 7*(3), 1–5.

Zull, J. E. (2002). *The art of changing the brain: Enriching the practice of teaching by exploring the biology of learning.* Sterling, VA: Stylus.

Chapter 6 Exercises

6.1 Quote Reflections

Review the sidebar quotes contained in this chapter and select two that were especially meaningful or inspirational to you.

For each quote, provide a three- to five-sentence explanation why you chose it.

6.2 Reality Bite

Too Fast, Too Frustrating: A Note-Taking Nightmare

Susan Scribe is a first-year student majoring in journalism. She's currently enrolled in an introductory course that is required for her major (Introduction to Mass Media). The instructor in this course lectures at a rapid rate and uses vocabulary that goes right over her head. Since she cannot get all her instructor's words down on paper and cannot understand half the words she does manage to write down, she becomes frustrated and stops taking notes. She wants to do well in this course because it's the first course in her major, but she's afraid she'll fail it because her class notes are so pitiful.

Reflection and Discussion Questions

1. Can you relate to this case personally, or do know any students who are in the same boat as Susan?

2. What would you recommend that Susan do at this point? Why?

6.3 Self-Assessment of Learning Habits

Look back at the ratings you gave yourself for effective note-taking (**Journal Entry 6.4, p. 133**), reading (**Journal Entry 6.7, pp. 139–140**), and studying (**Journal Entry 6.11, pp. 153–154**). Add up your total score for these three sets of learning strategies (the maximum score for each set is 28):

Note Taking = _____

Reading = _____

Studying = _____

Total Learning Strategy Score = _____

Self-Assessment Questions

1. In which learning strategy area did you score lowest?

2. Do you think the area in which you scored lowest has anything to do with your lowest course grade at this point in the term?

3. Of the seven strategies listed under the area you scored lowest, which could you immediately put into practice to improve your performance in the course you're having most difficulty with this term?

4. What's the likelihood that you will put the preceding strategies into practice this term?

6.4 Consulting with a Learning Specialist

Make an appointment to visit your Learning Center or Academic Support Center on campus to discuss the results of your note-taking, reading, and studying self-assessment in Exercise 6.1 (or any other learning self-assessment you may have taken). Ask for recommendations about how you can improve your learning habits in your lowest score area. Following your visit, answer the following questions.

Learning Resource Center Reflection

1. Who did you meet with in the Learning Center?

2. What steps were recommended to you for improving your academic performance?

3. How likely is it that you will take the steps mentioned in the previous question?

   (a) definitely,
   (b) probably,
   (c) possibly, or
   (d) unlikely. Why?

4. Do you plan to see a learning specialist again? (If yes, why? If no, why not?)

6.5 PEPS Learning Style Inventory Reflection

1. Looking at your PEPS preference chart, what surprises you the most? Why?

2. Is your dominant learning style visual, auditory, or kinesthetic? How can you use this to help you be successful in your classes?

3. According to the preference chart, do you prefer more or less structure when it comes to assignment details? How can you use this to your advantage in your college courses?

4. What area on the preference chart would you most like to improve upon? Why? Write a three- to five-step detailed action plan stating how you will improve in this area.

Chapter 6 Reflection

6.6 List and describe at least five principles discussed in this chapter that can help you take better notes in class and improve your reading comprehension.

1.

2.

3.

4.

5.

Now explain how you can put these principles into practice.

CHAPTER 7

Test-Taking Skills and Strategies

WHAT TO DO BEFORE, DURING, AND AFTER TESTS

This chapter supplies you with a systematic set of strategies for improving your performance on different types of tests that can be used before, during, and after exams, helping you to become more "test wise" and less "test anxious."

Chapter Preview

Acquire effective strategies to improve your performance on multiple-choice, true–false, and essay tests.

Learning Goal

 Think About It—Journal Entry 7.1

Thought Starter

On which of the following types of tests do you tend to perform better?

a) Multiple-choice tests

b) Essay tests

Why?

_____

_____

_____

_____

_____

Learning in college courses typically takes place in a three-stage process: (1) acquiring information from lectures and readings; (2) studying that information and storing it in your brain as knowledge; and (3) demonstrating that knowledge on exams. The following sections of this chapter contain strategies relating primarily to the third stage of this learning process and they are divided into three categories:

* Strategies to use *in advance* of a test,
* Strategies to use *during* a test, and
* Strategies to use *after* test results are returned.

Pre-Test Strategies: What to Do *in Advance* of Tests

Your ability to remember material on a test that you studied prior to the test depends not only on how long and how well you studied, but also on the type of test questions used to test your memory. You may be able to remember what you've studied if you're tested in one format (e.g., multiple-choice) but not if tested in a different format (e.g., essay). Thus, the type of questions that will appear on an upcoming test should influence the type of study strategies you use to prepare for the test. Test questions can be classified into the following two major categories, depending on the type of memory required to answer them.

1. *Recognition test questions* ask you to select or choose the correct answer from choices that are provided for you. Falling into this category are multiple-choice, true–false, and matching questions. These test questions don't require you to supply or produce the correct answer on your own; instead, you're asked to recognize or pick out the correct answer—similar to picking out the "correct" criminal from a lineup of potential suspects.
2. *Recall test questions* require you to retrieve information you've studied and reproduce it on your own. As the word "recall" implies, you have to re-call ("call back") information and supply it yourself—as opposed to picking it out from information supplied for you. Recall test questions include essay and short-answer questions that require you to provide your own answer—in writing.

Since recognition test questions (e.g., multiple-choice or true–false) ask you to recognize or pick out the correct answer from answers provided for you, reading your class notes and textbook highlights and identifying key information may be an effective study strategy—because it matches the type of mental activity you'll be performing on the exam—reading test questions and identifying correct answers provided to you.

On the other hand, recall test questions, such as essay questions, require you to retrieve information and generate your own answers. They don't involve answer recognition; they require answer *production*—you produce the answer in writing. If you study for essay tests by just looking over your class notes and reviewing your reading highlights, you're using a study strategy that doesn't align with or match what you'll be expected to do on the test itself, which is to supply the correct information yourself. To prepare for essay test questions, you need to practice *retrieval*—recalling the information on your own—without looking at it.

Two essay-test preparation strategies that ensure you engage in memory retrieval are: (a) recitation and (b) creation of retrieval cues. Each of these strategies is described below.

Recitation

Stating aloud the information we want to remember—without looking at that information—is a memory-improvement strategy known as *recitation*. Memory is strengthened substantially when we reproduce on our own what we're trying to remember, instead of simply looking it over or rereading it (Roediger & Karpicke, 2006). Research consistently indicates that this type of self-testing may be the most powerful of all test-preparation strategies (Carey, 2014). Recitation strengthens memory and better prepares you for essay tests because it:

- Requires *more mental effort* to dig out (retrieve) the answer on its own, which strengthens memory for the answer and allows the brain to practice exactly what it's expected to do on essay tests.

- Gives you clear *feedback* about whether or not you know the material. If you can't retrieve and recite it without looking at it, you know for sure that you won't be able to recall it at test time and need to study it further. You can provide yourself with this feedback by putting the question on one side of an index card and the answer on the flip side. If you find yourself flipping over the index card to look at the answer in order to remember it, this shows you can't retrieve the information on your own and you need to study it further. (To create electronic flash cards, see: www.studystack.com or studyblue.com)

- Encourages you to *use your own words*. If you can paraphrase it—rephrase what you're studying in your own words—it's a good indication you really understand it; and if you really understand it, you're more likely to recall it at test time.

Recitation can be done silently, by speaking aloud, or by writing out what you're trying to recall. Speaking aloud or writing out what you're reciting are particularly effective essay-test preparation strategies because they involve physical activity, which ensures that you're actively involved and engaged in the learning process.

Creating Retrieval Cues

Suppose you're trying to remember the name of a person you know; you know you know it, but just can't recall it. If a friend gives you a clue (e.g., the first letter of the person's name or a name that rhymes with it), it's likely to suddenly trigger your memory of that person's name. What your friend did was provide a retrieval cue. A *retrieval cue* is a type of memory reminder (like a string tied around your finger) that brings back to mind what you've temporarily forgotten.

Research shows that students who can't remember previously studied information are better able to recall that information if they're given a retrieval cue. In a classic study, students studied a long list of items, some of which were animals (e.g., giraffe, coyote, and turkey). After they finished studying, students were given a blank sheet of paper and asked to write down the names of those animals. None of the students were able to recall all of the animals that appeared on the list they previously studied. However, when the word "animals" was written on top of the answer sheet to provide students with a retrieval cue, they were able to recall many of the animals they had forgotten (Tulving, 1983). Research findings such as these suggest that category names can serve as powerful retrieval cues. By taking pieces of information you need to recall on an essay test and organizing it into categories, you can then use the category names as retrieval cues at test time. Retrieval cues work because memories are stored in the brain as part of an interconnected network. So, if you're able to recall one piece or segment of the network (the retrieval cue), it can trigger recall of other pieces of information linked to it in the same network (Willingham, 2009).

 Think About It—Journal Entry 7.2

Think about items of information you need to remember in a course you're taking this term. Group these items into a category that can be used as a retrieval cue to help you remember them.

1. What's the course?

    _____

    _____

    _____

    _____

2. What's the category you've created as a retrieval cue?

    _____

    _____

    _____

    _____

3. What items of information would this retrieval cue help you recall?

    _____

    _____

    _____

    _____

    _____

Another strategy for creating retrieval cues is to come up with your own catchword or catchphrase to "catch" or batch together all related ideas you're trying to remember. Acronyms can serve as catchwords, with each letter acting as a retrieval cue for a batch of related ideas. For instance, suppose you're studying for an essay test in abnormal psychology that will include questions testing your knowledge of different forms of mental illness. You could create the acronym SCOT as a retrieval cue to help you remember to include the following key elements of mental illness in your essay answers: Symptoms (S), Causes (C), Outcomes (O), and Therapies (T).

Strategies to Use *Immediately Before* a Test

1. **Before the exam, take a brisk walk or light jog.** Physical activity increases mental alertness by increasing oxygen flow to the brain; it also decreases tension by increasing the brain's production of emotionally "mellowing" brain chemicals (e.g., serotonin and endorphins).

2. **Come fully armed with all the test-taking tools you need.** In addition to the basic supplies (e.g., no. 2 pencil, pen, blue book, Scantron, calculator, etc.), bring backup equipment in case you experience equipment failure (e.g., an extra pen in case your first one runs out of ink or extra pencils in case your original one breaks).

> "Avoid flipping through notes (cramming) immediately before a test. Instead, do some breathing exercises and think about something other than the test."
>
> —*Advice to first-year students from a college sophomore*

3. **Get to the classroom as early as possible.** Arriving early allows you to take a few minutes to get into a relaxed pretest state of mind by thinking positive thoughts, taking slow, deep breaths and stretching your muscles.
4. **Sit in the same seat you normally occupy in class.** Research indicates that memory is improved when information is recalled in the same place where it was originally received or reviewed (Sprenger, 1999). Thus, taking a test in the same place where you heard the information delivered will likely improve your test performance.

Studies also show that when students take a test on material in the same environment where they studied the material, they tend to remember more of it at test time than do students who study the material in one place and take a test on that material in a different place (Smith & Vela, 2001). While it's unlikely you will be able to do all your studying in the same room where your test will be taken, it may be possible to do a short, final review session in your classroom or in an empty classroom with similar features. This should strengthen your memory because the physical features of the room become associated with the material you're trying to remember. Seeing these features again at test time can help trigger your memory of that material.

A classic, fascinating study supporting this recommendation was once conducted on a group of deep sea divers. Some divers learned a list of words on a beach, while the others learned the list underwater. They were later tested for their memory of the words. Half the divers who learned the words on the beach remained there to take the test; the other half were tested underwater. Half the divers who studied the words underwater took the test in the same place; the other half took the test on the beach. The results showed that the divers who took the test in the same place where they learned the list recalled 40% more of the items than the divers who did their learning and testing in different places (Godden & Baddeley, 1975). This study provides strong evidence that memory is strengthened when studying and testing takes place in the same location.

Other intriguing studies have shown that if students are exposed to a certain aroma while they're studying (e.g., the smell of chocolate) and they're later exposed to that same smell during a memory test for what they studied, they display better memory for the information they studied (Schab & Crowder, 2014). One possible, practical application of this finding to improve your memory during a test is to put on a particular cologne or perfume while studying, and put in on again on the day of the test. This may improve your memory for the information you studied by matching the scent of your study environment with the scent of your test environment. Although this strategy may seem silly, keep in mind that the area of the human brain where humans perceive smell has connections with the brain's memory centers (Jensen, 2005). These neurological connections probably explain why people often report that certain smells can trigger long-ago memories (e.g., the smell of a summer breeze triggering memories of summer games played during childhood).

Since smell is related to memory, you may be able to use smell as a retrieval cue to stimulate recall for information you've studied. In so doing, you may improve your performance on essay tests.

Box 7.1

Nutritional Strategies for Strengthening Academic Performance

Is there a "brain food" that can enhance our test performance? Can we "eat to learn" or "eat to remember"? Some animal studies suggest that memory can be improved by consumption of foods containing lecithin—a substance that helps the brain produce acetylcholine—a chemical that plays an important role in the formation of memories (Ueda, et al., 2011; Ulus & Wurtman, 1977). Fish contains high amounts of lecithin, which may explain why fish is sometimes referred to as "brain food."

Despite the results of some animal studies, not enough human research evidence is available to conclude that consuming certain foods will dramatically increase our ability to retain information or knowledge. However, the following nutritional strategies can improve mental performance on days when our knowledge is tested.

1. Eat breakfast on the day of the exam. Studies show that when students eat a nutritious breakfast on the day they are tested, they achieve higher test scores (Phillips, 2005; Schroll, 2006). Breakfast on the day of an exam should include grains, such as whole wheat toast, whole grain cereal, oatmeal, or bran, because those foods contain complex carbohydrates that deliver a steady stream of energy to the body throughout the day. These complex carbohydrates also help your brain produce a steady stream of serotonin—a brain chemical that reduces tension and anxiety.

> " No man can be wise on an empty stomach."
> —George Eliot, 19th-century English novelist

2. Make the meal you eat before a test a light meal. The meal you consume nearest test time should not be a large one because it will elevate your blood sugar to a high level, causing large amounts of insulin must be released into the bloodstream to reduce the blood sugar level. This draws blood sugar away from the brain, causing mental fatigue.

3. If you need an energy boost prior to a test, eat a piece of fruit rather than a candy bar. Candy bars are processed sweets that infuse synthetic sugar into the bloodstream, which provides a short and sudden burst of energy. That's the good news; the bad news is that this short-term rush of blood sugar and sudden jolt of energy can also increase bodily tension followed by a sharp drop in energy and feelings of sluggishness (Haas, 1994; Thayer, 1997). The key is to find a food that elevates energy without elevating tension and sustains this energy level over an extended period of time. The best nutritional option for producing such a steady, sustained state of higher energy is *natural* sugar contained organically in a piece of fruit, not processed sugar artificially slipped into a candy bar.

4. Avoid consuming caffeine before a test. Although caffeine increases alertness, it's a stimulant that elevates bodily tension and nervousness. These are feelings you don't want to experience during a test, particularly if you're prone to test anxiety. Also, caffeine is a diuretic, which means it will increase your urge to urinate. You certainly want to avoid this urge during an exam—when you're confined to a classroom and can't afford to take time to tend to urological needs (or be distracted by them).

Consuming large doses of caffeine or other stimulants before exams is likely to increase your alertness, but it's also likely to increase your level of stress and test anxiety.

Strategies to Use *During* Tests

1. Before you receive a copy of the test, write down any hard-to-remember terms, formulas, and equations and any memory-retrieval cues you may have created as soon as you start the exam. This will help ensure you don't forget this important information when you start focusing your attention on the test itself.

2. First answer questions you know well and carry the most points. Before automatically attacking the first question that appears on test, take a moment to check out the overall layout of the test and note the questions that are worth the most points and the questions you're best prepared to answer. Tackle these questions first. Put a checkmark next to questions whose answers you're unsure of and come back to them later—after you've answered the questions you're sure of—to ensure you get these points added to your total test score before you run out of test time.

3. If you experience "memory block" for information you know, use the following strategies to unlock it.
   * Mentally put yourself back in the environment in which you studied. Recreate the situation by mentally picturing the place where you first heard or saw the information and where you studied it—including sights, sounds, smells, and time of day. This memory-improvement strategy is referred to as *guided retrieval*, and research supports its effectiveness for recalling information of any kind, including information recalled by eyewitnesses to a crime (Glenberg, 1997; Glenberg, et al., 1983).
   * Think of any idea or piece of information that relates to the information you can't remember. Studies show that when students forget information they studied, they're more likely to suddenly remember that information if they first recall a piece related to it in some way (Reed, 2013). This strategy works because related pieces of information are typically stored in the same area of the brain—as part of an interconnected neural network.
   * Take your mind off the question by turning to another question. This frees your subconscious to focus on the forgotten information, which can suddenly trigger your conscious memory of it. Moving on to other test questions also allows you to find information included in later test questions that may enable you to recall information related to the earlier question that you previously forgot.

- Before turning in your test, carefully review and double-check your answers. This is the critical last step in the test-taking process. Sometimes the performance pressure and anxiety associated with test taking can cause students to overlook details, misread instructions, unintentionally skip questions, or make absentminded mistakes. So take time to look over your answers and check for any mindless mistakes you may have made. Avoid the temptation to immediately cut out of class after answering the last test question because you're pooped out or stressed out. When you think about the amount of time and effort you put into preparing for the exam, it's foolish not to take a little more time to detect and correct any silly mistakes you made that could cost you points and lower your test score.

Think About It—Journal Entry 7.3

I'm most likely to experience memory block during exams in the following subjects:

During tests, when I experience memory block, I usually . . .

Strategies for Answering Multiple-Choice Test Questions

You're likely to encounter multiple-choice questions on college tests (particularly in large classes), on certification or licensing exams for particular professions (e.g., nursing and teaching), as well as on admissions tests for graduate school (e.g., master's and doctoral degree programs) and professional school (e.g., law school and medical school). Since you're likely to take multiple-choice tests frequently in college and beyond, this section of the text is devoted to a detailed discussion of strategies for taking such tests. These strategies are also applicable to *true–false* questions, which are really essentially multiple-choice questions with two choices: true or false.

1. **Read the question and think of the answer in your head before looking at the possible answers.** If the answer you thought of is in the list of possible answers, it is likely that is the correct answer. However, if you see an answer that is similar but you feel is more correct, select that answer. Thinking of the answer in your head allows you to recall what you studied before recognizing it.

2. **Read all choices listed and use a** *process-of-elimination* **approach.** Search for the correct answer by first eliminating choices that are clearly wrong; continue to do so until you're left with one choice that represents the best option. Keep in mind that the correct answer is often the one that has the highest probability or likelihood of being true; it doesn't have to be absolutely true—just truer than all the other choices listed.

To be or not to be?
(a) Orange Julius
(b) Julius Erving ("Dr. J.")
(c) Julius Caesar
(d) Caesar Salad
(e) Casarean Section

A process-of-elimination approach is an effective test-taking strategy to use when answering difficult multiple-choice questions.

3. **For a choice to be correct, the** *entire statement* **must be true.** If any part of the statement is inaccurate or false, eliminate it because it's an incorrect answer.

4. **Use** *test-wise* **strategies when you cannot narrow down your choice to one answer.** Your first strategy on any multiple-choice question should be to choose an answer based on your knowledge of the material, not by guessing the correct answer based on how the question is worded. However, if you've relied on your knowledge, used the process-of-elimination strategy to eliminate clearly wrong choices, and you're still left with two or more answers that appear to be correct, then you should turn to being *test wise*—use the wording or placement of the test question itself to increase your chances of selecting the correct answer (Flippo & Caverly, 2009). Here are three test-wise strategies you can use for multiple-choice questions when more than one choice appears to be correct:

   • **Pick the answer that contains qualifying words.** Correct answers are more likely to contain modifying words such as "usually," "probably," "often," "likely," "sometimes," "perhaps," or "may." Knowledge often doesn't come neatly packaged as absolute or unqualified truths, so choices are more likely to be false if they make broad generalizations or contain words such as "always," "every," "never," "only," "must," and "completely."

   • **Pick the longest answer.** True statements often require more words to make them true.

- Pick a middle answer rather than the first or last answer. If you've narrowed down the correct answer to either "a" or "c," go with "c." Similarly, if you've narrowed your choices to "b" or "d," your best bet may be to go with "b." Studies show that instructors have a tendency to place the correct answer in the middle, rather than as the first or last choice (Miller, Linn, & Gronlund, 2012)—perhaps because they think the correct answer will be too obvious or stand out if it's placed at the top or bottom of the list.

5. **Check to be sure that your answers are aligned with the right questions.** When looking over your test before turning it in, search carefully for questions you may have skipped and intended to go back to later. Sometimes you may skip a test question on a multiple-choice test and forget to skip the number of that question on the answer form. This will throw off all your other answers by one space or line and result in a disastrous "domino effect" of wrong answers that can do major damage to your total test score. To prevent this from happening, check the alignment of all your answers to be sure there are no blank spaces on your column of answers and that your order of answers line up with the order or test questions.

6. **Don't feel that you must remain locked into your first answer.** When reviewing your answers on multiple-choice and true–false tests, don't be afraid to change an answer after you've given it more thought. Don't buy into the common belief that your first answer is always your best answer. There have been numerous studies on the topic of changing answers on multiple-choice and true–false tests, dating all the way back to 1928 (Kuhn, 1988). These studies consistently show that most changed test answers go from being incorrect to correct, resulting in improved test scores (Bauer, Kopp, & Fischer, 2007; Prinsell, Ramsey, & Ramsey, 1994). In one study of more than 1,500 students' midterm exams in an introductory psychology course, it was discovered that when students changed answers, 75% of the time they changed from an incorrect to correct answer (Kruger, Wirtz, & Miller, 2005). These results probably reflect the fact that students often catch mistakes when reading the question again or when they find some information later in the test that causes them to reconsider (and correct) their first answer to an earlier test question.

   If you have good reason to think an answer change should be made, don't be afraid to make it. The only exception to this general rule is when you find yourself changing many of your original answers; this may indicate that you were not well prepared for the exam and are just doing a lot of guessing and second-guessing.

Be sure you don't overthink the question and talk yourself into changing a correct answer. Sometimes "go with your gut" is the best decision if you are not sure. Don't change an answer if you are not sure the new answer is correct.

 ## Think About It—Journal Entry 7.4

On multiple-choice exams, do you ever change your original choice?

If you do make changes, what's your usual reason for doing so?

_____

_____

_____

_____

_____

Strategies for Answering Essay Questions

Along with multiple-choice questions, essay questions are among the most common types of test questions on college exams. The following strategies are recommended for strengthening your performance on essay questions.

1. **Look for "mental action" verbs in the question that point to the type of thinking your instructor expects you to demonstrate in your answer. Box 7.2** contains a list of thinking verbs you're likely to see in essay questions and the type of mental action typically called for by each of these verbs. As you read this list, place a check mark next to the verbs that represent a type of thinking you've rarely or never been asked to do in the past.

Box 7.2

Mental Action Verbs Commonly Found in Essay-Test Questions

Analyze. Break the topic down into its key parts and evaluate the parts in terms of their accuracy, strengths and weaknesses.

Compare. Identify the similarities and differences between major concepts.

Contrast. Identify the differences between ideas, particularly sharp differences and clashing viewpoints.

Describe. Provide details (e.g., who, what, where, and when).

Discuss. Analyze (break apart) and evaluate the parts (e.g., strengths and weaknesses).

Document. Support your judgment and conclusions with scholarly references or research evidence.

Explain. Provide reasons that answer the questions "why?" and "how?"

> I keep six honest serving men. They taught me all I knew. Their names are what and why and how and when and where and who."
> —*Rudyard Kipling*, "The Elephant's Child," The Just-So Stories

Illustrate. Supply concrete examples or specific instances.

Interpret. Draw your own conclusion and explain why you came to that conclusion.

Support. Back up your ideas with logical reasoning, persuasive arguments, or statistical evidence.

Think About It—Journal Entry 7.5

Which of the mental actions listed in **Box 7.2** was most often required on your high school writing assignments?

_____

_____

_____

_____

Which was least often (or never) required?

_____

_____

_____

_____

2. **Make an outline of your key ideas before you start writing sentences.** First, do a quick "information dump" by jotting down the main points you plan to make in your essay answer in outline form. Outlines are effective for several reasons:

    - **An outline ensures you don't forget to include your most powerful points.** The points listed in your outline serve as memory-retrieval cues that help you remember the "big picture" before getting lost in all the details.

    - **An outline earns you points by improving your answer's organizational quality.** In addition to reminding you of the points you need to make, an outline gives you a plan for ordering your ideas in a sequence that flows smoothly from beginning to middle to end. One factor instructors consider when awarding points for an essay answers is how well that answer is organized. An outline will make your answer's organization clearer and more coherent to the reader, which will increase the amount of points you're awarded.

    - **An outline helps reduce test anxiety.** By organizing your points ahead of time, you can focus on expressing (writing) those points without the added stress of figuring out *what* you're going to say at the same time you're trying to figure out *how* to say it.

    - **An outline can add points to answers you don't have time to complete.** If you run out of test time before writing out your full answer to an essay question, an outline shows your instructor what you planned to include in your written answer. The outline itself is likely to earn you some points because it demonstrates your knowledge of the major points called for by the question.

Exhibit 1

1. There are several different studies that scientists conduct, but one study that they conduct is to find out how genetics can influence human behavior in <u>identical twins</u>. Since they are identical, they will most likely end up very similar in behavior because of their identical genetic makeup. Although environment has some impact, genetics are still a huge factor and they will, more likely than not, behave similarly. Another type of study is with <u>parents and their family trees</u>. Looking at a subject's family tree will explain why a certain person is bipolar or depressed. It is most likely caused by a gene in the family tree, even if it was last seen decades ago. Lastly, another study is with adopted children. If an <u>adopted child</u> acts a certain way that is unique to that child, and researchers find the parents' family tree, they will most likely see similar behavior in the parents and siblings as well.

2. The monistic view of the mind-brain relationship is so strongly opposed and criticized because there is a belief or assumption that <u>free will</u> is taken away from people. For example, if a person commits a horrendous crime, it can be argued "monistically" that the chemicals in the brain were the reason, and that a person cannot think for themselves to act otherwise. This view limits responsibility.

   Another reason that this view is opposed is because it has been said that <u>there is no afterlife</u>. If the mind and brain are one and the same, and there is <u>NO</u> difference, then once the brain is dead and is no longer functioning, so is the mind. Thus, it cannot continue to live beyond what we know today as life. <u>And</u> this goes against many religions, which is why this reason, in particular, is heavily opposed.

Identical twins
Adoption
Parents/family tree
6/6

No freewill
No afterlife
6/6

A college sophomore's answers to short essay questions that demonstrate effective use of bulleted lists or short outlines (in the side margin) to ensure recall of key points.

3. **Get directly to the point on each question.** Avoid elaborate introductions that take up your test time (and your instructor's grading time) but don't earn you any points. An answer that begins with the statement "This is an interesting question that we had a great discussion on in class . . ." is pointless because it doesn't add points to your test score. Timed essay tests often leave you pressed for time; don't waste that time on flowery introductions that contribute nothing to your test grade.

   One effective way to get directly to the point on essay questions is to include part of the question in the first sentence of your answer. For example, suppose the test question asks you to, "Argue for or against capital punishment by explaining how it will or will not reduce the nation's homicide rate." Your first sentence could be, "Capital punishment will not reduce the homicide rate for the following reasons . . ." Thus, your first sentence becomes your thesis statement—it points you directly to the major points you're going to make in your answer and earns immediate points for your answer.

4. **Answer essay questions with as much detail as possible.** Don't assume that your instructor already knows what you're talking about or will be bored by details. Instead, take the approach that you're writing to someone who knows little or nothing about the subject—as if you're an expert teacher who is explaining it from scratch.

Note

As a general rule, it's better to over-explain than under-explain your answers to essay questions.

5. **Support your points with evidence—facts, statistics, quotes, or examples.** When you're answering essay questions, take on the mindset of a lawyer: make your case by presenting concrete evidence (exhibit A, exhibit B, etc.).

6. **Leave space between your answers to each essay question.** This strategy will enable you to easily add information to your original answer if you recall something later in the test that you would like to include.

7. **Proofread your answers for spelling and grammar.** Before turning in your test, proofread what you've written and correct any spelling or grammatical errors you find. Catching and correcting clerical errors will improve your test score. Even if your instructor doesn't explicitly state that grammar and spelling count toward your grade, these mechanical mistakes are still likely to influence your professor's overall evaluation of your written work.

8. **Neatness counts.** Many years of research indicate that neatly written essays are scored higher than sloppy ones, even if the answers are essentially the same (Huck & Bounds, 1972; Hughes, Keeling, & Tuck, 1983; Pai, et al., 2010). These findings aren't surprising when you consider that grading essay answers is a time-consuming, labor-intensive task that requires your instructor to plod through multiple answers written by students with multiple styles of handwriting—ranging from crystal clear to quasi-cryptic. If you make your instructor's job a little easier by writing as clearly as possible and cleaning up any sloppy markings before turning in your test, you're likely to earn more points for your answers.

Strategies for Online Tests

More instructors are using technology to enhance their courses. It is very possible that you could have to take an online test even when you are not taking an online course. When taking a test online, you should always read the instructions carefully. Below are some things you should consider when taking online tests.

1. **Online tests are often timed.** Because you are taking these tests outside of class, you are able to use your notes and books. For this reason, many instructors will place a time limit on the test. If you do not complete the test in time, it will shut off when your time is up and you won't be able to do the rest of the test. Be sure to study for online timed tests. You will not have enough time to look up all of the answers, and if you don't study, you won't do well.

2. **Backtracking might be prohibited.** Sometimes you have to answer a question before you can move on to the next question, and once you move on, you cannot go back and change an answer. If this is a timed test, be sure to use your time wisely and don't spend too much time on any one question.

If you have not taken an online test before, be sure to ask your instructor what to expect. Online tests can be created just like an in-class test. Don't assume that online tests will be made up of only multiple-choice and true–false questions.

Be sure you do not wait until the last minute to take your online test. Because you are dealing with technology something can (and often will) go wrong. Be prepared for something to go wrong (e.g., you lose your internet connection in the middle of the test) by giving yourself enough time to deal with any problems that might arise during the test.

When taking online tests, be sure you are using a reliable computer and you are free from anything that could take your focus away from the test (e.g., cell phone, children, etc.). If something does go wrong during the test, be sure to contact your instructor immediately.

Post-Test Strategies: What to Do *After* Receiving Your Test Results

Successful test performance involves both forethought (preparation before the test) and afterthought (reflection after the test). Often, when students get a test back, they check to see what grade they got, then stuff it in a binder or toss it into the nearest wastebasket. Don't fall prey to this unproductive habit; instead, use your test results as feedback to improve your future performance. Reflect on your results and ask yourself: How can I learn from this? How can I put it to use to correct my mistakes and repeat my successes? Remember: A test score isn't an end result; it may tell you where you are now, but it doesn't tell you where you'll end up. Use your results as a means to another end—a higher score on the next test.

> When you make a mistake, there are only three things you should do about it: admit it; learn from it; and don't repeat it."
>
> —Paul "Bear" Bryant, legendary college football coach

 ### Think About It—Journal Entry 7.6

What do you usually do with tests and assignments after they're returned to you? Why?

_____

_____

_____

_____

_____

_____

Note

If you do poorly on an exam, don't get bitter—get better. View your mistakes in terms of what they can do for you, not to you. A poor test performance can be turned into a productive learning experience, particularly if it occurs early in the course when you're still learning the rules of the game. You can use your test results as a valuable source of feedback for improving your future performance and final course grade.

In the movie and record industry, if the first cut isn't successful, additional "takes" ("take two," "take three," etc.) are made until it's done right. Successful students do the same thing: If they make a mistake on "take one," they stick with it and continue working to improve their performance on the next take.

©Lightspring/Shutterstock.com

 In the movies, a clipboard is used to signal the next take (shooting) if the previous take was unsuccessful. Take the same approach to your test performances. If you make a mistake, consider it "take one," learn from it, and approach the next take with the mindset that you're going to improve your previous performance.

> A man who has committed a mistake and doesn't correct it is committing another mistake."
>
> —Confucius, ancient Chinese philosopher and educator

Listed below are strategies you can use to transform your test results into performance-enhancing feedback.

1. **When you get a test back, determine where you gained points and lost points.** Pinpoint what went right so you do it again, and troubleshoot what went wrong so you don't make the same mistake again. On test questions where you lost points, use the strategies summarized in **Box 7.3** to pinpoint the source of the problem.

Box 7.3

Strategies for Pinpointing the Source of Lost Points on Tests

On test questions where you lost points, identify the stage in the learning process where the breakdown occurred by asking yourself the following questions.

- Did I have the information I needed to answer the question correctly? If you didn't have the information needed to answer the question, where should you have acquired it in the first place? Was it information presented in class that didn't get into your notes? If yes, consider adopting strategies for improving your classroom listening and note-taking (such as those found on p. 120). If the missing information was contained in your assigned reading, check whether you're using effective reading strategies (such as those listed on pp. 115–116).

- Did I have the information but didn't study it because I didn't think it was important? If you didn't expect the information to appear on the test, review the strategies for detecting the most important information delivered during class lectures and in reading assignments. (See strategies on p. 124.)

- Did I study it, but didn't retain it? Not remembering information you studied may mean one of three things:

  (a) You didn't learn it deeply and didn't lay down a strong enough memory trace in your brain for you to recall it at test time. This suggests you need to put in more study time or use a different study strategy to learn it more deeply. (See p. 166 for specific strategies.)

  (b) You may have tried to cram in too much study time just before the exam and may have not given your brain time enough to "digest" (consolidate) the information and store it in long-term memory. The solution may be to distribute your study time more evenly in advance of the next exam and take advantage of the "part-to-whole" study method. (See pp. 125–126.)

  (c) You studied hard and didn't cram, but you may need to study smarter or more strategically. (See strategies on p. 151.)

- Did I study the material but didn't really understand it or learn it deeply? This suggests you may need to self-monitor your comprehension more carefully while studying to track whether you're truly understanding the material and moving beyond "shallow" or "surface" learning. (See p. 132.)

- Did I know the material but lost points due to careless test-taking mistakes? If this happened, the solution may simply be to take more time to review your test after completing it and check for absent-minded errors before turning it in. Or, your careless errors may have resulted from test anxiety that interfered with your concentration and memory. If you think this was the factor, consider using strategies for reducing test anxiety. (See p. 154.)

2. **Get feedback from your instructor.** Start by noting any written comments your instructor made on your exam; keep these comments in mind when you prepare for the next exam. You can seek additional feedback by making an appointment to speak with your instructor during office hours. Come to the appointment with a positive mindset about improving your next test performance, not complaining about your last test grade.

3. **Seek feedback from professionals in your Learning Center or Academic Support Center.** Tutors and other learning support professionals can also be excellent sources of feedback about adjustments you can make in your test preparation and test-taking strategies. Ask these professionals to take a look at your tests and seek their advice about how to improve your test performance.

4. **Seek feedback from your classmates.** Your peers can also be a valuable source of information on how to improve your performance. You can review your test with other students in class, particularly with students who did well. Their test answers can provide you with models of what type of work your instructor expects on exams. You might also consider asking successful students what they did to be successful, such as how they prepared for the test and what they did during the test.

    Teaming up after tests and assignments *early in the term* is especially effective because it enables you to get a better idea of what the instructor will expect from students throughout the remainder of the course. You can use this information as early feedback to diagnose your initial mistakes, improve your next performance, and raise your overall course grade—while there's still plenty of time in the term to do so. (See **Box 7.4** for a summary of the type of feedback you should seek from others to best strengthen your academic performance.)

Box 7.4

Key Features of Performance-Enhancing Feedback

When asking for feedback from others on your academic performance, seek feedback that has the following performance-improvement features:

- Effective feedback is *specific*. Seek feedback that identifies precisely what you should do to improve your performance and how you should go about doing it. After a test, seek feedback that provides you with more than information about what your grade is, or why you lost points. Seek specific information about what particular adjustments you can make to improve your next performance.

- Effective feedback is *prompt*. After receiving your grade on a test or assignment, *immediately* review your performance and seek feedback as soon as possible. This is the time when you're likely most motivated to find out what you got right and wrong, and it's also the time when you're most likely to retain the feedback you receive.

- Performance-enhancing feedback is *proactive*. Seek feedback *early* in the learning process. Be sure to ask for feedback at the start of the term. This will leave you with plenty of time and opportunity to use the feedback throughout the term to accumulate points and earn a higher final grade.

Think About It—Journal Entry 7.7

How would you rate your general level of test anxiety during tests? (Circle one.) Explain.

high   moderate   low

What types of tests or subjects tend to produce the most test stress or anxiety for you?

_____

_____

_____

_____

Why?

_____

_____

_____

_____

Strategies for Reducing Test Anxiety

High levels of anxiety can interfere with the ability to recall information that's been studied and increases the risk of making careless concentration-related errors on tests—such as, overlooking key words in test questions (Fernández-Castillo & Caurcel, 2014; Tobias, 1993). Studies also show that students who experience high levels of test anxiety are more likely to use ineffective "surface"-level study practices that rely on memorization, rather than more effective "deep-learning" strategies that involve seeking meaning and understanding (Biggs & Tang, 2007; Ramsden, 2003). The strategies listed below can help you recognize and minimize test anxiety.

1. **Understand what test anxiety is and what it's not.** Don't confuse anxiety with stress. Stress is a physical reaction that prepares your body for action by arousing and energizing it; this heightened level of arousal and energy can actually strengthen your performance. In fact, to be totally stress-free during an exam may mean that you're too laid back and could care less about how well you're doing. Peak levels of performance—whether academic or athletic—are not achieved by completely eliminating stress. Research shows that experiencing a *moderate* level of stress (neither too high nor too low) during exams and other performance-testing situations serves to maximize alertness, concentration, and memory (Sapolsky, 2004). The key is to keep stress at a manageable

level so you can capitalize on its capacity to get you pumped up or psyched up, but prevent it from reaching a level where you become stressed out or psyched out.

If you often experience the following physical and psychological symptoms during tests, it probably means your stress level is too high and may be accurately called *test anxiety*.

- You feel bodily symptoms of tension during the test, such as pounding heartbeat, rapid pulse, muscle tension, sweating, or a queasy stomach.
- You have difficulty concentrating or maintaining your focus of attention while answering test questions.
- Negative thoughts and feelings rush through your head, such as fear of failure or self- putdowns (e.g., "I always mess up on exams.")
- You rush through the test just to get it over with and get rid of the uncomfortable feeling you're experiencing.
- Even though you studied and know the material, you go blank during the test and forget much of what you studied. However, after turning in the test and leaving the test situation, you're often able to remember the information you were unable to recall during the exam.

2. **Use effective test preparation strategies prior to the test.** Test-anxiety research indicates that college students who prepare well for tests and use effective study strategies prior to tests—such as those discussed in Chapter 6—experience less test anxiety during tests (Zeidner, 1995; Zohar, 1998). Studies also show that there is a strong relationship between test anxiety and procrastination—that is, students who put off studying to the very last minute are more likely to report higher levels of test anxiety (Carden, Bryant, & Moss, 2004). The high level of pretest tension caused by last minute rushing to prepare for an exam often carries over to the test itself, resulting in higher levels of tension during the exam. Furthermore, late night cramming deprives the brain of stress-relieving dream (REM) sleep (Voelker, 2004), causing the sleep-deprived student to experience higher levels of anxiety the following day—the day of the test.

3. **Stay focused on the test in front of you, not the students around you.** Don't spend valuable test time looking at what others are doing and wondering whether they're doing better than you are. If you came to the test well prepared and still find the test difficult, it's very likely that other students are finding it difficult too. If you happen to notice that other students are finishing before you do, don't assume they breezed through the test or that they're smarter than you. Their faster finish may simply reflect the fact that they didn't know many of the answers and decided to give up and get out, rather than prolong the agony.

4. **During the test, concentrate on the here and now.** Devote your attention fully to answering the test question that you're currently working on; don't spend time thinking (and worrying) about the test's outcome or what your grade will be.

5. **Focus on the answers you're getting right and the points you're earning, rather than worrying about what you're getting wrong and how many points you're losing.** Our thoughts can influence our emotions (Ellis, 2004), and positive emotions—such as those associated with optimism and a sense of accomplishment—can improve mental performance by enhancing the brain's ability to process, store, and retrieve information (Fredrickson & Branigan, 2005). One way to maintain a positive mindset is to keep in mind that college

tests are often designed to be more difficult than high school tests, so it's less likely that students will get 90% to 100% of the total points. You can still achieve a good grade on a college test without having to achieve a near-perfect test score.

6. **Don't forget that it's just a test, not a measure of your intelligence, academic ability, or self-worth.** No single test can measure your true intellectual capacity or academic talent. In fact, the test grade you earn may not be a true indicator of how much you've actually learned. A low test grade also doesn't mean you're not capable of doing better work or destined to end up with a poor grade in the course—particularly if you adopt a "growth mindset" that views mistakes as learning opportunities (see **p. 151**) and uses test results as feedback for improving future performance (see **p. 151**).

7. **If you continue to experience test anxiety after trying to overcome it on your own, seek assistance from a professional in your Learning (Academic Support) Center or Personal Counseling Office.** You can try to overcome test anxiety (or any other personal issue) through the use of self-help strategies. However, if the problem persists after you've done your best to overcome it, there's no need to keep struggling on your own; instead, it's probably time to seek help from others. This doesn't mean you're weak or incompetent; it means you have the emotional intelligence and resourcefulness to realize your limitations and capitalize on the support networks available to you.

Chapter Summary and Highlights

Effective performance on college tests involves strategies used in advance of the test, during the test, and after test results are returned. Good test performance starts with good test preparation and awareness of the type of test questions you will be expected to answer (e.g., multiple-choice or essay). Test questions can be classified into two major categories, depending on the type of memory required to answer them: (1) *recognition* questions and (2) *recall* questions. Each of these types of questions tests your knowledge and memory in a different way.

Recognition test questions ask you to select or choose the correct answer from choices provided for you. Falling into this category are multiple-choice, true–false, and matching questions. These test questions don't require you to supply or produce the correct answer on your own; instead, you recognize or pick out the correct answer. Since recognition test questions ask you to recognize or select the correct answer from among answers provided for you, reviewing your class notes and textbook highlights may be an effective study strategy for multiple-choice and true–false test questions because it matches the type of mental activity you'll be asked to perform on the exam—which is to read test questions and look for the correct answer.

Recall test questions, on the other hand, require you to retrieve information you've studied and reproduce it on your own. This means you have to recall (re-call or "call back") the information you studied and supply it yourself. Recall test questions include essay and short answer questions; these questions don't involve answer recognition, but answer *production*—you produce the answer in writing. Studying for these types of test questions require *retrieval*—such as reciting the information without looking at it.

Effective test performance not only involves effective test-preparation strategies, but also effective test-taking strategies. For multiple-choice tests, effective test-taking strategies include using a *process-of-elimination* approach to weed out incorrect answers before identifying the best option, and *test-wise* strategies that use the wording of test questions to increase the likelihood of choosing the correct answer (e.g., choosing the longest answer and eliminating answers that contain absolute truths or broad generalizations).

Lastly, effective test performance involves carefully reviewing test results and using them as feedback to improve your future performance and final course grade. When test results are returned, determine where you earned and lost points. Pinpoint what went right so you continue doing it, and troubleshoot what went wrong so you prevent it from happening again.

Learning More through the World Wide Web: Internet-Based Resources

For additional information on strategic test-taking and managing test anxiety, see the following websites:

Test-Taking Strategies:
https://miamioh.edu/student-life/rinella-learning-center/academic-counseling/self-help/test-taking/index.html

https://www.stmarys-ca.edu/academics/academic-resources-support/student-academic-support-services/tutorial-academic-skills-8

Overcoming Test Anxiety:
http://www.studygs.net/tstprp8.htm

http://www.sic.edu/files/uploads/group/34/PDF/TestAnxiety.pdf

References

Bauer, D., Kopp, V., & Fischer, M. R. (2007). Answer changing in multiple choice assessment: change that answer when in doubt—and spread the word! *BMC Medical Education, 7,* 28–32.

Biggs, J., & Tang, C. (2007) *Teaching for quality learning at university* (3rd ed.) Buckingham: SRHE and Open University Press.

Carden, R., Bryant, C., & Moss, R. (2004). Locus of control, test anxiety, academic procrastination, and achievement among college students. *Psychological Reports, 95*(2) 581–582.

Carey, B. (2014). *How we learn.* London: Random House.

Ellis, A. (2004) Rational emotive behavior Therapy: It works for me—It can work for you. Amherst, NY: Prometheus Books.

Fernández-Castillo, A., & Caurcel, M. J. (2014). State test-anxiety, selective attention and concentration in university students. *International Journal of Psychology, 50*(4), 265–271.

Flippo, R. F., & Caverly, D. C. (2009). *Handbook of college reading and study strategy research* (2nd ed.). New York: Lawrence Erlbaum Associates.

Fredrickson, B. L., & Branigan, C. (2005). Positive emotions broaden the scope of attention and thought-action repertoires. *Cognition & Emotion, 19,* 313–332.

Glenberg, A, M. (1997). What memory is for. *Behavioral and Brain Sciences, 20,* 1–55.

Glenberg, A. M., Schroeder, J. L., & Robertson, D. A. (1998). Averting the gaze disengages the environment and facilitates remembering. *Memory & Cognition, 26*(4), 651–658.

Godden, D., & Baddeley, A. (1975). Context dependent memory in two natural environments. *British Journal of Psychology, 66*(3), 325–331.

Haas, R. (1994*). Eat smart, think smart.* New York: HarperCollins.

Huck, S., & Bounds, W. (1972). Essay grades: An interaction between graders' handwriting clarity and the neatness of examination papers. *American Educational Research Journal, 9*(2), 279–283.

Hughes, D. C., Keeling, B., & Tuck, B. F. (1983). Effects of achievement expectations and handwriting quality on scoring essays. *Journal of Educational Measurement, 20*(1), 65–70.

Jensen, E. (2005). *Teaching with the brain in mind* (2nd ed.). Alexandria, VA: Association for Supervision and Curriculum Development.

Kruger, J., Wirtz, D., & Miller, D. (2005). Counterfactual thinking and the first instinct fallacy. *Journal of Personality and Social Psychology, 88,* 725–735.

Kuhn, L. (1988). What should we tell students about answer changing? *Research Serving Teaching, 1*(8).

Miller, M. D., Linn, R. L., & Gronlund, N. E. (2012). *Measurement and assessment in teaching* (7th ed.). Englewood Cliffs, NJ: Pearson.

National Resource Center for the First-Year Experience and Students in Transition (2004). *The 2003 Your First College Year (YFCY) Survey.* Columbia, SC: Author.

Pai, M. R., Sanji, N., Pai, P. G. & Kotian, S. (2010). Comparative assessment in pharmacology multiple choice questions versus essay with focus on gender differences. *Journal of Clinical and Diagnostic Research* [serial online], *4*(3), 2515–2520.

Phillips, G. W. (2005). Does eating breakfast affect the performance of college students on biology exams? *Bioscene, 30*(4), 15–19.

Prinsell, C. P, Ramsey, P. H., & Ramsey, P. P. (1994). Score gains, attitudes, and behaviour changes due to answer-changing Instruction. *Journal of Educational Measurement, 31*, 327–337.

Ramsden, P. (2003). *Learning to teach in higher education* (2nd ed.). London: RoutledgeFalmer.

Rankin CH, Abrams T, Barry RJ, Bhatnagar S, Clayton DF, Colombo J, Coppola G, Geyer MA, Glanzman DL, Marsland S, McSweeney FK, Wilson DA, Wu CF, Thompson RF (2009) Habituation revisited: an updated and revised description of the behavioral characteristics of habituation. Neurobiol Learn Mem 92:135–138

Reed, S. K. (2013). *Cognition: Theory and applications* (3rd ed.). Belmont, CA: Wadsworth/Cengage.

Roediger, H., & Karpicke, J. (2006). The power of testing memory: Basic research and implications for educational practice. *Perspectives on Psychological Science, 1*(3), 181–210.

Sapolsky, R. (2004). *Why zebras don't get ulcers*. New York: W. H. Freeman.

Schab, F. R., & Crowder, R.G. (2014). *Memory for odors*. New York: Psychology Press.

Schroll, R. M. (2006). Effects of breakfast on memory retention of students at the college level. *Saint Martin's University Biology Journal, 1*, 35–50.

Smith, S., & Vela, E. (2001). Environmental context-dependent memory: A review and meta-analysis. *Psychonomic Bulletin & Review, 8*(2), 203–220.

Sprenger, M. (1999). *Learning and memory: The brain in action*. Alexandria, VA: Association for Supervision and Curriculum Development.

Thayer, R. E. (1997). *The origin of everyday moods: Managing energy, tension, and stress*. New York: Oxford University Press.

Tobias, S. (1993). *Overcoming math anxiety*. New York: W.W. Norton.

Tulving, E. (1983). *Elements of episodic memory*. Oxford: Clarendon Press/Oxford University Press.

Ueda, Y., Wang, M. F., Irei, A. V., Sarukura, N., Sakai, T., & Hsu, T. F. (2011). Effect of dietary lipids on longevity and memory in SAMP8 mice. *Journal of Nutritional Science Vitaminol, 57*(1), 36-41.

Ulus, I. H., Scally, M. C., & Wurtman, R. C. (1977). Choline potentiates the induction of adrenal tyrosine hydroxylase by reserpine, probably by enhancing the release of acetylcholine. Life Sci 21:145–148.

Voelker, R. (2004). Stress, sleep loss, and substance abuse create potent recipe for college depression. *Journal of the American Medical Association, 291*, 2177–2179.

Willingham, D. B. (2009). *Cognition: The thinking animal*. Upper Saddle River, NJ: Pearson.

Zeidner, M. (1995). Adaptive coping with test situations: A review of the literature. *Educational Psychologist, 30*(3), 123–133.

Zohar, D. (1998). An additive model of test anxiety: role of exam-specific expectations. *Journal of Educational Psychology, 90*, 330–340.

Chapter 7 Exercises

7.1 Quote Reflections

Review the sidebar quotes contained in this chapter and select two that were especially meaningful or inspirational to you.

For each quote, provide a three- to five-sentence explanation why you chose it.

7.2 Reality Bite

Bad Feedback: Shocking Midterm Grades

Fred has enjoyed his first weeks on campus. He has met lots of people and really likes being in college. He's also very pleased to discover that, unlike high school, his college schedule doesn't require him to be in class for five to six hours per day. That's the good news. The bad news is that unlike high school, where his grades were all As and Bs, Fred's first midterm grades in college are three Cs, one D, and one F. He's stunned and a bit depressed by his midterm grades because he thought he was doing well. Since he never received grades this low in high school, he's beginning to think that he's not college material and may flunk out.

Reflection Questions

1. What factors may have caused or contributed to Fred's bad start?

2. What are Fred's options at this point?

3. What do you recommend Fred do right now to get his grades up and avoid being placed on academic probation?

4. What might Fred do in the future to prevent this midterm setback from happening again?

7.3 Self-Assessment of Test-Taking Habits and Strategies

Rate yourself in terms of how frequently you use these test-taking strategies according to the following scale:
4 = always, 3 = sometimes, 2 = rarely, 1 = never

1. I take tests in the same seat I usually sit in to take class notes.	4	3	2	1
2. I answer easier test questions first.	4	3	2	1
3. I use a process-of-elimination approach on multiple-choice questions to eliminate choices until I find one that is correct or appears to be the most accurate option.	4	3	2	1
4. Before answering essay questions, I look for key action words indicating what type of thinking I should display in my answer (e.g., "analyze," "compare").	4	3	2	1
5. On essay questions, I outline or map out the major ideas I'll include in my answer before I start writing sentences.	4	3	2	1
6. I look for information included on the test that may help me answer difficult questions or that may help me remember information I've forgotten.	4	3	2	1
7. I leave extra space between my answers to essay questions in case I want to come back and add more information later.	4	3	2	1
8. I carefully review my work, double-checking for errors and skipped questions before turning in my tests.	4	3	2	1

Self-Assessment Reflections

Which of the above strategies do you already use?

Of the ones you don't use, which one are you *most* likely to implement and *least* likely to implement? Why?

7.4 Midterm Self-Evaluation

At this point in the term, you may be experiencing the "midterm crunch"—a wave of midterm exams and due dates for assignments. This is a good time to step back and assess your academic progress.

Using the form below, list the courses you're taking this term and the grades you are currently receiving in each of these courses. If you don't know what your grade is, take a few minutes to check your syllabus for your instructor's grading policy and add up your scores on completed tests and assignments; this should give you at least a rough idea of where you stand in your courses. If you're having difficulty determining your grade in a course, even after checking your course syllabus and returned tests or assignments, ask your instructor how you could estimate your current grade.

	Course No.	Course Title	Grade
1.			
2.			
3.			
4.			
5.			

Reflection Questions

1. Were these the grades you *expected*? If not, were they better or worse than you anticipated?

2. Were these the grades you were *hoping* for? Are you pleased or disappointed?

3. Do you see any patterns in your performance that suggest what you're doing well and what you need to improve?

4. If you had to pinpoint one action you could immediately take to improve your lowest course grades, what would it be?

7.5 Calculating Your Midterm Grade Point Average

Use the information below to calculate what your grade point average (GPA) would be if your current course grades turn out to be your final grades for the term.

How to Compute Your Grade Point Average (GPA)

Most colleges and universities use a grading scale ranging from 0 to 4 to calculate a student's grade point average (GPA) or QPA (quality point average). Some schools use a grading system that involves only letters (A, B, etc.), while other institutions use letters as well as pluses and minuses (A–, B+, etc.). Check you college catalog or student handbook to determine what grading system is used at your campus.

The typical point value (points earned) by different letter grades are listed below.

Grade = Point Value

A = 4.0
A– = 3.7
B+ = 3.3
B = 3.0
B– = 2.7
C+ = 2.3
C = 2.0
C– = 1.7
D+ = 1.3
D = 1.0
D– = .7
F = 0

1. **Calculate the grade points you're earning in each of your courses this term by multiplying the course's number of units (credits) by the point value of the grade you're now earning in the course.** For instance, if you have a grade of B in a three-unit course, that course is earning you 9 grade points; if you have a grade of A in a two-unit course, that course is earning you 8 grade points.

2. **Calculate your grade point average by using the following formula:**

$$\text{GRADE POINT AVERAGE (GPA)} = \frac{\text{Total Number of Grade Points for all Courses}}{\text{Divided by Total Number of Course Units}}$$

For instance, see the fictitious example below:

Course	Units	×	Grade	=	Grade Points
Roots of Rock 'n' Roll	3	×	C (2)	=	6
Daydreaming Analysis	3	×	A (4)	=	12
Surfing Strategies	1	×	A (4)	=	4
Wilderness Survival	4	×	B (3)	=	12
Sitcom Analysis	2	×	D (1)	=	2
Love and Romance	3	×	A (4)	=	12
	16				48

$$\text{GPA} = \frac{48}{16} = 3.0$$

Reflection Questions

1. What is your GPA at this point in the term?

2. At the start of this term, was this the GPA you expected to attain? If there is a gap between the GPA you expected to achieve and the GPA you now have, what do you think accounts for this discrepancy?

3. Do you think your actual GPA at the end of the term will be higher or lower than it is now? Why?

Note: It's very typical for GPAs to be lower in college than they were in high school, particularly during the first year of college. Here are the results of one study that compared students' high school GPAs with their GPAs after their first year of college:

- A total of 29% of beginning college students had GPAs of 3.75 or higher in high school, but only 17% had GPAs that high at the end of their first year of college.

- A total of 46% had high school GPAs between 3.25 and 3.74, but only 32% had GPAs that high after the first year of college (National Resource Center for the First-Year Experience and Students in Transition, 2004).

Chapter 7 Reflection

What are some ways that you currently prepare for tests that do not seem to be working? Why do you think these methods of preparing for tests do not work?

List and explain three ways you can change your current methods of preparing for tests that you believe will help you perform better on tests.

1.

2.

3.

What are two things you can do during the test that will help you perform better?

1.

2.

What are two things you can do after you get your test back that can help you perform better on future tests?

1.

2.

Diversity and the Community College Experience

LEARNING ABOUT AND FROM HUMAN DIFFERENCES

This chapter clarifies what "diversity" truly means and demonstrates how experiencing diversity can deepen:

- Learning,
- Promote critical and creative thinking, and
- Contribute to your personal and professional development.

Simply stated, we learn more from people who differ from us than we do from people similar to us. There is more diversity among college students today than at any other time in history. This chapter will help you capitalize on this learning opportunity.

Gain greater appreciation of human differences and develop skills for making the most of diversity in college and beyond.

 Think About It—Journal Entry 8.1

Complete the following sentence:

When I hear the word *diversity*, the first thing that comes to my mind is . . .

What Is Diversity?

Literally translated, the word *diversity* derives from the Latin root *diversus*, meaning "various" or "variety." Thus, human diversity refers to the variety that exists in humanity (the human species). The relationship between humanity and diversity may be compared to the relationship between sunlight and the variety of colors that make up the visual spectrum. Similar to how sunlight passing through a prism disperses into the variety of colors that comprise the visual spectrum, the human species

FIGURE 8.1: Humanity and Diversity

"We are all brothers and sisters. Each face in the rainbow of color that populates our world is precious and special. Each adds to the rich treasure of humanity."

—*Morris Dees, civil rights leader and cofounder of the Southern Poverty Law Center*

HUMANITY →

SPECTRUM
of
DIVERSITY

Gender (male-female)
Age (stage of life)
Race (e.g., White, Black, Asian)
Ethnicity (e.g., Native American, Hispanic, Irish, German)
Socioeconomic status (job status/income)
National *citizenship* (citizen of U.S. or another country)
Native (first-learned) *language*
National *origin* (nation of birth)
National *region* (e.g., raised in north/south)
Generation (historical period when people are born and live)
Political ideology (e.g., liberal/conservative)
Religious/spiritual beliefs (e.g., Christian/Buddhist/Muslim)
Family status (e.g., single-parent/two-parent family)
Marital status (single/married)
Parental status (with/without children)
Sexual orientation (heterosexual/homosexual/bisexual)
Physical ability/disability (e.g., able to hear/deaf)
Mental ability/disability (e.g., mentally able/challenged)
Learning ability/disability (e.g., absence/presence of dyslexia)
Mental health/illness (e.g., absence/presence of depression)

_ _ _ _ _ _ = dimension of diversity

*This list represents some of the major dimensions of human diversity; it does not constitute a complete list of all possible forms of human diversity. Also, disagreement exists about certain dimensions of diversity (e.g., whether certain groups should be considered races or ethnic groups).

on planet earth is dispersed into a variety of different groups that comprise the human spectrum (humanity). **Figure 8.1** illustrates this metaphorical relationship between diversity and humanity.

As depicted in the above figure, human diversity is manifested in a multiplicity of ways, including differences in physical features, national origins, cultural backgrounds, and sexual orientations. Some dimensions of diversity are easily detectable, others are very subtle, and some are invisible.

Think About It—Journal Entry 8.2

Look at the diversity spectrum in Figure 8.1 and look over the list of groups that make up the spectrum. Do you notice any groups missing from the list that should be added, either because they have distinctive backgrounds or because they've been targets of prejudice and discrimination?

Diversity includes discussion of equal rights and social justice for minority groups, but it's a broader concept that involves much more than political issues. In a national survey of American voters, the vast majority of respondents agreed that diversity is more than just "political correctness" (National Survey of Women Voters, 1998). Diversity is also an *educational* issue—an integral element of a college education that contributes to the learning, personal development, and career preparation of *all* students. It enhances the quality of the college experience by bringing multiple perspectives and alternative approaches to *what* is being learned (the content) and *how* it's being learned (the process).

> Ethnic and cultural diversity is an integral, natural, and normal component of educational experiences for all students."
> —*National Council for Social Studies*

Note

Diversity is a human issue that embraces and benefits all people; it's not a code word for "some" people. Although one major goal of diversity is to promote appreciation and equitable treatment of particular groups of people who've experienced discrimination, it's also a learning experience that strengthens the quality of a college education, career preparation, and leadership potential.

What Is Racial Diversity?

A *racial group (race)* is a group of people who share distinctive physical traits, such as skin color or facial characteristics. The variation in skin color we now see among humans is largely due to biological adaptations that have evolved over thousands of years among groups of humans who migrated to different climatic regions of the world. Currently, the most widely accepted explanation of the geographic origin of modern humans is the "Out of Africa" theory. Genetic studies and fossil evidence indicate that all Homo sapiens inhabited Africa 150,000–250,000 years ago; over time, some migrated from Africa to other parts of the world (Mendez, et al., 2013; Meredith, 2011; Reid & Hetherington, 2010). Darker skin tones developed among humans who inhabited and reproduced in hotter geographical regions nearer the equator (e.g., Africans). Their darker skin color helped them adapt and survive by providing them with better protection from the potentially damaging effects of intense sunlight (Bridgeman, 2003). In contrast, lighter skin tones developed over time among humans inhabiting colder climates that were farther from the equator (e.g., Scandinavia). Their lighter skin color enabled them to absorb greater amounts of vitamin D supplied by sunlight, which was in shorter supply in those regions of the world (Jablonksi & Chaplin, 2002).

Currently, the U.S. Census Bureau has identified five races (U.S. Census Bureau, 2012):

White: a person whose lineage may be traced to the original people inhabiting Europe, the Middle East, or North Africa.

Black or African American: a person whose lineage may be traced to the original people inhabiting Africa.

American Indian or Alaska Native: a person whose lineage may be traced to the original people inhabiting North and South America (including Central America), and who continue to maintain their tribal affiliation or attachment.

Asian: a person whose lineage may be traced to the original people inhabiting the Far East, Southeast Asia, or the Indian subcontinent, including: Cambodia, China, India, Japan, Korea, Malaysia, Pakistan, the Philippine Islands, Thailand, and Vietnam.

Native Hawaiian or Other Pacific Islander: a person whose lineage may be traced to the original people inhabiting Hawaii, Guam, Samoa, or other Pacific islands.

It's important to keep in mind that racial categories are not based on scientific evidence; they merely represent group classifications constructed by society (Anderson & Fienberg, 2000). No identifiable set of genes distinguishes one race from another; in fact, there continues to be disagreement among scholars about what groups of people constitute a human race or whether distinctive races actually exist (Wheelright, 2005). In other words, you can't do a blood test or some type of internal genetic test to determine a person's race. Humans have simply decided to categorize themselves into races on the basis of certain external differences in their physical appearance, particularly the color of their outer layer of skin. The U.S. Census Bureau could have decided to divide people into "racial" categories based on other physical characteristics, such as eye color (blue, brown, and green), hair color (brown, black, blonde, or red), or body length (tall, short, or mid-sized).

AUTHOR'S EXPERIENCE

My father stood approximately six feet tall and had straight, light brown hair. His skin color was that of a Western European with a very slight suntan. My mother was from Alabama; she was dark in skin color with high cheekbones and had long curly black hair. In fact, if you didn't know that my father was of African American descent, you would not have thought he was black.

All of my life I've thought of myself as African American and all people who know me have thought of me as African American. I've lived half of a century with that as my racial identity. Several years ago, I carefully reviewed records of births and deaths in my family history and discovered that I had less than 50% African lineage. Biologically, I am no longer black; socially and emotionally, I still am. Clearly, my "race" has been socially constructed, not biologically determined.

— Aaron Thompson

While humans may display diversity in the color or tone of their external layer of skin, the reality is that all members of the human species are remarkably similar at an internal biological level. More than 98% of the genes of all humans are exactly the same, regardless of what their particular race may be (Bronfenbrenner, 2005). This large amount of genetic overlap accounts for our distinctively "human" appearance, which clearly distinguishes us from all other living species. All humans have internal organs that are similar in structure and function, and despite variations in the color of our outer layer of skin, when it's cut, all humans bleed in the same color.

AUTHOR'S EXPERIENCE

I was sitting in a coffee shop in the Chicago O'Hare airport while proofreading my first draft of this chapter. I looked up from my work for a second and saw what appeared to be a white girl about 18 years of age. As I lowered my head to return to work, I did a double-take and looked at her again because something about her seemed different or unusual. When I looked more closely at her the second time, I noticed that although she had white skin, the features of her face and hair appeared to be those of an African American. After a couple of seconds of puzzlement, I figured it out: she was an *albino* African American. That satisfied my curiosity for the moment, but then I began to wonder: Would it still be accurate to say she was "black" even though her skin was not black? Would her hair and facial features be sufficient for her to be considered or classified as black? If yes, then what would be the "race" of someone who had black skin tone, but did not have the typical hair and facial features characteristic of black people? Is skin color the defining feature of being African American or are other features equally important?

I was unable to answer these questions, but found it amusing that all of these thoughts were crossing my mind while I was working on a chapter dealing with diversity. On the plane ride home, I thought again about that albino African American girl and realized that she was a perfect example of how classifying people into "races" isn't based on objective, scientific evidence, but on subjective, socially constructed categories.

—*Joe Cuseo*

Categorizing people into distinct racial or ethnic groups is becoming even more difficult because members of different ethnic and racial groups are increasingly forming cross-ethnic and interracial families. By 2050, the number of Americans who identify themselves as being of two or more races is projected to more than triple, growing from 5.2 million to 16.2 million (U.S. Census Bureau, 2008).

Think About It—Journal Entry 8.3

What race(s) do you consider yourself to be?

Would you say you identify strongly with your racial identity, or are you rarely conscious of it?

Why?

What Is Cultural Diversity?

"Culture" may be defined as a distinctive pattern of beliefs and values learned by a group of people who share the same social heritage and traditions. In short, culture is the whole way in which a group of people has learned to live (Peoples & Bailey, 2011); it includes their style of speaking (language), fashion, food, art and music, as well as their beliefs and values. **Box 8.1** contains a summary of key components of culture that a group may share.

Box 8.1

Key Components of Culture

Language: How members of the culture communicate through written or spoken words; their particular dialect; and their distinctive style of nonverbal communication (body language).

Space: How cultural members arrange themselves with respect to social–spatial distance (e.g., how closely they stand next to each other when having a conversation).

Time: How the culture conceives of, divides, and uses time (e.g., the speed or pace at which they conduct business).

Aesthetics: How cultural members appreciate and express artistic beauty and creativity (e.g., their style of visual art, culinary art, music, theater, literature, and dance).

Family: The culture's attitudes and habits with respect to interacting with family members (e.g., customary styles of parenting their children and caring for their elderly).

Economics: How the culture meets its members' material needs, and its customary ways of acquiring and distributing wealth (e.g., general level of wealth and gap between the very rich and very poor).

Gender Roles: The culture's expectations for "appropriate" male and female behavior (e.g., whether or not women are able to hold the same leadership positions as men).

Politics: How decision-making power is exercised in the culture (e.g., democratically or autocratically).

Science and Technology: The culture's attitude toward and use of science or technology (e.g., the degree to which the culture is technologically "advanced").

Philosophy: The culture's ideas or views on wisdom, goodness, truth, and social values (e.g., whether they place greater value on individual competition or collective collaboration).

Spirituality and Religion: Cultural beliefs about a supreme being and an afterlife (e.g., its predominant faith-based views and belief systems about the supernatural).

Note

The reality of our own culture is not the reality of other cultures. Our perceptions of the outside world are shaped (and sometimes distorted) by our prior cultural experiences.

 Think About It—Journal Entry 8.4

Look at the components of culture cited in the previous list. Add another aspect of culture to the list that you think is important or influential. Explain why you think this is an important element of culture.

AUTHOR'S EXPERIENCE

I was watching a basketball game between the Los Angeles Lakers and Los Angeles Clippers when a short scuffle broke out between the Lakers' Paul Gasol—who is Spanish—and the Clippers' Chris Paul—who is African American. After the scuffle ended, Gasol tried to show Paul there were no hard feelings by patting him on the head. Instead of interpreting Gasol's head pat as a peace-making gesture, Paul took it as a putdown and returned the favor by slapping (rather than patting) Paul in the head.

This whole misunderstanding stemmed from a basic difference in nonverbal communication between the two cultures. Patting someone on the head in European cultures is a friendly gesture; European soccer players often do it to an opposing player to express no ill will after a foul or collision. However, this same nonverbal message meant something very different to Chris Paul—an African American raised in urban America.

—*Joe Cuseo*

What Is an Ethnic Group?

A group of people who share the same culture is referred to as an *ethnic group*. Thus, "culture" refers to *what* an ethnic group shares in common (e.g., language and traditions) and "ethnic group" refers to the *people* who share the same culture that's been *learned* through common social experiences. Members of the same racial group—whose shared physical characteristics have been *inherited*—may be members of different ethnic groups. For instance, white Americans belong to the same racial group, but differ in terms of their ethnic group (e.g., French, German, Irish) and Asian Americans belong to the same racial group, but are members of different ethnic groups (e.g., Japanese, Chinese, Korean).

Currently, the major cultural (ethnic) groups in the United States include:

* Native Americans (American Indians)
  * Cherokee, Navaho, Hopi, Alaskan natives, Blackfoot, etc.
* European Americans (Whites)
  * Descendents from Western Europe (e.g., United Kingdom, Ireland, Netherlands), Eastern Europe (e.g., Hungary, Romania, Bulgaria), Southern Europe (e.g., Italy, Greece, Portugal), and Northern Europe or Scandinavia (e.g., Denmark, Sweden, Norway)
* African Americans (Blacks)
  * Americans whose cultural roots lie in the continent of Africa (e.g., Ethiopia, Kenya, Nigeria) and the Caribbean Islands (e.g., Bahamas, Cuba, Jamaica)
* Hispanic Americans (Latinos)
  * Americans with cultural roots in Mexico, Puerto Rico, Central America (e.g., El Salvador, Guatemala, Nicaragua), and South America (e.g., Brazil, Columbia, Venezuela)
* Asian Americans
  * Americans whose cultural roots lie in East Asia (e.g., Japan, China, Korea), Southeast Asia (e.g., Vietnam, Thailand, Cambodia), and South Asia (e.g., India, Pakistan, Bangladesh)
* Middle Eastern Americans
  * Americans with cultural roots in Iraq, Iran, Israel, etc.

Think About It—Journal Entry 8.5

What ethnic group(s) are you a member of, or do you identify with? What would you say are the key cultural values shared by your ethnic group(s)?

_____

_____

_____

_____

"I'm the only person from my race in class."

—Hispanic student commenting on why he felt uncomfortable in his class on race, ethnicity, and gender

European Americans are still the majority ethnic group in the United States; they account for more than 50% of the American population. Native Americans, African Americans, Hispanic Americans, and Asian Americans are considered to be *minority* ethnic groups because each of these groups represents less than 50% of the American population.

As with racial grouping, classifying humans into different ethnic groups can be very arbitrary and subject to debate. Currently, the U.S. Census Bureau classifies Hispanics as an ethnic group rather than a race. However, among Americans who checked "some other race" in the 2000 Census, 97% were Hispanic. This finding suggests that Hispanic Americans consider themselves to be a racial group, probably because that's how they're perceived and treated by non-Hispanics (Cianciatto, 2005). It's noteworthy that the American media used the term "racial profiling" (rather than ethnic profiling) to describe Arizona's controversial 2010 law that allowed police to target Hispanics who "look" like illegal aliens from Mexico, Central America, and South America. Once again, this illustrates how race and ethnicity are subjective, socially constructed concepts that reflect how people perceive and treat different social groups, which, in turn, affects how members of these groups perceive themselves.

The Relationship between Diversity and Humanity

As previously noted, diversity represents variations on the same theme: being human. Thus, humanity and diversity are interdependent, complementary concepts. To understand human diversity is to understand both our differences and *similarities* (Public Service Enterprise Group, 2009). Diversity appreciation includes appreciating both the unique perspectives of different cultural groups as well as universal aspects of the human experience that are common to all groups—whatever their particular cultural background happens to be. Members of all racial and ethnic groups live in communities, develop personal relationships, have emotional needs, and undergo life experiences that affect their self-esteem and personal identity. Humans of all races and ethnicities experience similar emotions and reveal those emotions with similar facial expressions (see **Figure 8.2**).

FIGURE 8.2

Humans all over the world display the same facial expressions when experiencing and expressing different emotions. See if you can detect the emotions being expressed in the following faces.
(To find the answers, turn your book upside down.)

Answers: The emotions shown. Top, left to right: anger, fear, and sadness.
Bottom, left to right: disgust, happiness, and surprise.

Other characteristics that anthropologists have found to be shared by all humans in every corner of the world include: storytelling, poetry, adornment of the body, dance, music, decoration with artifacts, families, socialization of children by elders, a sense of right and wrong, supernatural beliefs, and mourning of the dead (Pinker, 2000). Although different cultural groups may express these shared experiences in different ways, they are universal experiences common to all human cultures.

Think About It—Journal Entry 8.6

In addition to those already mentioned, can you think of another important human experience that is universal—that is experienced by all humans?

_____

_____

_____

_____

_____

You may have heard the question: "We're all human, aren't we?" The answer to this important question is "yes and no." Yes, we are all the same, but not in the same way. A good metaphor for understanding this apparent contradiction is to visualize humanity as a quilt in which we're all united by the common thread of humanity—the universal bond of being human. (Much like the quilt below.) The different patches comprising the quilt represent diversity—the distinctive or unique cultures that comprise our shared humanity. The quilt metaphor acknowledges the identity and beauty of all cultures. It differs from the old American "melting pot" metaphor, which viewed cultural differences as something to be melted down and eliminated. It also differs from the old "salad bowl" metaphor that depicted America as a hodgepodge or mishmash of cultures thrown together without any common connection. In contrast, the quilt metaphor suggests that the unique cultures of different human groups should be preserved, recognized, and valued; at the same time, these cultural differences join together to form a seamless, unified whole. This blending of diversity and unity is captured in the Latin expression *E pluribus unum* ("Out of many, one")—the motto of the United States—which you'll find printed on all its currency.

"We are all the same, and we are all unique."

—Georgia Dunston, African American biologist and research specialist in human genetics

Note

When we appreciate diversity in the context of humanity, we capitalize on the variety and versatility of human differences while preserving the collective strength and synergy of human unity.

What Is Individuality?

©steven r. hendricks/Shutterstock.com

It's important to keep in mind that there are individual differences among members of any racial or ethnic group that are greater than the average difference between groups. Said in another way, there's more variability (individuality) within groups than between groups. For example, among

"We have become not a melting pot but a beautiful mosaic."

—Jimmy Carter, 39th president of the United States and winner of the Nobel Peace Prize

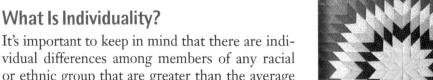
Cultural differences can exist within the same society (multicultural society), within a single nation (domestic diversity), or across different nations (international diversity).

When I was 12 years old and living in New York City, I returned from school one Friday and my mother asked me if anything interesting happened at school that day. I told her that the teacher went around the room asking students what they had for dinner the night before. At that moment, my mother became a bit concerned and nervously asked me: "What did you tell the teacher?" I said: "I told her and the rest of the class that I had pasta last night because my family always eats pasta on Thursdays and Sundays." My mother exploded and fired back the following question at me in a very agitated tone, "Why didn't you tell her we had steak or roast beef?" For a moment, I was stunned and couldn't figure out what I'd done wrong or why I should have lied about eating pasta. Then it dawned on me: My mom was embarrassed about being Italian American. She wanted me to hide our family's ethnic background and make it sound like we were very "American."

As I grew older, I understood why my mother felt the way she did. She grew up in America's "melting pot" generation—a time when different American ethnic groups were expected to melt down and melt away their ethnicity. They were not to celebrate their diversity; they were to eliminate it.

—*Joe Cuseo*

members of the same racial group, individual differences in their physical attributes (e.g., height and weight) and psychological characteristics (e.g., temperament and personality) are greater than any average difference that may exist between their racial group and other racial groups (Caplan & Caplan, 2008).

Note

While it's valuable to learn about differences between different human groups, there are substantial individual differences among people within the same racial or ethnic group that should neither be ignored nor overlooked. Don't assume that individuals with the same racial or ethnic characteristics share the same personal characteristics.

As you proceed through your college experience, keep the following key distinctions in mind:

- **Humanity.** All humans are members of the *same group*—the human species.
- **Diversity.** All humans are members of *different groups*—such as, different racial and ethnic groups.
- **Individuality.** Each human is a *unique individual* who differs from all other members of any group to which he or she may belong.

Major Forms or Types of Diversity in Today's World
Ethnic and Racial Diversity

America is rapidly becoming a more racially and ethnically diverse nation. Minorities now account for 36.6% of the total population—an all-time high; in 2011, for the first time in U.S. history, racial and ethnic minorities made up more than half (50.4%) of all children born in America (Nhan, 2012). By the middle of the 21st century, minority groups are expected to comprise 54% of the American population and more than 60% of the nation's children will be members of minority groups (U.S. Census Bureau, 2008).

More specifically, by 2050 the American population is projected to be more than 30% Hispanic (up from 15% in 2008), 15% Black (up from 13% in 2008), 9.6% Asian (up from 5.3% in 2008), and 2% Native Americans (up from 1.6% in 2008). The Native Hawaiian and Pacific Islander population is expected to more than double between 2008 and 2050. During this same timeframe, the percentage of white Americans will decline from 66% (2008) to 46% (2050). As a result of these demographic trends, today's ethnic and racial minorities will become the "new majority" of Americans by the middle of the 21st century (see **Figure 8.3**).

> "I realize that I'm black, but I like to be viewed as a person, and this is everybody's wish."
> —*Michael Jordan, Hall of Fame basketball player*

> "Every human is, at the same time, like all other humans, like some humans, and like no other human."
> —*Clyde Kluckhohn, American anthropologist*

The growing racial and ethnic diversity of America's population is reflected in the growing diversity of students enrolled in its colleges and universities. In 1960, whites made up almost 95% of the total college population; in 2010, that percentage had decreased to 61.5%. Between 1976 and 2010, the percentage of ethnic minority students in higher education increased from 17% to 40% (National Center for Education Statistics, 2011). This rise in ethnic and racial diversity on American campuses is particularly noteworthy when viewed in light of the historical treatment of minority groups in the United States. In the early 19th century, education was not a right, but a privilege available only to those who could afford to attend private schools. It was experienced largely by Protestants of European descent (Luhman, 2007).

FIGURE 8.3: The "New Majority"

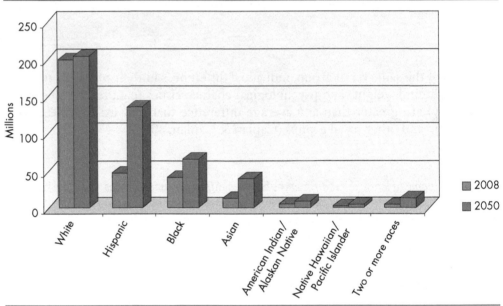

©Kendall Hunt Publishing Company

Northeast Iowa Community College; Diversity Facts, Academic Year 2015–16			
Gender			
Female	3712	56.8%	57.6%
Male	2828	43.2%	42.4%
Ethnicity			
White	6033	92.2%	92.4%
American Indian or Alaskan Native	21	0.3%	0.2%
Asian	31	0.5%	0.4%
Black	159	2.4%	2.4%
Hispanic	115	1.8%	1.6%
Multiple	32	0.5%	0.6%
Native Hawaiian or other Pacific Islander	12	0.2%	0.1%
No Response			
Age Ranges			
<18	1416	21.7%	20.1%
18–24	3874	59.2%	58.3%
>24	1250	19.1%	21.6%

Think About It—Journal Entry 8.7

1. What diverse groups do you see represented on your campus?

2. Are there groups on campus you didn't expect to see or to see in such large numbers?

3. Are there groups on campus you expected to see but don't see or, see in smaller numbers than you expected?

> Of all the civil rights for which the world has struggled and fought for 5,000 years, the right to learn is undoubtedly the most fundamental."
>
> —W. E. B. Du Bois, African American sociologist, historian, and civil rights activist

The rise in ethnic and racial diversity on American campuses is particularly noteworthy when viewed in light of the historical treatment of minority groups in the United States. Members of certain minority groups were left out of the educational process altogether, or were forced to be educated in racially segregated settings. For example, Americans of color were once taught in separate, segregated schools that were typically inferior in terms of educational facilities. It was not until the groundbreaking Supreme Court ruling in *Brown v. Board of Education* (1954) that the face of education for people of color changed with the ruling that "separate educational facilities are inherently unequal." The decision made it illegal for Kansas and 20 other states to deliver education in segregated classrooms.

Box 8.2

Diversity in America's Community Colleges

58% of community college students are women

53% are 22 years of age or older

Among full-time students, 50% are employed part-time and 27% are employed full-timeAmong part-time students, 50% are employed full-time and 33% are employed part-time

39% are the first in their family to attend college

36% are members of a minority ethnic or racial group

17% are single parents

Source: American Association of Community Colleges (2009)

AUTHOR'S EXPERIENCE

My mother was a direct descendent of slaves and moved with her parents from the Deep South at the age of 17. My father lived in an all-Black coal mining camp, into which my mother and her family moved in 1938. My father remained illiterate because he was not allowed to attend public schools in eastern Kentucky. In the early 1960s my brother, my sister, and I were integrated into the White public schools. Physical violence and constant verbal harassment caused many other Blacks to forgo their education and opt for jobs in the coal mines at an early age. But my father remained constant in his advice to me: "It doesn't matter if they call you n_____; but don't you ever let them beat you by walking out on your education." He would say to me, "Son, you will have opportunities that I never had. Just remember, when you do get that education, you'll never have to go in those coal mines and have them break your back. You can choose what you want to do, and then you can be free man."

My parents, who could never provide me with monetary wealth, truly made me proud of them by giving me the gift of insight and an aspiration for achievement.

—*Aaron Thompson*

Socioeconomic Diversity

Human diversity also exists among groups of people in terms of their socioeconomic status (SES), which is determined by their level of education, level of income, and the occupational prestige of the jobs they hold. Groups are stratified (divided) into lower, middle, or upper classes, and groups occupying lower social strata have less economic resources and social privileges (Feagin & Feagin, 2007).

> Being born in the elite in the U.S. gives you a constellation of privileges that very few people in the world have ever experienced. Being born poor in the U.S. gives you disadvantages unlike anything in Western Europe, Japan and Canada."
>
> *—David I. Levine, economist and social mobility researcher*

Young adults from high-income families are more than seven times likely to have earned a college degree and hold a prestigious job than those from low-income families (Olson, 2007). Sharp discrepancies also exist in income level among different racial, ethnic, and gender groups. In 2012, the median income for non-Hispanic white households was $57,009, compared to $39,005 for Hispanics and $33,321 for African Americans (DeNavas-Walt, Proctor, & Smith, 2013). From 2005 to 2009, household wealth fell by 66% for Hispanics, 53% for Blacks, and 16% for Whites, largely due to the housing and mortgage collapse—which had a more damaging effect on lower-income families (Kochlar, Fry, & Taylor, 2011).

Despite its overall wealth, the United States is one of the most impoverished of all developed countries in the world (Shah, 2008). The poverty rate in the United States is almost twice the rate of other economically developed countries around the world (Gould & Wething, 2013). In 2012, more than 16% of the American population, and almost 20% of American children, lived below the poverty line ($23,050 yearly income for a family of four) (U.S. Census Bureau, 2013).

 Think About It—Journal Entry 8.8

Are you the first in your family to attend college?

Whether yes or no, how does that make you feel?

International Diversity

If it were possible to reduce the world's population to a village of precisely 100 people, with all existing human ratios remaining about the same, the demographics of this world village would look something like this:

61 would be Asians; 13 would be Africans; 12 would be Europeans; 9 would be Latin Americans; and 5 would be North Americans (citizens of the United States and Canada)

50 would be male, 50 would be female

75 would be non-white; 25 white

67 would be non-Christian; 33 would be Christian

80 would live in substandard housing

16 would be unable to read or write

50 would be malnourished and 1 would be dying of starvation

33 would be without access to a safe water supply

39 would lack access to modern sanitation

24 would have no electricity (and of the 76 who have electricity, most would only use it for light at night)

8 people would have access to the Internet

1 would have a college education

1 would have HIV

2 would be near birth; 1 near death

5 would control 32% of the entire world's wealth; all 5 would be U.S. citizens

48 would live on less than $2 a day

20 would live on less than $1 a day (Family Care Foundation, 1997–2012).

In this world village, English would not be the most common language spoken—it would be third, following Chinese and Spanish (Lewis, Paul, & Fennig, 2014).

The need for American college students to develop an appreciation of international diversity is highlighted by a study conducted by an anthropologist who went "undercover" to pose as a student in a university residence hall. She found that the biggest complaint international students had about American students was their lack of knowledge of other countries and the misconceptions they held about people from different nations (Nathan, 2005). When you take the time to learn about other countries and the cultures of people who inhabit them, you move beyond being just a citizen of your own nation, you become *cosmopolitan*—a citizen of the world.

Generational Diversity

Humans are also diverse with respect to the historical time period in which they grew up. The term "generation" refers to a cohort (group) of individuals born during the same period in history whose attitudes, values, and habits have been shaped by events that took place in the world during their formative years of development. People growing up in different generations are likely to develop different attitudes and beliefs because of the different historical events they experienced during their upbringing.

Box 8.3 contains a brief summary of different generations, the key historical events they experienced, and the personal characteristics commonly associated with each generational group (Lancaster & Stillman, 2002).

Box 8.3

Generational Diversity: A Snapshot Summary

- The Traditional Generation (a.k.a. "Silent Generation") (born 1922–1945). This generation was influenced by events such as the Great Depression and World Wars I and II. Characteristics associated with people growing up at this time include loyalty, patriotism, respect for authority, and conservatism.
- The Baby Boomer Generation (born 1946–1964). This generation was influenced by events such as the Vietnam War, Watergate, and the civil rights movement. Characteristics associated with people growing up at this time include idealism, emphasis on self-fulfillment, and concern for social justice and equal rights.
- Generation X (born 1965–1980). This generation was influenced by Sesame Street, the creation of MTV, AIDS, and soaring divorce rates. They were the first "latchkey children"—youngsters who used their own key to let themselves into their home after school—because their mother (or single mother) was working outside the home. Characteristics associated with people growing up at this time include self-reliance, resourcefulness, and ability to adapt to change.
- Generation Y (a.k.a. "Millennials") (born 1981–2002). This generation was influenced by the September 11, 2001, terrorist attack on the United States, the shooting of students at Columbine High School, and the collapse of the Enron Corporation. Characteristics associated with people growing up at this time include a prefer-

ence for working and playing in groups, familiarity with technology, and willingness to engage in volunteer service in their community (the "civic generation"). This is also the most ethnically diverse generation, which may explain why they're more open to diversity than previous generations and are more likely to view diversity positively.

> "You guys [in the media] have to get used to it. This is a new day and age, and for my generation that's a very common word. It's like saying 'bro.' That's how we address our friends. That's how we talk."
>
> —Matt Barnes, 33-year-old, biracial professional basketball player, explaining to reporters after being fined for using the word "niggas" in a tweet to some of his African American teammates

- Generation Z (a.k.a. "The iGeneration") (born 1994–present). This generation includes the latter half of Generation Y. They grew up during the wars in Afghanistan and Iraq, terrorism, the global recession, and climate change. Consequently, they have less trust in political systems and industrial corporations than previous generations. During their formative years, the world wide web was in place, so they're quite comfortable with technology and rely heavily on the Internet, Wikipedia, Google, Twitter, MySpace, Facebook, Instant Messaging, image boards, and YouTube. They expect immediate gratification through technology and accept the lack of privacy associated with social networking. For these reasons, they're also referred to as the "digital generation."

 Think About It—Journal Entry 8.9

Look back at the characteristics associated with your generation. Which of these characteristics accurately reflect your personal characteristics and those of your closest friends? Which do not?

What is Sexual Diversity?
Sexual Diversity: LGBT, LGBTQ, LGBTQA, TBL

These acronyms refer to lesbian, gay, bisexual, transgender, queer or questioning, and asexual or ally but all of the different identities within "LGBT" are often grouped together. These groups are very present on college campuses and there are specific needs and concerns related to each individual identity.

Humans experience and express sexuality in diverse ways. "Sexual diversity" refers to differences in human *sexual orientation*—the gender (male or female) an individual is physically attracted to, and *sexual identity*—the gender an individual identifies with or considers himself or herself or to be. The spectrum of sexual diversity includes:

Heterosexuals—males who are sexually attracted to females, and females who are sexually attracted to males

Gays—males who are sexually attracted to males

Lesbians—females who are sexually attracted to females

Bisexuals—individuals who are sexually attracted to males and females

Transgender—individuals who do not identify with the gender they were assigned at birth, or don't feel they belong to a single gender (e.g., transsexuals, transvestites, and bigender) .

Other terms are often grouped and discussed in these diverse communities. They are:

Asexual: A person who generally does not feel sexual attraction or desire to any group of people. Asexuality is not the same as celibacy.

Ally: Typically any non-LGBT person who supports and stands up for the rights of LGBT people, although LGBT people can be allies, such as a lesbian who is an ally to a transgender person.

Cisgender: Types of gender identity where an individual's experience of their own gender matches the sex they were assigned at birth.

Coming Out: The process of acknowledging one's sexual orientation and/or gender identity to other people. For most LGBT people, this is a lifelong process.

Gender expression: A term that refers to the ways in which we each manifest masculinity or femininity. It is usually an extension of our "gender identity," our innate sense of being male, female, etc. Each of us expresses a particular gender every day—by the way we style our hair, select our clothing, or even the way we stand. Our appearance, speech, behavior, movement, and other factors signal that we feel—and wish to be understood as—masculine or feminine, or as a man or a woman.

Gender identity: The sense of "being" male, female, genderqueer, agender, etc. For some people, gender identity is in accord with physical anatomy. For transgender people, gender identity may differ from physical anatomy or expected social roles. It is important to note that gender identity, biological sex, and sexual orientation are separate and that you cannot assume how someone identifies in one category based on how they identify in another category.

Genderqueer: A term that refers to individuals or groups who "queer" or problematize the hegemonic notions of sex, gender, and desire in a given society. Genderqueer people possess identities that fall outside of the widely accepted sexual binary (i.e., "men" and "women"). Genderqueer may also refer to people who identify as both transgendered AND queer—that is, individuals who challenge both gender and sexuality regimes and see gender identity and sexual orientation as overlapping and interconnected.

Heterosexual: A person who is only attracted to members of the opposite sex. Also called "straight."

Homosexual: A clinical term for people who are attracted to members of the same sex. Some people find this term offensive.

Intersex: A person whose sexual anatomy or chromosomes do not fit with the traditional markers of "female" and "male." For example: people born with both "female" and "male" anatomy (penis, testicles, vagina, uterus); people born with XXY chromosomes.

In the closet: Describes a person who keeps their sexual orientation or gender identity a secret from some or all people.

Queer: 1) An umbrella term sometimes used by LGBTQA people to refer to the entire LGBT community. 2) An alternative that some people use to "queer" the idea of the labels and categories such as lesbian, gay, bisexual, etc. Similar to the concept of genderqueer. It is important to note that the word queer is an in-group term, and a word that can be considered offensive to some people, depending on their generation, geographic location, and relationship with the word.

Questioning: For some, the process of exploring and discovering one's own sexual orientation, gender identity, or gender expression.

Pansexual: A person who experiences sexual, romantic, physical, and/or spiritual attraction for members of all gender identities/expressions, not just people who fit into the standard gender binary (i.e., men and women).

Sexual orientation: The type of sexual, romantic, and/or physical attraction someone feels toward others. Often labeled based on the gender identity/expression of the person and who they are attracted to. Common labels: lesbian, gay, bisexual, pansexual, etc.

Transsexual: A person whose gender identity is different from their biological sex, who may undergo medical treatments to change their biological sex, oftentimes to align it with their gender identity, or they may live their lives as another sex.

For more information:
*   http://itspronouncedmetrosexual.com/2013/01/a-comprehensive-list-of
    -lgbtq-term-definitions/
*   http://gillfoundation.org/grants/gender-expression-toolkit/gender-expression/

College campuses across the country are increasing their support for GLBT (gay, lesbian, bisexual, transgendered) students, creating centers and services to facilitate their acceptance and adjustment. These centers and services play an important role in combating homophobia and related forms of sexual prejudice on campus, while promoting awareness and tolerance of all forms of sexual diversity.

By accepting individuals who span the spectrum of sexual diversity, we acknowledge and appreciate the reality that heterosexuality isn't the one-and-only form of human sexual expression (Dessel, 2012). This growing acknowledgment is reflected in the Supreme Court's historic decision to legalize same-sex marriage nationwide (Dolan & Romney, 2015).

The Benefits of Experiencing Diversity

Thus far, this chapter has focused on *what* diversity is; we now turn to *why* diversity is worth experiencing. National surveys show that by the end of their first year in college, almost two-thirds of students report "stronger" or "much stronger" knowledge of people from different races and cultures than they had when they first began college, and the majority of them became more open to diverse cultures, viewpoints and values (HERI, 2013, 2014). Students who develop more openness to and knowledge of diversity are likely to experience the following benefits.

Diversity Increases Self-Awareness and Self-Knowledge

Interacting with people from diverse backgrounds increases self-knowledge and self-awareness by enabling you to compare your life experiences with others whose experiences may differ sharply from your own. When you step outside yourself to contrast your experiences with others from different backgrounds, you move beyond ethnocentrism and gain a *comparative perspective*—a reference point that positions you to see how your particular cultural background has shaped the person you are today.

> "It is difficult to see the picture when you are inside the frame."
>
> —*An old saying (author unknown)*

A comparative perspective also enables us to learn how our cultural background has advantaged or disadvantaged us. For instance, learning about cross-cultural differences in education makes us aware of the limited opportunities people in other countries have to attend college and how advantaged we are in America—where a college education is available to everyone, regardless of their race, gender, age, or prior academic history.

Note

The more you learn from people who are different than yourself, the more you learn about yourself.

Diversity Deepens Learning

Research consistently shows that we learn more from people who differ from us than we do from people similar to us (Pascarella, 2001; Pascarella & Terenzini, 2005). Learning about different cultures and interacting with people from diverse cultural groups provides our brain with more varied routes or pathways through which to connect (learn) new ideas. Experiencing diversity "stretches" the brain beyond its normal "comfort zone," requiring it to work harder to assimilate something unfamiliar. When we encounter the unfamiliar, the brain has to engage in extra effort to understand it by comparing and contrasting it to something we already know (Acredolo & O'Connor, 1991; Nagda, Gurin, & Johnson, 2005). This added expenditure of mental energy results in the brain forming neurological connections that are deeper and more durable (Willis, 2006). Simply stated, humans learn more from diversity than they do from similarity or familiarity. In contrast, when we restrict the diversity of people with whom we interact (out of habit or prejudice), we limit the breadth and depth of our learning.

Diversity Promotes Critical Thinking

Studies show that students who experience high levels of exposure to various forms of diversity while in college—such as participating in multicultural courses and campus events and interacting with peers of different ethnic backgrounds—report the greatest gains in:

- thinking *complexity*—ability to think about all parts and sides of an issue (Association of American Colleges & Universities, 2004; Gurin, 1999),
- *reflective* thinking—ability to think deeply about personal and global issues (Kitchener, Wood, & Jensen, 2000), and
- *critical* thinking—ability to evaluate the validity of their own reasoning and the reasoning of others (Gorski, 2009; Pascarella, et al., 2001).

"When the only tool you have is a hammer, you tend to see every problem as a nail."

—Abraham Maslow, humanistic psychologist, best known for his self-actualization theory of human motivation

These findings are likely explained by the fact that when we're exposed to perspectives that differ from our own, we experience "cognitive dissonance"—a state of cognitive (mental) disequilibrium or imbalance that "forces" our mind to consider multiple perspectives simultaneously; this makes our thinking less simplistic, more complex, and more comprehensive (Brookfield, 1987; Gorski, 2009).

Diversity Stimulates Creative Thinking

"What I look for in musicians is generosity. There is so much to learn from each other and about each other's culture. Great creativity begins with tolerance."

—Yo-Yo Ma, French-born, Chinese-American virtuoso cellist, composer, and winner of multiple Grammy Awards

Cross-cultural knowledge and experiences enhance personal creativity (Leung, et al., 2008; Maddux & Galinsky, 2009). When we have diverse perspectives at our disposal, we have more opportunities to shift perspectives and discover "multiple partial solutions" to problems (Kelly, 1994). Furthermore, ideas acquired from diverse people and cultures can "cross-fertilize," giving birth to new ideas for tackling old problems (Harris, 2010). Research shows that when ideas are generated freely and exchanged openly in groups comprised of people from diverse backgrounds, powerful "cross-stimulation" effects can occur, whereby ideas from one group member trigger new ideas among other group members (Brown, Dane, & Durham, 1998). Research also indicates that seeking out diverse alternatives, perspectives, and viewpoints enhances our ability to reach personal goals (Stoltz, 2014).

Note

By drawing on ideas generated by people from diverse backgrounds and bouncing your ideas off them, divergent or expansive thinking is stimulated; this leads to synergy (multiplication of ideas) and serendipity (unexpected discoveries).

"When all men think alike, no one thinks very much."

—Walter Lippmann, distinguished journalist and originator of the term "stereotype"

In contrast, when different cultural perspectives are neither sought nor valued, the variety of lenses available to us for viewing problems is reduced, which, in turn, reduces our capacity to think creatively. Ideas are less likely to diverge (go in different directions); instead, they're more likely to converge and merge into the same cultural channel—the one shared by the homogeneous group of people doing the thinking.

Diversity Enhances Career Preparation and Career Success

Whatever line of work you decide to pursue, you're likely to find yourself working with employers, coworkers, customers, and clients from diverse cultural backgrounds. America's workforce is now more diverse than at any other time in history and will grow ever more diverse throughout the 21st century; by 2050, the proportion of American workers from minority ethnic and racial groups will jump to 55% (U.S. Census Bureau, 2008).

National surveys reveal that policymakers, business leaders, and employers seek college graduates who are more than just "aware" of or "tolerant" of diversity. They want graduates who have actual *experience* with diversity (Education Commission of the States, 1995) and are able to collaborate with diverse coworkers, clients, and customers (Association of American Colleges & Universities, 2002; Hart Research Associates, 2013). Over 90% of employers agree that all students should have experiences in college that teach them how to solve problems with people whose views differ from their own (Hart Research Associates, 2013).

The current "global economy" also requires skills relating to international diversity. Today's work world is characterized by economic interdependence among nations, international trading (imports/exports), multinational corporations, international travel, and almost instantaneous worldwide communication—due to rapid advances in the world wide web (Dryden & Vos, 1999; Friedman, 2005). Even smaller companies and corporations have become increasingly international in nature (Brooks, 2009). As a result, employers in all sectors of the economy now seek job candidates who possess the following skills and attributes: sensitivity to human differences, ability to understand and relate to people from different cultural backgrounds, international knowledge, and ability to communicate in a second language (Fixman, 1990; Hart Research Associates, 2013; National Association of Colleges & Employers, 2007; Office of Research, 1994).

As a result of these domestic and international trends, *intercultural competence* has become an essential skill for success in the 21st century (Thompson & Cuseo, 2014). Intercultural competence may be defined as the ability to appreciate and learn from human differences and to interact effectively with people from diverse cultural backgrounds. It includes "knowledge of cultures and cultural practices (one's own and others), complex cognitive skills for decision making in intercultural contexts, social skills to function effectively in diverse groups, and personal attributes that include flexibility and openness to new ideas" (Wabash National Study of Liberal Arts Education, 2007).

> "The benefits that accrue to college students who are exposed to racial and ethnic diversity during their education carry over in the work environment. The improved ability to think critically, to understand issues from different points of view, and to collaborate harmoniously with co-workers from a range of cultural backgrounds all enhance a graduate's ability to contribute to his or her company's growth and productivity."
> —*Business/Higher Education Forum*

> "Technology and advanced communications have transformed the world into a global community, with business colleagues and competitors as likely to live in India as in Indianapolis. In this environment, people need a deeper understanding of the thinking, motivations, and actions of different cultures, countries and regions."
> —*The Partnership for 21st Century Skills*

 Think About It—Journal Entry 8.10

What intercultural skills do you think you already possess?

_____

_____

_____

_____

_____

What intercultural skills do you think you need to develop?

_____

_____

_____

_____

_____

Note

The wealth of diversity on college campuses today represents an unprecedented educational opportunity. You may never again be a member of a community with so many people from such a wide variety of backgrounds. Seize this opportunity to strengthen your education and career preparation.

Overcoming Barriers to Diversity

Before we can capitalize on the benefits of diversity, we need to overcome obstacles that have long impeded our ability to appreciate and seek out diversity. These major impediments are discussed below.

Ethnocentrism

FIGURE 8.4:
Optical Illusion

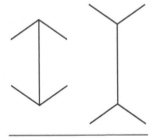

©Kendall Hunt Publishing
Company.

A major advantage of culture is that it builds group solidarity, binding its members into a supportive, tight-knit community. Unfortunately, culture not only binds us, it can also blind us from taking different cultural perspectives. Since culture shapes thought and perception, people from the same ethnic (cultural) group run the risk of becoming *ethnocentric*—centered on their own culture to such a degree they view the world solely through their own cultural lens (frame of reference) and fail to consider or appreciate other cultural perspectives (Colombo, Cullen, & Lisle, 2013). Optical illusions are a good example of how our particular cultural perspective can influence (and distort) our perceptions. Compare the lengths of the two lines in **Figure 8.4**.

If you perceive the line on the right to be longer than the one on the left, your perception has been shaped by Western culture. People from Western cultures, such as Americans, perceive the line on the right to be longer. However, both lines are actually equal in length. (If you don't believe it, take out a ruler and measure them.) Interestingly, this perceptual error isn't made by people from non-Western cultures—whose living spaces and architectural structures are predominantly circular (e.g., huts or igloos)—in contrast to rectangular-shaped buildings with angled corners that typify Western cultures (Segall, Campbell, & Herskovits, 1966).

The optical illusion depicted in Figure 8.4 is just one of a number of illusions experienced by people in certain cultures, but not others (Shiraev & Levy, 2013). Cross-cultural differences in susceptibility to optical illusions illustrate how strongly our cultural experiences can influence and sometimes misinform our perception of reality. People think they are seeing things objectively (as they actually are) but they're really seeing things subjectively—as viewed from their particular cultural perspective.

If our cultural experience can influence our perception of the physical world, it can certainly shape our perception of social events and political issues. Research in psychology indicates that the more exposure humans have to somebody or something, the more familiar it becomes and the more likely it will be perceived positively and judged favorably. The effect of familiarity is so prevalent and powerful that social psychologists have come to call it the "familiarity principle"—that is, what is familiar is perceived as better or more acceptable (Zajonc, 1968, 1970, 2001). Thus, we need to be mindful that the familiarity of our cultural experiences can bias us toward seeing our culture as normal or better. By remaining open to the viewpoints of people who perceive the world from different cultural vantage points, we minimize our cultural blind spots, expand our range of perception, and position ourselves to perceive the world with greater clarity and cultural sensitivity.

©James Michael Doresey/Shutterstock.com

People whose cultural experiences involve living and working in circular structures would not be fooled by the optical illusion in Figure 8.4.

Stereotyping

"Stereotype" derives from two different roots: *stereo*—to look at in a fixed way—and *type*—to categorize or group together, as in the word "typical." Thus, to stereotype is to view individuals of the same type (group) in the same (fixed) way.

Stereotyping overlooks or disregards individuality; all people sharing the same group characteristic (e.g., race or gender) are viewed as having the same personal characteristics—as in the expression: "You know how they are; they're all alike." Stereotypes can also involve *bias*—literally meaning "slant"—a slant that can tilt toward the positive or the negative. Positive bias results in favorable stereotypes (e.g., "Asians are great in science and math"); negative bias leads to unfavorable stereotypes (e.g., "Asians are nerds who do nothing but study"). Here are some other examples of negative stereotypes:

- Muslims are religious terrorists.
- Whites can't jump (or dance).
- Blacks are lazy.
- Irish are alcoholics.
- Gay men are feminine; lesbian women are masculine.
- Jews are cheap.
- Women are weak.

While few people would agree with these crass stereotypes, overgeneralizations are often made about members of certain groups. Such negative overgeneralizations malign the group's reputation, rob group members of their individuality, and can weaken their self-esteem and self-confidence (as illustrated by the following experience).

AUTHOR'S EXPERIENCE

When I was six years old, I was told by a six-year-old girl from a different racial group that all people of my race could not swim. Since I couldn't swim at that time and she could, I assumed she was correct. I asked a boy, who was a member of the same racial group as the girl, whether her statement was true. He responded emphatically: "Yes, it's true!" Since I was from an area where few other African Americans were around to counteract this belief about my racial group, I continued to buy into this stereotype until I finally took swimming lessons as an adult. After many lessons, I am now a lousy swimmer because I didn't even attempt to swim until I was an adult. Moral of this story: Group stereotypes can limit the confidence and potential of individual members of the stereotyped group.

—*Aaron Thompson*

Whether you are male or female, don't let gender stereotypes limit your career options.

Think About It—Journal Entry 8.11

1. Have you ever been stereotyped based on your appearance or group membership? If so, what was the stereotype and how did it make you feel?

2. Have you ever unintentionally perceived or treated a person in terms of a group stereotype rather than as an individual? What assumptions did you make about that person? Was that person aware of, or affected by, your stereotyping?

Prejudice

If all members of a stereotyped group are judged and evaluated in a negative way, the result is *prejudice*. The word "prejudice" literally means to "pre-judge." Typically, the prejudgment is negative and involves *stigmatizing*—ascribing inferior or unfavorable traits to people who belong to the same group. Thus, prejudice may be defined as a negative stereotype held about a group of people that's formed before the facts are known.

People who hold a group prejudice typically avoid contact with members of that group. This enables the prejudice to continue unchallenged because there's little opportunity for the prejudiced person to have a positive experience with members of the stigmatized group that could contradict or disprove the prejudice. Thus, a vicious cycle is established in which the prejudiced person continues to avoid contact with individuals from the stigmatized group; this, in turn, continues to maintain and reinforce the prejudice

> When you see me, do not look at me with disgrace. Know that I am an African-American Birthed by a woman of style and grace. Be proud To stand by my side. Hold your head high Like me. Be proud. To say you know me. Just as I stand by you, proud to be me.
>
> —Poem by Brittany Beard, first-year student

Think About It—Journal Entry 8.12

Prejudice and discrimination can be subtle and only begin to surface when the social or emotional distance among members of different groups grows closer. Rate your level of comfort (high, moderate, or low) with the following situations.

Someone from another racial group:

1. Going to your school	high	moderate	low
2. Working in your place of employment	high	moderate	low
3. Living on your street as a neighbor	high	moderate	low
4. Living with you as a roommate	high	moderate	low
5. Socializing with you as a personal friend	high	moderate	low
6. Being your most intimate friend or romantic partner	high	moderate	low
7. Being your partner in marriage	high	moderate	low

> See that man over there? Yes. Well, I hate him. But you don't know him. That's why I hate him."
>
> —Gordon Allport, influential social psychologist and author of The Nature of Prejudice

For any item you rated "low," what do you think was responsible for the low rating?

_____

_____

_____

_____

_____

> "We see what is behind our eyes."
>
> —*Chinese proverb*

Once prejudice has been formed, it often remains intact and resistant to change through the psychological process of *selective perception*—the tendency for biased (prejudiced) people to see what they *expect* to see and fail to see what contradicts their bias (Hugenberg & Bodenhausen, 2003). Have you ever noticed how fans rooting for their favorite sports team tend to focus on and "see" the calls of referees that go against their own team, but don't seem to react (or even notice) the calls that go against the opposing team? This is a classic example of selective perception. In effect, selective perception transforms the old adage, "seeing is believing," into "believing is seeing." This can lead prejudiced people to focus their attention on information that's consistent with their prejudgment, causing them to "see" what supports or reinforces it and fail to see information that contradicts it.

Making matters worse, selective perception is often accompanied by *selective memory*—the tendency to remember information that's consistent with one's prejudicial belief and to forget information that's inconsistent with it or contradicts it (Judd, Ryan, & Parke, 1991). The mental processes of selective perception and selective memory often work together and often work *unconsciously*. As a result, prejudiced people may not even be aware they're using these biased mental processes or realize how these processes are keeping their prejudice permanently intact (Baron, Byrne, & Brauscombe, 2008).

Think About It—Journal Entry 8.13

Have you witnessed selective perception or selective memory—people seeing or recalling what they believe is true (due to bias), rather than what's actually true? What happened and why do you think it happened?

_____

_____

_____

_____

_____

Discrimination

Literally translated, the term *discrimination* means "division" or "separation." Whereas prejudice involves a belief, attitude or opinion, discrimination involves an *act* or *behavior*. Technically, discrimination can be either positive or negative. A discriminating eater may only eat healthy foods, which is a positive quality. However, discrimination is most often associated with a harmful act that results in a prejudiced person treating another individual, or group of individuals, in an unfair manner. Thus, it could be said that discrimination is prejudice put into action. For instance, to fire or not hire people on the basis of their race, gender, or sexual orientation is an act of discrimination.

Box 8.4 below contains a summary of the major forms of discrimination, prejudice, and stereotypes that have plagued humanity. As you read through the following list, place a check mark next to any item that you, a friend, or family member has experienced.

Box 8.4

Stereotypes, Prejudices, and Forms of Discrimination: A Snapshot Summary

- **Ethnocentrism:** viewing one's own culture or ethnic group as "central" or "normal," while viewing different cultures as "deficient" or "inferior."

  Example: Viewing another culture as "abnormal" or "uncivilized" because its members eat animals our culture views as unacceptable to eat, although we eat animals their culture views as unacceptable to eat.

- **Stereotyping:** viewing all (or virtually all) members of the same group in the same way—as having the same personal qualities or characteristics.

  Example: "If you're Italian, you must be in the Mafia, or have a family member who is."

- **Prejudice:** negative prejudgment about another group of people.

  Example: Women can't be effective leaders because they're too emotional.

- **Discrimination:** unequal and unfair treatment of a person or group of people—prejudice put into action.

  Example: Paying women less than men for performing the same job, even though they have the same level of education and job qualifications.

- **Segregation:** intentional decision made by a group to separate itself (socially or physically) from another group.

  Example: "White flight"—white people moving out of neighborhoods when people of color move in.

- **Racism:** belief that one's racial group is superior to another group and expressing that belief in attitude (prejudice) or action (discrimination).

Example: Confiscating land from American Indians based on the unfounded belief that they are "uncivilized" or "savages."

- **Institutional Racism:** racial discrimination rooted in organizational policies and practices that disadvantage certain racial groups.

> Let us all hope that the dark clouds of racial prejudice will soon pass away and . . . in some not too distant tomorrow the radiant stars of love and brotherhood will shine over our great nation."
>
> —*Martin Luther King, Jr., Civil rights leader, humanitarian, and youngest recipient of the Nobel Peace Prize*

  Example: Race-based discrimination in mortgage lending, housing, and bank loans.

- **Racial Profiling:** investigating or arresting someone solely on the basis of the person's race, ethnicity, or national origin—without witnessing actual criminal behavior or possessing incriminating evidence.

  Example: Police making a traffic stop or conducting a personal search based solely on an individual's racial features.

- **Slavery:** forced labor in which people are considered to be property, held against their will, and deprived of the right to receive wages.

  Example: Enslavement of Blacks, which was legal in the United States until 1865.

- **"Jim Crow" Laws:** formal and informal laws created by Whites to segregate Blacks after the abolition of slavery.

(continued)

Box 8.4 *(continued)*

Example: laws in certain parts of the United States that once required Blacks to use separate bathrooms and be educated in separate schools.

- Apartheid: an institutionalized system of "legal racism" supported by a nation's government. (Apartheid derives from a word in the Afrikaan language, meaning "apartness.")

    Example: South Africa's national system of racial segregation and discrimination that was in place from 1948 to 1994.

> Never, never, and never again shall it be that this beautiful land will again experience the oppression of one by another."
>
> —*Nelson Mandela, anti-apartheid revolutionary, first Black president of South Africa after apartheid, and winner of the Nobel Peace Prize*

- Hate Crimes: criminal action motivated solely by prejudice toward the crime victim.

    Example: Acts of vandalism or assault aimed at members of a particular ethnic group or persons of a particular sexual orientation.

- Hate Groups: organizations whose primary purpose is to stimulate prejudice, discrimination, or aggression toward certain groups of people based on their ethnicity, race, religion, etc.

    Example: The Ku Klux Klan—an American terrorist group that perpetrates hatred toward all non-white races.

- Genocide: mass murdering of a particular ethnic or racial group.

    Example: The Holocaust, in which millions of Jews were systematically murdered during World War II. Other examples include the murdering of Cambodians under the Khmer Rouge regime, the murdering of Bosnian Muslims in the former country of Yugoslavia, and the slaughter of the Tutsi minority by the Hutu majority in Rwanda.

- Classism: prejudice or discrimination based on social class, particularly toward people of lower socioeconomic status.

    Example: Acknowledging the contributions made by politicians and wealthy industrialists to America, while ignoring the contributions of poor immigrants, farmers, slaves, and pioneer women.

- Religious Intolerance: denying the fundamental human right of people to hold religious beliefs, or to hold religious beliefs that differ from one's own.

Example: An atheist who forces nonreligious (secular) beliefs on others, or a member of a religious group who believes that people who hold different religious beliefs are infidels or "sinners" whose souls will not be saved.

> Rivers, ponds, lakes and streams— they all have different names, but they all contain water. Just as religions do— they all contain truths."
>
> —*Muhammad Ali, three-time world heavyweight boxing champion, member of the International Boxing Hall of Fame, and recipient of the Spirit of America Award as the most recognized American in the world*

- Anti-Semitism: prejudice or discrimination toward Jews or people who practice the religion of Judaism.

    Example: Disliking Jews because they're the ones who "killed Christ."

- Xenophobia: fear or hatred of foreigners, outsiders, or strangers.

    Example: Believing that immigrants should be banned from entering the country because they'll undermine our economy and increase our crime rate.

- Regional Bias: prejudice or discrimination based on the geographical region in which an individual is born and raised.

    Example: A northerner thinking that all southerners are racists.

- Jingoism: excessive interest and belief in the superiority of one's own nation—without acknowledging its mistakes or weaknesses—often accompanied by an aggressive foreign policy that neglects the needs of other nations or the common needs of all nations.

    Example: "Blind patriotism"—failure to see the shortcomings of one's own nation and viewing any questioning or criticism of one's own nation as being disloyal or "unpatriotic." (As in the slogan, "America: right or wrong" or "America: love it or leave it!")

> Above all nations is humanity."
>
> —*Motto of the University of Hawaii*

- Terrorism: intentional acts of violence committed against civilians that are motivated by political or religious prejudice.

    Example: The September 11, 2001, attacks on the United States.

(continued)

Box 8.4 *(continued)*

- **Sexism**: prejudice or discrimination based on sex or gender.

    Example: Believing that women should not pursue careers in fields traditionally filled only by men (e.g., engineering or politics) because they lack the innate qualities or natural skills to do so.
- **Heterosexism**: belief that heterosexuality is the only acceptable sexual orientation.

    Example: Believing that gays should not have the same legal rights and opportunities as heterosexuals.
- **Homophobia**: extreme fear or hatred of homosexuals.

    Example: Creating or contributing to anti-gay websites, or "gay bashing" (acts of violence toward gays).
- **Ageism**: prejudice or discrimination toward certain age groups, particularly toward the elderly.

    Example: Believing that all "old" people have dementia and shouldn't be allowed to drive or make important decisions.
- **Ableism**: prejudice or discrimination toward people who are disabled or handicapped (physically, mentally, or emotionally).

    Example: Intentionally avoiding social contact with people in wheelchairs.
- **Biphobia**: Aversion toward bisexuality and bisexual people as a social group or as individuals. People of any sexual orientation can experience such feelings of aversion. Biphobia is a source of discrimination against bisexuals, and may be based on negative bisexual stereotypes or irrational fear.
- **Transphobia**: The fear or hatred of transgender people or gender nonconforming behavior. Like biphobia, transphobia can also exist among lesbian, gay, and bisexual people as well as among heterosexual people.

Think About It—Journal Entry 8.14

As you read through the above list, did you, a friend, or family member experience any of the form(s) of prejudice listed? If yes, what happened and why do you think it happened?

> I grew up in a very racist family. Even just a year ago, I could honestly say 'I hate Asians' with a straight face and mean it. My senior AP language teacher tried hard to teach me not to be judgmental. He got me to be open to others, so much so that my current boyfriend is half Chinese."
>
> —First-year college student

Strategies for Overcoming Stereotypes and Prejudices

We may hold prejudices, stereotypes, or subtle biases that bubble beneath the surface of our conscious awareness. The following practices and strategies can help us become more aware of our unconscious biases and relate more effectively to individuals from diverse groups.

Consciously avoid preoccupation with physical appearances. Remember the old proverb: "It's what inside that counts." Judge others by the quality of their inner qualities, not by the familiarity of their outer features. Get beneath the superficial surface of appearances and relate to people not in terms of how they look but who they are and how they act.

Form impressions of others on a person-to-person basis, not on the basis of their group membership. This may seem like an obvious and easy thing to do, but

> Stop judging by mere appearances, and make a right judgment."
>
> —Bible, John 7:24

> You can't judge a book by the cover."
>
> —1962 hit song by Elias Bates, a.k.a. Bo Diddley (Note: a "bo diddley" is a one-stringed African guitar)

research shows that humans have a natural tendency to perceive individuals from unfamiliar groups as being more alike (or all alike) than members of their own group (Taylor, Peplau, & Sears, 2006). Thus, we need to remain mindful of this tendency and make a conscious effort to perceive and treat individuals of diverse groups as unique human beings, not according to some general (stereotypical) rule of thumb.

Note

It's valuable to learn about different cultures and the common characteristics shared by members of the same culture; however, this shouldn't be done while ignoring individual differences. Don't assume that all individuals who share the same cultural background share the same personal characteristics.

> "I am very happy with the diversity here, but it also frightens me. I have never been in a situation where I have met people who are Jewish, Muslim, atheist, born-again, and many more."
>
> —First-year student (quoted in Erickson, Peters, & Strommer, 2006)

Think About It—Journal Entry 8.15

Your comfort level while interacting with people from diverse groups is likely to depend on how much prior experience you've had with members of those groups. Rate the amount or variety of diversity you have experienced in the following settings:

1. The high school you attended	high	moderate	low
2. The college or university you now attend	high	moderate	low
3. The neighborhood in which you grew up	high	moderate	low
4. Places where you have been employed	high	moderate	low

Which setting had the *most* and the *least* diversity?

_____

_____

_____

_____

_____

What do you think accounted for this difference?

_____

_____

_____

_____

_____

_____

Place yourself in situations and locations on campus where you will come in

regular contact with individuals from diverse groups. Distancing ourselves from diversity ensures we'll never experience diversity and benefit from it. Research in social psychology shows that relationships are more likely to form among people who come in regular contact with one another (Latané, et al., 1995), and research on diversity reveals that when there's regular contact between members of different racial or ethnic groups, stereotyping is sharply reduced and intercultural friendships are more likely to develop (Pettigrew, 1997, 1998). You can create these conditions by making an intentional attempt to sit near diverse students in the classroom, library, or student café, and by joining them for class discussion groups or group projects.

Take advantage of social media to "chat" virtually with students from diverse groups on your own campus, or students on other campuses. Electronic communication can be a convenient and comfortable way to initially interact with members of diverse groups with whom you have had little prior experience. After interacting *online*, you're more likely to feel more comfortable about interacting *in person.*

Engage in co-curricular experiences involving diversity. Review your student handbook to find co-curricular programs, student activities, student clubs, or campus organizations that emphasize diversity awareness and appreciation. Studies indicate that participation in co-curricular experiences relating to diversity promotes critical thinking (Pascarella & Terenzini, 2005) and reduces unconscious prejudice (Blair, 2002).

Consider spending time at the multicultural center on your campus, or joining a campus club or organization that's devoted to diversity awareness (e.g., multicultural or international student club). Putting yourself in these situations will enable you to make regular contact with members of cultural groups other than your own; it also sends a clear message to members of these groups that you value their culture because you've taken the initiative to connect with them on "their turf."

If your campus sponsors multicultural or cross-cultural retreats, strongly consider participating in them. A retreat setting can provide a comfortable environment in which you can interact personally with diverse students without being distracted by your customary social circle and daily routine.

If possible, participate in a study abroad or travel study program that gives you the opportunity to live in another country and interact directly with its native citizens. In addition to coursework, you can gain international knowledge and a global perspective by participating in programs that enable you to actually *experience* a different country. You can do this for a full term or for a shorter time period (e.g., January, May, or summer term). To prepare for international experiences, take a course in the language, culture, or history of the nation to which you will be traveling.

Research on students who participate in study abroad programs indicates that these experiences promote greater appreciation of cross-cultural differences, greater interest in world affairs, and greater commitment to peace and international cooperation (Bok, 2006; Kaufmann, et al., 1992). Additional research shows that study abroad benefits students' personal development, including improved self-confidence, sense of independence, and ability to function in complex environments (Carlson, et al., 1990; IES Abroad News, 2002).

Incorporate diversity courses into your planned schedule of classes. Review your college catalog (bulletin) and identify courses that are designed to promote

> "Empirical evidence shows that the actual effects on student development of emphasizing diversity and of student participation in diversity activities are overwhelmingly positive."
>
> —*Alexander Astin,* What Matters in College

understanding or appreciation of diversity. These courses may focus on diverse cultures found within the United States (sometimes referred to as multicultural courses) or diverse cultures associated with different countries (sometimes referred to as international or cross-cultural courses).

In a national study of college students who experienced multicultural courses, it was discovered that students of all racial and ethnic groups made significant gains in learning and intellectual development (Smith, 1997; Smith, et al., 1997).

Taking courses focusing on international diversity can help you develop the global perspective needed for success in today's international economy and enhance the quality of your college transcript (Brooks, 2009; Cuseo, et al., 2013; National Association of Colleges & Employers, 2003).

> "The classroom can provide a 'public place' where community can be practiced."
> —*Susanne Morse*, Renewing Civic Capacity: Preparing College Students for Service and Citizenship.

Be on the lookout for diversity implications associated with topics you're reading about or discussing in class. Consider the multicultural and cross-cultural ramifications of material you're studying and use examples of diversity to support or illustrate your points. If you're allowed to choose a topic for a research project, select one that relates to diversity or has implications for diversity.

Seek out the views and opinions of classmates from diverse backgrounds. Discussions among students of different races and cultures can reduce prejudice and promote intercultural appreciation, but only if each member's cultural identity and perspective is sought out and valued by members of the discussion group (Baron, Byrne, & Brauscombe, 2008). During class discussions, you can demonstrate leadership by seeking out views and opinions of classmates from diverse backgrounds and ensuring that the ideas of people from minority groups are included and respected. Also, after class discussions, you can ask students from different backgrounds if there was any point made or position taken in class that they would have strongly questioned or challenged.

If there is little or no diversity among students in class, encourage your classmates to look at the topic from diverse perspectives. For instance, you might ask: "If there were international students here, what might they be adding to our discussion?" or, "If members of certain minority groups were here, would they be offering a different viewpoint?"

If you are given the opportunity to form your own discussion groups and group project teams, join or create groups composed of students from diverse backgrounds. You can gain greater exposure to diverse perspectives by intentionally joining or forming learning groups with students who differ in terms of gender, age, race, or ethnicity. Including diversity in your discussion groups not only creates social variety, it also enhances the quality of your group's work by allowing members to gain access to and learn from multiple perspectives. For instance, in learning groups that are diverse with respect to age, older students will bring a broad range of life experiences that younger students can draw upon and learn from, while younger students can provide a more contemporary and idealistic perspective to the group's discussions. Gender diversity is also likely to infuse group discussions with different learning styles and approaches to understanding issues. Studies show that males are more likely to be "separate knowers"—they tend to "detach" themselves from the concept or issue being discussed so they can analyze it. In contrast, females are more likely to be "connected knowers"—they tend to relate personally to concepts and connect them with their own experiences and the experiences of others. For example, when interpreting a poem, males are more likely to ask: "What techniques can I use to analyze it?" In contrast, females would be more likely to ask: "What is the poet trying to say to me?" (Belenky, et al., 1986). It's also been found that females are more likely to work collaboratively during group discussions and collect the ideas of other members; in contrast, males are more likely to adopt a competitive approach and debate the ideas of others (Magolda, 1992). Both of these styles of learning are valuable and you can capitalize on these different styles by forming gender-diverse discussion groups.

Form collaborative learning teams with students from diverse backgrounds. A learning *team* is more than a discussion group that tosses around ideas; it moves beyond discussion to *collaboration*—its members "co-labor" (work together) to reach the same goal. Research from kindergarten through college indicates that when students collaborate in teams, their academic performance and interpersonal skills are strengthened (Cuseo, 1996). Also, when individuals from different racial groups work collaboratively toward the same goal, racial prejudice is reduced and interracial friendships are more likely to be formed (Allport, 1954; Amir, 1976; Brown, et al., 2003; Dovidio, Eller, & Hewstone, 2011). These positive developments may be explained, in part, by the fact that when members of diverse groups come together on the same team, nobody is a member of an "out" group ("them"); instead, everybody belongs to the same "in" group ("us") (Pratto, et al., 2000; Sidanius, et al., 2000).

In an analysis of multiple studies involving more than 90,000 people from 25 different countries, it was found that when interaction between members of diverse groups took place under the conditions described in **Box 8.5**, prejudice was significantly reduced (Pettigrew & Tropp, 2000) and the greatest gains in learning took place (Johnson, Johnson, & Smith, 1998; Slavin, 1995).

Box 8.5

Tips for Teamwork: Creating Diverse and Effective Learning Teams

1. Intentionally form learning teams with students who have different cultural backgrounds and life experiences. Teaming up only with friends or classmates whose backgrounds and experiences are similar to yours can actually impair your team's performance because teammates can get off track and onto topics that have nothing to do with the learning task (e.g., what they did last weekend or what they're planning to do next weekend).

2. Before jumping into group work, take some time to interact informally with your teammates. When team members have some social "warm up" time (e.g., time to learn each other's names and learn something about each other), they feel more comfortable expressing their ideas and are more likely to develop a stronger sense of team identity. This feeling of group solidarity can create a foundation of trust among group members, enabling them to work together as a team, particularly if they come from diverse (and unfamiliar) cultural backgrounds.

    The context in which a group interacts can influence the openness and harmony of their interaction. Group members are more likely to interact openly and collaboratively when they work in a friendly, informal environment that's conducive to relationship building. A living room or a lounge area provides a warmer and friendlier team-learning atmosphere than a sterile classroom.

3. Have teammates work together to complete a single work product. One jointly created product serves to highlight the team's collaborative effort and collective achievement (e.g., a completed sheet of answers to questions, or a comprehensive list of ideas). Creating a common final product helps keep individuals thinking in terms of "we" (not "me") and keeps the team moving in the same direction toward the same goal.

4. Group members should work interdependently— they should depend on each other to reach their common goal and each member should have equal opportunity to contribute to the team's final product. Each teammate should take responsibility for making an indispensable contribution to the team's end product, such as contributing: (a) a different piece of *information* (e.g., a specific chapter from the textbook or a particular section of class notes), (b) a particular form of *thinking* to the learning task (e.g., analysis, synthesis, or application), or (c) a different *perspective* (e.g., national, international, or global). Said in another way, each group member should assume personal responsibility for a piece that's needed to complete the whole puzzle.

    Similar to a sports team, each member of a learning team should have a specific role to play. For instance,

(continued)

Box 8.5 *(continued)*

each teammate could perform one of the following roles:

- manager—whose role is to assure that the team stays on track and keeps moving toward its goal;
- moderator—whose role is to ensure that all teammates have equal opportunity to contribute;
- summarizer—whose role is to monitor the team's progress, identifying what has been accomplished and what still needs to be done;
- recorder—whose role is to keep a written record of the team's ideas.

5. After concluding work in diverse learning teams, take time to reflect on the experience. The final step in any learning process, whether it be learning from a lecture or learning from a group discussion, is to step back from the process and thoughtfully review it. Deep learning requires not only effortful action but also thoughtful reflection (Bligh, 2000; Roediger, Dudai, & Fitzpatrick, 2007). You can reflect on your experiences with diverse learning groups by asking yourself questions that prompt you to process the ideas shared by members of your group and the impact those ideas had on you. For instance, ask

yourself (and your teammates) the following questions:

What major similarities in viewpoints did all group members share? (What were the common themes?)

- What major differences of opinion were expressed by diverse members of our group? (What were the variations on the themes?)
- Were there particular topics or issues raised during the discussion that provoked intense reactions or emotional responses from certain members of our group?
- Did the group discussion lead any individuals to change their mind about an idea or position they originally held?

When contact among people from diverse groups takes place under the five conditions described in this box, group work is transformed into *teamwork* and promotes higher levels of thinking and deeper appreciation of diversity. A win-win scenario is created: Learning and thinking are strengthened while bias and prejudice are weakened (Allport, 1979; Amir, 1969; Aronson, Wilson, & Akert, 2013; Cook, 1984; Sherif, et al., 1961).

 Think About It—Journal Entry 8.16

Have you had an experience with a member of an unfamiliar racial or cultural group that caused you to change your attitude or viewpoint toward that group? Explain.

_____

_____

_____

_____

_____

Take a stand against prejudice or discrimination by constructively disagreeing with students who make stereotypical statements and prejudicial remarks. By saying nothing, you may avoid conflict, but your silence may be perceived by others to mean that you agree with the person who made the prejudicial remark. Studies show that when members of the same group observe another member of their own group making prejudicial comments, prejudice tends to increase among all group members—probably due to peer pressure of group conformity (Stangor, Sechrist, & Jost, 2001). In contrast, if a person's prejudicial re-mark is challenged by a member of one's own group, particularly a fellow member who is liked and respected, that person's prejudice decreases along with similar prejudices held by other members of the group (Baron, Byrne, & Brauscombe, 2008). Thus, by taking a leadership role and challenging peers who make prejudi-cial remarks, you're likely to reduce that person's prejudice as well as the prejudice of others who hear the remark. In addition, you help create a campus climate in which students experience greater satisfaction with with their college experience and are more likely to complete their college degree. Studies show that a campus climate which is hostile toward students from minority groups lowers students' level of college satisfaction and college completion rates of both minority and ma-jority students (Cabrera, et al., 1999; Eimers & Pike, 1997; Nora & Cabrera, 1996).

Note

By actively opposing prejudice on campus, you demonstrate diversity leadership and moral character. You become a role model whose actions send a clear message that valuing diversity is not only the smart thing to do, it's the right thing to do.

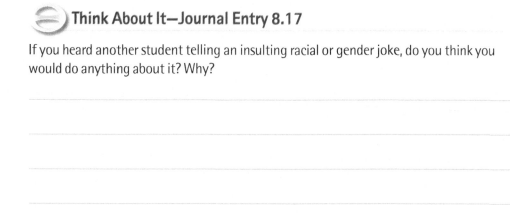

Think About It—Journal Entry 8.17

If you heard another student telling an insulting racial or gender joke, do you think you would do anything about it? Why?

_____

_____

_____

_____

_____

Chapter Summary and Highlights

Diversity refers to the variety of groups that comprise humanity (the human spe-cies). Humans differ from one another in multiple ways, including physical features, religious beliefs, mental and physical abilities, national origins, social backgrounds, gender, and sexual orientation. Diversity involves the important political issue of securing equal rights and social justice for all people; however, it's also an important *educational* issue—an integral element of the college experience that enriches learning, personal development, and career preparation.

When a group of people share the same traditions and customs, it creates a cul-ture that serves to bind people into a supportive, tight-knit community. However, culture can also lead its members to view the world solely through their own cul-tural lens (known as ethnocentrism), which can blind them to other cultural per-spectives. Ethnocentrism can contribute to stereotyping—viewing individual mem-bers of another cultural group in the same (fixed) way, in which they're seen as having similar personal characteristics.

Stereotyping can result in prejudice—a biased prejudgment about another person or group of people that's formed before the facts are known. Stereotyping and prejudice often go hand in hand because if the stereotype is negative, members of the stereotyped group are then judged negatively. Discrimination takes prejudice one step further by converting the negative prejudgment into behavior that results in unfair treatment of others. Thus, discrimination is prejudice put into action.

Once stereotyping and prejudice are overcome, we are positioned to experience diversity and reap its multiple benefits—which include sharper self-awareness, deeper learning, higher-level thinking, and better career preparation.

The increasing diversity of students on campus, combined with the wealth of diversity-related educational experiences found in the college curriculum and co-curriculum, presents you with an unprecedented opportunity to infuse diversity into your college experience. Seize this opportunity and capitalize on the power of diversity to increase the quality of your college education and your prospects for success in the 21st century.

Learning More through the World Wide Web: Internet-Based Resources

For additional information on diversity, see the following websites:

Stereotyping: ReducingStereotypeThreat.org at www.reducingstereotypethreat.org

Prejudice & Discrimination: Southern Poverty Law Center at www.splcenter.org/

Human Rights:
Amnesty International at www.amnesty.org/en/discrimination
Center for Economic & Social Justice at www.cesj.org

Sexism in the Media:
"Killing Us Softly" at www.youtube.com/watch?v=PTlmho_RovY

LGBT Acceptance & Support: "It Gets Better Project," at www.itgetsbetter.org

References

Acredolo, C., & O'Connor, J. (1991). On the difficulty of detecting cognitive uncertainty. *Human Development, 34,* 204–223.

Allport, G. W. (1954). *The nature of prejudice.* Cambridge, MA: Addison-Wesley.

Allport, G. W. (1979). *The Nature of prejudice* (3rd ed.). Reading, MA: Addison-Wesley.

American Association of Community Colleges (2009). 2009 Fact Sheet. Retrieved from http://www.aacc.nche.edu/About/Documents/factsheet2009.pdf.

Amir, Y. (1969). Contact hypothesis in ethnic relations. *Psychological Bulletin, 71,* 319–342.

Amir, Y. (1976). The role of intergroup contact in change of prejudice and ethnic relations. In P. A. Katz (Ed.), *Towards the elimination of racism* (pp. 245–308). New York: Pergamon Press.

Anderson, M. & Fienberg, S. 2000. *Race and ethnicity and the controversy over the US Census.* Current Sociology; 48(3): 87–110.

Aronson, E., Wilson, T. D., & Akert, R. M. (2013). *Social psychology* (8th ed.). Upper Saddle River, NJ: Pearson/Prentice Hall.

Association of American Colleges & Universities (AAC&U) (2002). *Greater expectations: A new vision for learning as a nation goes to college.* Washington, DC: Author.

Association of American Colleges & Universities (AAC&U) (2004). *Our students' best work.* Washington, DC: Author.

Baron, et. al., 2008. Social Psychology, 12th Edition. Allyn & Bacon, Boston, MA.

Belenky, M. F., Clinchy, B., Goldberger, N. R., & Tarule, J. M. (1986). *Women's ways of knowing: The development of self, voice, and mind.* New York: Basic Books.

Blair, I. V. (2002). The malleability of automatic stereotypes and prejudice. *Personality and Social Psychology Review, 6*(3), 242–261.

Bligh, D.A. (2000). *What's the use of lectures?* San Francisco: Jossey Bass.

Bok, D. 2006. *Our Underachieving Colleges: A Candid Look at How Much Students Learn and Why they Should be Learning More.* Princeton, New Jersey: Princeton University Press, 2006.

Bridgeman, B. 2003. Psychology and Evolution: The Origins of Mind. Thousand Oaks, Ca.: Sage Publications.

Bronfenbrenner, U. (Ed.) (2005). *Making human beings*

human: Bioecological perspectives on human development. Thousand Oaks, CA: Sage.

Brookfield, S. D. (1987). *Developing critical thinkers.* San Francisco: Jossey-Bass.

Brooks, I. 2009. Organisational Behaviour, 4th Edition. Englewood Cliffs, NJ: Prentice Hall.

Brown, T. D., Dane, F. C., & Durham, M. D. (1998). Perception of race and ethnicity. *Journal of Social Behavior and Personality, 13*(2), 295–306.

Brown, K. T, Brown, T. N., Jackson, J. S., Sellers, R. M., & Manuel, W. J. (2003).

Teammates on and off the field? Contact with Black teammates and the racial attitudes of White student athletes. *Journal of Applied Social Psychology, 33,* 1379–1403.

Cabrera, A., Nora, A., Terenzini, P., Pascarella, E., & Hagedorn, L. S. (1999). Campus racial climate and the adjustment of students to college: A comparison between White students and African American students. *The Journal of Higher Education, 70*(2), 134–160.

Caplan, P. J., & Caplan, J. B. (2008). *Thinking critically about research on sex and gender* (3rd ed.). New York: HarperCollins College Publishers.

Carlson, et al., 1990. Individual differences in the behavioral effects of stressors attributable to lateralized differences in mesocortical dopamine systems. *Society for Neuroscience absracts 16.*233.

Ciancotto, J. (2005). *Hispanic and Latino same-sex couple households in the United States: A report from the 2000 Census.* New York: The National Gay and Lesbian Task Force Policy Institute and the National Latino/a Coalition for Justice.

Colombo, G., Cullen, R., & Lisle, B. (2013). *Rereading America: Cultural contexts for critical thinking and writing* (9th ed.). Boston: Bedford Books of St. Martin's Press.

Cook, S. W. (1984). Cooperative interaction in multiethnic contexts. In N. Miller & M. B. Brewer (Eds.), *Groups in contact: The psychology of desegregation (pp. 291–302).* New York: Academic Press.

Cuseo, J. B. (1996). *Cooperative learning: A pedagogy for addressing contemporary challenges and critical issues in higher education.* Stillwater, OK: New Forums Press.

Cuseo, J. B. et al., 2013. *Thriving in Community College & Beyond: Strategies for Academic Success and Personal Development.* Kendall Hunt Publishing Company, Dubuque, Ia.

DeNavas-Walt, C., Proctor, B. D., & Smith, J. C. (2013). *Income, poverty, and health insurance coverage in the United States, 2012.* U.S. Census Bureau, Current Population Reports, P60–245, Washington, DC: U.S. Government Printing Office.

Dessel, A. (2012). Effects of intergroup dialogue: Public school teachers and sexual orientation prejudice. *Small Group Research, 41*(5), 556–592.

Dolan, M., & Romney, L. (2015). "Law in California is now a right for all." *Los Angeles Times.* June 27, pp. A1 & A8.

Dovidio, J. F., Eller, A., & Hewstone, M. (2011). Improving intergroup relations through direct, extended and other forms of indirect contact. *Group Processes & Intergroup Relations, 14,* 147–160.

Dryden, G., & Vos, J. (1999). *The learning revolution: To change the way the world learns.* Torrance, CA and Auckland, New Zealand: The Learning Web.

Education Commission of the States (1995). *Making quality count in undergraduate education.* Denver, CO: ECS Distribution Center.

Eimers, M. T., & Pike, G. R. (1997). Minority and nonminority adjustment to college: Differences or similarities. *Research in Higher Education, 38* (1), 77–97.

Erickson, B. L., Peters, C. B., & Strommer, D. W. (2006). *Teaching first-year college students.* San Francisco: Jossey-Bass.

Family Care Foundation. (1997–2012). *If the world were a village of 100 people.* Retrieved from http://www.familycare.org/special-interest/if-the-world-were-a-village-of-100-people/.

Feagin, J. R., & Feagin, C. B., 2007. Racial and Ethnic Relations, 8th Edition. Englewood Cliffs, NJ. Prentice Hall.

Fixman, C. S. (1990). The foreign language needs of U.S. based corporations. *Annals of the American Academy of Political and Social Science, 511,* 25–46.

Friedman, T. L. 2005. *The world is flat: A brief history of the twenty-first century: Revitalizing the civic mission of schools.* Alexandria, VA.

Gorski, P. C. (2009). *Key characteristics of a multicultural curriculum.* Critical Multicultural Pavilion: Multicultural Curriculum Reform (An EdChange Project). Retrieved from www.edchange.org/multicultural/curriculum/characteristics.html.

Gould, E. & Wething, H. 2013 *Health Care, the Market and Consumer Choice. Inquiry 50* (1):85–86.

Gurin, P. (1999). New research on the benefits of diversity in college and beyond: An empirical analysis. *Diversity Digest* (spring). Retrieved from http://www.diversityweb.org/Digest/Sp99/benefits.html.

Harris, 2010. Leading system transformation. *School Leadership and Management 30* (Jul).

Hart Research Associates (2013). *It takes more than a major: Employer priorities for college learning and student success.* Washington, DC: Author.

HERI (Higher Education Research Institute) (2013). *Your first college year survey 2012.* Los Angeles, CA: Cooperative Institutional Research Program, University of California-Los Angeles.

HERI (Higher Education Research Institute) (2014). *Your first college year survey 2014.* Los Angeles, CA: Cooperative Institutional Research Program, University of California-Los Angeles.

Hugenberg, K., & Bodenhausen, G. V. (2003). Facing prejudice: Implicit prejudice and the perception of facial threat. *Psychological Science, 14,* 640–643.

IES Abroad News (2002). Study abroad: A lifetime of benefits. Retrieved from www.iesabroad.org/study-abroad/news/study-abroad-lifetime-benefits.

Jablonski, N. G., & Chaplin, G. (2002). Skin deep. *Scientific American* (October), 75–81.

Johnson, D., Johnson, R., & Smith, K. (1998). Cooperative learning returns to college: What evidence is there that it works? *Change, 30,* 26–35.

Judd, C. M., Ryan, C. S., & Parke, B. (1991). Accuracy in the judgment of in-group and out-group variability. *Journal of Personality and Social Psychology, 61,* 366–379.

Kaufmann, N. L., Martin, J. M., & Weaver, H. D. (1992). *Students abroad: Strangers at home: Education for a global society.* Yarmouth, ME: Intercultural Press.

Kelly, K. (1994). *Out of control: The new biology of machines, social systems, and the economic world.* Reading, MA: Addison-Wesley.

Kitchener, K., Wood, P., & Jensen, L. (2000, August). *Curricular, co-curricular, and institutional influence on real-world problem-solving.* Paper presented at the annual meeting of the American Psychological *Associa*tion, Boston.

Kochlar, R., Fry, R., & Taylor, P. (2011). "Wealth gaps rise to record highs between Whites, Blacks, Hispanics, twenty-to-one." *Pew Research Social and Demographics Trends* (July). Retrieved from http://www.pewsocialtrends.org/2011/07/26/wealth-gaps-rise-to-record-highs-between-whites-blacks-hispanics/.

Lancaster, L., & Stilman, D. (2002). *When generations collide: Who they are. Why they clash.* New York: HarperCollins.

Latané, B., Liu, J. H., Nowak, A., Bonevento, N., & Zheng, L. (1995). Distance matters: Physical space and social impact. *Personality and Social Psychology Bulletin, 21,* 795–805.

Leung, A. K., Maddux, W. W., Galinsky, A. D., & Chie-yue, C. (2008). Multicultural experience enhances creativity: The when and how. *American Psychologist, 63*(3), 169–181.

Lewis, M., Paul, G. W., & Fenning, C. D. (Eds.) (2014). Ethnologue: languages of the world, seventeeth edition. Dallas, Texas: SIL International. Online version: http://www.ethnologue.com.

Luhman, R. (2007). *The sociological outlook.* Lanham, MD: Rowman & Littlefield.

Maddux, W.W. & Galinsky, A.D. 2009. *Cultural borders and mental barriers: the relationship between living abroad and creativity.* Journal of Personality and Social Psychology, 96(5):1047-61.

Magolda, M. B. B. (1992). *Knowing and reasoning in college.* San Francisco: Jossey-Bass.

Mendez, F., Krahn, T., Schrack, B., Krahn, A. M., Veeramah, K., Woerner, A., Fomine, F. L. M., Bradman, N., Thomas, M., Karafet, T., & Hammer, M. (2013). An African American paternal lineage adds an extremely ancient root to the human Y chromosome phylogenetic tree. *The American Journal of Human Genetics, 92,* 454–459. Meredith, M. (2011). *Born in Africa: The quest for the origins of human Life.* New York: Public Affairs.

Nagda, B. R., Gurin, P., & Johnson, S. M. (2005). Living, doing and thinking diversity: How does pre-college diversity experience affect first-year students' engagement with college diversity? In R. S. Feldman (Ed.), *Improving the first year of college: Research and practice* (pp. 73–110). Mahwah, NJ: Lawrence Erlbaum.

Nathan, R. (2005). *My freshman year: What a professor learned by becoming a student.* London: Penguin.

National Association of Colleges & Employers, 2003, 2007

National Association of Colleges and Employers (NACE). (2003). Job outlook 2003 survey. Bethlehem, PA: Author.

National Center for Education Statistics. (2011). *Digest of education statistics, table 237. Total fall enrollment in degree-granting institutions, by level of student, sex, attendance status, and race/ethnicity: Selected years, 1976 through 2010.* Alexandria, VA: U.S. Department of Education. Retrieved from http://neces.ed/gov/programs/digest/d11/tables/dt11_237.asp

National Association of Colleges and Employers (NACE). (2003). Job outlook 2003 survey. Bethlehem, PA: Author.

National Association of Colleges and Employers (NACE). (2007). Job outlook 2007 survey. Bethlehem, PA: Author

National Survey of Women Voters (1998). *Autumn overview report conducted by DYG Inc.* Retrieved from http://www.diversityweb.org/research_and_trends/research_evaluation_impact_/campus_community_connections/national_poll.cfm

Nhan, D. (2012). "Census: Minorities constitute 37 percent of U.S. population." *National Journal: The Next America-Demographics 2012.* Retrieved from http://www.nationaljournal.com/thenextamerica/demographics/census-minorities- constitute-37-percent-of-u-s-population-20120517

Nora, A., & Cabrera, A. (1996). The role of perceptions of prejudice and discrimination on the adjustment of minority college students. *The Journal of Higher Education, 67* (2), 119–148.

Office of Research (1994). *What employers expect of college graduates: International knowledge and second language skills.* Washington, DC: Office of Educational Research and Improvement, U.S. Department of Education.

Olson, L. (2007). What does "ready" mean? *Education Week, 40,* 7–12.

Pascarella, E. T. (2001, November/December). Cognitive growth in college: Surprising and reassuring findings from the National Study of Student Learning. *Change,* pp. 21–27.

Pascarella, E. T. & Terenzini, P. T. 2005. *How College Affects Students, Volume 2, A Third Decade of Research.* San Francisco, CA: Jossey-Bass.

Pascarella, E., Palmer, B., Moye, M., & Pierson, C. (2001). Do diversity experiences influence the development of critical thinking? Journal of College Student Development, 42(3), 257–291.

Peoples, J., & Bailey, G. (2011). *Humanity: An introduction to cultural anthropology.* Belmont, CA: Wadsworth, Cengage Learning.

Pettigrew, T. F. (1997). Generalized intergroup contact effects on prejudice. *Personality and Social Psychology Bulletin, 23,* 173–185.

Pettigrew, T. F. (1998). Intergroup contact theory. *Annual Review of Psychology, 49,* 65–85.

Pettigrew, T. F. & Tropp, L. R. (2000). Does intergroup contact reduce prejudice? Recent meta-analytic findings. S. Oskamp (Ed.), *Reducing prejudice and discrimination* (pp. 93–114). Mahwah, NJ: Lawrence Erlbaum Associates.

Pinker, S. (2000). *The language instinct: The new science of language and mind.* New York: Perennial.

Pratto, F., Liu, J. H., Levin, S., Sidanius, J., Shih, M., Bachrach, H., & Hegarty, P. (2000). Social dominance orientation and the legitimization of inequality across cultures. *Journal of Cross-Cultural Psychology, 31,* 369–409.

Public Service Enterprise Group (PSEG) (2009). *Diversity.* Retrieved from www.pseg.com/info/environment/ sustainability/2009/.../diversity.jsp

Reid, G. B. R., & Hetherington, R. (2010). *The climate connection: Climate change and modern evolution.* Cambridge, UK: Cambridge University Press.

Roediger, H. L., Dudai, Y., & Fitzpatrick, S. M. (2007). *Science of memory: concepts.* New York, NY: Oxford University Press.

Segall, M. H., Campbell, D. T., & Herskovits, M. J. (1966). *The influence of culture on visual perception.* Indianapolis: Bobbs-Merrill.

Shah, A. (2009). *Global issues: Poverty facts and stats.* Retrieved from http://www.globalissues.org/artoc;e/26/poverty-facts-and-stats.

Sherif, M., Harvey, D. J., White, B. J., Hood, W. R., & Sherif, C. W. (1961). *The Robbers' cave experiment.* Norman, OK: Institute of Group Relations.

Shiraev, E. D., & Levy, D. (2013). *Cross-cultural psychology: Critical thinking and contemporary applications* (5th ed.). Upper Saddle River, NJ: Pearson Education.

Sidanius, J., Levin, S., Liu, H., & Pratto, F. (2000). Social dominance orientation, anti-egalitarianism, and the political psychology of gender: An extension and cross-cultural replication. *European Journal of Social Psychology, 30,* 41–67.

Slavin, R. E. (1995). *Cooperative learning* (2nd ed.). Boston: Allyn & Bacon.

Smith, D. G., Guy L., Gerbrick, G. L., Figueroa, M. A., Watkins, G. H., Levitan, T., Moore L. C., Merchant, P. A., Beliak, H. D., & Figueroa, B. (1997). *Diversity works: The emerging picture of how students benefit.* Washington, DC: Association of American Colleges and Universities.

Stangor, C., Sechrist, G. B., & Jost, J. T. (2001). Changing racial beliefs by providing consensus information. *Personality and Social Psychology Bulletin, 27,* 484–494.

Stoltz, P. G. (2014). *Grit: The new science of what it takes to persevere, flourish, succeed.* San Luis Obispo: Climb Strong Press.

Taylor, S. E., Peplau, L. A., & Sears, D. O. (2006). *Social psychology* (12th ed.). Upper Saddle River, NJ: Pearson/ Prentice-Hall.

Thompson, A., & Cuseo, J. (2014). *Diversity and the college experience.* Dubuque, IA: Kendall Hunt.

U.S. Census Bureau (2008). *Bureau of Labor Statistics.* Washington, DC: Author.

U.S Census Bureau (2013). *Poverty.* Retrieved from https:// .www.census.gov/hhes/www/poverty/data/threshld/.

Wabash National Study of Liberal Arts Education (2007). *Liberal Arts outcomes.* Retrieved from http:www.liberalarts. wabash.edu/ study-overview/.

Wheelright, J. (2005, March). Human, study thyself. *Discover,* pp. 39–45.

Willis, J. (2006). *Research-based strategies to ignite student learning: Insights from a neurologist and classroom teacher.* Alexandria, VA: ASCD.

Zajonc, R. B. (1968). Attitudinal effects of mere exposure. *Journal of Personality and Social Psychology, 9,* Monograph Supplement, No. 2, part 2.

Zajonc, R. B. (1970). Brainwash: Familiarity breeds comfort. *Psychology Today,* (February), pp. 32–35, 60–62.

Zajonc, R. B. (2001). Mere exposure: A gateway to the subliminal. *Current Directions in Psychological Science, 10,* 224–228.

Chapter 8 Exercises

8.1 Quote Reflections

Review the sidebar quotes contained in this chapter and select two that were especially meaningful or inspirational to you.

For each quote, provide a three- to five-sentence explanation why you chose it.

8.2 Reality Bite

Hate Crime: A Racially Motivated Murder

Jasper County, Texas, has a population of approximately 31,000 people. In this county, 80% of the people are White, 18% are Black, and 2% are of other races. The county's poverty rate is considerably higher than the national average, and its average household income is significantly lower. In 1998, the mayor, the president of the Chamber of Commerce, and two councilmen were Black. From the outside, Jasper appeared to be a town with racial harmony, and its Black and White leaders were quick to state that there was no racial tension in Jasper.

However, one day, James Byrd Jr.—a 49-year-old African American man—was walking home along a road one evening and was offered a ride by three White males. Rather than taking Byrd home, Lawrence Brewer (age 31), John King (age 23), and Shawn Berry (age 23), three men linked to White-supremacist groups, took Byrd to an isolated area and began beating him. They then dropped his pants to his ankles, painted his face black, chained Byrd to their truck, and dragged him for approximately three miles. The truck was driven in a zigzag fashion to inflict maximum pain on the victim. Byrd was decapitated after his body collided with a culvert in a ditch alongside the road. His skin, arms, genitalia, and other body parts were strewn along the road, while his torso was found dumped in front of a Black cemetery. Medical examiners testified that Byrd was alive for much of the dragging incident.

When they were brought to trial, the bodies of Brewer and King were covered with racist tattoos; they were eventually sentenced to death. As a result of the murder, Byrd's family created the James Byrd Foundation for Racial Healing. A wrought iron fence that separated Black and White graves for more than 150 years in Jasper Cemetery was removed in a special unity service. Members of the racist Ku Klux Klan have since visited the gravesite of Byrd several times, leaving racist stickers and other marks that angered the Jasper community and Byrd's family.

Source: Louisiana Weekly (February 3, 2003).

Reflection Questions

1. What factors do you think were responsible for this incident?

2. Could this incident have been prevented? If yes, how? If no, why not?

3. How likely do you think an incident like this could take place in your hometown or near your college campus?

4. If this event happened to take place place in your hometown, how do you think members of your community would react?

8.3 Gaining Awareness of Your Group Identities

We are members of multiple groups at the same time and our membership in these overlapping groups can influence our personal development and identity. In the following figure, consider the shaded center circle to be yourself and the six unshaded circles to be six different groups you belong to and that you think have influenced your development.

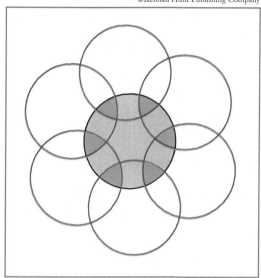

Fill in the unshaded circles with the names of groups to which you think you belong that have had the most influence on your personal development and identity. You can use the diversity spectrum (**p. 190**) to help you identify different groups to which you may be a member. Don't feel you have to fill in all six circles. What's more important is to identify those groups that you think have had a significant influence on your personal development or identity.

Reflection Questions:

1. Which one of your groups has had the greatest influence on your personal development or identity? Why?

2. Have you ever felt limited or disadvantaged by being a member of any your group(s) to which you belonged? Why?

3. Have you ever felt advantaged or privileged by your membership in any group(s)? Why?

8.4 Intercultural Interview

1. Identify a person on your campus who is a member of an ethnic or racial group that you've had little previous contact. Ask that person for an interview, and during the interview, include the following questions:

   - What does "diversity" mean to you?
   - What prior experiences have affected your current viewpoints or attitudes about diversity?
   - What would you say have been the major influences and turning points in your life?
   - Who would you cite as your positive role models, heroes, or sources of inspiration?
   - What societal contributions made by your ethnic or racial group would you like others to be aware of and acknowledge?
   - What do you hope will never again be said about your ethnic or racial group?

2. If you were the interviewee instead of the interviewer, how would you have answered the above questions?

3. What do you think accounts for the differences (and similarities) between your answers to the above questions and those provided by the person you interviewed?

8.5 Hidden Bias Test

Go to www.tolerance.org/activity/test-yourself-hidden-bias and take one or more of the hidden bias tests on this website. These tests assess subtle bias with respect to gender, age, ethnic minority groups, religious denominations, sexual orientations, disabilities, and body weight.

1. After completing the test, answer the following questions:

2. Did the results reveal any biases you weren't unaware of?

3. Did you think the assessment results were accurate or valid?

4. What do you think best accounts for or explains your results?

If your closest family member and best friend took the test, how do you think their results would compare with yours?

Chapter 8 Reflection

After reading this chapter, has your definition of diversity changed? Explain.

List and describe five ways appreciating diversity will assist you in being successful in college and/or life.

1.

2.

3.

4.

5.

Are there any areas of diversity you feel you need to be more comfortable with? What are the areas and HOW will you become more comfortable with them?

CHAPTER 9

Financial Literacy

MANAGING MONEY AND MINIMIZING DEBT

Chapter Preview

College students who accumulate high levels of debt are more likely to experience higher stress, lower academic performance, and greater risk of withdrawing or dropping out. The good news is that students who use effective money management strategies are able to minimize unnecessary spending, reduce accumulation of debt and stress, and improve the quality of their academic performance. This chapter provides you with specific strategies for tracking cash flow, minimizing and avoiding debt, balancing time spent on schoolwork and working for pay, and making wise spending and saving decisions while you're in college.

Learning Goal

Become more aware, knowledgeable, and strategic about managing money, financing your college education and handling your future finances.

Thought Starter

 Think About It—Journal Entry 9.1

Complete the following sentence with the first thought that comes to mind:

To me, money is . . .

_____

_____

_____

_____

For many students, starting college marks the start of greater personal independence and greater responsibilities for financial self-management and decision-making. The issue of money management for college students is growing in importance for a number of reasons. The rising cost of a college education has resulted in more students working more hours while attending college (Levine & Cureton, 1998; Perna & DuBois, 2010). The higher cost of a college education also requires more difficult fiscal decisions about what options (or combination of options) to use to meet college expenses. Unfortunately, research indicates that many students today are making decisions about financing their college education in ways that do not effectively promote their academic success and progress to graduation (King, 2005).

Another reason why money management is growing in importance for college students is the availability and convenience of credit cards. It's never been easier for college students to access, use, and abuse credit cards. Credit agencies and bureaus now closely monitor college students' credit card payments and routinely report their "credit score" to credit card companies and banks. Since research shows that there is a statistical relationship between using credit cards responsibly and being a responsible employee (Ring, 1997; Susswein, 1995), employers check these credit scores and use them as indicators or predictors of how responsible a student will be as an employee. Thus, being irresponsible with credit while in college can affect a student's ability to land a job after (or during) college. Students' credit scores also affect their likelihood of qualifying for car loans and home loans as well as their ability to rent an apartment (Pratt, 2011). College graduates today can do everything right while they are in college, such as get good grades, get involved on campus, and get work experience before graduating, but a poor credit history as college students can harm them after college—reducing their chance of obtaining credit and their job prospects (Nellie Mae, 2005; Sallie Mae, 2009).

Furthermore, accumulating high levels of debt while in college is associated with higher levels of student stress (Nelson, et al., 2008), lower academic performance (Susswein, 1995), and greater risk of withdrawing from college (Ring, 1997). On the positive side of the ledger, studies show that when college students learn to use effective money management strategies (such as those discussed below), they can reduce unnecessary spending, minimize accumulation of debt, and lower their overall level of stress (Health & Soll, 1996; Kidwell & Turrisi, 2004; Walker, 1996).

Sources of Income for Financing a College Education

College students' income typically comes from three sources:

- Loans that must be repaid,
- Scholarships or grants that are not repaid, and
- Salary earned from part-time or full-time work.

The *Free Application for Federal Student Aid (FAFSA)* is the application used by the U.S. Department of Education to determine financial aid eligibility for students. It asks for personal and family financial information to determine a student's eligibility for federal, state, and college-sponsored financial aid, including grants, loans, and work-study employment. A formula is used to determine the student's *estimated family contribution (EFC)*—the amount of money estimated by the government that a family can contribute to the educational costs incurred by a family member attending college.

No fee is charged to complete the application, so you should complete an application every year to determine your eligibility for financial aid. (See the Financial Aid Office on your campus for a copy of the FAFSA form and for help completing it.)

Student Loans

Loans need to be repaid after a student graduates from college. Listed below are some of the more well-known, federally funded student loan programs.

- *The Federal Perkins Loan*: a low-interest loan awarded to exceptionally needy students. Repayment of the loan begins nine months after a student is no longer enrolled at least half-time.
- *The Federal Subsidized Stafford Loan*: available to students enrolled at least half-time, has a fixed interest rate established each year on July 1. The federal govern-

ment pays the interest on the loan while the student is enrolled. Repayment for this loan begins six months after a student is no longer enrolled at least half-time.

- *The Federal Unsubsidized Stafford Loan*: a loan not based on need that has the same interest rate as the Federal Subsidized Stafford Loan. Students are responsible for paying the interest on this loan while they're enrolled in college. Repayment for this loan begins 6 months after a student is no longer enrolled at least half-time.

Keep in mind that federal loans and private loans differ in the following ways:

- *Federal* loans have fixed interest rates that are comparatively low (currently less than 7%) and cannot go higher.
- *Private* loans have variable interest rates that are very high (currently more than 15%) and can go higher at any time.

Despite the much higher interest rate of private loans, they're the fastest-growing type of loans taken out by college students—largely because of aggressive, and sometimes misleading, irresponsible, or unethical advertising on loan-shopping websites. Students sometimes think they're getting a federal loan only to find out later they've taken on a more expensive private loan (Hamilton, 2012; Kristof, 2008).

Keep in mind that not all loans are created equal. Compared to private loans, federally guaranteed student loans are relatively low-cost and may be paid off slowly after graduation. On the other hand, private lenders of student loans are like credit card companies; they charge extremely high interest rates (that can go even higher at any time) and the loans must be paid off quickly. Private loans should not be used as a primary loan to help pay for college and they should only be used as a last resort—when no other options are available for covering college expenses.

Also, keep in mind that federal and state regulations require that if you're receiving financial aid, you must maintain "satisfactory academic progress." In most cases this means you must do the following:

1. Maintain a satisfactory GPA—such as, 2.0 or above. Your entire academic record will be reviewed, even if you have paid for some of the classes with your own resources.
2. Make satisfactory academic progress—such as, 12 to 15 units per semester for full-time students and 6 to 9 hours for part-time students. You must successfully complete approximately 70% of the classes you attempt. Your academic progress will be evaluated at least once per year, usually at the end of each spring semester.
3. Complete a degree or certificate program with a reasonable number of units. There is a maximum number of course hours you can attempt per degree. (Check with your institution's Financial Aid Office for details.)

> "Apply for as much grant aid as possible before borrowing, and then seek lower-interest federal student loans before tapping private ones. There is a lot of student aid that can help make the expense [of college] more manageable."
>
> —*Sandy Baum, senior policy analyst, College Board (quoted in Gordon, 2009)*

NICC Satisfactory Academic Progress (SAP) Standards

Federal and state regulations require that if you are receiving financial aid, you must maintain "satisfactory academic progress." At NICC, you must do the following:

1. **Cumulative Grade Point Average Policy (Qualitative component)**—A student must maintain a cumulative grade point average of 2.0 (C average) or better.
2. **Student Pace Policy (Quantitative component – 67% completion)**—A student must successfully complete 67% or more of their cumulative attempted credit

hours including remedial and transfer credits at the end of the semester. A student's pace is calculated by taking the cumulative number of credits the student has successfully completed divided by the cumulative number of attempted credits.

3.   **Completion of Program 150% Policy (Maximum time frame component)—** To receive financial aid, a student must earn their degree within a maximum time frame. The maximum time frame for which students may receive financial aid is 150% of the published length of the program's credit hours.

For example, the length of an Associate's Degree is 60 credits. 60 credits x 150% = 90 credits. A student can receive financial aid for up to 90 credits in pursuit of this degree. Credits earned at another institution that have been accepted by NICC as transfer credit are included in this total even if financial aid was not awarded for these credits.

A student's satisfactory academic progress will be evaluated at the end of each academic semester (fall, spring and summer) once grades are reported. Upon evaluation of a student's satisfactory academic progress, a student will be assigned one of the three following statuses and notified through the student's Xpress email account:

Satisfactory
Financial Aid Warning
Financial Aid Suspension

A student will also have a SAP status assigned once a FAFSA is received by NICC if the student has a past academic record at NICC. This may include college credit classes that were earned while in high school (i.e., PSEO, concurrent enrollment, etc.). A student will have a status assigned even if those grades were earned without utilizing financial aid in the past.

Satisfactory

Student is meeting all satisfactory academic progress standards and is eligible to receive financial aid.

Financial Aid Warning

This is a warning to a student who is not meeting one or more of the satisfactory academic progress standards. The student remains eligible to receive financial aid for the upcoming semester, but must meet the satisfactory academic progress standards when it is evaluated at the end of that semester in order to maintain eligibility for the next semester. Students who fail to meet the requirements at the end of that semester will result in a Financial Aid Suspension status.

Financial Aid Suspension

Students who do not meet one or more of the satisfactory academic progress standards at the end of the semester after which they had been on Financial Aid Warning will no longer be eligible to receive financial aid. Students who complete any semester and receive only letter grades of F and or Withdrawals which result in 0.0 percent completion of all attempted credit hours, will automatically be placed on Financial Aid Suspension for the following semester and will not receive the semester of Financial Aid Warning.

If a student is placed on Financial Aid Suspension, they have the right to file for an appeal request or they may also re-establish their eligibility by meeting SAP Standards while paying on their own.

For assistance or for answers to questions regarding this process, visit with an NICC financial aid representative or your enrollment advisor. To access or view the appeal request form and to read the complete NICC SAP policy, visit www .nicc edu/appeal.

Student Loans and Credit Scores

Be aware that students loans are a type of loan and can affect your credit score. For many community college students, credit is now a reality and will be for the rest of you when you graduate from college. College loans can hurt or enhance your credit score depending on how you treat the loan.

Your credit score is a number that tells lenders and creditors how financially responsible you are. It assists them in judging the level of risk you present to them as a borrower.

This score will dictate how easily you can obtain credit cards, loans, houses, renting an apartment, etc. The score is based on the following percentages:

* 35% based on payment history: how consistently you pay bills on time
* 30% based on how much you currently owe
* 15% based on credit history: have you had credit before and handled it responsibly?
* 10% based on new credit: how many new applications and acceptances of other credit you've had
* 10% based on types of credit: credit card, student loan, auto loan, etc.

Thus, having loans (including student loans) can be good or bad and sometimes both, depending on how you use them and how you repay them. Making your student loan payments in full and on time each month will assist your credit score and help you to establish a good credit history. However, missing payments or not paying at all can be devastating to your credit and credit score.

Lastly, if you find yourself temporarily short of funds and need just a small loan to recover, many colleges have an *emergency student loan program*, whereby they provide students with an immediate, interest-free loan to help them cover short-term expenses (e.g., cost of textbooks) or deal with financial emergencies (e.g., accidents and illnesses). Emergency student loans are typically granted within 24 to 48 hours, sometimes even the same day, and usually need to be repaid within two months.

Student Loan Repayment

After graduation or being enrolled in less than six credit hours, your six-month grace period for loan repayment will begin. You will receive a letter from NICC which will require you to complete Entrance Counseling at www. studentloans.gov. If you do not complete Exit Counseling, it may result in a higher repayment amount. Student loans must be repaid even if you experience financial difficulties, so it is important to understand the repayment process for your federal and private student loans.

Know who your Loan Servicer and how to contact them. A loan servicer is the company that processes your federal student loans for the government. You will pay your Loan Servicer directly, and they can help you choose a payment plan, help you figure your interest and help you if you ever have trouble repaying your loan.

There are eight repayment plan options from which to choose:

Standard Repayment Plan
Graduated Repayment Plan
Extended Repayment Plan

Income-Based Repayment Plan
Pay As You Earn Repayment Plan
Income-Contingent Repayment Plan
Income-Sensitive Repayment Plan
REPAYE: Revised Pay As You Earn

For more information on student loan repayment or payment plan options, visit: www.studentaid.ed.gov/repay-loans.

Loan Deferment and Forbearance

Under certain circumstances, you can receive a deferment or forbearance that allows you to temporarily postpone or reduce your federal student loan payments.

If you can't make your scheduled loan payments, but don't qualify for a deferment, your loan servicer may grant you a forbearance. With forbearance, interest will continue to accrue on your subsidized and unsubsidized loans (including all PLUS loans). Continue to pay this interest if possible, even if granted a forbearance.

You will need to work with your loan servicer to apply for deferment or forbearance; be sure to keep making payments on your loan until the deferment or forbearance is in place. By working with your loan servicer, postponing or reducing your payments through deferment or forbearance may help you avoid loan default.

Think About It Journal Entry

For specific information about YOUR loan(s) and loan servicer(s), visit: www.nslds.ed.gov

My Loan Servicer(s) is (are):

Their contact information is:

My Loan Amount(s) is (are):

My monthly loan payment(s) will be:

Payments will begin on:

Also visit: www.finaid.org/calculators for loan calculation for repayment.

Default

Never ignore late payment notices from your loan servicer(s). If you fail to make your monthly loan payment, you will become delinquent on your student loans and put yourself and your credit at risk! Contact your loan servicer immediately if you are having difficulty in making timely payments.

Consequences of default can be severe, including a poor credit rating, resulting in your inability to buy a car, house, or even prevent employment. Further measures such as tax withholdings and wage garnishments (taken from your paycheck) may be taken by the government to collect on your overdue student loans!

Loan Consolidation

Loan consolidation can greatly simplify loan repayment by centralizing your loans to one bill and can lower monthly payments by giving additional years to repay your loans. However, by increasing the length of your repayment period, you will also make more payments and pay more in interest. Compare your current monthly payments to what monthly payments would be if you consolidated your loans.

You also should consider the impact of losing any borrower benefits offered with the original loans. Borrower benefits from your original loan, which may include interest rate discounts, principal rebates, or some loan cancellation benefits, can significantly reduce the cost of repaying your loans. You might lose those benefits if you consolidate.

To find out more about loan consolidation, visit: HYPERLINK "http://www.loanconsolidation.ed.gov/" www.loanconsolidation.ed.gov/

Contact NICC with changes to your:
* name, address, permanent address or phone number.

Contact your loan server when you:
* change your name, address, or phone number;
* need help making your loan payment;
* have a question about your bill; or
* have other questions about your student loan.

Scholarships

Scholarships are available from many sources, including Northeast Iowa Community College. They are awarded based on various criteria that may include a written essay, ACT or SAT scores, and high school grade point average (GPA). In addition to academic scholarships, scholarships are awarded based on organizations you may have been a part of, race or ethnicity, the region of the country you live in, athletics, artistic talents, and so on. It is important to remember that all scholarships are competitive and deadlines are observed by the awarding agencies or institutions. Be aware of the application material deadlines and submit your materials well in advance of these deadlines.

Northeast Iowa Community College awards over $100,000 annually to new and continuing students. The average scholarship award is between $500-$750. The priority deadline for NICC scholarship applications is April 1st, so be sure to apply early. Learn more about the NICC scholarship process and other local scholarhsips at nicc.edu/scholarships. You can also conduct an Internet search to find many sites that offer scholarship information (like www.fastweb.com), but it is important to remember that you should not enter credit card or bank account information on any site.

Grants

Grants are considered to be gift aid, which typically does not have to be repaid. About two-thirds of all college students receive grant aid, which, on average, reduces their tuition bills by more than half. The Federal Pell Grant is the largest grant program; it provides need-based aid to low-income undergraduate students. The amount of the grant depends on criteria such as: (1) the anticipated contribution of the family to the student's education (EFC), (2) the cost of the postsecondary institution that the student is attending, and (3) the enrollment status of the student (part-time or full-time). Even though grants do not need to be paid back, students must maintain certain academic standards to remain eligible to receive their grant money.

National Guard Education Assistance Program (NGEAP)

This is available to Iowa National Guard soldiers who are eligible for tuition assistance and other bonuses.

Veterans Benefits

If you are currently a veteran, you may be eligible for the GI Bill benefits.

What Is the Montgomery GI Bill—Active Duty?

The Montgomery GI Bill–Active Duty, called MGIB for short, provides up to 36 months of education benefits to eligible veterans. Benefits may include, but are not limited to, tuition and fees, a housing allowance, and a books and supplies stipend. Veterans must maintain certain academic standards to receive the benefits. Visit the Office of Veterans Affairs on your campus to get more information (see the following website for more detail: http://www.vba.va.gov/VBA/benefits/factsheets/index.asp#BM4).

Salary Earnings

If you're relying on salary from off-campus work to pay for college tuition, check with your employer to see if the company you're working for offers tuition reimbursement. Also, check with the Billing Office (sometimes referred to as the Cashier's Office) on your campus to determine whether payment plans are available that allow you to pay tuition costs on an installment schedule that aligns with the timing of your paychecks. These tuition-payment plans may provide you with some flexibility in terms of amount due per payment, deadlines for payments, and how remaining debt owed to the institution is dealt with at the end of the term. (Keep in mind that NICC will not allow you to register for the following term until tuition for the previous term has been completely paid.)

If possible, try to find work *on campus* rather than off campus. Research shows that when students work on campus they're more likely to succeed in college (Astin, 1993; Pascarella & Terenzini, 1991, 2005). This is probably due to the fact that they become more connected to the college (Cermak & Filkins, 2004; Tinto, 1993) and because on-campus employers are more flexible than off-campus employers in allowing students to meet their academic commitments (Leonard, 2008). For instance, on-campus employers are more willing to schedule students' work hours around their class schedule and allow students to modify their work schedule when their academic workload increases (e.g., at midterm and finals). Thus, if at all possible, rather than seeking work off campus, try to find work on campus and capitalize on its proven capacity to promote college success. NICC provides many opportunities for work study jobs for students.

Student Account Refunds

All accepted financial aid is first applied toward your tuition, fees, and bookstore charges. NICC uses a third party company to process any remaining balance, called a refund. It is extremely important to manage this refund, which can sometimes be very large, and to have a plan on how to use it in conjunction with your educational expenses. It is recommended that you have the refund selection setup to have the refund deposited directly into your personal bank account. Students receive information regarding this process in the beginning of their first semester with the college. Refunds are processed approximately 30 days after the start of the semester based on their attendance and enrollment status at that time. There are many factors, including class schedule, enrollment status, number of credits, the type of aid being received, etc. that may impact when students actually receive their refund. For example, students receiving a one-semester only student loan, will receive that refund in several intervals throughout the semester. It is best to meet directly with a Financial Aid Representative to determine when a refund should be expected and how to effectively budget that amount.

 ## Think About It—Journal Entry 9.2

If you're using any of the following financial resources to help pay for your college education, circle it: loans,   grants,   scholarships,   salary earnings,   savings,   monetary support from parents or other family members,   other resources.

Which of the above resources is the primary or main source of funding for your college education? Which of the resources above might you be able to use?

Developing a Money Management Plan

Gain Financial Self-Awareness

Development of any good habit begins with the critical first step of self-awareness. Developing effective money-management habits begins with awareness of your *cash flow*—the amount of money you have coming in and going out. As illustrated in **Figure 9.1**, cash flow is tracked by monitoring:

* Income—the amount of money you have coming in versus the amount going out (expenses or expenditures), and
* Savings—the amount of money you've earned and not spent versus the amount you've borrowed and haven't paid back (debt).

Once you're aware of the amount of money you have coming in (and from what sources) plus the amount of money you're spending (and for what reasons), your next step is to develop a plan for managing your cash flow. The bottom line is to ensure that the sum of money you have coming in (income)

FIGURE 9.1: **The Two-Way Street of Cash Flow**

Income ⟷ Expenses

Savings ⟷ Debt

©Kendall Hunt Publishing Company

is equal to or greater than the sum of money you have going out (expenses). If the amount of money going out exceeds the amount coming in, you're "in the red" or have "negative cash flow."

Track Your Cash Flow

You can track cash flow by using any of the following tools:

- Checking accounts
- Credit cards
- Charge cards
- Debit cards

Checking Accounts

Long before credit cards were created, a checking account was the method most people used to keep track of their money. Many people still use checking accounts in addition to (or instead of) credit cards. A checking account may be obtained from a bank or credit union; its typical costs include a deposit ($20–$25) to open the account, a monthly service fee (e.g., $10), and small fees for checks. Some banks charge customers a service fee based on the number of checks written; this is a good option if you don't plan to write many checks each month. Look for a checking account that doesn't charge you if your balance drops below a certain minimum figure. If you maintain a high enough *balance* (deposited money in your account) the bank may not charge any extra fees, and if you're able to maintain an even higher balance, some banks may also pay you interest—known as an interest-bearing checking account.

Along with your checking account, banks usually provide you with an automatic teller machine (ATM) card that you can use to get cash. Look for a checking account that offers a free service along with your checking account, rather than one that charges a separate fee for ATM transactions.

A checking account has several advantages:

- You can carry checks instead of cash.
- You have access to cash at almost any time through an ATM.
- You can keep a visible track record of your income and expenses in your checkbook.
- If you manage a checking account responsibly, it can serve as a good credit reference for future loans and purchases.

To make the best use of your checking account, apply the following strategies:

- Whenever you write a check or make an ATM withdrawal, immediately subtract its amount from your *balance* (the amount of money remaining in your account) and determine your new balance.
- Keep a running balance in your checkbook; this will ensure you know exactly how much money you have in your account at all times. It also reduces your risk of *bouncing* a check—writing a check for an amount that exceeds the total amount you have in your account. If you do bounce a check, you'll probably have to pay a charge to the bank and possibly to the business that attempted to cash your bounced check.
- Double-check your checkbook balance with each monthly statement you receive from the bank. Be sure to include the service charges your bank makes to your account; these charges will appear on your monthly statement. Checking your checkbook on a regular basis will enable you to catch errors that you've made or the bank has made. (Banks can and do occasionally make mistakes.)

Credit Cards

A credit card is basically money loaned to you by the credit card company issuing the card, which you pay back to the company on a monthly basis. You can pay the whole bill or a portion of the bill each month—as long as some minimum payment is made. However, for any remaining (unpaid) portion of your bill, you're charged a high interest rate—which can be as much as 30%. Consequently, if you decide to use a credit card, be sure you're able to pay off your whole bill (loan) each month.

If a credit card is used responsibly, it has some key advantages as a money management tool:

* It helps you track your spending habits because the credit card company sends you a monthly statement with an itemized list of all your card-related purchases. This list supplies you with a "paper trail" of what you purchase each month and when you purchased it.
* It provides a convenient way for you to purchase things you need online, which can save time and money that would otherwise be spent traveling to and from stores.
* It allows access to cash whenever and wherever you need it because any bank or ATM that displays your credit card's symbol will give you cash up to a certain limit (usually for a small transaction fee). Keep in mind that some credit card companies charge a higher interest rate for cash *advances* than credit card *purchases*.
* It enables you to establish a personal credit history. If you use a credit card responsibly, you can establish a good credit history that can be used later in life for big ticket purchases—such as a car or home. In effect, responsible use of a credit card shows others from whom you wish to seek credit (or borrow money) that you will pay it back. However, don't buy into the belief that the only way you can establish a good credit history is by using a credit card. It's not your only option; you can also establish a good credit history by responsible use of a checking account and by paying your bills on time.

If you decide to use a credit card, pay attention to its *annual percentage rate (APR)*—the interest rate you pay for previously unpaid monthly balances. This rate can vary from one credit card company to another. Credit card companies also vary in terms of their annual service fee. You'll find that companies charging higher interest rates also charge lower annual fees, and vice versa. As a general rule, if you expect to pay the full balance every month, you're probably better off choosing a credit card that doesn't charge you an annual service fee. On the other hand, if you think you'll need more time to make the full monthly payments, you're probably better off with a credit card company that offers a low interest rate.

Credit card companies also differ from one another in terms of whether they allow a *grace period*—the amount of time you have after receiving your monthly statement to pay back the company without paying additional interest fees. Some companies may allow you a grace period of a full month, while others may provide no forgiveness period and begin charging interest immediately after a payment isn't received by the bill's due date.

Credit cards also differ in terms of their *credit limit* (also known as a "credit line" or "line of credit"), which is the maximum amount of money the credit card company will make available to you. If you're a new customer, most companies will set a credit limit beyond which no additional credit will be granted.

There are advantages of using a credit card, but those advantages are only reaped by using credit cards strategically. If not, its advantages are quickly and greatly outweighed by its disadvantages. Listed here are some strategies for using a credit card in ways that maximize its advantages and minimize its disadvantages.

- Use a credit card for making purchases conveniently and for tracking the purchases you make; don't use it as a tool for obtaining a long-term loan. A credit card's main money-management advantage is that it enables you to make purchases with plastic instead of cash. It saves you the inconvenience of having to carry cash or checks and conveniently supplies you with a monthly statement of your purchases, making it easier for you to track and analyze your spending habits. The credit provided by a credit card should be seen simply as a short-term loan that must be paid back at the end of every month. Don't use credit cards for long-term credit or long-term loans because their interest rates are outrageously high. Paying such a high rate of interest for a loan is an ineffective (and irresponsible) money-management strategy.
- **Limit yourself to one credit card.** Having more than one credit card means having more accounts to keep track of and more opportunities to accumulate debt. You don't need additional credit cards from department stores, gas stations, or any other profit-making business because they duplicate what your personal credit card already does (plus they typically charge extremely high interest rates for late payments).
- **Make sure you know the specific terms of the agreement.** Credit card companies vary in terms of what they will charge you for not paying your full bill on time and what restrictions they will impose on further use of your card if you accumulate debt. Be sure to read the fine print on your contract; if you have any doubts or questions, contact a representative of the credit card company.
- **Pay off your balance each month** *in full* and *on time*. If you pay the full amount of your bill each month, this means you're using your credit card effectively to obtain an interest-free, short-term (1-month) loan. You're just paying *principal*—the total amount of money borrowed and nothing more. However, if your payment is late and you end up paying interest, you're paying more for the items you purchased than their actual ticket price. For instance, if you have an unpaid balance of $500 on your monthly credit bill for merchandise purchased the previous month and you're charged the typical 18% credit card interest rate for late payment, you end up paying $590: $500 (merchandise) + $90 (18% interest to the credit card company).

Credit card companies make their profit by the interest they collect from cardholders who don't pay back their credit on time. Just as procrastinating about completing schoolwork is a poor time-management habit that hurts your grades, procrastinating about paying your credit card bills is a poor money-management habit that hurts your pocketbook by forcing you to pay high interest rates.

Don't allow credit card companies to make profit at your expense. Pay your total balance on time and avoid paying exorbitantly high interest rates. If you can't pay the total amount owed at the end of the month, instead of making the minimum monthly payment, pay as much as you possibly can. If you keep making only the minimum payment each month, you'll begin piling up huge amounts of debt.

Note

If you keep making charges on your credit card while you have an unpaid balance (debt), you no longer have a grace period to pay back your charges; instead, interest is charged immediately on all your purchases.

"What I don't do that I know I should do is pay my bills on time, like my cell phone and credit cards."

—First-year student

"I need to pay attention to my balance more closely and actually allot certain amounts for certain things."

—First-year student

"You'll never get your credit card debt paid off if you keep charging on your card and make only the minimum monthly payment. Paying only the minimum is like using a Dixie cup to bail water from a sinking boat."

—Eric Tyson, financial counselor and national best-selling author of Personal Finance for Dummies

Box 9.1

Credit Cardholders' Bill of Rights Act of 2009

Congress passed legislation in 2009 that enacted certain protections for consumers who use credit cards. Here are the specific reforms that affect college students:

- Creditors are forbidden from offering credit to consumers under the age of 18 (unless they are emancipated under state law, or the consumer's parent or legal guardian is the primary account holder).

- College students without a cosigner will have their credit line limited to the greater amount of 20 percent of their annual gross income or $500. The collective amount of credit available on all credit cards will be limited to 30 percent of the student's annual gross income.
- Creditors are not allowed to open a credit-card account for a college student who does not have a verifiable annual gross income or already has a credit-card account with that creditor or any of its affiliates (Chan, 2009).

Think About It—Journal Entry 9.3

Do you have a credit card? Do you have more than one?

If you have at least one credit card, do you pay off your entire balance each month?

If you don't pay off your entire balance each month:

(a) What's your average unpaid balance per month?

(b) What changes would you have to make in your money-management habits to be able to pay off your entire balance each month?

Charge Cards (a.k.a Smart Cards)

A charge card works similar to a credit card in that you're given a short-term loan for one month; the only difference is that you must pay your bill in full at the end of each month and you cannot carry over any debt from one month to the next. Its major disadvantage relative to a credit card is that it has less flexibility—no matter what your expenses may be for a particular month, you must still pay up or lose your ability to obtain credit for the following month. However, if you're someone who consistently has trouble paying your monthly credit card bill on time, this is an advantage of a charge card because it will prevent you from accumulating debt.

Debit Cards

A debit card looks almost identical to a credit card (e.g., it has a *MasterCard* or *Visa* logo), but it works differently. When you use a debit card, money is immediately taken out or subtracted from your checking account. Like a check or ATM withdrawal, any purchase you make with a debit card is immediately subtracted from your balance. Thus, you can only use money that's already in your account (rather than borrowing money). At the end of the month, you don't receive a bill; instead, you get a statement with information about checks you deposited and cashed, as well as your debit card transactions. If you attempt to purchase something with a debit card that costs more than the amount of money you have in your account, your card will not allow you to do so. Similar to a bounced check, a debit card will not permit you to pay out any money that's not in your account.

Like a credit card, a major advantage of the debit card is that it provides you with the convenience of plastic; however, unlike a credit card, it prevents you from spending beyond your means and accumulating debt. For this reason, many financial advisors recommend using a debit card rather than a credit card (Knox, 2004; Tyson, 2012).

Box 9.2

Minimize Your Risk of Identity Theft

Identity thieves steal your personal information to make transactions or purchases in your name. This can damage your credit status and cost you time and money to restore your financial credibility. Listed below are key strategies for reducing your risk of identity theft.

- Don't share personal identity information over the phone with anyone you don't know and trust, especially your social security or credit card number.
- Don't share identity information over the phone with anyone who claims to be an Internal Revenue Service (IRS) agent and threatens you with arrest or deportation, or who requests personal information the purpose of sending you a refund. The IRS will contact you in writing if it needs anything.
- Don't respond to e-mails from anyone claiming to be from the IRS. This is always a scam because the IRS doesn't initiate contact with taxpayers by e-mail or social media to request personal or financial information. (The only legitimate communication you will receive from the IRS is through postal mail.)
- Don't click on links or open e-mail attachments from anyone unfamiliar to you. Scam artists create fake websites and send "phishing" e-mails—which are attempts to acquire personal information such as usernames, passwords, and credit card details, often using the names of trustworthy electronic sources (e.g., an Internet service provider).
- Don't enter your credit card or bank account information on any websites.
- Install firewalls and virus detection software on your computer, to protect yourself against "cyber crime."

- When using your laptop in public, shield your screen from "shoulder surfers."
- Don't carry your Social Security (SSN) card in your wallet or write it on your checks. Only give out your SSN to people you know and trust.
- Conceal your personal identification number (PIN). Don't supply it to anyone and don't keep it in your wallet.
- Shred documents containing personal information you no longer need. (Some identity thieves are "dumpster divers" who go through the garbage to get your personal information.)
- Compare your receipts with your account statements and credit card statements to be sure there are no transactions you didn't authorize. If you have an online account, you can check your account at any time. It's a good idea to get in the habit of checking it at least once a week (e.g., every Sunday evening).
- If you believe you've been victimized by identity theft, contact your local police department and any of the following credit reporting companies to place a fraud alert:

Experian: https://www.experian.com/freeze/center.html

TransUnion: https://freeze.transunion.com/sf/security-Freeze/landingPage.jsp

Equifax: https://www.freeze.equifax.com/Freeze/jsp/SFF_PersonalIDInfo.jsp

Sources:
Prevent and Report Identity Theft: https://www.irs.gov/Individuals/Identity-Protection

Identity Protection Tips - Internal Revenue Service: www.irs.gov/Individuals/Identity-Protection-Tips

Tips to Avoid Identity Theft: http://www.bbb.org/sacramento/news-events/consumer-tips/2015/03/how-to-avoid-identity-theft/

Developing a Plan for Managing Money and Minimizing Debt

The ultimate goal of money management is to save money and dodge debt. Here are some strategies for accomplishing both of these goals.

Prepare a personal budget. A budget is simply a plan for coordinating income and expenses in a way that ensures you're left with sufficient money to cover your expenses. It enables you to be your own accountant who keeps an accurate account of your own income and expenses.

Sources of expense for college students typically fall into three categories:

1. *Basic needs or essential necessities*—these are "fixed" expenses because you can't live without them—such as, expenses for food, housing, tuition, textbooks, phone, transportation to and from school, and health-related costs

2. *Incidentals or extras*—these are "flexible" expenses because they're optional or discretionary—you choose to spend at your own discretion or judgment. These expenses usually include:
   - money spent on entertainment, enjoyment, or pleasure (e.g., music, movies, and spring break vacations), and
   - money spent on promoting personal status or self-image (e.g., buying expensive brand name products, fashionable clothes, jewelry, and other personal accessories)

3. *Emergency expenses*—unpredicted, unforeseen, or unexpected expenditures (e.g., costs incurred by unanticipated car repairs or medical services)

Think About It—Journal Entry 9.4

What are your most expensive incidentals (optional purchases)?

_____

_____

_____

_____

What could you do to reduce or eliminate these expenses?

_____

_____

_____

_____

Similar to managing your time, the first step in planning and managing money is to prioritize. Identify your most important expenses—the indispensable necessities you can't live without—and separate them from incidentals—dispensable luxuries you can live without and can be reduced or eliminated if necessary. People easily confuse *essentials* (things they really *need*) with *desirables* (stuff they just *want*). For instance, if a piece of merchandise happens to be on sale, it may be a desirable purchase at that time because of its reduced price; however, it's not an essential purchase if you don't need that piece of merchandise at that particular time.

Note

Remaining aware of the distinction between essentials that must be purchased and incidentals that may or may not be purchased is an important first step toward budgeting effectively and minimizing debt.

Postponing short-term satisfaction of material desires is a key element of long-term financial success. Unfortunately, humans are often more motivated by short-range thinking because it produces quicker results and more immediate gratification (Goldstein & Hogarth, 1997; Lowenstein, Read, & Baumeister, 2003). This is why so many people pile up credit card debt; they choose to experience the short-term pleasure of the immediate purchase instead of postponing gratification to save money in the long run.

We need to remain mindful of whether we're spending money *impulsively* on what we want rather than *reflectively* on what we need. The truth is that humans spend money for a host of psychological reasons (conscious or subconscious), many of which are unrelated to actual need. Some people spend money to build their self-esteem or self-image, to combat personal boredom, or because of an emotional "high" they experience when they buy things for themselves (Dittmar, 2004; Furnham & Argyle, 1998). Other people can become obsessed with spending money, shop compulsively, and develop an addiction to purchasing products. Just as Alcoholics Anonymous (AA) functions as a support group for alcoholics, Debtors Anonymous serves as a support group for shopaholics and includes a similar 12-step recovery program.

AUTHOR'S EXPERIENCE

I was a student who had to manage my own college expenses, so I soon became an expert in managing small budgets. The first thing I always took care of was my tuition. I was going to go to school even if I starved. The next thing I budgeted for was food, housing, clothing, and transportation needs. If I ran out of money, I would then work additional hours if it didn't interfere with my school work.

Rather than making and spending money while I was in college, I was working to make a better future life for myself. To be successful, I had to be a great money manager because there was so little of it to manage. This took a lot of focus and strong will, but did it pay off? Absolutely.

—*Aaron Thompson*

Note

What you're willing to sacrifice and save for, and what you're willing to spend money on and go into debt for, says a lot about who you are and what you value.

Who's in Charge?

Financial Priorities

It is the first week of the term and you still don't have your books. You are getting irritated because your instructors are telling you that you are already falling behind and if you don't get your books soon, you will fail the class! You explain that you don't have the money right now and next week you need to get your nails done and buy an iPod® because your daughter broke yours. You think your instructors are plain mean and don't want to help you. Who is really at fault here? What could have been done differently in this situation?

_____

_____

_____

_____

Make all your bills visible and, if possible, pay them as soon as you see them. When bills are in your sight, they're on your mind and you're less likely to forget to pay them, or forget to pay them on time. Try to get in the habit of paying a bill as soon as you open it and have it in your hands, rather than setting it aside and running the risk of forgetting to pay it (or losing it altogether).

You can increase the visibility of your bill payments by creating and posting a financial calendar on which you record key fiscal deadlines for the academic year (e.g., due dates for tuition payments, residential bills, and financial aid applications). Also, consider setting up an online banking program that will enable you to visually track your transactions and make credit card payments automatically. The advantage of an online account is that it's paperless and you don't have to deal with bills sent to you through postal mail. However, its disadvantage is that it doesn't appear in tangible form in your mailbox—which provides you with clear, visual reminder to pay it. So, if you set up an online account, get into an ongoing habit of checking it. Otherwise, what's out of sight stays out of mind and your bills may not get paid on time.

Live within your means. Simply stated: Don't purchase what you can't afford. If you're spending more money than you're taking in, it means you're living *beyond* your means. To begin living *within* your means, you have two options:

1. Decrease your expenses (reduce your spending), or
2. Increase your income (earn more money).

AUTHOR'S EXPERIENCE

When I was young, my mom was always cutting out coupons and looking for what was on sale. If it was not on sale or she did not have a coupon, she usually did not buy it. As a child, it drove me nuts and I thought she was crazy! Now that I am older, I find I am a lot like her when it comes to money. I am always looking for coupons and I rarely buy anything if it is not on sale. Even when I do buy something I stop and think, "Do I really need this?" or "How much use will I get out of this?" It is because of this that I am able to save up some of my money and do things I really enjoy (season tickets for football games, traveling, etc.), and I am thankful my mom taught me how to save.

—*Julie McLaughlin*

Most college students work while attending college (Kingkade, 2014) and they work so many hours that it interferes with their academic performance and educational progress (King, 2005). Thus, for most college students who find themselves in debt, their best option is not to work more hours for more money, but to reduce their spending on nonessentials and live within their means.

> "We choose to spend more money than we have today. Choose debt, or choose freedom, it's your choice."
>
> —*Bill Pratt*, Extra Credit: The 7 Things Every College Student Needs to Know About Credit, Debt & Cash

 Think About It—Journal Entry 9.5

Are you working while attending college?

If you're working:

a)   How many hours per week do you currently work?

b)   Are you working for things you need or want?

c)   Do you think that working is interfering with your academic performance or progress? Why or why not?

Economize. Intelligent consumers use critical thinking skills when purchasing products. We can be frugal or thrifty without compromising the quality of our purchases. We could pay less to see the same movie in the late afternoon than to see it at night. Why pay more for brand name products that are exactly the same as less expensive products? For instance, why pay 33% more for Advil or Tylenol when we can get the same pain-relieving ingredient (ibuprofen or acetaminophen) from a generic brand? When we buy brand name products, what we're often paying for is all the advertising these brand name companies pay the media and celebrities to promote their products.

> "It is preoccupation with possessions, more than anything else, that prevents us from living freely and nobly."
>
> —*Bertrand Russell, British philosopher and mathematician*

Note

Advertising creates product familiarity, not product quality. The more money manufacturers pay for advertising and creating well-known brands, the more money we pay for their product.

Downsize. Cut down or cut out spending for products you don't need. Avoid conspicuous consumption or exhibitionistic (look-at-me) spending just to keep up with or show off to your friends. Don't allow peer pressure to determine your spending habits; your consumer decisions should reflect your ability to think critically, not your desire to conform socially.

Save money by living with others rather than living alone. You lose some privacy when you share living quarters, but you save a substantial amount of money. Living with others may also bring with it the fringe social benefit of spending time with people (roommates or housemates) with whom you're compatible and whose company you enjoy.

Give gifts of time instead of money. Spending money on gifts for family, friends, and romantic partners isn't the only way to show you care. The point of gift giving isn't to show others you aren't cheap, it's to show you care. You can demonstrate caring by making something special or doing something meaningful for those you care about. Gifts of time and kindness are often more personal and special than store-bought gifts.

Develop your own money-saving strategies and habits. You can save money by doing little things that eventually add up to big savings over time. The following tips for saving money were suggested by students in a first-year seminar class. Some of these strategies may work for you as well.

- Don't carry a lot of extra money in your wallet. (It's just like food; if it's easy to get to, you'll be more likely to eat it up.)
- Shop with a list—get in, get what you need, and get out.
- Put all your extra change in a jar.
- Put extra cash in a piggy bank that requires you to smash the piggy to get at it.
- Seal your savings in an envelope.
- When you get extra money get it immediately into the bank (and out of your hands).
- Bring (don't buy) your lunch.
- Hide your credit card or put it in the freezer so that you don't use it on impulse.
- Use cash (instead of credit cards) because you can set aside a certain amount of it for yourself and you can clearly see how much of it you have at the start of a week (as well as how much is left at any point during the week).

> "If you would be wealthy, think of saving as well as getting."
>
> —Benjamin Franklin, 18th-century inventor, newspaper writer, and cosigner of the Declaration of Independence

> "The safest way to double your money is to fold it over and put it in your pocket."
>
> —Kin Hubbard, American humorist, cartoonist, and journalist

AUTHOR'S EXPERIENCE

When my wife (Mary) and I were first dating, I was trying to gain weight because I was on the thin side. One day when I came home from school, I found this hand-delivered package in front of my apartment door. I opened it up and there was a homemade loaf of whole wheat bread made from scratch by Mary. That gift didn't cost her much money, but she took the time to do it and she remembered to do something that was important to me (gaining weight). That gift really touched me; it's a gift I've never forgotten. Since I eventually married Mary and we're still happily married, I guess you could say that inexpensive loaf of bread was a "gift that kept on giving."

—*Joe Cuseo*

 Think About It—Journal Entry 9.6

Do you use any of the money-saving strategies on the above list? Which one(s)?

What money-saving strategies do you use that could be added to the above list?

When I was a four-year-old boy living in the mountains of Kentucky, it was safe for a young lad to walk the roads and railroad tracks alone. Knowing this, my mother would send me to the general store to buy a variety of small items we needed for our household. Since we had very little money, she was very aware of the fact that we needed to be cautious and spend money only on the basic necessities for survival. I could only purchase items from the general store that my mother strictly ordered me to buy. In the early 1960s, most of these items cost less than a dollar and many times you could buy multiple items for a dollar. At the store's checkout counter there were jars with different kinds of candy or gum. You could buy two pieces for one cent. I didn't think there would be any harm in rewarding myself for completing my shopping errand with two pieces of candy. I could even devour the evidence of my disobedience during my slow walk home. When I returned home from the store, my mother—being the protector of the vault and the sergeant-of-arms in our household—would count each item I bought to make sure I had been charged correctly. My mother never failed to notice if I was even one cent short! She always found that I had either been overcharged by one cent or that I had spent one cent. After she gave me a scolding, she would say: "Boy, you better learn how to count your money if you're ever going to be successful in life." I learned the value of saving money and the danger of overspending at a very young age!

—*Aaron Thompson*

When making purchases, always factor in their total, long-term cost. Short-term thinking leads to poor long-term money management and financial planning. Those small (monthly) installment plans that businesses offer to entice you to buy expensive products may make the cost of those products appear attractive and affordable in the short run. However, when you factor in the interest rates you pay on monthly installment plans, plus the length of time (number of months) you're making installment payments, you get a more accurate picture of the product's total cost in the long run. Taking this long-range perspective can quickly alert you to the reality that a product's sticker price represents its partial and seemingly affordable short-term cost—not its total long-term cost—which is much less affordable and more likely to exceed your budget.

Furthermore, the total long-term cost for purchases sometimes involves additional "hidden costs" that don't relate directly to the product's initial price but must be paid to enable you to continue using the product. For example, the sticker price paid for clothes doesn't include the hidden, long-term costs of having those clothes dry-cleaned. By just taking a moment to check the inside label, you can save yourself this hidden, long-term cost by purchasing clothes that are machine washable. Similarly, deciding to buy a new car instead of a used car brings with it not only the cost of a higher sticker price, but also the higher hidden costs of licensing and insuring the new car (plus any interest fees that must be paid if the new car was purchased on an installment plan). When you add in these hidden, long-term payments to a new car's total cost, buying a good used car is clearly a much more effective money-management strategy.

"Ask yourself how much of your income is being eaten up by car payments. It may be time to admit you made a mistake . . . sell it [and] replace it with an older or less sporty model."

—*Bill Pratt,* Extra Credit: The 7 Things Every College Student Needs to Know About Credit, Debt & Cash

Long-Range Fiscal Planning: Financing Your College Education

Thus far, our discussion has focused primarily on short-range and mid-range financial planning strategies that will keep you out of debt on a monthly or yearly basis. We turn now to issues involving long-term financial planning for your entire college experience. While there's no one "correct" strategy for financing a college education, certain strategies are more effective than others. Studies show that financing a college education by obtaining a student loan and working no more than 15 hours per week is an effective long-range strategy for students at all income levels. Students who use this strategy are more likely to graduate from college, graduate in less time, and graduate with higher grades than full-time college students who work part-time for more than 15 hours per week or students who work full-time and attend college part-time (King, 2002; Perna & DuBois, 2010).

Unfortunately, less than 6% of all first-year students use the college-financing strategy of borrowing money in the form of a student loan, attending college full-time and working part time for 15 or fewer hours per week. Instead, almost 50% of first-year students choose a strategy that research indicates is the least likely to be associated with college success: borrowing nothing and trying to work more than 15 hours per week. Students who use this strategy increase their risk of lowering their grades significantly and withdrawing from college altogether (King, 2005), probably because they can't handle the academic work load required of a full-time student on top of all the hours they're working each week. Working longer hours also increases the likelihood that students switch from full-time and part-time enrollment, which delays their time to graduation and increases their risk of not graduating at all (Tinto, 2012). Thus, a good strategy for balancing learning and earning is to try to limit work for pay to 15 or fewer hours per week.

> "People don't realize how much work it is to stay in college. It's its own job in itself, plus if you've got another job you go to, too. I mean, it's just a lot."
> —*College student (quoted in Engle, Bermeo, & O'Brien, 2006)*

Some students decide to finance their college education by working full-time and attending college part-time. They believe it will be less expensive in the long run to attend college part-time because it will allow them to avoid any debt from student loans. However, studies show that when students use this strategy, it lengthens their time to degree completion and increases the risk that they will never complete a degree (Orszag, Orszag, & Whitmore, 2001).

Students who work more than 15 hours per week not only take longer to graduate from college, they end up losing money in the long run. The hourly pay most part-time jobs students earn while they're in college is less than half than what they'll earn from working in full-time positions as college graduates (King, 2005). Thus, the longer they take to graduate, the longer they must wait to enter higher-paying, full-time positions that a college diploma qualifies them for; this delays their opportunity to "cash in" on the monetary benefits of a college degree.

 Think About It—Journal Entry 9.7

Do you need to work part-time to meet your college expenses?

If you answered "yes" to the above question, are you working more than 15 hours per week?

If you answered "yes" to the above question, can you reduce your work time to 15 or fewer hours per week and still make ends meet?

_____

_____

_____

_____

_____

Furthermore, studies show that two out of three college students have at least one credit card and nearly one-half of students with credit cards carries an average balance of more than $2,000 per month (Nellie Mae, 2005; Sallie Mae 2009). A debt level this high is likely to force many students into working more than 15 hours a week to pay it off. ("I owe, I owe, so off to work I go.") These students often end up taking fewer courses per term so they can work more hours to pay off their credit card debt, which results in their taking longer to graduate and to start earning a college graduate's salary.

Instead of paying almost 20% interest to credit card companies for their monthly debt, these students would be better off obtaining a student loan at a much lower interest rate, which they will start paying back six months after graduation—when they'll be making more money in full-time positions as college graduates. Despite this clear advantage of student loans compared to credit-card loans, only about 25% of college students with credit cards take out student loans (King, 2002).

Note

Student loans are provided by the American government with the intent of helping its citizens become better educated. In contrast, for-profit businesses (such as credit card companies) lend students money with no intent of helping them become better educated, but with the clear intent of helping themselves make money—from the high rates of interest they collect from students who fail to pay off their debt in full at the end of each month.

Keep in mind that not all debt is bad. Debt can be good if it represents an investment in something that will appreciate with time—that is, something that will gain in value and eventually turn into profit for the investor. Purchasing a college education on credit is a good investment because you're investing in yourself and your future, which, over time, will *appreciate*—that is, increase its monetary return in the form of higher salaries and benefits accumulated over the remainder of your life. In contrast, purchasing a new car is a bad long-term investment because it begins to *depreciate* or lose monetary value immediately after it's purchased. The instant you drive that new car off the dealer's lot, you become the proud owner of a used car that's worth much less than what you just paid for it.

You may have heard the expression: "Time is money." One way to interpret this expression is that the more money you spend, the more time you must spend making money. College students who spend more time earning money to cover the costs of material things they want, but don't need, typically spend less time studying, complete fewer classes, and earn lower grades. You can avoid this negative cycle by viewing aca-

> "Unlike a car that depreciates in value each year that you drive it, an investment in education yields monetary, social, and intellectual profit. A car is more tangible in the short term, but an investment in education (even if it means borrowing money) gives you more bang for the buck in the long run."
>
> —Eric Tyson, financial counselor and national best-selling author of Personal Finance for Dummies

demic work as work that "pays" you back in terms of completed courses and higher grades. If you put in more academic time to earn more course credits in less time, you're paid back sooner by graduating sooner and beginning to earn the full-time salary of a college graduate—which will pay you about twice as much per hour than you'll earn doing part-time work without a college degree (plus additional "fringe benefits" like health insurance and paid vacation time). Furthermore, the time you put into earning higher grades in college will earn you more pay in your first full-time position after college because research shows that for students graduating in the same field, those with higher grades earn higher starting salaries (Pascarella & Terenzini, 2005).

> "If a man empties his purse into his head, no one can take it away from him. An investment in knowledge always pays the best interest."
>
> —*Benjamin Franklin, 18th-century scientist, inventor, and a founding father of the United States*

 Think About It—Journal Entry 9.8

In addition to college, what might be other good, long-term investments you could make now or in the near future?

_____

_____

_____

_____

_____

Box 9.3

Financial Literacy: Understanding the Language of Money Management

As you can tell from the number of financial terms used in this chapter, there's an entire language we must master to be *financially literate*. As you read the financial terms listed below, place a checkmark next to any term you didn't know.

Account. A formal business arrangement in which a bank provides financial services to a customer (e.g., checking account or savings account).

Annual Fee. Yearly fee paid to a credit card company to cover the cost of maintaining the cardholder's account.

Annual Percentage Rate (APR). Interest rate that must be paid when monthly credit card balances aren't paid in full.

Balance. Amount of money in a person's account or amount of unpaid debt.

Bounced Check. A check written for a greater amount of money than the amount contained in a personal checking account; it typically requires the person paying a charge to the bank and possibly to the business that attempted to cash the bounced check.

Budget. A plan for balancing income and expenses to ensure that sufficient money is available to cover personal expenses.

Cash Flow. Amount of money flowing in (income) and flowing out (expenses); "negative cash flow" occurs when the amount of money going out exceeds the amount coming in.

Credit. Money obtained with the understanding that it will be paid back.

Credit History. Past record of how timely and completely a credit card holder has paid off credit.

Credit Line (a.k.a. Credit Limit). The maximum amount of money (credit) made available to a borrower.

(continued)

Box 9.3 *(continued)*

Credit Score. Measure used by credit card companies to determine if someone applying for a credit card is "credit worthy," that is, likely to repay. (An applicant with a low credit score may be denied credit.)

Debt. Amount of money owed.

Default. Failure to meet a financial obligation (e.g., a student who fails to repay a college loan "defaults" on that loan).

Emergency Student Loan. Immediate, interest-free loan provided by a college or university to help financially strapped students cover short-term expenses (e.g., cost of textbooks) or deal with financial emergencies (e.g., accidents and illnesses). Emergency student loans are typically granted within 24 to 48 hours, sometimes even the same day, and usually need to be repaid within two months.

Deferred Student Payment Plan. A plan allowing student borrowers to temporarily defer or postpone loan payments for some acceptable reason (e.g., to pursue an internship or do volunteer work after college).

Estimated Family Contribution (EFC). Amount of money the government has determined a family can contribute to the educational costs of a family member attending college.

Fixed Interest Rate. A loan with an interest rate that stays the same for the entire term of the loan.

Free Application for Federal Student Aid (FAFSA). Free application that asks for personal and family financial information to determine a student's eligibility for federal, state, and college-sponsored financial aid, including grants, loans, and work-study employment.

Grace Period. Amount of time a credit card holder has—after a monthly credit card statement has been issued—to pay back the company without paying added interest fees.

Grant. Money received that doesn't have to be repaid.

Gross Income. Income generated before taxes and other expenses are deducted.

Identity Theft. A crime committed by obtaining someone's personal identity information and assumes that person's identity to make financial transactions or purchases.

Insurance Premium. Amount of money paid in regular installments to an insurance company to remain insured.

Interest. Amount of money paid to a customer for deposited money (as in a bank account) or paid by a customer for borrowed money (e.g., interest on a loan). Interest is usually calculated as a percentage of the total amount of money deposited or borrowed.

Interest-Bearing Account. A bank account that earns interest if the customer keeps a minimum amount of money in the bank.

Loan Consolidation. Consolidating (combining) separate student loans into one larger loan to make the process of tracking, budgeting, and repayment easier. Loan consolidation typically requires the borrower to pay slightly more interest.

Loan Premium. The amount of money loaned without interest.

Merit-Based Scholarship. Money awarded to a student on the basis of performance or achievement that doesn't have to be repaid.

Need-Based Scholarship. Money awarded to a student on the basis of financial need that doesn't have to be repaid.

Net Income. Money earned after all expenses and taxes have been paid.

Principal. Total amount of money borrowed or deposited, not counting interest.

Variable Interest Rate. An interest rate on a loan that can vary (up or down) over the term of the loan.

Work Study. Financial assistance that college students earned by working on campus (funded by the federal government).

Yield. Revenue gained beyond amount invested or paid. (For example, revenue gained by college graduates through higher lifetime salaries beyond the amount they paid for a college education.)

Think About It—Journal Entry 9.9

Which of the terms in Box 9.3 were unfamiliar to you?

_____

_____

_____

_____

Which of these unfamiliar terms apply to your current financial decisions or money management plans?

_____

_____

_____

_____

_____

_____

_____

Chapter Summary and Highlights

Similar to time management, if you manage your money effectively and gain control of how you spend it, you gain greater control over the quality of your life. Research shows that accumulating high levels of debt while in college is associated with higher levels of stress, lower academic performance, and greater risk of withdrawing from college. The good news is that research demonstrates that students who learn to use effective money-management strategies are able to reduce unnecessary spending, decrease their risk of debt and stress, and increase the quality of their academic performance.

In this chapter, effective strategies for money management were identified and discussed, such as the following:

- **Financing your college education wisely.** Explore all sources of income for financing your college education, including FAFSA, scholarships, grants, loans, salary earnings, and personal savings.
- **Utilizing your Financial Aid Office.** Check periodically to see if you qualify for additional sources of income, such as part-time employment on campus, low-interest loans, grants, or scholarships.
- **Gaining financial self-awareness.** Become aware of your cash flow—amount of money coming in versus going out.
- **Managing money effectively.** Use available financial tools and instruments to track and maximize cash flow, such as checking accounts, credit cards, or debit cards.
- **Preparing a personal budget.** Keep an accurate account of your money to ensure you have sufficient amount to cover your expenses.

- **Paying your bills when they arrive.** Take care of bills when you first get them to reduce the risk of forgetting to pay them or paying them late.
- **Living within your means.** Don't purchase what you can't afford.
- **Economizing.** Be an intelligent consumer who uses critical thinking skills to evaluate and prioritize purchases.
- **Downsizing.** Don't buy products you don't need and don't allow peer pressure to dictate your spending habits.
- **Working for better grades now and better pay later.** Taking out a student loan and working part-time for 15 or fewer hours per week is the most effective long-range financial and educational strategy for students at all income levels. It improves grades, enables students to earn their degree sooner, and allows them to gain earlier entry to higher-paying jobs that require a college degree.

Learning More through the World Wide Web: Internet-Based Resources

For additional information on fiscal literacy, money management, and financial planning, see the following websites.

Fiscal Literacy & Money Management:
www.360financialliteracy.org

www.cashcourse.org

Financial Aid & Federal Funding Sources for a College Education:
www.students.gov
https://studentloans.gov/myDirectLoan/index.action

Student Loan Management Strategies:
https://firsttechfed.studentchoice.org/.../managing.../student-loan-repayment strategies

Spending Habits & Consumer Self-Awareness:
beyondthepurchase.org

References

Astin, A. W. (1993). *What matters in college?* San Francisco: Jossey-Bass.

Cermak, K., & Filkins, J. (2004). *On-campus employment as a factor of student retention and graduation.* DePaul University. Retrieved from http://oipr.depaul.edu/open/gradereten/oce.asp

Cude, B. J., Lawrence, F.C., Lyons, A.C., Metzger, K., LeJeune, E., Marks, L., & Machtmes, K. 2006. College students and financial literacy: What they know and what we need to learn. *Proceedings of the Eastern Family Economics and Resource Management Association Conference* (pp. 102–109).

Dittmar, H. 2004. Understanding and diagnosing compulsive buying. In R. Coombs (Ed.), *Handbook of addictive disorders: A practical guide to diagnosis and treatment* (pp. 411–450). New York, NY: Wiley.

Engle, J. Bermeo, A., & O'Brien, C. (2006). *Straight from the source: What works for first-generation college students.* Washington, DC: The Pell Institute for the Study of Opportunity in Higher Education.

Furnham, A., & Argyle, M. (1998). *The psychology of money.* New York: Routledge.

Goldstein, W. M., & Hogarth, R. M. (Eds.) 1997. *Research on judgment and decision making,* Cambridge, UK: Cambridge University Press.

Gordon, L. (2009, Oct. 21). College costs up in hard times. *Los Angeles Times,* p. A13.

Hamilton, H. 2012. Student loan blues. *Los Angeles Times,* pp. B1, B8.

Health, C., & Soll, J. (1996). Mental budgeting and consumer decisions. *Journal of Consumer Research, 23,* 40–52.

Kidwell, B., & Turrisi, R. (2004). An examination of college student money management tendencies. *Journal of Economic Psychology, 25*(5), 601–616.

King, J. E. (2002). *Crucial choices: How students' financial decisions affect their academic success.* Washington, DC: American Council on Education.

King, J. E. (2005). Academic success and financial decisions: Helping students make crucial choices. In R. S. Feldman

(Ed.), *Improving the first year of college: Research and practice* (pp. 3–26). Mahwah, NJ: Lawrence Erlbaum.

Kingkade, T. (2014, August 27). "Sleepy college students are worried about their stress levels." *The Huffington Post*. Retrieved from http://www.huffingtonpost.com/2014/08/27/college-students-sleep-stress_n_5723438.html.

Knox, S. (2004). *Financial basics: A money management guide for students*. Columbus: Ohio State University Press.

Kristof, K. M., 2008. Hooked on debt: Students learn too late the costs of private loans. *Los Angeles Times*, pp. A1, A18-19.

Leonard, G. (2008). *A study on the effects of student employment on retention*. Retrieved from uc.iupui.edu/Portals/155/uploadedFiles/.../StudEmpRetentionRprt.pdf

Levine, A., & Cureton, J. S. (1998). *When hopes and fears collide*. San Francisco: Jossey-Bass.

Lowenstein, G., Read, D., & Baumeister, R. G. (Eds.) (2003). *Time and decision: Economic and psychological perspectives on intertemporal choice*. New York: Russell Sage Foundation.

Nellie Mae (2005). *Undergraduate students and credit cards in 2004: An analysis of usage rates and trend*. Wilkes-Barre, PA: Nellie Mae.

Nelson, M. C., Lust, K., Story, M., & Ehlinger, E. (2008). Credit card debt, stress and key health risk behaviors among college students. *American Journal of Health Promotion, 22*(6), 400–407.

Niederjohn, M.S. 2008. First-year experience course improves students' financial literacy. *ESource for College Transitions* [Electronic newsletter published by the National Resource Center for the First-Year Experiencee and Students in Transition], 6(1), 9–11.

Orszag, J. M., Orszag, P. R., & Whitmore, D. M. (2001). *Learning and earning: Working in college*. Retrieved from

http://www.brockport.edu/career01/upromise.htm.

Pascarella, E., & Terenzini, P. (1991). *How college affects students: Findings and insights from twenty years of research*. San Francisco: Jossey-Bass.

Pascarella, E., & Terenzini, P. (2005). *How college affects students: A third decade of research* (Vol. 2). San Francisco: Jossey-Bass.

Perna, L. W., & DuBois, G. (Eds.). (2010). *Understanding the working college student: New research and its implications for policy and practice*. Sterling, VA: Stylus.

Pratt, B. 2008. *Extra credit: The 7 things every college student needs to know about credit, debt, & cash*. Keedysville, MD: ExtraCreditBook.com.

Pratt, B. (2011). *Extra credit: The 7 things every college student needs to know about credit, debt & cash* (2nd ed.). Winterville, NC: Financial Relevancy.

Ring, T. (1997, October). Issuers face a visit to the dean's office. *Credit Card Management, 10*, 34–39.

Sallie Mae (2009, April). *How undergraduate students use credit cards: Sallie Mae's national study of usage rates and trends 2009*. Retrieved from http://static.mgnetwork.com/rtd/pdfs/20090830_iris.pdf.

Susswein, R. (1995). College students and credit cards: A privilege earned? *Credit World, 83*, 21–23.

Tinto, V. (1993). *Leaving college: Rethinking the causes and cures of student attrition* (2nd ed.). Chicago: University of Chicago Press.

Tinto, V. 2012. *Completing College: Rethinking Institutional Action*. University of Chicago Press, Chicago, IL.

Tyson, E. (2012). *Personal finance for dummies* (7th ed.). Hoboken, NJ: John Wiley & Sons. Walker, C. M. (1996). Financial management, coping, and debt in households under financial strain. *Journal of Economic Psychology, 17*,789–807.

Chapter 9 Exercises

9.1 Quote Reflections

Review the sidebar quotes contained in this chapter and select two that were especially meaningful or inspirational to you.

For each quote, provide a three- to five-sentence explanation why you chose it.

9.2 Reality Bite

Problems Paying for College

A college student posted the following message on the Internet:

"I went to college for one semester, failed some of my classes, and ended with $900 in student loans. Now I can't even get financial aid or a loan because of some stupid thing that says if you fail a certain amount of classes you can't get aid or a loan. And now since I couldn't go to college this semester they want me to pay for my loans already, and I don't even have a job."

Any suggestions?

Reflection and Discussion Questions

1. What suggestions do you have for this student? What should the student do immediately? Eventually?

2. What should the student have done to prevent this from happening in the first place?

3. Do you know of any students who are in a similar predicament or soon could be?

9.3 Self-Assessment of Financial Attitudes and Habits

Answer the following questions about yourself as accurately and honestly as possible.

	Agree	Disagree
1. I pay my rent or mortgage on time each month.	_____	_____
2. I avoid maxing out or going over the limit on my credit cards.	_____	_____
3. I balance my checkbook each month.	_____	_____
4. I set aside money each month for savings.	_____	_____
5. I pay my phone and utility bills on time each month.	_____	_____
6. I pay my credit card bills in full each month to avoid interest charges.	_____	_____
7. I believe it's important to buy the things I want when I want them.	_____	_____
8. Borrowing money to pay for college is a smart thing to do.	_____	_____
9. I have a monthly or weekly budget that I follow faithfully.	_____	_____
10. The thing I enjoy most about making money is spending money.	_____	_____
11. I limit myself to one credit card.	_____	_____
12. Getting a degree will get me a good job and a good income.	_____	_____

Sources: Cude, et al. (2006), Niederjohn (2008).

Give yourself one point for each item that you marked "agree"—except for items 7, 9, and 10. For these items, give yourself a point if you marked "disagree."

A perfect score on this short survey would be 12.

Reflection Questions:

1. What was your total score?

2. Which items lowered your score?

3. Do you detect any pattern across the items that lowered your score?

4. Do you see any realistic way(s) to improve your score on this test?

9.4 Financial Self-Awareness: Monitoring Money & Tracking Cash Flow

Step 1. Use the "Financial Self-Awareness" worksheet on the next page to *estimate* your income and expenses per month, and enter them in column 2.

Step 2. *Track* your actual income and expenses for a month and enter them in column 3. (To help you do this accurately, keep a file of your cash receipts, bills paid, and credit card or checking account records for the month.)

Step 3. After one month of tracking your cash flow, answer the following questions.

a. Were your estimates generally accurate?

b. On what items were there the largest discrepancies between your estimated cost and their actual cost?

c. Comparing your bottom-line total for income and expenses, are you satisfied with how your monthly cash flow is going?

d. What changes could you make to create more positive cash flow—that is, to increase your income or savings and reduce your expenses or debt?

e. How likely is it that you'll make the changes you mentioned in the previous question?

Financial Self-Awareness Worksheet

Financial Self-Awareness Worksheet

	Estimate	Actual
Income Sources		
Parents/Family		
Work/Job		
Grants/Scholarships		
Loans		
Savings		
Other:		
TOTAL INCOME		
Essentials (Fixed Expenses)		
Living Expenses: Food/Groceries		
Rent/Room & Board		
Utilities (gas/electric)		
Essentials (Fixed Expenses) *(continued)*		
Living Expenses (continued): Clothing		
Laundry/Dry Cleaning		
Phone		
Computer		
Household Items (dishes, etc.)		
Medical Insurance Expenses		
Debt Payments (loans/credit cards)		
Other:		

	Estimate	Actual
School Expenses:		
Tuition		
Books		
Supplies (print cartridges, etc.)		
Special Fees (lab fees, etc.)		
Other:		
Transportation:		
Public Transportation (bus fees, etc.)		
Car Insurance		
Car Maintenance		
Fuel (gas)		
Car Payments		
Other:		
Incidentals (*Variable* Expenses)		
Entertainment:		
Movies/Concerts		
DVDs/CDs		
Restaurants (eating out)		
Other:		
Personal Appearance/Accessories:		
Hairstyling/Coloring		
Cosmetics/Manicures		
Fashionable Clothes		
Jewelry		
Other:		
Hobbies:		
Travel (trips home, vacations)		
Gifts		
Other:		
TOTAL EXPENSES		

9.5 Chapter 9 Reflection

How are you financing your college education? Do you feel this is the best way for you to pay for college? Why or why not?

Do you feel you have good or poor money management skills? Explain.

List and describe at leave five principles discussed in this chapter that you can use to better manage your money.

1.

2.

3.

4.

5.

Now explain HOW you can put these principles into practice.

CHAPTER 10

Social and Emotional Intelligence

RELATING TO OTHERS AND REGULATING EMOTIONS

This chapter identifies effective strategies for communicating with and relating to others, as well as ways to understand and regulate our emotions—such as stress, anxiety, anger, and depression. Implementing the recommended strategies should improve the quality of your performance in college and your career, as well as enhance your overall quality of life.

Chapter Preview

Strengthen social intelligence through use of effective interpersonal communication and human relations skills, and enhance emotional intelligence by effectively recognizing one's own emotions and the emotions of others.

Learning Goal

 Think About It—Journal Entry 10.1

Thought Starter

When you think about someone being "intelligent," what personal characteristics come to mind?

"
The most important single ingredient in the formula of success is knowing how to get along with people."

—*Theodore (Teddy) Roosevelt, 26th president of the United States and winner of the Nobel Peace Prize*

If your answer to the preceding question focused on "intellectual" characteristics, your response reflected the traditional definition of intelligence. Human intelligence was once considered to be a general intellectual trait that could be measured by a single intelligence test score. Scholars have since discovered that the singular word "intelligence" needs to be replaced with the plural "intelligences" to reflect the fact that humans can and do display intelligence in many forms other than that measured by an IQ test. One of these other forms of human intelligence is referred to as *social intelligence* (a.k.a. "interpersonal intelligence"); it refers to the ability to communicate and relate effectively to others (Gardner, 1993, 1999; Goleman, 2006). It's been long known than interpersonal skills are essential for effective leadership (Avolio, Walumbwa, & Weber, 2009), and more recent research indicates

265

that social intelligence is a better predictor of personal and professional success than intellectual ability (Carneiro, Crawford, & Goodman, 2006; Goleman, 2006).

Another newly identified form of human intelligence is *emotional intelligence*—the ability to recognize our own emotions and the emotions of others, and behave in ways that have a positive impact on how others feel (Matthews, Zeidner, & Roberts, 2007; Salovey & Mayer, 1990). Research on emotional intelligence also reveals that it's a better predictor of personal and occupational success than performance on intellectual tests (Goleman, 1995, 2000). Research also shows that emotional self-awareness—a key element of emotional intelligence—is a characteristic of effective leaders (Avolio & Luthans, 2006; Goleman, Boyatzis, & McKee, 2013).

The Importance of Social Relationships and Social Intelligence

Studies show that people with stronger social support networks are happier (Myers, 1993, 2000) and live a longer life (Giles, et al., 2005). The need to develop strong social support networks is particularly important in today's high-tech world of virtual reality and online (vs. in-person) communication, both of which make it easier to avoid face-to-face interaction with other people and increase the risk of social isolation and loneliness (Putman, 2000).

 Think About It—Journal Entry 10.2

Who are the people in your life that you tend to turn to for social support when you're experiencing stress or need personal encouragement?

_____

_____

_____

_____

The quality of our social relationships rests heavily on two key skills:

- *interpersonal communication* skills—how well we communicate (verbally and nonverbally) when interacting with others, and
- *human relations* skills—how well we relate to and treat others (i.e., people skills).

Interpersonal Communication Skills

Listed below are strategies for strengthening interpersonal communication skills. Some of these strategies may seem very simple or obvious, but they are powerful. Perhaps it's because they're so simple that people simply overlook look them and forget to use them consistently. Don't be fooled by the seeming simplicity of the following suggestions and don't underestimate the positive impact they have on the quality of your interpersonal interactions and relationships.

1. **Take *listening seriously*.** When people hear the term "communication skills," the skills of speaking and writing usually come to mind. However, the root of the word "communicate" is *communicare, meaning* "to share or divide out," which suggests that communication is a two-way process that involves skills not only for delivering information, but receiving it as well. In fact, studies show that listening is the most frequently used communication skill; we spend more time listening than speaking, reading, and writing (Purdy & Borisoff, 1996). One study found that college students spend an average of 52.5% of each day listening (Barker & Watson, 2000). When people are asked to identify what they like most about their best friend, "a good listener" ranks among the top characteristics cited (Berndt, 1992). Effective listening skills is also a top-ranking characteristic of effective leaders (Johnson & Bechler, 1998), and it ranks among the top skills employers look for when hiring and promoting employees (Maes, Weldy, & Icenogle, 1997; Winsor, Curtis, & Stephens, 1997; Wolvin, 2010).

2. **Use *active* listening strategies.** We can listen to and understand spoken words at a rate four or more times faster than the average rate at which people speak (Barker & Watson, 2000). This leaves plenty of time for our attention to drift and fall into the trap of *passive listening*—hearing the words with our ears, but not thinking about those words with our mind because our mind is somewhere else. To combat this tendency, we need to engage in *active listening*, which involves: (a) making an effortful attempt to focus full attention on the speaker's message (as opposed to just waiting for our turn to talk or thinking about what we're going to say next); (b) being an empathic listener who attends to the speaker's feelings and nonverbal messages; and (c) being an engaged listener who checks for understanding, expresses interest, and encourages elaboration.

> "We have been given two ears and but a single mouth in order that we may hear more and talk less."
> —*Zeno of Citium, Ancient Greek philosopher and founder of Stoic philosophy*

Note

When you listen actively and closely to others, it sends them the message that you respect them and their thoughts and feelings are worthy of receiving your undivided attention.

Active listening doesn't happen naturally; it's a skill developed through effort and practice that eventually becomes a regular habit. To develop the habit of active listening, engage in the following practices:

* While listening, monitor your understanding of what's being said. Good listeners take personal responsibility for following the speaker's message; in contrast, poor listeners put all the responsibility on the speaker to make the message clear and interesting. One way to check if you've followed the message, is to occasionally summarize or paraphrase what you heard the speaker saying in your own words (e.g., "What I hear you saying is . . ."). This not only ensures you understand the message, it also sends the speaker the message that you're really listening to what's being said and taking it seriously.
* Check to be sure you're understanding what the person is *feeling* in addition to what the person is saying (e.g., I'm sensing that you're feeling . . ."). Be sensitive to nonverbal messages, such as tone of voice and body language; they can often provide clues to the feelings behind the speaker's words. (For instance, speaking at a high rate and with high volume may indicate frustration or anger and speaking at a low rate and with low volume may indicate dejection or depression.)
* When you ask questions, allow the speaker time to formulate a thoughtful response. Be patient with some period of silence. If the silence continues, rephrase the question in a different way.

- Avoid the urge to interrupt the speaker when you think you have something important to say. Wait until the speaker has paused or completed her train of thought.
- If the speaker pauses and you start to say something at the same time the speaker begins to speak again, don't overpower him by speaking louder; let him continue before you express your ideas.
- Be sure your nonverbal messages send the speaker the message that you're interested and non-judgmental. (For positive, nonverbal communication signals to send while listening, see **Box 10.1.**)

Box 10.1

Nonverbal Behaviors Associated with Active Listening

It's estimated that more than two-thirds of all human communication is nonverbal, and it's been found that nonverbal messages communicate stronger and truer messages than spoken language (Driver, 2010; Navarro, 2008). When there's inconsistency between an individual's verbal and nonverbal message (e.g., one shows interest, the other disinterest), we're more likely to perceive the nonverbal message as the true message (Ekman, 2009). Thus, "body language" may be the most powerful way a listener can communicate genuine interest in the speaker's message, as well as interest in and respect for the speaker. (Similarly, when we're speaking, awareness of our listeners' body language can provide us with important clues about whether we're holding or losing their interest.)

The most important thing in communication is to hear what isn't being said."

—*Peter F. Drucker, Austrian author and founder of the study of "management"*

Good listeners listen with their whole body and they use body language to signal their attention and interest. The different body language signals we should send while listening may be summarized in the acronym SOFTEN:

S = Smile. Smiling sends signals of acceptance and interest. However, smiling should be periodic, not continuous. (A sustained smile can come across as an insincere or artificial pose.)

Sit Still. Fidgeting or squirming sends the message that you're bored or growing inpatient (and can't wait to move onto something else).

O = Open Posture. Avoid closed-posture positions, such as crossing your arms or folding your hands; they can send the message that you're not open to what the speaker is saying or passing judgment on what's being said.

F = Forward Lean. Leaning *forward* sends the message that you're looking forward to what the speaker is going to say next. In contrast, leaning back can send a signal that you're backing off from (losing interest in) what's being said, or that you're evaluating (psychoanalyzing).

Face the Speaker Directly. Line up your shoulders with the speaker's shoulders rather than turning one shoulder away—which sends the message that you want to get away or are giving the speaker the "cold shoulder."

T = Touch. An occasional light touch on the arm or hand can be a good way to communicate warmth—but not repeated touching, stroking, or rubbing—which could be interpreted as inappropriate intimacy (or sexual harassment).

E = Eye Contact. Lack of eye contact sends the message that you're looking around for something more interesting or stimulating than the speaker. However, eye contact shouldn't be continuous because that borders on staring or glaring. Instead, strike a happy medium by making *periodic* eye contact.

N = Nod Your Head. Nodding slowly and periodically while listening sends the signal that you're following what's being said and affirming the person saying it. However, avoid rapid and repeated head nodding; this sends the message that you want the speaker to hurry up and finish up so you can start talking!

Sources: Barker & Watson (2000); Nichols (2009); Purdy & Borisoff (1996)

⊜ Think About It—Journal Entry 10.3

Are there any effective nonverbal listening messages cited in **Box 10.1** that you weren't already aware of, or that you need to work on? What are they? Why do you need to work on them?

_____

_____

_____

_____

_____

_____

An interesting exercise you can use to gain greater awareness of your nonverbal communication habits is to choose a couple of people whom you trust, and who know you well, and ask them to imitate your body language. This exercise can frequently be revealing (and sometimes very entertaining).

3. **Be open to listening to different conversational topics and viewpoints.** Don't be a close-minded or selective listener who listens to others like you're listening to a radio—selecting or tuning into only those stations that immediately capture your own interests or reinforce your opinions—while tuning out or turning off everything else. This is an issue of social etiquette and social ethics. It's also a learning issue because we learn the most from others whose interests and viewpoints don't duplicate our own. Thus, ignoring or blocking out information and ideas about topics that don't immediately interest you or support your particular perspective is not only a poor social skill; it's also a poor learning strategy.

When others express ideas you don't agree with, you still owe them the courtesy of listening to what they have to say (and not immediately shaking your head, frowning, or interrupting them). After others finish expressing their point of view, you should then feel free to express your own. You certainly have the right to express your viewpoints, as long as you don't express them in such an opinionated way that it makes others feel their views weren't heard or welcomed.

⊜ Think About It—Journal Entry 10.4

On what topics do you hold strong opinions?

_____

_____

_____

_____

When you express these opinions, how do others usually react to you?

_____

_____

_____

_____

> "Be sincere; be brief; be seated."
>
> —*Franklin D. Roosevelt, 32nd president of the United States*

> "It does not require many words to speak the truth."
>
> —*Chief Joseph, leader of the Nez Percé, Native American Indian tribe*

> "To talk without thinking is to shoot without aiming."
>
> —*An English proverb*

> "I have never been hurt by anything I didn't say."
>
> —*Calvin Coolidge, 30th U.S. president*

4. **Communicate your ideas precisely and concisely.** When we speak, our goal should be to get to our point, make it, get "off stage," and give someone else a chance to talk. Nobody appreciates "stage hogs" who dominate the conversation and gobble up more than their fair share of conversation time.

    You can make your spoken messages less time-consuming and more to the point by avoiding tangents, unnecessary details, and empty fillers (e.g., "like," "kinda like," "I mean," "I'm all," and "you know"). Fillers such as these just "fill up" time and waste conversation time while adding nothing substantial or meaningful to the conversation. Excessive use of fillers can also result in listeners losing patience, interest, and respect for the speaker (Daniels & Horowitz, 1997).

5. **Take time to gather your thoughts before expressing them.** It's better to think silently *before* speaking aloud than to think aloud *while* talking. Giving forethought to what you're going to say will enable you to speak economically and open up more time for others to speak.

6. **Be comfortable with silent spells that may take place during conversations.** Silence can sometimes make us feel uncomfortable (like being in an elevator with a stranger). To relieve the discomfort of silence, it's tempting to rush in and say anything to get the conversation going again. Although this may be well intended, it can result in speaking before (and without) thinking. Probably more often than not, it's better to hold back our words and think them through before blurting them out.

Silent spots in a conversation shouldn't always be viewed as a "communication breakdown." Instead, they may indicate that the people involved in the conversation are pausing to think deeply about what each other is saying and are comfortable enough with each other to allow these reflective pauses to take place.

Think About It—Journal Entry 10.5

Would you say that you're a good conversationalist?

_____

If yes, what makes you so?

_____

_____

_____

If no, what prevents you from being one?

_____

_____

_____

_____

Human Relations Skills (a.k.a. "People Skills")

In addition to communicating well with others, another key component of social intelligence is *human relations* skills—how well we relate to and treat others. Listed below are specific strategies for strengthening human relations skills.

Learn and remember the *names* of people you meet. When you refer to a person by name, you affirm that person's individuality and unique identity. You've likely heard people say they just don't have a good memory for names, which implies that they will never be good at remembering names. However, the truth is that the ability to remember names is not some kind of natural talent or inherited ability that you either have or don't have. Instead, it's an acquired skill that's developed through intentional effort and effective use of memory improvement strategies, such as those described below.

* Pay close attention to the names of people you meet when you first meet them. The key first step to remembering someone's name is to actually hear it and get it into our brain in the first place. As obvious as this may seem, when we first meet someone, instead of listening actively and carefully for their name, we're often more focused on the first impression we're making on the person, or what we're going to say next. Consequently, when we *forget* someone's name, what really happened is that we didn't *get* the name (into our brain) in the first place because we were distracted by other thoughts.
* Strengthen your memory for the person's name by saying it soon after you first hear it. For instance, if your friend Gertrude has just introduced you to Geraldine, you might say: "Geraldine, how long have you known Gertrude?" When you recall a person's name shortly after you've heard it, you prevent memory loss at the time when it's most likely to occur—during the first minutes after information is taken into the brain. Using the person's name soon after you've heard it also serves to make that person feel welcomed and validated.
* Associate the person's name with other information you've learned or know about the person. For instance, you can associate the person's name with (a) your first topic of conversation, (b) some physical characteristic of the person, or (c) the place where you met. By making a mental connection between the person's name and another piece of information, you capitalize on the brain's natural tendency to store (retain) information as part of an interconnected network, rather than as isolated bits of information.
* Keep a name journal that includes the names of new people you meet, along with information about them (e.g., what they do and what their interests are). We write down things we don't want to forget to do, so why not do the same for

> "We should be aware of the magic contained in a name. The name sets that individual apart; it makes him or her unique among all others. Remember that a person's name is to that person the sweetest and most important sound in any language."
>
> *—Dale Carnegie, author of the best-selling book,* How to Win Friends and Influence People, *and founder of* The Dale Carnegie Course—a worldwide leadership training program for business professionals

> "When I joined the bank, I started keeping a record of the people I met and put them on little cards, and I would indicate on the cards when I met them, and under what circumstances, and sometimes [make] a little notation which would help me remember a conversation."
>
> —*David Rockefeller, prominent American banker, philanthropist, and former CEO of the Chase Manhattan Bank*

the names of people we want to remember? Whenever you meet someone new, make note of that person's name by recording it in a name journal and accompany it with a short note of where you met and what you talked about.

Note

Remembering names is not only a social skill that can bring you friends and improve your social life, it's also a powerful professional tool that can promote your career success in whatever field you choose to pursue.

Refer to people by name when you greet and interact with them. Once you've learned a person's name, use it when you interact with the person. Saying, "Hi, Waldo" will mean a lot more to Waldo than simply saying "Hi" or the impersonal "Hi, there"—which sounds like you've just seen an unidentifiable entity "out there" in public space—similar to addressing a letter "to whom it may concern." By continuing to use people's names after you've learned them, you send the message you haven't forgotten who they are, and at the same time, you strengthen your memory of their names.

Remember information others share with you and refer to it when you interact with them. Ask people questions about their personal interests, plans, and experiences. Listen closely to their answers, especially to what seems most important to them, what they care about, or what interests them, and use this information in your future conversations with them. For one person that topic may be politics, for another it may be sports, for another it may be relationships.

When you see the person again, bring up something that was discussed in your last conversation. Get beyond the stock, generic questions that people routinely ask after they say "Hello" (e.g., "What's up? What's going on?"). Instead, ask about something specific you discussed with them last time you spoke (e.g., "How did you do on that math test last week?"). Our memories often reflect our priorities—we remember what's important to us. When you remember what others share with you, it shows them they're important to you.

Furthermore, when you show interest in others, you'll find that others start showing more interest in you. You're also likely to hear others say that you're a good listener and a great conversationalist.

Strategies for Meeting People and Forming Friendships

> "You can make more friends in 2 months by becoming interested in other people than you can in 2 years by trying to get other people interested in you."
>
> —*Dale Carnegie,* How to Win Friends and Influence People

An important aspect of the college experience is meeting new people, learning from them, and forming lifelong friendships. Listed below are practical strategies for increasing the number and variety of people you meet and the quality of friendships you form.

1. **Place yourself in situations and locations where you will come in regular contact with others.** Social psychologists have found that physical proximity is the first step in the process of forming friendships—that is, people are more likely to become friends if they continue to find themselves in the same place at the same time (Latané, et al., 1995). You can apply this principle by spending as much time on campus as possible and spending time in places where others are likely to be present (e.g., by eating your meals in the student cafeteria and studying in the college library). If you have the opportunity to live on campus, do so, because studies show that it helps students make social connections and increases their satisfaction with the college experience (Pascarella & Terenzini, 2005; Tinto, 2012). If you're a commuter student, make your college experi-

ence as similar as possible to that of a residential student. When your schedule permits, spend time on campus doing things other than attending class (e.g., study in the library and participate in campus events).

For more information about iMPACT, events on campus and how to get involved, go to www.nicc.edu/studentlife

Think About It—Journal Entry 10.6

Have you attended any events on campus?

If yes, what were they like?

If no, why haven't you?

2. **Put yourself in social situations where you're likely to meet people who share your interests, goals, and values.** Research supports the proverb: "Birds of a feather flock together." People tend to form friendships with others who share similar interests, values, or goals (AhYun, 2002). Friendships are more likely to form among people who have interests and values in common because they're more likely to spend time together doing things relating to their shared interests, and because they're more likely to validate each other's shared values (Festinger, 1954; Suls, Martin, & Wheeler, 2002).

One straightforward way to find others with whom you have something in common is by participating in campus clubs and organizations that reflect your interests and values. (If you can't find one, start one of your own.) Also, keep track of social events that are likely to attract others who share your interests, values, or goals by regularly checking your college newspaper, posted flyers on campus, and the Student Information Desk in your Student Activities Center. However as you know, meeting new people and "fitting in" doesn't mean blind conformity, caving into peer pressure, or doing things that conflict with your values and compromise your integrity.

"Open your arms to change, but don't let go of your values."
—*Dalai Lama, the current Dalai Lama, Tibetan Buddhist guru*

"I'm genuine. I don't change depending on who I'm around."
—*College sophomore*

Think About It—Journal Entry 10.7

Since you've begun college, have you experienced any "peer pressure" (good or bad)?

What was the situation?

How did you respond?

It's hard enough to have fun here with all the work you have to do. There's no reason to have the extra drama [of dating] in your life."

—College sophomore

Now all a guy has to do to hookup on a Saturday night is to sit on the couch long enough at a party. Eventually a girl will plop herself down beside him . . . he'll make a joke, she'll laugh, their eyes will meet, sparks will fly, and the mission is accomplished. And you want me to tell this guy to call a girl, spend $100 on dinner and hope for a goodnight kiss."

—College student

3. **Meet others through social websites.** Facebook and other social websites represent an additional way to meet new people, join groups on campus, and check for announcements of parties or other social events. However, the people you respond to, the screen name you use and the messages you post on your page or "wall." Don't forget that cyberspace is public space and it can be accessed by people beyond your social circle. For instance, some schools and employers review social networking sites (e.g., Facebook and Twitter) to check entries; they use the information they find to help them screen prospects and accept or reject applicants (Palank, 2006; Sinsky, 2011).

Dating and Romantic Relationships

Traditionally, romantic relationships begin through the process of dating. College students take different approaches to dating, ranging from not dating at all to dating with the intent of exploring or cementing long-term relationships. These different dating approaches are summarized in **Box 10.2**.

Box 10.2

Approaches to Dating

Postpone dating. Students who adopt this approach feel that the demands of college work and college life are too time-consuming to take on the additional social and emotional burden of dating while in college.

Student

Perspectives

"Relationships take time and patience, and in college, both of these can be very limited."
—*College student quoted in Kucewicz (2001)*

"It's hard enough to have fun here with all the work you have to do. There's no reason to have the extra drama [of dating] in your life."
—*College sophomore quoted in Sax (2003)*

Hooking up. Students who prefer this approach believe that formal dating is unnecessary; they feel that their social and sexual needs are better met more casually by associating with friends and acquaintances. Instead of going out on a one-on-one date, they prefer to fi rst meet and connect with romantic partners in larger group settings, such as college parties.

Casual dating. Students taking this approach go out on dates primarily for the purpose of enjoying themselves, but not getting "tied down" to any particular person. These "casual daters" prefer to go out on a series of successive dates with different partners, and they may date different individuals at the same time. Their primary goal is to meet new people and discover what characteristics they find attractive in others.

> "Now all a guy has to do to hookup on a Saturday night is to sit on the couch long enough at a party. Eventually a girl will plop herself down beside him . . . he'll make a joke, she'll laugh, their eyes will meet, sparks will fly, and the mission is accomplished. And you want me to tell this guy to call a girl, spend $100 on dinner and hope for a goodnight kiss."
>
> —*College student quoted in Beckett (2003)*

Exclusive dating. Students adopting this approach prefer to date only one person for an extended period of time. Although marriage is not the goal, exclusive dating takes casual dating one step further. This form of dating may help the partners develop a clearer idea of what characteristics they may seek in an ideal spouse or long-term mate.

Courtship. This form of dating is intended to continue the relationship until it cul-minates in marriage or a formal, long-term commitment.

Source: Adapted from research reviewed by Seirup (2004).

Think About It—Journal Entry 10.8

How would you define *love*? Would you say it's a feeling? An action? Both?

What do you think are the best signs that two people are "in love"?

What would you say are the most common reasons why people "fall out of love"?

_____

_____

_____

_____

Romantic Relationships

Dating relationships may eventually evolve into romantic relationships. Research on romantic relationships reveals they typically progress through the following stages (Bassham, et al., 2013; Ruggiero, 2011).

Stage 1. Passionate Love (Infatuation)

This is the very first stage of a romantic relationship, and it's characterized by the following features.

Happy Valentine's Day
I Love You
with All My Brain!

Despite expressions like "I love you with all my heart," romantic love takes place in the human brain and is accompanied by major changes in the production of brain chemicals.

- *Erotic* love: relationship involves intense physical arousal and passion; attention is focused primarily on the partner's physical appearance and physical attraction between the partners is at a peak.
- *Impulsivity*: partners can quickly "fall into" love or be suddenly "swept off their feet" (e.g., "love at first sight").
- *Obsession*: partners can't stop thinking about each other (they're "madly in love").
- *Intense emotions*: a surge of chemicals are released in the body and brain (similar to a drug-induced state), namely:
  1. a rush of adrenalin—a bodily hormone that triggers faster heart rate and breathing;
  2. increased production of dopamine—a brain chemical that triggers feelings of excitement, euphoria, joy, and general well being (Bartels & Zeki, 2000).
- *Idealism*: The partners perceive each other and the relationship as being "perfect." They may say things like: "We're made for each other." "Nobody else has a relationship like ours." "We'll be together forever." Such idealistic thinking can make love "blind"—the partner's flaws and weaknesses are not seen (although they may be obvious to those outside of the relationship). One or both of the partners may be in relationship *denial*, whereby problems that threaten the security of the relationship are simply denied (pushed out of conscious awareness).
- *Attachment and Dependency*: The lovers feel insecure without each other and can't bear being separated (e.g., "I can't live without him"). As a result of such attachment and dependency, love at this stage follows the principle: "I love you because I am loved" and "I love you because I need you." It's hard to determine if the person is in love with the other person or is in love with the idea or feeling of being in love (Fromm, 1970).
- *Possessiveness and Jealousy*: Each lover feels that he or she has exclusive rights to the partner and may quickly become suspicious about the partner's fidelity, as well as jealous of anyone else who interacts with the partner in a friendly or affectionate manner. This possessiveness can be unjustified and irrational ("insane jealousy"), whereby the lover suspects the partner is "cheating" when there's no real evidence that any cheating is taking place.

- *Love Sickness*: If the relationship breaks up, intense depression or "love withdrawal" tends to follow the breakup, similar to withdrawal from a pleasure-producing drug. Studies show that the most common cause of despair or depression among college students is a romantic breakup (Foreman, 2009).

Stage 2. Mature Love

The partners gradually "fall out" of first-stage (puppy) love and progress or "fall into" a more mature (advanced) stage of love that has the following characteristics.

- The partners become less selfish and self-centered and more selfless and other-centered. Love is no longer just a noun—an emotion or feeling within the person (e.g., "I'm in love"), but also an action verb—a way in which the partners act toward each other and treat one another (e.g., "we love each other"). More emphasis is placed on caring for the partner, rather than being cared for. This mature stage of love follows two principles:
    1. "I am loved because I love"—not, "I'm in love because I am loved" and
    2. "I need you because I love you"—not, "I love you because I need you" (Fromme, 1980).
- There's less of an emotional high experienced at this stage than early stages of the relationship. After the passage of time and experience with the partner, the original "mad rush" of hormones and euphoria-producing brain chemicals gradually levels off—similar to how the effects of a drug level off after it's been taken for an extended period of time (Fisher, 2004; Peele & Brodsky, 1991). The intense emotional "ups and downs" of early stage love are now replaced by feelings of emotional serenity (mellowness) and evenness—a less extreme, but more consistently pleasant emotional state characterized by slightly elevated levels of different brain chemicals (endorphins, rather than dopamine). Unlike infatuation or early-stage love, this pleasant emotional state does not decline with time; in fact, it may actually grow stronger as the relationship continues and matures (Bartels & Zeki, 2000).
- Physical passion decreases. The "flames of the flesh" don't burn as intensely as in first-stage love, but a romantic afterglow continues. This afterglow is characterized by more emotional intimacy or psychological closeness between the partners and greater self-disclosure, mutual trust, and interpersonal honesty—all of which enhance both the physical and psychological quality of the relationship (Viorst, 1998).
- Interest is now focused on the partner as a whole person, not just on the partner's physical qualities. The partners have a less idealistic, more realistic view of one another in which they recognize and accept each other's strengths and weaknesses. The partners genuinely like one another as persons (not just as lovers) and consider the other to be their "best" or "closest" friend.
- The partners have mutual trust and confidence in each other's commitment; they aren't plagued by feelings of suspicion, distrust, or petty jealousy. Each partner may have interests and close friends outside the relationship without the other becoming jealous (Hatfield & Rapson, 1993, 2000).
- The partners have mutual concern for each other's growth and fulfillment. Rather than being envious or competitive, they take joy in each other's personal successes and accomplishments.
- The relationship contains a balanced blend of independence and interdependence—is referred to as the "paradox (contradiction) of love"—because both partners maintain their independence and individuality yet feel more complete and fulfilled when they're together. The partners maintain their sense of personal identity and self-worth, but they're together, their respective identities become more complete.

> I learned love and I learned you. I learned that, in order to love someone, you must be blind to the physical and the past. You must see their emotional and mental strengths and weaknesses, passions and dislikes, hobbies and pastimes."
> —Letter written by first-year student

> Two become one, yet remain one."
> —Letter written by first-year student

Think About It—Journal Entry 10.9

Rate your degree of agreement or disagreement with the following statements:

1. "All you need is love."

   Strongly agree   Agree   Not sure   Disagree   Strongly disagree
   Reason for rating:

   _____

   _____

2. "Love is just a four-letter word."

   Strongly agree   Agree   Not sure   Disagree   Strongly disagree
   Reason for rating:

   _____

   _____

3. "Love stinks."

   Strongly agree   Agree   Not sure   Disagree   Strongly disagree
   Reason for rating:

   _____

   _____

   _____

Unhealthy Relationships

Love is Respect
866-331-9474
Text "campus" to 22522

National Sexual Violence
Resources Center
877-739-3895 Toll Free

National Domestic Violence
Hotline
1-800-799-SAFE (7233)

Relationships can become unhealthy and pose threats to our physical or psychological well-being. If you're in a relationship where you feel you're being repeatedly disrespected, excessively controlled, or are concerned for your safety, it's essential that you acknowledge and act upon these signals. Relationship abuse—whether emotional, psychological, physical, or sexual—is another threat to wellness and should *never* be tolerated. If you're in such a situation, or you have a friend who is, it's essential to address the issue immediately. See Box 10.3 for information on creating an environment of respect and Title IX.

Sometimes the victims and offenders of relationship abuse don't recognize that they are, in fact, involved in an abusive relationship. Behaviors that characterize relationship violence include, but are not limited to, degrading language, dominating or dictating a partner's actions, as well as physical and/or sexual assault (Murray & Kardatzke, 2007).

Without such recognition, victims and perpetrators are likely to remain in their current relationship or continue to get involved in such relationships in the future (Miller, 2011).

Unfortunately, the prevalence of relationship abuse is high among college-aged women and men. Studies show that 13% to 42% of college students have been involved in relationships where they were the victims or perpetrators of physical abuse (Luthra & Gidycz, 2006; Miller, 2011). In another study, 88% of females and 81% of males reported being in relationships where they were either the victim or perpetrator of psychological (emotional) abuse (White & Koss, 1991). It's important to note that relationship violence occurs among college students of all races, ethnicities, and socioeconomic groups (Malik, Sorenson, & Aneshensel, 1997). Comparable levels of relationship violence have also been found among victims and perpetrators who are gay, bisexual, or straight (Freedner, et al., 2002). Taken together, these data highlight the unfortunate fact that relationship abuse is all too common among college students and needs to be detected and addressed early in relationships—before it escalates to more violent levels.

Victims of relationship abuse are often reluctant to seek help because they fear embarrassment or retribution. If you find yourself in a violent relationship, it is important that you tell someone what's going on and get support. Don't let fear immobilize you. Talking to a trusted friend who has your health and safety in mind is a good place to start. Connecting with your college's counseling center is especially helpful because you can get professional assistance. Campus counseling centers are often staffed with professionals who have experience working with victims and perpetrators of relationship abuse, or they can refer you to professionals who do.

National Sexual Assault Hotline
800-656-4673

Riverview Center Hotline
888-557-0310

Sexual Harassment

This list explains various forms of abuse and violence experienced by both men and women. Note that these examples are not just physical or sexual in nature — emotional and psychological violence can be just as harmful to victims.

Sexual Harassment

Sexual harassment may be defined as unwelcome sexual advances or requests for sexual favors in exchange for a grade, job, or promotion. Harassment can take the following forms:

1. Verbal (e.g., sexual comments about your body or clothes; sexual jokes or teasing)
2. Nonverbal (e.g., staring or glaring at your body or obscene gestures)
3. Physical (e.g., contact by touching, pinching, or rubbing up against your body)

Recommendations for Dealing with Sexual Harassment

- Make your objections clear and firm. Tell the harasser directly that you are offended by the unwanted behavior and that you consider it sexual harassment.
- Keep a written record of any harassment. Record the date, place, and specific details about the harassing behavior.
- Become aware of NICC's sexual harassment policy which is part of the Student Conduct Code found in the college catalog.
- If you're unsure about whether you are experiencing sexual harassment, seek help from the College Title IX Coordinator or from the Counseling staff.

Box 10.3

Respectful Enviroment and Title IX Policy

Environment of Respect

At NICC, we value integrity, responsibility, and respect for the rights and interests of others. We are dedicated to establishing and maintaining a safe and inclusive campus where all have equal access to the educational and employment opportunities the College offers. We strive to promote an environment of sexual respect, safety, and well-being. In our policies and standards, the College demonstrates that sexual assault, gender-based harassment, domestic violence, dating violence, and other forms of sexual misconduct are not tolerated in our community.

You, as a student, are responsible for familiarizing yourself with the College civility standards and the NICC Student Conduct Code, which outlines expectations of appropriate behavior at www.nicc.edu/catalog. The campus community plays an important role in preventing acts that violate the dignity of an individual.

When you see or hear inappropriate actions, behaviors or comments, do something.

Report any incidence of concern to a College employee quickly.

What is Title IX?

Title IX of the Education Amendment of 1972 prohibits sex discrimination in educational programs and activities. Sexual harassment, sexual violence, sexual assault, and intimate partner violence are all forms of sex discrimination. Title IX provides that no person in the United States shall, on the basis of sex, be excluded from participation in, be denied the benefits, or be subjected to discrimination under any education program or activity receiving federal financial assistance.

NICC has a Title IX Coordinator who can provide assistance and resources if you or someone you know has been affected by sexual violence or discrimination.

Kelly McMahon
Executive Director for Risk Management
563.556.5110, ext. 477
mcmahonke@nicc.edu

The Title IX Coordinator is not the only person who can assist you. All staff and faculty at NICC can and will assist you if you or someone you know has been affected by sexual violence or discrimination. You are encouraged to ask for the help that you need.

What to do if you, or someone you know, has been affected by sexual violence, domestic violence, dating violence or stalking:

Get to a safe place. Your safety is the HIGHEST priority. Get away from the assailant quickly. Call 9-1-1, or someone you trust if you are not in immediate danger.

Know that what happened was not your fault. You are not responsible for the actions of others. No one deserves to be sexually assaulted. No one deserves to be stalked. No one has the right to hurt you or touch you against your will or without consent. It is not your fault.

Reach out for support. Call a friend, family member, or someone else you trust who can be with you and give you support.

Seek medical care. You have the right, and are encouraged, to seek medical care and assistance. After a physical or sexual assault, you may not know whether or not you have sustained any physical injuries. A healthcare provider can provide overall care; treat any injuries that may have occurred during the assault; provide emergency contraception; and/or offer preventive treatment for sexual transmitted infections (STIs).

Preserve any evidence. Evidence of sexual assault, dating violence, domestic violence, or stalking should be preserved as soon as possible, even if you are unsure about reporting to the College or filing criminal charges. Preservation of evidence is essential for both law enforcement and campus disciplinary investigations. Physical evidence should be preserved even if you choose not to go to the hospital for a forensic exam. Save all of the clothing you were wearing at the time of the assault. Put each item in a separate paper bag (do not use plastic bags). Save all bedding (blankets, sheets) and put each in a separate paper bag. Take photographs of any visible physical injuries (bruising, scratches) for use as evidence. If you report to law enforcement, they may want to take their own photos as evidence.

Write down, or have a friend write down, everything you can remember about the incident, including a physical description of the assailant. You should attempt to do this even if you are unsure about reporting the incident in the future. Evidence such as texts, emails, Facebook posts, chats, pictures, videos or other forms of electronic communication can be helpful in a college or criminal investigation. Download, save to a .pdf, take screen shots, or use other methods to preserve electronic evidence.

(continued)

Box 10.3 *(continued)*

Report the incident. You may choose to report the incident to your local law enforcement agency and/or NICC's Title IX Coordinator or to another campus staff or faculty member. The staff or faculty member can and will relay your report to the Title IX Coordinator. The College recognizes that deciding to make a report, either to the College or law enforcement, and choosing how to proceed are difficult decisions. The College

What is Sexual Violence?

Sexual violence is a significant problem in the United States. Sexual violence refers to any sexual activity where consent is not obtained or freely given. Anyone can experience or perpetrate sexual violence; however most victims of sexual violence are female. Perpetrators may be known to the victim and can be a friend, intimate partner, coworker, neighbor, family member of the victim, or a stranger. Sexual violence can include physical acts, such as unwanted sexual contact or unwanted sexual penetration. Sexual violence also includes acts that do not involve physical contact between the victim and the perpetrator—for example,

sexual harassment, threats, sexual exploitation and exposure.

According to 2014 statistics from the Centers for Disease Control:

An estimated 20% to 25% of college women in the United States were victims of attempted or completed rape during their college career and 5.2% in the past year.

Nearly 1 in 5 women and 1 in 59 men in the United States have been raped at some time in their lives.

An estimated 12.5% of women and 5.8% of men have experienced sexual coercion in their lifetime; and 27.3% of women and 10.8% of men have experienced unwanted sexual contact.

Healing takes time. Self-care can be an important component of one's healing. Adequate sleep, nutrition, and emotional self-care can help ensure your body and mind are able to participate fully in the healing process. Give yourself as much time as you need. Talking with supportive people may help you regain a feeling of control and help you feel less alone.

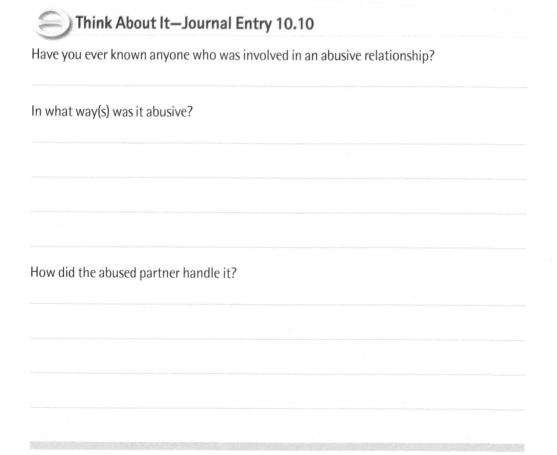

Think About It—Journal Entry 10.10

Have you ever known anyone who was involved in an abusive relationship?

In what way(s) was it abusive?

How did the abused partner handle it?

Managing Interpersonal Conflict

Disagreement and conflict among people are inevitable aspects of social life. Research shows that even the most happily married couples don't experience perpetual marital bliss; they have occasional disagreements and discord (Gottman, 1994, 1999).

Interpersonal conflict is something we can't expect to escape or eliminate; the best we can do is defuse it, contain it, and prevent it from reaching unmanageable levels. The interpersonal communication and human relations skills already discussed in this chapter can help minimize conflicts. In addition to these general social skills, the following set of specific strategies may be used to handle interpersonal conflicts constructively and compassionately.

1. **Approach the conflict with the attitude you're going to solve a problem, not win an argument.** Don't approach conflict with the attitude that you're going to get even or prove you're right. Winning the argument but not persuading the person to change the behavior that's causing the conflict is like winning a battle and losing the war. Instead, approach conflict resolution in a way that allows both parties to win—both of you can end up with a better relationship in the long run.

2. **Pick a private place and time to resolve the conflict.** Don't discuss the issue while others are present. As the old expression goes, "Don't air your dirty laundry in public." Criticizing someone in the presence of others is akin to a public stoning; it's likely to cause resentment and intensify the conflict.

Note

Things are better left unsaid until you find the right time and place to say them.

3. **Decompress emotionally before you express yourself verbally.** Sensitive issues shouldn't be discussed during a fit of anger (Daniels & Horowitz, 1997). Your objective should be to solve the problem and resolve the conflict, not release your emotions. Impulsively dumping on the other person and saying the first thing that comes to your mind may give you a short-lived sense of relief, but it's unlikely to improve the other person's attitude or behavior. Instead of unloading on the person, take the load off yourself—cool down by taking some downtime to gather your thoughts and respond rationally, not emotionally (e.g., count to 10 and give your emotions time to settle down). Taking the time to reflect, weigh your words, and respond in a mellow manner also communicates to the other person that you've given serious consideration to the matter and are not just storming in and firing away like a "loose cannon."

4. **Give the person a chance to respond.** Just because you're angry doesn't mean the person you're angry with must forfeit all rights to free speech and self-defense. By giving the other person a fair chance to be heard, you increase the likelihood that you'll receive a cooperative response. Don't jump the gun and pull the trigger before hearing the other side of the story and getting all the facts straight.

   After listening to the other person's response, check your understanding by summarizing it in your own words (e.g., "What I hear you saying is . . ."). This is an important step in the conflict-resolution process because conflicts often stem from a simple misunderstanding or failure to communicate. Sometimes just taking time to hear each other's side of the story can go a long way toward resolving the conflict.

5. **Acknowledge the person's perspectives and feelings.** After hearing the person's response, if you disagree with it, don't dismiss or discount the person's feelings. Avoid saying things like, "That's ridiculous!" or "That's no excuse!" Instead, acknowledge the persons' response by saying, "I can understand what you were thinking" or "I see how you might feel that way." Then follow by expressing how you believe your complaint is still justified.

> "Seek first to understand, then to be understood."
>
> —*Stephen Covey, international best-selling author of* Seven Habits of Highly Effective People

6. **If things begin to get nasty, call for a time-out or cease-fire and postpone the discussion to allow both of you time to cool off.** When emotions and adrenaline run high, logic and reason tend to run low. This can result in one person saying something during a fit of anger that triggers an angry response from the other person; then the anger of both combatants continues to escalate until it turns into a blow-by-blow volley of verbal punches and counterpunches. An emotionally heated conversation may end up going something like this:

Person A: "You're way out of control."
Person B: "I'm not out of control; *you're* the one that's overreacting."
Person A: "*I'm* overreacting? You're the one who's acting like a jerk!"
Person B: "I may be *acting* like a jerk, but you're a real jerk!"

Blow-by-blow exchanges such as these are likely to turn up the emotional heat to a level so high that resolving the conflict takes a back seat to winning the fight. Both boxers need to back off, retreat to their respective corners, and try again later when neither is about to throw a knockout punch.

7. **Avoid absolute judgments or blanket statements.** Compare the following three pairs of statements:

(a) "You're no help at all." versus "You don't help me enough."
(b) "You never try to understand how I feel." versus "You don't try hard enough to understand how I feel."
(c) "I always have to clean up." versus "I'm doing more than my fair share of the cleaning."

The first statement in each of the preceding pairs represents an absolute statement that covers all times, situations, and circumstances. Such extreme, blanket criticisms send the message that the person is doing nothing right with respect to the issue in question. The second statement in each of the above pairs phrases the criticism in terms of degree or amount—the person is doing something right, but needs to do more of it—which is likely to be less threatening or humiliating (and probably closer to the truth).

8. **Conclude your discussion of the conflict on a warm, constructive note.** End it by ensuring that there are no hard feelings, and by letting the person know you're optimistic that the conflict can be resolved and your relationship strengthened.

9. **If the person makes a change in response to your request, express your appreciation.** Even if your complaint was legitimate and your request justified, the person's effort to accommodate your request shouldn't be taken for granted. (The last thing you want to say is something like: "That's more like it" or "It's about time!")

Expressing appreciation to the other person for making a change is not only a socially sensitive thing to do, it's also a self-serving thing to do. By recognizing and reinforcing the other person's changed behavior, you increase the likelihood that the positive change in behavior will continue and you'll continue to benefit from the change.

> "To keep your marriage brimming with love . . . when you're wrong, admit it; when you're right, shut up."
>
> —Ogden Nash, American poet

How Do I Make My Point?

Make your point assertively—not passively, aggressively, or passive-aggressively. When you're passive, you don't stand up for your personal rights; you allow others to take advantage of you by letting them push you around. You say nothing when you should say something. You say "yes" when you want to say "no." Or, you make your point tentatively, timidly, or apologetically. When you handle conflict passively, you tend to become angry, bitter, or resentful because you keep it all inside (Alberti & Emmons, 2008).

In contrast, when you're *aggressive*, you stand up for your rights, but at the same time you violate the rights of the person with whom you have a conflict by threatening, dominating, humiliating, or bullying. You use a loud, intimidating voice and emotionally loaded words to attack the person (e.g., "You spoiled brat" or "You're a self-centered sociopath"). You may manage to get what you want but at the other person's expense and at the risk of losing a friend. Later, you tend to feel guilty about overreacting or coming on too strong (e.g., "I knew I shouldn't have said that").

Note

When dealing with interpersonal conflict, the goal should be reconciliation not retaliation.

When you're *passive–aggressive*, you get upset or angry but don't let the other person see it. Instead, you may openly agree with the person or a point the person is making, but you get angry behind the scenes and look for secret ways to get back at or get even with the other person by: (a) withholding or taking away something (e.g., not speaking to the other person or withdrawing attention and affection), or (b) indirectly hinting that you're angry (e.g., making cynical comments or using sarcastic humor).

When you're *assertive*, you're not aggressive, passive, or passive-aggressive. You handle conflict in a way that protects or restores your rights without taking away or stepping on the rights of others. You handle conflict in a direct, even-tempered manner, not in an angry or agitated fashion. Rather than yelling or screaming, you speak in a normal volume with a strong and sure tone that's not intimidating.

Listed below are specific strategies you can resolve conflicts *assertively*.

- **Focus on the *behavior* causing the conflict, not the person.** Avoid labeling the person as "selfish," "mean," or "inconsiderate." If you're upset because your roommate doesn't do his share of cleaning, stay away from aggressive labels such as "slob" or "slacker." Attacking with such negative labels makes the person feel like a verbal punching bag. This puts the person on the defensive and is likely to launch a counteroffensive assault on your personal flaws. Before you know it, you're likely to find yourself in a full-out war of words and mutual character assassinations that escalate well beyond a small-scale skirmish about the specific conflict in question.

  Rather than focusing on the person's general character, focus on the specific action or behavior that's causing the problem (e.g., failing to do the dishes or leaving dirty laundry around the room). This lets the other person know exactly what behavior needs to be changed to resolve the conflict. It's much easier to change a specific behavior than it is to change a person's entire character or personality.

- **Use "I" messages that focus on how the other person's behavior affects you.** Rather than targeting the other person, "I" messages focus on *you*—what you are perceiving and feeling. This sends a message that's less accusatory and threatening to the other person. For example, suppose you receive a course grade that's lower than what you actually earned. You think a mistake was made, so you decide to ask your instructor about it. The conversation should not begin by your saying to the instructor: "You made a mistake" or "You gave me the wrong grade." These messages are likely to put your professor immediately on the defensive and ready to defend the grade you received. Your professor will be less threatened and more likely to listen to and consider your complaint if you initiate the conversation with an "I" statement, such as: "I think an error may have been made in my final grade."

  "I" messages are less aggressive because you're targeting the issue and how it's affecting you, not the other person (McKay, Davis, & Fanning, 2009). By saying: "I feel angry when . . ." rather than "You make me angry when . . . ," you send the message that you're taking responsibility for the way you feel rather

> "Don't find fault. Find a remedy."
>
> —*Henry Ford, founder of Ford Motor Company and one of the most widely admired people of the 20th century*

than guilt-tripping the person for making you feel that way. In contrast, "you" messages are more likely to launch the person on a counter-offensive in an attempt to retaliate rather than cooperate (Bippus & Young, 2005).

Here are some specific tips for getting maximum mileage out of "I" messages.

a) Be *specific* about what *emotion* you're experiencing. Saying, "I feel neglected when you don't write or call" identifies what you're feeling more specifically than saying, "I wish you'd be more considerate." Describing what you feel in specific terms increases the persuasive power of your message and reduces the risk that the other person will misunderstand or discount it.

b) Communicate what you want the other person to do in the form of a firm *request* rather than a demand or ultimatum. Saying, "I would like you to . . ." is less likely to put the person on the defensive than saying, "I insist . . ." or "I demand . . ."

c) Be *specific* about what you want the person to *do* to resolve the conflict. Saying, "I would like for you to call me at least once a day" is more specific than saying, "I want you to keep in touch with me."

Think About It—Journal Entry 10.11

You're working on a group project and your teammates aren't carrying their weight. You're getting frustrated and angry because you're doing almost all of the work yourself.

Construct an "I" message that communicates your concern to your teammates in an assertive, nonthreatening way.

Emotional Intelligence

Excelling in college is a challenging task that will test your emotional strength and your ability to persist to task completion (graduation). Research indicates that college students who score higher on tests of emotional intelligence, such as the ability to identify their emotions and moods, are better able to focus their attention and stay absorbed ("in the zone") when completing challenging tasks and less likely to become frustrated or bored (Harris, 2006; Wiederman, 2007).

Research also indicates that experiencing positive emotions, such as optimism and excitement, promotes academic success. In one study involving nearly 4,000 first-year college students, it was found that students' level of optimism or hope for success during their first term on campus was a more accurate predictor of their first-year grades than was their SAT score or high school grade point average (Snyder, et al., 1991). In contrast, negative emotions—such as anxiety and fear—can interfere with the brain's ability to (a) store and retrieve memories, and (b) engage in higher-level thinking (Caine & Caine, 1994; Hertel & Brozovich, 2010).

The "fight-or-flight" reaction occurs when we're under stress because it's a throwback to the time when ancient humans needed to fight with or flee from potential predators. Unlike that of other animals, our hair doesn't rise up and appear more intimidating to foes (but we still get "goosebumps" when we're nervous, and we still refer to scary events as "hair-raising" experiences).

Discussed below are research-based strategies for minimizing negative emotions that sabotage success and maximizing positive emotions that promote success.

Stress and Anxiety

One of the most common emotions we must monitor and manage is stress. Students report experiencing higher levels of stress in college than they did in high school (Bartlett, 2002; Sax, 2003).

But what exactly is stress? Stress has its roots in the "fight-or-flight" response—an automatic physical reaction wired into the body that enabled our human ancestors to engage in fight (attack) or flight (run away) when confronted by life-threatening predators. The word *stress* derives from a Latin root that means "to draw tight." This suggests that stress isn't necessarily bad; in the right amount, it can actually be productive. For instance, a tightened guitar string generates better sound than a string that's too lax or loose, a tightened bow delivers a more powerful arrow shot, and a tightened muscle provides more strength or speed. Such productive stress is sometimes referred to as eustress—deriving from the root *eu* meaning "good"—as in the words "euphoria" (good mood) and "eulogy" (good words).

Keep in mind that stress can work for you as well as against you; it can either energize or sabotage your performance, depending on its level of intensity and the length of time it continues. Don't expect to stop or eliminate stress completely, nor should you want to; your goal should be to contain it and maintain it at a level where it's more productive than obstructive or destructive. Many years of research indicate that peak performance (mental and physical) is attained under conditions of *moderate* stress. (See **Figure 10.1.**) At an intermediate level, stress can enhance energy, attention, and motivation (Halvorson, 2010; Sapolsky, 2004).

FIGURE 10.1: **Relationship between Arousal and Performance**

Moderate challenge that produces moderate stress typically promotes maximum (peak) performance.

Source: Williams, Landers, & Boutcher (1993).

Think About It—Journal Entry 10.12

Can you think of a situation in which you performed at a higher level because you were slightly nervous or were experiencing a moderate amount of stress?

_____

_____

_____

However, if stress becomes intense, excessive, and persistent, it now may be defined as *anxiety* (Mayo Clinic, 2015a). Studies also show that students who experience high levels of academic stress and performance anxiety are more likely to use ineffective, "surface" approaches to learning that rely on memorization rather than effective, deep-learning strategies—such as reflection and seeking meaning (Biggs & Tang, 2011; Ramsden, 2003). Anxiety can interfere with mental performance on exams because anxious feelings and thoughts begin to preoccupy our mind, taking up valuable space in our limited attention span, leaving less room to process test information and engage in memory retrieval (Fernández-Castillo & Caurcel, 2014).

Anxiety experienced over an extended period of time can also suppress the immune system, leaving us more vulnerable to flu, colds, and other infectious diseases. Studies show that the immune system of college students is suppressed (produces fewer antibodies) at very stressful times during the academic term—such as midterms and finals (Bosch, et al., 2004; Deinzer, et al., 2000).

Box 10.4 provides a summary of the signs or symptoms of anxiety. If these symptoms are experienced for more than a week, help should be sought to reduce them.

Box 10.4

Recognizing the Symptoms of Anxiety

- Jitteriness or shaking—especially the hands
- Accelerated heart rate or heart palpitations (irregular heartbeat)
- Muscle tension. Tightness in the chest or upper shoulders or a tight feeling (lump) in the throat (the expressions "uptight" and "choking under pressure" derive from these symptoms of upper body tension)
- Body aches. Due to heightened muscle tension that can also lead to tension headaches, backaches, or chest pain (in extreme cases, it can feel like a heart attack)
- Sweating—especially sweaty (clammy) palms
- Cold, pale hands or feet. These symptoms are reflected in the expressions "white knuckles" and "cold feet," which have been used to describe someone who's highly anxious
- Dry mouth. Decreased production of saliva (hence, the expression "cotton mouth" and the tendency for nervous speakers to repeatedly sip water)
- Stomach discomfort or indigestion. Caused by increased secretion of stomach acid (as noted in the expression, "I feel like I have butterflies in my stomach")
- Gastrointestinal discomfort (e.g., stomach cramps, constipation, or diarrhea)
- Feeling faint or dizzy. Due to blood vessels constricting, which reduces oxygen flow to the brain
- Weakness and fatigue. A prolonged state of arousal and a sustained state of muscle tension can be physically exhausting
- Menstrual changes—missing or irregular menstrual periods
- Difficulty sleeping. Insomnia or interrupted (fitful) sleep
- Increased susceptibility to colds, flu, and other infections. Due to suppression of the body's immune system, resulting in lower production of antibodies

Think About It—Journal Entry 10.13

How would you rate your level of anxiety in the following situations?

1.	Taking tests or exams	high	moderate	low
2.	Interacting in social situations	high	moderate	low
3.	Making decisions about the future	high	moderate	low

Why did you rate them this way?

_____

_____

_____

_____

_____

_____

Box 10.5

Posttraumatic Stress Disorder: A Distinctive Form of Stress and Anxiety

Posttraumatic stress disorder (PTSD) is an anxiety disorder that arises after someone experiences a traumatic (dangerous or life-threatening) event, such as combat or sexual assault. It's natural to experience feelings of anxiety after such events, and the symptoms may last for weeks. However, if these feelings of anxiety do not gradually decline but remain or intensify over time and continue to interfere with the person's ability to carry out daily tasks, the person may be experiencing PTSD.

Symptoms of PTSD include the following:

- Constantly feeling tense or "on edge"
- Finding it difficult to concentrate
- Being easily startled
- Having difficulty sleeping
- Experiencing emotional numbness
- Having sudden outbursts of anger
- Blocking memories of the traumatic experience and events around the time of the experience
- Having flashbacks—reliving the trauma repeatedly and experiencing frightening thoughts and physical symptoms (e.g., a racing heart or sweating) that may occur spontaneously or be triggered by sights, sounds, or dreams that serve as reminders of the original traumatic experience
- Avoiding places, events, or objects that are reminders of the traumatic experience

If the preceding symptoms are occurring three or more months after a traumatic event, professional help should be sought. A good place to start would be the Counseling Center on campus or the PTSD Information Line at (802) 296-6300 (e-mail: ncptsd@va.gov).

Source: National Institute of Mental Health (2009).

Who's in Charge?

Stress

You have not done well on your first few assignments and tests in college, and it's really starting to get to you. You feel as though there is no hope–you have no future–and soon you stop eating and sleeping. Your life seems to be spinning out of control. You continue to tell yourself that you will amount to nothing and it doesn't matter what you do, the situation is not going to change–you just can't do this school thing! You are ready to give up! Are you in control of this situation, or is someone else? What could you have done to stop yourself from getting to the point where you want to give up? What are some resources you could use to help yourself through this situation?

_____

_____

_____

_____

_____

_____

_____

_____

Effective Methods for Managing Stress

If you perceive your level of stress reaching a point where it's beginning to interfere with the quality of your academic performance or your personal life, here are three key stress management methods that are well-supported by research in psychology and biology (Benson & Proctor, 2011; Lehrer, et al., 2007).

1. Deep (Diaphragmatic) Breathing

When people are experiencing excessive stress, their breathing pattern becomes fast, shallow, and irregular; they breathe through the mouth rather than the chest. Breathing associated with relaxation is just the opposite—slow, deep, and regular breathing that originates from the stomach.

Breathing is something we do involuntarily—without conscious awareness. However, with some concentration and effort, we can gain voluntary control of our breathing by controlling our diaphragm—the body's muscle that enables us to expand and contract our lungs. By intentionally controlling our diaphragm muscle, we slow our breathing rate, which, in turn, brings down our stress level. In fact, studies show that when we slow down our breathing rate, other systems of our body slow down—e.g., our heart rate and blood pressure drop (Benson & Proctor, 2011).

2. Progressive Muscle Relaxation

Similar to stretching exercises to relax and loosen muscles before and after physical exercise, total body (head-to-toe) muscle relaxation can be achieved by progres-

> "My stress has caused me to lose a lot of weight; my appetite is cut in half. My sleep pattern is off; I have trouble falling/ staying asleep. No matter how stressed I was in high school, this never happened [before]. What can I do to de-stress?"
>
> —First-term college student

sively tensing and releasing the five sets of muscles listed below. Hold tension in each muscle area for about five seconds and then release slowly.

1. Wrinkle your forehead muscles and then release them.
2. Shrug your shoulders up as if to touch your ears and then drop them.
3. Make a tight fist with both hands and then open them.
4. Tighten your stomach muscles and then release them.
5. Tighten your toes by curling them under your feet and then raise them as high as you can.

> "To relax, I like to stretch a lot."
> —First-year college student

When relaxing your muscles, take a deep breath and think or say: "Relax." By breathing deeply and thinking or hearing the word "relax" each time you release your muscles, the sound of the word "relax" becomes associated with your muscles being relaxed. When you find yourself in a stressful situation, take a deep breath and think or say the word "relax"; your stress level will drop because your muscles have been conditioned to relax in response to that word.

3. Mental Imagery

You can also reduce stress by *imagining* yourself in a calm, comfortable, and relaxing setting. Visualize images such as ocean waves, floating clouds, sitting in a warm sauna, or any sensory experience that tends to relax you. Try to use all of your senses—see it, hear it, smell it, touch it, and feel it. You can also create imaginary calming music in your head to accompany the visual image. The more senses you use, the more real the scene will seem and the more powerful its relaxing effects will be (Fezler, 1989).

AUTHOR'S EXPERIENCE

My wife, Mary, is a kindergarten teacher. Whenever her young students start misbehaving and the situation becomes especially stressful (e.g., during lunchtime when kids are running around wildly, arguing vociferously, and screaming at maximum volume), she "plays" relaxing songs in her head. Mary reports that her musical imagination always works to soothe her nerves, enabling her to remain calm and even-tempered when she must deal with children who are out of control, or need to be disciplined.

—*Joe Cuseo*

Think About It—Journal Entry 10.14

What are your most common sources or causes of stress?

What is your top strategy for coping with stress?

Would you say that you cope with stress well?

Simple Stress-Reduction Strategies and Habits

In addition to the formal stress-management techniques of diaphragmatic breathing, progressive muscle relaxation, and mental imagery, stress may be managed by simpler strategies and habits, such as those discussed below.

1. **Exercise.** Exercise reduces stress by increasing release of serotonin—a mellowing brain chemical that reduces feelings of tension (anxiety) and depression. It is for these reasons that counselors and psychotherapists recommend exercise for patients experiencing milder forms of anxiety or depression (Johnsgard, 2004). Exercise also elevates mood because it enhances self-esteem—by giving us a sense of accomplishment and an improved physical self-image. Studies show that people who exercise regularly tend to report feeling happier (Myers, 1993).
2. **Journaling.** Writing about our feelings in a personal journal helps us identify and express the emotions we're experiencing (a form of emotional intelligence), and provides us with a safe outlet for releasing stress (Seaward, 2011). Writing about our emotions also reduces the risk that we'll deny or repress them—(push them out of conscious awareness).

> There are thousands of causes for stress, and one antidote to stress is self-expression. That's what happens to me every day. My thoughts get off my chest, down my sleeves, and onto my pad."
>
> —Garson Kanin, American writer, actor, and film director

AUTHOR'S EXPERIENCE

I'm the kind of person who carries the worries of the day with me and it really affects my sleep. I'm also the type of person who juggles many balls during the day, which also adds to my stress level. By chance, I discovered a great strategy for managing my stress. I was doing a conflict resolution workshop about 15 years ago and I asked the participants to write down in a journal all the stressors they encountered during the day for 30 consecutive days. We would then come together as a group at the end of the 30 days to identify those stressors.

I decided to try this experiment on my own stressors. Every night before I went to bed I wrote down the categories or sources of stress I experienced during the day. After 30 days, I was able to recognize patterns in the causes of my stress and what strategies I could use to combat them. I also noticed was that over the 30 days my stress level decreased and the quality of my sleep improved. I still use this strategy whenever I'm under stress or not sleeping well.

—Aaron Thompson

3. **Substitute positive thoughts for negative thoughts.** Research indicates that the part of the human brain involved in thinking (the cortex) has many connections to the part of the brain responsible for emotions (the limbic system) (Goleman, 1995; Zull, 2002). Thus, our brain is wired in such a way that our thinking can directly influence our feelings. If thoughts influence emotions, then changing the way we think can change the emotions we experience, including our feelings of stress and anxiety.

   We can attack negative, anxiety-producing thoughts and replace them with positive, relaxing thoughts. For instance, you see some students turning in their tests before you're finished and you start having negative thoughts like: "They must all be smarter than I am." You can stop that anxiety-producing thought and substitute the following thought: "They're getting up and getting out because they're giving up." Or, "They're rushing out without taking the time to carefully review their answers before turning their test in."

   One of the keys to substituting positive for negative thoughts is to think about what you want to happen, not what you're afraid is going to happen (Halvorson, 2010). If you're a pitcher in a baseball game and you start thinking you're going to walk a batter, stop thinking about whether you're going to throw balls and start thinking about throwing strikes. Similarly, if you're taking a test, stop thinking (and worrying) about losing points and start thinking (and focusing) on earning points. This will reduce your level of test anxiety.

4. **Take time for humor and laughter.** Research on the benefits of humor for reducing tension is clear and convincing. In one study, college students were suddenly told they had to give an impromptu (off the top of their head) speech. This unexpected assignment typically caused students' heart rate to elevate to an average of 110 beats per minute during delivery of the speech. However, students who watched humorous episodes of sitcoms before delivering their impromptu speech had an average heart rate during the speech that was significantly lower (80–85 beats per minute)—indicating that experiencing humor reduces their level of anxiety (O'Brien, cited in Howard, 2014).

   Research also shows that humor strengthens our immune system after it's been suppressed or weakened. It does so by stress by blocking the body's production of the stress hormone cortisol—a biochemical that suppresses our immune system when we're under stress (Berk, cited in Liebertz, 2005b).

> "The arrival of a good clown exercises a more beneficial influence upon the health of a town than the arrival of twenty asses laden with drugs."
>
> —Thomas Sydenham, 17th-century physician

Depression

Along with anxiety, depression is the other major emotional problem that can afflict us. Research indicates that depression is associated with poorer academic performance in college and higher risk of withdrawing from college, even among highly motivated and academically well-prepared students (Eisenberg, Golberstein, & Hunt, 2009). Depression may be succinctly described as an emotional state characterized by a feeling of sadness accompanied by loss of interest, hope, and energy (Mayo Clinic, 2015b). As the term implies, when we're depressed, our mood is lowered or pushed down. In contrast to anxiety, which typically involves worrying about something that's currently happening or is about to happen, depression more often relates to something that has already happened, particularly a *loss*, such as a lost relationship (e.g., broken romance or death of a family member) or a lost opportunity (e.g., losing a job or being rejected by a school) (Bowlby, 1980; Price, Choi, & Vinokur, 2002).

It's natural and normal to feel dejected after losses such as these. However, if the dejection reaches a point where we can't concentrate and complete our day-to-day tasks, and if this continues for an extended period of time, we may be experiencing what psychologists call *clinical depression* or *depressive disorder*—that is, depression so serious that we should receive immediate professional help. **Box 10.6** provides a summary of symptoms or signs of depression. If these symptoms continue to occur for two or more weeks, you should take action to relieve them.

Box 10.6

Recognizing the Symptoms of Depression

- Feeling low, down, dejected, sad, or blue
- Pessimistic feelings about the future (e.g., expecting failure or feeling helpless or hopeless)
- Decreased sense of humor
- Difficulty finding pleasure, joy, or fun in anything
- Lack of concentration
- Loss of motivation and interest in things previously found to be exciting or stimulating (e.g., loss of interest in school, sudden drop in rate of class attendance or completion of course assignments)
- Stooped posture (e.g., hung head or drawn face)
- Slower and softer speech rate
- Decreased animation and slower bodily movements
- Loss of energy
- Changes in sleeping patterns (e.g., sleeping more or less than usual)
- Changes in eating patterns (e.g., eating more or less than usual)

- Social withdrawal
- Neglect of physical appearance
- Consistently low self-esteem (e.g., thinking "I'm a loser")
- Strong feelings of worthlessness or guilt (e.g., thinking "I'm a failure")
- Suicidal thoughts (e.g., experiencing thoughts such as: "I can't take it anymore," "People would be better off without me," or "I don't deserve to live")

Note: Depression and suicidal thoughts occur at alarmingly high rates among college students. In one national study of more than 26,000 students at 70 campuses, it was found that 15% of the students surveyed reported they "seriously considered" suicide and more than 5% reported they actually attempted suicide. Unfortunately, however, only half the students who had suicidal thoughts sought counseling or treatment (Drum, et al., 2009).

Note

There's a difference between feeling despondent or down and being depressed. When psychologists use the word "depression," they're usually referring to clinical depression—a mood state so low that it's interfering with a person's ability to cope with day-to-day tasks, such as getting to school or going to work.

Think About It—Journal Entry 10.15

Have you, or any member of your family, experienced clinical depression?

What do you think was the primary cause of it?

Strategies for Coping with Depression

Depression can vary widely in intensity. Moderate and severe forms of depression often require professional counseling or psychotherapy, and are often rooted in genetic or hereditary factors that cause imbalances in brain chemistry. The coping strategies described below can also be used for milder forms of depression that may be overcome through self-help and self-management. These strategies may be used in conjunction with professional help or medication to reduce the intensity and frequency of clinical depression.

1. **Focus on the present and the future, not the past.** Consciously combat the tendency to dwell on past losses or failures that can no longer be changed or controlled. Instead, focus on things you can control now.

2. **Make extra effort to engage in positive, emotionally uplifting behavior.** If our behavior is upbeat, our mind (mood) often follows suit. The expression, "Put on a happy face" can actually be an effective depression-reduction strategy because smiling produces changes in our facial muscles that trigger changes in brain chemistry—which, in turn, elevate our mood (Liebertz, 2005a). In contrast, frowning activates a different set of facial muscles that tend to interfere with production of mood-elevating brain chemicals (Myers, 1993).

3. **Continue to engage in activities that are fun and enjoyable.** When we're down, we can fall into the downward spiral of not doing the things that bring us joy (because we're too down to do them); this brings us down further because we fail to do the very things that bring us up. When we're emotionally low, we should try even harder to continue doing the things that bring us joy, such as socializing with friends and engaging in our usual recreational activities. Interestingly, the root of the word "recreation" means to re-create (create again), suggesting that recreational activity can revive, restore, and renew us—both physically and emotionally.

4. **Intentionally seek humor and opportunities to laugh.** In addition to reducing anxiety, laughter can lighten and brighten a dark mood. Furthermore, humor improves memory (Nielson, cited in Liebertz, 2005a), which can combat the memory loss that typically accompanies depression.

5. **Continue getting things done.** When we're feeling down, staying busy and accomplishing things helps boost our mood because it provides us with a sense of achievement. Helping others less fortunate than ourselves can also be a particularly effective way to boost our mood because it gets us outside ourselves, increases our sense of self-esteem, and helps us realize that our issues may be minor compared to the problems faced by others.

6. **Make a conscious effort to focus on personal strengths and accomplishments.** Another way to drive away the blues is by keeping track of the positive developments in our life. We can do this by keeping a "positive events journal" in which we note the good things that happen to us and for us, such as the fortunate experiences in our life, the things we're grateful for, and our personal accomplishments or achievements. Positive journal entries leave us with a visible uplifting record that we can review anytime we're feeling down.

7. **If you're unable to overcome depression on your own, seek help from others.** In some cases, we may be able to help ourselves overcome emotional problems through personal effort and use of effective coping strategies—particularly if we experience depression or anxiety in milder forms and for shorter periods of time. However, overcoming more serious and long-lasting episodes of depression or anxiety isn't as simple as people make it out to be when they insensitively use expressions like: "Just deal with it," "Get over it," or "Snap out

> " The best way to cheer yourself up is to try to cheer somebody else up."
>
> —*Samuel Clemens, a.k.a. Mark Twain, writer, lecturer, and humorist*

of it." More serious cases of depression and anxiety can be strongly associated with genetic factors, which are not completely within the person's control. In these cases, we shouldn't be reluctant to or embarrassed about seeking professional help.

Think About It—Journal Entry 10.16

If you thought you were experiencing a serious episode of anxiety or depression, would you feel comfortable seeking help from a professional? If yes, why? If no, why not?

How do you think other students would respond to the above question?

Using alcohol and/or other drugs to deal with stress, anxiety, or depression is not a healthy solution. Drugs and alcohol will be discussed further in the next chapter.

Chapter Summary and Highlights

Intellectual ability is only one form of human intelligence. Social and emotional intelligence are equally, if not more, important for living a successful, healthy, and happy life. The strategies discussed in this chapter should not be viewed merely as "soft skills," but as "hard core" skills essential for success in college and beyond.

Good communication skills (verbal and nonverbal) and good human relations skills ("people skills") are critical for the development of successful social relationships. We can improve our interpersonal interactions and relationships by working hard at remembering the names and interests of people we meet, being a good listener, and being open to different topics of conversation.

Interpersonal conflicts are an inevitable aspect of social life; we can't completely eliminate them, but we can minimize and manage them by using effective strategies to resolve conflicts assertively rather than aggressively, passively, or passive-aggressively.

Students report experiencing higher levels of stress in college than they did in high school. Strategies for reducing excess stress include formal stress-management techniques (e.g., deep, diaphragmatic breathing and progressive muscle relaxation), as well as simple stress-management strategies (e.g., exercising and journaling).

Along with anxiety, depression is the other major emotional problem that can afflict us.

Research on college students indicate that depression is associated with poorer academic performance in college and higher risk of withdrawing from college, even among highly motivated and academically well-prepared students. Mild depression may be overcome with a variety of self-help strategies. However, if symptoms of depression are severe and continue for two or more weeks, this suggests "clinical depression" or a "depressive disorder" is being experienced and professional help should be immediately sought.

Learning More through the World Wide Web: Internet-Based Resources

For additional information on social and emotional intelligence, see the following websites:

Social Intelligence and Interpersonal Relationships:
https://nationalvetcontent.edu.au/alfresco/d/d/workspace/SpacesStore/5c14c044-6d26-4ab8-aef1-530948605d36/ims/shared/resources/mag/web_conflict.htm

http://www.livestrong.com/article/132246-effective-interpersonal-communication-strategies/

http://www.yesintlcampus.com/index.asp?Cid=20&Tid=140&Sid=51680

Emotional Intelligence and Mental Health:
www.eqi.org/eitoc.htm

http://www.nimh.nih.gov/health/publications/depression-easy-to-read/index.shtml

http://www.activeminds.org/issues-a-resources/mental-health-resources/student-resources

References

AhYun, K. (2002). Similarity and attraction. In M. Allen, R. W. Preiss, B. M. Gayle, & N. A. Burrell (Eds.), *Interpersonal communication research* (pp. 145–167). Mahwah, NJ: Erlbaum.

Avolio, B., & Luthans, F. (2006). *The high impact leader*. New York: McGraw Hill.

Avolio, B. J., Walumbwa, F. O., &. Weber, T. J. (2009). *Leadership: Current theories, research, and future directions*. Annual Review of Psychology, 60, 421–449.

Barker, L., & Watson, K. W. (2000). *Listen up: How to improve relationships, reduce stress, and be more productive by using the power of listening*. New York: St. Martin's Press.

Bartels, A., & Zeki, S. (2000). The neural basis of romantic love. *European Journal of Neuroscience, 12*, 172–193.

Bartlett, T. (2002). Freshman pay, mentally and physically, as they adjust to college life. *Chronicle of Higher Education, 48*, 35–37.

Bassham, G., Irwin, W., Nardone, H., & Wallace, J. M. (2013). *Critical thinking: A student's introduction* (5th ed.) New York: McGraw-Hill.

Benson, H., & Proctor, W. (2011). *The relaxation revolution: The science and genetics of mind body healing*. New York: Scribner.

Berndt, T. J. (1992). Friendship and friends' influence in adolescence. *Current Directions in Psychological Science, 1*(5), 156–159.

Biggs, J., & Tang, C. (2011) *Teaching for quality learning at university*. New York: Open Education Press.

Biggs, J., & Tang, C. (2011) *Teaching for quality learning at university*. New York: Open Education Press.

Bippus, A. M., & Young, S. L. (2005). Owning your emotions: Reactions to expressions of self- versus other-attributed positive and negative emotions. *Journal of Applied Communication Research, 33*(1), 26–45.

Bowlby, J. (1980). *Attachment and loss: Vol. 3. Loss, sadness, and depression*. New York: Basic Books.

Caine, R., & Caine, G. (1994). *Making connections: Teaching and the human brain*. Menlo Park, CA: Addison-Wesley.

Carneiro, P., Crawford, C., & Goodman, A. (2006). *Which skills matter?* Centre for the Economics of Education,

London School of Economics, Discussion Paper 59. Retrieved from http://cee.lse.ac.uk/ceedps/ceedp59.pdf.

Daniels, D., & Horowitz, L. J. (1997). *Being and caring: A psychology for living*. Prospect Heights, IL: Waveland Press.

Driver, J. (2010). *You say more than you think: A 7-day plan for using the new body language to get what you want*. New York: Crown Publishers.

Drum, D., Brownson, C., Denmark, A.B., Smith, S.E. (2009). New data on the nature of suicidal crises in college students: Shifting the paradigm. *Professional Psychology: Research and Practice, 40*(3), 213–222.

Eisenberg, D., Golberstein, E., & Hunt, J. (2009). Mental health and academic success in college. *B.E. Journal of Economic Analysis & Policy, 9*(1), 1–40.

Ekman, P. (2009). *Telling lies: Clues to deceit in the marketplace, politics, and marriage* (revised ed.). New York: W. W. Norton.

Fernández-Castillo, A. & Caurcel, M. J., 2014. *State test-anxiety, selective attention and concentration in university students*. International Journal of Psychology, Vol 50, Issue 4, pp. 265-271.

Festinger, L. (1954). A theory of social comparison processes. *Human Relations, 7,* 117–140.

Fezler, W. (1989). *Creative imagery: How to visualize in all senses*. New York: Simon & Schuster.

Fisher, E. E. (2004). *Why we love: The nature and chemistry of romantic love*. New York: Henry Holt & Co.

Foreman, J. (2009, June 22). "Dear, I love you with all my brain." *Los Angeles Times*. Retrieved from http://www.latimes.com/features/health/la-he-love22-2009jun22,0,6897401.column.

Freedner, et al., 2002. Dating violence among gay, lesbian, and bisexual adolescents: Results from a community survey. *Journal of Adolescent Health, 31,* 469-474.

Fromm, E. (1970). *The art of loving*. New York: Bantam.

Fromme, A. (1980). *The ability to love*. Chatsworth, CA: Wilshire Book Company.

Gardner, H. (1993). *Frames of mind: The theory of multiple intelligences* (2nd ed.). New York: Basic Books.

Gardner, H. (1999). *Intelligence reframed: Multiple intelligences for the 21st century*. New York: Basic Books.

Giles, L. C., Glonek, F. V., Luszcz, M. A., & Andrews, G. R. (2005). Effect of social networks on 10-year survival in very old Australians: The Australia longitudinal study of aging. *Journal of Epidemiology and Community Health, 59,* 574–579.

Goleman, D. (1995). *Emotional intelligence: Why it can matter more than IQ*. New York: Random House.

Goleman, D. (2000). *Working with emotional intelligence*. New York: Bantam Dell.

Goleman, D. (2006). *Social intelligence: The new science of human relationships*. New York: Dell.

Goleman, D., Boyatzis, R., & McKee, A. (2013). *Primal leadership: Realizing the potential of emotional intelligence*. Boston, MA: Harvard Business School Press.

Gottman, J. (1994). *Why marriages succeed and fail*. New York: Fireside.

Gottman, J. (1999). *The seven principles for making marriage work*. New York: Three Rivers Press.

Halvorson, H. G. (2010). *Succeed: How we can reach our goals*. New York: Plume.

Harris, M. B. (2006). Correlates and characteristics of boredom and proneness to boredom. *Journal of Applied Social Psychology, 30*(3), 576–598.

Hatfield, E., & Rapson, R. L. (1993). *Love, sex, and intimacy: Their psychology, biology, and history*. New York: HarperCollins.

Hatfield, E., & Rapson, R. L. (2000). Love. In W. E. Craighead & C. B. Nemeroff (Eds.). *The concise Corsini encyclopedia of psychology and behavioral science* (pp. 898–901). New York: John Wiley & Sons.

Hertel, P. T., & Brozovich, F. (2010). Cognitive habits and memory distortions in anxiety and depression. *Current Directions in Psychological Science, 19,* 155–160.

Howard, P. J. (2014). *The owner's manual for the brain: Everyday applications of mind-brain research* (4th ed.). New York: HarperCollins.

Johnsgard, K. W. (2004). *Conquering depression and anxiety through exercise*. New York: Prometheus.

Johnson, S. D., & Bechler, C. (1998). Examining the relationships between listening effectiveness and leadership emergence: Perceptions , behaviors, and recall. *Small Group Research, 29*(4), 452–471.

Johnson, M. P., & Ferraro, K. J. (2000). Research on domestic violence in the 1990s: Making distinctions. *Journal of Marriage and the Family, 62,* 948–963.

Karjane, Fisher, & Cullen (2002, 2005). *Campus Sexual Assault.: How America's Institutions of Higher Education Respond*, final report to the National Institute of Justice, Oct. 2002, NCJ 196676.

Latané, B., Liu, J. H., Nowak, A., Bonevento, N., & Zheng, L. (1995). Distance matters: Physical space and social impact. *Personality and Social Psychology Bulletin, 21,* 795–805.

Lehrer, P., Barlow, D. H., Woolfolk, R. L., & Sime, W. E. (Eds.) (2007). *Principles and practice of stress management* (3rd ed.). New York: The Guilford Press.

Liebertz, C. (2005a). A healthy laugh. *Scientific American Mind, 16*(3), 90–91.

Liebertz, C. (2005b). Want clear thinking? Relax. *Scientific American Mind, 16*(3), pp. 88–89.

Liebertz, C. (2005b). A healthy laugh. *Scientific American Mind, 16*(4).

Luthra R, Gidycz CA. Dating violence among college men and women: Evaluation of a theoretical model. Journal of Interpersonal Violence. 2006;21:717–731.Maes, J. D., Weldy, T. G., & Icenogle, M. L. (1997). A managerial perspective: Oral communication competency is most important for business students in the workplace. *Journal of Business Communication, 34*(1), 67–80.

Malik, Sorenson, & Aneshensel, 1997. *Community and dating violence among adolescents: perpetration and victimization*. Journal of Adolescent Health Nov 1997(5): 291–302.

Matthews, G., Zeidner, M., & Roberts, R. D. (2007). *The science of emotional intelligence: Knowns and unknowns*. New York: Oxford University Press.

Mayo Clinic (2015a). *Anxiety: Definition*. Retrieved from http://www.mayoclinic.org/diseases-conditions/anxiety/basics/definition/con-20026282.

Mayo Clinic (2015b). *Depression: Definition*. Retrieved from http://www.mayoclinic.org/diseases-conditions/depression/basics/definition/con-20032977.

McKay, M., Davis, M., & Fanning, P. (2009). *Messages: The communication skills book* (2nd ed.). Oakland, CA: New Harbinbger.

Miller, L. M. (2011). Physical abuse in a college setting: A study of perception and participation in abusive dating relationships. *Journal of Family Violence*, 26(1), 71–80.

Murray, C.E. & Kardatzke, K.N. (2007). Dating violence among college students: Key issues for college counselors. Journal of College Counseling, 10 (1), 79+Myers, D. G. (1993). *The pursuit of happiness: Who is happy—and why?* New York: Morrow.

Myers, D. G. (2000). *The American paradox: Spiritual hunger in an age of plenty*. New Haven, CT: Yale University Press.

National Center for Victims of Crime (2012

Navarro, J. (2008). *What every BODY is saying*. New York: Harper Collins.

Nichols, M. P. (2009). *The lost art of listening*. New York: Guilford Press.

Ottens, A.J., and Hotelling, K. (2001). Sexual Violence on Campus: Politics, Programs, and Perspectives. New York: Springer Publishing Company, Inc.

Palank, J. (2006, July 17). *Face it: "Book" no secret to employers*. Retrieved from http://www.washtimes.com/business/20060717-12942-1800r.htm

Pascarella, E., & Terenzini, P. (2005). *How college affects students: A third decade of research* (Vol. 2). San Francisco: Jossey-Bass.

Peele, S., & Brodsky, A (1991). *Love and addiction*. New York: Signet Books.

Penfold, R. B. (2006). *Dragonslippers: This is what an abusive relationship looks like*. New York: Grove/Atlantic.

Price, R. H., Choi, J. N., & Vinokur, A. D. (2002). Links in the chain of adversity following job loss: How financial strain and loss of personal control lead to depression, impaired functioning, and poor health. *Journal of Occupational Health Psychology*, 7(4), 302–312.

Purdy, M., & Borisoff, D. (Eds.). (1996). *Listening in everyday life: A personal and professional approach*. Lanham, MD: University Press of America.

Putman, R. D. (2000). *Bowling alone: The collapse and revival of American community*. New York: Simon & Schuster.

Ramsden, P. (2003). *Learning to teach in higher education* (2nd ed.). London: RoutledgeFalmer.

Rohrbaugh, J. B. (April 2006). Domestic Violence in Same-Gender Relationships. *Family Court Review*, 44(2), 287–299.

Ruggiero, V. R. (2011). *Beyond feelings: A guide to critical thinking*. New York: McGraw-Hill Education.

Salovey, P., & Mayer, J. D. (1990). Emotional intelligence. *Imagination, Cognition, and Personality*, 9, 185–211.

Sapolsky, R. (2004). *Why zebras don't get ulcers*. New York: W. H. Freeman.

Sax, L. J. (2003). Our incoming students: What are they like? *About Campus* (July–August), 15–20.

Seaward, B. L. (2011). *Managing stress: Principles and strategies for health and well-being*. Burlington, MA: Jones & Bartlett Learning.

Senn CY, Eliasziw M, Barata PC, et al. Efficacy of a sexual assault resistance program for university women. N Engl J Med 2015;372:2326-2335Sinsky, R. (2011). "Reppler has a new way to rate your social network image." Retrieved from http://venturebeat.com/2011/09/27 /reppler/.

Snyder, C. R., Harris, C., Anderson, J. R., Holleran, S. A., Irving, L. M., Sigmon, S. T., et al. (1991). The will and the ways: Development and validation of an individual-differences measure of hope. *Journal of Personality and Social Psychology*, 60, 570–585.

Suls, J., Martin, R., & Wheeler, L. (2002). Social comparison: Why, with whom and with what effect? *Current Directions in Psychological Science*, 11(5), 159–163.

Tinto, V. (2012). *Completing college: Rethinking institutional action*. Chicago: The University of Chicago Press.

White, J.W. and Koss, M.P. Courtship violence: Incidence in a national sample of higher education students. Viol. Vict. 6: 247-256, 1991.Viorst, J. 1998. *Imperfect control: Our lifelong struggles with power and surrender*. New York: Simon Schuster.

Wiederman, M. W., 2007. Gender differences in sexuality. *Family Journal- Counseling and Therapy*. 9(4), 468–471.

Winsor, J. L., Curtis, D. B., & Stephens, R. D. (1997). National preferences in business and communication education: A survey update. *JACA*, 3 (September), 170–179.

Wolvin, A. D. (2010). *Listening and communication in the 21st century*. Malden, MA: Blackwell.

Zull, J. E. (2002). *The art of changing the brain: Enriching teaching by exploring the biology of learning*. Sterling, VA: Stylus.

Chapter 10 Exercises

10.1 Quote Reflections

Review the sidebar quotes contained in this chapter and select two that were especially meaningful or inspirational to you.

For each quote, provide a three- to five-sentence explanation why you chose it.

10.2 Reality Bite

Caught Between a Rock and a Hard Place: Romantic Involvement versus Academic Commitment

Lauren has been dating her boyfriend (Nick) for about two months. She's convinced this is the real thing and that she's definitely in love. Lately, Nick has been asking her to skip class to spend more time with him. He tells Lauren: "If you really love me, you would do it for our relationship." Lauren feels that Nick truly loves her and wouldn't do anything to intentionally hurt her or interfere with her goals. So she accommodates Nick's request and begins skipping some classes to spend time with him. However, Lauren's grades soon start to slip; at the same time, Nick continues to demand more of her time.

Reflection and Discussion Questions

1. What concerns you most about Lauren's behavior?
2. What concerns you most about Nick's behavior?
3. Would you agree with Lauren's decision to start skipping classes?
4. If you were Lauren's friend, what advice would you give her?
5. If you were Nick's friend, what advice would you give him?
6. What might Lauren do to keep her grades up and still keep her relationship with Nick strong?

10.3 Reality Bite—Case Study

Mental Wellness

Leo was really looking forward to college, but he was not prepared to handle the stress and anxiety that came along with it. In high school, his teachers always reminded him when things were due and he hardly had any homework. Now his instructors expect him to read that silly syllabus and he has so much homework he does not know where to start! He is starting to fall behind and gets anxious and nervous any time he goes to class. His heart starts to race and his palms get really sweaty. The further he falls behind, the worse his stress and anxiety get. Soon he stops going to class altogether because he gets so worked up he literally makes himself sick.

Discussion Questions

1. How realistic do you think this case is? Why?
2. What could Leo have done to calm himself down so that he was able to go to his classes and be successful?
3. What do you think is going to happen to Leo?

10.4 Identifying Major Ways of Handling Interpersonal Conflict

Think of a social situation or relationship that's currently causing the most conflict in your life. Describe how this conflict could be approached in each of the following ways:

1. Passively:

2. Aggressively:

3. Passive–aggressively:

4. Assertively:

(See **pp. 281–282** for descriptions of each of these four approaches.)

Practice the *assertive* approach by role-playing it with a friend or classmate and consider applying it to the actual situation or relationship that's currently causing you the most conflict.

10.5 College Stress: Identifying Sources and Solutions

Read through the following 29 college stressors and rate them in terms of how much stress each one is currently causing you—on a scale of 1 to 5 (1 = lowest, 5 = highest).

Potential Stressors	Stress Rating				
Tests and exams	1	2	3	4	5
Assignments	1	2	3	4	5
Class workload	1	2	3	4	5
Pace of courses	1	2	3	4	5
Performing up to expectations	1	2	3	4	5
Handling personal freedom	1	2	3	4	5
Time pressure (e.g., not enough time)	1	2	3	4	5
Organizational pressure (e.g., losing things)	1	2	3	4	5
Living independently	1	2	3	4	5
The future	1	2	3	4	5
Decisions about a major or career	1	2	3	4	5
Moral and ethical decisions	1	2	3	4	5
Finding meaning in life	1	2	3	4	5
Emotional issues	1	2	3	4	5
Physical health	1	2	3	4	5
Social life	1	2	3	4	5
Intimate relationships	1	2	3	4	5
Sexuality	1	2	3	4	5
Family responsibilities	1	2	3	4	5
Family conflicts	1	2	3	4	5
Family pressure	1	2	3	4	5
Peer pressure	1	2	3	4	5
Loneliness or isolation	1	2	3	4	5
Roommate conflicts	1	2	3	4	5
Conflict with professors	1	2	3	4	5
Campus policies or procedures	1	2	3	4	5
Transportation	1	2	3	4	5
Technology	1	2	3	4	5
Safety	1	2	3	4	5

Review your ratings and record your three, highest-rated stressors in the space below—along with: (a) a coping strategy you may use on your own to deal with that source of stress and (b) a campus resource you could use to obtain help with that source of stress.

Stressor #1: _____

Personal coping strategy:

Campus resource:

Stressor #2: _____

Personal coping strategy:

Campus resource:

Stressor #3: _____

Personal coping strategy:

Campus resource:

10.6 Do What You Are Reflection

Review your Do What You Are Report to answer the following questions.

1. What is your personality type?

2. What are the strengths of your personality type? How can you use these to assist in good communication with others?

3. What are the blind spots for your personality type? What can you do to improve in each of these areas to assist you in becoming a better communicator?

4. What are the strengths for your negotiation style? How can these help your negotiations with others?

5. What are the blind spots for your negotiation style? How could these impact your negotiations with others?

Chapter 10 Reflection

What is one healthy relationship you currently have that could positively affect your success in college? Explain.

What is one unhealthy relationship that could negatively affect your success in college? Explain. How can you make this relationship healthy, or what are other options you might have?

Think of a situation that is currently causing you stress. What is it? What are some ways you can address the situation so it will not cause you so much stress?

CHAPTER 11

Health and Wellness

BODY, MIND, AND SPIRIT

Chapter Preview

Humans cannot reach their full potential without attending to their physical well-being. Sustaining health and attaining peak levels of performance depend on how well we treat our body—what we put into it (healthy food), what we keep out of it (unhealthy substances), what we do with it (exercise), and how well we rejuvenate it (sleep). This chapter examines strategies for maximizing wellness by maintaining a balanced diet, attaining quality sleep, promoting total fitness, and avoiding risky behaviors that jeopardize our health and impair our performance.

Learning Goal

Acquire wellness strategies that can be immediately practiced in the first year of college and beyond.

Thought Starter

 Think About It—Journal Entry 11.1

What would you say are the three most important things that college students could do to preserve their health and promote peak performance?

1. _____

2. _____

3. _____

What Is Wellness?

Wellness may be defined as a high-quality state of health in which our risk of illness is minimized and the quality of our physical and mental performance is maximized. Research indicates that people who attend to multiple dimensions of self-development and live a well-rounded, well-balanced life are more likely to be healthy (physically and mentally) and successful (personally and professionally) (Covey, 2004; Goleman, 1995; Heath, 1977).

There's still some debate about the exact number and nature of the components that define the "whole self" (Miller & Foster, 2010; President's Council on Physical Fitness and Sports, 2001). However, the following eight dimensions of self-devel-

> "Wellness is a multidimensional state of being describing the existence of positive health in an individual as exemplified by quality of life and a sense of well-being."
>
> —Charles Corbin and Robert Pangrazi, President's Council on Physical Fitness and Sports

opment are commonly cited as the key elements of the "wellness wheel;" they provide the foundation for a well-rounded life.

1. **Intellectual:** acquiring broad-based knowledge, learning how to learn, and learning how to think critically.
2. **Emotional:** understanding, managing, and expressing emotions and feelings.
3. **Social:** improving the quality and depth of interpersonal relationships.
4. **Ethical:** building moral character—making sound ethical judgments, developing a clear value system for guiding personal decisions, and demonstrating consistency between your convictions (beliefs) and your commitments (actions).
5. **Physical:** acquiring knowledge about the human body and applying that knowledge to prevent disease, promote wellness, and achieve peak performance.
6. **Spiritual:** devoting attention to the "big questions," such as the meaning or purpose of life, the inevitability of death, and the origins of human life and the natural world.
7. **Vocational:** exploring career options and pursuing a career path that capitalizes on your talents, interests, and values.
8. **Personal:** developing a strong sense of personal identity, a coherent self-concept, and the capacity to manage personal affairs and resources.

For specific skills and qualities associated with each of these dimensions of wellness, see **Exercise 11.3, pp. 340**.

As can be seen in **Figure 11.1**, numerous elements of the self join together to form the wellness wheel. These elements of wellness correspond closely to the components of holistic ("whole person") development, which is a primary goal of the college experience. One of the multiple advantages of a college education is that college graduates are more likely to live longer, healthier lives and experience higher levels of psychological well-being. Apparently, students learn something important about wellness in college that improves the overall quality of their lives.

FIGURE 11.1: **Components of the Wellness Wheel**

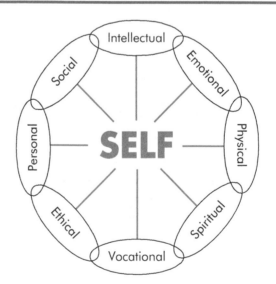

AUTHOR'S EXPERIENCE

On my office door, I posted a list of the key components of wellness to remind me to keep my life balanced. Every Sunday night I reflect on the previous week and ask myself if I've ignored any component of the holistic wheel. If I have, I try to make an earnest attempt to pay more attention to that aspect of my life during the upcoming week. For instance, if my previous week's activities reveal that I've neglected to spend enough time on my social self, I plan to spend more time the following week with family and friends. If I've neglected to attend to my physical self, I plan to exercise more consistently and eat more healthily the next week. Having the holistic wheel posted on my door provides me with a constant visual reminder to strive for "wholeness" and "balance" in my life.

—*Joe Cuseo*

> "Everyone is a house with four rooms: a physical, a mental, an emotional, and a spiritual. Most of us tend to live in one room most of the time but unless we go into every room every day, even if only to keep it aired, we are not complete."
> —*Native American proverb*

Physical Wellness

The physical component of wellness is the primary focus of this chapter. It could be said that physical health is a precondition or prerequisite that enables all other elements of wellness to be experienced. It's hard to grow intellectually and professionally if you're not well physically, and it's hard to become wealthy and wise without first being healthy.

> "Buono salute é la vera ricchezza ("Good health is true wealth.")"
> —*Italian proverb*

Physical wellness involves more than recovering from illness or disease after it occurs. Instead, it's engaging in health-promoting behaviors that proactively prevent illness from happening in the first place (Corbin, Pangrazi, & Franks, 2000). Wellness puts into practice two classic proverbs: "Prevention is the best medicine" and "An ounce of prevention is worth a pound of cure."

> "Health is a state of complete well-being, and not merely the absence of disease or infirmity."
> —*World Health Organization*

As depicted in **Figure 11.2**, there are three potential interception points for preventing illness, preserving health, and promoting peak performance; they range from reactive (after illness) to proactive (before illness). Wellness goes beyond maintaining physical health to attaining a higher quality of life that includes vitality (energy and vigor), longevity (longer life span), and life satisfaction (happiness).

During any major life transition, such as the transition to college, unhealthy

FIGURE 11.2: Potential Points for Preventing Illness, Preserving Health, and Promoting Peak Performance

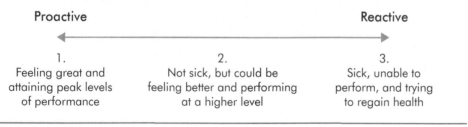

©Kendall Hunt Publishing Company

habits add to the level of transitional stress (Khoshaba & Maddi, 2005). In contrast, engaging in healthy habits is one way to manage and reduce stress at all stages of life—especially during stages of transition.

Think About It—Journal Entry 11.2

If you could single out one thing about your physical health right now that you'd like to improve or learn more about, what would it be? Why?

_____

_____

_____

_____

_____

Essential Elements of Physical Wellness

A healthy physical lifestyle includes three key components:

1. Supplying our body with effective fuel (nutrition) and transforming that fuel into bodily energy (exercise)
2. Giving our body adequate rest (sleep) so that it can recover and replenish the energy it has expended
3. Avoiding risky substances (alcohol and drugs) and risky behaviors that can threaten personal health and safety.

Nutrition

"Tell me what you eat and I'll tell you what you are."

—*Anthelme Brillat-Savarin, French lawyer, gastronomist, and founder of the low-carbohydrate diet*

"If we are what we eat, then I'm cheap, fast, and easy."

—*Steven Wright, award-winning comedian*

Similar to the way in which high-performance fuel improves the performance of an automobile, a high-quality (nutritious) diet improves the performance of the human body and mind, enabling each to operate at peak capacity. Unfortunately, we frequently pay more attention to the quality of fuel we put in our cars than to the quality of food we put into their bodies. We often eat without any intentional plan about what we should eat. We eat at places where we can get food fast conveniently without having to step out of our car (or off of our butts). America has become a "fast food nation"; we have grown accustomed to consuming food that can be accessed quickly, conveniently, cheaply, and in large (super-sized) portions (Schlosser, 2005). National surveys reveal that less than 40% of American college students report that they maintain a healthy diet (Sax, et al., 2004).

AUTHOR'S EXPERIENCE

When I first went away to college, I loved that I had the freedom to eat whatever I wanted, whenever I wanted. Food (and alcohol) were always readily available. During the first 18 years of my life, I never had any issues with my weight, so I didn't really think about what I was eating while in college. The late night pizza and ice cream runs caught up with me, and by the time I went home for the holiday break in December, I only had a few pairs of sweatpants that fit me. The fact that I was eating unhealthy foods and not exercising much had really caught up with me, and I gained over 20 pounds in four months. I have since learned how to eat healthier and exercise, but I have struggled with my weight ever since that first year of college.

—*Julie McLaughlin*

Think About It—Journal Entry 11.3

Have your eating habits changed since you've begun college? If yes, in what ways?

_____

_____

_____

_____

_____

_____

We should eat in a thoughtful, nutritionally conscious way, rather than solely out of convenience, habit, or pursuit of what's most pleasing to our taste buds. We should also "eat to win" by consuming the types of food that will best equip us to defeat disease and enables us to reach peak levels of physical and mental performance. The following nutrition management strategies may be used to enhance your body's ability to stay well and perform well.

Nutrition Management Strategies

1. **Develop a nutrition management plan that ensures your diet has variety and balance.** Planning what we eat is an essential step toward ensuring we eat what best preserves health and promotes wellness. If we don't plan in advance to obtain food we should eat, we're more likely to eat food that can be accessed conveniently and doesn't require advanced preparation. Unfortunately, the types of foods that are readily available, easily accessible, and immediately consumable are usually fast foods and prepackaged or processed foods, which are often the least healthy options. If we are serious about eating in a way that's best for our health and performance, we need to do more advanced planning.

   Figure 11.3 depicts the _MyPlate_ chart; this is the new version of the former Food Guide Pyramid created by the American Dietetic Association. Since foods vary in terms of the nature of nutrients they provide (carbohydrates, protein, and fat), no single food group can supply all the nutrients our body needs. Therefore, our diet should contain a balanced blend of all food groups, albeit in different proportions or percentages.

   To find the daily amount of food that should be consumed from each of the major food groups for your age and gender, go to _www.ChooseMyPlate.gov_ or _www.cnpp.usda.gov/dietaryguidelines_. You can use these guidelines to create a personal dietary plan that ensures you consume each of these food groups every day, which will result in a balanced diet that minimizes your risk of nutritional deficiencies and disorders, and maximizes your health and performance.

FIGURE 11.3: MyPlate

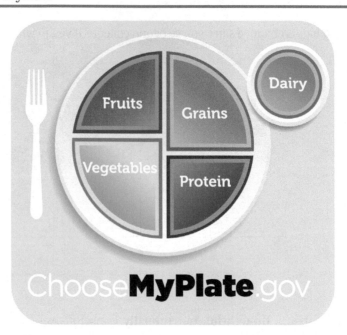

Source: USDA

"Eating the rainbow" is a phrase used by nutritionists to help people remember that including a variety of colorful fruits and vegetables in our diet is a simple way to get an ample amount of vitamins, minerals, and disease-fighting nutrients. The colors of certain fruits and vegetables can serve as indicators of the specific nutrients contained within them. For instance, fruits and vegetables that are:

- Orange and yellow (e.g., carrots, squash, melons): contain high amounts of vitamins A and C as well as nutrients that prevent cataracts and other types of eye disease
- Green (e.g., spinach, broccoli, avocado): contain high levels of vitamins B, E and K as well as anticancer agents
- Red (e.g., tomatoes, strawberries, cherries): contain an antioxidant that reduces the risk of cancer and heart disease.
- Purple and blue (e.g., grapes, eggplant, red cabbage): contain abundant amounts of vitamins C and K as well as antioxidants that reduce the risk of cancer and cardiovascular disease
- Brown and white (e.g., cauliflower, mushrooms, bananas): contain chemicals that reduce the risk of infectious diseases by attacking viruses and bacteria (Nutrition Australia, 2015).

What are your weakest categories? What could you eat, and would be willing to eat, to strengthen your weakest color category?

⊜ Think About It—Journal Entry 11.4

Do you eat fruits and vegetables regularly that fall into each of the above-five color categories? Why or why not?

_____

_____

_____

_____

_____

2. **Minimize your consumption of foods whose nutritional value is low (or zero) and that increase your risk of heart disease and cancer.**

    * Reduce intake of fried and fatty foods such as pizza, hamburgers, French fries, donuts, butter, and margarine. These foods not only contain lots of calories but also can increase the risk of heart disease because they contain saturated fats and trans fats—"bad" fats that tend to stick to blood vessel walls and increase the risk of blocking normal blood flow. Saturated fats also increase the risk of certain forms of cancer, such as breast and bowel cancer. Saturated fats should comprise less than one-tenth of the total number of calories you consume (National Research Council, 1989). Even if you exercise regularly and are physically active, you still have to be conscious of the food you put into your body. Well-conditioned athletes still can be at risk for heart disease and cancer if they consume foods containing high amounts of saturated fat.

    * Reduce consumption of processed foods. Processed foods were originally natural foods, but synthetic ingredients have been added to them so that they can be preserved, packaged, jarred, canned, or bottled and sold later to the public in large or bulk quantities. Processed foods contain additives that supplement natural food to preserve its shelf life, make it more pleasing to the eye, or make it more pleasing to the taste buds. These additives typically have no nutritional value and may have unknown or possibly unhealthy effects on the body. For example, processed foods often contain added sugar and salt, which tend to promote weight gain and elevate blood pressure, respectively.

    * Salt and sugar are often added to processed foods just to increase their taste appeal (and sales appeal). Why do humans often find sweeter and saltier processed foods tastier than natural foods? One theory is that processed foods haven't been around as long as unprocessed "natural" foods, which have been around for millions of years and were the only foods available to and consumed by our ancient ancestors. Therefore, our taste buds may find "newer" processed foods to be more stimulating because they're different from the "old" natural foods that have been eaten for millions of years (Eaton & Konner, 1985; Simopoulos & Pavlou, 1997). Ironically, humans may have developed or evolved a taste preference for the very foods that are

the least nutritious, least healthy, and highest in calories. The unfortunate consequence of all this is that the foods most likely to stimulate taste buds (and sense of smell) are the ones also most likely to inflate fat cells.

- Reduce consumption of high-fat dairy products (e.g., cheese, butter, margarine, cream, and whole milk). High-fat dairy products are high in saturated fat and sodium, both of which increase the risk of heart disease. The calcium contained in dairy products is good for you, but you're better off getting that calcium from low-fat dairy products, such as low-fat milk, yogurt, and cottage cheese.
- Minimize consumption of animal meat, particularly red meat such as hamburger and steak. Meat often contains a large amount of saturated fat, which poses a major risk for heart disease. Many people believe they must consume a substantial amount of red meat because the body needs protein. It's true that meat provides large amounts of protein, but protein should make up only 15 percent of your daily calories. Americans tend to consume about twice as much protein as their bodies need (National Research Council, 1989). Consequently, it's probably best to decrease the amount of protein you get from meat and increase the amount you get from sources that are low in saturated fat, such as plants (e.g., beans and peas), nuts (e.g., walnuts and almonds), and low-fat dairy products (e.g., low-fat milk and yogurt).

  If or when you consume meat, you can reduce its health risk by eating lean meat that has less fat and by removing any fatty skin from the meat (e.g., removing the skin from chicken or turkey). You can also reduce meat's unhealthy effects by not frying it, because the oils used in the frying process increase the concentration of saturated fat in the meat. Instead of frying, roast, grill, bake, or broil the meat you eat.

3. **Reduce calorie intake and control weight.**
   - Decrease or eliminate junk-food snacks. Replace sugary and salty snacks with healthier munchies, such as fruits, nuts, seeds, and raw vegetables. Many of these healthier snacks are as sweet, crispy, or crunchy as junk food snacks. Natural fruits can provide sweetness with more nutrients and fewer calories than processed sweets (e.g., candy bars and blended coffee drinks). Unfortunately, advertisers spend millions of dollars convincing consumers that processed sweets are "indescribably delicious." From a strictly economic standpoint, nutritious snacks represent a better financial investment because you get a bigger bang for your buck—that is, more nutrients (and less empty calories) for your snacking dollar.

 Think About It—Journal Entry 11.5

What type of junk food (if any) do you currently eat? Why?

If you do eat junk food, what's the likelihood that you'll continue to do so? Why?

_____

_____

_____

_____

What could you eat instead?

_____

_____

_____

_____

- Decrease the tendency to pack most of your calories into one or two large meals per day. Most nutritionists recommend that people eat large meals less often and small meals more often. No research evidence or dietary rule supports the American habit of eating three times a day as the best nutritional practice. Six smaller meals or healthy snacks per day may be a more effective way to fuel the body than three full-sized meals (Khoshaba & Maddi, 2004). When our ancient ancestors foraged for food, it's unlikely that they ate full meals three times a day; they probably ate more frequently and in smaller portions, which provided them with a steady stream of energy throughout the day.
- Decrease the amount of juices you consume daily. They contain a large amount of calories. Eliminate sodas as they contain a large amount of sugar and empty calories.
- Reduce the total number of calories consumed during your evening meal. The meal you eat closest to bedtime should be your lightest meal with the fewest calories because you're soon going to be lying down and not expending much physical energy for seven to eight hours. Remember that calories are measures of the amount of energy contained in food. One calorie may be described as one unit or degree of energy. If you consume a unit of energy and don't use it, you don't lose it; instead, you save it or store it—as fat. In other words, much like money, if you don't spend your income (caloric intake), you tend to save it in your body's bank of fat cells. Eating lots of calories in the evening and then lying down and sleeping soon thereafter means those evening calories don't get burned as physical energy, but are stored as body fat.

- Avoid rushing out at the beginning of the day and skipping or skimping on breakfast. As the term implies, a good breakfast provides energy that enables you to break your nighttime fast at the start of the day and sustain your energy throughout the day. (It also reduces your desire for unhealthy snacks later in the day.) Your first meal of the day should be the meal at which you consume most of your daily calories because you need energy for the next 16 or so hours that you'll be awake and moving. Unfortunately, Americans tend to do it backward by skipping or skimping at breakfast and piling on calories at dinner—a time of day when they don't need many calories because they'll soon be lying down and falling asleep.

4. **Make a conscious attempt to increase consumption of natural foods that have been available to humans throughout natural history.** The following foods aren't processed foods but natural foods that have been available to, and consumed by, humans for thousands of years. As a rule, the food that was good for our ancient ancestors and the survival of our species is good for us now. These are the foods that provide humans with the best protection against their two leading killers: heart disease and cancer.

    - Feast on fresh fruit. Fruit has multiple nutritional benefits, including high amounts of vitamins (especially A and C) and minerals. Many fruits also contain high amounts of fiber, which helps purify the bloodstream, lowers the bad type of cholesterol that causes heart disease, and rids the body of toxins found in the intestine. Other fruits, such as berries, are rich in antioxidants—substances known to lower the risk of cancer by attacking oxidants (toxins) in the body that can damage genetic DNA and weaken the immune system. (Blueberries are thought to contain the most antioxidants, followed by blackberries, raspberries, and strawberries.) Keep in mind that fresh fruit is superior to canned fruit, which has been processed and artificially preserved. Also, if weight control is an issue for you, fresh fruit is superior to dried fruit, which contains more calories.

    - Go for fresh (or frozen) vegetables. Fresh or frozen vegetables are superior to canned and processed vegetables. The natural oils in certain vegetables (e.g., olive, corn, avocado, and soy) are rich sources of unsaturated fat. Unsaturated fats, also known as essential fatty acids, are considered to be "good" fats because they don't congregate or coagulate in your bloodstream but remain in liquid form within your system; therefore, they don't degenerate into fat on the walls of blood vessels (Erasmus, 1993). Unsaturated fats also help wash away and flush out bad fats from your bloodstream. In addition to containing unsaturated fats, many vegetables—such as raw carrots and green beans—contain fiber that reduces the risk of heart disease and certain forms of cancer.

 Think About It—Journal Entry 11.6

Do you eat fresh fruit and vegetables daily?

Why or why not?

- Go wild on grains. Whole-wheat bread and pasta, whole-grain cereals, oat-meal, and bran are examples of healthy grains. Note that the word "whole" should appear in the product's name (e.g., "whole-wheat bread" and "whole-grain cereal"). This is the key to determining that the grain is natural and not processed; for example, whole-wheat bread is made from a natural grain, but wheat or white bread has been processed. Thus, if you're looking for unbleached, unprocessed grain bread, make sure it says "whole wheat."

  Natural grains contain complex carbohydrates, which the body uses to produce steady, ongoing energy. Complex carbohydrates are called "complex" because their molecular structure is harder for the body to digest and break down into blood sugar. Their more complex molecular structure slows the digestion process; as a result, they're absorbed into the bloodstream more slowly, which allows them to deliver energy to the body more gradually and evenly over an extended period (similar to a coated pill or time-released capsule). Thus, grains are an excellent source of food for producing the steady, long-term energy necessary for athletic activities that require endurance and stamina. Grains are also high in fiber, which helps fight heart disease and certain forms of cancer. Lastly, many complex carbohydrates contain an amino acid that helps manufacture serotonin, a brain chemical associated with relaxation and feelings of emotional serenity (Des-Maisons, 1998).

- Feed freely on fish. Fish are high in protein and low in saturated fat, and the natural oil in fish is high in unsaturated fat, which flushes out and washes away cholesterol-forming fats from the bloodstream (Khoshaba & Maddi, 2004). Thus, a diet high in unsaturated fats (and low in saturated fats) reduces risk for cardiovascular disease such as high blood pressure, heart attacks, and strokes. This explains why fish-eating Eskimos have a significantly lower rate of cardiovascular disease than non-Eskimos (Feskens & Kromhout, 1993). However, be cautious about eating too much fish that could contain high levels of mercury, such as shark, swordfish, red snapper, and orange roughy. Eating a variety of fish will help minimize this risk (American Heart Association, 2006).

- Consume lots of legumes. The word *legumes* derives from the Latin root *legumend*, meaning "to gather." This group includes plants and seeds, such as beans (black, red, and navy), lentils, Brussels sprouts, peas, and peanuts. Such foods are great sources of fiber, protein, iron, and B vitamins; plus, they are naturally cholesterol-free and low in saturated fat. The natural oil contained in these foods contains unsaturated fats—"good" fats that can reduce buildup of bad cholesterol in the bloodstream. It's interesting to note that in developing countries, where there is less affluence than in the United States, people rely mainly on legumes, grains, fruits, and vegetables. Despite their poorer economies and poorer medical care, people living in underdeveloped countries have significantly lower rates of heart disease and diet-related cancers than do people living (and eating) in the United States (U.S. Department of Health & Human Services, 2000).

- Drink more water. Most people don't get the recommended amount of water (seven 8-ounce glasses per day). You need to hydrate your body. The body uses water much like a car uses motor oil and transmission fluid, to drive nutrients (fuel) to their proper destinations and to drive waste products out of the system. Water also improves your nervous system's ability to conduct electrochemical signals, which may benefit the brain's ability to process information more easily and more rapidly. In addition to its internal benefits, water has the cosmetic benefit of improving the appearance of your skin. The multiple health benefits of water suggest that you shouldn't drink water only when you're feeling thirsty, but should get into a routine of drinking water regularly throughout the day.

- If you're a woman, make a conscious effort to consume more calcium. Females should take in at least 1,200 mg of calcium per day (Gershoff & Whitney, 1996) to reduce the risk of osteoporosis (thinning of bones and loss of bone mass or density), which increases risk for fractures and curvature of the upper spine. Although osteoporosis can happen in men as well as women, it occurs more often among females. It's estimated that one of three women over the age of 40 will develop osteoporosis (Bohme & Budden, 2001). Because societal pressures make women more weight-conscious than men, females may try to avoid high-calcium dairy products because they're high in calories. However, low-fat, low-calorie dairy products, such as cottage cheese and low-fat yogurt, can contain lots of calcium without lots of calories. Sizable amounts of calcium are also found in other low-calorie foods, such as certain fish (e.g., salmon), vegetables (e.g., broccoli), and fruit (e.g., oranges; Gershoff & Whitney, 1996). Women can also ensure that they get their optimum level of calcium each day by taking calcium dietary supplements.

5. Maintain self-awareness of your eating habits. In addition to planning our diet, effective nutrition management requires that we remain aware of our daily eating habits. We can monitor our eating habits by simply taking a little time to read the labels on food products before we put them into our shopping cart and into our body. Keeping a nutritional log or journal of what we eat in a typical week is an effective way to track the nutrients and caloric content of what we're consuming.

When choosing our diet, we should also be mindful of our family history. Are there members of your immediate and extended family who have shown tendencies toward heart disease, diabetes, or cancer? If so, intentionally adopt a diet that reduces your risk for developing the types of illnesses that you may have genetic tendencies to develop. (For regularly updated information on dietary strategies for reducing the risk of common diseases, see the following website: https://fnic.nal.usda.gov/diet-and-disease).

Think About It—Journal Entry 11.7

Are you aware of any disease or illness that tends to run in your family?

If yes, are you aware of how you may reduce your risk of experiencing this disease or illness through your diet?

Eating Disorders

While some students experience the "freshman 15"—a 15-pound weight gain during the first year of college (Brody, 2003)—others experience eating disorders related to weight loss and losing control of their eating habits. These disorders are more common among females (National Institute of Mental Health, 2014), largely because Western cultures place more emphasis and pressure on females to maintain lighter body weight and body size. Studies show that approximately one of every three college females reports worrying about her weight, body image, or eating habits (Leavy, Gnong, & Ross, 2009).

Box 11.1 provides a short summary of the major eating disorders experienced by college students. These disorders are often accompanied by emotional issues (e.g., depression and anxiety) that are serious enough to require professional treatment (National Institute of Mental Health, 2014). The earlier these disorders are identified and treated, the better the prognosis or probability of complete and permanent recovery.

Box 11.1

Major Eating Disorders

Anorexia Nervosa

Individuals experiencing anorexia nervosa are dangerously thin, yet they see themselves as overweight and have an intense fear of gaining weight. Anorexics typically deny that they're severely underweight; and even if their weight drops to the point where they may look like walking skeletons, they may continue to be obsessed with losing weight, eating infrequently, and eating extremely small portions. Anorexics may also use other methods to lose weight, such as compulsive exercise, diet pills, laxatives, diuretics, or enemas.

Bulimia Nervosa

This eating disorder is characterized by repeated episodes of "binge eating"—consuming excessive amounts of food within a limited period of time. Bulimics tend to lose

(continued)

Box 11.1 *(continued)*

self-control during their binges and then try to compensate for overeating by engaging in behavior to purge their guilt and prevent weight gain. They may purge themselves by self-induced vomiting, consuming excessive amounts of laxatives or diuretics, using enemas, or fasting. The binge–purge pattern typically takes place at least twice a week and continues for three or more months.

> I had a friend who took pride in her ability to lose 30 lbs. in one summer by not eating and working out excessively. I know girls that find pleasure in getting ill so that they throw up, can't eat, and lose weight."
>
> —*Comments written in a first-year student's journal*

Unlike anorexics, bulimics are harder to detect because their binges and purges typically take place secretly and their body weight looks about normal for their age and height. However, similar to anorexics, bulimics fear gaining weight, aren't happy with their body, and have an intense desire to lose weight.

Binge–Eating Disorder

Like bulimia, binge-eating disorder involves repeated, out-of-control episodes of consuming large amounts of food. However, unlike bulimics, binge eaters don't purge after binging episodes.

Those suffering from binge-eating disorder demonstrate at least three of the following symptoms, two or more times per week, for several months:

1. Eating at an extremely rapid rate
2. Eating until becoming uncomfortably full
3. Eating large amounts of food when not physically hungry
4. Eating alone because of embarrassment about others seeing how much they eat
5. Feeling guilty, disgusted, or depressed after overeating.

Sources: American Psychiatric Association (2015); National Institute of Mental Health (2014).

Exercise and Fitness

Wellness depends not only on fueling the body but using that fuel to move the body. We know that eating natural (unprocessed) foods is better for our health because those were the foods eaten by our ancient human ancestors, which has contributed to the survival of our species. Similarly exercise is another "natural" health-promoting activity that contributed to the health and survival of the human species (Booth & Vyas, 2001). Our ancient ancestors didn't have the luxury of motorized vehicles to transport them from point A to point B, nor could they stroll up leisurely to grocery stores and buy food or have food served to them while seated in restaurants. Instead, they had to roam and rummage for fruit, nuts, and vegetables, or chase down animals for meat to eat. Thus, exercise was part of their daily routine.

> If exercise could be packaged into a pill, it would be the single most widely prescribed and beneficial medicine in the nation."
>
> —*Robert N. Butler, former director of the National Institute of Aging*

The benefits of physical exercise for improving the longevity and quality of human life are simply extraordinary. If done regularly, exercise may well be the most effective "medicine" available to humans for preventing disease and preserving lifelong health. The major health-promoting benefits of exercise are described below.

Benefits of Exercise for the Body

1. **Exercise promotes cardiovascular health.** Simply stated, exercise makes the heart stronger. Since the heart is a muscle, like any other muscle in the body, its size and strength are increased by exercise. A bigger and stronger heart pumps more blood per beat, reducing the risk for heart disease and stroke (loss of oxygen to the brain) by increasing circulation of oxygen-carrying blood and increasing the body's ability to dissolve blood clots (Khoshaba & Maddi, 2005).

Exercise further reduces the risk of cardiovascular disease by: (a) decreasing the levels of triglycerides (clot-forming fats) in the blood, (b) increasing the levels of "good" cholesterol (high-density lipoproteins), and (c) preventing "bad" cholesterol (low-density lipoproteins) from sticking to and clogging up blood vessels.

2. **Exercise stimulates the immune system.** Exercise enables us to better fight off infectious diseases (e.g., colds and the flu) for the following reasons:

   * It reduces stress—which normally weakens the immune system.
   * It increases blood flow throughout the body, which increases circulation of antibodies that flush germs out of our system.
   * It increases body temperature, which helps kill germs in a way similar to how a low-grade fever kills germs when we're sick (Walsh, et al., 2011).

3. **Exercise strengthens muscles and bones.** Exercise reduces muscle tension, which helps prevent muscle strain and pain; (for example, strengthening abdominal muscles reduces the risk of developing lower back pain). Exercise also maintains bone density and reduces the risk of osteoporosis (brittle bones that bend and break easily). It's noteworthy that our bone density before age 20 affects the bone density we will have for the remainder of life. Thus, by engaging in regular exercise early in life, we minimize risk of bone deterioration throughout life.

AUTHOR'S EXPERIENCE

I kept in shape when I was young by playing sports such as basketball and baseball. Whenever time in my schedule would allow, I'd play these sports for hours at a time. I enjoyed it so much that I didn't even realize I was exercising. My body fat was practically nonexistent, energy was ever flowing, and my athletic skills were ever-growing. Age has caught up with me and I can no longer play these sports. At this point in my life, I attempt to remain active through regularly scheduled workouts to keep my body fat in a reasonable double-digit category. This requires effective planning, time management, and willpower.

—Aaron Thompson

Think About It—Journal Entry 11.8

Have your exercise habits changed (for better or worse) since you've begun college?

If yes, why has this change taken place?

> "I'm less active now than before college because I'm having trouble learning how to manage my time."
>
> *—First-year student*

4. **Exercise promotes weight loss and weight management.** In a study of 188 countries, the highest proportion of overweight and obese people live in the United States, and the rate is increasing (Ng & Associates, 2014). The national increase in overweight Americans is due not only to our consuming more calories but also to our lower levels of physical activity (NIDDK, 2010). We're now playing double jeopardy with our health by eating more and moving less. Much of our reduced level of physical activity has resulted from the emergence of modern technological conveniences that make it easier for us to go about our daily business without exerting ourselves in the slightest. TVs now come with remote controls; we don't have to move to change channels, change volume, or turn the TV on and off. We now have instant access to video games that can be played virtually without actually running, jumping, or even getting on our feet.

Intentional exercise is our best antidote to all the inactivity that characterizes modern life. As a weight-control strategy, it's superior to dieting in one key respect: It raises the body's rate of metabolism—the rate at which consumed calories are burned as energy rather than stored as fat. In contrast, dieting lowers the body's rate of metabolism and the rate at which calories are burned (Agus, et al., 2000; Leibel, Rosenbaum, & Hirsch, 1995). After two to three weeks of low-calorie dieting without exercising, the body "thinks" it's starving, so it compensates by conserving more calories as fat so that it can be used for future energy (Bennett & Gurin, 1983). In contrast, exercise speeds up basal metabolism—the body's rate of metabolism when it's resting. Thus, in addition to burning fat directly while exercising, exercise burns fat by continuing to keep the body's metabolic rate higher after we stop exercising and move on to do more sedentary things.

Benefits of Exercise for the Mind

In addition to its multiple benefits for the body, exercise benefits the mind. Here's a summary of the powerful effects that physical exercise has on our mental health and mental performance.

1. **Exercise increases mental energy and improves mental performance.** Have you noticed how red our face gets when we engage in strenuous physical activity? This rosy complexion occurs because physical activity pumps enormous amounts of blood into our head region and more oxygen into our brain. Exercise increases blood flow to all parts of the body, but since the brain uses more oxygen than any other organ of the body, it's the organ that benefits most from exercise. Moreover, aerobic exercise (exercise that increases respiratory rate and circulates oxygen throughout the body) has been found to: (a) enlarge the frontal lobe, the part of the brain responsible for higher-level thinking (Colcombe, et al., 2006; Kramer & Erickson, 2007); and (b) increase production of brain chemicals that enable neurological connections to form between brain cells (Howard, 2014; Ratey, 2013). As noted in Chapter 5, these are the connections that provide the biological basis of learning and memory. One well-designed study of more than 250 college students discovered that students who regularly engaged in vigorous physical activity had higher GPAs (Parker-Pope, 2010).

Furthermore, exercise is a stimulant whose stimulating effects are similar to those provided by popular energy drinks (e.g., Red Bull, Full Throttle, and Monster). However, exercise delivers these stimulating effects without the sugar, caffeine, and negative side effects of energy drinks—such as nervousness,

> "To keep the body in good health is a duty, otherwise we shall not be able to keep our mind strong and clear."
> —Buddha, founder of Buddhism

irritability, increased blood pressure, and a sharp drop in energy ("crash") after the drink's stimulating effects wear off (Malinauskas, et al., 2007).

2. **Exercise elevates mood.** Exercise stimulates release of: (a) endorphins—morphine-like chemicals found in the brain that produce a natural high; and (b) serotonin—a mellowing brain chemical that reduces feelings of tension, anxiety, and depression. It is for these reasons that psychotherapists often prescribe exercise for patients experiencing mild cases of anxiety and depression (Johnsgard, 2004). Studies show that people who exercise regularly report feeling happier (Myers, 1993).

3. **Exercise improves self-esteem.** Exercise can enhance our sense of self-worth by providing us with a feeling of accomplishment and improving our physical self-image (e.g., better weight control, muscle tone and skin tone).

4. **Exercise deepens and enriches the quality of sleep.** Sleep research indicates that if we engage in exercise at least three hours before bedtime, it helps us fall asleep, stay asleep, and sleep more deeply (Singh, Clements, & Fiatarone, 1997; Youngstedt, 2005). This is why exercise is a common component of treatment programs for people suffering from insomnia (Dement & Vaughan, 2000).

> "
> It is exercise alone that supports the spirits, and keeps the mind in vigor."
> —*Marcus Cicero, ancient Roman orator and philosopher*

Guidelines and Strategies for Maximizing the Effectiveness of Exercise

Although specific types of exercises benefit the body and mind in different ways, there are general guidelines that can be followed to maximize the positive impact of any exercise routine or personal fitness program. These guidelines are discussed below.

1. **Warm up before exercising and cool down after exercising.** Start with a 10-minute warm up of low-intensity movements similar to the ones you'll be using during the actual exercise. This will increase circulation of blood to the muscles you'll be exercising, which will reduce muscle soreness and risk of muscle pulls.

   Finish your exercise routine with a 10-minute cool down that involves stretching the muscles you used while exercising. Stretch the muscle until it burns a little bit, and then release it. By cooling down after exercise, you improve circulation to the muscles you exercised, enabling them to return more gradually to a tension-free state; this minimizes the risk of muscle tightness, cramps, pulls, and tears.

2. **Engage in cross-training to attain total body fitness.** A balanced, comprehensive fitness program includes cross-training—a combination of different exercises to achieve total body fitness. We should strive to combine exercises that enable us to achieve all of the following physical benefits:
   - Endurance and weight control (e.g., running, cycling, or swimming);
   - Muscle strength and tone (e.g., weight training, push-ups, or sit-ups); and
   - Flexibility (e.g., yoga, Pilates, or tai chi).

   Cross-training also entails exercising different muscle groups on a rotational basis (e.g., upper body muscles one day, lower body muscles the next). This gives different sets of muscle tissue extra time to rest, repair, and recover before they're exercised again.

3. **Include *interval training* as part of your exercise plan.** Interval training involves interspersing high-intensity exercise workouts with low-intensity exercise or short rest periods (Roxburgh, et al., 2014), such as interspersing walking with short bursts of running. Research indicates that alternating between

higher- and lower-intensity exercises effectively strengthen the heart muscle and increases its oxygen-carrying capacity; it also burns calories faster and enables you to exercise longer and at more intense levels (Mayo Clinic, 2015; Mazurek, et al., 2014).

4. **Exercise regularly, allowing strength and stamina to increase gradually.** The key to attaining fitness and avoiding injury is body training, not body straining. One strategy for ensuring you're not straining your body is to see if you can talk while you're exercising. If you can't continue speaking without stopping to catch your breath, this may indicate you're overdoing it. Drop the intensity level and allow your body to adapt or adjust to a less strenuous level. After continuing at this lower level for a while, try again at the higher level and try to talk simultaneously. If you can do both, you're ready to continue at that level for some time. Continue to use this strategy and gradually increase the intensity, frequency, or duration of your exercise routine to a level that produces maximum benefits with minimal post-exercise discomfort.

AUTHOR'S EXPERIENCE

I had a habit of exercising too intensely—to the point where my body felt sore for days after I worked out. I eventually discovered a way to avoid overdoing it. When listening to music through headphones while exercising, I'd see if I could sing along with the music without having to stop and catch my breath. If I could, I knew I wasn't overextending myself. This strategy has helped me manage my exercise intensity level and reduce my day-after exercise soreness. (Plus, I've gained more confidence as a vocalist because my singing sounds a lot better when my ears are covered with headphones.)

—Joe Cuseo

5. **Take advantage of exercise and fitness resources on your campus.** Your college tuition pays use of the campus gym or recreation center, so take advantage of it. Also, consider taking physical education courses offered by your college. They count toward your college degree, and typically they carry one unit of credit so that they can be easily added to your course schedule. If exercise groups or clubs meet on campus, join them; they can provide you with a motivational support group that converts exercise from a solitary routine into a social experience. (It's also a good way to meet people.)

6. **Take advantage of natural opportunities for physical activity that present themselves during the day.** Exercise can take place in places beyond a gym or fitness center and outside scheduled workout times. Opportunities for exercise are available to us as we go about our daily activities. If you can walk or ride your bike to class, do that instead of driving a car or riding a bus. If you can climb some stairs instead of taking an elevator, take the route that requires more bodily activity.

 Think About It—Journal Entry 11.9

Do you have a regular exercise routine?

If yes, what do you do and how often do you do it? If no, why not?

_____

_____

What more could you do to improve your:

(a) Endurance?

_____

_____

_____

(b) Strength?

_____

_____

_____

(c) Flexibility?

_____

_____

_____

Rest and Sleep

Sleep experts agree that humans in today's information-loaded, multitasking world aren't getting the quantity and quality of sleep needed to perform at peak levels (Mitler, Dinges, & Dement, 1994). We often underestimate the power of sleep and think we can cut down on the time we spend sleeping without compromising the quality of our lives. However, as discussed below, the amount of sleep we get plays a pivotal role for preserving our health and enhancing our performance.

> "Sleep deprivation is a major epidemic in our society. Americans spend so much time and energy chasing the American dream that they don't have much time left for actual dreaming."
>
> —William Dement, pioneering sleep researcher and founder of the American Sleep Disorders Association

The Value and Purpose of Sleep

Resting and reenergizing the body are the most obvious purposes of sleep. Listed below are other benefits of sleep that are less well known but equally important (Dement & Vaughan, 2000; Horne, 1988).

1. **Sleep restores and preserves the power of the immune system.** Studies show that when humans and other animals lose sleep, it lowers their production of disease-fighting antibodies, making them more susceptible to illness, such as common colds and the flu (Bryant, Trinder, & Curtis, 2004).

2. **Sleep helps us cope with daily stress.** Sleep research shows that when we're experiencing stress, we spend more time in the REM (rapid eye movement) stage of sleep, which is the stage when most dreaming takes place (Suchecki, Tiba, & Machado, 2012). This suggests that dreaming is our brain's natural way of coping with stress. When we lose dream sleep, emotional problems—such as anxiety and depression—worsen (Voelker, 2004). It's thought that the biochemical changes that take place in our brain during dream sleep help restore imbalances in brain chemistry that occur when we experience anxiety or depression. Thus, getting high-quality sleep (especially high-quality dream sleep) helps us maintain our emotional stability and keeps us in a positive frame of mind. Indeed, surveys reveal that people who report sleeping well also report feeling happier (Myers, 1993).

3. **Sleep helps the brain form and retain memories.** When we're sleeping, our brain isn't bombarded with sensory input from the outside world. This allows the brain—particularly during dream sleep—to devote more of its energy (metabolism) to processing and storing information taken in during the day (Willis, 2006). Studies show that loss of dream sleep at night results in poorer memory for information learned during the day (Peigneux, et al., 2001). For instance, teenagers who get less than adequate amounts of sleep have more difficulty retaining information they learn in school (Horne, 1988). Studies also show that increasing sleep time from six or fewer hours per night to eight hours can increase memory by as much as 25% (Frank, Issa, & Stryker, 2001). Additional research indicates that when students study before going to bed and stop studying when they begin to feel drowsy (rather than trying to continue studying after drowsiness sets in), their memory for the studied material is superior (Willis, 2006).

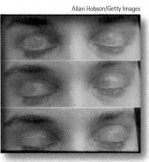

Allan Hobson/Getty Images

Studies show that dreaming during the REM stage of sleep helps us cope with stress and retain memories.

The Importance of Sleep for College Students

College students tend to have poorer sleep habits and experience more sleep problems than the general population. Heavier academic workloads, more opportunities for late-night socializing, and more frequent late-night (or all-night) study sessions often lead to more irregular sleep schedules and more sleep deprivation among college students. It's estimated that 60% of college students get an insufficient amount of sleep—a rate twice that of the general population (Kingkade, 2014).

How much sleep do we need and should we get? The answer lies in our genes and varies from person to person. On average, adults need seven to eight hours of sleep per day and teenagers need slightly more—about nine hours (Ohayon, et al., 2004). Research shows that college students get an average of less than seven hours of sleep each night (Hicks, cited in Zimbardo, Johnson, & McCann, 2012), which means they're not getting the amount of sleep needed for optimal academic performance.

Attempting to train our body to sleep less is likely to be an exercise in futility because it's attempting to make our body do something it's not naturally (genetically) "hard-wired" to do. When our body is deprived of the amount of sleep it's genetically designed to receive, it accumulates "sleep debt," which, like financial debt, must be paid back (Dement & Vaughan, 2000). If our sleep debt isn't repaid, it catches up to us and we pay for it by experiencing lower energy, lower mood, poorer health, and poorer performance (Van Dongen, et al., 2003). For example, studies show that the negative effects of sleep loss on driving an automobile are similar to the effects of drinking alcohol (Arnedt, et al., 2001; Fletcher, et al., 2003). Studies of sleep-deprived college students indicate that their academic performance is poorer than students who get sufficient sleep (Spinweber, cited in Zimbardo, Johnson, & McCann, 2012).

I'm not getting enough sleep. I've been getting roughly 6–7 hours of sleep on weekdays. In high school, I would get 8–9 hours of sleep."

—*First-year student*

First of all, you should probably know that your body will not function without sleep. I learned that the hard way."

—*Words written by a first-year student in a letter of advice to incoming college students*

The best way to open up more time for sleep is by using our time more effectively and efficiently to get things done during the day that are cutting into our sleep time at night. (For time management strategies, see Chapter 4.)

Think About It—Journal Entry 11.10

How much sleep do you think you need to perform at a peak level?

How many nights per week do you typically get this amount of sleep?

If you're not getting this optimal amount of sleep each night, what's preventing you from doing so?

Strategies for Improving Sleep Quality

Since sleep has such powerful benefits for both the body and mind, if you can improve the quality of your sleep, you can improve your physical and mental well-being. Listed below are specific strategies for improving sleep quality, which, in turn, should improve your health and performance.

1. **Become more aware of your sleep habits by keeping a sleep log or sleep journal.** Make note of what you did before going to bed on nights when you slept well or poorly. Tracking your sleep experiences in a journal may enable you to detect a pattern or relationship between certain things you do (or don't do) during the day on those nights when you sleep well. If you discover a pattern, you may have found yourself a routine to follow that gets you a good night's sleep on a consistent basis.
2. **Try to get into a regular sleep schedule by going to sleep and getting up at about the same time each day.** The human body functions best when it's on a biological rhythm of set cycles. If you can get your body on a regular sleep cycle, you can get into a biological rhythm that makes it easier for you to fall asleep, stay asleep, and wake up naturally from sleep— according to your body's own "internal alarm clock."

   Establishing a stable sleep schedule is particularly important around midterms and finals. Unfortunately, however, these are the times during the term when just the opposite happens. Normal sleep cycles are disrupted by cramming in last-minute studying, staying up later, getting up earlier, or pulling all-nighters and not sleeping at all. Sleep research shows that if students want to be at their physical and mental best for upcoming exams, they should get themselves on a regular sleep schedule of going to bed about the same time and getting up about the same time for at least one week before exams are to be taken (Dement & Vaughan, 1999). To help you get into this pattern, use the "distributed" practice strategies and the "part-to-whole" study method. (See Chapter 6 for a discussion of these techniques.)

3. **Attempt to get into a relaxing pre-bedtime ritual each night.** Taking a hot bath or shower, consuming a hot (noncaffeinated) beverage, or listening to relaxing music are bedtime rituals that can get you into a worry-free state before sleep and help you fall asleep sooner. Also, making a list of things you intend to do the next day before going to bed may help you relax and fall asleep because you know you're organized and ready to handle the following day's tasks.

   A light review of class notes or reading highlights just before bedtime can be a good nighttime ritual because sleep helps you retain what you experienced just before falling asleep. Many years of research indicate that the best thing you can do after attempting to learn information is to "sleep on it," probably because your brain can focus on processing and storing that information without interference from external stimulation or outside distractions (Jenkins & Dallenbach, 1924; Kuriyama, et al., 2008).

Think About It—Journal Entry 11.11

What do you do on most nights immediately before going to bed? Do you think this helps or hinders the quality of your sleep?

_____

_____

_____

_____

_____

4. **Avoid intense mental activity just before going to bed.** Light mental work may serve as a relaxing pre-sleep ritual, but cramming intensely for a difficult exam or doing intensive writing before bedtime will put you in a state of mental arousal, which can interfere with your ability to wind down and fall asleep.

5. **Avoid intense physical exercise before bedtime.** Physical exercise elevates muscle tension and increases oxygen flow to the brain, both of which will hinder your ability to fall asleep. If you like to exercise in the evening, it should be done at least three hours before bedtime (Epstein & Mardon, 2007).

6. **Avoid consuming sleep-interfering foods, beverages, or drugs in the late afternoon or evening.** In particular, avoid the following substances near bedtime:

   • **Caffeine.** It's a stimulant drug; for most people, it will stimulate their nervous system and keep them awake.

- **Nicotine.** Another stimulant drug that's also likely to reduce the depth and quality of your sleep. (Note: Smoking hookah through a water pipe delivers the same amount of nicotine as a cigarette.)
- **Alcohol.** It's a depressant (sedative) that makes you feel sleepy in larger doses; however, in smaller doses, it can have a stimulating effect. Furthermore, alcohol in any amount disrupts the quality of sleep by reducing the amount of time we spend in dream-stage sleep. (Marijuana does the same.)
- **High-fat foods.** Eating just before bedtime (or during the night) increases digestive activity in the stomach. This "internal noise" is likely to interfere with the soundness of our sleep. Peanuts, beans, fruits, raw vegetables, and high-fat snacks should especially be avoided because these are harder-to-digest foods.

Note

Substances that make us feel sleepy or cause us to fall asleep (e.g., alcohol and marijuana) typically reduce the quality of our sleep by interfering with dream sleep.

7. **Make sure the temperature in the room where you're sleeping is not warmer than 70 degrees (Fahrenheit).** Warm temperatures often make us feel sleepy, but they usually don't help us stay asleep or sleep deeply. This is why people have trouble sleeping on hot summer evenings. High-quality, uninterrupted sleep is more likely to take place at room temperatures around 65 degrees (Lack, et al., 2008).

Substance Abuse and Risky Behavior

In addition to putting healthy nutrients into our body, as well as exercising and resting it, there are two other important elements of physical wellness: (a) keeping risky substances out of our body and (b) avoiding risky behaviors that threaten our body's well-being.

Alcohol Use among College Students

In the United States, alcohol is a legal beverage (drug) for people 21 years of age and older. However, whether you're of legal age or not, it's likely that alcohol has already been available to you and will continue to be available to you as a college student. Since it's a substance commonly accessible at college parties and social gatherings, you'll be confronted with two choices:

1. To drink or not to drink
2. To drink responsibly or irresponsibly

If you decide to drink, here are some quick tips for drinking safely and responsibly:

- **Eat well before drinking and snack while drinking.** This will help lower the peak level of alcohol in your bloodstream.
- **Drink slowly.** Sip, don't gulp, and avoid "shot-gunning" or "chug-a-lugging" drinks.
- **Space out drinking over time.** (This gives the body time to metabolize the alcohol you've consumed and keeps your blood-alcohol level manageable.)
- **Alternate water and alcoholic drinks.**
- **Maintain awareness of how much you're drinking while you're drinking by monitoring your physical and mental state.** Slow down or stop drinking

after you've reached a state of moderate relaxation or a mild loss of inhibition. When folks drink to the point of slurring their speech, nodding out, or vomiting in the restroom, they're not exactly the life of the party.

Also, remember that alcohol is costly—both in terms of money and calories. Thus, reducing the amount we drink is not only a better way to manage our health; it's also a better way to manage our money and weight.

Research indicates that first-year college students drink more than they did in high school (Johnston, et al., 2005) and that alcohol abuse is higher among first-year college students than students at more advanced stages of their college experience (Bergen-Cico, 2000). The most common reason why first-year students drink is to "fit in" or to feel socially accepted (Meilman & Presley, 2005). However, college students overestimate the number of their peers who drink and the total amount they drink; this overestimation can lead them to believe that if they don't conform to this "norm," they're not "normal" (DeJong & Linkenback, 1999). If you choose to drink, make sure that it's *your* choice, not a choice imposed on you through social pressure or conformity.

Alcohol Abuse among College Students

FIGURE 11.4: Ethyl Alcohol: The Mind-Altering Ingredient Contained in Alcohol

©Kendall Hunt Publishing Company

College students' expectations that they should drink (or drink to excess) accounts, at least in part, for the fact that the number one drug problem on college campuses is *binge drinking*—periodic drinking episodes during which a large amount of alcohol (four to five drinks) is consumed in a short period of time, resulting in an acute state of intoxication, a.k.a., a "drunken state" (Marczinski, Estee, & Grant, 2009). Although alcohol is a legal substance (if you're 21 or older) and a substance that's consumed as a beverage rather than injected, smoked, or snorted, it still acts as a drug when consumed in large quantities (doses), and it does contain a mind-altering ingredient: ethyl alcohol (see **Figure 11.4**). Consumed in moderate amounts, alcohol is a relaxing beverage; in larger doses, it's a mind-altering drug. Like any other mind-altering substance, it has the potential to be addictive; approximately 7% to 8% of people who drink experience alcohol dependency (alcoholism) (Julien, Advokat, & Comaty, 2011). If there's a history of alcohol dependency in your family, be particularly cautious about your drinking habits.

Although binge drinking isn't necessarily a form of alcohol dependency, it's still a form of alcohol abuse because it has direct, negative effects on the health and well-being of the drinker (as well as others who have contact with the drinker). Research indicates that repeatedly getting drunk reduces the size and effectiveness of the part of the brain involved with memory formation (Brown, et al., 2000). These findings have led researchers to a simple conclusion: Each time we get drunk, the dumber we get (Weschsler & Wuethrich, 2002).

Binge drinking also reduces our inhibitions about engaging in risk-taking behavior, which, in turn, increases our risk of personal accidents, injuries, and illnesses. It's noteworthy that the legal age for consuming alcohol was once lowered to 18 years; it was raised back to 21 because the number of drunk-driving accidents and deaths among teenage drinkers increased dramatically when the legal age was lowered (NHTSA/FARS & U.S. Census Bureau, 2012). Traffic accidents still account for more deaths of Americans between the ages of 15 and 24 than any other single cause (Centers for Disease Control & Prevention, 2010).

Who's In Charge?

Drugs and Alcohol

It's "Thirsty Thursday" and your friend convinces you to go to a party with him. You tell him that you have class at 9:00 and you cannot miss it. He assures you that you will be home before midnight. You go to the party and you are having a great time. Everyone is drinking so you decide you should join in (even though you are underage). You drink more than your fair share and stumble in at 3 a.m. Your friend makes sure you get to bed OK and even sets your alarm for 8:30 so that you can make it to your 9:00 class. You are sick all night because you drank too much and you pass out on the bathroom floor. You finally get up around 11:00 and realize you missed class. You hear from a classmate that the teacher gave a pop quiz. You are irate with your friend because it is all his fault that you missed class and the quiz! Could you have handled this situation differently? If so, how? Who really is to blame for you missing class and the quiz?

_____

_____

_____

_____

_____

_____

_____

Arguably, no other drug reduces a person's inhibitions as dramatically as alcohol. When people consume a substantial amount of alcohol, they often become substantially less cautious about doing things they normally wouldn't do. This chemically induced sense of confidence—sometimes referred to as "liquid courage"—can override the process of logical thinking and decision making, increasing the drinker's willingness to engage in irrational, risk-taking behavior (e.g., engaging in dangerous stunts). Binge drinkers are also more willing to engage in reckless driving—increasing their risk of injury or death—and reckless (unprotected) sex—increasing their risk of accidental pregnancy or contracting sexual transmitted infections (STIs). It could be said that binge drinking leads drinkers to think they're invincible, immortal, and infertile.

This lack of inhibition happens because alcohol is a depressant drug, which depresses (slows down) signals normally sent from the upper, front part of the brain (the "human brain") that's responsible for rational thinking. This is the part of the brain that normally controls or inhibits the lower, middle part of the brain (the "animal brain")—which is responsible for basic animal drives, such as sex and aggression (see **Figure 11.5**). When the upper (rational) brain's messages are slowed by alcohol, the animal brain is freed from the signals that normally restrain or inhibit it, allowing its basic drives to be released or expressed. This is the underlying biological reason why excessive alcohol use increases the risk of aggressive behavior, such as: reckless driving, damaging property, fighting, sexual harassment, sexual abuse, and relationship violence (Abbey, 2002; Bushman & Cooper, 1990).

"If you drink, don't park.
Accidents cause people."
—Steven Wright, American comedian

FIGURE 11.5: How Alcohol Works in the Brain to Reduce Personal Inhibitions

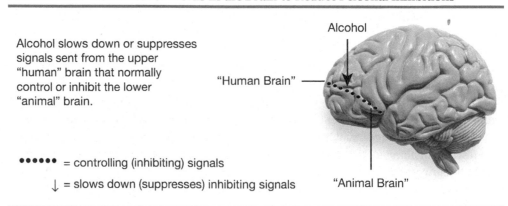

Alcohol slows down or suppresses signals sent from the upper "human" brain that normally control or inhibit the lower "animal" brain.

•••••• = controlling (inhibiting) signals

↓ = slows down (suppresses) inhibiting signals

©Kendall Hunt Publishing Company.

The point we're making here is not to scare you away from even thinking about drinking, nor is it to "guilt" you if you already drink. The point being made is: If you don't drink and don't care to drink, don't be pressured into drinking; and if you do drink, don't do it in excess or in binges.

Use and Abuse of Illegal Drugs

Alcohol can be legally used by anyone 21 years of age and older; other substances cannot be legally used by anyone at any age. While the college years are often a time for exploring and experimenting with different ideas, feelings and experiences, experimenting with illegal drugs can be risky. Even if we know how an illegal drug affects people in general, we don't know how it will affect us individually because each person has a unique genetic makeup. Furthermore, unlike legal drugs, which have to pass through rigorous testing by the Federal Drug Administration before being approved for public consumption, we don't have similar safeguards for the production and packaging of illegal drugs. For instance, we don't know if or what the drug may have been "cut" (mixed) with during the production process. Thus, we're not just taking a criminal risk by using an illegal substance, we're also taking a health risk by consuming an *unregulated* substance. Our bottom-line recommendation is: When in doubt, keep it out. Don't put anything into your body that's unregulated and whose impact may be unpredictable.

Listed below are the major types of illegal drugs, accompanied by a short description of their effects. Following the list, **Box 11.2** contains a summary of the major motives or reasons why people use drugs.

- Cocaine (coke, crack). A stimulant that's typically snorted or smoked and produces a strong "rush" (an intense feeling of euphoria)
- Amphetamines (speed, meth). A strong stimulant that increases energy and general arousal; it's usually taken in pill form but may also be smoked or injected
- Ecstasy (X). A stimulant typically taken in pill form that speeds up the nervous system and reduces social inhibitions
- Hallucinogens (psychedelics). Drugs that alter or distort perception—such as, LSD ("acid") and hallucinogenic mushrooms ("shrooms")

- **Narcotics (e.g., heroin and prescription pain pills).** Sedative drugs that slow down the nervous system and produce feelings of relaxation. (Heroin is a particularly powerful narcotic that's typically injected or smoked and produces an intense "rush" of euphoria.)
- **Marijuana (weed, pot).** Still an illegal drug in most states, it's primarily a depressant or sedative drug that slows down the nervous system and induces feelings of relaxation. It is important to note that while marijuana may be legal in some states, federal law (marijuana is illegal) overrides state law when institutions, etc. receive federal funds. Thus, marijuana is illegal on almost all college campuses regardless of the state law.
- **Date rape drugs.** Depressant (sedative) drugs that induce sleepiness, memory loss, and possible loss of consciousness; they're typically colorless, tasteless and odorless, so they can be easily mixed into a drink without the person noticing it, rendering that person vulnerable to rape or other forms of sexual assault. The most common date rape drugs are Rohypnol ("roofies") and GHB ("liquid E").
- **Synthetic drugs.** There has been a recent rise in the use of synthetic drugs (bath salts, K2, Spice, etc.). Legalities vary from state to state but there is no regulation on these chemical compounds. Because of this, these substance can be just as dangerous (if not more so) than traditional illegal drugs.

Think About It—Journal Entry 11.12

What drugs (if any) have you seen being used on your campus?

How would the type and frequency of drug use on your campus compare to what you saw in high school?

Box 11.2

Motives (Reasons) for Drug Use

People use drugs for a variety of reasons, the most common of which are listed below. If we remain aware of these motives, we reduce the risk that we'll do drugs for unconscious or subconscious reasons.

1. **Social Pressure.** To "fit in" or be socially accepted (e.g., drinking alcohol because everyone seems to be doing it)
2. **Recreational (Party) Use.** For fun, stimulation, or pleasure (e.g., smoking marijuana at parties to relax, loosen inhibitions, and have a "good time")

> For fun." "To party." "To fit in." "To become more talkative, outgoing, and flirtatious."
>
> To try anything once." "To become numb." "To forget problems." "Being bored."
>
> —*Responses of freshmen and sophomores to the question, "Why do college students take drugs?"*

3. **Experimental Use.** Doing drugs out of curiosity—to test out its effects (e.g., experimenting with LSD to see what it's like to have a psychedelic or hallucinogenic experience)
4. **Therapeutic Use.** Using prescription or over-the-counter drugs for medical purposes (e.g., taking Prozac for depression or Adderall to treat attention deficit disorder)
5. **Performance Enhancement.** To improve physical, mental, or social performance (e.g., taking steroids to improve athletic performance, stimulants to stay awake all night and cram for an exam, or alcohol to reduce social inhibitions and become more outgoing)
6. **Escapism.** To escape a personal problem or an unpleasant emotional state (e.g., taking ecstasy to escape depression or boredom)
7. **Addiction.** Physical or psychological dependence resulting from habitual use of a drug (e.g., continuing to use nicotine or cocaine because stopping triggers withdrawal symptoms such as anxiety and depression)

 Think About It—Journal Entry 11.13

What motives for drug use listed in **Box 11.2** would you say are the most common reasons for drug use on your campus?

_____

_____

_____

_____

_____

Any drug has the potential to be addictive (habit forming), especially if it's injected intravenously (directly into a vein), or smoked (inhaled through the lungs). These routes of delivery are particularly dangerous because they allow the drug to reach the brain faster and heighten its peak effect (the intensity of its highest point of impact). This rapid and high-peak effect is immediately followed by a rapid and sharp drop ("crash") (see **Figure 11.6**). This peak-to-valley, roller-coaster experience creates a greater risk for craving the drug again, thereby increasing the user's risk of dependency (addiction).

FIGURE 11.6: **Drugs Smoked Produce a Higher and More Rapid Peak Effect**

Here's a list of the most common signs that a person's drug use (including alcohol) is moving in the direction of *dependency* (*addiction*):

- Steadily increasing the amount (dose) of the drug and/or using it more often
- Difficulty cutting back (e.g., unable to use the drug less frequently or in smaller amounts)
- Difficulty controlling or limiting the amount taken after starting
- Keeping a steady supply of the drug on hand
- Spending more money on the drug than the person can afford
- Using the drug alone
- Hiding or hoarding the drug
- Lying about drug use to family and friends
- Reacting angrily or defensively when questioned about use of the drug
- Being "in denial" about abusing the drug (e.g., "I don't have a problem")
- Rationalizing drug abuse (e.g., "I'm just partying. It's a normal part of the college experience.")
- When continuing to use the drug matters more to the user than the personal and interpersonal problems caused by its use.
- Stealing from family, friends, anyone, in order to fund their habit

Sexually Transmitted Infections (STIs)

STIs represent a group of contagious infections spread through sexual contact that can threaten our health and well-being. Latex condoms provide the best protection against STIs (Holmes, Levine, & Weaver, 2004). Also, having sex with fewer partners reduces the risk of contracting an STI. Obviously, not engaging in sexual intercourse is the most foolproof way to eliminate the risk of an STI (and unwanted pregnancy). When it comes to sexual intercourse, we have three basic options: Do it recklessly, do is safely, or don't do it. If you choose the last option (abstinence), it doesn't mean you're a cold or unaffectionate prude. All it means is that you're choosing not to have sexual intercourse at this particular time in your life.

More than 25 types of STIs have been identified and virtually all of them are effectively treated if detected early. Listed below is a summary of the major forms of STIs. If ignored, some STIs can progress to the point where they result in serious infection and possible infertility (Cates, et al., 2004). Experiencing pain during or after urination, or unusual discharge from the penis or vaginal areas, are common

Last night I discovered a new form of oral contraceptive. I asked a girl to go to bed with me and she said no."

—Woody Allen, actor, writer, director, and comedian

early symptoms of STI. But the symptoms can sometimes be subtle and undetectable. If you have any doubt, play it safe and check it out immediately by visiting the Health Center on your campus. Any advice or treatment you receive there will remain confidential. If you discover that you have an STI, immediately inform anyone you've had sex with, so he or she can receive early treatment before the disease progresses. This isn't just a polite thing to do; it's the right (ethical) thing to do.

STIs Caused by Bacteria

Gonorrhea. This is a common STI with few symptoms but serious consequences if it is left untreated. In 2007, there were 355,991 cases reported; however, the Centers for Disease Control & Prevention (CDC) estimates there are nearly twice as many infections annually than the number reported (Weinstock, Berman, & Cates, Jr., 2004). Men typically experience creamy, yellow-colored, pus-like discharge from the penis, and burning when urinating. Women experience few early symptoms, but the disease can lead to later pelvic infections and possible infertility. The best way to detect gonorrhea, or any other STI that produces early symptoms that are not visible, is to have a laboratory test done by a doctor or health care provider. Gonorrhea can be treated and completely cured with antibiotics.

Chlamydia. This is the number one bacterial STI; it's estimated to infect more than 10% of college students. In 2007, there were 1,108,374 chlamydia diagnoses reported, the largest number of cases ever reported to the CDC for any condition. However, the CDC estimates that there are approximately 2.8 million new cases of chlamydia annually, meaning more than half of new cases go undiagnosed and unreported (Weinstock, et al., 2004). Symptoms include a clear, mucous-like discharge and a burning sensation when urinating. Men may experience pain in the testes, and women may experience pain in the abdomen. However, women typically experience few or no early symptoms.

Genital Herpes. Typically produces painful blisters on the genitals or in the anus, which may itch and burn, especially during and following urination. Symptoms may disappear and come back, but are never cured. Later attacks tend to be less severe than the first attack. The frequency and intensity of outbreaks can be reduced with prescription medication (e.g., acyclovir capsules).

Syphilis. Men first experience ulcers (open sores) on the penis. Women may first develop ulcers in the vagina, but they can be overlooked, allowing the disease to progress. Syphilis is totally curable with antibiotics.

STIs Caused by Viruses

Human Papilloma Virus (HPV). Overall, this is the most common STI among young, sexually active people. HPV is a virus that may cause warts in the genital area, but it typically does not produce noticeable symptoms in its early stages. Sometimes, the disease may also cause lesions (abnormal tissue changes) that are not visible, but when they appear, they look like small hard, cauliflower-like spots. Men can experience warts on the penis. HPV is treatable with laser or chemical treatment, which basically burn off the lesions. If untreated, HPV can lead to cancer of the cervix in women.

Human Immunodeficiency Virus (HIV). Early symptoms include fever, night sweats, swollen lymph nodes, diarrhea, chronic fatigue, and weight loss. About one-half of people with HIV experience these flu-like symptoms, but one-half show no symptoms at all. Thus, the disease may go undetected until the person is given a blood test for some other reason. Most cases of HIV are transmitted through sexual contact; however, the disease may also be contracted through the sharing of intravenous needles. The most serious form of HIV is acquired immune deficiency syndrome (AIDS), which is a life-threatening condition, because the person's immune system becomes severely impaired and leaves the infected person vulnerable to cancer and diseases of the nervous system.

Hepatitis B or Hepatitis C. About one-half of the people with hepatitis experience flu-like symptoms, and one-half show no symptoms at all. Thus, the disease may go undetected until the person is given a blood test for some other reason.

Pubic Lice (a.k.a. "Crabs"). Caused by tiny lice that are called "crabs" (because they look like sea crabs), which breed in pubic hair around the genitals. These creatures are not dangerous but can cause intense itching.

Who's In Charge?

STIs

You have been seeing a new guy for almost a month and decide you are ready have sex. He tells you not to worry because he has been tested for STIs and the test came back clean. Since you are both really into each other and have decided to be exclusive and you are on the pill, you decide there is no need to use a condom. Sex is so much better without them! A few weeks later you notice an odd-smelling discharge and go to the doctor only to find out you have an STI. What could you have done to prevent getting the STI? Many people blame the partner, but in this case, could the situation have been prevented? How?

_____

_____

_____

_____

_____

Unplanned Pregnancy and Community College Students

Understanding risky behaviors regarding sexual activity is important not only because of the risk of STIs but also because of the risk of unplanned pregnancy. Having a baby can be a wonderful experience, especially when he/she is planned. However, having an unplanned baby while in college could significantly decrease your chance of successfully completing college.

Although many might think this topic is not necessary to talk about for students in community colleges, it is! The rate of unplanned pregnancies is actually increasing (and not decreasing) among 20 to 24 year olds (Guttmacher Institute, 2009). Possibly the most important thing to know regarding community college students and unplanned pregnancy is that 61% of women who have children after enrolling in a community college do not finish their education. This number is 65% higher than for women who do not have children while in college (Bradburn, 2002).

Many students believe that preventing pregnancy while in school is important. Three-quarters of students report that preventing unplanned pregnancy is important to them, and 8 in 10 say that having a child while in school would make it harder to accomplish their goals. Research supports this belief. Students who are parents, particularly those who are single parents, often do not do as well in college as their peers without children (Prentice, Storin, & Robinson, 2012). Thus, having unprotected sex can lead to multiple unplanned outcome

---

Birth Control Facts

True or False: It is necessary to "take a break" from the pill every couple years.

True or False: An IUD can only be used by women who have already given birth.

True or False: It is okay to use petroleum jelly or Vaseline as a lubricant when using latex condoms.

True or False: A woman with a regular, 28-day cycle is most likely to get pregnant about two weeks after the first day of her period.

Among couples who have sex regularly, what percentage will get pregnant within one year if they use no birth control at all? 15%, 33%, 60%, 85%, or 97%.

If you would like more information refer to Bedsider.org to watch the "Fact or Fiction" videos about other myths.

Fog Zone (http://thenationalcampaign.org/sites/default/files/resource-supporting-download/myths.pdf) and Magical Thinking (http://thenationalcampaign.org/sites/default/files/resource-primary-download/magicalthinking.pdf) publications.

Answers: false, false, false, true, 85%.

Campus Safety

College campuses are generally safe and no more prone to crime than other locations or organizations. However, crimes do occur on campuses and one element of wellness is reducing your risk of being victimized by crimes, particularly crimes that threaten your physical well-being. Listed below are some top tips on doing so.

- After dark, don't walk alone; use a buddy system.
- At night or when walking alone, don't get so absorbed in texting or listening to iTunes that you tune out or block out what's going on around you.
- If you're carrying valuable electronics, keep them concealed.
- Check if your campus has an escort service at night; if it does, take advantage of it.
- Call ahead for campus shuttles and escort services to reduce the amount of time you're waiting for a ride.
- Have your keys out and ready before entering your building or your car, and double-check to be sure the door locks behind you.
- Know the phone number and location of the office for campus safety.
- Be aware of the location of emergency phones in academic buildings.
- Put emergency numbers in your cell phone.

(Sources: Lucler, 2015; "Staying Safe on Campus," 2012).

Mobile apps are also available to promote your safety. For instance, "Circle of 6" (www.circleof6app.com/) is a free mobile map that allows you to choose a network of six friends whom you can contact with emergency text messages, such as: "Call me immediately," "Come and get me," or "I need help getting home safely." When you text a message, your GPS location is included. This app was a co-winner of the national "Apps Against Abuse Challenge" sponsored by the White House (Rivera, 2015).

"ArcAngel" (www.patrocinium.com/arcangel) is another mobile safety app that notifies you within seconds of an emergency or if you're near danger (e.g., a crime scene, fire, or flood); it also provides ongoing status reports throughout the emergency and recommends evacuation routes as needed. If you need help, you can click a button that informs local authorities, campus security teams, and family members of your exact location.

Take advantage of these new safety technologies to lower your risk of being victimized by crime and avoiding dangerous situations.

Chapter Summary and Highlights

Wellness is a state of high-quality health and personal well-being that promotes peak physical and mental performance. It requires a healthy lifestyle that includes the following key elements: (a) supplying our body with effective fuel (nutrition) for optimal energy, (b) using energy to engage in heath-preserving exercise, (c) giving our body adequate rest (sleep) so that it can recover and replenish the energy it has expended.

Research findings and recommendations from health care professionals indicate that physical wellness is most effectively promoted by adopting the following strategies:

- **Watch what we eat.** In particular, we should increase consumption of natural fruits, vegetables, legumes, whole grains, fish, and water and decrease consumption of processed foods, fatty foods, fried foods, fast foods, and foods purchased from vending machines. Although the expression, "you are what you eat" may be a bit of an exaggeration, it contains a kernel of truth because the food we consume does affect our health, our emotions, and our performance.
- **Become more physically active.** To counteract the sedentary lifestyle created by life in modern society and attain total fitness, we should engage in a balanced blend of exercises that build stamina, strength, and flexibility.
- **Don't cheat on sleep.** Humans typically do not get the amount of sleep they need to perform at peak levels. College students, in particular, need to get more sleep than they usually do and develop more regular (consistent) sleep habits.
- **Drink alcohol responsibly or not at all.** Avoid excessive consumption of alcohol or other mind-altering substances that can threaten our physical health, impair our mental judgment, and reduce our inhibitions about engaging in dangerous, risk-taking behavior.
- **Avoid use of illegal substances that are unregulated**—particularly substances whose effects may be unpredictable and that pose a high risk for dependency (addiction).
- **Minimize the risk of contracting sexually transmitted infections.** There are three basic strategies for doing so: using latex condoms during sex, limiting the number of sexual partners, or choosing not to be sexually active.

- **Minimize the risk of unwanted pregnancy.** The rate of unwanted pregnancies is increasing among college-aged students; the risk can be reduced by engaging in protected sex or postponing sex.

The wellness-promoting strategies discussed in this chapter are effective ways to preserve health and promote peak performance, both in college and beyond.

Learning More through the World Wide Web: Internet-Based Resources

For additional information on health and wellness, see the following websites.

Nutrition:
www.eatright.org

Physical Activities & Fitness:
http://archive.ncppa.org/resources/coalitions/

Sleep:
www.sleepfoundation.org

Drugs & Abuse (including alcohol):
http://www.drugabuse.gov/drugs-abuse

http://www.wise-drinking.com/ (an app on responsible drinking)

Mental Health:
http://www.activeminds.org/issues-a-resources/mental-health-resources/student-resources

Sexual Harassment, Assault, & Abuse
http://uhs.princeton.edu/medical-services/sexual-health-and-wellness

Safer Sex
www.Bedsider.org/studentsexlife

References

Abbey, A. (2002). Alcohol-related sexual assault: A common problem among college students. *Journal of Studies on Alcohol, 14,* 118–128.

Agus M. S., Swain, J. F., Larson, C. L., Eckert, E. A., & Ludwig, D. S. (2000). Dietary composition and physiologic adaptations to energy restriction. *American Journal of Clinical Nutrition, 74*(4), 901–907.

American Psychiatric Association (2015). *Diagnostic and statistical manual of mental disorders, DSM-IV-TR* (5th ed.). Washington, DC: Author.

Arnedt, J. T., Wilde, G. J. S., Munt, P. W., & MacLean, A. W. (2001). How do prolonged wakefulness and alcohol compare in the decrements they produce on a simulated driving task? *Accident Analysis and Prevention, 33,* 337–344.

Bennett, W., & Gurin, J. (1983). *The dieter's dilemma.* New York: Basic Books.

Bergen-Cico, D. (2000). Patterns of substance abuse and attrition among first-year students. *Journal of the First-Year Experience and Students in Transition, 12*(1), 61–75.

Booth, F. W., & Vyas, D. R. (2001). Genes, environment, and exercise. *Advances in Experimental Medicine and Biology, 502,* 13–20.

Bradburn, E. M. (2002). *Short-term enrollment in postsecondary education: Student background and institutional differences in reasons for early departure, 1996-1998.* Washington, DC: National Center for Education Statistics, U.S. Department of Education. Brody, 2003

Brown, S. A., Tapert, S. F., Granholm, E., & Delis, D. C. (2000). Neurocognitive functioning of adolescents: Effects of protracted alcohol use. *Alcoholism: Clinical & Experimental Research, 24*(2), 164–171.

Bushman, B. J., & Cooper, H. M. (1990). Effects of alcohol on human aggression: An integrative research review. *Psychological Bulletin, 107*(3), 341–354.

Cates, J. R., Herndon, N. L., Schulz, S. L., & Darroch, J. E. (2004). *Our voices, our lives, our futures: Youth and sexually transmitted diseases.* Chapel Hill, NC: University of North Carolina at Chapel Hill School of Journalism and Mass Communication.

Centers for Disease Control & Prevention (2010). *Teen drivers fact sheet*. Retrieved from http://www.cdc.gov/motorvehiclesafety/teen_drivers/teendrivers_factsheet.html.

Colcombe, S. J., Erickson, K., Scalf, P. E., Kim, J. S., Prakash, R., & McAuley, E. (2006). Aerobic exercise training increases brain volume in aging humans. *Journal of Gerontology: Medical Sciences, 61A*(11), 1166–1170.

Corbin, C. B., Pangrazi, R. P., & Franks, B. D. (2000). Definitions: Health, fitness, and physical activity. *President's Council on Physical Fitness and Sports Research Digest, 3*(9), 1–8.

Covey, S. R. (2004). *Seven habits of highly effective people* (3rd ed.). New York: Fireside.

DeJong, W., & Linkenback, J. (1999). Telling it like it is: Using social norms marketing campaigns to reduce student drinking. *AAHE Bulletin, 52*(4), 11–13, 16.

Dement, W. C., & Vaughan, C. (2000). *The promise of sleep: A pioneer in sleep medicine explores the vital connection between health, happiness, and a good night's sleep*. New York: Dell.

Epstein, L., & Mardon. S. (2007). *The Harvard medical school guide to a good night's sleep*. New York:

Fletcher, A., Lamond, N., van den Heuvel, C. J., & Dawson, D. (2003). Prediction of performance during sleep deprivation and alcohol intoxication using a quantitative model of work-related fatigue. *Sleep Research Online, 5*, 67–75.

Frank, M., Issa, N., & Stryker, M. (2001). Sleep enhances plasticity in the developing visual cortex. *Neuron, 30*(1), 275-297.

Goleman, D. (1995). *Emotional intelligence: Why it can matter more than IQ*. New York: Random House.

Guttmacher Institute (2009). *A real-time look at the impact of the recession on women's family planning and pregnancy decisions*. New York: Guttmacher Institute.

Heath, H. (1977). *Maturity and competence: A transcultural view*. New York: Halsted Press.

Holmes, K. K., Levine, R., & Weaver, M. (2004). Effectiveness of condoms in preventing sexually transmitted infections. *Bulletin of the World Health Organization, 82*, 254–464.

Horne, J. (1988). *Why we sleep: The functions of sleep in humans and other mammals*. New York: Oxford University Press.

Howard, P. J. (2014). *The owner's manual for the brain: Everyday applications of mind-brain research* (4th ed.). New York: HarperCollins.

Jenkins, J. G., & Dallenbach, K. M. (1924). Oblivescence during sleep and waking. *American Journal of Psychology, 35*, 605–612.

Johnsgard, K. W. (2004). *Conquering depression and anxiety through exercise*. New York: Prometheus.

Johnston, L. D., O'Malley, P.M., Bachman, J. G., & Schulenberg, J. E. (2005). *Monitoring the future national survey results on drug use, 1975–2004:Vol 2. College students and adults ages 19–45*. National Institute on Drug Abuse: Bethesda, MD: 2005. NIH Publication No. 05-5728.

Julien, R. M., Advokat, C. D., & Comaty, J. E. (2011). *A primer of drug action*. New York: Worth.

Khoshaba, D., & Maddi, S. R. (2005). *HardiTraining: Managing stressful change* (4th ed.). Newport Beach, CA: Hardiness Institute.

Kingkade, T. (2014, August 27). "Sleepy college students are worried about their stress levels." *The Huffington Post*. Retrieved from http://www.huffingtonpost.com/2014/08/27/college-students-sleep-stress_n_5723438.html

Kramer, A. F., & Erickson, K. I. (2007). Capitalizing on cortical plasticity: Influence of physical activity on cognition and brain function. *Trends in Cognitive Sciences, 11*(8), 342–348.

Kuriyama, K., Mishima, K., Suzuki, H., Aritake, S., & Uchiyama, M. (2008). Sleep accelerates improvement in working memory performance. *The Journal of Neuroscience, 28*(4), 10145–10150.

Lack, L. C., Gradisar, M., Van Someren, E. J. W., Wright, H. R., & Lushington, K., (2008), The relationship between insomnia and body temperatures. *Sleep Medicine Reviews 12*(4), 307–317.

Leavy, P., Gnong, A., & Ross, L. S. (2009). Femininity, masculinity, and body image issues among college-age women: An in-depth and written interview study of the mind-body dichotomy. *The Qualitative Report, 14*(2), 261–292.

Leibel, R. L., Rosenbaum, M., & Hirsch, J. (1995). Changes in energy expenditure resulting from altered body weight. *New England Journal of Medicine, 332*, 621–628.

Lucler, K. L. (2015). "15 ways to stay safe while in college." Retrieved from http://collegelife.about.com/od/healthwellness/qt/SafetyTips.htm

Malinauskas, B. M., Aeby, V. G., Overton, R. F., Carpenter-Aeby, T., & Barber-Heidal, K. (2007). A survey of energy drink consumption patterns among college students. *Nutrition Journal, 6*(1), 35.

Marczinski, C., Estee, G., & Grant, V. (2009). *Binge drinking in adolescent and college students*. New York: Nova Science Publishers.

Mayo Clinic (2015). "Rev up your workout with interval training: Interval training can help you get the most out of your workout." Retrieved from http://www.mayoclinic.org/healthy-living/fitness/in-depth/interval-training/art-20044588?pg=1

Mazurek K., Karwczyk K., Zemijeeski, P., Norkoski H., & Czajkowska, M. (2014). Effects of aerobic interval training versus continuous moderate exercise programme on aerobic and anaerobic capacity, somatic features and blood lipid profile in collegiate females. *Annals of Agricultural and Environmental Medicine, 21*(4), 844–849.

Meilman, P. W., & Presley, C. A. (2005). The first-year experience and alcohol use. In M. L. Upcraft, J. N. Gardner, & B. O. Barefoot, and Associates, *Challenging and supporting the first-year student: A handbook for improving the first year of college* (pp. 445–468). San Francisco: Jossey-Bass.

Miller, G. D. & Foster, L. T. (2010). *Critical synthesis of wellness literature*. Victoria: University of Victoria. Retrieved from http://www.geog.uvic.ca/wellness.

Mitler, M. M., Dinges, D. F., & Dement, W. C. (1994). Sleep medicine, public policy, and public health. In M. H. Kryger, T. Roth, & W. C. Dement (Eds.), *Principles and practice of sleep medicine* (2nd ed.). Philadelphia: Saunders.

Myers, D. G. (1993). *The pursuit of happiness: Who is happy—and why?* New York: Morrow.

National Institute of Mental Health (2014). *What are eating disorders?* Washington, DC: U.S. Department of Health and Human Services. Retrieved from http://www.nimh.nih.gov/health/publications/eating-disorders-new-trifold/index.shtml.

Ng, M. & Associates (2014). Global, regional, and national prevalence of overweight and obesity in children and adults during 1980–2013: a systematic analysis for the Global Burden of Disease Study 2013. *The Lancet, 384* (No. 9945), pp. 766–781.

NHTSA/FARS & U.S. Census Bureau (2012).*Underage drunk driving fatalities*. Retrieved from www.centurycouncil.org/drunk-driving/underage-drunk-driving-fatalities.

NIDDK (National Institute of Diabetes & Digestive Kidney Diseases) (2010). *Overweight and obesity statistics*. Washington, DC: U.S. Department of Health and Human Services.

Nutrition Australia (2015). *Eat a rainbow*. Retrieved from http://www.nutritionaustralia.org/national/resource/eat-rainbow.

Ohayon, M. M., Carskadon, M. A. , Guilleminault, C., & Vitiello, M. V. (2004). Meta-analysis of quantitative sleep parameters from childhood to old age in healthy individuals: developing normative sleep values across the human lifespan. *Sleep, 27*, 1255–1273.

Parker-Pope, T. (2010). "Vigorous exercise linked with better grades." Retrieved from http://query.nytimes.com/gst/fullpage.html?res=9A03EEDE103EF93BA35755C0A9669D8B63.

Peigneux, P., Laureys, S., Delbeuck, X., and Maquet, P. (2001). Sleeping brain, learning brain. The role of sleep for memory systems. Neuroreport 12, A111–A124.

Prentice. M., Storin, C., & Robinson, G. (2012). *Make it personal: How pregnancy planning and prevention help students complete college*. Washington, DC : American Association of Community Colleges.

President's Council on Physical Fitness and Sports. (2001). Toward a uniform definition of wellness: A commentary. *Research Digest, 3*(15), 1–8.

Ratey, J. J. (2013). *Spark: The revolutionary new science of exercise and the brain*. New York: Little, Brown & Company.

Rivera, C. (2015, July 1). "College safety gets a tech boost." *Los Angeles Times*, p. B2

Roxburgh, et al., 2014. *Is moderate intensity exercise training combined with high intensity interval training more effective a t improving cardiorespiratory fitness than moderate intensity exercise training alone?* Journal of Sports Science and Medicine, *13*(3):702-707.

Sax, L. J., Bryant, A. N., & Gilmartin, S. K. (2004). A longitudinal investigation of emotional health among male and female first-year college students. *Journal of the First-Year Experience and Students in Transition, 16*(2), 29–65.

Schlosser, E. (2005). *Fast food nation: The dark side of the all-American meal*. New York: Harper Perennial.

Singh, N. A., Clements, K. M., & Fiatarone, M. A. (1997). A randomized controlled trial of the effect of exercise on sleep. *Sleep, 20*, 95–101.

"Staying Safe on Campus" (2012 July 20). Retrieved from http://www.nytimes.com/2012/07/20/education/edlife/students-fear-venturing-out-alone-at-night-on-campus.html?pagewanted=all.

Suchecki, D., Tiba, P. A., & Machado, R. B. (2012). REM sleep rebound as an adaptive response to stressful situations. *Frontiers in Neurology, 3*, 41.

Van Dongen, H. P. A., Maislin, G., Mullington, J. M., & Dinges, D. F. (2003). The cumulative cost of additional wakefulness: Dose–response effects on neurobehavioral functions and sleep physiology from chronic sleep restriction and total sleep deprivation. *Sleep, 26*, 117–126.

Voelker, R. (2004). Stress, sleep loss, and substance abuse create potent recipe for college depression. *Journal of the American Medical Association, 291*, 2177–2179.

Walsh, N. P., Gleeson, M., Shephard, R. J., Woods, J. A., Bishop, N. C., Fleshner, M., Green, C., Pedersen, B. K., Hoffman-Goetz, L., Rogers, C. J., Northoff, H., Abbasi, A., & Simon. P. (2011). Position statement. Part one: Immune function and exercise. *Exercise Immunology Review, 17*, 6–63.

Weinstock, H., Berman, S., & Cates, W. Jr. (2004). Sexually transmitted diseases among American youth: incidence and prevalence estimates, 2000. *Perspectives on Sexual and Reproductive Health, 36*(10), 6–10.

Weschsler, H., & Wuethrich, B. (2002). *Dying to drink: Confronting binge drinking on college campuses*. Emmaus, PA: Rodale.

Willis, J. (2006). *Research-based strategies to ignite student learning: Insights from a neurologist and classroom teacher*. Alexandria, VA: ASCD.

Youngstedt, S. D. (2005). Effects of exercise on sleep. *Clinical Sports Medicine, 24*(2), 355–365.

Zimbardo, P. G., Johnson, R. L., & McCann, V. (2012). *Psychology: Core concepts* (7th ed.). Boston: Pearson.

Chapter 11 Exercises

11.1 Quote Reflections

Review the sidebar quotes contained in this chapter and select two that were especially meaningful or inspirational to you.

For each quote, provide a three- to five-sentence explanation why you chose it.

11.2 Reality Bite

Concerns about Eating: Too Much or Too Little?

The following e-mail message was sent by an underweight, 25-year-old woman (Nancy) who was seeking advice:

I have a big worry: I eat normally during the day but I eat two scoops of ice cream at the end of the day followed by a large package of cookies. I am not exaggerating the situation. Last week, I could only stuff myself with two scoops of ice cream after dinner, but these days it's getting worse—now that I can add bread and buttery cookies (a whole packet, not those mini ones, mind you). What should I do? I know that I should gain weight but I should be getting the extra pounds by more normal means like meat or milk—and I am really worried that once this binge and indulgence becomes a habit, it's difficult to get rid of.

Discussion Questions

Nancy goes on to ask the following questions about her condition. As you read each question, respond to it with the advice you think would be best.

1. Is it okay that I eat that much at the end of each day rather than distributing it equally throughout the day? (Though the former way seems better, I can tell myself, "Hey, girl, after all, you are eating less than your sister!")

2. I am eating junk food—ice cream, loads of biscuits, bread, those Garden chocolate roll cakes, chocolate fingers, chocolate McVita's, buttery cookies...It seems that this is not as healthy as gaining weight by eating meat, milk, or carbohydrates. Is this true?

3. Is it unhealthy to eat just before bed?

4. Could it become difficult to stop?

5. Am I controlled by food?

6. Now that I am eating more than my sister, I am really scared indeed, not only because I am eating far more than her but also because I am having fat deposited in undesirable parts of my body and getting a totally worse figure than she has— that fat which I had tried so hard for three years to get rid of. Any advice?

11.3 Holistic Development Needs and Priorities: A Self-Assessment

Development of the whole self is an essential goal of the liberal arts and general education. As you read through the specific skills and qualities associated with the following dimensions of holistic ("whole person") development, rate each one in terms of its *importance to you* on a scale of 1 to 5, with 5 being highest and 1 lowest.

Skills and Qualities Associated with the Dimensions of Holistic (Whole-Person) Development

1. ***Intellectual* Development:** acquiring a broad base of knowledge, learning how to learn deeply and think critically.

   Specific Objectives & Attributes:

   ____ Becoming aware of your intellectual abilities, interests, and learning styles

   ____ Improving your focus of attention and concentration

   ____ Moving beyond memorization to learning at a deeper level

   ____ mproving your ability to retain knowledge on a long-term basis

   ____ Acquiring effective research skills for finding information from a variety of sources and systems

   ____ Learning how to view issues from multiple angles or perspectives (psychological, social, political, economic, etc.)

   ____ Responding constructively to differing viewpoints or opposing arguments

   ____ Critically evaluating ideas in terms of their truth and value

   ____ Detecting and rejecting persuasion tactics that appeal to emotion rather than reason

   ____ hinking creatively and innovatively

   > Intellectual growth should commence at birth and cease only at death."
   > —*Albert Einstein, Nobel Prize-winning physicist*

2. **Emotional Development:** understanding, managing, and expressing emotions.

   Specific Objectives and Attributes:

   ____ Dealing with personal emotions in an honest, nondefensive manner

   ____ Maintaining a healthy balance between emotional control and emotional expression

   ____ Responding with empathy and sensitivity to emotions experienced by others

   ____ Using effective stress management strategies to control anxiety and reduce tension

   ____ Dealing effectively with depression

   ____ Dealing effectively with anger

   ____ Responding constructively to frustrations and setbacks

   ____ Dealing effectively with fear of failure and lack of self-confidence

   ____ Maintaining optimism and enthusiasm

   ____ Accepting feedback from others in a constructive, nondefensive manner

   > It's not stress that kills us, it is our reaction to it."
   > —*Hans Selye, Canadian endocrinologi and author of* Stress Without Distress

3. **Social Development:** Improving the quality and depth of interpersonal relationships.

   Specific Objectives and Attributes:

   ____ Increasing social self-confidence

   ____ Improving listening and conversational skills

   ____ Overcoming shyness

   ____ Relating to others in an open, nondefensive and nonjudgmental manner

   ____ Forming meaningful friendships

   ____ Learning how to resolve interpersonal conflicts effectively

   ____ Developing greater empathy for others

   ____ Relating effectively to others from different cultural backgrounds and lifestyles

   ____ Collaborating effectively with others when working in groups or teams

   ____ Strengthening leadership skills

   > Chi rispetta sara rippetato."
   > ("Respect others and you will b respected.")
   > —*Italian proverb*

342

4. **Ethical (Character) Development:** Developing a clear value system for guiding personal decisions, making sound ethical judgments, and demonstrating consistency between convictions (beliefs) and commitments (actions).

Specific Objectives and Attributes:

___ Gaining deeper awareness of your personal values and ethical priorities

___ Making personal choices and life decisions based on a meaningful value system

___ Developing the capacity to think and act with personal integrity and authenticity

___ Resisting social pressure to act in ways that are inconsistent with your values

___ Treating others in a fair and just manner

___ Exercising personal freedom responsibly without infringing on the rights of others

___ Increasing awareness of and commitment to human rights and social justice

___ Developing the courage to challenge or confront others who violate human rights and social justice

___ Using electronic technology in a civil and ethical manner

___ Becoming a more engaged and responsible citizen

> If you don't stand for something you will fall for anything."
> —*Malcolm X, African American Muslim minister, public speaker, and human rights activist*

5. **Physical Development:** Acquiring knowledge about the human body and how to apply that knowledge to prevent disease, preserve wellness, and promote peak performance.

Specific Objectives and Attributes:

___ Becoming more aware of your physical condition and state of health

___ Applying knowledge about exercise and fitness to improve your physical and mental health

___ Developing sleep habits that maximize physical and mental well-being

___ Maintaining a healthy balance between work, recreation, and relaxation

___ Applying knowledge about nutrition to reduce risk of illness and promote peak performance levels

___ Becoming knowledgeable about nutritional imbalances and eating disorders

___ Developing a positive physical self-image

___ Increasing knowledge about the effects of drugs and how they affect the body and mind

___ Becoming more knowledgeable about human sexuality and sexual diversity

___ Understanding how biological differences between the sexes affect how males and females communicate and relate to each other

> A man too busy to take care of his health is like a mechanic too busy to take care of his tools."
> —*Spanish proverb*

6. **Spiritual Development:** Devoting attention to the "big questions" about the meaning or purpose of life, the inevitability of death, and the origins of human life and the natural world.

Specific Objectives and Attributes:

___ Developing or refining your philosophy of life

___ Exploring the unknown or what cannot be completely understood scientifically

___ Appreciating the mysteries associated with the origin of the universe

___ Searching for the connection between the self and the larger world or cosmos

___ Searching for the mystical or supernatural—that which transcends the boundaries of the natural world

___ Examining questions relating to death and life after death

___ Exploring questions about the possible existence of a supreme being or higher power

___ Gaining knowledge about different approaches to spirituality and their underlying beliefs or assumptions

___ Understanding the difference and relationship between faith and reason

___ Becoming more aware and accepting of diverse religious beliefs and practices

> We are not human beings having a spiritual experience. We are spiritual beings having a human experience."
> —*Pierre Teilhard de Chardin, French philosopher, geologist, paleontologist, and Jesuit priest*

7. **Vocational Development:** Exploring career options and pursuing a career path that is compatible with your interests, talents, and values.

Specific Objectives and Attributes:

___ Understanding the relationship between majors and careers

___ Using effective strategies for exploring and identifying potential careers

___ Identifying career options that capitalize on your personal interests, talents, needs, and values

___ Acquiring work experience related to your vocational interests

___ Creating an effective resume or portfolio

___ Developing effective strategies for selecting personal references and acquiring letters of recommendation

___ Implementing effective job search strategies

___ Learning how to write persuasive letters of inquiry and letters of application for employment positions

___ Acquiring networking skills for connecting with potential employers

___ Developing strategies for performing successfully in job interviews

> Your work is to discover your work and then with all your heart to give yourself to it."
> —Hindu Siddhartha Prince Gautama Siddharta, a.k.a. Buddha, founder of the philosophy and religion of Buddhism

8. **Personal Development:** Developing a strong sense of personal identity, a coherent self-concept, and the ability to manage personal affairs and resources.

Specific Objectives and Attributes:

___ Discovering your identity and clarifying your self-concept (Answering the question: Who am I?)

___ Finding a sense of purpose and direction in life (Answering the question: Who will I become?)

___ Developing greater self-respect and self-esteem

___ Increasing self-confidence

___ Developing self-efficacy—belief that the outcomes of your life are within your control and can be influenced by personal initiative and effort

___ Strengthening skills for managing personal resources (e.g., time and money)

___ Becoming more independent, self-directed, and self-reliant

___ Setting realistic goals and priorities

___ Developing the self-motivation and self-discipline needed to reach long-term goals

___ Developing the resiliency to overcome obstacles and convert setbacks into comebacks

> Remember, no one can make you feel inferior without your consent."
> —Eleanor Roosevelt, former United Nations diplomat and humanitarian

Based on your total score in each area, what aspect(s) of self-development appear to be most and least important to you? How would you explain (or what do you think accounts for) this discrepancy?

Add up your total score for each of the eight areas of holistic development.

a) Do your totals in each of the eight areas suggest that all aspects of self-development are about equally important to you and that you're striving to become a well-rounded person?

b) If yes, why? If no, why not?

11.4 Wellness Self-Assessment for Self-Improvement

For each aspect of wellness listed below, rate yourself in terms of how close you are to doing what you should be doing (1 = furthest from the ideal, 5 = closest to the ideal).

	Nowhere Close to What I Should Be Doing		Not Bad but Should Be Better		Right Where I Should Be
Nutrition	1	2	3	4	5
Exercise	1	2	3	4	5
Sleep	1	2	3	4	5
Alcohol and Drugs	1	2	3	4	5

For each area in which there's a gap between where you are now and where you should be, identify the best action you could take to reduce or eliminate the gap.

11.5 Nutritional Self-Assessment and Self-Improvement

1. Go to: *www.ChooseMyPlate.gov.*

2. For each of the five food groups listed below, record in the first column the amount you *should* be consuming daily; in the second column, estimate the amount you *do* consume daily.

Basic Food Type	Amount Recommended	Amount Consumed
Fruits		
Vegetables		
Grains		
Protein Foods		
Dairy		

3. For any food group that you're consuming less than the recommended amounts, use the website to find foods that would enable you to meet the recommended daily amount. Write down those food items, and answer the following questions about each of them:

   (a) How likely is it that you'll actually add these food items to your regular diet?

   Very Likely   Possibly   Very Unlikely

   (b) For those food items you identified as "very unlikely," why would you be unlikely to add these items to your regular diet?

Chapter 11 Reflection

What is the one area of your health that could most affect your success in college. Explain?

What are three action steps you can take to improve in this area?

1.

2.

3.

Write three health goals you have set for yourself. (Remember to use the goal-setting strategies you learned about in Chapter 3.)

Educational and Career Planning and Decision Making

MAKING WISE CHOICES ABOUT A COLLEGE MAJOR, COLLEGE TRANSFER, AND FUTURE CAREER

Making strategic choices about your courses and your major is essential to reaching your educational goals. You want to be sure your choice of a major is compatible with your personal interests, talents, and values. You should also have a strategic plan in mind (and in hand) to explore your options and decide on a major field of study and transfer options to a four-year campus.

Chapter Preview

Even though career entry may be years away, career exploration and preparation should begin in the first term of college. Career planning gives you a practical, long-range goal to strive for and gets you thinking about how the skills you're using and developing in college align with the skills that promote your professional success beyond college. This chapter will help you develop a plan for making educational and career decisions that will best enable you to reach your long-term goals.

Equip you with effective strategies for pursuing an educational and career path that's compatible with your personal interests, talents, and goals.

Learning Goal

Think About It—Journal Entry 12.1

Ignite Your Thinking

At this point in your college experience, are you decided or undecided about a major?

1. If you're undecided, what subjects are you considering as possible majors?

2. If you're decided:

    a) What's your choice?

b)   What led you to this choice?

_____

_____

_____

_____

c)   How sure are you about this choice? (Circle one.)

absolutely sure   fairly sure   not too sure   likely to change

To Be or Not to Be Decided: What Research Shows about Students' Choice of a College Major

"What's your major?" is a question that students are asked over and over again—even before they've stepped foot on a college campus. You probably also saw this question on every one of your college applications and you're likely to hear it again during your very first term in college.

Studies of student decisions about a college major show that:

* Fewer than 10% of new college students feel they know a great deal about the field they intend to major in;
* As students proceed through the first year of college, they grow more uncertain about the major they chose when they entered college;
* More than one-third of new students change their mind about their major during their first year of college;
* Only one in three college seniors eventually major in the same field they had in mind when they began college (Cuseo, 2005; HERI, 2014).

These findings demonstrate that the vast majority of first-year students are uncertain about their academic specialization. Typically, they don't make a final decision about their major _before_ starting college; instead, they reach that decision _during_ their college experience.

Thus, being initially undecided about a major isn't something you should be worried or embarrassed about; it doesn't mean you're clueless. It may just mean you're open-minded. In fact, studies show that new students are often undecided for very good reasons. Some are undecided because they have multiple interests; this is a healthy form of indecision indicating they have a wide range of interests and a high level of intellectual curiosity. Students may also be undecided because they are reflective and deliberate decision-makers who prefer to explore their options carefully before making a firm and final commitment. In a national study of students who were undecided about a major at the start of college, 43% of them had some majors in mind but weren't quite ready to make a final commitment to one of them (Gordon & Steele, 2003).

For new students to be at least somewhat uncertain about their educational goals at the start of their college experience is only natural because they haven't yet experienced the variety of subjects included in the college curriculum. One goal of general education courses is to help new students develop the critical thinking skills

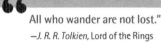

"All who wander are not lost."
—_J. R. R. Tolkien_, Lord of the Rings

needed to make wise choices and well-informed decisions, including their decision about a college major.

The college curriculum will introduce you to new fields of study, some of which you never experienced before and all of which represent possible choices for a college major. A key benefit of experiencing the variety of courses in the general education curriculum is that they help you become more aware of the range of academic disciplines and subject areas available to you as potential majors, while at the same time, helping you become more aware of yourself. As you gain experience with the college curriculum, you will gain greater self-insight into your academic interests, strengths, and weaknesses. Take this self-knowledge into consideration when choosing a major because you want to pursue a field that capitalizes on your intellectual curiosity, abilities, and talents.

The Importance of Long-Range Educational Planning

If you haven't declared a major, it doesn't mean you're indecisive or a hopeless procrastinator. However, it also doesn't mean you can put all thoughts about your major on the back burner and simply drift along until you're forced to make a choice. Being undecided doesn't mean you have no plan; your plan is to find out what your major will be. Now is the time to start the major selection process by testing your interests and narrowing down your choices. If you're planning to transfer, it's better to reach a sound decision about a major sooner rather than later because you will probably have to declare a major at the time you apply to a four-year campus and begin major-specific coursework almost immediately after you're accepted (Miller & Nadler, 2004). Thus, it's important to develop an educational plan during your first term in college so that you can immediately begin to select and enroll in transferable courses.

Note

Developing a long-range educational plan takes time so make an appointment to meet with an advisor at a time other than during the mad rush of course registration. This will give you both the opportunity to focus on your transfer plans and long-range goals, rather than focusing on short-term scheduling of next term classes.

On the other hand, if you've already chosen a major, this doesn't mean that you'll never have to give any more thought to that decision. Instead, you should continue the exploration process by carefully testing your first choice, making sure it's a choice that is compatible with your abilities and interests. Take the approach that this is your *current* choice; whether it becomes your firm and *final* choice will depend on how well you perform (and how interested you are) in the first courses you take in the field.

Developing a long-range educational plan enables you to take a *proactive* approach to your education—you take charge of it by taking early and preemptive action that anticipates your future. Rather than waiting and passively letting your educational future happen *to* you, advanced planning makes it happen *for* you.

Note

Keep in mind that a long-range educational plan isn't something set in stone. As you gain more educational experience, your specific academic and career interests may change and so may the specifics of your long-range plan. The purpose of a plan is not to tie you up or pin you down, but provide you with a roadmap to keep you on track and moving along the right pathway.

> You have brains in your head. You have feet in your shoes. You can steer yourself any direction you choose.
>
> —*Theodore Seuss Giesel (a.k.a. Dr. Seuss)*, Oh the Places You'll Go

> Some people make things happen, while others watch things happen or wonder what has happened."
>
> —*Author unknown*

> When you have to make a choice and don't make it, that is in itself a choice."
>
> —*William James, philosopher and one of the founders of American psychology*

Educational Pathways for Community College Students

As a beginning community college student, you have two primary educational paths to choose from: Career Technical Education or Transfer Preparation.

1. *Career Technical Education* Pathway. This pathway prepares you for a specific particular occupation or trade and immediate employment after completing either (a) a short-term (e.g., one year or less) credential or certificate program, or (b) a two-year associate degree—such as an *Associate of Applied Science (AAS)* or an *Associate of Applied Technology (AAT)* degree. Some community colleges offer "stackable credentials" that allow you to earn a short-term credential that you can build on later by taking additional courses to earn longer-term credentials that allow you to move up a career ladder and advance to higher-paying positions. For example, you can continue to earn educational credits along the pathway to an associate degree by completing a series of shorter credentials that focus on mastering skills for specific technologies, which prepare them to gain entry level work in the field of information technology and eventually advance to higher positions in that field.

2. *Transfer Preparation* Pathway. This pathway prepares you for transfer to a four-year college or university and a four-year (bachelor's) degree. These programs typically lead to degrees such as an *Associate of Arts (AA)* or an *Associate of Science (AS)*. Some community colleges offer *Inverted Degree* programs, whereby students can complete a degree in a career technical education program (e.g., an AAS degree) and then transfer to a four-year college to complete general education to earn a bachelor's degree. Many community colleges also have *Reverse Transfer* programs whereby students who transfer to a four-year college before completing an associate degree are allowed to transfer credits completed at the four-year campus back to their previous two-year campus to receive the Associate Degree.

Think About It—Journal Entry 12.2

Are you currently planning to pursue a career technical education pathway or a transfer preparation pathway? How sure are you about this choice?

A Checklist of Course-Recognition Registration Reminders for Community College Students

Achieving your educational goals requires both long- and short-range planning. Your long-range plan involves completing your degree, and your short-range plan involves continuing your enrollment in college from term to term. When planning to register for the next academic term, keep the following list of reminders handy to ensure that your term-to-term transition proceeds smoothly.

- Check the registration dates and be prepared to register at the earliest date that's available to you.
- Check with an academic adviser to be sure that you're planning to take the right classes for your program, major, and any four-year school you plan to transfer to.

- Let your advisor know what your educational goals are and if you've changed your goals since the last time you registered.
- Let your advisor know the total number of hours per week you plan to work so that you create a schedule that will allow you to successfully balance schoolwork and for-pay work.
- If you're receiving financial aid, meet with a financial aid counselor or advisor to be sure that you have adequate funds to cover next term's tuition, book costs, and parking fees.
- Once you've registered periodically check the status of your courses, because last-minute changes can occur in the time and day when courses meet and it's possible that one of your courses might be canceled (e.g. due to insufficient enrollment).

Factors to Consider When Choosing a Major or Field of Study

Self-awareness is the critical first step in the process of making any effective personal decision or choice. You need to know yourself well before knowing what major is best for you. When choosing a major, self-awareness should include awareness of your:

- Mental abilities and talents
- Personal interests and curiosities

Research indicates that students who choose majors that are compatible with their personal characteristics are more likely to be academically successful in college and complete their degree (Leuwerke, et al., 2004; Pascarella & Terenzini, 2005).

Multiple Intelligences: Becoming Aware of Your Mental Abilities and Talents

One personal characteristic you should be aware of when choosing a major is your mental strengths, abilities, and talents. Intelligence was once considered to be a single, general trait that could be identified by one intelligence test score. Scholars have since discovered that intelligence doesn't come conveniently wrapped in a one-size-fits-all package. The singular word "intelligence" has been replaced by the plural word "intelligences" to reflect the fact that humans display intelligence (mental ability) in a variety of forms other than that measured by their score on an IQ or SAT test.

Based on studies of gifted and talented individuals, experts in different lines of work, and research on the human brain, psychologist Howard Gardner (1993, 1999, 2006) has identified the multiple forms of intelligence listed in **Box 12.2**. Keep these forms of intelligence in mind when you're choosing a college major because different majors emphasize different intellectual skills (Brooks, 2009). Ideally,

> Exceptional individuals have a special talent for identifying their own strengths and weaknesses."
>
> —*Howard Gardner*, Extraordinary Minds

you want to pursue an academic field that allows you to utilize your strongest mental attributes and talents. If you do, you're likely to master the concepts and skills required by your major more efficiently and more deeply, excel in courses required by your major, and experience a higher level of academic self-confidence and motivation to continue your education.

Box 12.2

Multiple Forms of Intelligence

As you read through the following forms of intelligence, place a checkmark next to the type that you think represents your strongest ability or talent. (You can possess more than one type.)

1. *Linguistic* Intelligence: ability to comprehend the meaning of words and communicate through language (e.g., verbal skills relating to speaking, writing, listening, and learning foreign languages).

2. *Logical-Mathematical* Intelligence: aptitude for understanding logical patterns (e.g., making and following logical arguments) and solving mathematical problems (e.g., working well with numbers and quantitative calculations).

3. *Spatial* Intelligence: aptitude for visualizing relationships among objects arranged in different spatial positions and ability to perceive or create visual images (e.g., forming mental images of three-dimensional objects; detecting detail in objects or drawings; drawing, painting, sculpting, and graphic design; strong sense of direction and capacity to navigate unfamiliar places).

4. *Musical* Intelligence: ability to appreciate or create rhythmical and melodic sounds (e.g., playing, writing, or arranging music).

5. *Interpersonal (Social)* Intelligence: ability to relate to others and accurately identify their needs, motivations, or emotional states; effective at expressing emotions and feelings to others (e.g., interpersonal communication skills, ability to accurately "read" the feelings of others and meet their emotional needs).

6. *Intrapersonal (Self)* Intelligence: ability to introspect and understand your own thoughts, feelings, and behaviors (e.g., capacity for personal reflection; emotional self-awareness; self-insight into personal strengths and weaknesses).

7. *Bodily–Kinesthetic (Psychomotor)* Intelligence: ability to control one's own body skillfully and learn through bodily sensations or movements; skilled at tasks involving physical coordination, working well with hands, operating machinery, building models, assembling things, and using technology.

> I used to operate a printing press. In about two weeks I knew how to run it and soon after I could take the machine apart in my head and analyze what each part does, how it functioned, and why it was shaped that way.
>
> —*Response of college sophomore to the questions: "What are you really good at? What comes easily or naturally to you?"*

8. *Naturalist* Intelligence: ability to carefully observe and appreciate features of the natural environment; keen awareness of nature or natural surroundings; ability to understand causes and consequences of events occurring in the natural world.

9. *Existential* Intelligence: ability to conceptualize phenomena and ponder experiences that go beyond sensory or physical evidence, such as questions involving the origin of human life and the meaning of human existence.

Sources: Gardner (1993, 1999, 2006).

Think About It—Journal Entry 12.3

Look back at the nine forms of intelligence listed in **Box 12.2.**

Which of these types of intelligence do you think represents your strongest talent(s)?

_____

_____

_____

_____

Which college major(s) do you think may best match your natural talents?

_____

_____

_____

_____

Discovering a Major that's Compatible with Your Personal Interests and Talents

In addition to knowing your intellectual strengths and learning styles, another key to factor into your decisions about a college major are your *interests*. Here are some specific strategies for exploring and confirming whether a major is compatible with your educational interests.

Reflect on past learning experiences you found stimulating and were productive. Think about previous classes that piqued your curiosity and in which you produced your best work. The subjects of these courses may be major fields of study that match up well with your interests, talents, and learning style.

At the website *www.mymajors.com*, you can enter information about your academic performance in high school courses. Your inputted information will be analyzed and you'll receive a report on what college majors appear to be a good match for you. You can do the same analysis for the first courses you complete in college.

Take a look at introductory textbooks in the field you're considering as a major. Review the table of contents and read a few pages of the text to get some sense of the writing style used in the field and whether the topics are compatible with your educational interests. You should be able to conveniently find introductory textbooks for different fields of study in your college bookstore.

Seek out students majoring in the subject you're considering and ask them about their experiences. Talk to several students to get a different and balanced perspective on what the field is like. You can find these students by visiting student clubs on campus related to the major (e.g., psychology club or history club). You could also check the class schedule to see when and where classes in that major are meeting. Go there and speak with students about the major, either before or after class. The following questions may be good ones to ask students in a major you're considering:

- What attracted you to this major?
- What would you say are the advantages and disadvantages of majoring in this field?
- Knowing what you know now, would you choose the same major again?

Also, ask students about the quality of teaching and advising in the department offering the major. Studies show that different departments within the same college or university can vary greatly in terms of the quality of teaching as well as their educational philosophy and attitude toward students (Pascarella & Terenzini, 1991, 2005).

Sit in on some classes in the field you're considering as a major. If the class you'd like to visit is large, you may be able to just slip into the back row and listen. If the class is small, ask the instructor for permission. When visiting a class, focus on the content or ideas being covered rather than the instructor's personality or teaching style. Remember: you're trying to decide whether to major in the subject, not the teacher.

Discuss the major you're considering with an academic advisor or career counselor. To get unbiased feedback about the pros and cons of majoring in a particular field, it's probably best to speak with an academic advisor who works with students from a variety of majors. If you're still interested, you can follow up by getting more detailed information by consulting with an advisor who works primarily with students in that particular major.

Speak with faculty members in the department. Consider asking them the following questions:

- What academic skills or qualities are needed for a student to be successful in your field?
- What are the greatest challenges faced by students majoring in your field?
- What can students do with a major in your field after graduation?
- What types of graduate programs or professional schools would a student in your major be well prepared to enter?

Surf the website of the professional organization associated with the field you're considering as a major. These websites often contain useful information for students interested in pursuing a major in the field. To locate the professional website for a field you would like to explore as a major, ask a faculty member in that field or complete a search on the web by simply entering the name of the field followed by the word "association." For example, if you're thinking about becoming an anthropology major, check out the website of the American Anthropological Association. If you're considering history as a major, take a look at the website of the American Historical Association. The website of the American Philosophical Association contains information about nonacademic careers for philosophy majors, and the American Sociological Association's website identifies various careers that sociology majors are qualified to pursue.

Use your elective courses to test your interest in subjects that you might major in. As its name implies, "elective" courses are those you elect or choose to take. They come in two forms: free electives and restricted electives. *Free electives* are any courses you take that count toward your college degree but aren't required for general education or a major. *Restricted electives* are courses you must take, but you get to choose them from a restricted list (menu) of possible courses that have been specified by your college to fulfill a requirement in general education or a major. For example, your campus may have a general education requirement in the social or behavioral sciences that stipulates you must take two courses in this field, but you choose what those two courses are from a list of options (e.g., anthropology, economics, political science, psychology, or sociology). If you're considering one of these fields as a possible major, you can take an introductory course in that subject to test your interest in the subject while simultaneously fulfilling a general education requirement needed for graduation. This strategy allows you to use general education as the main highway for travel toward your final destination (a college degree) while using your restricted electives to explore side roads (potential majors) along the way. You can use the same strategy with your free electives.

> I took it (Biology) to satisfy the distribution requirement and I ended up majoring in it."
> — *Pediatrician (quoted in Brooks, 2009)*

Be sure you're aware of all courses required for the major you've chosen or are considering. You can find this information in your college catalog, university bulletin, or campus website. If you're in doubt, seek assistance from an academic advisor.

Sometimes college majors require courses you would never expect to be required. Students interested in majoring in the field of forensics are often surprised by the number of science courses for this major. Keep in mind that college majors often require courses in fields outside of the major that are designed to support the major. For instance, psychology majors are often required to take at least one course in biology, and business majors are often required to take calculus.

If you're interested in majoring in a particular field, be sure you are fully aware of such outside requirements and are comfortable with them. Once you've accurately identified all courses required for the major you're considering, ask yourself the following two questions:

1. Do the course titles and descriptions appeal to my interests and values?
2. Do I have the abilities or skills needed to do well in these courses?

AUTHOR'S EXPERIENCE

As an academic advisor, I often see students who are confused about what they want to major in, especially traditional (18 to 24 year old) students. I can relate to these students because I changed my major multiple times before I reached a final decision. The first piece of advice I give students about choosing majors is to use their resources (e.g., academic advisement) and to do some research on the courses required for the majors they're considering. Over the last few years, I've seen many students who want to major in forensic science—largely due to the popularity of the CSI shows. I then ask them how they feel about science and math, and many of these students tell me they hate those subjects. When I inform them that becoming forensic scientist involves a minimum of a master's in chemistry, they decide to look at other majors. Fewer surprises like this would occur if students did at least some research on what courses are required for the majors and careers they're considering.

—*Julie McLaughlin*

When completing your bachelor degree, consider the possibility of completing a college minor in a field that complements your major. A college minor usually requires about half the number of credits (units) required for a major. Most campuses allow you the option of completing a minor along with your major. Check your course catalog or consult with an academic advisor for college minors that may interest you.

If you have a strong interest in two different fields, a minor will allow you to major in one of these fields while minoring in the other. Thus, you're able to pursue two fields of interest without having to sacrifice one for the other. Another advantage of a minor is that it can usually be completed with a major without delaying your time to graduation. In contrast, a double major is likely to lengthen your time to graduation because it requires completing all requirements for both majors.

Another way to complete a second field of study without increasing your time to graduation is by completing a "concentration" or "cognate area"—an academic specialization that requires fewer courses to complete than a minor (e.g., four to five courses vs. seven to eight courses). A concentration area may have even fewer requirements (only three to four courses).

Taking a cluster of courses in a field outside your major can be an effective way to strengthen your resume and your employment prospects; it demonstrates your versatility and ability to acquire knowledge and skills in areas that may be missing or underemphasized in your major. For example, by taking a cluster of courses in fields such as mathematics (e.g., statistics), technology (e.g., computer science), and business (e.g., economics), students majoring in the fine arts (e.g., music or theater) or humanities (e.g., English or history) can acquire knowledge and skills in areas not strongly emphasized by their major, thereby increasing their prospects for employment after graduation.

 Think About It—Journal Entry 12.4

Consider the following statement: "Choosing a major is a life-changing decision because it will determine what you will do for the rest of your life."

Would you agree or disagree?

Why?

Myths about the Relationship between Majors and Careers

Numerous misconceptions exist about the relationship between college majors and careers, some of which can lead students to make uninformed or unrealistic decisions about a major. Here are four common myths about the major–career relationship you should be aware of and factor into your decision about a college major.

Myth 1. When you choose your major, you're choosing your career.

While some majors lead directly to a specific career, most do not. Majors leading directly to specialized careers are often called preprofessional or pre-vocational majors; they include such fields as accounting, engineering, and nursing. However, the relationship between most college majors and future careers is often not direct or linear; you don't travel on a monorail straight from your major to a single career that's directly connected to your major. For instance, all physics majors don't become physicists, all philosophy majors don't become philosophers, all history majors don't become historians, and all English majors don't become Englishmen (or Englishwomen). Instead, the same major typically leads you to a variety of career options.

The truth is that for most college students the journey from college major to future career(s) is less like scaling a vertical pole and more like climbing a tree. As illustrated in **Figure 12.1**, you begin with the tree's trunk (the foundation provided by general education (the liberal arts); this leads to separate limbs (choices for college majors), which, in turn, lead to different branches (different career paths or options). Note that different sets of branches (careers) grow from the same limb (major).

> "Linear thinking can keep you from thinking broadly about your options and being open-minded to new opportunities."
>
> —*Katharine Brooks, author,* You Majored in What?

FIGURE 12.1: **The Relationship between General Education (Liberal Arts), College Majors, and Careers**

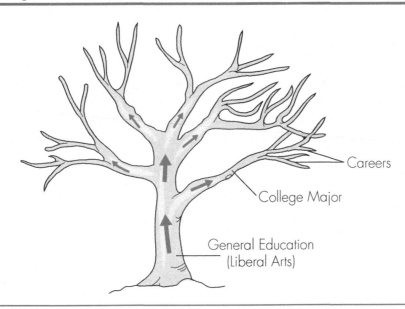

Careers

College Major

General Education
(Liberal Arts)

Similarly, different career clusters or "career families" grow from the same major. An English major can lead to a variety of careers that involve writing (e.g., editing, journalism, or publishing), and a major in Art can lead to different careers that involve visual media (e.g., illustration, graphic design, or art therapy).

Furthermore, different majors can lead to the same career. For instance, a variety of majors can lead a student to law school and a career as a lawyer; in fact, there's really no such thing as a "law major" or "pre-law major." Students with a variety of majors (or minors) can also enter medical school as long as they have a solid set of foundational courses in biology and chemistry and score well on the medical college admissions test.

Studies show that today's workers change jobs 10 times in the two decades following college and the job-changing rate is highest for younger workers (AAC&U, 2007). Research also indicates that only half of new college graduates expect to be working in the same field in which they're currently employed (Hart Research Associates, 2006); they frequently change positions during their first two decades of

> "I intend on becoming a corporate lawyer. I am an English major. The reason I chose this major is because while I was researching the educational backgrounds of some corporate attorneys, I found that a lot were English majors. It helps with writing and delivering cases."
>
> —*College sophomore*

employment following college completion, and the further along they proceed in their career path, the more likely they are to be working in a field that's unrelated to their college major (Millard, 2004).

So, don't assume that your major *is* your career, or that your major automatically turns into your lifelong career. It's this belief that can result in some students procrastinating about choosing a major; they think they're making a lifelong decision and fear that if they make the "wrong" choice, they'll be stuck doing something they hate for the rest of their life. Although it's important to think about how your choice of a college major will affect your career path, for most college students—particularly those not majoring in preprofessional fields—choice of a major and choice of a career are not identical decisions made at the same time. Choosing a specific major is a decision that should be made by your sophomore year; choosing a career is a decision that can be made later.

Note

Don't assume that choosing your college major means you're choosing what you'll be doing for the remainder of your working life. Deciding on a major and deciding on a career are not identical decisions that must be made simultaneously.

Myth 2. If you want to continue your education after college graduation, you must continue in the same field as your college major.

After graduating with a four-year (baccalaureate) degree, you have two primary paths available to you: (a) enter the workforce immediately, and/or (b) continue your education in graduate school or professional school. (**See Figure 12.2** for a visual map of the stages and milestones in the college experience and the paths available to you after college.)

FIGURE 12.2: **A Snapshot of the College Experience and Beyond**

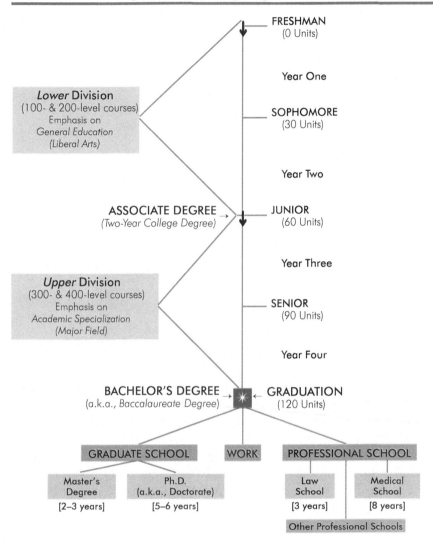

Notes

1. On average, about one-third of the courses required for a college degree are general education courses selected from the liberal arts curriculum. However, the number of required general education courses varies from campus to campus and can vary at the same campus depending on the student's major.

2. The word "freshman" originated in England in 1596, when every college student was a "fresh" (new) "man." Today, the term "freshman" is frequently being replaced by "first-year student" because this is a more gender-neutral term.

3. The term "baccalaureate" derives from "Bacchus"— the Greek god of wine and festive celebration, and "laurel"—a wreath made from the laurel plant that ancient Greeks draped around the neck of Olympic champions.

4. It often takes college students longer than four years to graduate due to a variety of reasons, such as working part-time and taking fewer courses per term, needing to repeat courses that were failed or dropped, or making a late change to a different major and needing to fulfill additional requirements for the new major.

5. Graduate and professional schools are options for continuing to higher levels of education after completion of an undergraduate (college) education.

6. Students going to graduate school on a full-time basis can sometimes support themselves financially by working part-time as a teaching assistant (TA) or research assistant (RA). It's also possible to enroll in some graduate or professional school programs on a part-time basis while holding a full-time job.

7. The term "Ph.D." refers to "Doctor of Philosophy," respecting the fact that the first scholars were the ancient Greek philosophers (e.g., Socrates, Plato, and Aristotle). However, a Ph.D. can be earned in many different academic fields (Mathematics, Music, Economic, etc.).

8. Compared to graduate school, professional school involves advanced education in more "applied" professions (e.g., pharmacy or public administration).

Think About It—Journal Entry 12.5

Reflect back on the timeline depicted in Figure 12.2, which suggests that an associate degree is designed to be completed in two years and a bachelor's degree in four years.

Do you see yourself completing an associate degree in two years? A bachelor's degree in four years? Why or why not?

"The first week of law school, one of my professors stressed the importance of 'researching, analyzing and writing.' I thought this was an interesting thing to say, because English majors learn and practice these skills in every class."

—*English major attending law school*

Once you earn a college diploma, you can continue your education in a field that's not directly related to your college major. This is particularly true for students majoring in liberal arts fields that don't lead directly to a specific career after graduation (Pascarella & Terenzini, 1991, 2005). For example, an English major can go to graduate school in a subject other than English, or go to law school, or get a master's degree in business administration. In fact, most students who attend graduate school in the field of business (e.g., MBA programs) were not business majors when they were in college (Zlomek, 2012).

Myth 3. Since most college graduates are employed in business organizations or corporations, you should major in business.

Most college graduates are employed in business settings, so students (and their parents) often conclude that if students are going to work for a business, they better major in business. This belief likely explains why business is the most popular major among college students (National Center for Education Statistics, 2014). However, college graduates now working in business settings have majored in variety of fields besides business, and many CEOs of today's most profitable companies did not major in business (Elliot, 2015). Certainly, if you have an interest in and passion for majoring in business, by all means major in business; however, don't choose a business major because you think it's the only major that will qualify you to work for and succeed in a business organization after graduation.

AUTHOR'S EXPERIENCE

My undergraduate degree was in political science and sociology. When I graduated from college, I spent the first eight years of my professional life becoming a corporate manager. I did not major in business, but found that my liberal arts background gave me the problem-solving and communication skills that were crucial in working with a variety of people in my profession. You do not need to major in business to be a successful business person. Indeed, employers are telling us that they are looking for those who can solve, critically think, write and speak well, and work with a diversity of people and thoughts.

—Aaron Thompson

Myth 4. If you major in a liberal arts field, the only career available to you is teaching.

A commonly held myth is that all you can do with a major in a liberal arts subject is to teach the subject you majored in (e.g., math majors become math teachers; history majors become history teachers). The truth is that students majoring in different liberal arts fields go on to enter, advance, and prosper in a wide variety of careers. College graduates with degrees in the liberal arts who went on to achieve professional success in careers other than teaching include:

- Jill Barad (English major), CEO, Mattel Toys
- Willie Brown (liberal studies major), Mayor of San Francisco
- Ken Chenault (History major), CEO, American Express
- Christopher Connor (Sociology major), CEO, Sherwin Williams
- Robert Iger (Communications major), CEO, Walt Disney Company

Significant numbers of liberal arts majors are also employed in positions relating to marketing, human resources, and public affairs (Bok, 2006; Useem, 1989). An experienced career counselor once tracked the majors of college graduates working in the insurance industry. She found an art history major working at a major insurance firm whose job was to value oriental carpets and art holdings. She found a geology major working for an insurance company whose job was to evaluate beach properties and determine the odds of hurricanes or other natural phenomena causing property damage. This former geology major spent much of her work time traveling to beachfront communities to review new developments and assessing damages after hurricanes or other tragic events (Brooks, 2009).

Research also reveals that the career mobility and career advancement of liberal arts majors working in the corporate world are comparable to business majors. For example, liberal arts majors are just as likely to advance to the highest levels of corporate leadership as majors in such preprofessional fields as business and engineering (Pascarella & Terenzini, 2005). The point we're making here is that if you have a passion for and talent in a liberal arts field, don't dismiss it as being "impractical," and don't be dismayed or discouraged by those who challenge your choice by asking: "What are you going to do with a degree in that major?" (Brooks, 2009).

> They asked me during my interview why I was right for the job and I told them because I can read well, write well and I can think. They really liked that because those were the skills they were looking for."
>
> *—English major hired by a public relations firm*

My brother, Vinny, was a philosophy major in college. He came home one Christmas wearing a tee-shirt on which was printed the message: "Philosophy major. Will think for food." With his major in philosophy, my brother went to graduate school, completed a Master's degree in higher education, and is now making a six-figure salary working as a college administrator. Looking back, his old tee-shirt should have read: "Philosophy major. Will think for money."

—*Joe Cuseo*

Think About It—Journal Entry 12.6

Look back at the four myths about the relationships between majors and careers. Which of these four myths did you know were false? Which myths did you previously think were true? Explain.

Do What You Are (DWYA)

1. According to your DWYA report, what are your career satisfiers? Do you agree or disagree with these? Explain.

2. Look at your DWYA report and your "pretty interested" or "somewhat interested" career suggestions. Of these careers, which are your top three choices? Why are these your top three choices?

3. How do your career satisfiers tie in with the three careers you chose in question two?

_____

_____

_____

_____

Strategies for Successful Transfer to a Four-Year College or University

Almost one-half of all people in this country with a bachelor's degree started their college education at a two-year college before transferring to and graduating from a four-year college or university (National Student Clearing House Research Center, 2015). Listed below are strategies you can use to prepare for successful transfer and join the ranks of Americans who began their college education at a two-year college and went on to complete a four-year degree.

Connect early and often with an academic advisor. National surveys show that community college students rank academic advising higher than any other student support service: Almost two-thirds of community college students rate it as a "very important" service. However, only about one-third of community college students report using advising "often" and over one-third report using advising "rarely or never" (Center for Community College Engagement, 2008, 2010).

Research indicates that successful transfer depends on students taking the right courses in the right sequence (Hagedorn, et al., 2006; Zamani, 2001). Students who enroll in courses that are nontransferable or require a prerequisite they haven't completed end up losing transfer credit; the fewer credits students have at the time they transfer, the less likely they are to complete a four-year degree (CCRC, 2014).

To maximize your number of transferable course credits, ask an advisor about whether your community college has any of the following programs that ensure transfer credit:

- Transfer Articulation Agreements or Transfer Agreement Pacts. Agreement between two-year and four-year colleges that allow for "Block Transfer"—transfer of a whole group (block) of courses at the same time (e.g., all general education courses taken at a community college are accepted for credit at a four-year college).
- Guaranteed Admission Agreement (aka, Joint Admissions or "2+2 Agreement"). Agreement between a two-year and four-year college that allows students who complete the general education program at their community college with a satisfactory GPA to be automatically admitted to the four-year college campus as upper-division students (junior status) without having to complete a formal application for admission and acceptance.
- Concurrent Enrollment Program: An agreement between two- and four-year colleges that allows potential transfer students at the two-year college to cross-register for courses offered by the four-year college. For instance, a four-year university may offer courses to community college students that allows them to obtain "advanced transfer credit."

If you are an adult student who has received credit at your community college for experiential learning that took place in noncollege settings (e.g., previous work or military experiences), ask an advisor if your community college has any agreements that allow you to transfer these experiential credits to four-year colleges.

Lastly, keep in mind that community college courses may transfer to fulfill a general education requirement, a requirement in your major, or as elective credit. If possible, you want your transferable courses to fulfill general education requirements or requirements in your intended major. Check with your advisor to see if your community college has *Major-Specific (aka, Program-Major-to-Program-Major) Agreements*, which ensure that community college courses taken in your intended major are automatically accepted as fulfilling graduation requirements in your major at the four-year college to which you intend to transfer.

Save your course syllabi and course assignments. You may be able to use materials to answer any questions a four-year college may have about the nature and transferability of your courses.

Capitalize on available resources to help you prepare for successful transfer. Transfer resources may be available to you online, in print, and in person. They include the following resources.

- *Common Course Numbering System*: a computer-based system offered in some states that places the same number and prefix on courses that count for credit at both the community college and the four-year college to which you intend to transfer.
- Checklists or worksheets developed by advisors at your community college that make it easy for you to identify general education requirements and required courses in specific majors at different four-year colleges.
- Transfer workshops and transfer events on campus, especially "Transfer Days" or "Transfer Fairs" at which transfer advisors and college admissions representatives from four-year institutions help community college students plan for successful transfer.
- Campus visits and tours of four-year colleges provided by your community college.
- Transfer student clubs, committees, councils, and honor associations (e.g., Phi Theta Kappa).

Complete your associate degree before transferring. Studies consistently show that transfer students who complete an associate degree before transferring to a four-year college perform better after transferring and are more likely to complete a four-year degree (Community College Research Center, 2014; Thurmond, 2007). Listed below are key advantages of an associate degree that probably account for why transfer students who complete this degree are more successful.

Advantages of Completing an Associate Degree Prior to Four-Year College Transfer

1. Many four-year campuses give priority admission to transfer students who have completed an associate degree (CSU Student Transfer, 2015; Washington State Board for Community & Technical Colleges, 2015). Thus, earning an associate degree will increase your transfer chances and options. It also allows you to capitalize on articulation agreements between two- and four-year campuses that grant "block transfer" of all general education credits earned for an associate degree. Research shows that students with more transfer

credits at the time they enter a four-year college are more likely to complete a bachelor's degree (CCRC, 2014).

2. **By completing an associate degree, you buy extra time and advising support to reach a final decision about your college major and what four-year college you'll transfer to.** If you're unsure about what major you want to declare, or what four-year college you want to attend, returning to your community college for your sophomore year provides an additional year of time and advising support to reach both of these important decisions.

    What field of study you major in and what four-year college you attend are often interrelated decisions. Some majors may only be offered at certain colleges, and the nature and quality of the same major may vary from one campus to the next. A second year at your community college can provide the time and support you need to reach a well-informed decision about what four-year campus is the best choice for your major.

3. **Research shows that students who complete an associate degree make a smoother academic transition to four-year campuses.** Students who transfer before completing an associate degree tend to experience more "transfer shock"—a sharper drop in GPA after transferring to a four-year institution—than do students who transfer after completing an associate degree (Laanan, 2001). The superior post-transfer performance of students who complete an associate degree may be due to the fact that they (a) develop a stronger set of transferable skills by completing more academic skill-building courses (writing, math, oral communication) prior to transfer and (b) acquire a broader base of knowledge by completing the wide range of general education courses required for the associate degree. In addition, completing an associate degree allows you to complete all these academic skill-building courses and general education requirements at a community college—where classes are smaller and courses are taught by experienced instructors whose primary responsibility is teaching, not research. (At larger universities, first- and second-year courses are often taught by the least experienced professors or graduate students.)

4. **Earning an associate degree opens up more opportunities for you to obtain internships, part-time employment during the academic year, or full-time employment during the summers in between your junior and senior years of college.** Having an associate degree increases your chances of being hired and also increases the amount you're paid for the work you're hired to do (Gagliardi & Heimstra, 2013; Mullin & Phillippe, 2013). Employees possessing an associate degree earn substantially more money than individuals with a high school diploma (Ganzglass, 2014; Tinto, 2012). This may be particularly advantageous if, for some reason, you're unable to complete a four-year degree or have to postpone its completion.

5. **Completing an associate degree supplies you with more time and opportunity to accumulate academic awards and honors prior to transfer (e.g., graduating with honors and participating in Phi Theta Kappa—national honor society for two-year college student).** Such awards increase your chances of receiving scholarships and grants from four-year colleges. Furthermore, since these accomplishments remain on your permanent college record after completing a bachelor's degree, they strengthen your job prospects after college graduation, as well as your chances of acceptance to graduate or professional school.

6. **Completing an associate degree provides you with more opportunity for leadership development and recognition during your sophomore year.** As a community college student, you become eligible for a variety of resume-

building and character-building leadership opportunities during your second year (e.g., orientation week leader, peer tutor, or peer mentor). At four-year colleges and universities, sophomores are often unable to assume these leadership positions because they may be reserved for more experienced juniors and seniors. At two-year colleges, sophomores are the "seniors" and you can engage in leadership experiences during your sophomore year that will: (a) increase your chances of acceptance at four-year colleges, (b) qualify you for similar leadership positions at the four-year college to which you transfer, and (c) enhance your job prospects during your last two years of college and after completing your four-year degree.

7. **Completing an associate degree gives you the opportunity to participate in your community college's graduation ceremony.** Even if you plan to transfer and graduate from a four-year college with a bachelor's degree, don't underestimate the importance of celebrating your attainment of an associate degree. This is a significant achievement because:

    *   It indicates you have survived and thrived during the two most critical years of the college experience. (Research shows that almost 75% of those students who withdraw from college will do so during the freshman and sophomore years [American College Testing, 2015]). Your attainment of an associate degree serves as evidence to four-year colleges and employers that you had the grit to persist and complete these two critical years.

    *   It signifies that you've successfully completed the general education component of the college experience. In many ways, this is the most important component of your college career because it represents the acquisition of breadth of knowledge and the development of essential, transferable skills (e.g., writing, speaking, critical thinking, and quantitative reasoning) that spell success in all majors and all careers. Surveys indicate that these are the type of lifelong learning skills that employers look for and value most in employees (AAC&U, 2013).

    *   It's an opportunity for you to be recognized publicly—in front of family, friends, faculty, and fellow students. Research indicates that student involvement in college rituals or ceremonial events (such as graduation) reinforces their commitment to continue their education and reach their educational goal (Kuh, et al., 2005). Thus, participating in your community college's graduation ceremony isn't only an opportunity for you to celebrate achievement of your associate degree; it's also an opportunity to receive a motivational "shot in the arm" that propels you toward completion of a four-year degree. Proof of the power of the graduation experience is illustrated in the following excerpt of a letter written by a student who graduated with an associate degree from a two-year college and transferred to a four-year campus to complete her bachelor's degree.

        "I just wanted to get in touch and let you know how I am doing. I successfully graduated from USF [a four-year college]. Looking back, the two-year college experience helped me achieve successful habits that brought me to where I am today. Also, during the graduation ceremony for my associate degree, I saw some fellow students wearing the yellow shawl that represented walking with honors. I thought to myself, 'I am going to walk with honors when I get my B.A.' And that I did! Who would have ever thought? [Now] I have decided that I want to go to graduate school."

        —Letter from a two-year college graduate received by Joe Cuseo

Think About It—Journal Entry 12.7

If you're planning to transfer to a four-year college or university, do you intend to complete an associate degree before transferring? Why or why not?

Factors to Consider when Choosing a Four-Year College for Transfer

Keep in mind that not all four-year colleges and universities are created equal. Some are more "transfer student friendly" than others; they welcome and value transfer students by reaching out to recruit them and supporting them once they've been recruited. Listed below are key things to look for, ask about, and factor into your decision about what four-year campuses to apply to and attend.

Outreach to Community College Students:
- Does the four-year college show interest in transfer students by supplying community college students with transfer information in the form of transfer websites, brochures, newsletters, guides, or handbooks?
- Has a representative from the four-year college visited your community college campus to recruit transfer students?
- Does the four-year college hold transfer fairs and campus visits for transfer students?

Financial Aid:
- Does the four-year college set aside financial aid, scholarships, grants, and campus employment opportunities for transfer students?
- Does the four-year college provide transfer students with early notification about how much financial aid they will receive?
- Does the four-year college offer specialized financial counseling for transfer students?

Transfer Audit (aka Transfer Credit Evaluation): Does the four-year campus provide early evaluation of transfer students' transcripts so they know exactly how many courses will be accepted for transfer credit and where the credit will be applied (e.g., toward general education, the major, or electives).

Registration: Are transfer students allowed to register at the same time as other students, or must they wait until all other students at the college (freshman through seniors) have already registered?

Housing:
- Does the college reserve on-campus housing spaces for transfer students?
- Does the college help transfer students find off-campus housing?

Transfer Student Orientation: Does the college offer an orientation program designed specifically for new transfer students? (Or, must transfer students participate in the same orientation program designed for freshmen?)

Transfer Advisors: Does the college offer specialized academic advising for transfer students?

Transfer Center: Does the college have a transfer resource center that provides a place for transfer students to gather and receive support?

Peer Support: Does the college have peer mentors for transfer students to help them navigate their new environment and develop social networks?

Transfer Orientation Course (aka, Transfer Student Seminar): Does the college offer a first-term course specifically for new transfer students that's designed to promote their success?

Transfer Honors Program: Does the college have an honors program specifically designed for transfer students (e.g., Tau Sigma Honor Society—a national honors and scholarship program for transfer students who earn a 3.5 GPA after their first term on campus or rank among the top 20% of their entering transfer class in academic performance).

How Four-Year Colleges and Universities Evaluate Transfer Students

The following criteria are those that four-year colleges will most likely use to evaluate your application and decide on your acceptance.

Academic Record. Four-year colleges will look at your overall GPA, as well as your grades for courses in your major. (Be sure to have the registrar's office send your academic record in the form of an *official transcript*—a verified record of your completed course work that's signed and date-stamped by the registrar's office to verify that the information contained in it is up-to-date, accurate, and hasn't been altered.)

Out-of-class Experiences. Your involvement in leadership activities and volunteer experience in the community or on campus can play a role in your acceptance at a four-year college.

Personal Statement. In your letter of application for college admission, demonstrate your knowledge of:
- *Yourself* (e.g., your personal interests, abilities, and values),
- Your intended *major* (e.g., why you're interested in it and what you might do with it after graduation), and
- The *college* to which you're applying to show that you know something specific about the school—such as its mission, philosophy, and specific programs—especially the particular program to which you're applying.

Letters of Recommendation (Letters of Reference)

Letters of recommendation can come from course instructors, academic advisors, or other student support professionals. Provide the following courtesies for those you ask to write letters for you:
- Give the person advanced notice (at least two weeks).
- Provide a *fact sheet* about yourself that will enable them to cite concrete examples or specific evidence of your achievements and contributions—(this will make the letter much more powerful).
- If your letter is to be mailed, supply a *stamped*, *addressed* envelope (a personal courtesy that makes the job a little easier for your reference).
- Send a *thank you note* close to the date the letter is due. This isn't only the polite thing to do, it also serves as a gentle reminder for the person to write your letter.

The Importance of Career Planning

Most of the remaining hours of your life will be spent working; the only other single activity you'll spend more time doing is sleeping. Since such a sizable portion of your life is spent on your vocation, it's easy to see why your career can have such a strong influence on your identity and personal happiness. Choosing a career path is one of the most important decisions you'll make in your life, so the process of career exploration and choice should begin right now—during your first year in college. The need to do so is highlighted by a national survey of first-year college student: almost 60% of them strongly agreed that it's important to be thinking about their career path; however, only 25% reported they had a clear idea on how to achieve their career goals (HERI, 2014).

Even if you have decided on a career that you've been dreaming about since you were a preschooler, you still need to confirm this choice and will likely need to decide on a specialization within your chosen field. For instance, if you're interested in pursuing a career in law, you'll need to decide what branch of law you will practice (criminal law, corporate law, family law, etc.). You will also need to decide what employment sector or type of industry you'd like to work in (e.g., nonprofit, for-profit, education, or government). Thus, no matter how certain or uncertain you are about your career path, you still need to explore specific career options and begin to devise a career development plan.

> "Love and work . . . work and love . . . what else is there really? Love and work are the cornerstones to our humanness."
>
> *—Sigmund Freud, famous psychologist, responding to the question: What do you humans need to be happy?*

Strategies for Career Exploration and Preparation

Reaching an effective decision about a career path involves four key steps:

1.

Awareness of *yourself*—insight into your personal, interests, talents, needs, and values

↓

2.

Awareness of your *career options*—knowing the different career choices available to you

↓

3.

Awareness of what career options provide the *best "fit"* for you—knowing what career(s) best match your personal interests, talents, needs, and values

↓

4.

Awareness of the key *steps and strategies* needed to reach your career goal—knowing how to prepare for and gain entry to the career of your choice

In short, effective career decision-making begins with a clear understanding of who you are, where you can go, where you will go, and how you will get there.

Step 1. Awareness of Self

The career you decide to pursue says a lot about who you are, what you want from life, and how you want to impact the lives of _____, self-awareness is the critical first step in the _____ or career planning _____ career choice begins with a clear unde_____ of who you are from there _____ determine where you want to go and _____ to get there. You must know yourself _____ you know what career is best for yo_____ _____ _____ self-awareness and self-discovery are often overl_____ _____ in the career planning/seeking process. By deepening your self-aware_____ you can _____ and better position to choose a career path that's true to the p_____ _____ _____ _____ _____ _____ to be.

Self-awaren_____ _____ step in the career planning process. Me_____ _____ and effective career choices are built on a deep underst_____ _____

You can i_____ your self-awareness by ask_____ yourself questions that stimulate introspection—_____ reflection on your inner qualities and personal priorities. Introspective questions l_____ _____ you on an inner quest for self-insight and self-discovery which leads you to a career that's consistent with who you are and who you want to be. You can begin _____ this introspective process by asking yourself questions relating to your personal:

- **Interests:** what you *like* doing;
- **Talents:** what you're *good* at doing;
- **Needs:** what you find personally *satisfying* or *fulfilling;* and
- **Values:** what you believe is *important* to do or is *worth* doing.

 Think About It—Journal Entry 12.8

Complete the following sentences:

- My primary interests are . . .

_____

_____

_____

- My strongest abilities or talents are . . .

_____

_____

_____

- What brings me the greatest sense of personal satisfaction and fulfillment is ...

_____

_____

_____

_____

- What I value the most is ...

_____

_____

_____

_____

How do your above answers compare with results from the "Your Career Satisfiers" section of your _Do What You Are_ report?

_____

_____

_____

_____

One way to gain greater self-awareness is by taking psychological tests or assessments. These assessments allow you to see how your interests and values compare with other students and with working professionals who are satisfied and successful with their careers. This comparative perspective provides you with an important reference point for assessing whether your level of interest in a career is high, average, or low relative to other students and to professionals working in that field. To take a career interest test, as well as other career exploration assessments, consult the Career Development Office on your campus.

In addition to your personal interests, another factor you should consider when choosing a career is your personal needs. A _need_ may be described as something stronger than an interest. When you do something that satisfies a personal need, you're doing something that you find highly motivating and personally fulfilling (Melton, 1995). Psychologists have identified several important human needs that vary in strength or intensity from person to person (Ryan, 1995; Ryan & Deci, 2000). Listed in **Box 12.3** are personal needs that are especially important to consider when making a career choice.

> "I believe following my passion is more crucial than earning money. I think that would come itself eventually."
>
> —_College sophomore responding to the question, "What are you looking for in a career?"_

Box 12.3

Personal Needs to Consider When Making Career Choices

After reading about each need in this box, make a note indicating how strong that need is for you (high, moderate, or low).

1. Autonomy. Need for working independently without close supervision or control. Individuals with a high need for autonomy experience greater fulfillment working in careers that allow them to be their own boss, make their own choices or decisions, and control their own work schedule. Individuals low in this need may experience greater satisfaction working in careers that are more structured and allow them to work with a supervisor who provides direction, assistance, and frequent feedback.

Our research [on happiness] indicates prosperity is not the most important factor. Personal freedom is more important, and it's freedom in all kinds of ways... political freedom and freedom of choice."
—Ronald Inglehart, happiness researcher, University of Michigan

AUTHOR'S EXPERIENCE

As a college junior with half of my degree completed, I had an eye-opening experience. I wish this experience had happened in my first year, but better late than never. When I chose a career during my first year of college, my decision-making process was not systematic and didn't involve critical thinking. I chose a major based on what sounded prestigious and would pay me the most money. Although these are not necessarily bad factors, my failure to use a systematic and reflective process to evaluate my career choice. In my junior year I asked one of my professors why he decided to get his Ph.D. and become a professor. He simply answered, "I wanted autonomy." This was an epiphany for me. He explained that when he reflected on what mattered most to him, he realized that he needed a career that offered independence. So, he began looking at career options that would allow him to work independently. After hearing his explanation, "autonomy" became my favorite word, and this story became a guiding force in my life. After going through a critical introspective process, I determined that autonomy was exactly what I desired and a professor is what I became.

—*Aaron Thompson*

2. Affiliation (Belongingness). Need for social interaction, a sense of belonging, and the opportunity to collaborate with others. Individuals with a high need for affiliation experience greater fulfillment working in careers that involve teamwork and frequent interpersonal interaction with coworkers. Individuals low in this need are more likely to be satisfied working alone or in competition with others.

To me, an important characteristic of a career is being able to meet new, smart, interesting people."
—First-year student

3. Achievement (Competence). Need to experience challenge and a sense of personal accomplishment. Individuals with high achievement needs feel a more fulfilled working in careers that push them to solve problems, generate creative ideas, and continually learn new information or master new skills. Individuals with a low need for achievement are likely to be more satisfied with careers that don't continually test their abilities and don't repeatedly challenge them to stretch their skills with new tasks and different responsibilities.

I want to be able to enjoy my job and be challenged by it at the same time. I hope that my job will not be monotonous and that I will have the opportunity to learn new things often."
—First-year student

4. Recognition. Need for prestige, status, and respect from others. Individuals with high recognition needs are likely to feel satisfied working in high-status careers that society perceives as prestigious. Individuals with a low need for recognition would feel comfortable working in a career that they find

(continued)

Box 12.3 *(continued)*

self-satisfying, regardless of how impressive or enviable their career appears to others.

5. **Sensory Stimulation.** Need for experiencing variety, change, and risk. Individuals with high sensory stimulation needs are more likely to be satisfied working in careers that involve frequent changes of pace and place (e.g., travel), unpredictable events (e.g., work tasks that require them to think on their feet), and some stress (e.g., working under pressure of competition or deadlines). Individuals with a low need for sensory stimulation may feel more comfort-

able working in careers that involve regular routines, predictable situations, and minimal risk or stress.

> For me, a good career is very unpredictable and interest-fulfilling. I would love to do something that allows me to be spontaneous."
> *—First-year student*

Sources: Baumeister & Leary (1995); Chua & Koestner (2008); Deci & Ryan (2002); Ryan (1995)

 Think About It—Journal Entry 12.9

Looking back at the five needs listed in **Box 12.3,** which one(s) did you identify as being strong needs for you?

What career or careers do you think would best match your strongest needs?

> Don't expect a recluse to be motivated to sell, a creative thinker to be motivated to be a good proofreader day in and day out, or a sow's ear to be happy in the role of a silk purse."
> *—Pierce Howard, author of* The Owner's Manual for the Brain

_____

_____

_____

_____

_____

_____

_____

In sum, four key personal characteristics should be considered when exploring and choosing a career: abilities, interests, values, and needs. As illustrated in **Figure 12.3**, these core characteristics are the pillars that provide the foundational support for making effective career choices and decisions. Ideally, you want to be in a career that you're good at, interested in, passionate about, and brings you a sense of personal satisfaction and fulfillment.

FIGURE 12.3: **Personal Characteristics Providing the Foundation for Effective Career Choice**

©Kendall Hunt

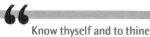

> "Know thyself and to thine own self be true."
>
> —*Polonius in* Hamlet, *a play by William Shakespeare*

The opportunity to make a reasonable amount of money is certainly one factor to consider when choosing a career, but a good career choice involves more factors than just starting salary. It's a decision that should also involve deep awareness and strong consideration of your special abilities, what you're passionate about, and what is meaningful to you. It's noteworthy that the word *vocation* derives from the Latin "vocatio" meaning "a calling." This suggests that a career is more than a money-making venture; it should call out to you and call forth your true talents and interests.

Step 2. Awareness of Career Options

In addition to self-awareness and knowledge about yourself, effective career decision- making requires knowledge about your range of career options and the realities of the work world. If you were to ask people to name as many careers as they could, they would not come close to naming the 900 career titles listed by the federal government in its Occupational Information Network. There are many more career choices in today's work world than there were for our early ancestors. When you look at the list of occupations in **Box 12.4**—none of which existed ten years ago—you can see how the nature of today's work world is changing more rapidly than at any other time in history.

Box 12.4

Occupations that Didn't Exist Ten Years Ago

1. **App developer:** When you hear "there's an app for that" it's because a career track emerged for program developers who have professional knowledge and skills into the world of mobile devices.
2. **Market research data miner:** Ever wonder how retailers know how to create customized advertisements especially for you? Market researcher data miners collect data on consumer behaviors and predict trends for advertisers to use to develop marketing strategies.
3. **Educational or admissions consultant:** Some parents take extra steps to ensure their children are accepted at the "right" school (from preschool to college). Educational or admissions consultants are hired to guide families through the application and interview process.
4. **Millennial generation expert:** It's now very common to find people from different generations working together in the same organization. Millennial generation experts help employers maximize the potential of their staff by providing advice on working with their youngest employees and mentoring them for future success.
5. **Social media manager:** The business world now makes greater use of social media to market and advertise their products and services. Social media managers target their marketing to users of different social media sites.
6. **Chief listening officer:** Similar to a social media manager, a chief listening officer uses social media to monitor consumer discussions and shares this information with marketing agents so they can design strategies that appeal to various segments of the population.
7. **Cloud computing services:** Most websites used every day by consumers store incredibly large amounts of data. Computer engineers with expertise in data management, store and index tremendous volumes of bytes for companies—about a quadrillion!
8. **Elder care:** Life expectancy is increasing and along with it the need for individuals who possess the knowledge, skills and compassion to serve the elderly, their families, and the agencies and companies that assist them.
9. **Sustainability expert:** For environmental and economic reasons, companies are now seeking ways to minimize their carbon emissions. This has created a demand for professionals with expertise in the science of sustainability and the ability to develop "green" business practices that are also cost-effective.
10. **User experience design:** User experience designers do exactly what their titles suggest: they create experiences for consumers through technology. These designers use current technology to create color, sound and images by using tools like HTML, Photoshop, and CSS.

Source: Casserly (2012)

Career Information Resources

Listed below are some of the best sources of information about careers. The primary place on campus for locating these sources is likely to be your Career Center. In addition to helping you assess your career interests and abilities, this is also the place where you can learn about the nature of different careers and locate career-related work experiences. Your College Library is another campus resource where you can find a wealth of reading material on careers, either in print or online.

NICC Career Services (www.nicc.edu/careerservices). Access resources online with NICC career services. You will find information on career decision making, job search and other useful career planning websites.

Occupational Outlook Handbook (OOH) (www.bls.gov/oco). This is one of the most widely available and used resource on careers. It contains descriptions of approximately 250 positions, including information on: the nature of the work; work conditions; places of employment; training or education required for career entry and advancement; salaries and benefits; and additional sources of information about particular careers (e.g., professional organizations and governmental agencies associated with a career). A distinctive feature of this resource is that it also contains information about the *future employment outlook* for different careers.

Fergusons Career Guidance

This is an excellent NICC library database for searching careers. The information is helpful when exploring career trends and job searches. See the career videos and take a career interest assessment here as well!

Occupational Information Network (O*NET) Online (www.online.onetcenter.org). This is America's most comprehensive online source of online information about careers. It contains up-to-date descriptions of almost 1,000 careers, plus lots of other career-related information similar to what you would find in the *Dictionary of Occupational Titles*.

In addition to these general sources of information, your Career Development Center and College Library should have resources relating to specific careers or occupations (e.g., careers for English majors). You can also learn a great deal about specific careers by simply reading advertisements for position openings in your local newspaper or online (e.g., www.careerbuilder.com and college.monster.com). When reading position descriptions, make special note of the tasks, duties, or responsibilities they involve and ask yourself whether these positions are compatible with your personal talents, interests, needs, and values.

NICC Career coach (https://nicc.emsicareercoach.com/). Check out this resource for regional career projections, salary data and details about NICC programs.

Career Planning and Development Workshops

Periodically during the academic year, your campus is likely to offer programs devoted to career exploration and career preparation. For example, the Career Center may sponsor career exploration or career planning workshops that you can attend for free. Research indicates that career development workshops are effective in helping students plan for and choose careers (Brown & Krane, 2000; Hildenbrand & Gore, 2005). Your Career Center may also organize career fairs, at which professionals working in different career fields have booths where you can visit with them and ask questions about their careers. (See **p. 405** for interview questions you can ask working professions about their career.)

Career Development Courses

Your college may offer career development courses for elective credit. These courses typically include self-assessments of your career interests, information about different careers, and strategies for career preparation. Since you need to do career planning while you're enrolled in college, why not do it by enrolling in a career planning course that gives you college credit for doing it? Studies show that students benefit from participating in these courses (Pascarella & Terenzini, 2005).

You may also be able to explore career interests in a writing or speech course that allows you to choose the topic that you write or speak about. If you're given the freedom to choose any topic to research, consider researching a career you're exploring and make that the topic of your paper or presentation.

Information Interviews

One of the best and most overlooked ways to get accurate information about a career is to interview professionals working in that career. Career development specialists refer to this strategy as information interviewing. Don't assume that working professionals aren't interested in taking time to speak with a student; most are open to being interviewed and many report they like doing it (Crosby, 2002).

Information interviews provide you with "inside information" about what the career is really like because you're getting it directly from the horse's mouth—the person actually working in the career on a day-to-day basis. Information interviewing also helps you gain experience and confidence in interview situations, which may help you prepare for future job interviews. Furthermore, if you make a good impression during information interviews, the people you interview may suggest that you contact them again after graduation to see if there's a position opening. If there is an opening, you might find yourself being the interviewee instead of the interviewer, and find yourself being hired.

Because interviews can supply you with valuable information about careers and provide possible contacts for future employment, we strongly encourage you to complete the information interview assignment at the end of this chapter.

Career Observation (Shadowing)

In addition to reading about careers and interviewing professionals, you can also learn about careers by observing professionals performing their daily duties in their place of work. Two college-sponsored programs may be available on your campus that will allow you to observe working professionals:

Job Shadowing Program. Following (shadowing) and observing a professional during a typical workday.

Externship Program. An extended version of job shadowing that lasts for a longer time period (e.g., two to three days).

Visit your Career Development Center to learn about what job shadowing or externship programs may be available on your campus. If you're unable to find a campus program for the career field you're exploring, consider finding one on your own by using strategies similar to the recommendations for information interviews at the end of this chapter. It's basically the same process; the only difference is that instead of asking the person for an interview, you're asking if you could observe that person at work. In fact, you could ask the person who granted you an information interview if you could observe (shadow) that person at work. Just a day or two of job shadowing can give you valuable information about a career.

AUTHOR'S EXPERIENCE

When my sister was in the last year of her nursing degree, she decided she wanted to be a pediatric nurse and work at one of the top 10 pediatric hospitals in the country. At the time, I lived in a city with an excellent pediatric hospital. My sister decided to come visit me for an extended weekend and made appointments to shadow different units in that hospital on her visit. She fell in love with the place and decided she definitely wanted to work there! A few months later, when she was in her last semester of school, that hospital called her and asked if she wanted to come and interview for jobs on all four units. They'd been just as impressed with her when she shadowed as she was with them, and they made a note on her resume to call her when she was close to graduating. She interviewed and was offered all four jobs! It turned out her shadowing experience actually ended up being a "pre-interview," and she had a job before she even graduated!

—Julie McLaughlin

Think About It—Journal Entry 12.10

If you were to interview or observe a working professional in a career that interests you, what type of work would that person be doing?

_____

_____

_____

_____

_____

_____

Information interviewing, job shadowing, and externships supply you with great information about a career. However, information is not experience. To get career-related work *experience*, you've got four major options:

- Internships
- Cooperative education programs
- Volunteer work or service learning
- Part-time work

Internships

In contrast to job shadowing and externships—which involve observing someone at work—an internship actively involves you in the work itself and gives you an opportunity to perform career-related work duties. A distinguishing feature of internships is that you can receive academic credit and sometimes financial compensation for the work you do. Usually, an internship involves a total of 120 to 150 work hours, which may be completed at the same time you're enrolled in classes, or at a time when you're not taking classes (e.g., summer internship).

A key advantage of internships is that they enable you to escape the classic catch-22 situation that college graduates often run into when interviewing for their first career position. The interview scenario usually goes something like this: The potential employer asks the college graduate, "What work experience have you had in this field?" The recent graduate replies, "I haven't had any work experience because I've been a full-time student." You can avoid this scenario by completing an internship during your college experience. Participating in at least one internship while you're enrolled in college will enable you to beat the "no experience" rap after graduation and distinguish yourself from other college graduates. Surveys show that more than 75% of employers prefer candidates with internships (National Association of Colleges & Employers, 2010); students with internships are more likely to acquire career-relevant work skills while in college and find immediate employment after college (Hart Research Associates, 2006, 2014; Pascarella & Terenzini, 2005).

> "Give me a history major who has done internships and a business major who hasn't, and I'll hire the history major every time."
>
> —*William Ardery, senior vice president, Investor Communications Company*

Internships are typically available to college students during their junior or senior year; however, some campuses offer internships for first- and second-year students as well. Check with your Career Center if this option may be available to you. You can also pursue internships on your own by consulting published guides that list various career-related internships and provide information on how to apply for them (e.g., Peterson's Internships and the Vault Guide to Top Internships). You can also find internships on websites such as www.internships.com or www.vaultreports.com. Lastly, information on internships may be available from the local chamber of commerce in your hometown, or in the city where your college is located.

Cooperative Education (Co-op) Programs

Co-op programs are similar to internships but involve work experiences that last longer than one academic term and often require students to stop their coursework temporarily to participate in the program. Some co-op programs, however, allow you to continue to take classes while working part time at a co-op position; these are sometimes referred to as "parallel co-ops." Students are paid for participating in co-op programs and their co-op experience is officially noted on their college transcript (Smith, 2005).

Typically, co-ops are only available to juniors or seniors, or students in technical programs, but you can begin now to explore co-op programs by reviewing your college catalog and visiting your Career Development Center to see if co-op programs are available in a career field you're pursuing. If you find one, build it into your educational plan because it can provide you with authentic and extensive career-related work experience.

The value of co-ops and internships is strongly supported by research, which indicates that students who have these experiences during college:

Are more likely to report that their college education was relevant to their career;

- Receive higher evaluations from employers who recruit them on campus;
- Have less difficulty finding an initial position after graduation;
- Are more satisfied with their first career position following graduation; and
- Earn higher starting salaries (Gardner, 1991; Knouse, Tanner, & Harris, 1999; Pascarella & Terenzini, 1991, 2005).

When employers are asked to rank various factors they consider important when hiring new college graduates, internships or cooperative education programs receive the highest ranking (National Association of Colleges & Employers, 2012, 2014). Employers also report that when full-time positions open up in their organization or company, they usually turn first to their own interns and co-op students (National Association of Colleges & Employers, 2013).

Volunteer Work or Service Learning

Volunteer service not only gives you the opportunity to serve your community, it also gives you the opportunity to explore different work environments and gain work experience in career fields relating to your area of service. For example, volunteer work performed for different age groups (children, adolescents, or the elderly) and in different work environments (hospital, school, or laboratory) provides you with firsthand, resume-building experience and the opportunity to test your interest in careers related to these age groups and work environments. Volunteer experience also enables you to network with professionals who can serve as personal references for you and provide you with letters of recommendation. Furthermore, if these professionals are impressed with your service they may hire you on a part-time basis while you're still in college, or full-time after you graduate.

To get an idea of the wide range of career-related service opportunities that may be available to you, go to: www.usa.service.org. You may also get volunteer experience through *service learning* courses at your college that integrate these experiences into coursework. Volunteer service may be incorporated into the course as a required or optional assignment whereby you participate in the volunteer experience and then reflect on your experience in a paper or class presentation.

Another course-integrated option for gaining work experience is by enrolling in courses that include a *practicum* or *field work*. For instance, if you're interested in working with children, courses in child psychology or early childhood education may offer experiential learning opportunities in a preschool or daycare center on campus.

Lastly, it may be possible to do volunteer work on campus in different college offices, or by assisting a faculty member. Volunteering as a research or teaching assistant can be a very valuable experience if you intend to go to graduate school. If you have a good relationship with faculty members in an academic field that interests you, consider asking them whether they would like some assistance with their teaching or research responsibilities. You might also check out your professors' web pages to find out what type of research projects they're working on; if any of these projects interest you or relate to a career path you're considering, contact the professor and offer your help. Volunteer work done for a college professor could lead to your making a presentation with your professor at a professional conference or may even result in your name being included as a coauthor on an article published by the professor.

AUTHOR'S EXPERIENCE

I was once advising two first-year students, Kim and Christopher. Kim was thinking about becoming a physical therapist and Chris was thinking about becoming an elementary school teacher. To help Kim get a better idea if physical therapy was the career for her, I suggested that she visit a hospital near our college to inquire about whether she could do volunteer work in the physical therapy unit. As it turned out, the hospital did need volunteers, so she volunteered in the physical therapy unit and loved it. That volunteer experience confirmed for Kim that a physical therapist is what she wanted to be. She completed a degree in physical therapy and is now a professional physical therapist.

Similarly, I suggested to Chris that he test his interest in possibly becoming an elementary school teacher by visiting some local schools to ask about whether they could use a volunteer teacher's aide. One of the schools did need his services, so Chris volunteered as a teacher's aide for about 10 weeks. About two weeks into his volunteer experience, he came into my office to tell me that the kids were just about driving him crazy and he no longer had any interest in becoming a teacher! He ended up majoring in communications.

Kim and Chris were the first two students I advised to get involved in volunteer work to test their career interests. Their volunteer experiences proved to be so useful in helping them identify their career path that I continued to encourage all students I advised to get volunteer experience in the career field they were considering.

—*Joe Cuseo*

Think About It—Journal Entry 12.11

If you have participated in volunteer experiences, what did you learn about yourself from these experiences that might influence your career plans, or acquire skills that could be applied to a future career?

_____

_____

_____

_____

_____

_____

Part-Time Work

Jobs you hold during the academic year or summer break shouldn't be overlooked as career development experiences. Part-time work can supply you with opportunities to develop skills and personal qualities that may be relevant to any future career you decide to pursue, such as organizational skills, communication skills, and ability to work effectively with coworkers from diverse backgrounds and cultures. It's also possible that work in a part-time position may eventually turn into a full-time career—as illustrated in the following story.

AUTHOR'S EXPERIENCE

While he was enrolled in college, a former student of mine (Matt), an English major, worked part time for an organization that provides special assistance to mentally handicapped children. After he completed his English degree, the organization offered him a full-time position that he accepted. While working full-time at this position with handicapped children, Matt decided to go to graduate school part-time and eventually completed a master's degree in special education. This degree qualified him for a promotion to a more advanced position in the organization, which he also accepted. Moral of the story: Part-time work in college can play an important role in opening up a future career path.

—Joe Cuseo

It might also be possible for you to obtain part-time work experience on campus through your school's work-study program. Work-study jobs can be done in a variety of campus settings (e.g., Financial Aid Office, Library, Public Relations Office, or Computer Services Center), and they can be built around your course schedule. Just like off-campus work, on-campus work can provide you with valuable career exploration and resume-building experiences, and the professionals for whom you work can also serve as excellent references for letters of recommendation to future employers. To see whether you are eligible for your school's work-study program, visit the Financial Aid Office on your campus. If you don't qualify for work-study jobs, ask about other forms of campus employment that are not funded through the work-study program.

There's simply no substitute for gaining knowledge about careers than direct, hands-on learning experience in actual work settings—such as shadowing, intern-

"As entertainment, TV shows are great. As reality, they fall a little short. So enjoy your TV and movies, but don't make career decisions based on them."

—Katharine Brooks, author, You Majored in What? Mapping Your Path from Chaos to Career ships, volunteer services, and part-time work. These firsthand experiences represent the ultimate career "reality test." They allow you direct access to what careers are really like—as opposed to the glamorized and unrealistic picture of them portrayed in the media.

Note

A key characteristic of effective goal setting is to set goals that are realistic. In the case of career goals, getting firsthand experience in actual work settings allows you to get a much more realistic view of what work in a field is really like—before committing to that field as your career goal.

Tying it altogether, experiencing work in real-life work settings has five powerful career advantages:

- You get a realistic picture of what work is like in a particular field
- You get to test your interests and skills for certain types of work
- You strengthen your resume by adding experiential learning to academic (classroom) learning
- You acquire contacts who can serve as personal references and sources for letters of recommendation
- You network with employers who may hire you or refer you for a position after graduation.

In addition, getting work experience *early* in college makes you a more competitive candidate for internships and part-time positions you may apply for later in your college experience.

To locate and participate in work experiences that relate to your career interests, use all resources available to you, including campus resources (e.g., the Career Development Center and Financial Aid Office), local resources (e.g., Chamber of Commerce), and personal contacts (e.g., family and friends). Take these experiences seriously, learn as much as you can from them, and build relationships with the people you work with—these are the people who can provide you with future contacts, references, and referrals. Don't forget that almost three of every four jobs are obtained through personal relationships, aka "networking" (Brooks, 2009).

Think About It—Journal Entry 12.12

1. Have you had work experiences that may influence your future career plans, or provided you with skills you can include on your resume? What are they?

2. If you could get work experience in any career field right now, what would it be? Why?

Step 3. Awareness of Career Options that Provide the Best "Fit" for You

As we've emphasized throughout this chapter, the factor that should carry the greatest weight in career decision-making is the match between your career choice and your personal talents, interests, needs, and values. Since a career choice is a long-range decision that affects your life well beyond college, the process of self-awareness should not only involve reflection on who you are now, but also on how your career choice relates to where you see yourself in the future.

Think About It—Journal Entry 12.13

Answer the following questions about a career you're considering or have chosen:

1. Why are you attracted to this career? (What led or caused you to become interested in it?)

2. Would you say that your interest in this career is characterized primarily by *intrinsic* motivation—something "inside" of you, such as your personal abilities, interests, needs, and values? Or, would you say that your interest in the career is driven by *extrinsic* motivation—something "outside" of you, such as starting salary, pleasing your family, or meeting expectations of your gender (i.e., an expected career role for a male or female)? Explain.

> More people today have the means to live, but no meaning to live for."
>
> —Viktor Frankl, Austrian neurologist, psychiatrist, and Holocaust survivor

> I think that a good career has to be meaningful for a person. It should give a person a sense of fulfillment."
>
> —First-year student

_____

_____

_____

3. If money weren't an issue and you could earn a comfortable living working in another
    career, would you still continue to pursue the same career you're currently considering?
    Why or why not?

_____

_____

_____

_____

Step 4. Awareness of the Major Steps Needed to Reach Your Career Goal

Whether you're keeping your career options open or you think you've already decided on a particular career, you can start now by taking early steps for successful
entry into any career by using the following strategies.

Self-Monitoring: Watching and Tracking Your Skills and Attributes

Keep in mind that the *academic* skills you're developing in college are also *professional* skills you'll use beyond college. Said in another way, learning skills become
earning skills. When you're engaged in the process of completing academic tasks—
such as note-taking, reading, writing papers and taking tests—you're also developing career-relevant skills—such as listening, interpreting, analyzing, and problem
solving.

What matters more to employers of college graduates than their degree credentials or the courses on their transcript are the skills and personal qualities
they've developed and can bring to the position (Education Commission of the
States, 1995; Figler & Boles, 2007) You can start building these skills and qualities
through effective *self-monitoring*—that is, monitoring (watching) yourself and tracking the skills you're using and developing during your college experience. Skills are
habits, and like other habits which are repeatedly practiced, their development can
be so gradual and subtle that you may not even notice how much growth has taken
place (like watching grass grow). Thus, career development specialists recommend
that you consciously and carefully reflect on the skills you're using so you remain
aware of their development and are able to articulate them to potential employers
(Lock, 2004).

One way to track your developing skills is by keeping a *learning journal* in which
you reflect on the academic tasks and assignments you've completed, along with the

skills you developed while completing them. Your journal should also include skills developed outside the classroom—such as those acquired through co-curricular experiences, leadership development programs, volunteer experiences, and part-time jobs.

Since skills are actions, it's best to track and record them in your journal as *verbs*. You're likely to find that many of these action verbs reflect the type of work-related skills that employers seek in today's job candidates. **Box 12.5** contains a sample of action-oriented career skills you're likely to develop in college that are relevant to successful performance in a variety of careers.

Box 12.5

Transferable Skills Relevant to Successful Career Performance

The following behaviors represent a sample of flexible skills that are relevant to success in virtually all careers (Bolles, 1998; Figler & Bolles, 2007) As you track your learning experiences in college, remain mindful of whether you're developing these (and other) skills, both inside and outside the classroom.

advise	create	initiate	present	sequence
assemble calculate	delegate	measure	produce	summarize
coach	design evaluate	motivate	research	supervise
coordinate	explain	negotiate	resolve	synthesize

In addition to tracking your skills, also keep track of the positive traits and attributes you're developing. While skills are best recorded as *verbs* because they represent actions you can perform for anyone who hires you, personal attributes are best recorded as *adjectives* because they describe who you are and what positive qualities you can bring to any position. **Box 12.6** below identifies examples of personal traits and attributes that are relevant to successful performance in any career.

Box 12.6

Personal Traits and Attributes Relevant to Successful Career Performance

As you proceed through college, keep track of these and other personal attributes or character traits you are developing.

collaborative	conscientious	considerate	curious	dependable
determined	energetic	enthusiastic	ethical	flexible
imaginative	industrious	loyal	observant	open-minded
outgoing	patient	persuasive	positive	precise
prepared	productive	prudent	punctual	reflective
sincere	tactful	team player	thorough	thoughtful

Think About It—Journal Entry 12.14

Look back at the personal skills and traits listed in **Boxes 12.5** and **12.6**. Underline or highlight those that you think are relevant to the career(s) you're considering.

AUTHOR'S EXPERIENCE

After class one day, I had a conversation with a student of mine (Max) about his personal interests. He said he was considering a career in the music industry and was working part-time as a disc jockey at a night club. I asked him what it took to be a good disc jockey, and in less than five minutes of talking about his part-time work, we discovered that there were many transferable career skills embedded in his job than he realized. Each night he worked he was responsible for organizing three to four hours of music; he had to read the reactions of his audience (customers) and adapt or adjust his selections to their musical tastes; he had to arrange his selections in a sequence that varied the tempo of music he played throughout the night; and he had to continually research and update his music collection to track the latest trends in hits and popular artists. His job also required him to deliver public announcements, which enabled him to overcome his fear of public speaking.

Although we were just having a short, friendly conversation after class about his part-time work, Max ended up reflecting on and identifying multiple skills he was developing on the job. We both agreed that it would be a good idea for him to get these skills down in writing so that he could use them as selling points for future jobs in the music field, or any other line of work he might eventually pursue.

—*Joe Cuseo*

Note

Embedded in your work and class experiences are transferable skills and personal qualities that are applicable to a variety of careers. Tracking these skills and qualities and articulating them to potential employers is as important to successful entry into a future career as the courses listed on your transcript and the major listed on your resume.

Self-Marketing: Packaging and Presenting Your Personal Strengths and Achievements

"Man who stand on hill with mouth open will wait long time for roast duck to drop in."

—*Confucius, Chinese philosopher who emphasized sincerity and social justice*

Studies show that students who convert their college degree into a successful career have two common characteristics: personal initiative and a positive attitude (Pope, 1990). They don't take a passive approach and assume a good position will just fall into their lap; nor do they believe they are owed a position simply because they have a college degree or credential. Instead, they take an active role involved in defining their strengths and showcasing them in the job-search process (Brown & Krane, 2000).

One way you can convert your college degree into gainful employment is to view yourself (a college graduate) as a product and view employers as customers who may be interested in purchasing your product (your skills and attributes). As a first-year student, it could be said that you're in the early stages in the process of developing your product. Begin the process now by identifying and packaging your skills and attributes so by the time you graduate you'll have a well-developed product that potential employers will be interested in purchasing.

By developing an effective self-marketing plan, you give employers a clear idea of what you can bring to the table and do *for them*. You can market your personal skills, qualities, and achievements to future employers through the following formats.

> The bottom line for most employers is 'Will this person fit in our environment?' One of the keys to marketing yourself is to make a connection, to get out of your mindset and into your audience's.
>
> *—Katharine Brooks, author,* You Majored in What? Mapping Your Path from Chaos to Career

Course Transcript

Your course transcript is a listing of all courses you enrolled in and the grades you received in those courses. Two pieces of information included on your college transcript can strongly influence employers' hiring decisions or admissions committee decisions about your acceptance to a graduate or professional school: (a) the grades you earned in your courses and (b) the types of courses you completed.

Simply stated, the better the grades you earn in college, the better are your employment prospects after college. Research on college graduates indicates that the higher their grades, the higher:

- The prestige of their first job
- Their total earnings (salary and fringe benefits)
- Their job mobility (ability to change jobs or positions).

This relationship between higher college grades and career advantages holds true for students at all types of colleges and universities, regardless of the perceived reputation or prestige of the school they attended (Pascarella & Terenzini, 1991, 2005).

Co-curricular Experiences

Participation in student clubs, campus organizations, and other types of co-curricular activities represent a valuable source of experiential learning that complements classroom-based learning and contributes to career preparation and development. A sizable body of research supports the power of these experiences for career success (Astin, 1993; Hart Research Associates, 2006, 2014; Kuh, 1993; Pascarella & Terenzini, 1991, 2005). Co-curricular experiences that are especially relevant to career development and career success are those that:

- Allow you to develop leadership and mentoring skills—such as, participating in leadership retreats, student government, college committees, peer counseling, or peer tutoring.
- Enable you to interact with others from diverse ethnic and racial groups—such as, multicultural or international clubs and organizations.
- Relate to your academic major or career interests—such as, involvement in student clubs in your college major or intended career field.

Don't forget that co-curricular experiences are also resume-building experiences; they serve as evidence of social responsibility to your communities on and off campus. Be sure to showcase these experiences to prospective employers. Also, don't forget that campus professionals with whom you may interact while participating in co-curricular activities (e.g., the director of student activities or dean of students) can serve as valuable references and provide you with letters of recommendation to future employers, graduate schools, or professional schools.

Personal Resume

A resume may be described as a listed or bulleted summary of your most important accomplishments, skills, and credentials. If you haven't yet accumulated enough experiences to construct a fully developed resume, you can start building a "skeletal resume" that contains major categories or headings (the skeleton) which you'll eventually flesh out with your specific experiences and accomplishments. (See **Box 12.7** for a sample skeleton resume.)

Box 12.7

Constructing a Skeletal Resume

Use this skeletal resume as an outline or template or blueprint to begin constructing your personal resume and setting future goals. (If you have already created a resume, use this template to identify and add categories that may be missing from your current one.)

NAME
(First, Middle, Last)

Current Addresses: *Permanent* Addresses:
Postal address   Postal address
E-mail address   E-mail address
Phone no.   Phone no.

EDUCATION: Name of College or University, City, State
               Degree Name (e.g., Bachelor of Science)
               College Major (e.g., Accounting)
               Graduation Date
               GPA (if 3.0 or higher)

RELATED WORK   Position Title, City, State   Start and stop dates
EXPERIENCES: (Begin the list with your most recent experiences.)
(List skills you used or developed.)

VOLUNTEER (COMMUNITY SERVICE) EXPERIENCES
(List skills you used or developed.)

NOTABLE COURSEWORK
(e.g., leadership, interdisciplinary, or intercultural courses; study abroad experiences)

CO-CURRICULAR EXPERIENCES
(e.g., student government or peer leadership)
(List skills used or developed.)

PERSONAL SKILLS AND POSITIVE QUALITIES
(List as bullets; be sure to include those that are especially relevant to the position for which you're applying.)

HONORS AND AWARDS
(Include those received prior to college and outside of college)

REFERENCES
(Names and contact information for those who can speak to your work experience)

Portfolio

Unlike a resume, which simply lists your experiences, a portfolio contains actual products or samples of your work. You may have heard the word "portfolio" referred to as a collection of artwork that professional artists put together to showcase or advertise their artistic ability. However, the term *portfolio* has a broader meaning; it can be a collection of any material that depicts a person's skills and talents, or demonstrates educational and personal development. For example, a portfolio could include items such as:

- Outstanding papers, exam performances, research projects, and lab reports
- Work samples and photos from study abroad experiences, service learning, and internships
- Video footage of oral presentations and public performances
- Performance evaluations received from professors, student development professionals, and employers
- Letters of recognition or commendation from professors, student development professionals, and employers.

As a first-year student, you can begin the process of portfolio development right now by saving your best work and performances, including those done in classes, co-curricular experiences on campus, or service and work experiences off campus. Store them in a traditional portfolio folder, or save them on a flash drive to create an electronic portfolio. You could also create a website and upload your materials there. Eventually, you should be able to build a well-stocked portfolio that showcases your skills and demonstrates your achievements to future employers or future schools.

Think About It—Journal Entry 12.15

What do you predict will be your best work products in college—those that you would most likely showcase in a portfolio?

_____

_____

_____

Why?

_____

_____

_____

_____

Letters of Recommendation (Letters of Reference)

The quality of your letters of recommendation will be strengthened if you give careful thought to (a) who will serve as your references, (b) how to approach them, and (c) what to provide them. Specific strategies for doing so are summarized in **Box 12.8.**

Box 12.8

The Art and Science of Requesting Letters of Recommendation: Effective Strategies and Common Courtesies

1. Select recommendations from people who know you well. Think about individuals with whom you've had an ongoing relationship, who know you by name, and who have observed your strongest performances and skills. Good candidates are instructors who you've had for more than one course, an academic advisor whom you see often, or an employer who has witnessed your work habits for an extended period of time.

2. Seek a balanced blend of letters from people who have observed your performance in different settings or situations. The following are performance-based settings where people may have observed how well you performed:
   - The classroom—a professor who can speak to your academic performance
   - On campus—a student life professional who can comment on your contributions to a club or organization
   - Off campus—a professional for whom you've performed volunteer service, part-time work, or an internship

3. Pick the right time and place to make your request. Be sure to request letters of recommendation well in advance of the letter's deadline date (at least two weeks). First, ask the person if he or she is willing to write you a letter of recommendation. Don't approach the person with the form in your hand because it may send the message that you have assumed the person will say yes or are pressuring the person to say yes. This isn't the most socially sensitive message to send someone whom you're about to ask a favor.

    Also, pick a place and time where the person can give full attention to your request. Make a personal visit to the person's office, rather than making the request in a busy hallway or in front of a classroom full of students.

4. Provide your references with a fact sheet about yourself. Include your experiences and achievements—both inside and outside the classroom. This will help make your references' job a little easier by providing points for them to focus on. It's also likely to make your letter stronger because it will contain specific examples that draw directly from your personal experiences and accomplishments. On your fact sheet, be sure to include high grades you may have earned in certain courses, as well as volunteer services, leadership experiences, awards or forms of recognition, and special interests or talents relevant to your academic major and career choice. Your fact sheet is the place to "toot your own horn," so don't fear coming across as a braggart. You're not being boastful or showboating; you're just highlighting your strengths.

5. If the letter is to be mailed, provide your references with a stamped, addressed envelope. This is a simple courtesy that makes their job easier and demonstrates your social sensitivity.

6. Waive your right to see the letter. If you have the option to waive (give up) your right to see the letter of recommendation, waive your right—as long as you feel reasonably certain that you will receive a good letter of recommendation. By waiving your right to see the letter, you show confidence that the letter will be positive and assures the person reading the letter that you didn't inspect or screen it to ensure it was good before sending it.

7. Follow up with a thank you note. Send this note at about the time your letter of recommendation should be sent. This is the right thing to do because it shows your appreciation; it's also the smart thing to do because if the letter hasn't been sent, the thank you note serves as a gentle reminder to your reference that the letter should be sent soon.

8. Let your references know the outcome of your application. If you've been offered the position or been admitted to the school to which you applied, let your references know. This is the socially sensitive thing to do, and your references are likely to notice and remember your social sensitivity—which should strengthen the quality of any future letters of recommendation you may request from them.

Think About It—Journal Entry 12.16

Have you met anyone on campus who you could be in a position to write a letter of recommendation for you?

If you have, who is this person, and what position does he or she hold on campus?

If you haven't, who might be a good future candidate?

Networking

Would it surprise you to learn that 80% of jobs are never advertised? This means that jobs you see listed in a classified section of the newspaper and posted in a Career Development Center or employment center represent only 20% of available openings at any given time. Almost one-half of all job hunters find employment through people they know or have met, such as friends, family members, and casual acquaintances. When it comes to locating positions, *who* you know can be as important as *what* you know or how good your resume looks. Consequently, it's important to continually expand the circle of people who are aware of your career interests and abilities, because they can be a valuable source of information about employment opportunities.

Also, be sure to share copies of your resume with friends and family members, just in case they come in contact with employers who are looking for somebody with your career interests and qualifications.

Personal Interview

A personal interview is your opportunity to make a positive in-person impression. You can make a strong first impression during any interview by showing that you've done your homework and have come prepared. In particular, you should come to the interview with knowledge about yourself and your audience.

You can demonstrate knowledge about yourself by bringing a mental list of your strongest selling points to the interview and being ready to speak about them when the opportunity arises. You can demonstrate knowledge of your audience by doing some homework on the organization you are applying to, the people who are likely to be interviewing you, and the questions they are likely to ask you. Try to acquire as much information about the organization and its key employees as is available to you online and in print. When you know your audience (who your interviewers are likely to be and what they're likely to ask), and when you know yourself well (what about yourself you're going to say), you should then be ready to answer what probably is the most important interview question of all: "What can *you* do for *us*?"

To prepare for interviews, visit your Career Development Center and inquire about questions that are commonly asked during personal interviews. You might also try to speak with seniors who have interviewed with recruiters and ask them whether certain questions tended to be frequently asked. Once you begin to participate in actual interviews, make note of the questions you are asked. Although you may be able to anticipate some of the more general questions that are asked in almost any interview, there likely will be unique questions asked of you that relate specifically to your personal qualifications and experiences. If these questions are asked in one of your interviews, there's a good chance they'll be asked in a future interview. As soon as you complete an interview, mentally review it and attempt to recall the major questions you were asked before they slip your mind. Consider developing an index card catalog of questions that you've been asked during interviews, with the question on one side and your prepared response on the reverse side. By being better prepared for personal interviews, you'll increase the quality of your answers and decrease your level of anxiety. You should also have a list of questions to ask at the interview. This shows that you are interested and did your homework. Finally, remember to dress appropriately for an interview. If you are unsure how to dress, consult a professional you trust on campus.

Lastly, remember to send a thank you note to the person who interviewed you. This is not only the courteous thing to do, but also the smart thing to do because it demonstrates your interpersonal sensitivity and reinforces the person's memory of you.

Technology and Career Placement

Once you start looking for a job, internship, or co-op, it is very important to consider how you use technology:

1. **Your e-mail address.** Make sure it is professional and would not offend anyone.
2. **Your cell phone.** Consider your "ring-back tone." If it is music that has offensive language, remove it. Also, make sure your voicemail message is short and professional. Time is precious and people don't want to listen to a two-minute voicemail message, no matter what it is about.
3. **Facebook, Twitter, etc.** Make sure anything you post would not turn off any potential employers. Even if your page is marked "private," employers are hiring people to get all the dirt on you!

It is important when you are looking for a job to put your best self out there—this includes your digital self.

Chapter Summary and Highlights

Studies show that the vast majority of students entering college are uncertain about their academic specialization. Most students do not reach a final decision about their major *before* starting college; typically, they make that decision *during* their college experience. As you gain experience with the college curriculum, you will gain greater self-insight into your academic interests, strengths, and weaknesses. Take this self-knowledge into consideration when choosing a major to help you select a field that capitalizes on your personal interests, abilities, and talents.

To make a well-informed choice of a college major, there are several myths you should be aware of:

- When you choose your major, you're choosing your career.
- After you graduate with a college degree, any further education you pursue must be in the same field as your college major.
- Since most college graduates work in business settings, you should major business.
- If you major in a liberal arts subject, the only career available to you is teaching.

Reaching an effective decision about a career path involves four forms of awareness: involved in setting

1. Awareness of *self*—insight into your personal interests, talents, needs, and values
2. Awareness of your *career options*—knowledge of different career fields available to you
3. Awareness of what options provide the *best "fit" for you*—knowing what careers most closely match your personal interests, talents, needs, and values
4. Awareness of the major *steps needed to reach your career goal*—knowing how to prepare for and gain entry into the career of your choice

You can gain valuable information about careers by:

- Accessing printed and online career resources (e.g., *Dictionary of Occupational Titles; Occupational Outlook Handbook*)
- Taking career development courses
- Attending career fairs on campus
- Conducting information interviews with professionals in careers that interest you
- Shadowing (observing) professionals at work
- Engaging in service learning, internships, or cooperative education programs

Learning More through the World Wide Web: Internet-Based Resources

For additional information related to educational planning and choosing a major, see the following websites.

Identifying and Choosing College Majors:
www.mymajors.com

www.princetonreview.com/majors.aspx

Relationships between Majors and Careers:
http://uncw.edu/career/WhatCanIDoWithaMajorIn.html

Developing a Personalized Career Plan: www.mapping-your-future.org

Navigating the Job Market: www.mymajors.com

Career Descriptions and Future Employment Outlook: www.bls.gov/

Position Openings & Opportunities:
www.rileyguide.com
www.monster.com

Resume Writing & Job Interviewing: www.quintcareers.com

References

AAC&U (Association of American Colleges and Universities) (2007, 2013). *It takes more than a major: Employer priorities for college learning and success*. Washington, DC: Author.

American College Testing (2015). *College student retention and graduation rates from 2000 through 2015*.

Astin, A. W. (1993). *What matters in college?* San Francisco: Jossey-Bass.

Baumeister, R., & Leary, M. R. (1995). The need to belong: Desire for interpersonal attachments as a fundamental human motivation. *Psychological Bulletin, 117*, 497–529.

Bok, D. (2006). *Our underachieving colleges*. Princeton, NJ: Princeton University Press.

Bolles, R.N., 1998. *The new quick job-hunting map*. Toronto, Ontario, Canada: Ten Speed Press.

Brooks, K. (2009). *You majored in what? Mapping your path from chaos to career*. NY: Penguin.

Brown, S. D., & Krane, N. E. R. (2000). Four (or five) sessions and a cloud of dust: Old assumptions and new observations about career counseling. In S. D. Brown & R. W. Lent (Eds.), *Handbook of counseling psychology* (3rd ed., pp. 740–766). New York: Wiley.

Casserly, M. (2012). "10 jobs that didn't exist 10 years ago." *Forbes*. Retrieved from http://www.forbes.com/sites/meghancasserly/2012/05/11/10-jobs-that-didnt-exist-10-years-ago/.

Center for Community College Student Engagement (2008). *High expectations and high support* (2008 CCSSE findings). Austin, Texas: The University of Texas at Austin, Community College Leadership Program.

Center for Community College Student Engagement (2010). *The heart of student success: Teaching, learning, and college completion* (2010 CCSSE findings). Austin, TX: The University of Texas at Austin, Community College Leadership Program.

Chua, S. N., & Koestner, R. (2008). A Self-Determination Theory perspective on the role of autonomy in solitary behavior. *The Journal of Social Psychology, 148*(5), 645–647.

Community College Research Center (CCRC) (2014). "Earning an associate degree increases likelihood of completing bachelor's degree." Retrieved from http://ccrc.tc.columbia.edu/press-releases/earning-associate-before-transfer-press-release.html.

Crosby, O. (2002). Informational interviewing: Get the scoop on careers. *Occupational Outlook Quarterly* (Summer), 32–37.

CSU Student Transfer (2015). "The student transfer achievement reform act." Retrieved from http://www.calstate.edu/transfer/degrees/.

Cuseo, J. B. (2005). "Decided," "undecided," and "in transition": Implications for academic advisement, career counseling, and student retention. In R. S. Feldman (Ed.), *Improving the first year of college: Research and practice* (pp. 27–50). Mahwah, NJ: Lawrence Erlbaum.

Deci, E., & Ryan, R. (Eds.). (2002). *Handbook of self-determination research*. Rochester, NY: University of Rochester Press.

Education Commission of the States. (1995). *Making quality count in undergraduate education*. Denver, CO: ECS Distribution Center.

Elliott, M. (2015). *CEOs who didn't pursue undergrad business degrees*. Retrieved from http://www.usatoday.com/story/money/business/2015/03/29/cheat-sheet-ceos-college-business/70442270/.

Figler, H., & Bolles, R. N. (2007). *The career counselor's handbook*. Berkeley, CA: Ten Speed Press.

Gagliardi, J., & Hiemstra, H. (2013). *College still pays*. Kentucky Postsecondary Education Policy Brief. Retrieved from http://cpe.ky.gov/NR/rdonlyres/8DE2CF1E-51A2-4C27-8C2B-41FB126252FE/0/CollegeStillPayspolicybrief.pdf.

Ganzglass, E. (2014). Scaling "stackable credentials": Implications for implementation and policy. Center for Postsecondary and Economic Success. Retrieved from http://www.clasp.org/resources-and-publications/files/2014-03-21-Stackable-Credentials-Paper-FINAL.pdf.

Gardner, P. D. (1991, March). *Learning the ropes: Socialization and assimilation into the workplace*. Paper presented at the Second National Conference on the Senior Year Experience, San Antonio, TX.

Gardner, H. (1993). *Frames of mind: The theory of multiple intelligences* (2nd ed.). New York: Basic Books.

Gardner, H. (1999). *Intelligence reframed: Multiple intelligences for the 21st century*. New York: Basic Books.

Gardner, H. (2006) *Changing Minds. The art and science of changing our own and other people's minds*. Boston MA.: Harvard Business School Press.

Gordon, V. N., & Steele, G. E. (2003). Undecided first-year students: A 25-year longitudinal study. *Journal of the First-Year Experience and Students in Transition, 15*(1), 19–38.

Hagedorn, L. S., Moon, H. S., Cypers, S., Maxwell, W. E., & Lester, J. (2006). Transfer between community colleges and four-year colleges: The all-American game. *Community College Journal of Research and Practice*, 30(3), 223–242.

Hart Research Associates. (2006). *How should colleges prepare students to succeed in today's global economy?* Based on surveys among employers and recent college graduates. Conducted on behalf of the Association of American Colleges and Universities. Washington, DC: Author.

Hart Research Associates. (2014. July). *How should colleges prepare students to succeed in today's global economy?* Retrieved from http://dpdproject.info/details/how-should-colleges-prepare-students-to-succeed-in-todays-global-economy-peter-d-hart-research-associates/.

HERI (Higher Education Research Institute) (2014). *Your first college year survey 2014.* Los Angeles, CA: Cooperative Institutional Research Program, University of California-Los Angeles.

Hildenbrand, M., & Gore, P. A., Jr. (2005). Career development in the first-year seminar: Best practice versus actual practice. In P. A. Gore (Ed.), *Facilitating the career development of students in transition* (Monograph No. 43, pp. 45–60). Columbia: National Resource Center for the First-Year Experience and Students in Transition, University of South Carolina.

Knouse, S., Tanner, J., & Harris, E. (1999). The relation of college internships, college performance, and subsequent job opportunity. *Journal of Employment Counseling, 36,* 35–43.

Kuh, G. D. (1993). In their own words: What students learn outside the classroom. *American Educational Research Journal, 30,* 277–304.

Kuh, G. D., Kinzie, J., Schuh, J. H., Whitt, E. J., et al (2005). *Student success in college: Creating conditions that matter.* San Francisco, CA: Jossey-Bass.

Laanan, F. S. (2001). Transfer student adjustment. In F. S. Laanan (Ed.), *Transfer students: Trends and issues* (pp. 5–13). New Directions for Community Colleges, No. 114. San Francisco: Jossey-Bass.

Leuwerke, W. C., Robbins, S. B., Sawyer, R., & Hovland, M. (2004). Predicting engineering major status from mathematics achievement and interest congruence. *Journal of Career Assessment, 12,* 135–149.

Lock, R. D. (2004). *Taking charge of your career direction* (5th ed.). Belmont, CA: Brooks Cole. Melton, 1995

Millard, B. (2004, November 7). *A purpose-based approach to navigating college transitions.* Preconference workshop presented at the Eleventh National Conference on Students in Transition, Nashville, Tennessee.

Miller, M. T., & Nadler, D. P. (2004). Transfer trends in the future of higher education. In B. C. Jacobs (Ed.), *The college transfer student in America: The forgotten student* (pp.

188–201). Washington, DC: American Association of Collegiate Registrars and Admissions Officers.

Mullin, C., & Phillippe, K. (2013). *Community college contributions* (No. AACC Policy Brief 2013-01PB). American Association of Community Colleges. Retrieved from http://www.aacc.nche.edu/Publications/Briefs/Documents/2013PB_01.pdf.

National Association of Colleges & Employers (2012). *Internship and co-op survey.* Bethlehem, PA: Author.

National Association of Colleges & Employers (2013). *Job outlook: The candidate skills/qualities employers want.* Retrieved from http://www.naceweb.org/s10022013/job-outlook-skills-quality.aspx.

National Association of Colleges & Employers (2014). *2014 Internship and co-op survey,* **executive summary.** Retrieved from https://www.naceweb.org/uploadedFiles/Content/static-assets/downloads/executive-summary/2014-internship-co-op-survey-executive-summary.pdf.

National Center for Education Statistics (2014). *Fast facts: Most popular majors.* Washington, DC: U.S. Department of Education. Retrieved from http://nces.ed.gov/fastfacts/display.asp?id=37.

National Student Clearing House Research Center (2015). *Contribution of two-year institutions to four-year completions.* Retrieved from https://nscresearchcenter.org/snapshotreport-twoyearcontributionfouryear completions17/.

Pascarella, E., & Terenzini, P. (1991). *How college affects students: Findings and insights from twenty years of research.* San Francisco: Jossey-Bass.

Pascarella, E., & Terenzini, P. (2005). *How college affects students: A third decade of research* (Vol. 2). San Francisco: Jossey-Bass.

Pope, L. (1990). *Looking beyond the Ivy League.* New York: Penguin Press.

Ryan, R. (1995). Psychological needs and the facilitation of integrative processes. *Journal of Personality, 63,* 397–427.

Ryan, R. M., & Deci, E. L. (2000). Self-determination theory and the facilitation of intrinsic motivation, social development, and well-being. *American Psychologist, 55,* 68–78.

Smith, D. D. (2005). Experiential learning, service learning, and career development. In P. A. Gore (Ed.), *Facilitating the career development of students in transition* (Monograph No. 43, pp. 205–222). Columbia: National Resource Center for the First-Year Experience and Students in Transition, University of South Carolina.

Thurmond, K. C. (2007). Transfer shock: Why is a term forty years old still relevant? Retrieved from *NACADA Clearinghouse of Academic Advising Resources* website: http://www.nacada.ksu.edu/Resources/Clearinghouse/View-Articles/Dealing-with-transfer-shock.aspx.

Tinto, V. (2012). *Completing college: Rethinking institutional action.* Chicago: The University of Chicago Press.

Useem, M. (1989). *Liberal education and the corporation: The hiring and advancement of college graduates.* Piscataway, NJ: Aldine Transaction.

Washington State Board for Community & Technical Colleges (2015). *Transfer associate degrees.* Retrieved from http://www.sbctc.ctc.edu/college/_e-transferdegrees.aspx

Zamani, E. (2001). Institutional responses to barriers to the transfer process. In F. Laanan (Ed.), *Transfer students: Trends and issues* (pp. 15–24). New Directions for Community Colleges, No. 114. San Francisco: Jossey-Bass.

Zlomek, E. (2012, March 26). As MBA applicants, business majors face an uphill battle. *Bloomburg Business.* Retrieved from http://www.bloomberg.com/bw/articles/2012-03-26/as-mba-applicants-business-majors-face-an-uphill-battle.

Chapter 12 Exercises

12.1 Quote Reflections

Review the sidebar quotes contained in this chapter and select two that were especially meaningful or inspirational to you.

For each quote, provide a three- to five-sentence explanation why you chose it.

12.2 Reality Bite

Career Choice: Conflict and Confusion

Josh is a first-year student whose family has made a great financial sacrifice to support his college education. He deeply appreciates the sacrifice his family members has made and wants to pay them back as soon as possible. Consequently, he's been looking into careers that offer the highest starting salaries immediately after graduation. Unfortunately, none of these careers seem to match Josh's natural abilities and personal interests. He's now conflicted, confused, and worried. He knows he'll have to make a decision soon because the careers with high starting salaries involve majors that have many course requirements. If he expects to graduate in four years, he'll have to start taking some of these courses next semester.

Reflection and Discussion Questions

1. If you were Josh, what would you do?
2. Do you see any way that Josh might balance his desire to pay back his family as soon as possible with his desire to pursue a career that's compatible with his interests and talents?
3. What questions or factors do you think Josh should consider before making his decision about a career?
4. Can you relate to Josh's story, or do you know of students in a similar predicament?

12.3 Gaining Self-Awareness of Personal Interests, Talents, and Values

No one is in a better position to discover who you are, and who you want to be, than *you*. One effective way to gain deeper self-insight is through self-questioning. You can become more self-aware by asking yourself questions that cause you to think carefully about your inner qualities and characteristics. Responding honestly to the following questions can sharpen awareness of your true interests, abilities and values, and help you determine what major or career is a good "fit" for you. As you read each question, briefly note what thought(s) come to mind about yourself.

Personal Interests

1. What tends to grab your attention and hold it for long periods of time?
2. What sorts of things are you naturally curious about or frequently intrigue you?
3. What do you really enjoy doing and do as often as you possibly can?
4. What do you look forward to, or get excited about?
5. What are your favorite hobbies or pastimes?
6. When you're with your friends, what do you like to talk about or spend time doing?
7. What has been your most stimulating or enjoyable learning experience?
8. If you've had previous work or volunteer experience, what jobs or tasks did you find most interesting or stimulating?
9. When time seems to "fly by" for you, what are you usually doing?

10. What do you like to read about?

11. When you open a newspaper or log onto the Internet, where do you tend to go first?

12. When you find yourself daydreaming or fantasizing about your future, what is it usually about?

From your responses to the above questions, identify a career that appears to be most compatible with your personal *interests*? In the space below, note the career and your interests that are compatible with it.

Personal Talents and Abilities

1. What seems to come naturally to you?

2. What would you say is your greatest talent or personal gift?

3. What are your most advanced or well-developed skills?

4. What seems to come easily to you that others have to work harder to do?

5. What would you say has been your greatest personal accomplishment or achievement in life thus far?

6. What about yourself are you most proud of, or that you take most pride in doing?

7. When others come to you for advice or assistance, what is it usually for?

8. What would your best friend(s) say is your best quality, trait, or characteristic?

9. When you've done something that left you feeling like you really were successful, what was it that you did?

> Never desert your line of talent. Be what nature intended you for and you will succeed."
>
> —Sydney Smith, 18th-century English writer and defender of the oppressed

10. If you have received awards or other forms of recognition, what have they been for?

11. On what types of learning tasks or activities have you experienced the most success?

12. In what types of courses do you tend to earn the highest grades?

From your responses to the above questions, identify a career that appears to be most compatible with your personal *talents and abilities*? In the space below, note the career and your talents and abilities that are compatible with it.

Personal Values

> To love what you do and feel that it matters—how could anything be more fun?"
>
> —Katharine Graham, former CEO of the Washington Post and Pulitzer Prize-winning author

1. What matters most to you?

2. If you were to single out one thing you really stand for or believe in, what would it be?

3. What would you say are your highest priorities in life?

4. Whenever you get the feeling you've done what was good or right, what was it that you did?

5. If there were one thing in the world you could change, improve, or make a difference in, what would it be?

6. When you have extra spending money, what do you usually spend it on?

7. When you have free time, what do you usually find yourself doing?

8. What does living a "good life" mean to you?

> Success is getting what you want. Happiness is wanting what you get."
>
> —Dale Carnegie, author of the best-selling book, How to Win Friends and Influence People and founder of The Dale Carnegie Course—a worldwide program for business based on his teachings

9. How would you define success? (What would it take for you to feel that you achieved success?)

10. How do you define happiness? (What would it take for you to be happy?)

11. Do you have a hero or anyone you admire, look up to, or feel has set an example worth following? (If yes, who and why?)

12. Would you rather be thought of as:

    (a) smart,

    (b) wealthy,

    (c) creative, or

    (d) caring?

(Rank from 1 to 4, with 1 being the highest)

From your responses to the above questions, identify a career that appears to be most compatible with your personal *values*? In the space below, note the career and your values that are compatible with it.

Do what you value; value what you do."

—*Sidney Simon, author of* Values Clarification and In Search of Values

MI Advantage

1. According to your MI report, what are your top three ranked intelligences? Do you agree or disagree with these? Why?

2. Looking at your MI report, of your top suggested careers, which three are most appealing to you? Why?

3. How do your top three intelligences fit with your top three careers?

4. How can you strengthen the intelligence areas you scored lower in?

12.4 Developing a Long-Range Academic Plan for Your Coursework

This exercise is designed to help you design a detailed yet flexible, two-year academic plan. While it may seem a bit overwhelming to develop a long-range plan at this stage of your college experience, you will receive guidance from your course instructor. This is an opportunity to begin customizing your college experience and mapping your educational future. Remember: an educational plan isn't something set in stone, it can change depending on changes in your academic and career interests. As you create, shape, and follow your plan, consult frequently with an academic advisor. If you're planning to transfer to a particular four-year college or university, be aware of its requirements as you develop this academic plan.

Overview of Courses Comprising Your Plan

Your trip through the college curriculum will involve taking courses in the following three key categories:

1. *General education* courses required of all college graduates regardless of their major

2. *Required courses in your chosen major*

3. *Elective* courses you choose to take from any listed in your college catalog.

What follows are planning directions for each of these types of courses. By building these three sets of courses into your educational plan, you can create a roadmap that guides your future coursework. Once you've reserved slots for these three key categories of courses you will have a blueprint to guide (not dictate) your educational future. If you later change your mind about a particular course you originally planned to take, you can do so without interfering with your educational progress by substituting another course from the same category. For instance, if your original plan was to take psychology to fulfill a general education requirement in the Social and Behavioral Sciences, but you decide later to take anthropology instead, you have a space reserved in your plan to make the switch.

As you gain more educational experience, your specific academic and career interests are likely to change and so may the specifics of your long-range plan. The purpose of this plan is not to tie you up or pin you down, but to supply you with a map that keeps you on course and moving in the right direction. Since this is a flexible plan, it's probably best to complete it in pencil or electronically so you can make future changes as needed.

Once you've developed your plan, hold onto it, and keep an up-to-date copy of it throughout your time in college. Bring it with you when you meet with advisors and career development specialists, and come prepared to discuss your progress on the plan as well as any changes you'd like to make to your plan.

Part A. Planning for General Education

Step 1. Use your course catalog (bulletin) to identify the general education requirements for graduation. You're likely to find these requirements organized into general divisions of knowledge (Humanities, Natural Sciences, etc.). Within each of these divisions, courses will be listed that you can take to fulfill the general education requirement(s) for that particular division. (Course catalogs can sometimes be tricky to navigate or interpret; if you run into any difficulty, seek help from your course instructor or an academic advisor.) You'll probably be able to choose courses from a list of different options. Use your freedom of choice to choose general education courses whose descriptions capture your curiosity and contribute to your personal development and career plans. You can use general education courses not only to fulfill general education requirements, but also to test your interest and talent in different fields—one of which may end up becoming your major (or minor).

Step 2. Identify courses in the catalog you plan to take to fulfill your general education requirements and list them on the following form. Some courses you're taking this term may be fulfilling general education requirements, so be sure to list them as well.

Planning Grid for *General Education* Courses

Course Title	Units	Course Title	Units

Total Number of Units Required for *General Education* = _____

Part B. Planning for a College Major

The point of this portion of your educational plan is not to force you to commit to a major right now, but to develop a flexible plan that will allow you to reach a well-informed decision about your major. If you have already chosen a major, this exercise will help you lay out exactly what's ahead of you and confirm whether the coursework required by your major is what you expected and "fits" well with your interests and talents.

Step 1. Go to your college catalog and locate the major you've chosen or are considering. If you're completely undecided, select a field that you might consider as a possibility. To help you identify possible majors, peruse your catalog or go online and answer the questions at *www.mymajors.com.*

Another way to identify a major for this exercise is to first identify a career you might be interested in and work backward to find a major that leads to this career. If you would like to use this strategy, the following website will guide you through the process: *http://uncw.edu/career/WhatCanIDoWithaMajorIn.html.*

Step 2. After you've selected a major, consult with an academic advisor about what courses are required for that major. The advising center on campus may have "major planning sheets" that list the specific course requirements for different majors.

A college major will require all students majoring in that field to complete specific set of courses. For instance, all business majors are required to take microeconomics and macroeconomics. Other courses required for a major may be chosen from a menu or list of options (e.g., "choose any three courses from the following list of six courses"). Such courses are often called "major electives." For these major electives, read their course descriptions carefully and use your freedom of choice wisely to select courses that interest you and are most relevant to your future plans.

Note: You can "double dip" by taking courses that fulfill a major requirement and a general education requirement at the same time. For instance, if your major is psychology, you may be able to take a course in General or Introductory Psychology that counts simultaneously as a required major course and a required general education course in the area of Social and Behavioral Sciences.

Step 3. Identify courses you plan to take to fulfill your major requirements and major electives and list them on the following form. Courses you're taking this term may be fulfilling requirements in the major you've selected, so be sure to list them as well.

Planning Grid for Courses in Your *Major*

Course Title	Units	Course Title	Units

Total Number of Units Required for Your *Major* = _____

Plan C. Planning Your Free Electives

Now that you've built general education courses and major courses into your educational map, you're well positioned to plan your *free electives*—courses not required for general education or your major but that are needed to reach the minimum number of units required for your degree or program. These are courses you are free to choose from any listed in the college catalog.

To determine how many free elective units you have, add up the number of course units you're taking to fulfill general education and major requirements, then subtract this number from the total number of units you need to graduate. The number of course units remaining represents your total number of free electives.

Planning Grid for Your *Free Electives*

Course Title	Units	Course Title	Units

Total Number of *Free Elective* Units = _____

Part D. Putting It Altogether: Developing a Comprehensive Graduation Plan

In the previous three sections, you built three key sets of college courses into your plan: general education courses, major courses, and free elective courses. Now you're positioned to tie these three sets of courses together and create a comprehensive graduation plan.

Using the "Long-Range Graduation Planning Form" on **p. 399,** enter the courses you selected to fulfill general education requirements, major requirements, and free electives. In the space provided next to each course, use the following shorthand notations to designate its category:

GE = *general education* course

M = *major* course

E = *elective* course

Notes:

1. If there are courses in your plan that fulfill two or more categories at the same time (e.g., a general education requirement and a major requirement), note both categories.

2. To complete an associate degree (approximately 60 units) in two years, you should plan to complete about 30 course credits each academic year. Keep in mind that you can take college courses in the summer as well as the fall and spring.

Note

Unlike high school, taking summer courses in college doesn't mean you've fallen behind or need to retake a course you failed during the "normal" school year (fall and spring terms). Instead, summer term can be used to get ahead and reduce your time to graduation. Adopt the mindset that summer term is a regular part of the college academic year; use it strategically to stay on track to complete your degree in a timely fashion.

3. Keep in mind that the number associated with a course indicates the year in the college experience when the course is usually taken. Courses numbered in the 100s (or below) are typically taken in the first year of college and 200-numbered courses in the sophomore year.

4. If you haven't decided on a major, a good strategy is to focus on completing general education requirements during your first year of college. This first-year strategy will open more slots in your course schedule during your sophomore year—by that time, you may have a better idea of what you'll major in and what four-year college you want to attend, so you can fill these open slots with courses required for the major you've chosen. (This first-year strategy will also allow you to use general education courses in different subjects to test your interest in majoring in one of these subjects.)

5. Be sure to check whether the course you're planning to take has any *prerequisites*—courses that need to be completed *before* you can enroll in the course you're planning to take. For example, before you can enroll in literature course, you may need to complete at least one prerequisite course in writing or English composition.

6. Your campus may have a *degree audit program* that allows you to electronically track the courses you've completed and the courses you still need to complete a degree in your chosen major. If such a program is available, take advantage of it.

7. You're not locked into taking all your courses in the exact terms you originally placed them in your plan. You can trade terms if it turns out that the course isn't offered during the term you were planning to take it, or if it's offered at a time that conflicts with another course in your schedule.

8. Keep in mind that not all college courses are offered every term, every year. Typically, college catalogs do not contain information about when courses will be scheduled. If you're unsure when a course will be offered, check with an academic advisor. Some colleges develop *a projected plan of scheduled courses* that shows what academic term(s) courses will be offered for the next few years. If such a projected schedule of courses is available, take advantage of it. It will enable you to develop an educational plan that not only includes *what* courses you will take, but also *when* you will take them.

9. Don't forget to include out-of-class learning experiences as part of your educational plan, such as co-curricular experiences on campus and volunteer work or internships.

FRESHMAN YEAR
Fall Term

Course Title	Course Type General Ed. (GE), Major (M), Elective (E)	Course Units

Total Units = _____

Spring Term

Course Title	Course Type General Ed. (GE), Major (M), Elective (E)	Course Units

Total Units = _____

Summer Term

Course Title	Course Type General Ed. (GE), Major (M), Elective (E)	Course Units

Total Units = _____

SOPHOMORE YEAR
Fall Term

Course Title	Course Type General Ed. (GE), Major (M), Elective (E)	Course Units

Total Units = _____

Spring Term

Course Title	Course Type General Ed. (GE), Major (M), Elective (E)	Course Units

Total Units = _____

Summer Term

Course Title	Course Type General Ed. (GE), Major (M), Elective (E)	Course Units

Total Units = _____

Reflection Questions:

1. What is the total number of credits in your graduation plan? Does it equal or exceed the total number of credits needed to graduate with an associate degree?

2. How many credits will you be taking in the following areas?

   a) General Education =
   b) Major =
   c) Free Electives =

3. Look over the course required for the major you selected:

   a) Are there required courses you were surprised to see or didn't expect would be required?
   b) Are you still interested in majoring in this field?
   c) How likely is it that you will change the major you selected?
   d) If you were to change your major, what would "Plan B" likely be?

4. Did completing this long-range graduation plan help you clarify your educational goals?

Why or why not?

12.5 Conducting an Information Interview

One of the best ways to acquire accurate information about a career is to interview a working professional in that career. This career exploration strategy is known as an *information interview*. An information interview enables you to (a) get an insider's view of what the career is really like, (b) network with a professional in the field, and (c) gain confidence in interview situations that prepares you for future job interviews.

Steps in the Information Interview Process

1. Select a career you may be interested in pursuing. Even if you're currently keeping your career options open, pick a career that might be a possibility. You can use the resources cited on **pp. 373–374** in this chapter to help you identify a career that may be most appealing to you.

2. Find someone in the career you've selected and set up an information interview with that person. To locate possible interview candidates, consider members of your family, friends of family members, and family members of your friends. Any of these people may be working in the career you are considering and may be good interview candidates, or they may know others who could be good candidates. The Career Development Center on your campus, as well as the Alumni Association may also be able to provide you with contacts who are willing to talk about their careers with students—such as alumni or professionals working in the local community near your campus. The Internet may be another source for locating interview candidates.

3. Once you've identified someone you would like to interview, send that person a short letter or e-mail, or give them a call, asking about the possibility of scheduling a short interview and mention that you would be willing to conduct the interview in person or by phone—whichever would be more convenient. If you don't hear back within a reasonable period (7–10 days), send a follow-up message. If you don't receive a response to the follow-up message, try contacting someone else.

4. After you have found someone to interview, here are some strategies for conducting the interview:

   - Thank the person for taking the time to speak with you. This should be the first thing you do after meeting the person—before you officially begin the interview.
   - Prepare your interview questions in advance. Here are some questions that you might consider asking:

     1) During a typical day's work, what tasks occupy most of your time?
     2) What do you like most about your career?
     3) What are the most difficult or frustrating aspects of your career?
     4) What personal skills or qualities do you see as being critical for success in your career?
     5) How did you decide on your career?
     6) What personal qualifications or prior experiences enabled you to enter your career?
     7) How does someone find out about openings in your field?
     8) What steps did you take to locate your current position?
     9) What advice would you give first-year students about what they might do at this stage of their college experience to begin preparing for a career in your field?
     10) How does someone advance in your career?
     11) Are there any moral issues or ethical challenges that tend to arise in your career?
     12) Are members of diverse groups likely to be found in your career? (This is an especially important question to ask if you're a member of an ethnic, racial, or gender group that is underrepresented in the career field.)
     13) What impact does your career have on your home life or personal life outside of work?
     14) If you had to do it all over again, would you choose the same career?
     15) Would you recommend that I speak with anyone else to obtain additional information or a different perspective on your career field? (If the answer is "yes," you may follow up by asking: "May I mention that you referred me?") It's always a good idea to obtain more than one person's perspective before making any important choice, such as your career choice.

- **Take notes during the interview.** This not only helps you remember what was said, it also sends a positive message to the persons you interview because it shows them that their ideas are important and noteworthy (worth taking notes on).
- **If the interview goes well, consider asking if it might be possible to observe or shadow that person at work.**

Self-Assessment Questions

After completing your interview, take a moment to reflect on it and answer the following questions:

1. What information did you receive that impressed you about the career?

2. What information did you receive that distressed (or depressed) you about the career?

3. What was the most useful piece of information you took away from the interview?

4. Based on the information you acquired during the interview, would you still be interested in pursuing a career in this field? Why?

Chapter 12 Reflection

What is your ideal career?

What would your work day be like?

Make a detailed plan for how you can get this career.

What are some things you can utilize from this chapter to make it happen?

End-of-Course Reflection

Now that your First Year Experience course is coming to an end, take some time to reflect on and answer the following questions.

1. Look back at the three things you wanted to learn or accomplish through completing this course on p. xxix of the Introduction. What were they? Have you learned or accomplished them? Explain.

2. Think back to the first day of this course. What type of person and student were you? How have you changed over the semester?

3. Has your approach to college changed as a result of this course? Explain.

Learning the Language of Higher Education

A GLOSSARY AND DICTIONARY OF COLLEGE VOCABULARY

Academic Advisors: faculty or professional staff who advise college students on course selection, help them understand college procedures, and guide their academic progress toward completion of a college degree.

Academic Affairs: unit or division of the college that deals primarily with the college curriculum, course instruction, and campus services supporting academic success (e.g., library and learning center).

Academic Calendar: the scheduling system used by a college or university to divide the academic year into shorter terms (e.g., semesters, trimesters, or quarters).

Academic Credits (Units): how students receive credit for courses counting toward completing a college degree. Academic credit is typically counted in terms of how many hours the class meets each week (e.g., a course that meets for three hours per week counts for three credits).

Academic Discipline: a field of study (biology, psychology, philosophy, etc.).

Academic Dismissal: a student is denied enrollment at a college because of a cumulative GPA that is below a minimum standard (e.g., below 2.0).

Academic Probation: a period of time (usually one term) during which students with a grade point average that does not meet the college's minimum requirement for graduation (e.g., less than 2.0) are given a chance to improve their grades. If grades improve to the point that they meet or exceed the college's minimum requirement, probation is lifted; if not, the student may be academically dismissed from the college.

Academic Standing: where a student stands academically (cumulative GPA) at a given point in the college experience (e.g., after one term or one year of coursework).

Academic Support Center: place on campus where students can obtain individual assistance from professionals and trained peers to support and strengthen their academic performance.

Academic Transcript: an official list of all courses a student has enrolled in, the grades received in those courses, and the student's grade point average for all courses.

ACE Military Credit: credit granted toward a college degree based on previous military experience (Army, Navy, Air Force, Coast Guard, Department of Defense, or Marine Corps).

Active Involvement (aka Engagement): the amount of *time* a student devotes to learning in college and the degree of personal *effort* or *energy* (mental and physical) the student puts into the learning process.

Advanced Placement (AP) Tests: tests designed to measure knowledge and skills mastered in high school. If a student scores high enough, college credit is awarded in the subject area tested, or the student is granted advanced placement in a college course.

Analysis (Analytical Thinking): a form of higher-level thinking, which involves breaking down information and identifying its key parts or underlying elements, and detecting what's most important or relevant.

APA Style: a particular style of citing references in a research report or term paper that is endorsed by the American Psychological Association (APA) and is most commonly used in fields that comprise the Behavioral Sciences (e.g., Psychology and Sociology) and Natural Sciences (e.g., Biology and Chemistry).

Aptitude: ability to do something well or to the potential to do it well.

Associate of Applied Science Degree (AAS Degree): community college degree in science-related fields that lead directly to a job rather than transfer to a 4-year college or university.

Associate of Applied Technology Degree (AAT Degree): community college degree in technology-related fields that lead directly to a job rather than transfer to a four-year college or university.

Associate of Arts Degree (AA Degree): community college degree that represents completion of general education and premajor requirements needed for transfer to a four-year college or university with a major in a nonscience field(arts).

Associate of Science Degree (AS Degree): community college degree that represents completion of general education and pre-major requirements needed for transfer to a four-year college or university in a science-related field.

Bachelor's (Baccalaureate) Degree: degree awarded by four-year colleges and universities that represents completion of general education requirements and requirements for a major.

Career: the sum total of vocational experiences throughout an individual's work life.

Career Advancement: working up the career ladder to higher levels of authority and socioeconomic status.

Career Development Center: key campus resource where students learn about the nature of different careers and acquire strategies for locating career-related work experiences.

Career Development Courses: college courses that typically include self-assessment of career interests, information about different careers, and strategies for career preparation.

Certificate: credential received by students at a community or technical college to signify completion of a vocational or occupational training program, which qualifies them for a specific job or occupation.

Citation: an acknowledgment of the source of any piece of information included in a written paper or oral report that is not the writer's original work.

Co-curricular Experiences: student learning and development that results from experiences taking place outside the classroom.

College Catalog (aka College Bulletin): an official publication of a college or university that identifies its mission, curriculum, academic policies and procedures, as well as the names and educational background of its faculty.

Commuter Students: college students who do not live on campus.

Concept: a system or network of related ideas.

Concept (Idea) Map: a diagram that represents or maps out main categories of ideas and depicts their relationships in a visual–spatial format.

Cooperative Education (Co-op) Program: program in which students gain work experience relating to their college major, either by stopping their course work temporarily to work full-time at the co-op position, or by continuing to take classes while working part-time at the co-op position.

Core Courses: courses required of all students, regardless of their particular major.

Counseling Services: personal counseling provided by professionals with expertise in promoting self-awareness and self-development, particularly with respect to social and emotional aspects of life.

Cover (Application) Letter: letter written by an applicant applying for an employment position or admission to a school.

Cramming: packing study time into one study session immediately before an exam.

Creative Thinking: a form of higher-level thinking that generates unique ideas, strategies, or products.

Critical Thinking: a form of higher-level thinking that involves making well-informed evaluations or judgments.

Cross-registration: a collaborative program offered by two colleges or universities that allow students enrolled at one institution to register for and take courses at another institution.

Culture: a distinctive pattern of beliefs and values learned by a group of people who share the same social heritage and traditions.

Cum Laude: graduating "with honors" (e.g., achieving a cumulative GPA of 3.5).

Cumulative GPA: a student's grade point average for all academic terms combined.

Curriculum: the total set of courses offered by a college or university.

Dean: a college or university administrator who is responsible for running a particular unit of the college (e.g., Dean of Fine Arts).

Dean's List: achieving an outstanding GPA for a particular term (e.g., 3.5 or higher).

Developmental Education Courses (aka Transitional or Foundation Courses): noncredit courses in reading, writing, or mathematics that student must completed before being able to take college credit–earning courses.

Distance Learning: courses taken online rather than in person.

Diversity: the variety of different groups that comprise the human species (humanity).

Diversity Appreciation: valuing the experiences of different groups of people and interest in learning from their experience.

Diversity (Multicultural) Courses: courses designed to promote diversity awareness and appreciation of multiple cultures.

Doctoral Degree: an advanced degree obtained after completion of the bachelor's (baccalaureate) degree, which typically requires five to six years of full-time study in graduate school, including completion of a thesis or doctoral dissertation.

Documentation: sources of information that serve as references to support or reinforce conclusions in a written paper or oral presentation.

Double Major: a bachelor's degree in two majors that is attained by meeting the course requirements in both fields of study.

Drop/Add: the process of changing an academic schedule by dropping courses or adding courses to a preexisting schedule.

Electives: courses that students are not required to take, but which they elect (choose) to take.

Ethnic Group (Ethnicity): a group of people who share the same culture.

Experiential Learning: out-of-class experiences that promote learning and development.

Faculty: the collection of instructors on campus whose primary role is to teach courses offered in the college curriculum.

FAFSA (Free Application for Federal Student Aid): a form prepared annually by current and prospective college students (undergraduate and graduate) in the United States to determine their eligibility for student financial aid.

Fine Arts: a division of the liberal arts curriculum that focuses largely on artistic performance and appreciation of artistic expression by pursuing such questions as: What is beautiful? How do humans express and appreciate aesthetic (sensory) experiences, imagination, creativity, style, grace, and elegance?

Free Electives: courses that students may elect to enroll in, which count toward a college degree, but are not required for general education or an academic major.

Freshman Fifteen: a phrase commonly used to describe the 15-pound weight gain that some students experience during their first year of college.

Full-time Student: a student enrolled in at least 12 units of coursework during the academic term.

General Education Curriculum: collection of courses designed to provide breadth of knowledge and transferable skills needed for success in any major or career.

Grade Points: number of points earned for a course, which is calculated by multiplying the course grade by the number of credits carried by the course.

Grade Point Average (GPA): translation of students' letter grades into a numeric system, whereby the total number of grade points earned in all courses is divided by the total number of course units.

Graduate Assistant (GA): a graduate student who receives financial assistance to pursue graduate studies by working in a university office or for a college professor.

Graduate Record Examination (GRE): a standardized test for admission to graduate schools, similar to how SAT and ACT tests are used for admission to undergraduate colleges and universities.

Graduate School: education pursued after completing a bachelor's degree.

Graduate Student: student who has completed a four-year (bachelor's) degree and is enrolled in graduate school to obtain an advanced degree (e.g., Master's or Ph.D.).

Grant: money received that does not have to be repaid.

Guaranteed Admission Agreement (aka, Joint Admissions or "2+2 Agreements"): Agreement between a two-year and four-year college that stipulates if students complete the general education program at their community college with a satisfactory GPA, they are automatically admitted to the four-year college campus as upper division students (junior status) without having to complete a formal application for admission and acceptance.

Health Services: on-campus services to treat students experiencing physical illnesses or injuries, and to educate students on matters relating to health and wellness.

Higher Education: formal education beyond high school.

Higher-Level Thinking: thinking at a higher or more complex level than merely acquiring factual knowledge or memorizing information.

Holistic (Whole Person) Development: development of the total self, which includes intellectual, social, emotional, physical, spiritual, ethical, and vocational aspects of personal development.

Honors Program: a special program of courses and related learning experiences designed for students who have demonstrated exceptionally high levels of academic achievement.

Humanities: division of the liberal arts curriculum that focuses on the human experience, human culture, and questions relating to the human condition, such as: Why are we here? What is the meaning or purpose of our existence? How should we live? What is the good life? Is there life after death?

Humanity: common elements of the human experience shared by all human beings.

Hypothesis: an informed guess that might be true, but still needs to be tested to confirm or verify its truth.

Impacted Major: a college major in which there are more students wishing to enter the program than there are spaces available in the program; thus, students must formally apply and qualify for admission to the major by going through a competitive screening process. Might have a waiting list for admission to the major.

Independent Study: a project in which students receive academic credit for in-depth study of a topic of their choice by working independently with a faculty member, rather than enrolling in a classroom-based course.

Informational Interview: an interview with a professional currently working in a career to obtain inside information about what the career is really like.

Intellectual (Cognitive) Development: acquiring knowledge, learning how to learn, and learning to think deeply.

Intercultural Competence: ability to appreciate and capitalize on human differences, and to interact effectively with people from diverse cultural backgrounds.

Interdisciplinary: courses or programs that are designed to help students integrate knowledge from two or more academic disciplines (fields of study).

International Student: a student attending college in one nation, but who is a citizen of another nation.

International Study (Study Abroad) Program: taking courses at a college or university in a foreign country.

Internship: work experience related to a college major for which students receive academic credit and, in some cases, financial compensation.

Interpret: to draw a conclusion about something and support that conclusion with evidence.

Job Shadowing: a program that allows a student to follow (shadow) and observe a professional during a typical workday.

Leadership: ability to influence people in a positive way (e.g., motivating peers to do their best), or the ability to produce positive change in an organization or institution (e.g., improving the quality of a school, business, or political organization).

Learning Community: a program in which the same group of students takes the same block of courses together during the same academic term.

Learning Habits: the usual approaches, methods, or techniques a student uses while learning.

Learning Style: the way in which an individual prefers to perceive information (receive or take it in) and process information (deal with it once it has been taken in).

Liberal Arts: the component of a college education that represents the essential foundation or backbone for the college curriculum, which is designed to equip students with a versatile set of skills that promotes their success in any academic major or career.

Lifelong Learning: learning how to learn and how to continue learning throughout life.

Lower-Division Courses: courses taken by college students during their freshman and sophomore years.

Magna Cum Laude: graduating with "high honors" (e.g., achieving a cumulative GPA of 3.8).

Major: the academic field students choose to specialize in while in college.

Major-Specific (aka, Program-Major-to-Program-Major) Agreements: courses taken by students at community college in a field they intend to major in after transferring to a four-year college are automatically accepted by the four-year college as fulfilling graduation requirements in that major.

Master's Degree: degree obtained after completion of the bachelor's (baccalaureate) degree that typically requires two to three years of full-time study in graduate school.

Mentor: someone who serves as a role model and personal guide to help students reach their educational or occupational goals.

Merit-Based Scholarship: money awarded on the basis of performance or achievement that does not have to be repaid.

Metacognition: thinking about how you are thinking while you are thinking.

Midterm: the midpoint of an academic term.

Minor: a field of study designed to complement and strengthen a major, which usually consists of about half the number of courses required for a college major (e.g., six to seven courses for a minor).

MLA Style: a style of citing references adopted by the Modern Language Association (MLA) and commonly used by academic fields in the Humanities and Fine Arts (e.g., English and Philosophy).

Mnemonic Device (Mnemonic): a memory improvement method for retaining and recalling information (e.g., an acronym or rhyming pattern).

Multicultural Center: place on campus designed for interaction among and between members of diverse cultural groups.

Multidimensional Thinking: a form of higher-level thinking that involves taking multiple perspectives and vantage points.

Multiple Intelligences: the theory that humans display intelligence and mental ability in a variety of ways (e.g., social intelligence and emotional intelligence).

Natural Sciences: a division of the liberal arts curriculum that focuses on the systematic observation of the physical world and underlying explanations of natural phenomena, asking such questions as: "What causes the physical events that take place in the natural world?" "How can we predict and control natural events?"

Need-Based Scholarship: money awarded to students on the basis of financial need that does not have to be repaid.

Netiquette: applying principles of social etiquette and interpersonal sensitivity when communicating online.

Nonresident Status: out-of-state students who typically pay higher tuition than in-state students because they are not residents of the state in which their college is located.

Nontraditional Students (aka Re-entry Students): students who do not begin college immediately after high school.

Official Transcript: college transcript signed and date-stamped by the registrar's office to verify that the information contained in it is up-to-date, accurate, and not altered by the student. For students intending to transfer, an official transcript must be sent by the registrar's office to the colleges to which the student intends to transfer.

Orientation: an educational program experienced before the first academic term in college that's designed to help new students make a smooth transition to higher education.

Oversubscribed (aka Impacted) Major: a major that has more students interested in it than there are openings for it.

Paraphrase: restating or rephrasing information in your own words.

Part-Time Student: a college student who enrolls in fewer than 12 units during an academic term.

Part-to-Whole Study Method: a study strategy in which material to be learned is divided into smaller parts and studied in a series of short sessions in advance of an exam; on the day before the exam, the previously studied parts are reviewed as a whole.

Pass/Fail (Credit/No Credit) Grading: a grading option offered in some courses whereby students can choose to receive a grade of "pass" (credit) or "fail" (no credit), rather than a letter grade (A–F).

Phi Beta Kappa: a national honor society that recognizes outstanding academic achievement of students at four-year colleges and universities.

Phi Theta Kappa: a national honor society that recognizes outstanding academic achievement of students at two-year colleges.

Placement Tests: tests administered to new students upon entry to a college or university that are designed to assess their basic academic skills (e.g., reading, writing, mathematics) and place them in courses that are neither too advanced nor too elementary for their particular level of skill development.

Plagiarism: intentional or unintentional use of someone else's work without acknowledging it, giving the impression that it is one's own work.

Portfolio: a collection of work materials or products that illustrates an individual's skills and talents, or demonstrates educational and personal development.

Postsecondary Education: formal education beyond secondary (high school) education.

Prerequisite Course: a course that must be completed before a more advanced course can be taken.

Prewriting: an early stage in the writing process where the focus is on generating and organizing one's own ideas, rather than expressing or communicating ideas to someone else.

Process-of-Elimination Method: test-taking strategy for multiple-choice exams whereby choices that are clearly wrong are "weeded out" or eliminated until the best possible answer is identified.

Professional School: formal education pursued after a bachelor's degree in a school that prepares students for an "applied" profession (e.g., Pharmacy, Medicine, or Law).

Proofreading: final stage of editing that focuses on detecting mechanical errors relating to referencing, grammar, punctuation, and spelling.

Quarter System: a system for scheduling courses in which the academic year is divided into four quarters (fall, winter, spring, and summer terms), each of which lasts approximately 10–11 weeks.

Recall Test Question: a type of test question that requires students to generate or produce the correct answer on their own (e.g., essay question).

Recitation (Reciting): a study strategy that involves recalling and speaking aloud information to be remembered without looking at it.

Recognition Test Question: a type of test question that requires students to select or choose a correct answer from answers that are provided to them (e.g., multiple-choice, true–false, and matching questions).

Reference (Referral) Letter: a letter of reference typically written for students who are applying for entry into positions or schools after college, and for students applying for special academic programs, student leadership positions on campus, or part-time employment.

Reflection: a thoughtful review of what one has already done, is in the process of doing, or is planning to do.

Registrar's Office: campus office that maintains college transcripts and other official records associated with student coursework and academic performance.

Research Skills: ability to locate, access, retrieve, organize, and evaluate information from a variety of sources, including library and technology-based (computer) systems.

Resident Status: in-state students who typically pay lower tuition than out-of-state students because they are residents of the state in which their college is located.

Residential Students: students who live on campus or in a housing unit owned and operated by the college.

Restricted Electives: courses that students choose to take from a restricted set or list of possible courses that have been specified by the college.

Resume: a list of an individual's credentials, accomplishments, skills, and awards.

Reverse Transfer Agreement: community college students who transfer to a four-year college before completing an associate degree are allowed to transfer credits completed at the four-year campus back to their previous two-year campus to receive the associate degree.

Rough Draft: an early stage in the writing process whereby the writer's major ideas are expressed without close attention to the mechanics of writing (e.g., punctuation, grammar, or spelling).

Scholarly: a criterion or standard for evaluating the quality of an information source; typically, a source is considered "scholarly" if it has been reviewed by a panel or board of impartial experts in the field before being published.

Self-Assessment: the process of reflecting on and evaluating personal characteristics, such as personality traits, personal interests, or learning habits.

Self-Monitoring: maintaining self-awareness of what you're doing and how well you're doing it.

Self-Regulation: adjusting one's learning strategies in a way that best meet the specific demands of the subject being learned.

Semester System: a system for scheduling courses in which the academic year is divided into two terms (fall and spring) that are approximately 15–16 weeks long.

Semester (Term) GPA: GPA calculated for one semester or academic term.

Senior Seminar (Capstone) Course: course designed to put a "cap" or final touch on the college experience, helping seniors to tie ideas together in their major and to make a smooth transition from college to post-college life.

Service Learning: a form of experiential learning in which students serve or help others while also acquiring skills through hands-on experience that can be used to strengthen their resumes and explore potential careers.

Sexually Transmitted Infections (STIs): a group of contagious infections spread through sexual contact.

Shallow (Surface) Learning: an approach to learning in which the student's study time is spent repeating and memorizing information in the exact form in which it's presented, rather than transforming it into words that are meaningful to the student.

Social and Behavioral Sciences: a division of the liberal arts curriculum that focuses on the observation of human behavior, individually and in groups, asking such questions as: What causes humans to behave the way they do? How can we predict, control, or improve human behavior?

Socially Constructed Knowledge: knowledge that is built up through interaction and dialogue with others.

Stackable Credentials: short-term credentials that students can earn at a community colleges that can eventually be built on by taking additional courses to longer-term credentials that allow students to advance up a career ladder or across career pathways to higher-paying jobs. (For example, students can continue to earn educational credits along the pathway to an associate degree by completing a series of shorter credentials that focus on mastering skills for specific technologies, which prepare them to gain entry-level work in the field of information technology and eventually advance to higher positions.)

Student Activities: co-curricular experiences offered outside the classroom designed to promote student involvement in campus life.

Student Development Services (Student Affairs): division of a college or university that provides student support on issues relating to social and emotional adjustment, involvement in campus life outside the classroom, and leadership development.

Student Handbook: an official college publication that identifies student roles and responsibilities, violations of campus rules and policies, and opportunities for student involvement in co-curricular programs, such as student clubs, campus organizations, and student leadership positions.

Summa Cum Laude: graduating with "highest honors" (e.g., achieving a cumulative GPA of 4.0 or higher).

Summer Session: courses offered during the summer between spring and fall terms, which typically run on a shorter timeframe (e.g., eight weeks).

Syllabus: an academic document that outlines course requirements, attendance policies, grading scale, course topics by date, test dates and dates for completing reading and other assignments, as well as information about the instructor (e.g., office location and office hours).

Synthesis: a form of higher-level thinking that involves integrating (connecting) smaller, separate pieces of information into a more comprehensive and coherent product.

Tau Sigma Honor Society: a national honors and scholarship program offered at some four-year colleges that is specifically designed for transfer students. To be eligible, transfer students must earn at least a 3.5 GPA after their first term on campus or rank among the top 20% of their entering transfer class in academic performance.

Test Anxiety: a state of emotional tension that can weaken test performance by interfering with concentration, memory, and ability to think at a higher level.

Test-Wise: using characteristics of the test question itself (e.g., its wording or format) to increase the probability of choosing the correct answer.

Theory: a body of conceptually related concepts and general principles that help organize, understand, and apply knowledge that has been acquired in a particular field of study.

Thesis Statement: a one- to three-sentence statement contained in the introduction to a paper, which serves as a summary of the key point or main argument the writer intends to make and support with evidence.

Transfer Advisors (aka Transfer Counselors): professionals working at either two-year or four-year colleges who specialize in advising transfer students.

Transfer Articulation Agreements (aka, Transfer Agreement Pacts): agreements between two-year and four-year colleges about how course credit will be transferred from one college to the other.

Transfer Articulation Officer: person in charge of determining if and how academic credit will be transferred from one college to another.

Transfer Audit (aka Transfer Transcript Evaluation): process whereby a four-year college evaluates a transferring student's transcript to determine how many courses will be accepted for transfer credit and where the credit will be applied (e.g., as credit toward general education, a college major, or an elective).

Transfer Fair: an event held at a two-year or four-year campus whereby transfer advisors and college admissions representatives from four-year institutions help community college students plan for successful transfer.

Transfer of Experiential Credit: college credit granted for prior learning experiences that took place in noncollege settings (e.g., previous work or military experiences).

Transfer Program (aka Transfer Track): two-year college program that provides general education and premajor coursework to prepare students for successful transfer to a four-year college or university.

Transfer Ready: community college students who have completed all course requirements needed to be ready for transfer to a four-year college.

Transfer Shock (aka Transfer Dip): cultural adjustment and dip in GPA typically experienced by transfer students during their first term on the four-year campus; however, after surviving this initial adjustment and dip, transfer students' grades improve and their graduation rates are similar to students who begin their college education at four-year colleges.

Transfer-Student Orientation: program offered at a four-year college designed specifically for new transfer students to facilitate their transition to the college.

Transfer-Student Orientation Course (aka, Transfer Student Seminar): course offered at a four-year college specifically for new transfer students during their first term on campus to facilitate their transition to the college.

Transferable Skills: skills that can be transferred or applied across different subjects, careers, and life situations.

Trimester System: a system for scheduling courses in which the academic year is divided into three terms (fall, winter, and spring) that are approximately 12–13 weeks long.

Undeclared: students who have not declared (committed to) a college major.

Undergraduate: student enrolled in a two-year or four-year college.

Upper-division Courses: courses taken by college students during their junior and senior years.

Visual Aids: charts, graphs, diagrams, or concept maps that improve learning and memory by enabling the learner to organize information into a picture or image.

Visual Memory: memory that relies on the sense of vision.

Visualization: a memory improvement strategy that involves creating a mental image or picture of what is to be remembered, or by imagining it in a familiar site or location.

Vocational (Occupational) Development: exploring career options, making career choices wisely, and developing skills needed for career success.

Vocational/Technical Programs: community college programs of study that train students for a particular occupation or trade and immediate employment after completing a two-year associate degree (e.g., Associate of Applied Science) or a one-year certificate program.

Volunteerism: volunteering personal time to help others without being rewarded with pay or academic credit.

Waive: to give up one's right to access information (e.g., waiving the right to see a letter of recommendation).

Wellness: a state of optimal health, peak performance, and positive well-being that results from balancing and integrating different dimensions of the "self" (body, mind, and spirit).

Withdrawal: dropping a class after the drop/add deadline, which results in a student receiving a "W" for the course and no academic credit.

Work-Study Program: a federal program that supplies colleges and universities with funds to provide on-campus employment for students who are in financial need.

Writing Center: a campus support service where students receive assistance at any stage of the writing process, whether it be collecting and organizing ideas, composing a first draft, or proofreading a final draft.

Index